# U. S. Trade Tokens

# 1866-1889

### By Russell Rulau

### Includes Unlisted 1861-1865 Tokens

A catalog of the private coinage and
advertising tokens of an industrializing
America, from the close of the Civil War
to the centennial of Washington's inaugural.
With sections on Mavericks and confusing
British and Canadian pieces.

**Special Consultants**

Byron Johnson
Joseph Schmidt
David Schenkman
Steve Tanenbaum
George Fuld
Gregory Brunk

**First Edition**

IOLA, WISCONSIN 54990

COPYRIGHT MCMLXXXIII
by Krause Publications Inc.
Library of Congress Catalog Card Number: 83-81009
International Standard Book Number: 0-87341-035-1

# TABLE OF CONTENTS

| | Page |
|---|---|
| Introductory text | 5 |
| Centennial token dies | 8 |
| Numbering system | 16 |
| Abbreviations | 11 |
| Billiard token makers | 13 |
| Contributors to the catalog | 14 |
| Bibliography of reference sources | 15 |

**Catalog**

| | |
|---|---|
| Alabama | 17 |
| Arkansas | 17 |
| California | 17 |
| Colorado | 22 |
| Connecticut | 23 |
| District of Columbia | 25 |
| Georgia | 26 |
| Idaho | 26 |
| Illinois | 27 |
| Indiana | 42 |
| Iowa | 43 |
| Kansas | 44 |
| Kentucky | 45 |
| Louisiana | 47 |
| Maine | 49 |
| Maryland | 51 |
| Massachusetts | 59 |
| Michigan | 69 |
| Minnesota | 71 |
| Mississippi | 72 |
| Missouri | 73 |
| Montana | 77 |
| Nebraska | 78 |
| Nevada | 79 |
| New Hampshire | 79 |
| New Jersey | 81 |
| New Mexico | 84 |
| New York | 84 |
| North Carolina | 109 |
| Ohio | 110 |
| Oklahoma | 119 |
| Oregon | 120 |
| Pennsylvania | 120 |
| Rhode Island | 143 |
| South Carolina | 143 |
| South Dakota | 144 |
| Tennessee | 145 |
| Texas | 147 |
| Utah | 160 |
| Vermont | 160 |
| Virginia | 162 |
| Washington | 164 |
| Wisconsin | 165 |
| Wyoming | 168 |
| Non-local | 169 |
| Mavericks | 169 |
| Miscellaneous U.S. counterstamps | 184 |
| Love tokens | 199 |

**Foreign**

| | |
|---|---|
| Canada | 202 |
| Ceylon | 214 |
| France | 214 |
| Germany | 216 |
| Great Britain | 208 |
| Ireland | 212 |
| Peru | 216 |
| Trinidad | 216 |

*Broadway, New York, with the 100's and 200's in foreground, shows the tangle of electrification overhead in the mid-1870's. After the great Blizzard of 1888 such wires went underground. This section of Broadway was an emporium for jewelers. (Courtesy New York Historical Society)*

A special feature of the post-Civil War period is the Centennial of the United States celebrations which took place in Philadelphia in 1876. The Centennial spawned a large number of special tokens -- made as much for collectors as for the general public -- carrying the names of many prominent merchants of the Seventies.

This series is dominated by such stock devices as the Liberty Bell, Libertas Americana medal, Continental Army soldier, Independence Hall, etc. An attractive Abraham Lincoln bust by Bolen was also introduced at about the same time or somewhat earlier.

The so-called "Centennial cards" were in many respects a throwback to the Golden Age of token issuance in the late 1850's -- they are decorative, and not needed (or used) as money. There are several independent series of 1876 Centennial cards, by Lingg, by Kline, by Bolen, etc., and all of them are covered in this reference.

At the same time, though, the burgeoning needs of trade were calling for an ever-widening issuance of trade tokens, which were utilitarian in appearance and worth a fixed amount -- 25 cents, one drink, one shave, one admittance, one cigar, one tune.

In this new reference catalog, *U.S. Trade Tokens 1866-1889*, the user will discover that it contains pieces in all of these categories:
   Store cards
   Advertising checks
   Work, Job, Picker and Railroad checks and talleys
   Saloon and Billiard tokens
   Checks for value
   Exposition and Festival medalets
   Counterstamped coins
   Other related items

There are a number of post-Civil War series which are **not** included in this book, principally because good references already exist for them and this book is intended to serve the interests of collectors of the many series listed above. Those series not included are:
   Transportation tokens
   Hard Rubber tokens and medals
   Embossed Shell and Mirror cards
   Military and Sutler tokens
   Political campaign tokens (except Store Card mules)

# The Role of Aluminum

Very few trade tokens, store cards or medals were made of aluminum prior to 1890. A small number of commemorative medals were struck in the 1880's, and the U.S. Mint used aluminum even earlier for pattern coins and for assay medals.

There is good reason for the sparsity of aluminum used in the period covered by this reference, 1866-1889. In 1854 aluminum was worth $17 an ounce (gold was $20 at the time), but there wasn't a pound of it in the world available for the coining process. By 1859 the only aluminum refinery in the world (in France), had produced a total of 60 pounds of aluminum and was selling it at $17 a pound. It was much more expensive than silver at this time.

In the United States, during the 1860's, 1870's and early 1880's, aluminum was selling at about $2 an ounce — twice the price of silver. When the first U.S. electrolytic process for refining aluminum began in November, 1888, aluminum was being offered at "several dollars a pound."

Then in 1889 its price stood at $3 a pound; by 1891 it had dropped to $1.50 a pound, and in 1893 to 75 cents per pound. During 1889 the plant was producing 50 pounds a day, but there was almost no market for the metal.

Thus it can be seen that aluminum, expensive before the 1888 breakthrough in refining the metal from its ores, was suitable only for certain medals and a few store cards (such as presentation pieces for employees) before 1889. Almost all the aluminum tokens listed by Dr. Wright, therefore, can be assumed — safely — to emanate from the 1890's, and the number of aluminum pieces included in this catalog is minimal (some that are included properly belong to the 1890-on period but complete some series or literary thought and thus find space herein.)

Interestingly, by 1910 aluminum had become so cheap — and its novelty had by then worn off — that there was a retreat from its use in preparing medals and store cards, though its use in tokens continued. This situation was not reversed until about 1950, after the aluminum industry had begun an "education" program to induce aluminum's use in almost every conceivable form. A byproduct of the propaganda campaign is that aluminum medals once more became fashionable.

For the collector concerned with "dating" his elusive tokens, the history of aluminum's use is most helpful. The simple rule: If it's aluminum, it's post-1889. (The few exceptions, we trust, are cataloged in these pages.)

## Genealogical Research

A number of basic historical source documents were used to enhance the data included in this book. The facts are presented, wherever possible, after digestion and editing.

Once while going over the notes extracted from the tedious chore of studying aging books and reading microfilm, I said silently to myself, "It's a good thing you've got 44 years of numismatic background. This is hard stuff to absorb."

When one assembles a catalog such as this, one finds the necessity of dealing with names — thousands of them. America is rich in source material, however, so it becomes a matter of examining enough printed material, over enough time, to sift out useful tidbits of information.

The primary source documents include the decennial census records, city directories, county history books, directories of specialized professions, and books containing rosters of certain professions known to be active in token-making or counterstamping: silversmiths, gunsmiths, stencil cutters and sealmakers, daguerreotypers, for example.

We owe a special debt of gratitude to the Mormon Genealogical Library in Salt Lake City, Utah, a repository of more than 60 million family names. Nowhere else in North America can one find such a wealth of census records, graves records, very early city directories and other business directories, land registrations, etc. I spent a number of days there deeply immersed in the "people history" of our nation.

Many token collectors are amateur historians. Their breadth of knowledge on Commercial America might astound professional historians. Some of these who were especially helpful in this catalog are: Byron Johnson, Gary Pipher, Steve Tanenbaum, Bruce W. Smith, Dave Schenkman, Bob Schuman, Mike Pfefferkorn, Joe Schmidt, Damia Francis.

## Foreign Tokens

A substantial number of the tokens of Great Britain and Canada and a few pieces from Ireland, France, Germany, Trinidad, Ceylon, Peru etc. are catalogued in this reference. Users may wonder why.

The answer is: Convenience. Many Canadian and British tokens have been confused as American issues, especially the merchant counterstamps. The U.S. Large cent was a popular planchet on which merchants advertised their wares and services — north of the border and across the Atlantic as well.

Excellent writers of the past have confused the token output of Pears' Soap, Empire Theatre and other issuers as U.S. pieces, and for this reason we've appended a "primer" on such issues in catalog format. The counterstamp listing is reasonably complete for Canada and may find favor with our continental neighbors as a result.

Coins and tokens tended to ignore the U.S.-Canada frontier in the 19th century, circulating rather freely on both sides. U.S. coins may still today be found in Canadian circulation, and vice versa, especially in the lower denominations.

## Maverick Counterstamps

Appended to this reference book is an alphabetized listing of maverick counterstamps appearing on American and some foreign coins which could possibly be frivolous in nature. Many of them will be found, ultimately, to be merchant pieces, and publication here may hasten the attribution process.

Counterstamped coins which bear locales of the issuer, or for which the locale has been deduced by research, are included in their proper place under state listings. Those maverick counterstamps which suggest mercantile reasons for their existence, or which have been found on several different coins, appear under the Maverick section if their locale is not known.

All pieces in the Miscellaneous Counterstamps addendum have been examined by the author or one of his major collaborators, so their existence is verified, and many of these have been photographed. The listing thus is supplemental to — rather than inclusive of — lists published earlier in *The Numismatist* such as those by Gould or Hallenbeck. The accumulations of counterstamps of all these specialists have been examined: Steve Tanenbaum, Frank Kovacs, David Schenkman, John Cheramy, Roy Van Ormer, Hank Spangenberger, Kurt R. Krueger, Rich Hartzog, Dr. Gregory Brunk, Gary Pipher, Chester L. Krause, Byron Johnson, Joseph Schmidt, Stanley L. Steinberg.

Cross-references to the published lists of Dr. Gregory Brunk, Kenneth Hallenbeck, Maurice M. Gould, Stanley Steinberg, Joseph Schmidt, Frank Duffield and others are included in the lengthy list and throughout the catalog.

To keep confusion to a minimum, the Foreign Section of this catalog also contains alphabetized listings of miscellaneous maverick counterstamps (which could be frivolous) of Canada, Great Britain and Ireland — a first anywhere in a single reference, so far as we are aware.

One theme that recurs frequently on American counterstamped coins employs certain words, such as CAST STEEL, CAST STEEL WARRANTED, WARRANTED, PATENT, etc. Sometimes these words are accompanied by initials, names, locales or dates.

We believe these terms may be associated with the manufacture of firearms, and may have been parts of the punches used to mark lock-plates and other metallic portions of muskets, rifles, revolvers etc.

Another possibility is that these terms are associated with punches used to mark knives, axes, cutlery or tools. The number of counterstamps using such terms is large enough to admit of other possibilities as well. As time passes, more of these maverick stampings will be attributed by collectors.

It is not likely the "cast steel" type of counterstamp was used for advertising purposes. More likely is that handy coins were used to test the punches — or to create personal pocket pieces for workmen.

# CENTENNIAL DIES

| A | B | C | D |
| E | F | G | H |
| J | K | L | OV |

Memorial Hall

V     W     X     Y     Z

# Arrangement of the Centennial Cards

A special feature of this catalog is the inclusion of all those store cards issued before and during the Centennial of the United States in 1876. This grouping of store cards, which has always had special relevance for historically minded collectors, is very perplexing to the novice collector. Partly this is due to the early efforts of Wright, Adams and others to list all the issuers and pieces known to them — mostly without benefit of illustration.

In 1981 Arlie R. Slabaugh cleared up much of the confusion in his booklet on the Lingg-struck cards, and in this reference we are detailing a good number more of Lingg pieces than were included in Slabaugh, as well as cataloguing all those Kline, Bolen and other Centennial-type cards known to the author and his contributors.

The Kline, Bolen and other cards are treated as all other tokens, with full narrative description after each listing. A special arrangement of our own has been adopted for the Lingg cards — those which recur most frequently and which are usually thought of when the term "Centennial cards" is used.

There are 11 obverse dies measuring 23 millimeters (slightly larger than U.S. nickel size); 5 obverse dies measuring 19mm (U.S. cent size); and 1 oval die measuring 25 by 20mm. Each Lingg die is assigned a letter. (A few special obverse dies, SM, SP etc., are described under their issuer.)

Here is a listing of the Lingg Centennial dies; the date shown is the latest date appearing on the die.

### 23 Millimeter Dies

| Die A | Libertas Americana | 1776 |
| Die B | Liberty Bell, 13 stars | 1776 |
| Die C | Liberty Bell, dashes | 1776 |
| Die D | Two heads | No date |
| Die E | Continental soldier | 1876 |
| Die F | Maryland arms | No date |
| Die G | Carpenters' Hall | 1774 |
| Die H | Independence Hall | 1776 |
| Die J | Public Buildings | No date |
| Die K | Capitol | No date |
| Die L | Watch | 1857 |

### 19 Millimeter Dies

| Die V | Memorial Hall | 1876 |
| Die W | Liberty Bell, small letters | 1876 |
| Die X | Liberty Bell, large letters | 1876 |
| Die Y | Independence Hall | 1776 |
| Die Z | New Masonic Hall | No date |

### Oval 25 by 20 Millimeter Dies

| Die OV | Independence Hall | 1876 |

There are well over 600 design and metal varieties in this series, plus at least 30 mulings of obverse dies with each other (no issuer name on token). In addition, there are a number of minor die varieties and die striation variations (not catalogued) which would push this total higher.

Most of the Centennial cards are scarce. It is doubtful if any merchant ordered as many as 1,000 pieces of any one type. Many of the specimens made for collectors by the token-makers were in the 5 to 25 mintage range.

The cards are generally priced in this volume for EF and Unc. only, since few actually received wear. Some did serve as pocket pieces (as they were intended to do) and show much wear, but these are the exceptions. In a few cases, F and VF specimens are priced where these are known to exist.

All Centennial tokens have plain edges and most are well struck up.

The Libertas Americana design (die A) is probably the most common occurring motif in the series. Yet it is also the most sought after by token collectors who are not specialists in the Centennial series. The device is a reduced-size imitation of the DuVivier medal struck at the Paris Mint to honor "American Liberty" on the occasion of the 1776 Declaration of Independence. The flowing hair Liberty head also was captured on the U.S.' earliest Large cent designs in 1793.

As one of America's favorite medallic design concepts, it is only natural that collectors should seek out the Libertas Americana type in preference to the stodgier dies with buildings (G, H, J, K, OV, V, Y and Z) or Liberty Bells (B, C, W and X).

A plate of Lingg Centennial card obverse dies appears here. The cards are listed in this manner under their issuers, and each reverse die (text side) is described under the issuer. In this manner line listings which save space and are easy to use are applied to the Lingg-struck series. (See Lingg & Bro., Philadelphia, for more details on the Centennial cards in the catalog itself.)

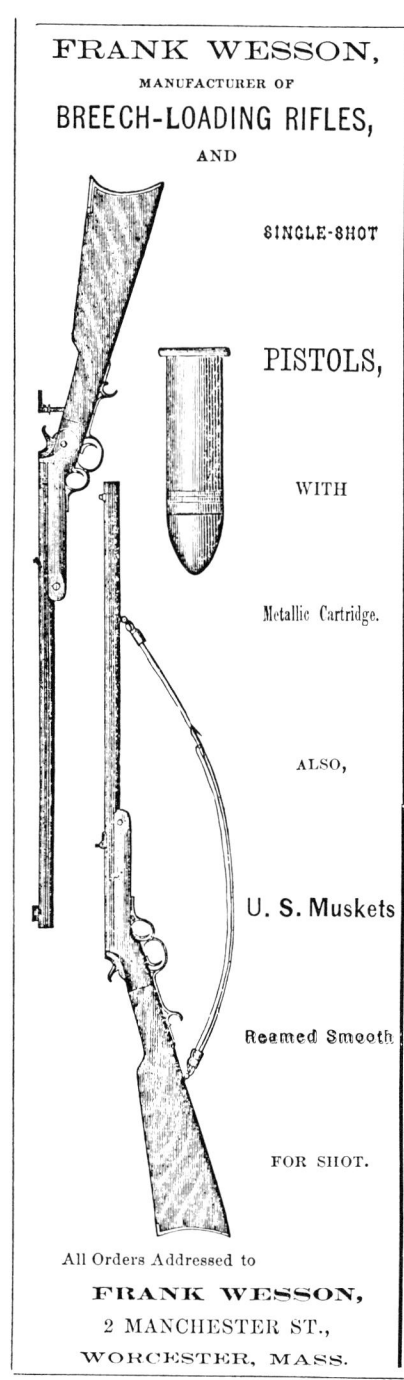

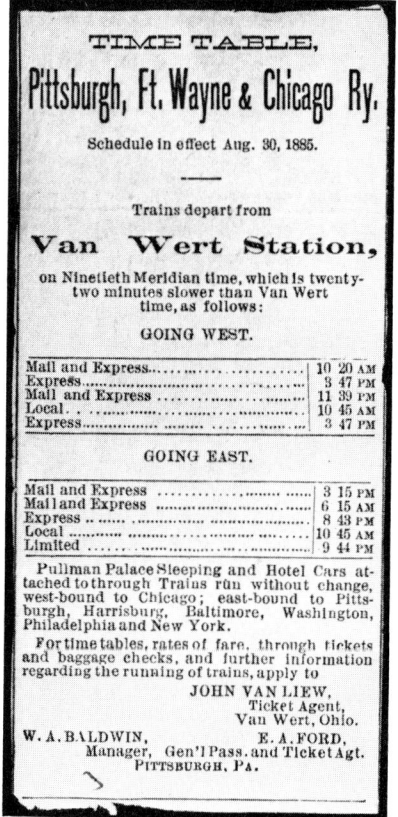

*Collectors can learn much about the period after the Civil War by reference to such things as old railway time tables. Van Wert is in west central Ohio, near the Indiana line.*

*Gunsmiths of New England were among the most prolific issuers of counterstamped coins. This is an 1868 advertisement of Frank Wesson, riflemaker of Worcester, Mass.*

# Abbreviations

| | | | |
|---|---|---|---|
| alum | aluminum | oct. | octagonal |
| Can. | Canadian | PF | proof |
| CN | cupronickel | P-L | proof-like |
| coll. | collection | poss. | possibly |
| ctsp | counterstamped | R | rarity (number) |
| CW | Civil War | rect. | rectangular |
| CWT | Civil War token | rev. | reverse |
| diff. | different | Rv: | reverse |
| EAT | Early American Tokens | sc | scalloped |
| EF | extremely fine | scal | scalloped |
| ex- | out of (collection) | Scrc | scarce |
| F | fine | S/Br | silvered brass |
| F.E. | Flying Eagle | S/Brass | silvered brass |
| G | good | S/Copper | silvered copper |
| G/Br | gilt brass | SL | small letters |
| G/Cop | gilt copper | S.L. | seated Liberty |
| G/WM | gilt white metal | slvd | silvered |
| Gilt/B | gilt brass | Span.-Am. | Spanish-American |
| Gilt/C | gilt copper | | |
| GS | German silver | S/WM | silvered white metal |
| hex. | hexagonal | Unc | uncirculated |
| HT | Hard Times | USMT | U.S. Merchant Tokens |
| HTT | Hard Times token | | |
| LL | large letters | USTT | U.S. Trade Tokens |
| Mex. | Mexican | VF | very fine |
| mm | millimeters | VG | very good |
| N/Steel | nickel-plated steel | WM | white metal |
| obv. | obverse | | |

*The Fulton fish market in New York, 1869, on the north side of Fulton Street between South and Front Streets, was built 1821 and replaced by a new building 1882. When this view was sketched the wholesale fish business was thriving; the 14 firms of the market ran a fleet of 111 ships and annually sold over $2 million worth of fish of all varieties — brought from as far away as Canada and North Carolina.*

# DATES OF ISSUE FOR SOME BILLIARD TOKEN TYPES

| | |
|---|---|
| Brunswick Bros. | 1875-1876 |
| Brunswick & Co. | 1877-1894 |
| J. M. Brunswick Billiard Mfg. Co. | 1872-1873 |
| J. M. Brunswick & Balke Co. | 1874-1884 |
| Brunswick Balke Collender Co. | 1884-1900 or later |
| H. W. Collender Co. | 1875-1884 |
| E. Brunswick Billiard Table Co. | 1887-1889 |
| Jacob Strahle & Co. | 1883-1891 |
| Estate of St. Germain | 1892 |
| St. Germain Billiard Co. | 1892-1900 or later |
| August Jungblut & Co. | ca. 1883-1891 |
| Chas. Pick & Co. | ca. 1880-1915 |

# CONTRIBUTORS

It would not be possible to name every numismatist upon whose research this catalog was constructed. Virtually all who wrote on the subject of post-Civil War trade tokens over the years would have to be thanked. The Bibliography mentions some of the more prominent of these sources.

Many of those named below provided direct assistance on this project, which began in earnest in 1981. Pricing input is due almost entirely to these collectors and dealers, without whose cooperation such evaluations would have had less credibility.

Edward Ahern
Anne Arundel County Historical Society
Dr. Herman Aqua
Bary Bender
Fred Borgmann
Richard Bottles Jr.
Q. David Bowers
Erwin E. Brauer
Walter Breen
Kenneth E. Bressett
Gregory G. Brunk
R. F. Buckley
Lester Burzinski
Carl W. A. Carlson
Garry Charman
John Cheramy
Alva Christensen
R. W. Colbert
Louis Crawford
James J. Curto
Jack R. Detwiler
Rich Eckebrecht
Lewis Egnew
John J. Ford
William E. Fowler
Damia R. Francis
Dave Freed
Dr. George Fuld
Melvin Fuld
Charlotte Gale
David M. Gale
Harvey Gamer
Thomas P. Gardner
David Gladfelter
Joe Gregory
Cindy Grellman

Dick Grinolds
Jay P. Guren
Kenneth Hallenbeck
N. Neil Harris
Jim Hartman
Rich Hartzog
Roy N. P. Hawkins
James H. Holtel
Lea Hornbeck
Byron Johnson
Charles V. Kappen
Chris Keogh
Charles E. Kirtley
Paul Koppenhaver
Frank L. Kovacs
Kurt R. Krueger
Larry Laevens
Robert D. Leonard
H. Joseph Levine
Donald R. Lewis
Gaylor Lipscomb
William Massey
Donald M. Miller
Ralph A. Mitchell
Montana Historical Society
Mormon Genealogical Library
Thomas Mulrooney
Su Nadin-Davis
Mike O'Brien
Benjamin Odesser
Kenneth A. Palmer
Mike Pfefferkorn
Gary Pipher
Robert M. Ramsay
Lou Rasera

Fred Reed
Jeff Rock
Glenn A. Rome
Richard Rossa
Jerry Roughton
Dean M. Ryder
David Schenkman
Joseph Schmidt
Donald T. Schmidt
Dr. Robert Schuman
J. Gavin Scott
Neil Shafer
Arlie R. Slabaugh
Bruce W. Smith
Hank Spangenberger
Stanley L. Steinberg
Elizabeth Steinle
John H. Stribhei
Harry L. Strough
Charles Sullivan
Emil Szauer
Steve Tanenbaum
Dr. Sol Taylor
Terry Trantow
Edmund Tylenda
Roy H. Van Ormer
Robert A. Vlack
Tom Wall
Douglas Watson
Thomas Wehner
Randy Weir
R. B. White
William Williges
Michael B. Zeddies
Charles Ziegler

And to those who preceded us ....

Edgar H. Adams
C. Wyllys Betts
P. Napoleon Breton
Charles I. Bushnell
Raymond Byrne
Dr. James Courteau
J. Doyle DeWitt
Gordon Dodrill
Frank G. Duffield
William F. Dunham
Thomas L. Elder
Milton Fishgold

Ralph Goldstone
Maurice M. Gould
Paul Hamm
John W. Haseltine
Richard D. Kenney
Lyman Haynes Low
C. Mathis
Donald M. Miller
Waldo C. Moore
Stuart Mosher
George R. Owen
Fred Pridmore

Wayte Raymond
Alfred Z. Reed
Lionel Rudduck
Alfred H. Satterlee
John W. Scott
Dr. Horatio Storer
Malcolm Storer
Isaac F. Wood
William Woodside
W. Eliot Woodward
Dr. Benjamin P. Wright
Farran Zerbe

# BIBLIOGRAPHY

Adams, E. H., "United States Store Cards," New York, 1920.

Anon., "A Missouri Record, in Missouri Numismatic Society bulletin for 1981-82. (A continuing report on numismatic items related to Missouri)

Baker, W. S., "Medallic Portraits of Washington," 1885. (Reprint, Iola, Wis., 1965)

Briggs & Co., "The New Hampshire Business Directory for 1868," Boston, 1868.

Brunk, G. G., "A Preliminary Listing of Merchant Advertising Countermarks," University, Ala., 1982.

Brunk, G. G., "World Countermarks on Medieval and Modern Coins," Lawrence, Mass., 1976.

Caldwell, W. "Coal Company Scrip," Fayetteville, W. Va., 1969.

Carey, A. M., "American Firearms Makers," New York, 1953.

Colbert, R. W., "Georgia Trade Tokens on Parade." In *Georgia State Token Exonumia Association Bulletin* for June, 1982.

Cooke, D. B. & Co., "City Directory for the Year 1859-60," Chicago, 1859.

Crawford, L., Farber, G. V., and Tylenda, E., "Louisiana Trade Tokens," Jackson, Miss., 1983.

Davison, C. W., "Minneapolis City Directory for 1880-81," Minneapolis, 1880.

DeWitt, J. D., "A Century of Campaign Buttons 1789-1889," Hartford, Conn., 1959.

Duffield, F. G., "A Trial List of the Countermarked Modern Coins of the World." In *The Numismatist* for 1919-1922. (With supplements)

Duffield, F. G., "The Merchant Cards and Tokens of Baltimore." In *The Numismatist* for March, 1907.

Dusterberg, R. B., "Cincinnati Mother of Expositions." In *TAMS Journal* for Aug., 1980.

Elrod, J. H., "Oswego Starch Factory." In *TAMS Journal* for Aug., 1982.

First National Bank of Mobile, "Highlights of 100 Years in Mobile," Mobile, Ala., 1965.

Ford, J., "The Cambridge Directory and Almanac for 1852," Cambridge, Mass., 1852.

Fowler, W. E. and Strough, H. L., "The Trade Tokens of Texas," in *TAMS Journal* for April, 1973 and Feb., 1979.

Fuld, G. and M., "U.S. Civil War Store Cards," 2nd ed., Lawrence, Mass., 1975.

Fuld, M. and G., "Token Collectors Pages." In *The Numismatist* for 1948-1971. (Reprint 1972)

Gluckman, A., and Satterlee, A. D., "American Gun Makers," Harrisburg, Pa., 1953.

Gluckman, A., "Identifying Old U.S. Muskets, Rifles and Carbines," Harrisburg, Pa., 1965.

Gould, M. M., "Counterstamped or Countermarked U.S. Large Cents." In *The Numismatist* for July, 1947 and Nov., 1957.

Gould, M. M., "Merchant Counterstamps on American Silver Coins," Wayland, Mass., 1962.

Grellman, C., "World's Industrial & Cotton Centennial Exposition Medals," Vandenberg AFB, Calif., 1982.

Hallenbeck, K. L., "Counterstamped U.S. Large Cents." In *The Numismatist* for Aug., 1965 and Aug., 1967.

Hoch, A. D., ed., "American Token Reprints," 1969. (Selected articles from *The Numismatist* 1904-1938)

Houghton, H. O. & Co., "United States Official Postal Guide," Boston, 1877.

Houghton Mifflin & Co., "United States Official Postal Guide," Boston, 1882.

Johnson, G., "Trade Tokens of Wisconsin," Wisconsin Rapids, Wis., 1967. (Supplement 1977)

Kappen, C. V., "California Tokens," El Cajon, Calif., 1976.

Kenney, R. D., "Struck Copies of Early American Coins," New York, 1952.

King, R. P., "Lincoln in Numismatics." In *The Numismatist* for 1924, 1927 and 1933. (Reprint 1966)

Lippincott, J. B. & Co., "History of Monroe County, New York," Philadelphia, 1877.

McCabe, James D., "The Illustrated History of the Centennial Exhibition," Philadelphia, 1876.

Miller, D. M., "A Catalogue of U.S. Store Cards or Merchants Tokens," Indiana, Pa., 1962.

Raymond, W., "Standard Catalogue of United States Coins and Tokens," New York, 1942.

Rulau, R. and Fuld, G., "American Game Counters." Iola, Wis., 1972. (With supplements 1973 and 1974)

Rulau, R., "Early American Tokens," Iola, Wis., 1981.

Rulau, R., "Hard Times Tokens," 2nd ed., Iola, Wis., 1981.

Rulau, R., "U.S. Merchant Tokens 1845-1860," Iola, Wis., 1982.

Rulau, R., "Early Tokens of the Queen City, Cincinnati." In *TAMS Journal* for April and June, 1974.

Rulau, R., "Numismatics of Old Alabama." In *Numismatic Scrapbook Magazine* for Feb. through Dec., 1971.

Rulau, R., "Money Evolution in West Ohio, from Barter to Credit Card." In *Numismatic Scrapbook Magazine* for Dec. 1969 through Dec. 1970.

Rulau, R., and Wigington, H., "Gold Dust Banking in Montana Territory." In *Numismatic Scrapbook Magazine* for Aug., 1969, et seq.

Schell, F. R., "Idaho Merchants' Tokens 1865-1970," 2nd ed., Twin Falls, Idaho, 1970.

Schenkman, D. E., "A Survey of American Trade Tokens," Lawrence, Mass., 1975. (Anthology of *The Numismatist* articles 1902-1968)

Schenkman, D. E., "Virginia Tokens," Hampton, Va., 1980.

Schenkman, D. E., "Joseph H. Merriam Die Sinker." In *The Numismatist* for April, 1980.

Schenkman, D. E., "The Heenan-Sayers Championship Prize Fight," in *TAMS Journal* for Dec., 1978.

Schmidt, J., "19th Century Illinois Exonumia." In *TAMS Journal* for Dec., 1977.

Schmidt, J., and Owen, G., "Businesses Merchants and Products on Counterstamped Coins," undated (1979).

Slabaugh, A. R., "American Centennial Tokens and Medals," Tecumseh, Mich., 1981.

Union Historical Co., "History of Buchanan County Missouri," 1881.

Walker, L. C., "Catalog of Oklahoma Tokens," Lawton, Okla., 1978.

Wright, B. P., "The American Store or Business Cards." In *The Numismatist* for 1898-1901. (Reprints 1963 et seq.)

Wyler, S. B., "The Book of Old Silver," New York, 1937.

## Numbering System

An entirely new numbering system has been devised for this reference book. Only a tiny fraction of the pieces catalogued herein were listed in the references by Adams and Miller, and thus an adaptation of the Adams-Miller numbering system was not considered appropriate.

The Rulau numbers used throughout this catalog constitute a system in which the state and city of issue (where known) are abbreviated as part of the number, and then a numerical system has been applied which takes into account some peculiarities of the 1866-1889 token-issuing period.

Cross-reference in the catalog to the numbers previously assigned to the same tokens by Adams-Miller, Wright, Kappen, Storer, King, Rulau-Fuld, Duffield, Brunk, Gould and other cataloguers, is extensive. Users of the catalog should have little difficulty in checking out this new catalog with entries on their token envelopes or in their collection ledgers.

The Rulau numbering system uses two letters to identify the state of issue, separated by a hyphen from two letters to identify the community of issue. Numerals are then added to each state-city breakdown. For example:

**Al-Bi 7** identifies the Dude Saloon one drink token of the 1880's issued in Birmingham, Alabama.

**Ca-Va 3** identifies the Will J. Shinn counterstamped quarter dollar of Vallejo, Calif., circa 1870's.

**Il-Ch 14** identifies the Dacosta 75-cent token of the 1880's issued in Chicago, Ill.

Special numbers have also been applied to non-local issues (**NL-12**, for example), and to mavericks, those unattributed pieces which plague every collector (**Mv 3**, etc.).

Tokens of other nations which are catalogued herein have a single-letter code: **C** for Canada, **B** for Great Britain, **F** for France, **I** for Ireland, **P** for Peru, etc. Thus, for example, **C15** or **B22**.

## Metals

| | |
|---|---|
| Brass | copper-zinc alloy, yellowish |
| Bronze | copper-tin alloy, brownish |
| Copper | pure copper, reddish |
| Cupronickel | copper-nickel alloy * |
| Galvanized Iron | zinc-iron, grayish |
| German Silver | copper-nickel-zinc alloy * |
| Gold | gold-copper alloy |
| Iron | pure iron, grayish |
| Nickel | pure nickel, magnetic * |
| Oroide | copper-zinc alloy, golden |
| Pot Metal | lead-based alloy, dark |
| Silver | silver-copper alloy |
| Steel | iron alloy, silvery |
| Tin | pure tin ** |
| Vulcanite | hardened rubber |
| White Metal | lead-tin alloy |

\* It is frequently difficult to tell nickel and its principal alloys apart. New, they all resemble silver and look much alike. Pure nickel is magnetic, however, and only a small amount of impurity removes the magnetic quality. Cupronickel resists tarnish, while German silver (also called nickel-silver, argentan and other names) tarnishes much like silver. The catalog may well be in error in describing some of these nickel-alloy pieces.

\*\* Pure tin is almost never used in token manufacture. Old catalogs frequently refer to "tin" pieces; what is meant is generally silvered white metal.

NOTE: Certain other substances are catalogued herein, namely Leather, Cardboard, Celluloid, Bone, Ivory, Mother-of-Pearl, etc. These terms are self-explanatory and should cause little trouble.

# ALABAMA

### THE DUDE SALOON
### Birmingham, Ala.

| Rulau | Date | Metal | Size | VG | F | VF | Unc |
|---|---|---|---|---|---|---|---|
| Al-Bi 7 | (1880's) | CN | 29mm | — | — | 150. | — |

Man with top hat, tails, monocle, cigarette, walking stick. THE DUDE SALOON. Rv: IOU / ONE / DRINK. Plain edge. (Dick Grinolds 1982 sale)

### B. M. GREGORY
### Mobile, Ala.

| Rulau | Date | Metal | Size | VG | F | VF | EF |
|---|---|---|---|---|---|---|---|
| Al-Mo 12 | 1872 | Silver | 39mm | — | — | 300. | — |

B. M. GREGORY. / MOBILE ALA. / 1872. ctsp on Bolivia silver 1835-PTS-IM 8-sueldos. (John Ford coll.)

# ARKANSAS

### S.B.

| Rulau | Date | Metal | Size | VG | F | VF | EF |
|---|---|---|---|---|---|---|---|
| Ar-Un 1 | (?) | Copper | 29mm | — | — | 40.00 | — |

S. B. ARKANSAS ctsp on U.S. Large cent. (Hallenbeck 1.760)

# CALIFORNIA

### C. ANCHARDOQUI
### Las Cruces, Calif.

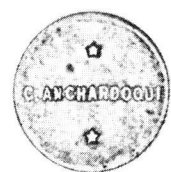

| Rulau | Date | Metal | Size | VG | F | VF | Unc |
|---|---|---|---|---|---|---|---|
| Ca-Lc 1 | (?) | Brass | 21mm | — | 15.00 | 30.00 | — |

* / C. ANCHARDOQUI / *. Rv: * GOOD FOR * / 1 / SHEEP SHEAR. Plain edge. (Kappen LC 1)

Sheep shearing tokens used on the Anchardoqui ranch at Las Cruces in Santa Barbara County.

### AMERICAN HOTEL BAR
### Petaluma, Calif.

| Rulau | Date | Metal | Size | VG | F | VF | Unc |
|---|---|---|---|---|---|---|---|
| Ca-Pe 1 | (1874-84) | Brass | 24mm | — | — | 25.00 | — |

THE J. M. BRUNSWICK & BALKE CO. Rv: AMERICAN HOTEL BAR, 1 DRINK, PETALUMA. Plain edge. (Brunswick 2009)

### J.B.
### (Jotham Bixby)
### Rancho Los Cerritos, Calif.

| Rulau | Date | Metal | Size | VG | F | VF | Unc |
|---|---|---|---|---|---|---|---|
| Ca-RC 1 | (1866-81) | Copper | 19mm | — | 20.00 | 35.00 | — |

J B. Rv: Blank. Plain edge. Irregularly round planchet. (Kappen Rancho Los Cerritos 1)

These were sheep shearing tallies used by Jotham Bixby on his Rancho Los Cerritos spread in Los Angeles County, from 1866 to 1881. Los Cerritos was located near present Long Beach.

## SIEBERT & VASSALO
## Columbia, Calif.

| Rulau | Date | Metal | Size | VG | F | VF | Unc |
|---|---|---|---|---|---|---|---|
| Ca-CO 7 | (1874-84) | Brass | 24mm | — | — | 25.00 | — |

Liberty Head left in central circle, THE J.M. BRUNSWICK & BALKE COS. / .CHECK. around. Rv: GOOD FOR 12 1/2 ¢ SIEBERT & VASSALO. Plain edge.

Siebert and Vassalo ran the Big Tree Saloon in Columbia.

## R.A. AYERS
## Los Angeles, Calif. (?)

| Rulau | Date | Metal | Size | VG | F | VF | Unc |
|---|---|---|---|---|---|---|---|
| Ca-LA 1 | (?) | Copper | 29mm | — | — | — | — |

R.A. AYERS ctsp on U.S. Large cent. (Hallenbeck 1.763; Brunk 14)

| Ca-LA 2 | (?) | Copper | 29mm | — | — | — | — |

R.A. AYERS / L.A. ctsp on U.S. Large cent. (Hallenbeck 1.759; Brunk 15)

The attribution to Los Angeles is arbitrary, based on the 'L.A.' punch on number 2, and needs verification. The initials could have a totally different meaning, for example LA for Louisiana.

## GEORGE LEE
## Rocklin, Calif.

| Rulau | Date | Metal | Size | VG | F | VF | Unc |
|---|---|---|---|---|---|---|---|
| Ca-RK 3 | (1883-91) | Brass | 26mm | — | — | 40.00 | — |

Billiard table. JACOB STRAHLE & CO. / BILLIARD M'F'R'S / 515 MARKET ST. / SAN FRANCISCO, CAL. Plain edge. (Wright 588)

## G. F. BOCHOW
## San Diego, Calif.

| Rulau | Date | Metal | Size | VG | F | VF | Unc |
|---|---|---|---|---|---|---|---|
| Ca-SD 1 | (1887-89) | Brass | 25mm | — | — | 40.00 | — |

THE E. BRUNSWICK BILLIARD TABLE CO. Rv: GOOD FOR / 12 1/2 ¢ / G. F. BOCHOW / 1427 H. ST. / BET. 5TH & 6TH. Plain edge. (Brunswick 1001)

## TILL A. BURNS
## San Diego, Calif.

| Rulau | Date | Metal | Size | VG | F | VF | Unc |
|---|---|---|---|---|---|---|---|
| Ca-SD 2 | (1874-84) | Brass | 24mm | — | — | 40.00 | — |

Billiard table at bottom. Above: THE / J.M. BRUNSWICK / AND / BALKE CO. Rv: GOOD FOR / 1 / TILL A. BURNS / SAN DIEGO / * DRINK *. Plain edge. (Brunswick 2052)

## BROWN BROS. & CO.
## San Francisco, Calif.

| Rulau | Date | Metal | Size | VG | F | VF | Unc |
|---|---|---|---|---|---|---|---|
| Ca-SF 7 | (1882-86) | Copper | 31mm | 8.50 | 15.00 | 25.00 | 40.00 |

Eagle at center, head turned right, SILVER SAVING SALE above, SOUVENIR below. Rv: BROWN BROS. & CO. / WHOLESALE / MANUFACTURERS / OF / CLOTHING / RETAILING / AT / WHOLESALE / PRICES / 121-123 SANSOME ST. S.F. Plain edge. Two die varieties. (Kappen S.F. 334)

Brown Brothers & Co. (Morris & Lewis Brown and Bernard Bahr Sheideman) were first listed 1868-69 as agents of Oregon Woolen Mills, and capitalists, with offices at the southeast corner of Sansome and Sacramento Sts. In 1870 the address was 4 Battery St.; in 1871, 24 Sansome; 1872-80, 24 and 26 Sansome; after 1880 they were at 121-123 Sansome St., the address on the tokens. When last listed in 1885-86, Ralph Brown had been added to the company's ownership.

## W. BUCKLEY
## San Francisco, Calif.

| Rulau | Date | Metal | Size | VG | F | VF | EF |
|---|---|---|---|---|---|---|---|
| Ca-SF 16 | (?) | Bronze | 23mm | — | — | 55.00 | — |

W. BUCKLEY / S. F. ctsp on U.S. 1864 2-Cent piece.

## CERCLE FRANCAIS
## San Francisco, Calif.

| Rulau | Date | Metal | Size | VG | F | VF | Unc |
|---|---|---|---|---|---|---|---|
| Ca-SF 20 | (1888-1905) | Brass | 25mm | 5.00 | 7.50 | — | — |

CERCLE / FRANCAIS. Rv: GOOD FOR ONE / 25 ¢ / CIGAR. Plain edge.

The Cercle Francais ("French Club") appears in the directories for 1888 through 1905.

## CERCLE M. S.
## (San Francisco, Calif.?)

| Rulau | Date | Metal | Size | VG | F | VF | EF |
|---|---|---|---|---|---|---|---|
| Ca-SF 22 | (?) | GS | 27.5mm | — | — | — | — |

Eagle with drooping wings on plain field. Rv: CERCLE / 1 / M. * S.

This token was first reported by Schmidt & Owen in *TAMS Journal* for Oct. 1980, page 192. It is apparently a companion to the Mauduit & Co. 'Cercle de San Francisco' and the Cercle Francais pieces. Just what social or fraternal role these 'cercles' (clubs) served is yet to be discovered.

## CHUNG JAN
## San Francisco, Calif.

| Rulau | Date | Metal | Size | F | VF | Unc |
|---|---|---|---|---|---|---|
| Ca-SF 25 | (ca 1885) | Brass | 28mm | 12.50 | — | — |

* / CHUNG / JAN / 1438 1/2 / L. H. MOISE S.F. Rv: Similar to obverse, but from differing die; no signature of tokenmaker. Plain edge.

Struck by L. H. Moise of San Francisco. The attribution to San Francisco is unverified, but probable. (See *The Numismatist* for Jan. 1951, page 52.)

## CORNELL WATCH CO.
## San Francisco, Calif.

| Rulau | Date | Metal | Size | F | VF | EF | Unc |
|---|---|---|---|---|---|---|---|
| Ca-SF 28 | 1875 | S/WM | 30.5mm | 18.50 | 25.00 | 40.00 | 75.00 |

Clock face, CORNELL WATCH CO. / SAN FRANCISCO in upper part of face. Rv: TENTH INDUSTRIAL FAIR / SAN FRANCISCO / 1875 / * OF THE MECHANICS INSTITUTE *. Plain edge. (Wright 1379) (Kappen S.F. 576)

Cornell Watch Co. apparently was in business only 1875-1877. Paul Cornell was president and Henry Cox secretary; the works were at West 4th between Bryant and Harrison. R.H. French became secretary in 1877. In the 1877-78 directory, French was listed as secretary of the California Watch Co. at 120 Sutter St.

## DEUTSCHE FRIEDENSFEIER
## San Francisco, Calif.

| Rulau | Date | Metal | Size | VF | EF | Unc Proof |
|---|---|---|---|---|---|---|
| Ca-SF 30 | 1871 | Silver | 30mm | — | — | — 175. |

Seated Germania facing, with six flags around her. Around: ZUR ERINNERUNG A. D. DEUTSCHE FRIEDENSFEIER. Below: .IN SAN FRANCISCO. Rv: Crossed German flag and sword within oak and olive wreath. Around: EINIGKEIT MACHT STARK. DURCH KAMPF ZUM SIEG. Below: D. 22. MAERZ / 1871. Plain edge. Weight 11.7 grams.

In commemoration of the German peace celebration following the Franco-Prussian war. Dies cut by Albrecht Kuner, the maker of many dies for territorial gold coin issues. (See *The Numismatist*, 1910, page 107.)
Specimens appeared in the Garrett IV sale in 1981 and the Clifford sale in 1982.
(See background notes under Milwaukier Friedens-Feier, Milwaukee, Wis.)

## EUREKA (Hotel)
## San Francisco, Calif.

| Rulau | Date | Metal | Size | VG | F | VF Unc |
|---|---|---|---|---|---|---|
| Ca-SF 33 | 1867 | Brass | 20mm | — | 20.00 | — 40.00 |

(Three rosettes) / EUREKA / * 1867 *. Rv: 5 / CENTS. 11 stars around. Toothed borders on each side. Plain edge. (Kappen S.F. 784)

| Ca-SF 34 | 1867 | Brass | 20mm | — | 20.00 | — 40.00 |

Similar, but 10 / CENTS on reverse. 12 stars around. Plain edge. (Kappen S.F. 785)

| Ca-SF 35 | 1867 | Brass | 22mm | — | 20.00 | — 40.00 |

Similar, but 50 / CENTS on reverse. 11 stars around. Plain edge. (Wright 296; Kappen S.F. 786; Fuld NC-12b)

Eureka Hotel on Sansome Street was under the proprietorship of Jacob Levy, 1864-1868. The attribition is circumstantial.

## W. FRANK & CO.
## San Francisco, Calif.

| Rulau | Date | Metal | Size | VG | F | VF | Unc |
|---|---|---|---|---|---|---|---|
| Ca-SF 38 | (1867-70) | Brass | 27mm | 85.00 | 100. | 140. | 250. |

Eagle with U.S. shield on its breast at center. Around: THE LARGEST STOCK OF BAS-

| Rulau | Date | Metal | Size | VG | F | VF | Unc |
|---|---|---|---|---|---|---|---|

KETS AND WILLOW WARE *. Rv: W. FRANK & CO. / JMPORTERS / OF / TOYS AND FANCY / GOODS / SAN FRANCISCO / CAL. Plain edge. (Kappen S.F. 887; Miller Calif. 4)

| Ca-SF 39 | (1867-70) | WM | 27mm | 35.00 | 45.00 | 75.00 | 175. |

As 4. Plain edge. (Not in Kappen; Miller Calif. 4A)

William Frank & Co. were at 406 and 408 Stockton in 1867. Then at 406 and 408 Battery St. 1868-69, and at 406 Battery St. in 1870.

## N. J. HYMAN
## San Francisco, Calif.

| Rulau | Date | Metal | Size | VG | F | VF | Unc |
|---|---|---|---|---|---|---|---|
| Ca-SF 42 | (1876-77) | Copper | 32mm | 15.00 | 25.00 | 75.00 | 150. |

N. J. HYMAN / S.F. CAL / SOLE AGENTS FOR / — HYMAN'S — / ENGLISH BLACK / GARNET JEWELLER / WHOLESALE / & RETAIL / 205 KEARNY ST. Rv: N. J. HYMAN / S.F. CAL / IMPORTER OF WATCHES / * FINE JEWELLERY / FRENCH ENGLISH / JAPANESE & CHINESE / FANCY GOODS / — &C — 205. KEARNY ST. (Wright 483) (Kappen S.F. 1191; Miller Calif. 5)

| Ca-SF 43 | 1878 | Copper | 32mm | 20.00 | 30.00 | 75.00 | 150. |

Similar to 5, but the address has been removed from the die. (Kappen S.F. 1191A; Miller Calif. 5A)

Nathan J. Hyman in 1875 was at the S.W. Corner of Montgomery and Pine Streets, then 1876-77 at 205 Kearny St. where the tokens were issued. In 1878 he was at 307 Kearny St.
Hyman was a clerk for Joseph Brothers, also token issuers 1854-60, in 1860-61. He was a salesman in 1867.

## MAUDUIT & CO.
## San Francisco, Calif.

| Rulau | Date | Metal | Size | VG | F | VF | Unc |
|---|---|---|---|---|---|---|---|
| Ca-SF 45 | (?) | WM | 27.5mm | 250. | 300. | 400. | — |

MAUDUIT / ¢ (sic) / COMPNIE. Rv: CERCLE DE SAN FRANCISCO / 1/2 / DOLLAR / (ornament). Plain edge. (Wright 675; Kappen S.F. 465; Miller Calif. 8)

This token was missing from all the great 19th century token collections, Dr. Wright says. Thus far, Mauduit & Co.'s "San Francisco Club" has eluded attribution. Some authorities feel it may be a Latin American token.

## NEWMAN BROS.
## San Francisco, Calif.

| Rulau | Date | Metal | Size | VG | F | VF | Unc |
|---|---|---|---|---|---|---|---|
| Ca-SF 50 | (1865-66) | Brass | 20mm | 20.00 | 50.00 | 125. | 250. |

Liberty head with 13 stars around, COMP. S. MARKE below. Rv: NEWMAN BROS. /

| Rulau | Date | Metal | Size | VG | F | VF | Unc |
|---|---|---|---|---|---|---|---|

IMPORTERS / OF TOYS & / BASKETS / SAN FRANCISCO. Plain edge. (Miller Calif. 8½)

| Rulau | Date | Metal | Size | VG | F | VF | Unc |
|---|---|---|---|---|---|---|---|
| Ca-SF 51 | (1865-66) | WM | 20mm | 45. | 60. | 140. | 250. |

As 8½. Plain edge. (Miller Calif. 8½A)

Thomas and Edward Newman established a brush factory in May 1856 at 74 Sansome St. In 1858 they were at 74 Battery St., then at 303 Battery St. in 1864-65, and at 406 & 408 Battery St. in 1865-66. They imported, manufactured and dealt in brushes. In 1865-66 they also advertised themselves as "importers and jobbers of wood and willow ware, etc." The partnership apparently dissolved in 1868.

The game counter-type tokens are believed to emanate from the 1865-66 period.

## WEIL & LEVY
### San Francisco, Calif.

| Rulau | Date | Metal | Size | VG | F | VF | Unc |
|---|---|---|---|---|---|---|---|
| Ca-SF 60 | (1864-70) | Brass | 22mm | — | — | 75.00 | 150. |

Spread eagle, U.S. shield on its breast, head turned left, scroll above reads IMPORTERS OF FANCY GOODS. Above: WEIL & LEVY. Below: SAN FRANCISCO. Rv: Laurel wreath, the center blank. Plain edge. (R-F Sca-16; Miller Calif. 12A). Rarity 9.

| Ca-SF 61 | (1864-70) | Brass | 22mm | — | — | 60.00 | 150. |

Obverse as 60. Rv: Liberty Head left in circle of 11 stars, SP. MARKE below. Plain edge. (Kurth 28; R-F Sca-17; Miller Calif. 12B). Rarity 7.

| Ca-SF 62 | (1864-70) | Brass | 27.5mm | — | — | 60.00 | 150. |

As 61, but in larger size. Plain edge. (Kurth 29; R-F Sca-18; Miller Calif. 12). Rarity 7.

| Ca-SF 63 | (1864-70) | Brass | 33.5mm | — | — | 75.00 | 150. |

Similar to 60, but in larger size. Plain edge. (Kurth 30; R-F Sca-19; Miller Calif. 12D). Rarity 8.

| Ca-SF 64 | (1864-70) | Brass | 34mm | — | — | 75.00 | 150. |

Obverse similar to 60. Rv: WEIL & LEVY below eagle. Plain edge. (R-F Sca-20; Miller Calif. 12C). Rarity 8. (This piece has not been examined)

Meyer Weil and Solomon A. Levy, in partnership 1864-1870, were at the northwest corner of Sacramento and Battery Streets 1864-1865. By 1870 they were at 113 Battery Street. In 1871 the firm name became Weil & Woodleaf.

In the listing above, all the tokens are store card-game counters for use in card games. Ca-SF 60 and 61 are $5 size, Ca-SF 62 $10 size, and Ca-SF 63 and 64 are $20 gold piece size. All are quite rare.

## GALL & MADDENS
### Stockton, Calif.

| Rulau | Date | Metal | Size | VG | F | VF | Unc |
|---|---|---|---|---|---|---|---|
| Ca-St 4 | (1874-84) | CN | 24mm | — | — | 40.00 | — |

Pool table at center, THE J.M. BRUNSWICK / & / BALKE COS above, CHECK below. Rv: GOOD FOR / 1 / DRINK / GALL & MADDENS / STOCKTON, CAL. Plain edge. (Brunswick 2132)

| Rulau | Date | Metal | Size | VG | F | VF | Unc |
|---|---|---|---|---|---|---|---|
| Ca-St 6 | (1874-85) | Brass | 25mm | — | — | 40.00 | — |

Liberty head left within central circle, THE J.M. BRUNSWICK & BALKE COS. around, .CHECK. below. Rv: GOOD FOR / 1 / DRINK / J.D. GALL. Plain edge. (Brunswick 2133)

There may be no connection between the J.D. Gall maverick and the Gall & Maddens piece, though the coincidence seems pretty good. The J.D. Gall piece is probably the earlier.

## NEW ESS(EX) SALOON
### Truckee, Calif.

| Rulau | Date | Metal | Size | VG | F | VF | Unc |
|---|---|---|---|---|---|---|---|
| Ca-Tk 4 | (1874-84) | Brass | 25mm | — | — | 40.00 | — |

THE J.M. BRUNSWICK & BALKE CO. Rv: GOOD FOR / 1 / NEW ESS SALOON / TRUCKEE, CALIF. Plain edge. (Brunswick 2263)

## WILL J. SHINN
### Vallejo, Calif.

| Rulau | Date | Metal | Size | VG | F | VF | EF |
|---|---|---|---|---|---|---|---|
| Ca-Va 3 | (?) | Silver | 25mm | — | — | 100. | — |

WILL. J. / SHINN / VALLEJO. ctsp on U.S. 1868-S Liberty Seated quarter. (Dr. Sol Taylor collection)

Vallejo, in Sonoma County, is just north of San Francisco, on San Francisco Bay. In 1877 it was in Solano County.

## A. ZELLER
### (probably California)

| Rulau | Date | Metal | Size | VG | F | VF | Unc |
|---|---|---|---|---|---|---|---|
| Ca-Un 1 | (1883-91) | Brass | 24mm | — | 30.00 | 40.00 | — |

GOOD FOR / A 5¢ / A. ZELLER / * DRINK *. Rv: Pool table in center. AUG. JUNGBLUT & CO. / MANUFACTURERS / — OF — above; SAN FRANCISCO, CAL. below. Beaded rim. Plain edge. (Not in Kappen)

August Jungblut & Co., San Francisco manufacturers of pool tables and supplies, prepared tokens for their clients in the 1883-1891 period. Zeller has not been located.

*Advertisement from B. F. Stilwell & Co.'s San Francisco Business Directory and Mercantile Guide for 1864.*

# COLORADO

## KNOX BROS.
## Canon City, Colo.

| Rulau | Date | Metal | Size | F | VF | EF | Unc |
|---|---|---|---|---|---|---|---|
| Co-Ca 3 | (?) | WM | 38mm | — | 75.00 | — | — |

Seated female next to a broken column, looking at the sun rising over the sea. A harp at the female's side. All enclosed by a wreath of shamrocks, a star near the wreath's top opening. Rv: KNOX BROS. / KB (monogram) / * CANON CITY COLO. *. Rare. (Wright 1490)

The seated female and sun undoubtedly represents Ireland awaiting deliverance. The Fenian movement was strong in the American West in the 1866-1875 period; this piece might mourn the failure of the two Fenian raids into Canada in 1866 and 1870.

## C. C. R. R.
## (Colorado Central Railroad)
## Central City, Colo.

Wood hauler tokens of the C.C.C.R. in various fractional card denominations were listed by Dr. P. Whiteley in *The Numismatist* in error. The tokens were actually issues of M.C.R.R. (Michigan Central Railroad), which see.

## L.T. NOSSAMAN
## Central City, Colo.

| Rulau | Date | Metal | Size | VG | F | VF | EF |
|---|---|---|---|---|---|---|---|
| Co-CC 12 | (?) | Silver | 28.3mm | — | — | 250. | — |

L.T. NOSSAMAN / (star) / CENTRAL / (three leaves) CITY, / (star) / (three leaves) COL. TER. (three leaves) ctsp on Spanish-American 1783-Mo-FF 2-reales, which has been broadened by the striking from 27 to 28.3mm. There is also an engraved circle of diamonds struck to form a border around the counterstamping. Holed flan. (Spangenberger coll.)

Colorado was a territory only from 1861 to August 1, 1876, when it was admitted to the Union as a state.

## HUBERT MINE
## Cripple Creek, Colo.

| Rulau | Date | Metal | Size | VG | F | VF | EF |
|---|---|---|---|---|---|---|---|
| Co-Cp 3 | (1880's) | Brass | ---mm | — | — | 150. | — |

(All incused) HUBERT MINE / 1/4 / * CORD *. Rv: Blank. Plain edge.

| Co-Cp 5 | (1880's) | Brass | ---mm | — | — | 150. | — |

HUBERT MILL (in relief in recessed arc) / 1/3 (incused) / 1/4 CORD (in relief in recessed arc). Rv: Blank. Plain edge.

These are ore haulers' tokens or chips, ore being measured in cords rather than weighed. A "cord" of ore in Gilpin County, Colo. equaled 7 to 10 tons of weight. A quarter cord filled a light wagon; the third cord a somewhat heavier wagon; and a "half cord" wagon had wheels over 50 inches in diameter, and high sideboards.

(See "Numismatic Reminiscences from the Shining Mountains" by Dr. Philip Whitely, in *The Numismatist* for June, 1967)

## JOSLIN & PARK
## Leadville, Colo. and
## Salt Lake City, Utah

| Rulau | Date | Metal | Size | VG | F | VF | Unc |
|---|---|---|---|---|---|---|---|
| Co-Le-5 | (?) | ? | ---mm | — | — | 75.00 | — |

JOSLIN & PARK / JEWELERS / LEADVILLE, COLO. & SALT LAKE, UTAH.

An advertising whist counter. (Stanley Steinberg 1982 sale number 85, lot 35).

## LEADVILLE, COLO.

| Rulau | Date | Metal | Size | F | VF | EF | Unc |
|---|---|---|---|---|---|---|---|
| Co-Ld 7 | 1880 | Gold | 15mm | — | — | — | Unique |

LEADVILLE. / COLO. / 1880 engraved on obverse of U.S. 1871 gold dollar.

Generally engraved pieces (love tokens) are excluded from this reference, but this Colorado Territory piece provides an exception.

## EV. LUTH. CHURCH
### Brighton, Colo.

| Rulau | Date | Metal | Size | VG | F | VF | Unc |
|---|---|---|---|---|---|---|---|
| Co-Br 1 | (1844-1900) | CN | 29mm | — | 40.00 | — | — |

Pool table, THE BRUNSWICK BALKE / COLLENDER / COMPY. above, CHECK in exergue. Rv: EV. LUTH. CHURCH / (ornament) / BRIGHTON / COLO. Plain edge. (Brunswick 5201) Scalloped flan.

## NATIONAL MINING AND INDUSTRIAL EXPOSITION
### Denver, Colo.

| Rulau | Date | Metal | Size | F | VF | EF | Unc |
|---|---|---|---|---|---|---|---|
| Co-De 5 | 1882 | Silver | 31mm | — | — | — | 125. |

Mountainous mining scene fills entire field. The scene includes a cutaway of the underground workings. Rv: Buildings across center, small E. JACCARD JEWELRY CO. ST. LOUIS MO. underground line. Above: NATIONAL MINING. Below: DENVER CO. 1882 / (arm and hammer) / AND INDUSTRIAL EXPOSITION. Plain edge.

The workmanship on this medalet is superb. Probably much more rare than price indicates.

## HY. CZARNOWSKY
### Silver Plume, Colo.

| Rulau | Date | Metal | Size | VG | F | VF | Unc |
|---|---|---|---|---|---|---|---|
| Co-SP 2 | (1887-94) | Brass | 25mm | — | 40.00 | — | — |

-.- / CHECK / -.- in central circle, BRUNSWICK & COMPANY. above, CHICAGO. below. Rv: GOOD FOR / 5¢ / HY. CZARNOWSKY / .IN. / TRADE. Plain edge. (Brunswick 19)

# CONNECTICUT

## ALFRED S. ROBINSON
### Hartford, Conn.

| Rulau | Date | Metal | Size | F | VF | Unc | Proof |
|---|---|---|---|---|---|---|---|
| Ct-Ha 10 | (?) | Copper | 28mm | — | — | — | Unique |

Building of C.G. Day & Co. at 56 Asylum Street, before which are pedestrians and carriages. Rv: ALFRED S. ROBINSON. / BANKER / BROKER / AND / NOTARY PUBLIC / DEALER IN / STOCKS BONDS NOTES / LAND WARRENTS / UNCURRENT MONEY AND / ALL KINDS OF AMERICAN / & FOREIGN / SPECIE / 309 MAIN ST HARTFORD CONN. (The only specimen is in Wadsworth Athenaeum, Hartford). (Miller Conn. 6)

| Ct-Ha 11 | 1861 | Silver | 28mm | — | 75.00 | 250. | 350. |

Imitation of Higley threepence (standing deer left, VALUE. ME. AS. YOU. PLEASE around, (hand) III (star) below. Rv: ALFRED S. ROBINSON / BANKER / NUMISMATIST & / NOTARY PUBLIC / DEALER IN / STOCKS. BONDS. NOTES. / LAND WARRANTS / UNCURRENT MONEY / & ALL KINDS OF / AMERICAN & FOREIGN / SPECIE / HARTFORD, CONN. 1861. (Miller Conn. 7)

| Rulau | Date | Metal | Size | F | VF | EF | Unc |
|---|---|---|---|---|---|---|---|
| Ct-Ha 12 | 1861 | S/Copper | 28mm | — | 25.00 | 50.00 | 100. |

As 11. (Miller Conn. 7A)

| Ct-Ha 13 | 1861 | Copper | 28mm | — | 20.00 | 40.00 | 100. |

As 11. Mintage: 150. (Miller Conn. 8)

| Ct-Ha 14 | 1861 | Brass | 28mm | — | 20.00 | 40.00 | 100. |

As 11. (Miller Conn. 9)

| Ct-Ha 15 | 1861 | WM | 28mm | — | 25.00 | 50.00 | 100. |

As 11. Mintage: 150. Two specimens appeared in the Dec. 17, 1981 Springfield sale. (Miller Conn. 10)

| Ct-Ha 16 | 1861 | CN | 28mm | — | 30.00 | 65.00 | 100. |

As 11. (Miller Conn. 11)

| Ct-Ha 19 | (1860's) | WM | 41mm | — | — | 20.00 | 45.00 |

Bust facing at center, ROBERT FULTON above, BORN 1765 DIED 1815 below. Rv: Steamship at center. Above: (13 stars) / STEAM NAVIGATION / WAS FIRST ESTABLISD (sic) IN THE / UNITED STATES. Below: ON THE / HUDSON RIVER / 1807 / ALFRED S. ROBINSON'S HISTORICAL SERIES NO 2. Plain edge.

## LITCHFIELD S. CO.
### Litchfield, Conn.

| Rulau | Date | Metal | Size | G | VG | F | EF |
|---|---|---|---|---|---|---|---|
| Co-Li 1 | (?) | Bronze | 23mm | — | — | 40.00 | — |

LITCHFIELD / S CO. in closed arc, ctsp on U.S. 1866 2-cent piece. (Stanley L. Steinberg coll., Malden, Mass.)

[23]

# C.W. BETTS
## New Haven, Conn.

| Rulau | Date | Metal | Size | F | VF | EF | Unc |
|---|---|---|---|---|---|---|---|
| Ct-NH 3 | (1880's) | Copper | 32mm | — | — | — | Rare |

C.W. BETTS, NUMISMATIST. Rude impression. (Miller Conn. 16)

| Ct-NH 4 | (?) | Lead | 32mm | — | — | — | Rare |

As 16. (Miller Conn. 17)

| Ct-NH 6 | (?) | Copper | 28mm | — | — | — | Rare |

C.W. BETTS, COINS, MEDALS (etc.). Rude impression. (Miller Conn. 18)

| Ct-NH 7 | (?) | Lead | ---mm | — | — | — | Rare |

As 18. (Miller Conn. 19)

C.(harles) Wyllys Betts was a collector of great imagination and creativity, who is responsible for a number of Colonial imitations and concoctions. He is best known, though, for his book *American Colonial History Illustrated by Contemporary Medals* (New York, 1894; Quarterman reprint 1972). This book is based upon Bett's manuscript, which was left unfinished at his death in 1887. His brother Frederic H. Betts and nephew Wyllys Rosseter Betts, plus editors Lyman Haynes Low and William T. R. Marvin finished the work and enlivened it with copious footnotes and line illustrations. The 1972 reprint added photographs of many specimens.

| Rulau | Date | Metal | Size | F | VF | EF | Unc |
|---|---|---|---|---|---|---|---|
| Ct-NH 8 | (1880's) | — | 23mm | — | — | — | Rare |

CHAS WYLLYS / BETTS. Center blank. Rv: Blank. Plain edge. (Kenneth Bressett coll.)

| Rulau | Date | Metal | Size | F | VF | EF | Unc |
|---|---|---|---|---|---|---|---|
| Ct-NH 9 | (?) | — | 29mm | — | — | — | Rare |

CONNECTICUT / NEW . HAVEN (boss). Ornament at center. Four leaf-like ornaments at bottom. Rv: Radiant shield. (Kenneth Bressett coll.)

Bressett says that Ct-NH 9 is a modern fantasy made by C. Wyllys Betts. Betts made dozens of imitations of Colonial coins and created other concoctions. His own store cards are quite rare.

# HUSSEY & MURRAY
## New Haven, Conn.

| Rulau | Date | Metal | Size | | | |
|---|---|---|---|---|---|---|
| Ct-NH 10 | (?) | — | 31mm | — | — | Rare |

HUSSEY & MURRAY / BAKERS / CHOCOLATE / (rosette of dots). Beaded rim. Rv: Intaglio of obverse. Plain edge. (Kenneth Bressett coll.)

Another Betts fantasy concoction, Kenneth Bressett says. As all Betts imitations, it is very scarce and not well known in numismatic circles.

# WILCOX
## New Haven, Conn.

| Rulau | Date | Metal | Size | VG | F | VF | EF |
|---|---|---|---|---|---|---|---|
| Ct-NH 20 | (?) | Copper | 29mm | — | — | 40.00 | — |

WILCOX NEW HAVEN ctsp on U.S. Large cent. (Hallenbeck 23.514).

# LESLIE WHITE
## Waterbury, Conn.

| Rulau | Date | Metal | Size | VG | F | VF | EF |
|---|---|---|---|---|---|---|---|
| Ct-Wb 7 | (?) | CN | 22mm | — | — | 40.00 | — |

LESLIE WHITE, WATERBURY, CT. ctsp on U.S. 1887 Liberty Head nickel.

# DISTRICT OF COLUMBIA

### A. DITTRICH
### Washington, D.C.

| Rulau | Date | Metal | Size | VG | F | VF | Unc |
|---|---|---|---|---|---|---|---|
| DC-Wa 10 | 1875 | Brass | 26mm | — | 25.00 | — | — |

Grecian head with coronet left, 11 stars around, 1875 below. Rv: A. DITTRICH / HATTER / — AND — / FURRIER / 724 / 7TH. ST. / WASHINGTON. D.C. Plain edge. Scarce. (Wright 252)

### KNIGHTS OF THE GOLDEN EAGLE
### Washington, D.C.

| Rulau | Date | Metal | Size | F | VF | EF | Unc |
|---|---|---|---|---|---|---|---|
| DC-Wa 17 | 1888 | Brass | 25.5mm | — | — | — | 20.00 |

Capitol at center, ANNUAL CONVOCATION OF SUPREME CASTLE / KNIGHTS OF THE GOLDEN EAGLE above, WASHINGTON / MAY 22. / . 1888. . below. Rv: Laurel wreath around rim surrounds blank center, apparently for inscribing. Plain edge.

### H. SCHWARZENBERG
### Washington, D.C.

| Rulau | Date | Metal | Size | VG | F | VF | Unc |
|---|---|---|---|---|---|---|---|
| DC-Wa 23 | (?) | Brass | 25mm | — | — | — | — |

Harp. A FINE ORCHESTRION WILL PERFORM / EVERY / AFTERNOON / AND / EVENING. Rv: H. SCHWARZENBERG'S / TERRITORIAL / * / HOUSE / 468 / PENN AVE / WASHINGTON, D.C. Plain edge. (Wright 964)

### SOCIETY ARMY OF THE CUMBERLAND
### Washington, D.C.

| Rulau | Date | Metal | Size | VG | F | VF | Unc |
|---|---|---|---|---|---|---|---|
| DC-Wa 25 | 1879 | WM | 23mm | — | — | — | Scarce |

Wreath encloses: THOMAS / 1870. Rv: SOCIETY ARMY OF THE CUMBERLAND / WASHINGTON / CITY / 1879. Plain edge. (Wright 1138)

### SOCIETY ARMY OF THE TENNESSEE
### Washington, D.C.

| Rulau | Date | Metal | Size | F | VF | EF | Unc |
|---|---|---|---|---|---|---|---|
| DC-Wa 27 | 1876 | WM | 21mm | — | — | 17.00 | 27.50 |

Mounted officer at center, McPHERSON above, 1864 in exergue. Tiny G H L at rim at 8 o'clock. Rv: SOCIETY ARMY OF THE TENNESSEE / WASHINGTON / CITY / 1876. Plain edge.

| | | | | | | | |
|---|---|---|---|---|---|---|---|
| DC-Wa 27A | 1876 | Copper | 21mm | — | — | 17.00 | 27.50 |

As 27. Plain edge.

| | | | | | | | |
|---|---|---|---|---|---|---|---|
| DC-Wa 27B | 1876 | Brass | 21mm | — | — | 17.00 | 27.50 |

As 27. Plain edge.

### W.C. TAX
### (Washington City Dog Tax)
### Washington, D.C.

| Rulau | Date | Metal | Size | F | VF | EF | Unc |
|---|---|---|---|---|---|---|---|
| DC-Wa 32 | 1880 | CN | *22 by 25.5mm | — | — | — | — |

Dog. W. C. D. C. around: TAX in exergue. Rv: NO. / 1880. (Wright 1211)

There is space on reverse to stamp in a number.

*Shield-shaped flan.

# GEORGIA

## SPRAGUE & BLODGETT
### Georgia

| Rulau | Date | Metal | Size | G | VG | F | EF |
|---|---|---|---|---|---|---|---|
| Ga-Un 7 | (?) | Silver | 31mm | — | — | — | 200. |

SPRAGUE & BLODGETT'S / ADMIT / ONE / GEORGIA MINSTRELS ctsp on U.S. Liberty Seated 1876 half dollar. (Gould 64; Brunk 354)

The attribution to Georgia is purely arbitrary based on the legend. For comparison, Daniel Emmett's Virginia Minstrels played primarily in New York.

## PIEDMONT EXPOSITION
### Atlanta, Ga.

| Rulau | Date | Metal | Size | F | VF | EF | Unc |
|---|---|---|---|---|---|---|---|
| Ga-At 4 | 1889 | WM | 32mm | — | 60.00 | — | — |

Phoenix rising from flames at center, RESURGENS above, * 1864 * ATLANTA, GA. * 1889 * below. Rv: Buildings at center, PIEDMONT EXPOSITION above, MAIN BUILDING / (U.S. shield between four draped flags). There is an ornate border on each side of this medalet. Plain edge.

## RESURGENS
### Atlanta, Ga.

| Rulau | Date | Metal | Size | F | VF | EF | Unc |
|---|---|---|---|---|---|---|---|
| Ga-AT 8 | 1865 | Brass | 14.5mm | — | — | 75.00 | — |

Phoenix rising from flames at center, 1847 RESURGENS 1865 around, ATLANTA, GA. below. Rv: Blank. Plain edge. (Tom Wall coll.)

Resurgens is a Latin word meaning recovering or reawakening and the phoenix rising from its own ashes as a favorite mythical theme used by many governments and movements, including the Greek government in the 1820's and Henri Christophe of Haiti about the same time.

## J. NALLE (et al)
### Macon, Ga.

| Rulau | Date | Metal | Size | VG | F | VF | EF |
|---|---|---|---|---|---|---|---|
| Ga-Ma 3 | (?) | Copper | 29mm | — | 30.00 | — | — |

J. NALLE — N. YORK — M. BENEDICT J. A. & S. S. VIRGIN MACON, GEO. ctsp on a U.S. 1835 Large cent.

## ELDORADO SALOON
### Savannah, Ga.

 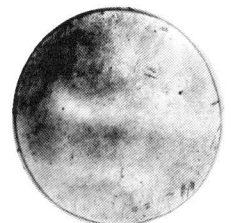

| Rulau | Date | Metal | Size | VG | F | VF | Unc |
|---|---|---|---|---|---|---|---|
| Ga-Sa 4 | (1870's) | GS | 28.2 mm | 25.00 | 40.00 | 100. | — |

(All incused, and the incused letters enameled black) ELDORADO SALOON / 10 / SAVANNAH, GA. Rv: Blank. Plain edge. (Miller Ga 4)

## HAYWOODS SALOON
### Savannah, Ga.

| Rulau | Date | Metal | Size | VG | F | VF | Unc |
|---|---|---|---|---|---|---|---|
| Ga-Sa 8 | (1870's) | GS | 28mm | 25.00 | 40.00 | 100. | — |
| Ga-Sa 9 | (1870's) | GS | 28mm | 25.00 | 40.00 | 100. | — |

HAYWOODS SALOON. Numeral 10 in center. (Miller Ga 5)

Similar, but numeral 25 in center. (Miller Ga 6)

# IDAHO

## (Swan) AND ANDERSON
### Burke, Idaho

| Rulau | Date | Metal | Size | VG | F | VF | Unc |
|---|---|---|---|---|---|---|---|
| Id-Bu 2 | (?) | Brass | 21mm | — | — | Scrc | — |

Swan across top, AND / ANDERSON below. Rv: GOOD FOR / —.— / *ONE* / —.— / DRINK. Plain edge. Recessed dentilated rim on reverse. Rarity 7.

## HEDLUND & OLSON
### Burke, Idaho

| Rulau | Date | Metal | Size | VG | F | VF | Unc |
|---|---|---|---|---|---|---|---|
| Id-Bu 2 | (?) | Brass | 21mm | — | — | Scrc | — |

HEDLUND & OLSON / (ornament) / BURKE, / — / — IDAHO. Rv: GOOD FOR / — / 12 1/2 ¢ / — / —IN TRADE—. Plain edge. Rarity 7.

## HOTEL DE FRANCE
### Lewiston, Idaho

| Rulau | Date | Metal | Size | VG | F | VF | Unc |
|---|---|---|---|---|---|---|---|
| Id-Le 2 | (?) | Copper | 35mm | — | — | 40.00 | — |

(All incused) HOTEL DE FRANCE / ONE / MEAL / LEWISTON, IDAHO. Rv: Blank. Plain edge.

## J. W. LIEUALLENS BAKERY
### Moscow, Idaho

| Rulau | Date | Metal | Size | VG | F | VF | Unc |
|---|---|---|---|---|---|---|---|
| Id-Md 1 | (?) | WM | 24mm | — | — | Scrc | — |

(All incused, crude) J. W. LIEUALLENS / BAKERY—. Rv: ONE / 1 / LOAF. Plain edge.

## HOTEL LEMHI BAR
### Salmon, Idaho

| Rulau | Date | Metal | Size | VG | F | VF | Unc |
|---|---|---|---|---|---|---|---|
| Id-Sa 2 | (?) | CN | Rect. 31 by 19mm | — | — | 40.00 | — |

HOTEL LEMHI / BAR / WM ANDERSON BROS. Rv: GOOD FOR / 12 1/2 ¢ / IN TRADE. Plain edge.

William Anderson still ran this hotel in 1918. Rarity 7.

## THE NEW RESORT
### Shoshone, Idaho

| Rulau | Date | Metal | Size | VG | F | VF | Unc |
|---|---|---|---|---|---|---|---|
| Id-Sh 2 | (?) | Brass | 29mm | — | — | — | — |

THE NEW RESORT / (flowers) / SHOSHONE, / —IDA.—. Rv: GOOD FOR. / CENTS / * 12 1/2 * / CENTS / .IN TRADE. Plain edge. Rarity 7.

# ILLINOIS

## H.N. KENDALL
### Alton, Ill.

| Rulau | Date | Metal | Size | VG | F | VF | Unc |
|---|---|---|---|---|---|---|---|
| Il-At 3 | (1870's) | Brass | 26mm | — | 20.00 | 25.00 | — |
| Il-At 4 | (1870's) | Brass | 23mm | — | 20.00 | 25.00 | — |

H.N. KENDALL / 1 / BREAD. Rv: Blank. Plain edge. Rarity 9. (Wright 542; Schmidt K46)

H.N. KENDALL & CO. / 1 / BREAD (all incused). Rv: No. Plain edge. Rarity 9. (Schmidt K47)

H.N. Kendall and Co. was primarily a baker of crackers. The building is still standing today, with its brick ovens still in the basement.

## A.F. MILLER
### Alton, Ill.

| Rulau | Date | Metal | Size | VG | F | VF | Unc |
|---|---|---|---|---|---|---|---|
| Il-At 7 | (1889-90) | Alum | 23mm | 5.00 | 10.00 | 15.00 | — |

A.F. MILLER / ALTON / ILLS. Rv: GOOD FOR / 2 1/2 ¢ / IN TRADE. Plain edge. (Schmidt M31)

Augustus F. Miller was a tobacco maker located at 3rd and Langdon in Alton, according to the 1886-87 directory for Alton and Madison County. However, aluminum was not used in tokens before 1888-89 except rarely.

## SHURTLEFF COLLEGE
### Alton, Ill.

| Rulau | Date | Metal | Size | VG | F | VF | Unc |
|---|---|---|---|---|---|---|---|
| Il-At 11 | 1867 | Bronze | 31mm | 5.00 | 7.00 | 10.00 | 25.00 |

Male bust facing at center, CHILDRENS PROFESSORSHIP / * 1867 *. Rv: View of college at center, SHURTLEFF COLLEGE CHARTRD 1835. Plain edge. (Schmidt S29)

Shurtleff College became part of Southern Illinois University in the late 1950's.

## E.B. YOUNG
### Alton, Ill.

| Rulau | Date | Metal | Size | VG | F | VF | Unc |
|---|---|---|---|---|---|---|---|
| Il-At 15 | (1889) | Aluminum | 23mm | — | 15.00 | 20.00 | — |

HOPPE'S CHINA HALL / ALTON, ILL. Rv: (Incuse) E. B. YOUNG / (relief) GOOD FOR 1 PINT MILK. Plain edge. (Schmidt)

Emily B. Young was the proprietor, according to the Bradstreet Directory for 1890. The obverse was one used by several merchants in the area. The city of Alton was named for Alton Easton, son of its founder, Rufus Easton.

## COFFEY & HARRISON
### Ashley, Ill.

| Rulau | Date | Metal | Size | VG | F | VF | Unc |
|---|---|---|---|---|---|---|---|
| Il-As 3 | 1881 | WM | 31mm | 7.50 | 10.00 | 15.00 | — |

COFFEY & HARRISON / * (rosette) * / 1881 / ASHLEY, ILL. / * (rosette) *. Rv: (Flowers) / 100 / C.B. Plain edge. (Schmidt C58) Rarity 8.

Coffey, Brown & Co. had a general store and a mill, according to the 1866 *Bradstreet Directory*. In the 1870 *Bradstreet*, this had become Coffey, Brown & Harrison, mill.

## MUSCHLER & WILLIS
### Aurora, Ill.

| Rulau | Date | Metal | Size | VG | F | VF | Unc |
|---|---|---|---|---|---|---|---|
| II-AU 5 | (1886-90) | Brass | 23mm | 10.00 | 15.00 | 20.00 | — |

(All incused) MUSCHLER & WILLIS / GOOD FOR / 5¢ / IN TRADE. Rv: Blank. Plain edge. Rarity 8. (Schmidt M80)

George F. Muschler and James H. Willis ran a saloon on North Broadway from 1886 to 1890, selling Schlitz' Milwaukee beer.

## JACK SHORT
### Aurora, Ill.

| Rulau | Date | Metal | Size | VG | F | VF | Unc |
|---|---|---|---|---|---|---|---|
| II-AU 12 | (1881-1893) | Brass | 24mm | 12.00 | 17.00 | 25.00 | — |

JACK SHORT AURORA, ILL. / GOOD FOR / 5¢ / IN TRADE. Rv: Large 5. Plain edge. Rarity 8. (Schmidt S36)

John M. Short opened his saloon in 1881 as a "sample room," a commonly used term in those days which fooled no one. In 1887 he moved one block to Fox Street, operating the saloon until his death in 1898.

Earlier, about 1870, Short may have run a saloon with a partner as Short & Evans. Old timers recalled Shorts' as a fine, clean saloon with a discreet "family entrance" at the rear of the building.

## NEWTON WAGON CO.
### Batavia, Ill.

| Rulau | Date | Metal | Size | VG | F | VF | Unc |
|---|---|---|---|---|---|---|---|
| II-Bv 7 | (1880's) | Copper | 25mm | 5.00 | 7.50 | 10.00 | 25.00 |

WAgon and team, NEWTON HIGH GRADE WAGONS. Rv: NOTHING BUT WAGONS SINCE 1854. NEWTON WAGON CO. BATAVIA. ILL. Plain edge. Rarity 6. (Schmidt N19)

The 1890 *Bradstreet Directory* said this firm had $250,000 surplus capital, a great amount in those days. The firm also appears in the 1866 and 1870 directories.

## BAKER & THOMAS
### Belleville, Ill.

| Rulau | Date | Metal | Size | VG | F | VF |
|---|---|---|---|---|---|---|
| II-Bv 2 | (1871) | | 23mm | — | — | 1 Known |

(All incused) BAKER & THOMAS / DRUGGISTS / BELLEVILLE. Rv: SODA. Plain edge. (Rich Hartzog coll.)

These druggists appear in the 1871 directory, but have disappeared by the 1878 edition.

## P. HAUSCHILD
### Benson, Ill.

| Rulau | Date | Metal | Size | VG | F | VF | Unc |
|---|---|---|---|---|---|---|---|
| II-Be 4 | (1880-86) | Brass | 26mm | 7.50 | 15.00 | 20.00 | — |

GOOD FOR / 5¢ / P. HAUSCHILD / BENSON, ILL. / IN / TRADE. Rv: Goblet and crossed utensils at center, CHAS. PICK & CO. / DEALERS IN above, — CHICAGO — below. Plain edge. (Schmidt H11)

## J.F. ILLGEN
### Bloom, Ill.

| Rulau | Date | Metal | Size | VG | F | VF | Unc |
|---|---|---|---|---|---|---|---|
| II-Bm 1 | (1874-84) | Brass | 24mm | — | 20.00 | 35.00 | — |

Pool table, three balls and a cuestick, THE J.M. BRUNSWICK / & / BALKE COS. Rv: GOOD FOR / 5¢ / J. F. ILLGEN / BLOOM. ILL. / IN TRADE. Plain edge. Rarity 8. (Schmidt I39; Brunswick 2176)

This is a token of Bloom and not Bloomington, as one might believe.

## M. CHATFIELD
### Bloomington, Ill.

| Rulau | Date | Metal | Size | VG | F | VF | EF |
|---|---|---|---|---|---|---|---|
| II-Bl 2 | (?) | Silver | 27mm | — | — | 125. | — |

M. CHATFIELD / BLOOMINGTON / — ILL. — ctsp on Span.-Am. 1821-Mo 2-reales. (Brunk 84)

| | | | | | | | |
|---|---|---|---|---|---|---|---|
| II-Bl 2A | (?) | Silver | 25mm | — | — | 125. | — |

Similar ctsp on U.S. 1853 A&R Seated Liberty quarter.

Chatfield does not appear in the 1866-1870 directories.

## WM. H. SCHUTTER
### Cairo, Ill.

| Rulau | Date | Metal | Size | VG | F | VF | Unc |
|---|---|---|---|---|---|---|---|
| II-Cr 4 | (1870's) | Brass | 24mm | — | — | 35.00 | Rare |

Liberty head, 12 stars around. Rv: WM H. SCHUTTER / CAIRO / 10 / CENTS. Plain edge. Rarity 7. (Schmidt S15)

| | | | | | | | |
|---|---|---|---|---|---|---|---|
| II-Cr 4F | (1875-80) | Brass | 34mm | 18.50 | 30.00 | 45.00 | — |

(All incused). Within circle: WM. H. SCHUTTER / NO. 4 / SPRINGFIELD / BLOCK. Rv: 50 / CTS. Plain edge.

| Rulau | Date | Metal | Size | VG | F | VF | Unc |
|---|---|---|---|---|---|---|---|
| II-Cr 4G | (1870's) | Brass | 25mm | — | 30.00 | 45.00 | — |

Indian head left surrounded by stars, 50 C in exergue. Rv: As obverse of 15. Plain edge. (Wright 960)

This liquor and cigar merchant appears in the 1866-1870 directories.

## J. O. CONKLIN
## Champaign, Ill.

| Rulau | Date | Metal | Size | VG | F | VF | Unc |
|---|---|---|---|---|---|---|---|
| II-Cm 5 | 1865 | Brass | 22mm | 15.00 | 25.00 | 35.00 | 50.00 |

Dog in center, CHAMPAIGN, ILL. 1865. Rv: J.O. CONKLIN 10 / BAR CHECK. Plain edge. Rarity 6. (Schmidt C-52)

Joseph O. Conklin, saloon and eating house, appears in the 1866 *Bradstreet Directory* but has vanished by the 1870 edition.

## L. BIGGIO
## Chicago, Ill.

| Rulau | Date | Metal | Size | VG | F | VF | EF |
|---|---|---|---|---|---|---|---|
| II-Ch 1 | (1886-87) | Copper | 29mm | — | — | 50.00 | — |

L. BIGGIO ctsp on U.S. 1951 Large cent. (Rich Hartzog coll.)

Lawrence Biggio had a saloon at 30 West Randolph St. listed in the 1887 directory. By 1893 Biggio Brothers' saloon was located at 6 South Canal St.

## L. BOCHE
## Chicago, Ill.

| Rulau | Date | Metal | Size | VG | F | VF | Unc |
|---|---|---|---|---|---|---|---|
| II-Ch 2 | (1880's) | GS | 25mm | — | — | 25.00 | 40.00 |

Owl facing, seated on sword and scepter, all within wreath. L. BOCHE, CHECK M'F'R above, CHICAGO. below. Rv: Large ornate numeral 25 within beaded circle. Plain edge.

Boche struck tokens for firms in eight states, from the late 1870's to about 1905. A 15-cent token in reported.

## BUHLERT & STEPHANY
## Chicago, Ill.

| Rulau | Date | Metal | Size | VG | F | VF | Unc |
|---|---|---|---|---|---|---|---|
| II-Ch 3 | 1881 | Brass | 25mm | 5.00 | 10.00 | 15.00 | — |

Large star at center, with 1881 on it. Around: BUNDES SANGERFEST / CHICAGO. Rv: BUHLER & STEPHANY 5 CENTS. Plain edge. Rarity 4. (Schmidt B88)

## BUTCHERS N. P. A.
## Chicago, Ill.

 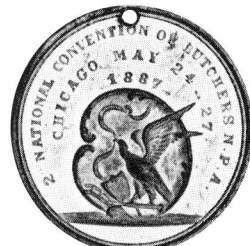

| Rulau | Date | Metal | Size | F | VF | EF | Unc |
|---|---|---|---|---|---|---|---|
| II-Ch 4 | 1887 | WM | 33mm | — | 25.00 | 32.50 | 40.00 |

Bull's head left. Rv: Eagle, shield and plow at lower center. Above: 2.. NATIONAL CONVENTION OF BUTCHERS N. P. A. / CHICAGO MAY 24-27 / 1887. Plain edge.

| II-Ch 4D | 1887 | WM | 34mm | — | 20.00 | 30.00 | 40.00 |

Butcher and steer standing, facing, in central circle, SOUVENIR above, BUTCHERS CONVENTION below. Rv: CHICAGO / MAY 24-27-87. / UNDER THE / AUSPICES / OF / B.N.P.A. OF U.S. Plain edge.

B.N.P.A. = Butchers National Protective Association.

## CANALPORT AVE. POLICE STATION
## Chicago, Ill.

| Rulau | Date | Metal | Size | VG | F | VF | Unc |
|---|---|---|---|---|---|---|---|
| II-Ch 5 | 1886 | WM | 30mm | — | — | Rare | — |

Crossed billy clubs with thongs at center, IN MEMORY OF THE DEDICATION / OF / CANALPORT AVE. above, POLICE STATION. / * AUG. 5. 1886. * below. Rv: (Ornament) / JOHN REHM / —*— / LIEUTENANT / (ornament). Plain edge. Rarity 9. (Schmidt C18)

There are only two specimens known, one of which has a recut 6 in the date. The famous Haymarket Massacre took place May 4, 1886, but anarchist troubles continued into the summer.

## CENTENNIAL OF OUR NATION
## Chicago, Ill.

| Rulau | Date | Metal | Size | F | VF | EF | Unc |
|---|---|---|---|---|---|---|---|
| II-Ch 7 | 1889 | WM* | 37mm | 5.00 | 10.00 | 15.00 | 30.00 |

Naked bust of George Washington left, UNITED STATES OF AMERICA / IN GOD WE TRUST. Rv: THE CENTENNIAL OF OUR NATION CHICAGO COMMEMORATION

| Rulau | Date | Metal | Size | F | VF | EF | Unc |
|---|---|---|---|---|---|---|---|

1789 APRIL 30. 1889. Plain edge. Issued holed. Rarity 4. Issued with a red, white and blue suspension ribbon. (Schmidt C42)

II-Ch8  1889  WM*  37mm  10.00  20.00  25.00  40.00
As 7, except E PLURIBUS UNUM replaces CHICAGO COMMEMORATION on obverse. Plain edge. Issued holed. 5 known. (Schmidt C42a)

\* Actually pot metal, a lead alloy.

## CHICAGO EXPOSITION
### Chicago, Ill.

| Rulau | Date | Metal | Size | VG | F | VF | Unc |
|---|---|---|---|---|---|---|---|
| II-Ch 9 | 1874 | WM | 31mm | 5.00 | 9.00 | 13.00 | 18.00 |

Building at center, CHICAGO EXPOSITION. Rv: INTERSTATE — INDUSTRIAL EXPOSITION MEDAL, 1874, SECOND ANNUAL EXPOSITION, CHICAGO. ILLS. Plain edge. Rarity 6. (Schmidt C53)

II-Ch 10  1875  WM  30mm  7.50  10.00  15.00  50.00
Eagle with wings outstretched, points down, 13 stars around, 1875 below. Rv: Building at center, THIRD ANNUAL above, CHICAGO / . / EXPOSITION MEDAL below. Plain edge. Rarity 8. (Schmidt C57)

II-Ch 11  1876  WM  30mm  7.00  15.00  20.00  35.00
Building at center, CENTENNIAL EXPOSITION above, * 1876 * / OF CHICAGO. below. Rev: Eagle at center, head turned left, HAPPY / .—. below, all within central circle. Around: EAT GUNTHER'S CANDY / * AND YOU WILL BE *. Plain edge. Rarity 7. (Schmidt C40)

**Foil-wrapped chocolate "coin" of 1876.**

## THE CHICAGO HERALD
### Chicago, Ill.

| Rulau | Date | Metal | Size | F | VF | EF | Unc |
|---|---|---|---|---|---|---|---|
| II-Ch 13 | 1889 | WM | 37mm | — | 20.00 | 25.00 | 50.00 |

Man standing, leaning against high-front-wheel bicycle, THE CHICAGO HERALD above, CHAMPION below. Rv: SOUVENIR / OF / TOM ROE'S / BICYCLE TOUR / SAN FRANCISCO / TO CHICAGO / 1889 (on plaque) / SEPT. 21 - DEC. 3 / ON A / "LIGHT CHAMPION". Plain edge. Rarity 7. (Schmidt C61)

About 20 pieces known, including six Unc.

## S.D. CHILDS & CO.
### Chicago, Ill.

| Rulau | Date | Metal | Size | VG | F | VF | Unc |
|---|---|---|---|---|---|---|---|
| II-Ch 14 | (1875-85) | GS | 24mm | 7.50 | 15.00 | 20.00 | — |

Eagle at center, head turned left. E PLURIBUS UNUM above, CHILDS, CHICAGO below. Rv: Mounted Indian left at top, large 5 ¢ at center, fan-shaped ornament at bottom. Plain edge. Rarity 7. (Schmidt C76)

II-Ch 15  (1880's)  Brass  32mm  6.50  9.00  12.50  20.00
Indian head right, superimposed on a pelt pierced by an arrow. S.D. CHILDS & CO. above, *** CHICAGO. *** below. Rv: THIS COIN / MADE BY / S.D. CHILDS & CO. / 200 CLARK ST. / CHICAGO. Reeded edge. Rarity 6. (Schmidt (C70)

II-Ch 16  (1880's)  Gilt/B  32mm  6.50  9.00  12.00  25.00
Indian bust in full headdress right, S.D. CHILDS & CO. above, *** CHICAGO *** below. Rev: Same as 15. Reeded edge. Rarity 6. (Schmidt C72)

| Rulau | Date | Metal | Size | VG | F | VF | Unc |
|---|---|---|---|---|---|---|---|
| II-Ch 16F | (1880's) | Gilt/B | 32mm | 6.50 | 9.00 | 12.00 | 25.00 |

Obverse as 16 (Indian bust right). Rv: ADVERTISING NOVELTIES / COINS / CHARMS / FOBS / BUTTONS / \*\*\*\* Reeded edge. Rarity 6. (Schmidt C74)

## CUDDY
### Chicago, Ill.

| Rulau | Date | Metal | Size | VG | F | VF | EF |
|---|---|---|---|---|---|---|---|
| II-Ch 16T | (1886-87) | Copper | 28mm | — | — | 50.00 | — |

CUDDY / 80 ctsp on worn copper coin.

J. Cuddy and Co. were commission merchants at 62 Water St. listed in the 1887 directory. This item may have been used as a tally or work check.

## DACOSTA'S
### Chicago, Ill.

| Rulau | Date | Metal | Size | VG | F | VF | Unc |
|---|---|---|---|---|---|---|---|
| II-Ch 17 | (1880's ?) | Brass | 24mm | 15.00 | 20.00 | 30.00 | 40.00 |

DACOSTA'S / ESTABLISHED / 1877 / \*.\*.\*.\*.\* / .+. CHICAGO .+. Rv: Large numeral 75 within circle formed of alternating stars and ornate crosses. Plain edge. Rarity 7. (Schmidt D17)

## DALLEMAND & CO.
### Chicago, Ill.

| Rulau | Date | Metal | Size | F | VF | EF | Unc |
|---|---|---|---|---|---|---|---|
| II-Ch 18 | (1888-95) | Aluminum | 40mm | 5.00 | 7.50 | 12.50 | 20.00 |

Large D&C monogram within central circle, small TRADE MARK below. Around: DALLEMAND & CO. / \* CHICAGO. \*. Rv: CREAM (in script) / PURE RYE / RICH AND MELLOW. Plain edge. (Wright 225; Schmidt D20)

## W. DEAKIN
### Chicago, Ill.

| Rulau | Date | Metal | Size | VG | F | VF | EF |
|---|---|---|---|---|---|---|---|
| II-Ch 19 | 1863 | Copper | 29mm | — | — | 150. | — |

W. DEAKIN DEALER IN BOOK & COIN 131 WELLS ST. CHICAGO 1863 ctsp on planed-down early English copper coin.

The only piece known, sold 1975 for $125, was dug up 1973. The 1863 date is contemporary with issuance. He does not appear in 1866-70 directories.

## DOUGLAS MONUMENT ASSOCIATION
### Chicago, Ill.

| Rulau | Date | Metal | Size | F | VF | EF | Unc |
|---|---|---|---|---|---|---|---|
| II-Ch 20 | 1866 | WM | 34mm | — | — | 45.00 | 60.00 |

Naked bust left of Stephen A. Douglas, three stars below bust. Around: BORN APRIL 23. 1813. DIED JUNE 8. 1861. Rv: DOUGLAS MONUMENT ASSOCIATION / CORNER STONE / LAID (on tablet) / SEPTEMBER 6. / 1866 / \*. Plain edge. Rarity 9. (Schmidt D70)

## F. & M. (and) J.R.M.
### Chicago, Ill.

| Rulau | Date | Metal | Size | VG | F | VF | Unc |
|---|---|---|---|---|---|---|---|
| II-Ch 22 | (1874-84) | Brass | 24mm | — | 15.00 | — | — |

Liberty Head left in beaded circle. Around: THE J.M. BRUNSWICK & BALKE COS. / .CHECK. Rv: GOOD FOR / 5 ¢ / F. & M. / 170 S. CLARK ST. Plain edge. (Brunswick 2113)

| | | | | | | | |
|---|---|---|---|---|---|---|---|
| II-Ch 22C | (1874-84) | Brass | 24mm | — | 15.00 | — | — |

Pool table in central beaded circle. Around: THE J.M. BRUNSWICK & BALKE COS. / CHECK. Rv: GOOD FOR / \* 5 ¢ \* / J.R.M. (on scroll) / .—. 170 CLARK ST. / (19 alternating dots and stars). Plain edge. (Brunswick 2182)

The attribution to Chicago is tentative.

## P.C. DUNN SALOON
### Chicago, Ill.

| Rulau | Date | Metal | Size | VG | F | VF | Unc |
|---|---|---|---|---|---|---|---|
| II-Ch 21 | (1876-83) | Copper | 29mm | — | — | 210. | — |

P.C. DUNN / SALOON / CHICAGO / ILLS. ctsp on U.S. 1855 (?) Large cent. (Rich Hartzog coll.)

Peter C. Dunn appears in the 1876 and 1883 directories.

## FIRST INTERNATIONAL MILITARY ENCAMPMENT
### Chicago, Ill.

| Rulau | Date | Metal | Size | VG | F | VF | Unc |
|---|---|---|---|---|---|---|---|
| II-Ch 23 | 1887 | WM | 29mm | — | — | 15.00 | 25.00 |

Mounted officer at center, tents at left, soldiers at attention at right. Rv: INTERNATIONAL MILITARY ENCAMPMENT AT CHICAGO. ILL. U.S.A. SOUVENIR OCTOBER 1887. Plain edge. Rarity 6. (Schmidt F30)

| II-Ch 23B | 1887 | Gilt/B | 32mm | 5.00 | 10.00 | 15.00 | 25.00 |
|---|---|---|---|---|---|---|---|

Soldier in kneeling rifle position within central circle, INTERNATL MILITARY ENCAMPMENT CHICAGO OCT. / 1887 around. Rv: Crossed rifles as supporters and military helmet as crest surround shield, on which a sentry guards tents. Plain edge.

## COL. JAMES FISK JR.
### Chicago, Ill.

| Rulau | Date | Metal | Size | VG | F | VF | Unc |
|---|---|---|---|---|---|---|---|
| II-Ch 23F | (1871) | Brass | 23mm | 3.00 | 4.00 | 6.00 | 10.00 |

Bust right, tiny A. WILLEMIN under truncation. Around: COL. JAMES FISK JR. Rv: Railroad engine to right, RELIEF FOR above, CHICAGO. below. Plain edge. (Bruce Smith coll.)

Col. James Fisk Jr. (1834-1872) was a partner of financier Jay Gould. Together they attempted to corner the gold market in 1869, bringing on the Panic of '69 and, after Fisk's death, the grim Panic of 1873 was an offshoot result, some say.

In this token, however, Fisk is a hero. He donated use of his railroad trains to carry food, medical supplies and other goods to survivors of the Great Chicago Fire of 1871. Smith reports he has owned three specimens, all of which have been holed. The Unc. price above would pertain to an unpierced specimen.

Nearly 5,000 tokens were issued, some from a reengraved die. As late as 1950 in Chicago, these were still considered "junk box" items. Specimens exist in silvered brass and copper.

## FRENCH PALACE
### Chicago, Ill.

| Rulau | Date | Metal | Size | VG | F | VF | Unc |
|---|---|---|---|---|---|---|---|
| II-Ch 24 | (1880's) | CN | 24mm | — | — | — | Rare |

FRENCH PALACE / 5 / 81 UNION ST. Rv: Blank. Plain edge.

The Rich Hartzog collection specimen has a pedigree back to 1915, ex-Morris Thacker, Benjamin Odesser, Joseph Schmidt, Hartzog. The establishment may have been a bawdy house.

## J.W. GEHRIG
### Chicago, Ill.

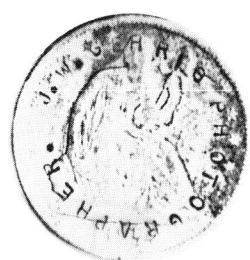

| Rulau | Date | Metal | Size | VG | F | VF | EF |
|---|---|---|---|---|---|---|---|
| II-Ch 25 | (1872-83) | Silver | 31mm | — | — | 175. | — |

J.W. GEHRIG PHOTOGRAPHER. ctsp in a circle on U.S. 1849 Liberty Seated half dollar.

Gehrig appears in the 1872 and 1883 directories.

## GENIN THE HATTER
### Chicago, Ill.

| Rulau | Date | Metal | Size | VG | F | VF | Unc |
|---|---|---|---|---|---|---|---|
| II-Ch 26 | 1872 | GS | 24mm | 35.00 | 50.00 | Rare | — |

Hat with buckled band, 1872. Rv: GENIN THE HATTER / 175 W. MADISON ST. / CHICAGO. Plain edge. Thin planchet. Rarity 7. (Schmidt G20)

Genin in 1853 had a store at 214 Broadway in New York, next door to Barnum's American Museum.

## GILES BRO. & CO.
### Chicago, Ill.

| Rulau | Date | Metal | Size | VG | F | VF | Unc |
|---|---|---|---|---|---|---|---|
| II-Ch 27 | 1883 | WM | 32mm | — | — | 20.00 | 50.00 |

Locomotive, SOUVENIR NATL. R.R. EXPOSITION / CHICAGO 1883. Rv: Pocket watch within wreath at center. Around: GILES BRO. & CO. WATCHES, DIAMONDS. Plain edge. Rarity 7. (Schmidt G35)

## GRAND CENTRAL CLOTHING HOUSE
### Chicago, Ill.

| Rulau | Date | Metal | Size | VG | F | VF | Unc |
|---|---|---|---|---|---|---|---|
| II-Ch 28 | (1870-90) | GS | 24mm | 5.00 | 10.00 | 15.00 | 30.00 |

GRAND CENTRAL / ONE PRICE / CLOTHING HOUSE / 142 & 144 / STATE ST. / CHICAGO. Rv: THIS MEDAL / GOOD FOR / ONE DOLLAR / ON EACH / TWENTY DOLLARS / PURCHASED AT / 142 & 144 STATE ST. / CHICAGO. Thick planchet. Plain edge. Rarity 2. (Wright 398; Schmidt G60a)

| II-Ch 28A | (1870-90) | Brass | 24mm | — | — | Rare | — |
|---|---|---|---|---|---|---|---|

As 28. Plain edge. Rarity 9. (Schmidt G60)

| II-Ch 28B | (1870-90) | Copper | 24mm | — | — | Rare | — |
|---|---|---|---|---|---|---|---|

As 28. Plain edge. Rarity 8.

## GRENIER'S LYCEUM
## Chicago, Ill.

| Rulau | Date | Metal | Size | F | VF | EF | Unc |
|---|---|---|---|---|---|---|---|
| II-Ch 29 | (1880's) | Brass | 24mm | 6.00 | 10.00 | 15.00 | 30.00 |

\* GRENIER'S LYCEUM \* / VARIETY / .—. / PALACE / —\*— GOLD MINE / —NO 1 —. Rv: \* GRENIER'S GARDEN \* / CHICAGO'S / —\*— / GREATEST / — RESORT— / GOLD MINE / NO 2. Plain edge. Rarity 2. (Schmidt G75)

| II-Ch 29A | (1880's) | Copper | 24mm | 7.00 | 12.50 | 17.50 | 40.00 |

As 29. Plain edge. Rarity 5. (Schmidt G75a)

| II-Ch 29B | (1880's) | Nickel | 24mm | 10.00 | 15.00 | 20.00 | 50.00 |

As 29. Plain edge. Rarity 6. (Schmidt G75b)

Grenier's Lyceum and Grenier's Garden were entertainment houses of the 1880's. The text's use as "gold mine" (of entertainment) is unusual.

## HANNAH AND HOGG
## Chicago, Ill.

| Rulau | Date | Metal | Size | VG | F | VF | Unc |
|---|---|---|---|---|---|---|---|
| II-Ch 30 | (1870-90) | GS | 24mm | 3.00 | 6.00 | 8.50 | 20.00 |

Scotch thistle with three blooms. Rv: HANNAH / AND (on ribbon) / \* HOGG \*. This planchet. Plain edge. (Wright 421; Schmidt H12)

| II-Ch 30A | (1870-90) | Copper | 24mm | — | — | 11.50 | 25.00 |

As 30. Plain edge. (Schmidt H12a)

| II-Ch 31 | (1870-90) | GS | 24mm | 5.00 | 7.50 | 12.00 | 20.00 |

Scotch thistle with one blossom. Rv: HANNAH / AND (on ribbon) / \* HOGG \*. Thick planchet. Plain edge. (Schmidt H12b)

| Rulau | Date | Metal | Size | VG | F | VF | Unc |
|---|---|---|---|---|---|---|---|
| II-Ch 32 | (1880-99) | GS | 24mm | 2.00 | 5.00 | 7.00 | 15.00 |

Scotch thistle with three blooms above HANNAH / \* HOGG (all in script) / 222 & 224 CLARK ST. / —151— / RANDOLPH ST. / HOTEL BREVOORT / STOCK EXCHANGE / FISHER BUILDING / 83 MADISON ST. / CHICAGO. in eight lines.

| Rulau | Date | Metal | Size | VG | F | VF | Unc |
|---|---|---|---|---|---|---|---|

Thin planchet. Plain edge. There are five die varieties of this piece. (Miller Ill 13; Schmidt H12c to H12g)

**Schmidt H12c Variety**

| II-Ch 33 | (1880-99) | GS | 24mm | 2.00 | 5.00 | 7.00 | 15.00 |

As 32, but centrally holed planchet. Plain edge. There are three major obverse die varieties of this token, with differing thistle arrangements; all are Rarity 3. (Schmidt H12h to H12j)

Hannah and Hogg were proud Scotsmen who used their national flower, the thistle, liberally on their tokens. They operated a chain of saloons in Chicago for about 40 years before 1919 — many in choice locations as II-Ch 32 above indicates.

Each Hannah and Hogg piece catalogued here was worth 2½ Cents in trade, it is theorized.

In 1918, Hannah & Hogg Inc. were listed in the R.G. Dun directory as being in the wholesale wine and liquor business. But the business had changed hands in 1914. Both Hannah and Hogg were dead by 1919.

All Hannah and Hogg taverns had a stone man at the entranceway. It was at once their symbol, trademark and advertisement.

The name still graces a rather poor grade of whiskey sold in Chicago and environs.

## ILLINOIS MILITARY & MECHANICAL TRAINING SCHOOL
## Chicago, Ill.

| Rulau | Date | Metal | Size | F | VF | Unc | Proof |
|---|---|---|---|---|---|---|---|
| II-Ch 50 | 1887 | SWM | 30mm | — | — | 22.50 | |

Building across center; ILLINOIS MILITARY / & / MECHANICAL above; TRAINING SCHOOL / FOR / POOR / BOYS / CHICAGO. Rv: Within central circle: SOUVENIR / 1837 1887 / (ornament) / (star). Plain edge. Issued holed at top for suspension from red ribbon.

The 1837 date is puzzling. The school was founded in the 1850's. Such schools did exaggerate their founding date to add to prestige.

## F.A. JENSCH
## Chicago, Ill.

| Rulau | Date | Metal | Size | F | VF | EF | Unc |
|---|---|---|---|---|---|---|---|
| II-Ch 53 | 1857 | Copper | 25mm | 10.00 | 15.00 | 25.00 | 50.00 |

Mounted bell inscribed: F.A. JENSCH / BELL FOUNDER / CHICAGO, ILL. Above: MADE TO ORDER FROM 1 TO 50,000 LBS.

| Rulau | Date | Metal | Size | F | VF | EF | Unc |
|---|---|---|---|---|---|---|---|
| | | In exergue: ESTAB'D 1857. Rv: F.A. JENSCH / BELL / FOUNDER / (ornament) / 105 S. WELLS ST. / CHICAGO. Plain edge. (Miller III 18; Schmidt J28b) | | | | | |
| II-Ch 54 | 1857 | Brass | 25mm | 12.50 | 20.00 | 35.00 | 75.00 |
| | | As 53. Plain edge. (Miller III 19; Schmidt J28) | | | | | |
| II-Ch 54A | 1857 | S/Br | 25mm | — | — | — | Rare |
| | | As 53. Plain edge. (Schmidt J28c) | | | | | |
| II-Ch 55 | 1857 | WM | 25mm | — | — | — | Rare |
| | | As 53. Plain edge. (Wright 508; Miller III 20; Schmidt J28d) | | | | | |
| II-Ch 56 | 1857 | Copper | 25mm | — | — | — | Rare |
| | | Similar to 53, but no address on reverse. Bell is smaller, and no 'ESTAB'D 1857' on obverse. (Miller III 20A; Schmidt J28e | | | | | |

Probably issued in the 1865-1880 period. The date 1857 refers to the firm's founding.

## LYCEUM THEATRE
### Chicago, Ill.

| Rulau | Date | Metal | Size | VG | F | VF | Unc |
|---|---|---|---|---|---|---|---|
| II-Ch 60 | (1870-90) | GS | 24mm | 2.00 | 3.50 | 5.00 | 10.00 |

LYCEUM THEATRE / FINEST / VAUDEVILLE / HOUSE / ON EARTH / CHICAGO. Rv: LAUGHING HEADQUARTERS / BURLESQUE / NOVELTY / MINSTRELS / SPECTACULAR / COMEDY. Thin planchet. Plain edge. There are three varieties, all Rarity 5. (Schmidt L92)

## MALLORY COMMISSION CO.
### Chicago, Ill.

| Rulau | Date | Metal | Size | F | VF | EF | Unc |
|---|---|---|---|---|---|---|---|
| II-Ch 61 | (?) | Bronze | 27mm | — | 25.00 | | |

Steer left, MALLORY COMMISSION CO. above, tiny S.D. CHILDS & CO. CHICAGO. below. Rv: LIVE STOCK COMMISSION / CHICAGO / KANSAS CITY / SO. ST. JOSEPH / SO. OMAHA / SIOUX CITY / SO. ST. PAUL / . ESTABLISHED 1862. Plain edge.

| Rulau | Date | Metal | Size | F | VF | EF | Unc |
|---|---|---|---|---|---|---|---|
| II-Ch 61c | (?) | Bronze | 37mm | — | 25.00 | | |

Similar to last, but LIVE STOCK COMMISSION above steer on obverse. Rv: Similar to last, but first line reads: MALLORY COMMISSION CO. Flourishes have been added throughout legend. Plain edge.

## N. MATSON & CO.
### Chicago, Ill.

| Rulau | Date | Metal | Size | VG | F | VF | Unc |
|---|---|---|---|---|---|---|---|
| II-Ch 62 | (1870's) | Silver | 26mm | — | 35.00 | 45.00 | |

N. MATSON & CO. / JEWELERS / 117 / LAKE ST. / CHICAGO ILL. Rv: JEWELRY / (Counterstamped numeral) / CHECK. Reeded Edge. Rarity 8. (Schmidt Chicago M12)

The specimen in the collection of James H. Holtel, Nelsonville, Ohio, is stamped with the numeral '499' on reverse. Only five pieces are known.

Matson & Hoes, jewelry, appears in the 1866 directory. N. Matson & Co. is listed in 1870.

## NORTHWESTERN DENTAL INFIRMARY
### Chicago, Ill.

| Rulau | Date | Metal | Size | VG | F | VF | Unc |
|---|---|---|---|---|---|---|---|
| II-Ch 66 | (1870-90) | GS | 24mm | — | 15.00 | 25.00 | 40.00 |

NORTH WESTERN / * / DENTAL / INFIRMARY / CHICAGO / OPERA HOUSE. / Rv: ALL WORK FREE / SMALL / * CHARGE * / FOR / MATERIAL. Thin planchet. Plain edge.

## N. W. SHOW CASE MFG. CO.
### Chicago, Ill.

| Rulau | Date | Metal | Size | VG | F | VF | Unc |
|---|---|---|---|---|---|---|---|
| II-Ch 69 | (1872) | GS | 23mm | — | 10.00 | 15.00 | 25.00 |

Curved front showcase, RE ESTABLISHED above, AT / 59 & 61 S. CANAL ST. / CHICAGO. Rv: NICKEL / FROM THE / RUINS / OF THE / N.W. SHOW CASE MF'G CO. / OCT. 9TH. Thin planchet. Plain edge. Rarity 6. (Wright 1544; Schmidt N57)

Four square miles of Chicago, including the business district, were destroyed by a great fire on Oct. 8-9, 1871. Canal St. lies along the south branch of the Chicago River and this area was thoroughly burned out, the flames even leaping the river northeastward and dying out only when they reached the lake on the north side.

| Rulau | Date | Metal | Size | VG | F | VF | Unc |
|---|---|---|---|---|---|---|---|
| II-Ch 70 | (1870's) | CN | 21mm | 3.00 | 5.00 | 7.50 | 20.00 |

Large 10 C. at center. Around: N. W. SHOWCASE MF'G CO. / 59 & 61 SO CANAL ST. CHICAGO. Rv: RE'D'M'BLE IN SUMS NOT EX'C'D'G 10 PR CT ON PURCHASE / GOOD FOR / 10 C. / IN MDSE. Plain edge. Rarity 4. (Schmidt N58)

## 22 NORD-AMER. SANGERFEST
### Chicago, Ill.

| Rulau | Date | Metal | Size | F | VF | EF | Unc |
|---|---|---|---|---|---|---|---|
| II-Ch 65 | 1881 | WM | 30mm | 20.00 | 25.00 | — | — |

Woman with lyre standing half right. Around: DER MENSCHHEIT WURDE IST IN EURE HAND GEGEBEN, BEWAHRT SIE. Rv: Within wreath: 22 / NORD-AMER. / SANGERFEST / CHICAGO. / 1881 / JUNI 29. JULY 3. Plain edge.

Commemorated the 22nd North American Singing Festival in Chicago in 1881. The 19th century German immigrants retained their cultural ties with Germanism through singing festivals, turner (gymnastic) fests and other events honored on medalets and tokens.

## PALMER HOUSE
### Chicago, Ill.

| Rulau | Date | Metal | Size | VG | F | VF | Unc |
|---|---|---|---|---|---|---|---|
| II-Ch 71 | (1880-93) | CN* | 38mm | — | — | 25.00 | 40.00 |

* Cupronickel, with black enameled letters. (All incused) PALMER HOUSE / 10¢ / 66 / BARBER SHOP. Rv: Blank. Plain edge. Issued holed. Only 5 pieces known.

| II-Ch 72 | (1880's) | Brass | 26mm | 7.50 | 15.00 | 20.00 | 30.00 |
|---|---|---|---|---|---|---|---|

Crossed billiard cues within central circle, N-B-M-C in angles. Around: NATIONAL BILLIARD MFG. CO. Rv: PALMER HOUSE / GOOD FOR / 5 C / IN TRADE / * BAR *. Plain edge.

## PETER SCHUTTLER
### Chicago, Ill.

| Rulau | Date | Metal | Size | F | VF | EF | Unc |
|---|---|---|---|---|---|---|---|
| II-Ch 100 | 1876 | Brass | 32mm | 5.00 | 10.00 | 15.00 | 25.00 |

Manufacturing plant at center, THE PIONEER WAGON WORKS / OF THE WEST. above, ESTABLISHED / — 1843 — / PETER SCHUTTLER CHICAGO. below. Rv: Wagon at center, * MFR. OF FARM, FREIGHT & SPRING WAGONS * / FIRST PREMIUM above, PARIS 1867 / PHILADELPHIA / .1876. / FACTORY 45 W. MONROE ST. CHICAGO below. Plain edge. (Schmidt S20). There are four die varieties.

| II-Ch 100A | 1876 | Brass | 32mm | 9.00 | 15.00 | 25.00 | 35.00 |
|---|---|---|---|---|---|---|---|

As 100, but Thick planchet. Plain edge. (Schmidt S20a)

| II-Ch 100B | 1876 | S/Brass | 32mm | 20.00 | 25.00 | 35.00 | 50.00 |
|---|---|---|---|---|---|---|---|

As 100. Plain edge. (Schmidt S20b)

| II-Ch 100C | 1876 | WM | 32mm | 9.00 | 15.00 | 25.00 | 40.00 |
|---|---|---|---|---|---|---|---|

As 100. Plain edge. (Schmidt S20c). Thick flan.

## BRANCH AGENCY TOKENS

Most of these tokens used an obverse die similar to II-Ch 100, with minor die variations. Some reverse dies substituted "dealer in agricultural implements" for "first premium," etc. The name of the agent is inscribed with the city of issue. All agency store cards are 33mm, plain edge, Rarity 7 through Rarity 10.

| Rulau | Date | Metal | Agent | F | VF | EF | Unc |
|---|---|---|---|---|---|---|---|
| II-Ch 104 | 1876 | Brass | M.C. Hawley & Co., San Francisco | 12.00 | 20.00 | 25.00 | 40.00 |
| II-Ch 104A | 1876 | WM | do | 20.00 | 25.00 | 40.00 | 60.00 |

| II-Ch 106 | (1876) | Brass | John J. Maxey Denver, Col. | 12.00 | 20.00 | 25.00 | 40.00 |
|---|---|---|---|---|---|---|---|
| II-Ch106A | (1876) | WM | do | 20.00 | 25.00 | 40.00 | 60.00 |

| Rulau | Date | Metal | Agent | F | VF | EF | Unc |
|---|---|---|---|---|---|---|---|
| II-Ch 108 | 1876 | Brass | Thos. C. Carson, Iowa City, Ia. | 12.00 | 17.00 | 25.00 | 35.00 |

| | | | | | | | |
|---|---|---|---|---|---|---|---|
| II-Ch 110 | 1876 | Brass | Smith & Keating, Kansas City, Mo. | 12.00 | 17.00 | 25.00 | 35.00 |
| II-Ch 112 | 1876 | Brass | Dodd & Co. Portland, Or. | 12.00 | 17.00 | 25.00 | 35.00 |
| II-Ch 114 | 1876 | Brass | Austin, Tx. | — | — | 200. | — |
| II-Ch 115 | 1876 | Brass | A.B. Tabor, Dallas, Tx. | 12.00 | 17.00 | 22.50 | 33.00 |
| II-Ch 115A | 1876 | WM | do | 20.00 | 25.00 | 40.00 | 60.00 |
| II-Ch 116 | 1876 | Brass | Byers Bros., Sherman, Tx. | 12.00 | 17.00 | 22.50 | 33.00 |

| | | | | | | | |
|---|---|---|---|---|---|---|---|
| II-Ch 117 | 1876 | Brass | George A. Lowe, Salt Lake City, Ut. | 12.00 | 17.00 | 22.50 | 33.00 |
| II-Ch 117A | 1876 | WM | do | | | | Unique |
| II-Ch 118 | 1876 | Brass | Herman Hass, Cheyenne, Wy | 35.00 | 45.00 | 67.50 | 100. |

## SCHUTTLER & HOTZ
## Chicago, Ill.

| Rulau | Date | Metal | Size | F | VF | EF | Unc |
|---|---|---|---|---|---|---|---|
| II-Ch 120 | 1878 | Copper | 34mm | 10.00 | 15.00 | 20.00 | 35.00 |

Obverse similar to 100, with minor differences. The 1843 is larger. Rv: Wagon at center, * SCHUTTLER & HOTZ, MANUFACTURERS OF THE * / FIRST PREMIUM. PARIS 1867. / PHILADELPHIA 1876 / PARIS 1878 above, ESTABLISHED / 1843 / OFFICE 45 W. MONROE ST. / CHICAGO, ILL. / OLD RELIABLE SCHUTTLER WAGON below. Plain edge. Thick planchet. (Schmidt S22)

| II-Ch 122 | (1889) | Aluminum 34mm | 5.00 | 10.00 | 15.00 | 25.00 |
|---|---|---|---|---|---|---|

Obverse similar to 120, with minor differences. Rv: Wagon right, its right side wheels appearing tilted inward. Above: FIRST PREMIUM. Below: WHEREVER EXHIBITED; all within central circle. Around: SCHUTTLER & HOTZ, MANUFACTURERS OF . / THE OLD RELIABLE SCHUTTLER WAGON. Plain edge. (Schmidt S23)

| II-Ch 123 | (1889) | Aluminum 34mm | 5.00 | 10.00 | 15.00 | 25.00 |
|---|---|---|---|---|---|---|

As 122, but wheels on reverse appear normal. Plain edge. (Schmidt S23a)

## SEA'S MILLINERY DEPT.
## Chicago, Ill.

| Rulau | Date | Metal | Size | VG | F | VF | Unc |
|---|---|---|---|---|---|---|---|
| II-Ch 73 | 1885 | WM | --mm | — | — | 15.00 | 30.00 |

Eagle with U.S. shield on its breast at center, SEA'S MILLINERY DEPT. around, 1885. below. Rv: SEA'S / MILLINERY / DEPT. / SOUVENIR / OF THE OPENING / 20TH SEASON. Plain edge.

## E.H. STEIN
## Chicago, Ill.

| Rulau | Date | Metal | Size | VG | F | VF | Unc |
|---|---|---|---|---|---|---|---|
| II-Ch 74 | (1866-69) | Nickel | 21mm | | | | 2 Known |

E.H. STEIN / $1.00 / STORE / CITY OF PARIS / 83. S. CLARK. ST (all lettering incuse). Rv: Blank. Plain edge. (Rulau-Miller III 107)

The address could fix this concern as early as 1845. The "City of Paris" was a block in Chicago which boasted many shops handling the exotic wares of the world before and during the Civil War. The token's crudeness seemed to indicate a date before 1860, and thus it was included in our 1845-60 reference.

Joseph Schmidt, the Illinois token expert, points out that Stein was at 83 Clark St. as late as 1871-1876. David Schenkman thought this piece dates from about 1870.

The 1869 Chicago directory may have cleared up the matter. It lists "E.H. Stein, proprietor of City of Paris One Dollar Store" at 81 So. Clark, probably another entrance to the same building. So we are reassigning the token to this 1866-1889 reference.

E.H. Stein does not appear in either the 1859 or 1865 directories.

## ROBERT TARRANT
## Chicago, Ill.

| Rulau | Date | Metal | Size | F | VF | EF | Unc |
|---|---|---|---|---|---|---|---|
| II-Ch 75 | (1889?) | Alum | 38mm | 10.00 | 20.00 | 25.00 | 40.00 |

Steamboat to left, MARINE ENGINE above, WORKS in exergue. Tiny CHILDS CHICAGO below exergue line. Rv: COMPLIMENTS / —OF— / ROBERT TARRANT / CHICAGO / —.— / 52 TO 56 ILLINOIS ST. Plain edge. Rarity 8. (Wright 1091; Schmidt T10)

## TERRILL BROS.
## Chicago, Ill.

| Rulau | Date | Metal | Size | VG | F | VF | EF |
|---|---|---|---|---|---|---|---|
| II-Ch 76 | (1885) | Brass | 29mm | — | — | 2 Known | |

(All incused) TERRILL BROS., 196 & 198 S. WATER ST., 50 1 COOP. Rv: Blank. Plain edge. (Schmidt T20)

Terrill Brothers became defunct by 1896.

## DANIEL G. TRENCH & CO.
## Chicago, Ill.

| Rulau | Date | Metal | Size | F | VF | EF | Unc |
|---|---|---|---|---|---|---|---|
| II-Ch 77 | (1883-93) | Brass | --mm | — | 9.00 | 15.00 | — |

DANIEL G. TRENCH & CO. / CANNING / FACTORY / OUTFITTERS / * / CHICAGO. Rv: Blank. Plain edge. (Schmidt T33)

The Trench store card was muled with many other tokens of the period. This is the only known piece mentioning Trench alone.

## VAUGHAN'S SEED STORE
## Chicago, Ill.

| Rulau | Date | Metal | Size | F | VF | EF | Unc |
|---|---|---|---|---|---|---|---|
| II-Ch 78 | 1887 | CN | 31mm | 10.00 | 15.00 | 20.00 | 40.00 |

Six-story building at center, VAUGHAN'S SEED STORE above, CHICAGO below. Rv: + 3RD ANNUAL MEETING + / SAF / COMPLIMENTS / OF / J. C. VAUGHAN / 1887. Plain edge. Rarity 7. (Wright 1186; Schmidt V10)

Dr. Wright called this piece rare in 1901! SAF = Society of American Florists. There are two die varieties.

## WALDRON'S PRESCRIPTION STORE
## Chicago, Ill.

| Rulau | Date | Metal | Size | F | VF | EF | Unc |
|---|---|---|---|---|---|---|---|
| II-Ch 79 | (1885) | Brass | 25mm | — | — | 2 Known | |

Eagle facing, head turned left. WALDRON'S PRESCRIPTION STORE around, .CHICAGO. below. Rv: GOOD FOR ONE GLASS OF SODA WATER / AT / WALDRON'S / RANDOLPH / & / FIFTH AVE. / —.— / .CHICAGO. Plain edge. (Schmidt W12)

## CONCORDIA
## Elgin, Ill.

| Rulau | Date | Metal | Size | VG | F | VF | Unc |
|---|---|---|---|---|---|---|---|
| II-El 3 | (1885) | Brass | 25mm | 3.00 | 5.00 | 10.00 | 20.00 |

Indian head left within central beaded circle. Around: L. BOCHE ENGRAVER, DIE SINKER & MANUF'R OF CHECKS, 166 RANDOLPH ST. CHICAGO. Rv: CONCORDIA / * / ELGIN / ILLS. surrounded by circle of 35 stars. Plain edge. (Schmidt C58)

## ELGIN NATIONAL WATCH CO.
## Elgin, Ill.

The Elgin National Watch Co. gave away attractive 30mm white metal tokens with their watches. Most were identical, except that an incuse watch movement number has been placed on reverse, and the watch model name is included on many of the pieces following the word NAME. Though many thousands of these tokens must have been issued, they are not particularly common in numismatic channels and we suspect that a great many of them are still resting in homes among other old oddments.

| Rulau | Date | Metal | Size | F | VF | EF | Unc |
|---|---|---|---|---|---|---|---|
| II-El 5 | (1870's) | WM | 30mm | 5.00 | 9.00 | 15.00 | 25.00 |

Winged nude man with scythe and large Elgin watch striding right, THE ELGIN NATIONAL WATCH COMPANY OF ELGIN

| Rulau | Date | Metal | Size | F | VF | EF | Unc |
|---|---|---|---|---|---|---|---|

ILLS / * INCORPORATED 1865 *. Rv: ELGIN NATIONAL WATCH CO / THIS / CERTIFIES THAT / LEVER MOVEMENT / NO. 205091 (numerals incused; these change on each token) / ENGRAVED / MANF'D ELGIN, ILLS. / WAS MANUFACTURED BY US / OF THE BEST MATERIALS / AND IS / WARRANTED / A GOOD / TIME-KEEPER. Plain edge. (Schmidt Not Listed)

| Rulau | Date | Metal | Size | F | VF | EF | Unc |
|---|---|---|---|---|---|---|---|
| II-El 6 | (1870's) | WM | 30mm | 5.00 | 9.00 | 15.00 | 25.00 |

Obverse as 5. Rv: As 5, except fifth and sixth lines of central legend read: NAMED / ELGIN NAT. WATCH CO. instead of: ENGRAVED / MANF'D ELGIN, ILLS. Plain edge. Rarity 5. (Wright 287; Miller Ill. 42; Schmidt E27)

II-El 6 is the most readily available token in this series. The following varieties are the same as II-El 6 except that they bear one of 13 watch model names in the sixth line on reverse, following NAMED on the fifth line. Each variety is Rarity 5 or 6, apparently, ranging in price about $1 to $2 more than comparable conditions in II-El 6. (Other watch model names may exist)

II-El 6A   T.M. AVERY (reverse watch name)
II-El 6B   GAIL BORDEN
II-El 6C   H.Z. CULVER
II-El 6D   DEXTER ST.
II-El 6E   CHAS. FARGO
II-El 6F   W.H. FERRY
II-El 6G   LADY ELGIN
II-El 6H   M.D. OGDEN
II-El 6I   B.W. RAYMOND
II-El 6J   J.T. RYERSON
II-El 6K   H.H. TAYLOR (Miller Ill 43)
II-El 6L   C.M. WHEELER

| II-El 7 | (1870's) | SB | 16mm | | | | Rare |

"Trademark" on pedestal, on which stands winged nude Father Time similar to that on II-El 5 and 6. Rv: Intaglio of obverse. Plain edge. Rarity 8. (Schmidt E29) A bangle?

| Rulau | Date | Metal | Size | VG | F | VF | Unc |
|---|---|---|---|---|---|---|---|
| II-El 8 | 1873 | WM | 30mm | 5.00 | 9.00 | 15.00 | 30.00 |

Exposition building in center, CHICAGO EXPOSITION above, 1873 / * below. Tiny V.S. WEBER below ground. Rv: Clock face in center, hands at 3:02 1/2 position. Around: MADE BY THE NATIONAL ELGIN WATCH CO / * IN EXPOSITION BUILDING *. Thick planchet. Plain edge. Rarity 6. (Schmidt C50)

| II-El 9 | 1873 | | WM | 30mm | 10.00 | 15.00 | 20.00 | 35.00 |

As 8, but CONTRIBUTION TO 1873 / YELLOW FEVER SUFFERERS added to reverse. Clock hands at 3:38 position. Plain edge. Rarity 6. (Schmidt C50a)

| Rulau | Date | Metal | Size | F | VF | EF | Unc |
|---|---|---|---|---|---|---|---|
| II-El 10 | 1874 | WM | 30mm | 4.50 | 9.00 | 15.00 | 30.00 |

Exposition building, CHICAGO EXPOSITION above, 1000 FT. LONG 240 FT. W. / * 1874 * / * below. Tiny V.S. WEBER CHICAGO below ground. Rv: As obverse of II-El 5 (Winged nude Father Time). Plain edge. Rarity 6. (Schmidt C53)

| Rulau | Date | Metal | Size | VG | F | VF | Unc |
|---|---|---|---|---|---|---|---|
| II-El 11 | (1875) | WM | 30mm | 5.00 | 9.50 | 15.00 | 30.00 |

Obverse as II-El 5. Rv: Building at center, THIRD ANNUAL above, CHICAGO / EXPOSITION MEDAL below. Plain edge. Rarity 6. (Schmidt C55)

| II-El 14 | (1898-1930) | Brass | 31mm | 7.50 | 11.50 | 14.00 | 18.00 |

Winged Father Time right, holding aloft a large watch, and ELGIN ADVENTURERS' CLUB across the standing figure's legs — all within a clock face. Rv: (8 stars) / THIS IS TO / CERTIFY THAT / A. RUSSELL (incused; or another name) / IS A CHARTER / MEMBER / IF FOUND PLEASE RETURN TO THE ELGIN NATIONAL WATCH CO. ELGIN, ILL. Plain edge. Issued holed.

Dr Wright in 1898 called the figure on II-El 5 "Father Time," but the more familiar figure of Father Time today does appear on the last token listed above, II-El 14. The figure on 5 is unique to Elgin — a compelling representation.

The Chicago Exposition tokens perhaps should have been listed under Chicago in this catalog, but we preferred to keep all the Elgin National Watch Co. pieces together. Non-Elgin exposition pieces may be found under Chicago.

## ELGIN TURNVEREIN
### Elgin, Ill.

| Rulau | Date | Metal | Size | VG | F | VF | Unc |
|---|---|---|---|---|---|---|---|
| II-El 16 | (1880's) | Br Oct. | 23mm | — | — | 15.00 | 20.00 |

Owl facing, perched on crossed torch and sword, all within wreath. Above: L. BOCHE, CHECK M ' F ' R. Below: CHICAGO. Rv: ELGIN / —.— / TURN / —.— / VEREIN within corded circle. Plain edge. (Schmidt E32)

## FREJA
### Elgin, Ill.

| Rulau | Date | Metal | Size | VG | F | VF | Unc |
|---|---|---|---|---|---|---|---|
| II-El 18 | (1880's) | Brass | 25mm | — | 20.00 | 25.00 | |

Obverse as II-El 3, the Concordia token (Indian head left, L. BOCHE). Rv: FREJA / ELGIN / ILL. surrounded by stars. Plain edge. (Schmidt F70)

## SVEA SOCIETY
### Elgin, Ill.

| Rulau | Date | Metal | Size | VG | F | VF | Unc |
|---|---|---|---|---|---|---|---|
| II-El 40 | (1885) | Brass | 27mm? | — | 20.00 | 25.00 | — |

Three stars in relief within depressed circular center. SVEA SOCIETY / ELGIN (all incused) around. Rv: Blank. Plain edge.

| II-El 42 | (1885) | Brass | 27mm? | — | 20.00 | 25.00 | — |

Blank depressed circular center. (All incused) SVEA HALL / ELGIN around. Rv: Blank. Plain edge.

Svea = Swedish. Both pieces are in Rich Hartzog coll. The Svea Society was large; a hoard of tokens could exist.

## P. HERMAN JR.
### Freeburg, Ill.

| Rulau | Date | Metal | Size | VG | F | VF | Unc |
|---|---|---|---|---|---|---|---|
| II-Fr 5 | (1880's) | Brass | 28mm | — | 10.00 | — | — |

10 / ¢ within central circle, P. HERMAN JR. above, FREEBURG, ILL. below. Rv: Blank. Plain edge.

| II-Fr 6 | (1880's) | Brass | 33mm | — | 10.00 | — | — |

Similar, but 25 / ¢. Plain edge.

| II-Fr 7 | (1880's) | Brass | 36mm | — | 15.00 | — | — |

Similar, but 50 ¢. Plain edge.

| II-Fr 8 | (1880's) | Brass | 39mm | — | 25.00 | — | — |

Similar, but $ 1. Plain edge.

## T.B. ROWIN
### Kirkland, Ill.

| Rulau | Date | Metal | Size | VG | F | VF | Unc |
|---|---|---|---|---|---|---|---|
| II-Kk 3 | (1874-84) | Brass | 24mm | — | 20.00 | 30.00 | — |

Female head left in central circle, THE J.M. BRUNSWICK & BALKE COS. around, CHECK. below. Rv: GOOD FOR / 5¢ / T.B. ROWIN / KIRKLAND / IN / TRADE / *. Plain edge. (Schmidt R74)

## JOHN BERNER
### Lyons, Ill.

| Rulau | Date | Metal | Size | VG | F | VF | Unc |
|---|---|---|---|---|---|---|---|
| II-Ly 3 | (1880's) | Nkl Oct. | 25mm | — | — | 17.50 | 30.00 |

(All incused) JOHN BERNER / GOOD FOR / 5 ¢ / * DRINK * / LYONS. Rv: Blank. Plain edge. Only 3 known.

## BLANCHARD HOUSE
### Monmouth, Ill.

| Rulau | Date | Metal | Size | VG | F | VF | EF |
|---|---|---|---|---|---|---|---|
| II-Mn 3 | (1870-82) | Copper | 29mm | — | 100. | — | — |

BLANCHARD HOUSE / MONMOUTH / ILL ctsp on U.S. 1847 Large cent. Five specimens known.

| II-Mn 4 | (1870-82) | Silver | 27mm | — | 125. | — | — |

Similar ctsp on Spanish-American 1786-Mo 2-reales. (Gould 321; Brunk 48)

| II-Mn 5 | (1870-82) | Silver | 27mm | — | 125. | — | — |

Similar ctsp on Spanish-American Carlos III 2-reales. Also there is a small 'E' incused below. (Frank Kovacs coll.)

These pieces are probably related to the 1865 token of the Ed. Blanchard bar, II-Mn 6. Note that Blanchard used only coins already obsolete as money for his counterstamps.

E. Blanchard appears as a saloon keeper in the 1866 and 1870 *Bradstreet Directories*.

## ED. BLANCHARD
## Monmouth, Ill.

| Rulau | Date | Metal | Size | VG | F | VF | Unc |
|---|---|---|---|---|---|---|---|
| II-Mn 6 | 1865 | Brass | 22mm | 10.00 | 15.00 | 30.00 | 60.00 |

Horse. ED BLANCHARD — BAR CHECK. Rv: Dog. MONMOUTH, ILLS. — 1865. (Wright 1340; Schmidt B37)

## J. W. GAUL
## Monmouth, Ill.

| Rulau | Date | Metal | Size | VG | F | VF | Unc |
|---|---|---|---|---|---|---|---|
| II-Mn 9 | (?) | Brass | 25mm | 20.00 | 25.00 | 30.00 | 50.00 |

Elephant standing right. Rv: J. W. GAUL / * 5 * / MONMOUTH, ILLS. Plain edge. Rarity 6.

Compare this elephant with that on Maverick number MV 450 in this book. While resembling each other, they are definitely from different dies. The John W. Gaul restaurant was still in business in 1918.

## W. S. STITELY
## Mount Carroll, Ill.

| Rulau | Date | Metal | Size | VG | F | VF | Unc |
|---|---|---|---|---|---|---|---|
| II-MC 7 | (?) | Brass | 24mm | 9.00 | 15.00 | 20.00 | — |

(All incused) W. S. STITELY / GOOD FOR / 5 ¢ / LOAF OF BREAD / MT. CARROLL ILL. Rv: Blank. Plain edge. Beaded, incised rim on both sides.

| II-MC 7A | (?) | Alum | 24mm | — | — | — | — |

As 7. Plain edge. (Probably 1890's)

## M. WACHTER
## O'Fallon, Ill.

| Rulau | Date | Metal | Size | VG | F | VF | Unc |
|---|---|---|---|---|---|---|---|
| II-Of 7 | (1880-87) | Brass | 23mm | — | 15.00 | 20.00 | — |

(Incuse) M. WACHTER / (relief) GOOD FOR / (relief) 5 C / (relief) DRINK / (incuse) ornament. Rv: (All relief) F. MESSMER / — . — / FAUCET CO. / —.— / ST. LOUIS. Plain edge. 5 known. (Schmidt W10)

| II-Of9 | (1880-87) | Br sc | 23mm | — | 15.00 | 20.00 | — |

(Incuse) M. WACHTER / (relief) GOOD FOR / (relief) 5 ¢ / (relief) LOAF BREAD. Rv: Blank. Plain edge. Rarity 8. (Schmidt W12)

## F. X. MAYER
## Oregon, Ill.

| Rulau | Date | Metal | Size | VG | F | VF | Unc |
|---|---|---|---|---|---|---|---|
| II-Or 5 | (1880's) | Br Oct. | 26mm | 15.00 | 20.00 | 25.00 | — |

F. X. MAYER / (stylized flower) / OREGON / ILL. Rv: GOOD FOR / 5 / CENTS / —AT— / *** X.'S. ***. Plain edge.

Mayer was in business 1880-1895, and evidently his place was known as 'X's' after his middle initial. (Likely his name was Francis Xavier Mayer — common among German Catholics).

## BOWMAN
## Ottawa, Ill.

| Rulau | Date | Metal | Size | VG | F | VF | EF |
|---|---|---|---|---|---|---|---|
| II-Ot 2 | (1870-81) | Silver | 31mm | — | 240. | 275. | — |

BOWMAN / PHOTOGRAPHER / OTTAWA. ILL. ctsp on U.S. 1860 Liberty Seated half dollar. (Bill Rodgers collection; Schmidt B57)

| II-Ot 3 | (1870-81) | | | — | — | — | — |

Similar ctsp on several different, unspecified coins. (Brunk 53)

| II-Ot 3A | (1870-81) | Silver | 31mm | — | — | — | — |

Similar ctsp on U.S. 1857 Liberty Seated half dollar.

| II-Ot 5 | (1870-81) | | | — | — | — | — |

BOWMAN ctsp on several different, unspecified coins. (Brunk 52)

W. E. Bowman, born in Pennsylvania Apr. 28, 1834, studied photography in 1857 under Dewitt Rawson and settled in LaSalle, Ill. in 1865. His photography won him six silver medals at state fairs. The counterstamps date from 1870-1881, most likely, but could be as early as 1866.

## CHILD & BRO.
## Ottawa, Ill.

| Rulau | Date | Metal | Size | VG | F | VF | EF |
|---|---|---|---|---|---|---|---|
| II-Ot 9 | (1866-76) | Silver | 31mm | 125. | — | 150. | — |

CHILD & BRO / OTTAWA ILL ctsp on U.S. 1854-O with Arrows Liberty Seated half dollar. (Brunk 85) (Seven specimens known.)

| II-Ot 10 | (1866-76) | Silver | 25mm | — | — | 225. | — |

Similar ctsp on U.S. 1859 Seated Liberty quarter.

Child & Brother are listed as shoemakers in the 1866, 1870, 1871 and 1876 directories.

## CENTENNIAL OF OUR NATION
## Peru, Ill.

| Rulau | Date | Metal | Size | F | VF | EF | Unc |
|---|---|---|---|---|---|---|---|
| II-Pu 4 | 1889 | WM* | 37mm | — | — | 2 Known | |

Obverse same as II-Ch 7 (Washington bust left). Rv: As II-Ch 7, but .PERU, ILLS. COMMEMORATION. at bottom in place of CHICAGO COMMEMORATION. Plain edge. Issued holed. (Schmidt C42)

*Actual pot metal, a lead alloy.
The Schmidt specimen, the finest known, is shown above. The Phil Klabel specimen has been dug up. (See same issuer under Chicago and Springfield). This type could have been issued for other towns as well.

## H. S. M.
## (H. S. Moody)
## Shawneetown, Ill.

| Rulau | Date | Metal | Size | VG | F | VF | Unc |
|---|---|---|---|---|---|---|---|
| II-Sh 4 | (1878-83) | Brass | 31mm | — | 15.00 | 20.00 | — |

H. S. M. / SHAWNEETOWN, ILS. Rv: Blank. Plain edge. Rarity 9. (Schmidt H9)

H. S. Moody appears in the 1878 and 1883 directories.

## CENTENNIAL OF OUR NATION
## Springfield, Ill.

| Rulau | Date | Metal | Size | VG | F | VF | Unc |
|---|---|---|---|---|---|---|---|
| II-Sp 3 | 1889 | WM* | 37mm | — | — | Rare | — |

* Actually pot metal, another lead alloy. Obverse same as II-Ch 7 (Washington bust left). Rv: As II-Ch 7, but SPRINGFIELD, ILL. COMMEMORATION at bottom in place of CHICAGO COMMEMORATION. Plain edge. Issued holed with a red, white and blue ribbon for suspension. 3 known. (Schmidt C42)

For similar pieces of the same issue, see under Chicago and Peru, Ill.

## ILLINOIS WATCH CO.
## Springfield, Ill.

| Rulau | Date | Metal | Size | VG | F | VF | Unc |
|---|---|---|---|---|---|---|---|
| II-Sp 9 | (?) | WM | 28mm | — | — | 20.00 | 30.00 |

Clock face. In upper area: I W C. Rv: ILLINOIS WATCH Co / ——— / KEY / — & — / STEM WIND / WATCHES / —— / SPRINGFIELD. Plain edge.

## KINGMAN & CO.
## Peoria, Ill. & St. Louis, Mo.

| Rulau | Date | Metal | Size | VG | F | VF | Unc |
|---|---|---|---|---|---|---|---|
| II-Pe 6 | 1885 | WM | 31mm? | — | — | Rare | — |

Plough at center, KINGMAN & CO. / WHOLESALE above, FARM / MACHINERY / PEORIA, ILL. * ST. LOUIS, MO. below. Rv: HIGHEST AWARD / FOR / BEST DISPLAY / AT / ST. LOUIS FAIR, 1885. (Wright 554)

Kingman, Hotchkiss & Co., farm implements, appears in 1870 directories.

## KITTINGERS
## Upper Alton, Ill.

| Rulau | Date | Metal | Size | VG | F | VF | Unc |
|---|---|---|---|---|---|---|---|
| II-Ua 2 | (1880-1900) | Brass sc, 23mm | | — | 15.00 | 25.00 | — |

KITTINGERS / 1 / LOAF. Rv: EXCELSIOR, 113 OLIVE ST., ST. LOUIS. Plain edge. Rarity 8. (Schmidt K32)

Daniel B. Kittinger had a grocery store in Upper Alton, at College Avenue near Manning Street, in the 1880's and 1890's.
The Excelsior firm in St. Louis struck his tokens.

## A. NESBIT
## Whitehall, Ill.

| Rulau | Date | Metal | Size | VG | F | VF | Unc |
|---|---|---|---|---|---|---|---|
| II-Wt 3 | (1870's) | Brass | 25mm | — | 15.00 | 20.00 | — |

(All incused) A. NESBIT / 10¢ / BREAD. Rv: Blank. Plain edge. Rarity 9. (Schmidt N20)

Archibald Nesbit, born in Ireland, traveled extensively before settling in Whitehall (which was once known as Loafer's Grove). Nesbit's bakery was operated in the 1870's.

## HAYWARD'S BILLIARD PARLOR
## Illinois ?

| Rulau | Date | Metal | Size | VG | F | VF | Unc |
|---|---|---|---|---|---|---|---|
| II-Un 1 | (1880-86) | Brass | 25mm | — | 15.00 | 20.00 | — |

HAYWARD'S BILLIARD PARLOR / GOOD FOR / 15¢ / AT BAR. Rv: Crossed goblet, tongs and ladle. Above: CHAS. PICK & CO. / DEALERS IN. Below: (Diamond) CHICAGO. (diamond). Plain edge. All devices and lettering incused.

Charles Pick & Company was a manufacturer of supplies for billiard parlors, restaurants, etc. Its tokens, unlike those of the Brunswick and other billiard supply houses, are less often encountered. Pick made tokens for concerns in 11 states and Canada, using at least 13 different stock dies in the 1880-1915 period. That used here is the oldest type, circa 1880-86.

## PETER CARLSON
## Utica, Ill.

| Rulau | Date | Metal | Size | VG | F | VF | Unc |
|---|---|---|---|---|---|---|---|
| II-Ut 3 | (1880) | Br Oct. 26mm | | — | 10.00 | — | Rare |

(All incuse) PETER CAELSON / GOOD FOR / 5¢ / DRINK / AT BAR / UTICA, ILLS. Rv: Blank. Plain edge. Only 4 specimens known.

### C. E. HENSEN
### Virden, Ill.

| Rulau | Date | Metal | Size | VG | F | VF | Unc |
|---|---|---|---|---|---|---|---|
| Il-Vi 3 | (1880's) | Brass | 25mm | — | — | 20.00 | 30.00 |

Rooster left, C. E. HENSEN above, VIRDEN, ILL. below. Rv: Large 15 within circle of 16 alternating stars and rosettes, each of 5 points. Plain edge.

### W. C. McDONALD
### Virginia, Ill.

| Rulau | Date | Metal | Size | VG | F | VF | Unc |
|---|---|---|---|---|---|---|---|
| Il-Vg 5 | (?) | CN | 25mm | 15.00 | 20.00 | 25.00 | 35.00 |

W. C. McDONALD / BILLIARD / * / PARLOR / VIRGINIA ILL. Rv: GOOD FOR 5 CENTS / UNCLE BEN ? . * . / * CIGAR * / + 5 + / O IN TRADE O. Plain edge. (Hartzog coll.)

# INDIANA

### C.S. HILDEBRAND & CO.
### Crawfordsville, Ind.

| Rulau | Date | Metal | Size | VG | F | VF | Unc |
|---|---|---|---|---|---|---|---|
| In-Cr 3 | (?) | Brass | 23mm | 10.00 | 18.00 | 30.00 | — |

*O* / C.S. HILDEBRAND / — & CO — / WATCHMAKERS / — / & / JEWELERS / CRAWFORDSVILLE, IND. Rv: JAMES MURDOCK, JR. / STAMPS / BURNING / BRANDS / AND / STENCILS / 139 / W. 5TH ST., CINCINNATI. Plain edge. (Wright 452; Miller Ind 1)

### WHITNEY SEWING MACHINE
### Indianapolis, Ind.

| Rulau | Date | Metal | Size | VG | F | VF | Unc |
|---|---|---|---|---|---|---|---|
| In-Ip 9 | 1874 | WM | 29mm | 7.50 | 10.00 | 15.00 | 30.00 |

Buildings across center, tiny CHAS. H. COX. at right under ground line. Above: EXPOSITION BUILDINGS. Below: INDIANAPOLIS. / *. Rv: Within wreath at center: INDIANA / STATE FAIR / & / EXPOSITION / * / 1874. Around: * BUY THE WHITNEY SEWING MACHINE & GET FOR THIS $10. Plain edge. (Brunk coll.)

### B.W. SMITH & CO.
### Lafayette, Ind.

| Rulau | Date | Metal | Size | VG | F | VF | Unc |
|---|---|---|---|---|---|---|---|
| In-La 6 | 1882 | Brass | 25mm | — | — | 10.00 | — |

Man cutting tree at right, bison charging left, sun rising over mountains in background. DOG TAG / 1882 above. Rv: Number 183 in relief on open book; B.W. SMITH & CO. / LAFAYETTE. / IND. below. Plain edge. Issued holed. (Wright 995)

Dr. Wright's piece was numbered '89.'

### C.S. STEEL
### Mishawaka, Ind.

| Rulau | Date | Metal | Size | VG | F | VF | EF |
|---|---|---|---|---|---|---|---|
| In-Mk 7 | (?) | Copper | 29mm | — | — | 40.00 | — |

C.S. STEEL / MISHAWAKA ctsp on U.S. Large cent. (Hallenbeck 19.771)

### J.W. COTTON (and)
### WILLIS COTTON
### Walkerton, Ind.

| Rulau | Date | Metal | Size | VG | F | VF | EF |
|---|---|---|---|---|---|---|---|
| In-Wa 3 | 1875 | — | — | — | — | 40.00 | — |

J.W. COTTON, WALKERTON, IND. / 1875 ctsp on unspecified coins / obverse. Rv: GOOD HEALTH IS MORE WEALTH THAN MUCH MONEY on coins' reverse. (Brunk 109)

| | | | | | | | |
|---|---|---|---|---|---|---|---|
| In-Wa 4 | 1875 | — | — | — | — | 40.00 | — |

WILLIS COTTON, WALKERTON, IND. / 1875 ctsp on unspecified coins' obverse. Rv: INDUSTRY AND ECONOMY SHOULD GO HAND IN HAND on coins' reverse. (Brunk 110)

### P. HUFFMAN
### Warsaw, Ind.

| Rulau | Date | Metal | Size | VG | F | VF | EF |
|---|---|---|---|---|---|---|---|
| In-Ww 4 | (?) | Silver | 39mm | — | — | 150. | — |

P. HUFFMAN / WARSAW, INDIANA ctsp on Mexico 8-reales. (Gould 98)

## INDIANA ASBURY UNIVERSITY
### Indiana

| Rulau | Date | Metal | Size | VG | F | VF | Unc |
|---|---|---|---|---|---|---|---|
| In-Un 2 | 1866 | Brass | 30mm | — | — | 12.50 | |

Male bust in clerical garb to right, CENTENNIAL MEDAL above, 1866 below. Rv: INDIANA / ASBURY / UNIVERSITY within wreath. Outside wreath: SUNDAY SCHOOL CENTENARY CHAIR. Plain edge. Issued holed.

## ALBION COLLEGE
### Indiana

| Rulau | Date | Metal | Size | F | VF | EF | Unc |
|---|---|---|---|---|---|---|---|
| In-Un 4 | 1884 | WM | 35mm | — | — | 35.00 | |

Building within central circle. Above: ASBURY CENTENARY LIBRARY ASSOCIATION. Below: ** ALBION * 1884 * COLLEGE **. Rv: Rev. Coke administering oath to kneeling Asbury within central circle, ASBURY at left, COKE at right. Around: FRANCIS ASBURY ORDAINED BISHOP OF THE METHODIST EPISCOPAL CHURCH DEC 27 / 1784. Plain edge. (Brunk coll.)

Francis Asbury, subject of numbers 2 and 4, was born Aug. 20, 1745 at Handsworth, Staffordshire, England. A preacher, he emigrated to America in 1771 and soon became John Wesley's general assistant in the Methodist Church. He favored American independence and became a citizen of Delaware in 1778. In 1784 he was elected superintendent of the Methodist Church in America and its first bishop consecrated in this country. It is due to his diligent travel as head of the church that it grew from 3 to 412 congregations by the time of his death March 31, 1816, at Spottsylvania, Va.

# IOWA

## C. CANNON
### Dubuque, Iowa

| Rulau | Date | Metal | Size | VG | F | VF | EF |
|---|---|---|---|---|---|---|---|
| Ia-Du 3 | (?) | ? | --mm | — | — | 200. | — |

C. CANNON / GROCER / NO. 41 / DUBUQUE, IOWA ctsp on various different, unspecified coins. (Brunk 76)

| Ia-Du 4 | (?) | Silver | 27mm | — | — | 200. | — |

Similar ctsp on Spanish-American 2-reales.

## A. KOHN & CO.
### McGreger, Iowa

**1876 Centennial Tokens**

Reverse type 1: A. KOHN & CO. / (star) / CLOTHING / HALL / HATS & CAPS / McGREGER, IOWA. (All 23mm; plain edge)

| Rulau | Obv | Rev | Metal | F | VF | EF | Unc |
|---|---|---|---|---|---|---|---|
| Ia-Mc 3 | G | 1 (Miller Iowa 1) | WM | — | — | — | 150. |
| Ia-Mc3 A | G | 1 (ANS coll.) | Copper | — | — | — | 150. |
| Ia-Mc 3 B | G | 1 (ANS coll.) | Brass | — | — | — | 150. |

## J.B. ADLON
### Oskaloosa, Iowa (?)

| Rulau | Date | Metal | Size | VG | F | VF | EF |
|---|---|---|---|---|---|---|---|
| Ia-Os 1 | 1876 | Silver | 26mm | — | — | 45.00 | — |

J.B. ADLON. / 1876. / OSKLOOSA ctsp on 1853 Arrows and Rays quarter dollar. (Krause coll.)

The attribution to Oskaloosa, Iowa is uncertain. It could be a much smaller place, Oskloosa, Kansas. There does not appear to be an 'Oskloosa' in the United States. The 1877 Postal Guide also listed an Oskaloosa in Clay County, Ill.

## CORN PALACE
### Sioux City, Iowa

| Rulau | Date | Metal | Size | F | VF | EF | Unc |
|---|---|---|---|---|---|---|---|
| Ia-SC 7 | 1888 | Gilt Brass | 25mm | — | — | 12.00 | |

Building at center, CORN PALACE above, SIOUX CITY, IA. below. Rv: SOUVENIR / OF / THE CORN PALACE / CITY OF THE WORLD / 1888., all within flourishes. Plain edge.

| Rulau | Date | Metal | Size | F | VF | EF | Unc |
|---|---|---|---|---|---|---|---|
| Ia-SC 16 | (1880's) | —mm | — | — | — | 12.00 | 15.00 |

Obverse: Rv: Crossed ears of corn at center. SIOUX / CORN -- PALACE / CITY. Plain edge. Issued holed.

Corn Palace tokens bearing dates 1887, 1890 and 1891 are also reported. Apparently all Corn Palace pieces were originally issued as badges suspended from ribbons, or intended for such use.

| Rulau | Date | Metal | Size | F | VF | EF | Unc |
|---|---|---|---|---|---|---|---|
| Ia-SC 8 | 1888 | Gilt Brass | 25mm | — | — | 12.00 | — |

Indian head left, KING CORN on its headband. Above: SECOND ANNUAL HARVEST FESTIVAL. Below: SOUVENIR / + 1888 +. Rv: Building at center, CORN PALACE above. SIOUX CITY in exergue. Plain edge.

## CASPER BENESK
### Spillville, Iowa

| Rulau | Date | Metal | Size | VG | F | VF | Unc |
|---|---|---|---|---|---|---|---|
| Ia-Sp 1 | (1877-94) | Brass | 24mm | — | — | 40.00 | — |

—.— / CHECK / —.— within central circle. Around: BRUNSWICK & COMPANY. / CHICAGO. Rv: GOOD FOR / 5 ¢ / CASPER BENESK. Plain edge. (Brunswick page 16, no number)

| Rulau | Date | Metal | Size | F | VF | EF | Unc |
|---|---|---|---|---|---|---|---|
| Ia-SC 9 | 1888 | SWM | 30mm | — | — | 15.00 | 20.00 |

Liberty head in Phrygian cap right, ears of corn at either side. SIOUX CITY on headband. M on truncation of bust. Rv: Corn Palace in center, . CORN PALACE . above, SEP. 24. OCT. 6. 1888. below. Plain edge. Issued holed.

## PUTZEL'S CLOTHING HALL
### Winterset, Iowa

**1876 Centennial Tokens**

| Rulau | Date | Metal | Size | F | VF | EF | Unc |
|---|---|---|---|---|---|---|---|
| Ia-SC 14 | 1889 | Gilt Brass | 26mm | — | — | 12.00 | 17.00 |

Corn Palace within central circle, SIOUX CITY CORN PALACE around, . 1889 . below. Rv: Crossed ears of corn surrounded by wreath. CORN IS KING around. Plain edge. Issued holed.

Reverse type 1: PUTZEL'S / (star) / CLOTHING / HALL / HATS CAPS / WINTERSET, IOWA. (All 23mm; plain edge)

| Rulau | Obv | Rev | Metal | F | VF | EF | Unc |
|---|---|---|---|---|---|---|---|
| Ia-Wi 3 | H | 1 (Miller 2) | WM | — | — | — | 150. |
| Ia-Wi 3 A | H | 1 (ANS coll.) | Brass | — | — | — | 150. |

# KANSAS

## SWENSON BROTHERS
### Cleburne, Kansas

| Rulau | Date | Metal | Size | VG | F | VF | Unc |
|---|---|---|---|---|---|---|---|
| Ks-Cl 5 | 1888 | Brass | Oct. 22.5mm | — | — | 20.00 | — |

Triangle with large 1 inside, at center. Around: SWENSON BROTHERS / A 1888 D. Rv: Triangle with 1 inside, GOOD FOR above, MDSE. below. Plain edge. Two die varieties (large dots and small dots).

| Rulau | Date | Metal | Size | VG | F | VF | Unc |
|---|---|---|---|---|---|---|---|
| Ks-Cl 6 | 1888 | Brass | 21mm | — | — | 20.00 | — |
| Ks-Cl 10 | 1888 | Alum | 39mm | — | — | 25.00 | — |

Similar, but 5. Plain edge.

Similar, but large S inside each triangle, and 500 on three sides around it. Plain edge.

Aluminum was still a somewhat 'noble' metal in 1888, accounting for its use on the $5 denomination. (See "The Swenson Brothers" by Kent Johnson in *TAMS Journal* for Oct., 1977).

These tokens could have been issued later than the date they bear.

*Court House Square, Lexington, Kentucky, 1887.*

# KENTUCKY

### HARNESS & CLAY
### Hopkinsville, Ky.

| Rulau | Date | Metal | Size | VG | F | VF | Unc |
|---|---|---|---|---|---|---|---|
| Ky-Ho 1 | (?) | Gilt/B | 23mm | — | 75.00 | — | — |

HARNESS & CLAY / PHARMACISTS / — / HOPKINSVILLE / KY. Rv: — / 5 ¢ / SODA. / —. Rim of beaded dots on both sides. Plain edge. Square planchet. (Miller Ky. 1/2A)

### H. WILSON
### Lexington, Ky.

| Rulau | Date | Metal | Size | VG | F | VF | EF |
|---|---|---|---|---|---|---|---|
| Ky-Lx 10 | (?) | Silver | 30mm | — | — | 100. | — |

H. WILSON LEX. KY. ctsp on Canada 1870 Queen Victoria half dollar.

### WINCHESTER
### Lexington, Ky.

| Ky-Lx 12 | (?) | Silver | 31mm | — | — | 100. | — |
|---|---|---|---|---|---|---|---|

WINCHESTER, LEX. KY ctsp on U.S. 1838 Bust half dollar.

### COOK & SLOSS
### Louisville, Ky.

| Rulau | Date | Metal | Size | VG | F | VF | Unc |
|---|---|---|---|---|---|---|---|
| Ky-Lo 4 | (?) | Brass | 26mm | 10.00 | 20.00 | 30.00 | 60.00 |

Exposition buildings, LOUISVILLE INDUSTRIAL EXPOSITION. Rv: COOK & SLOSS, JEWLERS, LOUISVILLE. Plain edge. (Miller Ky. 5)

| Ky-Lo 5 | (?) | Brass | 26mm | — | — | 20.00 | 30.00 |
|---|---|---|---|---|---|---|---|

Railroad locomotive right, spewing smoke, PROGRESS above. Rv: As 5. Plain edge. (Miller Ky. 6)

### HOWE MACHINE CO.
### Louisville, Ky.

| Rulau | Date | Metal | Size | VG | F | VF | Unc |
|---|---|---|---|---|---|---|---|
| Ky-Lo 10 | (?) | Brass | 26mm | — | 20.00 | 30.00 | 60.00 |

Bust right within circle. Around: THE HOWE MACHINE CO. Below: * ELIAS HOWE JR. *. Rv: Railroad locomotive right, spewing smoke from its chimney. Above: PROGRESS. Plain edge. (Wright 1461; Miller Ky. 15)

| Rulau | Date | Metal | Size | VG | F | VF | Unc |
|---|---|---|---|---|---|---|---|
| Ky-Lo 11 | (?) | WM | 26mm | 9.00 | 20.00 | 30.00 | 60.00 |

As 15. Plain edge. (Miller Ky. 15A)

| Ky-Lo 12 | (?) | Brass | 26mm | 9.00 | 20.00 | 30.00 | 60.00 |
|---|---|---|---|---|---|---|---|

Exposition buildings, LOUISVILLE INDUSTRIAL EXPOSITION. Rv: Large $10 at center. Inscription: BUY A HOWE MACHINE FOR CASH & RECEIVE FOR THIS / AT 166 FOURTH ST., LOUISVILLE, KY. Plain edge. (Miller Ky. 16)

| Ky-Lo 13 | (?) | Brass | 26mm | 9.00 | 20.00 | 30.00 | 60.00 |
|---|---|---|---|---|---|---|---|

Obverse as reverse of Ky 15 (Locomotive). Rv: As 16. Plain edge. (Wright 1462; Miller Ky. 17)

| Ky-Lo 14 | (?) | Brass | 26mm | — | — | 20.00 | 30.00 |
|---|---|---|---|---|---|---|---|

Obverse as 16 (Exposition buildings). Rv: As 15 (Locomotive). Plain edge. Muling: no name on token. (Miller Ky. 18)

The Exposition Buildings or Locomotive stock dies were also used on other Louisville cards — of F. S. Kirtland, Cook & Sloss, Preuser & Wellenvoss, and J. W. Quest.

In the 1880's Louisville moved to rebuild the shattered industry of the South following the Civil War and was greatly aided in this by the extension of the Louisville & Nashville Railroad, referred to on the tokens as 'PROGRESS'.

## DEPPEN'S HATTERS
### Louisville, Ky.

| Rulau | Date | Metal | Size | VG | F | VF | Unc |
|---|---|---|---|---|---|---|---|
| Ky-Lo 7 | 1888 | Alum | 23mm | — | — | — | — |

Flowers over entire field. Across center is a bar inscribed: LOUISVILLE, KY. Around: COMMERCIAL AND FLORAL CELEBRATION / 1888. Rv: DEPPEN'S / HATTERS / ** / CLOTHIERS / HABERDASHERS / xx / TAILORS / * LOUISVILLE *. Plain edge. (Wright 242)

## F. S. KIRTLAND
### Louisville, Ky.

| Rulau | Date | Metal | Size | VG | F | VF | Unc |
|---|---|---|---|---|---|---|---|
| Ky-Lo 17 | (?) | Brass | 26mm | 9.00 | 20.00 | 30.00 | 60.00 |

Exposition buildings, LOUISVILLE INDUSTRIAL EXPOSITION. Rv: F. S. KIRTLAND / * / CLOTHING / N. E. COR. FOURTH / & JEFFERSON / * / LOUISVILLE, KY. Plain edge. (Miller Ky. 20)

| Ky-Lo 18 | (?) | Brass | 26mm | 9.00 | 20.00 | 30.00 | 60.00 |
|---|---|---|---|---|---|---|---|

Railroad locomotive right, spewing, PROGRESS above. Rv: As 20. Plain edge. (Wright 558); Miller Ky. 21)

## PREUSER & WELLENVOSS
### Louisville, Ky.

| Rulau | Date | Metal | Size | VG | F | VF | Unc |
|---|---|---|---|---|---|---|---|
| Ky-Lo 20 | (?) | Brass | 26mm | 9.00 | 20.00 | 30.00 | 60.00 |

Exposition buildings, LOUISVILLE INDUSTRIAL EXPOSITION. Rv: Hat. PREUSER & WELLENVOSS / 56 MARKET ST. BET. 2ND & 3RD ST / * LOUISVILLE KY. *. Plain edge. (Wright 847; Miller Ky. 27)

| Ky-Lo 21 | (?) | Brass | 26mm | 9.00 | 20.00 | 30.00 | 60.00 |
|---|---|---|---|---|---|---|---|

Railroad locomotive right, spewing smoke, PROGRESS above. Rv: As 27. Plain edge. (Miller Ky. 28)

## J. W. QUEST
### Louisville, Ky.

| Rulau | Date | Metal | Size | VG | F | VF | Unc |
|---|---|---|---|---|---|---|---|
| Ky-Lo 24 | (1880's) | Brass | 25mm | 9.00 | 20.00 | 30.00 | 60.00 |

Buildings, LOUISVILLE INDUSTRIAL EXPOSITION. Rv: J. W. QUEST / BOOTS & SHOES / (boot) / 80 WEST MARKET ST. / LOUISVILLE, KY. Plain edge. (Miller Ky. 30)

| Ky-Lo 25 | (1880's) | Brass | 25mm | 9.00 | 20.00 | 30.00 | 60.00 |
|---|---|---|---|---|---|---|---|

Locomotive spewing smoke right, PROGRESS above. Rv: As Ky. 30. Plain edge. (Wright 864; Miller Ky. 31)

## SOUTHERN EXPOSITION
### Louisville, Ky.

| Rulau | Date | Metal | Size | F | VF | Unc |
|---|---|---|---|---|---|---|
| Ky-Lo 30 | 1883 | Bronze | —mm | — | 10.00 | 30.00 |

Aerial view of exposition building complex, mountains in background. Rv: SOUTHERN EXPOSITION / AUG. 1ST 1883 / SOUVENIR (on scroll) / 100 DAYS / LOUISVILLE, KY. Plain edge.

| Ky-Lo 32 | 1883 | S/WM | 32mm | — | — | — | 60.00 |
|---|---|---|---|---|---|---|---|

Two men shaking hands within a shield, ribbon below reads: UNITED WE STAND DIVIDED WE FALL. Below: SOUTHERN EXPOSITION, LOUISVILLE, KENTUCKY. Rv: Building across center, OPENS AUG. 1ST 1883 above, CONTINUES / ONE HUNDRED DAYS below. Plain edge.

## WAYT DENTAL CO.
### Louisville, Ky.

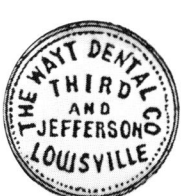 

| Rulau | Date | Metal | Size | VG | F | VF | Unc |
|---|---|---|---|---|---|---|---|
| Ky-Lo 35 | (?) | GS | 25mm | — | — | — | 75.00 |

THE WAYT DENTAL CO / THIRD / AND / JEFFERSON / LOUISVILLE. Rv: FOUR EXPERIENCED / DENTISTS / AND A KIND / —AND— / EFFICIENT / LADY / ATTENDANT. (Wright 1133)

## F. B.
### Newport, Ky.

| Rulau | Date | Metal | Size | VG | F | VF | Unc |
|---|---|---|---|---|---|---|---|
| Ky-Ne 3 | (?) | Br Sq. | 23.5mm | — | — | 20.00 | — |

— * — / F. B. / NEWPORT, KY. / (ornament), all within central circle. Rv: — * — / POST OFFICE / — * — / EXCHANGE / — * — / UNSER FRITZ / — * — / I. (All arranged in diamond shape.) There is a beaded border on each side. Plain edge.

## JOHN H. JENKINS
### Silver Grove, Ky.

| Rulau | Date | Metal | Size | VG | F | VF | EF |
|---|---|---|---|---|---|---|---|
| Ky-Si 4 | (?) | Silver | 31mm | — | 150. | — | 250. |

JOHN H. JENKINS / SILVER GROVE ctsp on U.S. 1865 Liberty Seated half dollar. (Gould 33; Brunk 195)

Silver Grove is in Campbell County near the Ohio River, a suburb of Newport, upriver from Cincinnati. No Silver Grove, however, appeared in the 1877 Postal Guide.

# LOUISIANA

## CHARLES H. RICHARDSON
### Baton Rouge, La.

| Rulau | Date | Metal | Size | VG | F | VF | EF |
|---|---|---|---|---|---|---|---|
| La-BR 7 | (?) | ? | —mm | | | | |

CHARLES H. RICHARDSON / BATON ROUGE, LA. ctsp on several different, unspecified coins. (Brunk 315)

| La-BR 8 | (?) | Silver | 38mm | | | | |

Similar ctsp on U.S. 1860 Liberty Seated dollar. (Gould 6)

| La-BR 9 | (?) | Silver | 38mm | | | | |

Similar ctsp on U.S. 1867 Liberty Seated dollar. (Gould 6)

| La-BR 11 | (?) | ? | —mm | | | | |

RICHARDSON / BATON ROUGE, LA. ctsp on several different, unspecified coins. (Brunk 314)

## G. W. BENNETT
### Bennettville, La.

| Rulau | Date | Metal | Size | F | VF | EF | Unc |
|---|---|---|---|---|---|---|---|
| La-Be 1 | 1871 | GS | 30mm | 50.00 | 65.00 | — | Rare |

(All lettering incuse). G. W. BENNETT / GOOD FOR / x 25¢ x / IN GOODS / BENNETTVILLE, LA. 1871. Rv: Same as obverse. Plain edge.

| La-Be 2 | 1871 | GS | 32mm | | | | V. Rare |

As 1, but 50¢. Plain edge.

| La-Be 3 | 1871 | GS | 35mm | | | | V. Rare |

As 1, but $100. Plain edge.

This was a general store in Rapides Parish, probably associated with sugar plantations, which closed in 1905. Bennettville was located between Bunkie and Cheneyville. It is possible that 5 and 10-cent tokens were issued, but none have been reported.

At present only one or two specimens of each token are known. The 25-cent piece illustrated (Rulau coll., ex-Fuld) is in VF-plus condition.

## JULIUS LEVIN & CO.
### Levin, La.

| Rulau | Date | Metal | Size | VG | F | VF | Unc |
|---|---|---|---|---|---|---|---|
| La-Lv 1 | (1880-95) | Brass | 23mm | — | — | Rare | — |

JULIUS LEVIN & CO. (incuse) / GOOD FOR / 5 C. / IN MDSE. / LEVIN, LA. (incuse). Rv: W.H. HASKELL / 713 / OLIVE ST. / ST. LOUIS. Plain edge.

| La-Lv 4 | (1880-95) | Brass | 28mm | — | — | Rare | — |

Similar, but 1.00. Plain edge.

Julius Levin operated a sawmill at what is known today as Tioga in Rapides Parish.

## ALF J. MAYER
### Marksville, La.

| Rulau | Date | Metal | Size | VG | F | VF | Unc |
|---|---|---|---|---|---|---|---|
| La-Ma 4 | (1880) | Brass | —mm | — | — | — | — |

ALF. J. MAYER, / . . . . . . / — * — / MARKSVULLE / — LA. — . Rv: MERCHANDISE / 25 / CHECK. Plain edge.

| La-Ma5 | (1880) | Brass Oct. | —mm | — | — | — | — |

Similar, but 10 instead of 25. Plain edge.

## GEO. L. MAYER
### Marksville, La.

| Rulau | Date | Metal | Size | VG | F | VF | Unc |
|---|---|---|---|---|---|---|---|
| La-Ma 9 | (1880's) | Brass | 30mm | — | — | — | — |

GOOD FOR MERCHANDISE / GEO. L. / MAYER / — . — / MARKSVILLE / LA. Rv: 1oo. Beaded rims on both sides. Plain edge.

| Rulau | Date | Metal | Size | G | VG | F | EF |
|---|---|---|---|---|---|---|---|
| La-Ma 13 | (1880's) | Br | Oc. 23mm | 5.00 | 10.00 | — | — |

GOOD FOR MERCHANDISE / GEO. L. / MAYER / —.— / MARKSVILLE / LA. Rv: Large 10. Plain edge.

In 1918 there was a firm, Mayer Brothers, in the auto and supply business in Marksville, Avoyelles Parish, which may have been a successor firm. In 1918 Marksville had 1,076 people.

## HENRY KLINE
### Monroe, La.

| Rulau | Date | Metal | Size | VG | F | VF | Unc |
|---|---|---|---|---|---|---|---|
| La-Mo 3 | (1889-90) | GS | 29mm | — | — | 40.00 | — |

COMMERCIAL / SALOON / HENRY KLINE, / PRO. / MONROE, LA. Rv: I O U / ONE / DRINK. Plain edge.

## CASSIDY'S
### New Orleans, La.

| Rulau | Date | Metal | Size | VG | F | VF | Unc |
|---|---|---|---|---|---|---|---|
| La-No 8 | (1880's ?) | Brass | 31mm | — | 13.50 | 22.50 | — |

CASSIDY'S / $5.00 / 174 / GRAVIER ST. Rv: Blank. (Wright 146)

## CRESCENT CITY ATHLETIC CLUB
### New Orleans, La.

| Rulau | Date | Metal | Size | F | VF | EF | Unc |
|---|---|---|---|---|---|---|---|
| La-No 15 | 1883 | ? | ---mm | — | 20.00 | — | — |

Building at center, CRESCENT CITY ATHLETIC CLUB above, AMPHITHEATER below. Rv: Two men boxing. HALL VS. FITZSIMMONS / $40,000 / MARCH 8TH, 1883. Plain edge. (Wright 1383)

The token description in Wright is incomplete.
Robert Fitzsimmons (called "Bob" or "Ruby Robert") was born in Helston, Cornwall, England, June 4, 1862, and died in Chicago, Oct. 22, 1917. He became world boxing champion in three separate weight divisions, middleweight, light heavyweight and heavyweight (respectively in 1891, 1903 and 1897). Born in Cornwall, he grew up in New Zealand and emigrated to America in 1890 after visiting there in 1883. He won the middleweight championship from Nonpareil Jack Dempsey (13 rounds) in New Orleans, Jan. 14, 1891. He won the heavyweight championship from Jim Corbett (14 rounds) in Carson City, Nev. on March 17, 1897 (resigning his middleweight crown). He lost the heavyweight crown to James J. Jeffries (11 rounds) at Coney Island, N.Y., June 9, 1899.
Fitzsimmons won the light heavyweight crown at the age of 41 when he defeated George Gardner (20 rounds) in San Francisco, Nov. 25, 1903. He lost this crown in a knockout (13 rounds) in San Francisco on Dec. 20, 1905 by Jack O'Brien. Fitzsimmons weighed only about 170 pounds in his fighting career but had the chest and shoulder development of a much larger man.

## MARDI GRAS
### New Orleans, La.

| Rulau | Date | Metal | Size | F | VF | EF | Unc |
|---|---|---|---|---|---|---|---|
| La-No 25 | 1884 | Gilt Brass | 16mm | 10.00 | 16.00 | 22.00 | 28.00 |

NEW ORLEANS / 1884 / FEBRUARY. Rv: MARDI GRAS / (ornament) / SOUVENIR. Plain edge.

## A. FATTERS
### New Orleans, La.

| Rulau | Date | Metal | Size | VG | F | VF | Unc |
|---|---|---|---|---|---|---|---|
| La-NO 20 | (?) | Brass | 23mm | — | — | 30.00 | — |

Pool table at center, POOL above, CHECK below. Rv: A. FATTERS / GOOD FOR / 5¢ / DRINK / NEW ORLEANS. Plain edge.

Anthony Fatter's billiard parlor was located at 841 Royal St. from the 1880's to about 1907.

## NORTH, CENTRAL AND SOUTH AMERICAN EXPOSITION
### New Orleans, La.

| Rulau | Date | Metal | Size | F | VF | EF | Unc |
|---|---|---|---|---|---|---|---|
| La-NO 29 | 1886 | S/WM | 31.5mm | — | — | 60.00 | — |

Building across center, THE MAIN BUILDING above, 1378 BY 905 FEET / (U.S. shield flanked by four flags). Globe at center showing Western Hemisphere, 1885 at North Pole and 1886 at South Pole. Around all: NORTH, CENTRAL & SOUTH * AMERICAN EXPOSITION / * NEW ORLEANS *. Plain edge.

## ROBINSON MUSEUM & THEATRE
### New Orleans, La.

| Rulau | Date | Metal | Size | VG | F | VF | Unc |
|---|---|---|---|---|---|---|---|
| La-No 33 | 1884 | WM | 24mm | — | — | — | — |

ROBINSON MAMMOTH MUSEUM & THEATRE. ONE DIME. Rv: OPENING SOUVENIR PRESENTED BY E. ROBINSON PROPRIETOR, NEW ORLEANS LA. OCT. 30, 1884. Loop attached. Plain edge.

## WORLD'S INDUSTRIAL AND COTTON CENTENNIAL EXPOSITION
### New Orleans, La.

| Rulau | Date | Metal | Size | F | VF | EF | Unc |
|---|---|---|---|---|---|---|---|
| La-NO 50 | 1885 | WM | 21mm | — | — | — | 20.00 |

Large 5-pointed star above exposition building, all within starred wreath. Rv: Bale of cotton within circular laurel wreath at center. THE WORLDS INDUSTRIAL / AND COTTON CENTENNIAL above; * EXPOSITION * / * NEW ORLEANS . 1884 . 1885 * below. Plain edge. (Grellman coll.)

| | | | | | | | |
|---|---|---|---|---|---|---|---|
| La-NO 52 | 1885 | Brass | 26mm | — | — | 20.00 | — |

Defiant eagle standing above three shields, stars and rays around. Above: WORLDS INDUSTRIAL AND COTTON CENTENNIAL. In a cartouche below: 1884-5 / EXPOSITION / NEW ORLEANS. Rv: SOUVENIR at center, wreath around. Plain edge. (Grellman coll.)

| Rulau | Date | Metal | Size | F | VF | EF | Unc |
|---|---|---|---|---|---|---|---|
| La-NO 55 | 1885 | WM | 31.5mm | — | — | — | 40.00 |

Pelican feeding its young at center, FROM DEC. 16. 1884 TO above, MAY 31, 1885 below. All within a wreath of corn, cotton, tobacco, etc. Around the rim: THE WORLDS INDUSTRIAL AND COTTON CENTENNIAL EXPOSITION / NEW ORLEANS. Rv: Building across center, 1378 BY 905 FEET under the ground line. Above: THE MAIN BUILDING. Below: U.S. shield flanked by flags. Plain edge. (Grellman coll.)

La-NO 57  1885  WM  31.5mm  — — — 30.00
Building across center, THE MAIN BUILDING above, NEW ORLEANS / 1884 ' 85 / (crescent) below. Rv: Within wreath: SOUVENIR / OF THE / WORLDS / INDUSTRIAL / AND / COTTON / EXPOSITION. Plain edge.

There are at least 11 other medalets under 35mm honoring this exposition, plus another 11 larger pieces in the So-Called Dollars category not listed in this reference. Those listed here are representative of the store card-sized pieces commemorating this important event, which brought New Orleans back to world attention after its Civil War and Reconstruction decline.

## E. L. CHARROPPIN
### Port Allen, La.

| Rulau | Date | Metal | Size | VG | F | VF | Unc |
|---|---|---|---|---|---|---|---|
| La-PA 2 | 1882 | Brass | 28mm | — | — | Rare | — |

Bottle at center, E. L. CHARROPPIN, above, PORT ALLEN, LA. below. Rv: Star at center, VELVET BOWEN above, 1882 below. Plain edge.

Charroppin's general store was in business from the 1870's to about 1900. 'Velvet Bowen' was a brand of whiskey. Port Allen is in West Baton Rouge Parish.

## CHAS. WISE
### Waterproof, La.

| Rulau | Date | Metal | Size | VG | F | VF | Unc |
|---|---|---|---|---|---|---|---|
| La-Wt 1 | (1888-90) | Brass | 28mm | — | — | Rare | — |

CHAS. WISE, / WATERPROOF. Rv: GOOD FOR / ONE / DRINK. Plain edge.

Charles Wise was listed as a general merchant in Waterproof (Tensas Parish) in the 1890 business directory.

## F. A. DUNN
### Wilson, La.

| Rulau | Date | Metal | Size | VG | F | VF | Unc |
|---|---|---|---|---|---|---|---|
| La-Wi 2 | (?) | Brass | 24mm | — | — | 30.00 | — |

F. A. DUNN / GOOD FOR / 1 / SHAVE / WILSON LA. Rv: In small circle: AUG. KERN B. S. CO. / ST. LOUIS. (Wright 270)

The August Kern firm in St. Louis made many of the nation's "shave checks." Wilson is in East Feliciana Parish. The 1910 population was 762.

# MAINE

## B. PARKER
### Bangor, Maine

| Rulau | Date | Metal | Size | VG | F | VF | EF |
|---|---|---|---|---|---|---|---|
| Me-Ba 10 | (1862-69) | Copper | 29mm | — | — | — | — |

B. PARKER ctsp on U.S. Large cent. (Duffield 1431; Hallenbeck 16.500; Brunk 288)

Me-Ba 11  (1862-69)  Copper  29mm
Similar ctsp on U.S. 1853 Large cent, with additional ctsp on each side: A: S. Mc P. (Kovacs coll.)

Ben Parker had a brass foundry and metalworking business at 3 Columbia St. in the 1862-69 period and probably earlier. He made stencils for marking lumber, and had a sideline business of countermarking Large cents (and other coins) with people's names or initials for his customers.

Collector Walter B. Gould of Bangor, who knew Parker when Gould was a youth, once possessed 200 Large cents with the B. PARKER stamp upon them. Parker made the T.J.S. — marked cents for Thomas J. Stewart of Bangor (which see).

## C. V. RAMSDELL
### Bangor, Maine

| Rulau | Date | Metal | Size | G | VG | F | EF |
|---|---|---|---|---|---|---|---|
| Me-Ba 14 | (?) | Copper | 29mm | — | — | — | — |

C.V. RAMSDELL ctsp on U.S. 1850. Large cent.

Ramsdell was a general gunsmith.

## T. J. S.  (Thomas J. Stewart)
### Bangor, Maine

| Rulau | Date | Metal | Size | VG | F | VF | EF |
|---|---|---|---|---|---|---|---|
| Me-Ba 17 | (1862-69) | Copper | 29mm | — | — | — | — |

T. J. S. ctsp on U.S. Large cent. (Duffield 1451; Hallenbeck 20.251)

Me-Ba 18  (1862-69)  Copper  29mm
T. J. STEWART ctsp on U.S. Large cent. (Hallenbeck 19.757)

Thomas J. Stewart manufacturered birch bark shooks, which he exported to the Mediterranean area for oranges and lemons. The T.J.S. counterstamp was his business mark for the shooks.

The stencils for Stewart's mark were made by metalworker Ben Parker of Bangor (which see).

## J. W. STRANGE and C. A. STRANGE
### Bangor, Maine

| Rulau | Date | Metal | Size | VG | F | VF | EF |
|---|---|---|---|---|---|---|---|
| Me-Ba 20 | (1850's-69) | Copper | 29mm | — | — | — | — |
| | | J. W. STRANGE ctsp on U.S. Large cent. | | | | | |
| Me-Ba 22 | (1860-69) | Copper | 29mm | — | — | — | — |
| | | C. A. STRANGE ctsp on U.S. Large cents. Dates examined: 1851. (Duffield 1431; Hallenbeck 19.761; Brunk 370) | | | | | |

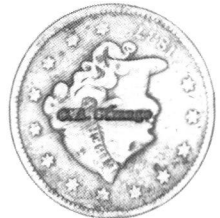

| Me-Ba 23 | (1860-69) | Copper | 29mm | — | 25.00 | — | — |
|---|---|---|---|---|---|---|---|
| | | Similar ctsp on U.S. 1837 Large cent. (Rulau coll.) | | | | | |

J.W. Strange and his son, C.A. Strange, had a brass foundry, diesinking and stencil making business in Bangor, on Central Street. They manufactured brass candlesticks, andirons, etc.

The Stranges countermarked copper cents and other coins, some of them artistically, usually in small script letters. Some of their products include: HUNT & MOORE: C. A. SWIFT / C. BIGNAL; W. WILLEY / S. S., and their own pieces.

Collector Walter B. Gould of Bangor in 1921 wrote: "In the 1850's and 60's it seems to have been a common practice to mutilate, mark and hole coins. There was no law against it, and the mutilated coins . . . were equally as desirable as the perfect and clumsy coins of the period." In the 1860's Gould personally knew two of the countermarkers of Bangor — Ben Parker of 3 Columbia St. and J. W. Strange of Central St., both metalworkers and brass founders.

## G. L. BAILEY
### Portland, Maine

| Rulau | Date | Metal | Size | VG | F | VF | EF |
|---|---|---|---|---|---|---|---|
| Me-Po 1 | (1865-1905) | Silver | 32.5mm | 100. | 150. | — | — |
| | | G. L. BAILEY / (flintlock pistol) / ctsp on U.S. Bust type half dollar. (Gould 3) | | | | | |

Gilbert L. Bailey was a sporting goods dealer in business from about the time of the Civil War until the early 1900's.

## G. L. BAILEY & J. W. SAWYER
### Portland, Maine

| Rulau | Date | Metal | Size | G | VG | F | EF |
|---|---|---|---|---|---|---|---|
| Me-Po 4 | (?) | Copper | 29mm | | | | |
| | | G. L. BAILEY / J. W. SAWYER ctsp on U.S. 1839 Large cent. (Collection S. L. Steinberg, Malden, Mass.) | | | | | |

G. L. Bailey and J. W. Sawyer were gunsmiths.

## J. T. BROWN
### Portland (Maine ?)

| Rulau | Date | Metal | Size | VG | F | VF | EF |
|---|---|---|---|---|---|---|---|
| Me-Po 6 | 1867 | Silver | 38mm | — | 34.50 | — | — |
| | | J. T. BROWN / PORTLAND CO. 1867 ctsp on Mexico 1866 Maximilian peso. | | | | | |

There are no Portland Counties in the United States, so the 'CO.' must indicate 'company' or some other word.

## A. S. RICHMOND
### Winthrop, Maine

| Rulau | Date | Metal | Size | VG | F | VF | EF |
|---|---|---|---|---|---|---|---|
| Me-Wi 6 | (?) | Copper | 29mm | — | — | 150. | — |
| | | A. S. RICHMOND / WINTHROP, ME. ctsp on U.S. 1853 Large cent. (Tanenbaum coll.) | | | | | |

A. S. Richmond is listed in the 1866 edition of *Bradstreet's Directory* as being in the shoe business.

## F. QUEBE
### York, Maine

| Rulau | Date | Metal | Size | F | VF | EF | Unc |
|---|---|---|---|---|---|---|---|
| Me-Yo 1 | (1865) | WM | 22.5mm | — | — | | 2 Known |

Washington head right, HUGHES on truncation of bust. Rv: Wide depressed rim around edge; raised central area blank. Within depressed rim: F. QUEBE / (three dots) YORK ME (three dots). Plain edge. (Miller Me 7)

Struck by J. A. Hughes, diesinker of Cincinnati, Ohio.

## G. A. R. 19 ANNUAL ENCAMPMENT
### Portland, Maine

| Rulau | Date | Metal | Size | F | VF | EF | Unc |
|---|---|---|---|---|---|---|---|
| ME-Po 8 | 1885 | Bronze | 27mm | — | — | 30.00 | 50.00 |
| | | Grant head left above laurel sprays, ULYSSES S. GRANT above. Rv: CAMP / GRANT / PORTLAND MAINE / 19, ANNUAL / ENCAMPMENT / G.A.R / JUNE 24 25 1885. Plain edge. | | | | | |

The G.A.R. (Grand Army of the Republic) was the principal veterans' organization of the Union forces following the Civil War. This campout took place 20 years after the Civil War ended, while the bulk of the veterans were still vigorous and at the peak of their influence in life.

## G. F. FISHER
### (Maine ?)

| Rulau | Date | Metal | Size | VG | F | VF |
|---|---|---|---|---|---|---|
| Me-Un 1 | 1879 | Copper | 29mm | — | 175. | |

1879 / G. F. FISHER is ctsp on a U.S. Large cent which has previously been ctsp DR / SHATTUCK'S / WATER CURE / WATERFORD / ME.

## A. D. SWEETSIR
### (Maine ?)

| Rulau | Date | Metal | Size | VG | F | VF | EF |
|---|---|---|---|---|---|---|---|
| Me-Un 3 | ca 1862-69 | Copper | 29mm | 20.00 | — | 40.00 | — |

A. D. SWEETSIR ctsp on U.S. 1833 Large cent. (Tanenbaum coll.) (Duffield 1431; Hallenbeck 19.766; Brunk 374)

| Me-Un 4 | ca 1862-69 | Copper | 29mm | 20.00 | — | 40.00 | — |

Similar ctsp on later U.S. Large cents. (Dates examined: 1845, 1847.

# MARYLAND

## W. R. BAKER
### Annapolis, Md

| Rulau | Date | Metal | Size | VG | F | VF | Unc |
|---|---|---|---|---|---|---|---|
| Md-An 2 | (1870's) | Brass | 25mm | — | 10.00 | 15.00 | — |

Coronet Liberty head left, four stars on coronet, within a wreath, a star above. Rv: W. R. BAKER / * / FRUIT / — *1* — / PACKER / * / ANNAPOLIS, MD. Plain edge. (Miller Md 1; Duffield 3)

| Md-An 4 | (1870's) | Brass | 18mm | — | — | 15.00 | — |

Eagle. Rv: As 2, no denomination. Plain edge. (Miller Md 1A)

## J. H. R.
### (John Henry Robinson)
### Anne Arundel County, Md.

The 1874-1885 picker checks of this issuer are catalogued in *U.S. Merchant Tokens 1845-1860*, which see.

## L. R. S.
### (Larkin R. Shipley)
### Anne Arundel County, Md.

The 1874-1885 picker checks of this issuer are catalogued in *U.S. Merchant Token 1845-1860*, which see.

## L. A.
### (Louis Asbeck)
### Baltimore, Md.

| Rulau | Date | Metal | Size | F | VF | EF | Unc |
|---|---|---|---|---|---|---|---|
| Md-Ba 1 | (1870-78) | Brass | 20mm | 3.00 | 5.00 | 8.00 | — |

MYSTIC / L. A. Rv: Numeral 5 within wreath, star at wreath opening at top. Plain edge. (Miller Md 4; Dufield 2)

Louis Asbeck was the proprietor of the Mystic Restaurant at 13 So. Eutaw St. from 1864 through 1878.

## B. L.
### (Baltimore Liederkranz)
### Baltimore, Md.

| Rulau | Date | Metal | Size | VG | F | VF | Unc |
|---|---|---|---|---|---|---|---|
| Md-Ba 2 | (1870's) | Brass | 20mm | 3.00 | 5.00 | 8.50 | 11.00 |

Script monogram B.L. Rv: Numeral 5 in oak and olive wreath, star at top opening. Plain edge. (Miller Md 5; Duffield 4)

| Md-Ba 2C | (1870's) | GS | 20mm | 3.00 | 5.00 | 8.50 | 11.00 |

As last, but numeral 25. Plain edge. (Miller Md 6; Duffield 5)

The Baltimore Liederkranz, organized 1836, was the oldest of many German singing societies in Baltimore. In 1899 it was merged with the Germania Maennerchor. The B.L. headquarters were at 274 (later 661) West Lexington St.

Baltimore building addresses were completely renumbered in 1886.

## H. C. B.
### (Charles Betch)
### Baltimore, Md.

| Rulau | Date | Metal | Size | VG | F | VF | Unc |
|---|---|---|---|---|---|---|---|
| Md-Ba 4 | (1870's) | Brass | 21mm | — | — | 8.50 | — |

H. C. B. in an arc incused at center of blank field. Rv: Blank. Beaded, incised rim on each side. Plain edge. Rarity 5.

Charles Betch was an oyster packer located at McElderberry's Wharf in Baltimore in the 1870's. His tokens were oyster shucker's checks.

## BALTIMORE
### Baltimore, Md.

| Rulau | Date | Metal | Size | VG | F | VF | EF |
|---|---|---|---|---|---|---|---|
| Md-Ba 5 | 1868 | Copper | 29mm | — | — | 15.00 | — |

BALTIMORE 1868 ctsp on U.S. Large cent. (Hallenbeck 2.507)

## BALTIMORE FESTIVAL
### Baltimore, Md.

| Rulau | Date | Metal | Size | F | VF | EF | Unc |
|---|---|---|---|---|---|---|---|
| Md-Ba 6 | 1881 | WM | 25mm | — | 5.00 | — | 15.00 |

Statue, BALTIMORE FESTIVAL. Rv: Bird, ORIOLE, 1881. Issued holed. Plain edge.

## BALTIMORE ORIOLE CELEBRATION
### Baltimore, Md.

| Rulau | Date | Metal | Size | F | VF | EF | Unc |
|---|---|---|---|---|---|---|---|
| Md-Ba 6C | 1882 | WM | 32.5mm | — | 25.00 | — | — |

Statue atop memorial. Rv: Oriole flying left at center, BALTIMORE ORIOLE . CELEBRATION above, + SEP. 12. 13. 14. 1882. + below. Plain edge. (Brunk coll.)

## THE B. C. BIBB STOVE CO.
### Baltimore, Md.

| Rulau | Date | Metal | Size | F | VF | EF | Unc |
|---|---|---|---|---|---|---|---|
| Md-Ba 7 | (1889) | Brass | 25mm | 3.00 | 7.00 | 10.00 | 25.00 |

Cook stove at center, .THE B. C. BIBB STOVE CO. / BALTIMORE, MD around. Rv: ESTABLISHED 1851 / THE / B. C. BIBB STOVE CO / FIREPLACE HEATERS / COOKSTOVES RANGES / FURNACES &C. / (ornament) / BALTIMORE MD. Plain edge. (Wright 1103; Duffield 12; Miller Md. 13)

| Md-Ba 8 | (1889) | Copper | 25mm | 5.00 | 10.00 | 15.00 | 35.00 |
|---|---|---|---|---|---|---|---|

As 7. Plain edge. (Duffield 12; Miller Md. 14)

Bentley C. Bibb and H. P. Robbins formed a partnership to manufacture stoves in 1851. It was Bibb & Robbins 1851-1855; Bibb & Co. 1855-1877; Bibb & Son 1877-1889, and B. C. Bibb Stove Co. 1889 to 1918 or later. Bentley C. Bibb died June 23, 1894, aged 79. From 1851 until 1907 or later its location was the same — 39-41 Light St. (renumbered 107-109 in 1886).

## S. S. BARNES & CO.
### Baltimore, Md.

| Rulau | Date | Metal | Size | F | VF | EF | Unc |
|---|---|---|---|---|---|---|---|
| Md-Ba 9 | (1867-68) | Brass | 21mm | — | — | 20.00 | 45.00 |

Two oyster shells within a circle of 16 stars. Rv: S. S. BARNES & CO. / OYSTER PLANTERS & / PACKERS / ELLICOTS WHARF / CR WEST & / JACKSON ST / BALTIMORE, MD. Plain edge. (Miller Md 10; Duffield 9)

S. S. Barnes and Co. were in the oyster planting and packing business only from 1867 to 1868. Nothing can be learned from the directories about Barnes in the 1869-74 period, but he was part of the firm of Hunt, Barnes & Co. at 66 Boston St. 1875-1879.

The token is of superb workmanship, one of the most attractive shucker checks of Maryland.

## CARROLLTON CLOTHING HOUSE
### Baltimore, Md.

| Rulau | Date | Metal | Size | VG | F | VF | Unc |
|---|---|---|---|---|---|---|---|
| Md-Ba 10 | 1876 | Brass | 25mm | — | — | 12.50 | — |

Liberty head left, wearing coronet bearing four stars, 1876 in exergue. Rv: THE CARROLLTON / 171 / W BALTO ST. / NEXT TO THE / CARROLLTON / HOTEL / CLOTHING HOUSE. Plain edge. (Wright 1661; Miller Md 23; Duffield 20)

The Carrollton Clothing House, as such, does not appear in any of the directories. In that of 1876, and in that year only, is found: 'G. C. Norris, retail clothing, 171 W. Baltimore St.' This would indicate Norris' years of activity were limited to 1875-76.

Dr. Wright called this piece rare in 1900, and Frank G. Duffield did not dispute this claim in 1907. The Fulds, in the 1950's, knew of only two specimens, including their own. The die work is that of J. F. W. Dorman.

## CONCORDIA
### Baltimore, Md.

| Rulau | Date | Metal | Size | F | VF | EF | Unc |
|---|---|---|---|---|---|---|---|
| Md-Ba 11 | (1870's) | Copper | 22mm | 2.75 | 5.00 | 7.50 | 15.00 |

Eagle with drooping wings, head turned right, shield on breast, 17 stars above. Rv: CONCORDIA / 5 / .BALTIMORE. (Wright 185; Duffield 31; Miller Md. 39)

| Md-Ba 12 | (1870's) | Brass | 22mm | 2.75 | 5.00 | 7.50 | 15.00 |
|---|---|---|---|---|---|---|---|

Similar to 39, but numeral 10 on reverse. (Miller Md. 40)

| Md-Ba 13 | (1870's) | CN | 22mm | — | — | 15.00 | 35.00 |
|---|---|---|---|---|---|---|---|

Similar to 39, but numeral 25 on reverse. (Duffield 32; Miller Md. 41)

The Concordia German Association was founded 1847 at Western Hall, corner Howard and Lexington Streets. In 1865 its new home — Concordia Opera House and Hall — opened at corner Eutaw and German Streets. The Concordia Opera House burned down June 10, 1892, and the association passed out of existence. In 1868 Charles Dickens gave readings there.

## COX
### Baltimore, Md

| Rulau | Date | Metal | Size | VG | F | VF | Unc |
|---|---|---|---|---|---|---|---|
| Md-Ba 15 | (1870) | Copper | 19.5mm | — | — | — | Rare |

Eagle with drooping wings atop mound of olive branches, 12 stars around. Rv: COX within circular wreath tied with a bow at bottom. Dentilated rims on both sides.

## CASINO NO. 3
### Baltimore, Md.

| Rulau | Date | Metal | Size | VG | F | VF | Unc |
|---|---|---|---|---|---|---|---|
| Md-Ba 16 | (1870-75) | Brass | 19mm | — | — | 15.00 | 35.00 |

Eagle with outstretched wings at center, CASINO NO. 3. above, * BALTO * below. Rv: Numeral 5 within wreath, star in opening at top. Plain edge. (Miller Md) Rarity 6.

| Md-Ba 17 | (1870-75) | Copper | 19mm | — | — | — | — |
|---|---|---|---|---|---|---|---|

Obverse as last. Rv: Similar to last, but numeral 10. Plain edge. (Miller Md 25). Rarity 6.

| Md-Ba 18 | (1870-75) | GS | 19mm | — | — | 15.00 | 35.00 |
|---|---|---|---|---|---|---|---|

Similar to last, but numeral 25. Plain edge. (Miller Md 24; Duffield 21). Rarity 6.

The Casino Clubrooms were located at 216 (later 1122) Hartford Ave. and served as headquarters for a political club during the 1870-75 period. The significance of 'No. 3' has not been learned. The striking is by J. F. W. Dorman.

## DORMAN'S STENCIL & STAMP WORKS
### Baltimore, Md.

| Rulau | Date | Metal | Size | F | VF | EF | Unc |
|---|---|---|---|---|---|---|---|
| Md-Ba 22 | (1869-71) | Brass | 24mm | 5.00 | 7.50 | 10.00 | 20.00 |

J. F. W. DORMAN / — / MAN'F'R OF / PRINTING / — PRESSES — / 21 GERMAN ST. / —*— / BALTIMORE. Rv: DORMAN'S STENCIL & STAMP WORKS / 25 / BALTIMORE . (Duffield 35; Miller Md. 44)

| Rulau | Date | Metal | Size | F | VF | EF | Unc |
|---|---|---|---|---|---|---|---|
| Md-Ba 23 | (1869-71) | SB | 20mm | 4.00 | 6.50 | 9.00 | 20.00 |

Obverse similar to 22, but PRINTING PRESSES on two scrolls. Rv: Large numeral 5 surrounded by rays. (Duffield 36; Miller Md. 45)

| Rulau | Date | Metal | Size | F | VF | EF | Unc |
|---|---|---|---|---|---|---|---|
| Md-Ba 25 | 1875 | Brass | 20mm | 4.00 | 7.50 | 10.00 | 20.00 |

Liberty head in coronet left, 1875 below, 13 stars around. Rv: DORMAN'S STENCIL / & / STAMP / WORKS / 19 / GERMAN ST. / BALTIMORE. (Wright 267; Duffield 33; Miller Md. 42)

| Md-Ba 26 | 1875 | Brass | 20mm | 4.00 | 7.50 | 10.00 | 20.00 |

As 25, but 19 GERMAN ST. in larger letters. (Duffield 34; Miller Md. 43)

John F. W. Dorman was proprietor of Dorman's Stencil & Stamp Works 1874-1891. This firm was known as Dorman & Thomas 1866-1869 (Dorman and James S. Thomas); J. F. W. Dorman & Co. 1869-1871 (Dorman and William F. Sutz); United States Mfg. Co. 1871-1878, and The J. F. W. Dorman Co. 1891-1918 or later.

The above tokens were issued on the occasion of Dorman occupying his new building at 19 German Street in 1875.

John F. W. Dorman was born in Warsaw, Kentucky in 1836, later moving to St. Louis, where he engaged in several trades. Before the Civil War he was an actor and was associated with others in managing other actors. During the war he was a sutler, and for a time was confined in the Confederates' Libby Prison.

In 1866 in partnership with J. S. Thomas, he opened a stencil cutting and rubber stamp manufacturing business in Baltimore, at 97 West Lombard St. Thomas withdrew in 1869 and William F. Sutz became a partner. The name United States Manufacturing Co. was adopted in 1870 and this was continued until 1879, when Dorman began manufacturing printing presses. In 1874 he erected a large 5-story building at 19 German St., where his enterprises were located until his death on March 26, 1893.

After Dorman's death the business was conducted by a stock company in the Equitable Building at 121 East Fayette St., until that building burned about 1904.

Both the United States Manufacturing Co. and Dorman's Stencil & Stamp Works were in business at the same time in the 1870-1879 period. Dorman was president and principal stockholder of both firms.

(For full information on Dorman, see "The Tokens and Medals Relating to Numismatists and Coin Dealers" in *The Numismatist* for 1905, by Albert R. Frey.)

## WM. L. ELLIS & CO.
### Baltimore, Md.

| Rulau | Date | Metal | Size | F | VF | EF | Unc |
|---|---|---|---|---|---|---|---|
| Md-Ba 28 | (1865-70) | Nickel | 19mm | — | — | 10.00 | 20.00 |

Square, compass and G at center, WM. L. ELLIS & CO. around, 6-pointed star below. Rv: 10 / GALL'S at center, 13 stars around. Plain edge.

William L. Ellis was a ship's carpenter at Orleans near Broadway through 1864. In 1865 he formed William L. Ellis & Co., moving to Orleans between Broadway and Ann on Fells Point. The oyster packing firm consisted of Ellis and F.M. Ketchum. The business lasted until 1888.

## G. FALKENSTEIN
### Baltimore, Md.

| Rulau | Date | Metal | Size | F | VF | EF | Unc |
|---|---|---|---|---|---|---|---|
| Md-Ba 30 | (1870's) | Copper | 20mm | 4.00 | 6.00 | 9.00 | 20.00 |

Tree at center, GREENWOOD PARK / G. FALKENSTEIN around. Rv: Numeral 10 within wreath. (Duffield 39; Miller Md. 47½)

| Md-Ba 31 | (1870's) | Brass | 20mm | 4.00 | 6.00 | 9.00 | 20.00 |

As 30. (Miller Md. 48)

| Md-Ba 32 | (1870's) | Brass | — | 4.00 | 6.00 | 9.00 | 20.00 |

As 30, but numeral 5 on reverse. (Miller Md. 49)

| Md-Ba 33 | (1870's) | GS | 20mm | 4.00 | 6.00 | 9.00 | 20.00 |

Similar to 30, but numeral 25 on reverse. (Wright 304; Duffield 40; Miller Md. 50)

George Falkenstein operated a restaurant at 32 East Pratt St. 1867-70, then at Gay and Frederick Streets 1870-90. The Greenwood Park Brewery was located at Belair Road and Oliver St. J. F. W. Dorman cut these tokens.

## FOUNDING OF THE CITY
### Baltimore, Md.

| Rulau | Date | Metal | Size | F | VF | EF | Unc |
|---|---|---|---|---|---|---|---|
| Md-Ba 35 | 1880 | Brass | 32mm | — | — | 25.00 | — |

Facing bust of Calvert, * GEORGE CALVERT * above, THE FIRST LORD OF BALTIMORE below. Rv: Monument at center. 150TH ANNIVERSARY OF THE FOUNDING OF THE CITY / 1730 1880 / OCT. 11TH / OF / * BALTIMORE *. Plain edge.

## FREE POOL
### (Joseph Beard Jr.)
### Baltimore, Md.

| Rulau | Date | Metal | Size | VG | F | VF | Unc |
|---|---|---|---|---|---|---|---|
| Md-Ba 36 | (1883-85) | CN | 25mm | 4.50 | 6.00 | 9.00 | 20.00 |

(All incused) Elephant at center, FREE above, POOL below. rv: 33 & 35 / E. BALTIMORE.

## GOSMAN & CO.
### Baltimore, Md.

| Rulau | Date | Metal | Size | F | VF | EF | Unc |
|---|---|---|---|---|---|---|---|
| Md-Ba 37 | (1868-78) | GS | 22mm | 5.00 | 10.00 | 20.00 | 40.00 |

Urn fountain at center, GOSMAN & CO. around, * BALTO. * below. Rv: Numeral 10 within wreath. Plain edge. (Wright 391; Miller Md 63; Duffield 52)

Adam J. Gosman appears as a druggist in 1858 at 194 East Fayette St. In 1860 he moved to 66 No. Eden. Then in 1863-64 he was a Gay and Baltimore Sts., the address of the well-established MacKenzie & Co. drug firm, which he succeeded in 1865, establishing a "family medicine and prescription store."

The name Gosman & Co. was announced in 1868 when he became associated with another token-issuing druggist, John J. Myer (which see), who had joined MacKenzie & Co. in 1856. The address now was 191 Madison Ave. (Myer kept his own business at Fremont and Townsend 1873-78 though associated with Gosman.)

## GREENWOOD PARK
### Baltimore, Md.

| Rulau | Date | Metal | Size | VG | F | VF | Unc |
|---|---|---|---|---|---|---|---|
| Md-Ba 40 | (1870's) | Brass | 16mm | — | — | 9.00 | 20.00 |

Numeral 5 on reverse. (Miller Md. 64½)

| Rulau | Date | Metal | Size | VG | F | VF | Unc |
|---|---|---|---|---|---|---|---|
| Md-Ba 41 | (1870's) | Brass | 19mm | — | — | 9.00 | 20.00 |

Numeral 10 on reverse. (Miller Md. 64½A)

| Rulau | Date | Metal | Size | | | | |
|---|---|---|---|---|---|---|---|
| Md-Ba 3 | (1870's) | Brass | 23mm | — | — | 300. | — |

Tree with spreading branches separates G --- B. Rv: GREENWOOD PARK / 25 / BALTO. Beaded rim on each side. Plain edge.

The G.B. equals George Bauernschmidt. George Fuld dates this piece to the late 1870's.
This piece appeared as lot 4402 in the Chesterfield sale in Indianapolis, April 3-4, 1981. It is obviously related to the later (1867-1875) George Falkenstein tokens of the Greenwood Park Brewery (Miller 47 1/2) — all using the tree with spreading branches motif. The 25-cent denomination realized $300 in the 1983 AB&R sale.

## GREISENHEIM
### Baltimore, Md.

| Rulau | Date | Metal | Size | F | VF | EF | Unc |
|---|---|---|---|---|---|---|---|
| Md-Ba 44 | 1885 | Bronze | 32mm | — | — | 15.00 | — |

Building at center, GREISENHEIM above, BALTIMORE / 1885. below. Rv: ZUM ANDENKEN / AN DIE / EIN WEIHUNG / DES DEUTSCHEN / GREISENHEIM / IM MAI / 1885 / GEGRUNDET JUNI 30, 1881. Plain edge. Issued holed.

The word 'Greisenheim' means 'Home for the Aged'. The reverse legend translates: 'In memory of the consecration of the German Home for the Aged, May 1885, Founded June 30, 1881'.

## CHAS. W. HAMILL & CO.
### Baltimore, Md.

| Rulau | Date | Metal | Size | F | VF | EF | Unc |
|---|---|---|---|---|---|---|---|
| Md-Ba 46 | 1880 | S/WM | 29mm | — | 10.00 | 15.00 | 40.00 |

Morgan-type Liberty head left, F. X. KOHLER on truncation of neck. Around: CHAS. W. HAMILL & CO. MF. SILVER PLATED WARE. Rv: Baltimore Monument at center, 150TH ANNIVERSARY BALTIMORE CITY around, OCTOBER / 1880 below. Plain edge. (Wright 417; Miller Md 67)

| Md-Ba 46A | 1880 | Gilt/WM | 29mm | — | — | — | 50.00 |

As 46. Plain edge.

The head is a remarkably close copy of the Morgan silver dollar's head. The Morgan dollar had been introduced only two years earlier at this point and was still a popular novelty.

## SAMUEL JACKSON
### Baltimore, Md.

| Rulau | Date | Metal | Size | VG | F | VF | EF |
|---|---|---|---|---|---|---|---|
| Md-Ba 49 | (?) | Copper | 29mm | — | — | 50.00 | — |

SAMUEL / JACKSON / BALTIMORE ctsp on U.S. Large cent. (Hallenbeck 10.504)

## KENSETT
### Baltimore, Md.

| Rulau | Date | Metal | Size | F | VF | EF | Unc |
|---|---|---|---|---|---|---|---|
| Md-Ba 55 | (1865-75) | Brass | 24mm | 3.00 | 5.00 | 8.00 | 20.00 |

(Ornament) / KENSETT / (ornament). Rv: Same as obverse. (Wright 545; Duffield 68; Miller Md. 80)

Thomas Kensett, founder of Kensett & Co., was born in Cheshire, Conn. on Feb. 12, 1814. He came to Baltimore in 1840 and established an oyster and fruit packaging business, using a secret process invented by his father in 1819. At first he was on York Street, then in 1852 he erected a large building on West Falls Avenue, where the business remained. In 1855 Ira B. Wheeler became a partner of Thomas Kensett for a short time. Kensett died Aug. 6, 1877. The business was carried on by his sons and nephews.

## LYON-HALL & CO.
### Baltimore, Md.

| Rulau | Date | Metal | Size | F | VF | EF | Unc |
|---|---|---|---|---|---|---|---|
| Md-Ba 65 | (1884-94) | Brass | 25mm | — | — | 350. | — |

CHINA — LYON-HALL & CO. — JAPAN / BALTIMORE ctsp on border of China 1-cash coin of Ch'ing dynasty. Rv: CHINA-INDIA-JAPAN / MATTING IMPORTERS. ctsp on opposite side border of the coin. Plain edge. Only 4 known.

Lyon & Co. (J. Crawford Lyon and William A. Lyon) traded in carpets at 236 W. Baltimore St. from 1881 on. In 1884 they admitted John W. Hall and the business became Lyon-Hall & Co. and began trading in imports.
They moved to 8 W. Baltimore St. in 1887 and to 105 Hopkins Place in 1890 and to 6 South St. in 1892. John W. Hall withdrew in 1895 and the name became Lyon Bros. (still J. Crawford and William A. Lyon), importers of matting, fur rugs and linoleum.
Great quantities of the cheap Chinese cash (face value only 1/10 cent) were imported by Chinese-Americans for gambling pieces and as decorations for wicker sewing baskets, etc., so these coins provided a convenient and cheap flan for Lyon-Hall's advertising tokens.
Specimens examined have been 1-cash of Chia Ch'ing (1796-1820), Tientsin Mint, and Ch'ien Lung (1736-95), Peking Board of Revenue Mint. Both cash types were once exceedingly common.

## L. McMURRAY & CO.
### Baltimore, Md.

| Rulau | Date | Metal | Size | F | VF | EF | Unc |
|---|---|---|---|---|---|---|---|
| Md-Ba 66 | (1860-69) | Brass | 19mm | — | — | 20.00 | 35.00 |

L. McMURRAY & CO. / 5 / CENT / CHECK. Rv: Numeral 5 surrounded by rays. Plain edge.

| Md-Ba 67 | (1870-80) | Brass | 20mm | — | — | 10.00 | 15.00 |

L. Mc. M. / & CO. / *. Rv: Numeral 5 within circular wreath. Plain edge.

| Md-Ba 67A | (1870-80) | Copper | 20.5mm | — | — | 10.00 | 15.00 |

As last, but slightly larger flan. Plain edge.

L. McMurray and Co. (Louis McMurray, Charles E. Houghton and A.B. Ellis), oyster and fruit packers, were located at 1, 3, 5 and 7 Cross St. from 1860 to 1870.

The Baltimore directories listed the firm as L. Mc.M. & Co. at 254-256 West Biddle St. 1870-1889. At the same time, Louis McMurray & Co. was listed at 1-7 Cross St., 1870-89. After 1889 the companies became vegetable packers; a branch packed corn in Frederick, Md. The company does not appear in the 1890 directory.

None of these McMurray checks (used for tallying oyster shucking, etc.) were listed in Wright, Adams-Miller or Duffield.

Baltimore had 27 oyster and fruit packers in 1860, 85 in 1871, 101 in 1879, 110 in 1881, 86 in 1889, and only 15 in 1890. The demise of oyster packing affected most packer firms by ending their business lives; McMurray switched to vegetable canning.

By 1918 McMurray was no longer listed in either Baltimore or Frederick. A Frederick City Packing Co., fruit and vegetable packers, was listed in 1918, but there may be no connection.

(See "The Canning Industry in Baltimore" by M. and G. Fuld in *Token Collector's Pages* (Boston, 1972, pages 125-129) for an excellent exposition on this subject.

## J.J. MEYER & CO.
### (Actual name: Myer)
### Baltimore, Md.

| Rulau | Date | Metal | Size | F | VF | EF | Unc |
|---|---|---|---|---|---|---|---|
| Md-Ba 69 | (1873-78) | GS | 22mm | 7.00 | 9.50 | 20.00 | 40.00 |

Urn fountain at center, J.J. MEYER & CO. above, .BALTO. below. Plain edge. (Miller Md 89A)

Myer's name is misspelled on the token. For details, see under Gosman & Co., Baltimore.

## B. MOMENTHY
### Baltimore, Md.

| Rulau | Date | Metal | Size | VG | F | VF | Unc |
|---|---|---|---|---|---|---|---|
| Md-Ba 70 | (1870) | Copper | 20mm | — | 10.00 | — | — |

B. MOMENTHY / FAYETTE HALL / BALTIMORE. Rv: Numeral 5 within wreath. Plain edge. (Miller Md 91; Duffield 85)

| Md-Ba 70C | (1870) | Brass | 20mm | — | 10.00 | — | — |

Obverse as 70. Rv: Similar to 70, but no numeral at center. (Miller Md 92)

Bruno Momenthy was proprietor about 1870 of Fayette Hall (also known as Central Hall) at 28 No. Gay St.

Bruno Momenthy (the same man, or a successor?) was listed in 1917-1918 as a "wholesale liquor dealer and restaurateur'" in the *R.G. Dun Business Register*.

## MOORE & BRADY
### Baltimore, Md.

| Rulau | Date | Metal | Size | VG | F | VF | Unc |
|---|---|---|---|---|---|---|---|
| Md-Ba 71 | (1875) | Brass | 24mm | 12.00 | 16.00 | 22.00 | 45.00 |

Coronet Liberty head left, four stars on coronet, circle of stars around. Rv: Raised rectangle at center (a can?) between ornaments, MOORE & BRADY above, BALTIMORE below. Plain edge. (Miller Md 95; Duffield 88)

| Md-Ba 71B | (1875) | Brass | 24mm | — | 16.00 | 22.00 | 45.00 |

As 71, but ctsp on obverse: #3 Y (probably for 'Number 3 Yard'). Plain edge. (Miller Md 96)

| Md-Ba 72 | (1875) | Brass | 18mm | 12.00 | 21.00 | 30.00 | 45.00 |

MOORE & BRADY / * / FIVE / * / BALTIMORE. Rv: Blank. Plain edge. (Miller Md 96A; Duffield 89)

George W. Moore formed Geo. W. Moore & Co. in 1871 at 54 No. High St., oyster packers. In 1875 he admitted James H. Brady and the firm became Moore & Brady, located at the foot of Montgomery St. Francix X. Koehler struck their tokens. The business survived to 1906 or later.

## NEW YORK CLOTHING HOUSE
### Baltimore, Md.

| Rulau | Date | Metal | Size | VG | F | VF | Unc |
|---|---|---|---|---|---|---|---|
| Md-Ba 79 | 1889 | WM | 40mm | 5.00 | 8.00 | 10.00 | 35.00 |

Baltimore Battle Monument at center, between SEPT 12 / 1814 and SEPT. 12 / 1889. Above: * ANNIVERSARY *. Below: BATTLE OF NORTH POINT. Rv: SOUVENIR (on scroll) / OF THE / NEW YORK / CLOTHING / HOUSE / BALTIMORE, MD. Plain edge. (Miller Md 101; Duffield 90)

New York Clothing House was established in 1875. In 1887 it relocated at 102 East Baltimore St. It was still in business in 1918, owned by the Rosenfeld Brothers.

## NONPAREIL
### Baltimore, Md.

| Rulau | Date | Metal | Size | F | VF | EF | Unc |
|---|---|---|---|---|---|---|---|
| Md-Ba 80 | (1867-70) | Nickel | 20mm | 5.00 | 7.00 | 10.00 | 20.00 |

Liberty head in Phrygian cap left, 13 stars around. Small PJH below head. Rv: NONPAREIL / * 5 * / BALTIMORE. (Wright 762; Miller Md 99)

| Md-Ba 81 | (1867-70) | Nickel | 20mm | 7.00 | 9.00 | 12.00 | 20.00 |

As 80, but ctsp B.A. (Miller Md 100)

Struck by Peter H. Jacobus of Philadelphia. The Nonpareil Association was a social club from 1867 to 1870, headquartered at the corner of Bond and Bank Streets. The French word "nonpareil" means matchless, or unparalleled.

## WM. NUMSEN & SONS
### Baltimore, Md.

| Rulau | Date | Metal | Size | VG | F | VF | Unc |
|---|---|---|---|---|---|---|---|
| Md-Ba 83 | (1870's) | Brass | 24mm | — | — | 8.00 | 20.00 |

Coronet Liberty head left within wreath. Rev: Large radiant N at center, WM NUMSEN & SONS around, ornament below. Plain edge.

| MD-Ba 84 | (1870's) | Brass | 21mm | — | — | 6.00 | 20.00 |

Large N in chief of U.S. shield, at center, palm wreath around. Rv: W. N. / & / SONS within circle of 13 6-pointed stars. Plain edge. (Wright 1259; Miller Md 102)

Probably both tokens were struck by Dorman in Baltimore.

William Numsen & Sons Inc. were still in the oyster and fruit packing business in Baltimore in 1918. They had a branch at Asbestos in Carroll County, and other branches. In 1918 there was another Baltimore firm, Numsen & Davis, vegetable packing and canned goods. N&D had a branch at Benedict in Charles County.

## O'NEILL & CO.
### Baltimore, Md.

| Rulau | Date | Metal | Size | VG | F | VF | Unc |
|---|---|---|---|---|---|---|---|
| Md-Ba 200 | (1869-73) | CN | 25mm | 5.00 | 10.00 | 15.00 | 30.00 |

O'NEILL & CO. / * 1 * / GAL. / CANTON. Rv: REDEEMABLE / * / FROM / SHUCKERS / * / ONLY. Plain edge. (Miller Md 106; Duffield 95; Wright 788)

Canton was the southeastern section of Baltimore, between Patterson Park and the harbor, Boston Street being the main thoroughfare.

O'Neill and Co. was formed in 1869 by James H. O'Neill, F. Wehr and H. Wehr. The Wehrs withdrew in 1870. The business was at 112 Boston St. until 1873, when it apparently ended its corporate life.

This is one of the most explicit shucker checks of Baltimore as regards redemption. Dr. Wright called it rare in 1898.

## PATAPSCO FRUIT BUTTER CO.
### Baltimore, Md.

#### 1876 Centennial Tokens

Reverse type 1: * PATAPSCO FRUIT BUTTER CO. * / NO. 27 / SOUTH / * / LIBERTY ST / BALTIMORE, / MD. (All 23mm; plain edge)

| Rulau | Obv | Rev | Metal | F | VF | EF | Unc |
|---|---|---|---|---|---|---|---|
| Md-Ba 205 | A | 1 | WM | 5.00 | 8.00 | 15.00 | 50.00 |

(Wright 795; Miller Md 113; Duffield 100)

| Rulau | Obv | Rev | Metal | F | VF | EF | Unc |
|---|---|---|---|---|---|---|---|
| Md-Ba 206 | B | 1 | WM | 5.00 | 8.00 | 15.00 | 50.00 |

(Miller 109; Duffield 97)

| | | | | | | | |
|---|---|---|---|---|---|---|---|
| Md-Ba 206 A | B | 1 | Copper | — | — | 17.50 | 55.00 |
| Md-Ba 206 B | B | 1 | Brass | — | — | 20.00 | 55.00 |
| Md-Ba 207 | D | 1 | WM | — | — | 17.50 | 55.00 |
| Md-Ba 208 | E | 1 | WM | — | — | 15.00 | 50.00 |

(Miller 114; Duffield 101)

| | | | | | | | |
|---|---|---|---|---|---|---|---|
| Md-Ba 209 | F | 1 | WM | — | — | 15.00 | 50.00 |

(Miller 115; Duffield 102)

| | | | | | | | |
|---|---|---|---|---|---|---|---|
| Md-Ba 210 | G | 1 | WM | — | — | 15.00 | 50.00 |

(Miller 112; Duffield 99)

| Rulau | Obv | Rev | Metal | F | VF | EF | Unc |
|---|---|---|---|---|---|---|---|
| Md-Ba 211 | H | 1 | WM | — | — | 15.00 | 50.00 |

(Miller 110; Duffield 98)

| | | | | | | | |
|---|---|---|---|---|---|---|---|
| Md-Ba 211 A | H | 1 | Brass | — | — | 20.00 | 55.00 |

(Miller 111)

| | | | | | | | |
|---|---|---|---|---|---|---|---|
| Md-Ba 212 | J | 1 | WM | — | — | 20.00 | 55.00 |

(Miller 117)

| | | | | | | | |
|---|---|---|---|---|---|---|---|
| Md-Ba 213 | K | 1 | WM | | | | Not confirmed |

The Patapsco Fruit Butter Co. apparently existed under that name only in the Centennial year, 1876. It comprised Mrs. L.F. Munder and Maurice P. Munder. It was a subsidiary of C.F. Munder & Brother, confectioners, at the same address, 27 So. Liberty St., which advertised that year it was "also proprietors of the Patapsco Fruit Butter Co."

Charles F. Munder, a baker and confectioner, founded the parent firm about 1820. From 1856 to 1878 it was known as C.F. Munder & Bro. The firm, at the same address for 58 years, was dissolved in 1878.

## POST OFFICE
### Baltimore, Md.

| Rulau | Date | Metal | Size | F | VF | EF | Unc |
|---|---|---|---|---|---|---|---|
| Md-Ba 220 | 1889 | Gilt/B | 25.5mm | — | — | — | 20.00 |

Building at center, POST OFFICE BALTIMORE, MD. above, DEDICATED SEP. 12, 1889 below. Rv: Sailing war vessels at sea bombarding fortress in foreground. Above: BOMBARDMENT OF FORT McHENRY. Below: 1814. Plain edge.

## PRICE BROS.
### Baltimore, Md.

| Rulau | Date | Metal | Size | VG | F | VF | Unc |
|---|---|---|---|---|---|---|---|
| Md-Ba 85 | 1866 | CN | 19.4mm | — | — | 10.00 | — |

Oyster at center, ONE GALLON above, * OYSTERS * below. Rv: PRICE BROS. / 1866 / * BALTO. *. Plain edge. Rarity 6. (Miller Md. 122; Wright 848; Duffield 105)

| | | | | | | | |
|---|---|---|---|---|---|---|---|
| Md-Ba 86 | 1866 | CN | 19.4mm | — | — | 10.00 | — |

Obverse as last. Rv: PRICE BROS. & CO. / 1866 / * BALTO. *. Plain edge. Rarity 6. (Miller Md. 123; Wright 849; Duffield 123)

John S. and Joseph Price were members of the firm of Price Brothers, oyster and fruit packers, at the foot of Cross Street, from 1866-1869. The 1866 date in the first instance is probably the date of issue as well as the establishment date of the firm; the second token was probably issued one or more years later.

## PRINGSHEIM
### Baltimore, Md.

| Rulau | Date | Metal | Size | VG | F | VF | Unc |
|---|---|---|---|---|---|---|---|
| Md-Ba 87 | (1865-66) | S/Brass | 15mm | — | — | 35.00 | — |

Cylindrical object within circle of 12 stars at center, PRINGSHEIM above, BALTIMORE below. Rv: ONE / WHITE within wreath. Plain edge. (Miller Md 124; Duffield 107)

"One White" equaled "One Beer." Moritz Pringsheim about 1865-66 was a brewer of Berlin White Beer. He was also proprietor of a Restaurant at 16 So. Frederick St.

## P.J. REID
### Baltimore, Md.

| Rulau | Date | Metal | Size | VG | F | VF | Unc |
|---|---|---|---|---|---|---|---|
| Md-Ba 89 | (1885-90) | CN | 30mm | 5.00 | 10.00 | 15.00 | — |

(All incuse) P.J. REID / 65 (numeral very large). Rv: Blank. Plain edge. (Miller Md 129; Duffield 110)

Patrick J. Reid ran a restaurant at 2 McClellan St. from 1885 to 1890. Probably other incuse numerals exist, but none have been reported. This piece may be quite scarce.

## SCHUTZEN PARK
### Baltimore, Md.

| Rulau | Date | Metal | Size | F | VF | EF | Unc |
|---|---|---|---|---|---|---|---|
| Md-Ba 90 | (?) | Copper | 20mm | 2.50 | 4.00 | 7.50 | 20.00 |

Crossed rifles above a target. No wreath. SCHUTZEN PARK BALTO. around. Rv: Large 5 in wreath, star at top. (Duffield 121; Miller Md. 141)

| | | | | | | | |
|---|---|---|---|---|---|---|---|
| Md-Ba 91 | (?) | Copper | 20mm | 5.00 | 8.00 | 10.00 | 20.00 |

Obverse as 141. Rv: Blank. (Miller Md. 141A)

## 6 BALTM.
### Baltimore, Md.

| Rulau | Date | Metal | Size | VG | F | VF | EF |
|---|---|---|---|---|---|---|---|
| Md-Ba 94 | (?) | | | — | — | 9.00 | |

6 (four dotted lines) / BALTM. ctsp on unspecified coins. (Brunk 28)

The four dotted lines in the ctsp represent either a fireplace grate or an oyster crate. If the latter, this might be a work check.

## CHAS. TREUSCH
### Baltimore, Md.

| Rulau | Date | Metal | Size | F | VF | EF | Unc |
|---|---|---|---|---|---|---|---|
| Md-Ba 97 | (1868-70) | Brass | 20mm | 4.00 | 6.00 | 9.00 | 20.00 |

Liberty head in Phrygian cap left; small P.H.J. below truncation of neck. 13 stars around. Rv: CHAS. TREUSCH / 5 / * BALTIMORE *. (Wright 1160; Duffield 145; Miller Md. 170)

| Md-Ba 98 | (1868-70) | Lead | — | — | — | — | Rare |

Flower with 12 petals. Rv: As reverse of 97. (Duffield 146; Miller Md. 171)

Struck by Peter H. Jacobus of Philadelphia. Charles Treusch began business 1868 as an oyster and fruit packer. Previously for several years he had been a member of the firm of Treusch, Schoenberg & Co. He died Feb. 9, 1903, having been born in Germany in 1828.

## ROBERT TURNER & SON
### Baltimore, Md.

| Rulau | Date | Metal | Size | G | VG | F | EF |
|---|---|---|---|---|---|---|---|
| Md-Ba 105 | (1867) | Silver | 38mm | — | 125. | — | — |

ROBERT TURNER & SON ctsp on U.S. silver dollar reverse. (Gould 7; Duffield 147; Brunk 393; Miller Md 172)

Robert Turner was engaged in the flour, feed and lime business at 43 So. Frederick St. In 1867 Harry F. Turner, a son, was admitted to the business, which may have been honored by this counterstamp. The firm survived to 1907 or later. In 1918 Turner & Owens, commission merchants, were apparent successors.

## U.S. MANF/G. CO.
### BALTIMORE, Md.

| Rulau | Date | Metal | Size | VG | F | VF | Unc |
|---|---|---|---|---|---|---|---|
| Md-Ba 110 | 1872 | GS | 20mm | — | 8.00 | 15.00 | 27.50 |

U.S. MANF'G CO / STEEL / STAMPS , / STENCILS &C / 97 / W. LOMBARD ST. / BALTIMORE. Rv: MARYLAND INSTITUTE / 25TH / EXHIBITION / OCT. 1872. BALTO. MD. Plaine edge. (Wright 1172; Duffield 149; Miller Md 174)

| Md-Ba 110 A | 1872 | Brass | 20mm | — | 8.00 | 15.00 | 27.50 |

As 110. Plain edge. (Miller Md 175)

| Md-Ba 111 | 1872 | Brass | 20mm | — | — | 20.00 | 30.00 |

As 110A, but ctsp with numeral '5'. Plain edge. (Duffield 149; Miller Md 176)

See J.F.W. Dorman under Baltimore in this reference.

## MILLIGAN & SON
### Crisfield, Md.

| Rulau | Date | Metal | Size | F | VF | EF | Unc |
|---|---|---|---|---|---|---|---|
| Md-Cr 12 | 1875 | Brass | 20mm | 10.00 | 20.00 | 25.00 | 35.00 |

Coronet Liberty head left, 1875. Rv: MILLIGAN & SON / 1 GAL. Plain edge. (Miller Md 184a)

E.W. Milligan and Son were oyster packers. This shucker's check is for one gallon of oysters.

## F.A. WAIDNER & CO.
### Baltimore, Md.

| Rulau | Date | Metal | Size | VG | F | VF | Unc |
|---|---|---|---|---|---|---|---|
| Md-Ba 115 | (1879-82) | Copper | 23.5mm | — | — | 15.00 | — |

F.A. WAIDNER & CO. / (ornament) around blank center. Rv: Blank. Plain edge. Rarity 8.

## A.C. CO.
### (Aughinbaugh Canning Co.)
### Baltimore, Md.

| Md-Ba 118 | (1882-88) | Copper | 19.3mm | — | — | 10.00 | — |

(Wavy line) / A.C. Co. / (wavy line). Rv: 1 / BKT. Plain edge. Rarity 5.

F.A. Waidner & Co. were oyster, fruit and vegetable packers at 2307-2311 Boston St., established in 1879. In 1882 Waidner was incorporated with the Aughinbaugh Canning Co., with C.R. Aughinbaugh, manager. The oysters and fruit of this company had an enviable reputation in Europe for uniform good quality, and more than 500 employees were working. In 1886, more than 3,500,000 cans of oysters, fruits and vegetables were processed, and exports were made to Australia, Mexico, South America, Canada and all over the U.S. By 1918 Aughinbaugh was a subsidiary of Torsch Packing Co.

Both tokens were "shucker checks" for oysters.

## E.J.H.
### (Edward J. Hines)
### Bodkin Point, Md.

| Rulau | Date | Metal | Size | VG | F | VF | Unc |
|---|---|---|---|---|---|---|---|
| Md-Bo 3 | (1880's) | Brass Oc | 19mm | — | 5.00 | — | — |

E.J.H stamped on plain flan with recessed rim all around. Rv: Blank, but recessed rim. Plain edge.

Edward James Hines III (1822-1926), used these picker checks about the 1880's and perhaps later.

## MACGILL & MOORE
### Hagerstown, Md.

| Rulau | Date | Metal | Size | VG | F | VF | Unc |
|---|---|---|---|---|---|---|---|
| Md-Ha 7 | (1889-90) | Brass | 18mm | 5.00 | 9.50 | 15.00 | 30.00 |

Eagle with U.S. shield on breast. Rv: Radiate numeral 3 at center, MACGILL & MOORE above, HAGERSTOWN, MD. below Plain edge. Thin flan. (Miller Md 188A)

| Md-Ha 8 | (1889-90) | Brass | 20mm | 5.00 | 8.50 | 11.00 | 17.50 |

Liberty head. Rv: Similar, but radiate numeral 5. Plain edge. (Duffield 78; Miller Md 188)

## R.E.O.
### (Robert E. Owens)
### Hanover, Md.

| Rulau | Date | Metal | Size | VG | F | VF | Unc |
|---|---|---|---|---|---|---|---|
| Md-Hn 3 | (1889) | Fiber | 23mm | — | — | 7.50 | — |

R.E.O. / 1 stamped on plain flan. Rv: Blank. Thick flan. Plain edge. The fiber flans are colored red.

## E.K.
### (Egbert Kelly)
### Harmans, Md.

| Rulau | Date | Metal | Size | VG | F | VF | Unc. |
|---|---|---|---|---|---|---|---|
| Md-Hr 3 | (1885) | Brass | 21mm | — | 7.00 | — | — |

E.K. / 2 stamped in center, beaded rim around. Rv: Blank, but beaded rim. Plain edge.

| Rulau | Date | Metal | Size | VG | F | VF | Unc |
|---|---|---|---|---|---|---|---|
| Md-Hr 4 | (1890's) | Brass | 20mm | — | 5.00 | — | — |
| | | E.K. / 1 stamped in center, recessed dentilated rim. Rv: Blank, but recessed dentilated rim. Plain edge. | | | | | |
| Md-Hr 5 | (1890's) | Brass Oc | 19mm | — | 5.00 | — | — |
| | | E.K. / 5 stamped in center, recessed rim around. Rv: Blank, but recessed rim. Plain edge. | | | | | |
| Md-Hr 6 | (1890's) | Brass Oc | 19mm | — | 5.00 | — | — |
| | | E.K. / 10. Similar to last. Plain edge. | | | | | |

Egbert J. Kelly was born in 1863 and died in 1945.

## H.N.K.
## (Hezron N. Kelley)
## Harmans, Md.

The 1874-1880 picker checks of this issuer are catalogued in *U.S. Merchant Tokens 1845-1860*, which see.

## T.F.B.
## (Thomas F. Bottomley)
## Magothy, Md.

| Rulau | Date | Metal | Size | VG | F | VF | Unc |
|---|---|---|---|---|---|---|---|
| Md-Mg 1 | (1880's ?) | Brass Sc | 22mm | — | 7.00 | — | — |
| | | T.F.B. / 1 1/2 stamped at center. Rv: Blank. Recessed beaded rim on each side. Plain edge. | | | | | |
| Md-Mg 2 | | Similar, 7 1/2 | Octagonal, 22mm | | | | |
| Md-Mg 3 | | Similar, 10 | Round, 23mm | | | | |
| Md-Mg 4 | | Similar, 15 | Round, 23mm | | | | |
| Md-Mg 5 | | Similar, 20 | Octagonal, 22mm | | | | |
| Md-Mg 6 | | Similar, 30 | Scalloped, 25mm | | | | |
| Md-Mg 7 | | Similar, 75 | Round, 29mm (dentilated, non-recessed rim) | | | | |

Thomas F. Bottomley farmed on Fortsmall Wood Road, Magothy. Robert Wesley Chard, another chit issuer, apparently was his illegitimate son.

## J.S.H.
## (John S. Hawkins)
## Wellhams, Md.

| Rulau | Date | Metal | Size | VG | F | VF | Unc |
|---|---|---|---|---|---|---|---|
| Md-Wm 4 | (1880's) | Brass | 20mm | — | 5.00 | — | — |
| | | J.S.H / 1 stamped on plain flan with recessed, dentilated rim. Rv: Blank, but recessed rim. Plain edge. | | | | | |

John Sterling Hawkins Sr. (1865-1894) farmed at Wellhams, Maryland, in Anne Arundel County.

## MARYLAND PICKER CHITS

The following list of initials covers known picker chit issuers from 1853 to 1945. It was compiled with the aid of the Anne Arundel County Historical Society in Maryland.

| | |
|---|---|
| TFB | Thomas F. Bottomley — MAGOTHY |
| UWB | Ulysses W. Brooks (a Black) |
| WB | William Brossius — CROWNSVILLE |
| FWC | Unidentified |
| RWC | Robert Wesley Chard |
| TMC | Thomas M. Cole — HARMANS (used 1889-1945) |
| WD | William C. Dotson |
| EK | Egbert J. Kelly (born 1863, died 1945) |
| EHH | Egbert H. Hawkins — HARMANS (born 1893, still alive 1966) |
| EJH | Edward Hines III — HARMANS (born 1822, died 1926) |
| JAH | John Asbury Hancock — BODKIN POINT (born 1837, married 1861; tokens used 1853-61 for strawberries) |
| JSH | John Sterling Hawkins Sr. — WELLHAMS (born 1865, died 1894) |
| HNK | Hezron Nehemiah Kelley (born 1818, died 1880) |
| REO | Robert E. Owens (used 1889 only) |
| CBP | Charles B. Pumphrey — MARLEY (1880's ?) |
| R | Unidentified |
| BTR | Benjamin T. Ray — HARMANS (born 1846, died 1921) |
| JHR | John Henry Robinson (born a Negro slave 1844, freed 1864) |
| RR on WD | A son of W.C. Dotson |
| AAS | Adam Alexander Shipley |
| BHS | Basil Hamilton Smith — SEVERN |
| CLS | Charles L. Solley — SOLLEY |
| JWS | John Wilson Shipley — WELLHAMS (used 1902-03 only) |
| LRS | Larkin Rodolphus Shipley — HARMANS (born 1841, died 1890; tokens used 1874-1940) |
| ROS | Roderick Octavius Shipley |
| WES | William Elbridge Shipley (born 1870, died 1930; tokens used 1890-1930) |
| BFT | Benjamin F. Thomas — HAMMONDS LANE |
| PSW | Penrhyn Stanley Watts — ADMERIAL FT. MEADE & SEVERN (born 1890, died 1970) |
| WW | William Ware (a Black) |

For additional reading, consult "Builder Uncovers Tin Box Containing Servants' checks Used by Pumphrey" by Melvin Fuld, in *Coin World* for March 9, 1966, page 46.

## B. F. SHRIVER & CO.
## Westminster, Md.

| Rulau | Date | Metal | Size | F | VF | EF | Unc |
|---|---|---|---|---|---|---|---|
| Md-Ws 6 | (1870's) | GS | 25mm | 5.00 | 10.00 | 15.00 | 30.00 |
| | | Liberty head within wreath. Rv: Large numeral 5, radiant, at center, B. F. SHRIVER & CO., WESTMINSTER, MD. around. Plain edge. (Miller Md 189; Duffield 129) | | | | | |
| Md-Ws 6 | (1870's) | WM | 20mm | 8.00 | 12.00 | 20.00 | 40.00 |
| | | Obverse as 6. Rv: Similar to 6, but numeral 3. Plain edge. (Miller Md 190) | | | | | |

## SOVEREIGNS OF INDUSTRY
## Woodberry, Md.

| Rulau | Date | Metal | Size | VG | F | VF | Unc |
|---|---|---|---|---|---|---|---|
| Md-Wb 3 | 1876 | Brass | 25mm | — | 17.50 | 25.00 | 35.00 |
| | | Coronet Liberty head left, four stars in its coronet. Eleven stars around. Rv: SOVEREIGNS OF INDUSTRY, EXCELSIOR COUNCIL / WOODBERRY, MD. Incused numeral at center within beaded circle. (Numerals examined: 1). Plain edge. (Miller Md 191; Duffield 137) | | | | | |
| Md-Wb 4 | 1876 | Lead | 25mm | — | 17.50 | 25.00 | 35.00 |
| | | As 3. (Numerals examined: 15). Plain edge. | | | | | |

Probably an identification check for a society. Woodberry was incorporated into Baltimore 1888.

# MASSACHUSETTS

### A.P. KNOWLES
### Ashland, Mass.

| Rulau | Date | Metal | Size | VG | F | VF | EF |
|---|---|---|---|---|---|---|---|
| Ma-As 4 | 1873 | Copper | 29mm | — | — | 75.00 | — |

STENCILS, STEEL STAMPS, KEY CHECKS JC. / MADE BY A.P. KNOWLES / ASHLAND, MASS. / 1873 ctsp on U.S. Large cent, date worn off.

### G. GERRY
### Athol, Mass.

| Rulau | Date | Metal | Size | VG | F | VF | EF |
|---|---|---|---|---|---|---|---|
| Ma-At 1 | (?) | Copper | 29mm | — | 50.00 | — | 100. |

G. GERRY / ATHOL MASS. ctsp on U.S. Large cent. (Hallenbeck 7.511; Brunk 161)

| Ma-At 1A | (?) | Copper | 29mm | — | 50.00 | — | 100. |

Similar ctsp on U.S. 1847 Large cent.

| Ma At 2 | (?) | Copper | 29mm | — | 50.00 | — | 100. |

G. GERRY ctsp on reverse of U.S. 1836 Large cent. (Tanenbaum coll.)

In 1918 George Gerry & Son, machinery manufacturers, were probable successors. Athol is in Worcester County.

### BERNARD & FRIEDMAN
### Boston, Mass.

| Rulau | Date | Metal | Size | F | VF | EF | Unc |
|---|---|---|---|---|---|---|---|
| Ma-Bo 12 | (?) | Cop. | 22x26mm | — | 5.00 | 10.00 | 18.00 |

Shield of arms at center (Shield divided per bend; in chief three horseshoes; in base three nails). Above: BERNARD & FRIEDMAN.; below: BOSTON. Rv: BERNARD & FRIEDMAN. / TITAN / CALF / BOSTON. Plain edge. Horseshoe-shaped flan. (Wright 1337)

In 1918 The Bernard Co. were leather makers.

### BOSTON NUMISMATIC SOCIETY
### Boston, Mass.

| Rulau | Date | Metal | Size | F | VF | EF | Unc |
|---|---|---|---|---|---|---|---|
| Ma-Bo 13 | 1875 | Brass | 31mm | — | — | — | 40.00 |

Both sides of New England shilling above pine tree on a hill, INSTITUTED / 1860 above, all within central circle. Around, in two concentric circles: PRESIDENCY OF ULYSSES S. GRANT / **** 1875 **** / BOSTON NUMISMATIC SOCIETY / INCORPORATED 1870. Rv: Society seal in central circle. Around, in two concentric circles: TWIN DELVERS IN THE GARDEN OF HISTORY / (ISAAC F. WOODS / MEMORIAL SERIES) / N. E. HISTORIC GENEALOGICAL / * SOCIETY *. Plain edge. (Wright 89)

Isaac F. Wood's memorial series. This is the same I. F. Wood of New York who issued the Cogan "English Daddy" pieces of Brooklyn, N.Y. (See NY-Bk 7 through 10)

### HENRY W. BURR & CO.
### Boston, Mass.

| Rulau | Date | Metal | Size | VG | F | VF | Unc |
|---|---|---|---|---|---|---|---|
| Ma-Bo 14 | (1870's) | WM | 31mm | — | — | — | Rare |

HENRY W. BURR & CO / RUBBER / GOODS / OF EVERY / DESCRIPTION / AT WHOLESALE & RETAIL. Rv: BOSTON RUBBER EMPORIUM / NO. 37 / MILK ST. / * / BOSTON / MASS. Plain edge. (Tanenbaum coll.)

This token is normally molded in hard rubber. Only one white metal example has been seen.

### L.J. COLBY
### Boston, Mass.

| Rulau | Date | Metal | Size | VG | F | VF | EF |
|---|---|---|---|---|---|---|---|
| Ma-Bo 15 | (?) | Silver | 24mm | 30.00 | — | 60.00 | — |

(5-pointed star in circle) / L.J. COLBY in circle / (5-pointed star in circle) / BOSTON MASS in circle — ctsp on reverse of England 1817 Shilling. (Tanenbaum coll.)

### HENRY COOK
### Boston, Mass.

| Rulau | Date | Metal | Size | F | VF | EF | Unc |
|---|---|---|---|---|---|---|---|
| Ma-Bo 19 | (1861-2) | Copper | 43mm | — | 25.00 | 35.00 | 50.00 |

Scroll inscribed CONSTITUTION. NO SURRENDER OF THE FORT SUMTER OF THE NORTH. Thirteen stars. Under scroll: THE GIFT OF OUR PATRIOT SIRES / WE NEVER WILL / SURRENDER / TO / TRAITORS AND REBELS. Rv: Wreath around: HENRY COOK / MONEY BROKER / AND DEALER

| Rulau | Date | Metal | Size | F | VF | EF | Unc |
|---|---|---|---|---|---|---|---|
| | | IN / RARE AND ANTIQUE / COINS / MEDALS / AUTOGRAPHS / CURIOSITIES, RELICS / &C &C / NO. 74 FRIEND ST., / BOSTON. Plain edge. (Wright 205; Miller Mass 28) | | | | | |
| Ma-Bo 19A | (1861-2) | WM | 43mm | — | 25.00 | 35.00 | 57.50 |
| | | As last. Plain edge. (Miller Mass 29) | | | | | |
| Ma-Bo 20 | (1860's) | Copper | 28mm | 600. | — | — | — |
| | | Eagle on apothecary's mortar (Haviland Stevenson card, Miller SC 3). Rv: HENRY COOK, MONEY BROKER. Only 2 pieces known. (Woodward Oct. 25, 1886 sale, lot 1342) | | | | | |

## FOREIGN EXHIBITION
### Boston, Mass.

| Rulau | Date | Metal | Size | F | VF | EF | Unc |
|---|---|---|---|---|---|---|---|
| Ma-Bo 26 | 1883 | WM | 29mm | — | — | 35.00 | |
| | | Four 18th century gentlemen gathered around a table for a signing ceremony. Above: TREATY OF PEACE BETWEEN GREAT BRITAIN AND THE UNITED STATES / SEPT 3D. Below: SIGNED AT / PARIS FRANCE. / .1783. Rv: . FOREIGN EXHIBITION . / OPENED / SEPTEMBER 3D. / 1883. / BOSTON, MASS. U.S.A. Plain edge. | | | | | |

This medalet honors the centennial of the Paris Treaty, by which the United States achieved formal recognition of its independence.

## GEORGE FERA
### Boston, Mass.

| Rulau | Date | Metal | Size | F | VF | EF | Unc |
|---|---|---|---|---|---|---|---|
| Ma-Bo 22 | 1864 | Copper | 27mm | — | 30.00 | — | 75.00 |
| | | SOLDIERS' FAIR DEC. 1864. SPRINGFIELD MASS. within laurel wreath. Rv: GEORGE FERA / * STUDIO BUILDING * / MERRIAM (tiny) Plain edge. (Miller Mass 42) | | | | | |
| Ma-Bo 23 | 1864 | WM | 27mm | — | — | — | 75.00 |
| | | As Ma-Bo 22. (Miller Mass 43) | | | | | |
| Ma-Bo 24 | (1867-71) | Copper | 27mm | — | 30.00 | — | 75.00 |
| | | APOLLO GARDENS / 576 / WASHINGTON ST. / GOOD FOR / 6 / CENTS. / * HESS & SPEIDEL * (reverse of Mass 4). As reverse of (Ma-Bo 22.) Plain edge. (Miller Mass 44.) | | | | | |

The regular Fera store cards appear in my 1845-1860 reference. These are mulings made in the 1867-71 period.

## HAPGOOD
### Boston, Mass.

| Rulau | Date | Metal | Size | VG | F | VF | EF |
|---|---|---|---|---|---|---|---|
| Ma-Bo 28 | (?) | Copper | 29mm | — | — | 35.00 | — |
| | | HAPGOOD BOSTON ctsp on U.S. Large cent. (Hallenbeck 8.501) | | | | | |

## HESS & SPEIDEL, APOLLO GARDENS
### Boston, Mass.

| Rulau | Date | Metal | Size | F | VF | EF | Unc |
|---|---|---|---|---|---|---|---|
| Ma-Bo 30 | (1860's) | Copper | 27mm | — | — | Ex. Rare | |
| | | Lincoln bust right. ABRAHAM LINCOLN above. BORN FEB. 12, 1809. below. Tiny MERRIAM under bust. Rv: APOLLO GARDENS / 576 / WASHINGTON ST. / GOOD FOR / 6 / CENTS. / * HESS & SPEIDEL *. Plain edge. (Miller Mass 9; DeWitt AL 1860-45 (F) | | | | | |
| Ma-Bo 31 | (1860's) | WM | 27mm | — | — | Ex. Rare | |
| | | As last. Plain edge. (Miller Mass 10) | | | | | |

| Rulau | Date | Metal | Size | F | VF | EF | Unc |
|---|---|---|---|---|---|---|---|
| Ma-Bo 33 | (1870's) | WM | 27mm | — | — | Ex. Rare | |
| | | Obverse as last (Lincoln). Rv: Apollo bust right, within oak wreath. APOLLO. above. Plain edge. (Schenkman B1; Miller Mass 10A) | | | | | |
| Ma-Bo 34 | (1860's) | WM | 27mm | — | — | 35.00 | 100. |
| | | Obverse as reverse of Miller Mass 9 (HESS & SPEIDEL card). Rv: Card of George Fera, Studio Building. Plain edge. (Miller Mass 11) | | | | | |
| Ma-Bo 36 | (1870's) | WM | 27mm | — | — | 50.00 | 100. |
| | | George Washington bust left, J.A. BOLEN under truncation. WASHINGTON above. Rv: As obverse of last (HESS & SPEIDEL card). Plain edge. (Miller Mass 12) | | | | | |
| Ma-Bo 37 | (1870's) | Copper | 27mm | — | — | 50.00 | 75.00 |
| | | As last. Plain edge. (Miller Mass 12A0 | | | | | |

| Rulau | Date | Metal | Size | F | VF | EF | Unc |
|---|---|---|---|---|---|---|---|
| Ma-Bo 39 | 1862 | Copper | 27mm | — | — | 35.00 | 100. |
| | | Obverse as reverse of Miller Mass 9 (HESS & SPEIDEL card). Rv: MADE FROM COPPER / - TAKEN FROM / THE RUINS OF / - THE - / TURPENTINE WORKS / NEWBERN / - N.C. - /DESTROYED BY THE / REBELS / MERRIAM (tiny) / MARCH 14, 1862. Plain edge. (Miller Mass 15; Schenkman B10) | | | | | |

| Rulau | Date | Metal | Size | F | VF | EF | Unc |
|---|---|---|---|---|---|---|---|
| Ma-Bo 41 | 1864 | Copper | 27mm | — | — | — | Rare |
| | | Washington head right within oak branches, WASHINGTON above. Rv: MADE FROM A COPPER BOLT / TAKEN FROM / - THE - / WRECK OF THE / FRIGATE CONGRESS / - BY - / G.W. WILLIAMS / - / CO. C. 25. REG. M.V. / JAN. 1. 1864. Plain edge. (Schenkman B28) | | | | | |
| Ma-Bo 43 | (1870's) | Copper | 27mm | — | — | 35.00 | 100. |
| | | Obverse as reverse of Miller Mass 9 (HESS & SPEIDEL card). Rv: As reverse of George Fera card (PARTIES SUPPLIED). Plain edge. (Miller Mass 16) | | | | | |
| Ma-Bo 44 | (1870's) | WM | 27mm | — | — | 35.00 | 100. |
| | | As last. Plain edge. (Miller Mass 17) | | | | | |
| Ma-Bo 46 | (1870's) | CN | 27mm | — | — | — | 100. |
| | | Beardless Lincoln bust right, ABRAHAM LINCOLN above, BORN FEB. 12, 1809. below. Tiny MERRIAM BOSTON below truncation. Rv: Obverse as reverse of Miller Mass 10A (Apollo bust). Plain edge. (Miller Mass 17A; King 598; DeWitt AL 1860-45(E) | | | | | |

## INTERNATIONAL MARITIME EXHIBITION
### Boston, Mass.

| Rulau | Date | Metal | Size | VG | F | VF | Unc |
|---|---|---|---|---|---|---|---|
| Ma-Bo 50 | 1889-90 | Silver | 25mm | — | — | 15.00 | 30.00 |
| | | A ship, MARITIME EXHIBITION above, BOSTON MASS below. Rv: Buildings, INTERNATIONAL / MARITIME / EXHIBITION / 1889-90. Plain edge. (Wright 661) | | | | | |
| Ma-Bo 51 | 1889-90 | G/Silver | 25mm | — | — | 15.00 | 30.00 |
| | | As last. (Stanley Steinberg 1982 sale) | | | | | |

## MASONIC TEMPLE
## Boston, Mass.

| Rulau | Date | Metal | Size | VG | F | VF | EF |
|---|---|---|---|---|---|---|---|
| Ma-Bo 55 | 1864 | Silver | 31mm | — | — | — | 100. |

BOSTON/ENCAMPMENT ctsp on obverse of U.S. 1864. Seated Liberty half dollar. TAKEN FROM THE RUINS OF MASONIC TEMPLE / APRIL 6'' 1864. ctsp on reverse of the coin. All ctsp letters are in script.

| Ma-Bo 57 | 1864 | Silver | 31mm | — | — | — | 100. |

Similar ctsp to last, but HAMILCAR RICE in script added to obverse, on 1864 Liberty Seated half dollar.

| Ma-Bo 59 | 1864 | Silver | 31mm | — | — | — | 100. |

S. N. FURBER / MASONIC HALL BT. / APRIL 5TH / 1864 (all in script) ctsp on U.S. 1864 Liberty Seated half dollar.

All these counterstamps, which resemble engravings, were done by the same fine hand in excellent style. All are on new, or near-new coins. All above reposed in personal collection of Kurt R. Krueger, Iola, Wis. in 1982; ex-Maurice M. Gould collection.

The Boston Masonic Hall burned April 5, 1864. From the inscription, it would appear these then-new half dollars were salvaged from the ruins the next day. What purpose these souvenirs served is conjecture at this point, though it seems likely they were a fund-raising receipt of some kind to rebuild the hall. Just who Hamilcar Rice and S.N. Furber are must also be determined, but it seems safe to assume they were Masons of the Civil War period.

St. Andrew's Royal Arch Chapter was founded Aug. 12, 1769. Paul Revere was made a Mason in Massachusetts in 1760; he was Master of this lodge 1770-71, 1777-79 and 1780-82. Later Revere was Grand Master of the Grand Lodge of Massachusetts 1794-97. Bronze medals were struck in 1894 for the 125th anniversary of this lodge (King 153). Two volumes of the history of this lodge were published in 1882 by Alfred F. Chapman.

| Rulau | Date | Metal | Size | VG | F | VF | EF |
|---|---|---|---|---|---|---|---|
| Ma-Bo 60 | 1867 | WM | 31mm | — | — | — | 20.00 |

Temple at center, MASONIC TEMPLE above, BOSTON below. Rv: NEW MASONIC TEMPLE / (radiant seeing eye) / DEDICATED / JUNE 24. A. L. 5867 / CHAS. C. DAME / (square and compass) / GRAND MASTER. Plain edge. (Schenkman C12-C13)

## JOS. H. MERRIAM
## Boston, Mass.

| Rulau | Date | Metal | Size | F | VF | EF | Unc |
|---|---|---|---|---|---|---|---|
| Ma-Bo 65 | (1860) | Copper | 32mm | — | — | 50.00 | 75.00 |

Daniel Webster. Rv: As reverse of Miller Mass 58. Plain edge.

| Ma-Bo 66 | (1860) | Brass | 32mm | — | — | 50.00 | 75.00 |

As Ma-Bo 65. Plain edge. (Miller Mass 60)

| Ma-Bo 67 | (1860) | WM | 32mm | — | — | 50.00 | 75.00 |

As Ma-Bo 65. Plain edge. (Miller Mass 61)

| Ma-Bo 69 | (1860) | Copper | 32mm | — | — | 50.00 | 75.00 |

Albert Edward, Prince of Wales. Rv: As Ma-Bo 65. Plain edge. (Miller Mass 62)

| Ma-Bo 70 | (1860) | Brass | 32mm | — | — | 50.00 | 75.00 |

As 69. Plain edge. (Miller Mass 63)

| Ma-Bo 71 | (1860) | WM | 32mm | — | — | 50.00 | 75.00 |

As 69. Plain edge. (Miller Mass 64)

| Ma-Bo 72 | (1860) | Copper | 32mm | — | — | — | Unique |

Head of Everett left, EDWARD EVERETT above, BORN APRIL 11, 1794. below. Rv: As Ma-Bo 65. Plain edge. (Springfield sale, Dec. 17, 1981)

| Ma-Bo 72A | (1860) | WM | 32mm | — | — | — | 100. |

Same as last. (Schenkman C-7)

| Ma-Bo 73 | (1860) | Copper | 32mm | — | — | 50.00 | 75.00 |

Bust of Merriam left, LABOR OMNIA VICIT above. Rv: As 65. Plain edge. (Miller Mass 65)

| Ma-Bo 74 | (1860) | Brass | 32mm | — | — | 50.00 | 75.00 |

As 73. Plain edge. (Miller Mass 66)

| Ma-Bo 75 | (1860) | WM | 32mm | — | — | 50.00 | 75.00 |

As 73. Plain edge. (Miller Mass 67)

| Ma-Bo 77 | 1859 | Copper | 32mm | — | — | 20.00 | 50.00 |

Bust of Sayers left, THOMAS SAYERS / CHAMPION OF ENGLAND 1859. Rv: As 65. Plain edge. (Wright 693A; Miller Mass 68)

| Ma-Bo 78 | 1859 | Copper | 32mm | — | — | 20.00 | 50.00 |

Bust of Heenan right, JOHN C. HEENAN / CHAMPION OF AMERICA 1859. Rv: As 65. Plain edge. (Wright 693; Miller Mass 69)

| Ma-Bo 79 | (1860) | WM | 32mm | — | — | 20.00 | 50.00 |

Bust of Apollo. Rv: As 65. Plain edge. (Miller Mass 68A)

| Rulau | Date | Metal | Size | VG | F | VF | Unc |
|---|---|---|---|---|---|---|---|
| Ma-Bo 81 | 1862 | Copper | 27mm | — | — | — | Rare |

Washington head in wreath right, WASHINGTON above (obverse of Mass 55). Rv: MADE FROM COPPER / — TAKEN FROM — / THE RUINS OF / — THE — / TURPENTINE WORKS / NEWBERN / —N.C.— / DESTROYED BY THE REBELS / MARCH 14, 1862 (reverse of Miller Mass 15). Rarity 9. (Baker 622)

Merriam store cards of the 1859-1860 period may be found in *U.S. Merchant Tokens 1845-1860*. Those true store cards of the Civil War period appear in *Civil War Store Cards* by the Fulds.

---

ADVERTISING DEPARTMENT. 215

## MERRIAM & CO.
## SEAL ENGRAVERS,
Make Numbers for Pews, Streets, &c.,

### Cheaper than any other Live Men !!!

SEALS FOR LODGES, NOTARIES, &c.,

19 Brattle Square, . . . . . . . BOSTON.

---

*Advertisement for Merriam & Co., Boston, in 1868.*

## E. R. MORSE
### Boston, Mass.

| Rulau | Date | Metal | Size | VG | F | VF | EF |
|---|---|---|---|---|---|---|---|
| Ma-Bo 83 | (?) | Copper | 29mm | — | 200. | — | — |

E. R. MORSE UNION ST. / BOSTON ctsp on U.S. 1802 Large cent. (Hallenbeck 13.752)

## NATIONAL PEACE JUBILEE
### Boston, Mass.

| Rulau | Date | Metal | Size | F | VF | EF | Unc |
|---|---|---|---|---|---|---|---|
| Ma-Bo 88 | 1869 | G/Br | 28mm | — | 5.00 | 10.00 | 15.00 |

Large building at center. Above: NATIONAL PEACE JUBILEE / LET US HAVE / PEACE. Below: COLISEUM / BOSTON JUNE 17. 69. Rv: U.S. eagle displayed, UNITED STATES above, THE BIRTH PLACE OF FREEDOM below. Plain edge. (Wright 1371)

| Rulau | Date | Metal | Size | F | VF | EF | Unc |
|---|---|---|---|---|---|---|---|
| Ma-Bo 89 | 1869 | G/Br | 28mm | — | 5.00 | 10.00 | 15.00 |

Obverse as last. Rv: P.S. GILMORE, / STATISTICS / LENGTH 500 FT / WIDTH 300 FT / HEIGHT 100 FT / LUMBER 2000000 / NAILS 23 TONS / GAS PIPE 25000 FT / SEATS 50000 / *** ORIGINATOR. ***. Plain edge.

## H. M. RICHARDS & CO.
### Boston, Mass.

| Rulau | Date | Metal | Size | F | VF | EF | Unc |
|---|---|---|---|---|---|---|---|
| Ma-Bo 94 | (1879) | N/Steel* | 31mm | — | — | 300. | — |

H. M. RICHARDS & CO. / MANUFRS OF / JEWELRY, / SOCIETY & / MILITARY / BADGES, / EMBLEMS &C. / *7 GREEN ST. BOSTON. *. Rv: * PAY AT * / 50 / THE COUNTER. Plain edge.

*The steel token has nickel plating on the edge and rim and on all lettering. The field is enameled black.

According to the patent application accompanying the only known specimen of this token, Hervey M. Richards of North Attleboro, Mass. (the same man who manufactured Hard Times tokens more than 40 years earlier) on June 29, 1878 filed this token with his application for a new design of "lunch and baggage checks." Patent No. 218.577 was granted Aug. 12, 1879.

In 1918 in Attleboro a probable successor firm, W. E. Richards Co., were manufacturing jewelers.

## C. W. RICHARDSON
### Boston, Mass.

| Rulau | Date | Metal | Size | VG | F | VF | EF |
|---|---|---|---|---|---|---|---|
| Ma-Bo 95 | (?) | Silver | 25mm | — | — | 75.00 | — |

C. W. RICHARDSON, BOSTON ctsp on U.S. 1853 Arrows & Rays Seated Liberty quarter.

## DR. RIDGE'S FOOD
### Boston, Mass.

| Rulau | Date | Metal | Size | VG | F | VF | Unc |
|---|---|---|---|---|---|---|---|
| Ma-Bo 93 | 1872 | WM | 32mm | — | — | — | — |

* DR. RIDGE'S FOOD FOR * / (embossed) 4 — 1 — 2 — 3 (At four compass points) / (raised boss, for spinning) / INFANTS & INVALIDS. Rv: WORLD'S PEACE JUBILEE & MUSICAL FESTIVAL / DR. RIDGE'S FOOD FOR / (raised boss) / INFANTS & INVALIDS / * 1872 *. Plain edge. (Wright 896 variety: Horatio Storer 3025 or 3026). Rarity 9.

In *Medicina in Nummis*, Dr. Storer mentions three varieties of this very early spinner token, one of which is 34mm in diameter.

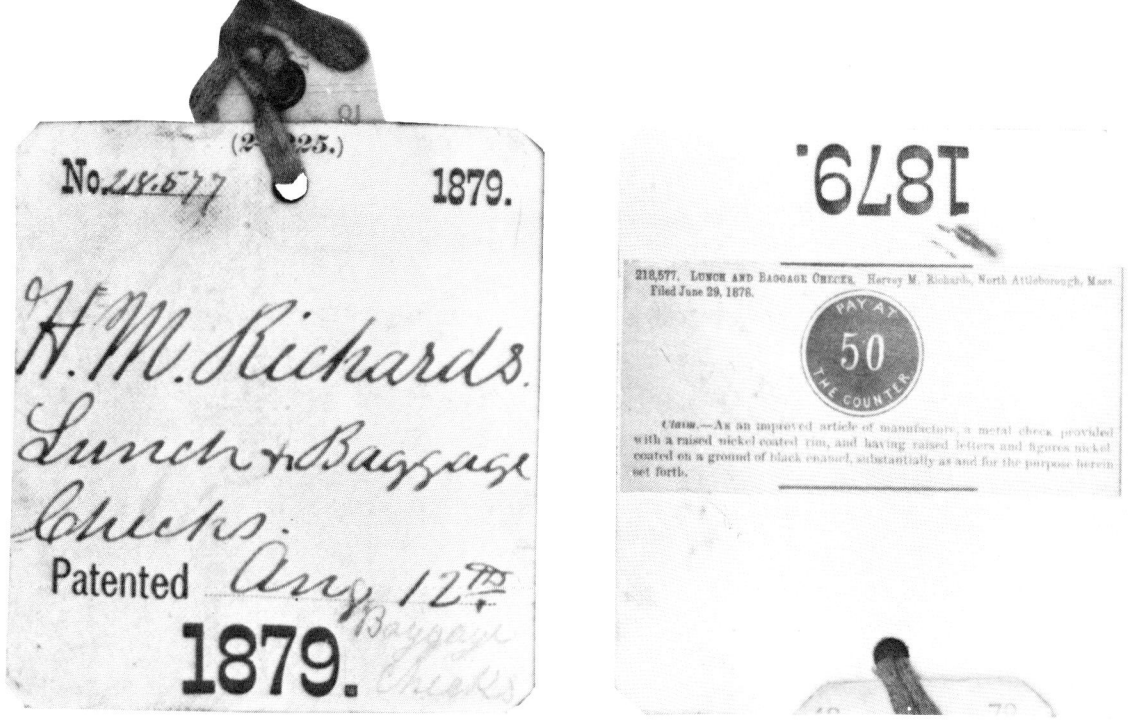

**1879 Patent granting tag, cloth.**

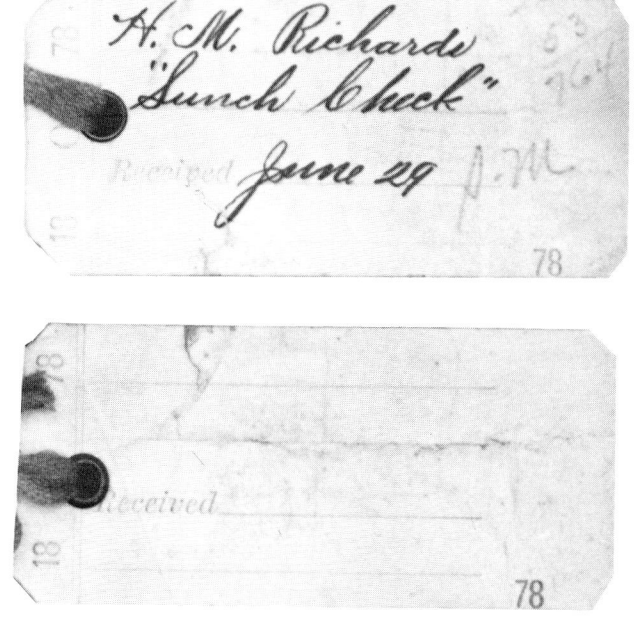

**1878 Patent application tag, cardboard.**

## F. W. SNOW
### Boston, Mass.

| Rulau | Date | Metal | Size | VG | F | VF | EF |
|---|---|---|---|---|---|---|---|
| Ma-Bo 96 | (?) | Bronze | 31mm | — | — | 75.00 | — |

F. W. SNOW BOSTON ctsp on Great Britain 1865 Victoria penny.

It is possible that the F. SNOW counterstamp on a Large cent, Hallenbeck 19.750, is connected with this issuer.

## T. P. SPITZ
### Boston, Mass.

| Rulau | Date | Metal | Size | VG | F | VF | EF |
|---|---|---|---|---|---|---|---|
| Ma-Bo 97 | (?) | GS | Oval 35x21.5mm | — | — | — | Scrc |

Eagle. On three scrolls: T. P. SPITZ / 28 PORTER ST. / BOSTON. Rv: Blank. (Wright 1029)

## THROUGH THE FIRE
### Boston, Mass.

| Rulau | Date | Metal | Size | VG | F | VF | EF |
|---|---|---|---|---|---|---|---|
| Ma-Bo 100 | 1872 | Bronze | 23mm | — | — | 20.00 | — |

THROUGH . THE FIRE. / BOSTON. / NOV. / 9 / 1872. ctsp on U.S. 1867 2-cent piece.

The great fire of 1872 destroyed much of the heart of Boston.

## F. G. WINNETT
### Cambridge, Mass.

| Rulau | Date | Metal | Size | VG | F | VF | Unc |
|---|---|---|---|---|---|---|---|
| Ma-Cm 7 | (?) | CN | Oval 35x19mm | 2.00 | 3.50 | 5.00 | 11.50 |

Eagle. Inscribed: F.G. WINNETT / 25 MILL ST. / CAMBRIDGE / MASS. Rv: Blank. Plain edge. (Wright 1731)

## MASS. ARMS CO.
### Chicopee Falls, Mass.

| Rulau | Date | Metal | Size | VG | F | VF | EF |
|---|---|---|---|---|---|---|---|
| Ma-CF 3 | (1860's) | Copper | 29mm | — | — | 150. | — |

MANUFACTURED BY / MASS. ARMS CO. / CHICOPEE FALLS ctsp on U.S. Large cent. (Hallenbeck 13.502; Brunk 250)

| | | | | | | | |
|---|---|---|---|---|---|---|---|
| Ma-CF 6 | (1860's) | Silver | 31mm | — | — | 150. | — |

Similar ctsp on U.S. Liberty Seated 1857 half dollar (Kurt Krueger coll.)

The counterstamp is the stamp used to mark Smith breech-loading percussion carbines made by the firm during the Civil War. Massachusetts Arms Co. was incorporated March 5, 1850; the Smith carbine was patented 1856-1857. The firm also made Maynard and Greene carbines and Wesson and Leavitt revolvers. The business failed after the war and was taken over Feb. 1, 1876 by Lamb Knitting Machine Co.

## ROBINSON & HEATH
### Chicopee, Mass.

| Rulau | Date | Metal | Size | VG | F | VF | Unc |
|---|---|---|---|---|---|---|---|
| Ma-Cp 4 | (1880's) | Br Oct. | 26mm | — | — | 35.00 | 45.00 |

Indian head left in central circle. Around: L. BOCHE, ENGRAVER, DIE SINKER & MANUF'R OF CHECKS, 166 RANDOLPH ST. CHICAGO. Rv: GOOD FOR 5 CENTS / ROBINSON / & / HEATH / ... / CHICOPEE / MASS / * IN TRADE *. Plain edge. (Hartzog coll.)

Boche introduced the Indian head stock die about 1885. (See a similar card under Concordia, Elgin, Ill.)

## F. BLODGETT
### Gardner, Mass.

| Rulau | Date | Metal | Size | VG | F | VF | EF |
|---|---|---|---|---|---|---|---|
| Ma-Gr 2 | (?) | Copper | 29mm | — | — | 75.00 | — |

F. BLODGETT / GARDNER, MASS. ctsp on U.S. Large cent. (Hallenbeck 2.545)

## ROGERS & BRO.
### Gloucester, Mass.

| Rulau | Date | Metal | Size | VG | F | VF | Unc |
|---|---|---|---|---|---|---|---|
| Ma-Gc 7 | (?) | Brass | 19mm | — | 10.00 | — | 20.00 |

Closed hand emitting electric discharges. ROGERS & BRO TRIPLE PLATE. Rv: Blank. Plain edge. (Wright 910)

J. S. Rogers & Brother were manufacturing jewelers.

## W. A. C.
### Lowell, Mass.

| Rulau | Date | Metal | Size | VG | F | VF | Unc |
|---|---|---|---|---|---|---|---|
| Ma-Lo 4 | 1876 | WM | 25mm | — | — | 10.00 | — |

Female seated right, in her hand a distaff for spinning. SHE SEEKETH / WOOL AND FLAX AND WORKETH WILLINGLY WITH HER HANDS 1776. Rv: Large monogram. W.A.C. at center. ART IS THE HAND MAID OF HUMAN GOOD / LOWELL 1876. Plain edge. (Wright 1194)

## A. LAWRENCE
### Lowell, Mass.

| Rulau | Date | Metal | Size | VG | F | VF | EF |
|---|---|---|---|---|---|---|---|
| Ma-Lo 8 | (?) | CN | 19mm | — | — | 150. | — |

A. LAWRENCE / DENTIST / LOWELL ctsp on U.S. 1857 Flying Eagle cent.

## PALMER, MASS.

| Rulau | Date | Metal | Size | VG | F | VF | EF |
|---|---|---|---|---|---|---|---|
| Ma-Pa 1 | (?) | Silver | 38mm | 25.00 | — | 50.00 | — |

PALMER, MASS. ctsp on U.S. 1879 Morgan silver dollar. (Koppenhaver Aug. 1982 sale)

## G. S. GATES
### Rutland, Mass.

| Rulau | Date | Metal | Size | VG | F | VF | EF |
|---|---|---|---|---|---|---|---|
| Ma-Ru 5 | (?) | Silver | 25mm | — | — | 75.00 | — |

G. S. GATES / RUTLAND, MASS. ctsp on U.S. 1875 Liberty Seated quarter dollar. (Gould 82)

# BEE HIVE
## Salem, Mass.

| Rulau | Date | Metal | Size | VG | F | VF | Unc |
|---|---|---|---|---|---|---|---|
| Ma-Sa 3 | (?) | WM | 28.5mm | — | — | 20.00 | — |

BEE HIVE / 5. Rv: Same as obverse. Plain edge.

Attributed by association with a business card with which it was discovered. The card reads: FRANK COUSINS — BEE HIVE — SALEM, MASS. — XMAS & NEW YEAR GIFTS.

# J. A. BOLEN
## Springfield, Mass.

| Rulau | Date | Metal | Size | F | VF | EF | Unc |
|---|---|---|---|---|---|---|---|
| Ma-Sp 4 | 1862 | Copper | 28.3mm | — | — | — | 150. |

Boy with flag riding a flying eagle, YOUNG AMERICA around, 1862 below. Border of dots and stars around rim. Rv: J. A. BOLEN / DIE SINKER / AND / MEDALIST / SPRINGFIELD, MASS. Plain edge. Only 75 struck. (Wright 127; Miller Mass 101)

| Ma-Sp 5 | 1862 | Brass | 28.3mm | — | — | — | 150. |

As 4. Plain edge. Only 75 struck. (Miller Mass 102)

| Ma-Sp 6 | 1862 | Silvered | 28.3mm | — | — | — | 150. |

As 4. Plain edge. (Miller Mass 102A)

| Ma-Sp 7 | 1862 | Copper | 28.3mm | — | — | 75.00 | 100. |

Obverse as 4. Rv: Building with flag flying, tiny J. A. BOLEN on truncation. Below: U.S. / ARSENAL. Plain edge. (Miller Mass 101A)

| Ma-Sp 8 | 1862 | WM | 28.3mm | — | — | 75.00 | 100. |

As 101A. Plain edge. (R. B. White collection). This piece was not recorded by Adams or Miller.

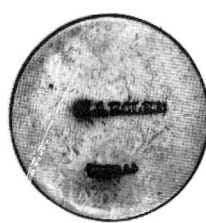

| Ma-Sp 10 | (1860's) | Copper | 29mm | — | 100. | — | — |

J. A. BOLEN ctsp on U.S. Large cent. Also, J. A. BOLEENN ctsp in mirror-image in smaller letters on same side of cent. Plain edge. (R. B. White collection)

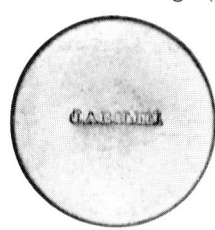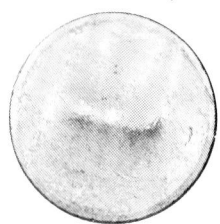

| Ma-Sp 12 | (1860's) | Alum | 28.7mm | — | — | 75.00 | — |

J. A. BOLEN ctsp on blank aluminum disc. Plain edge. (R. B. White collection)

The two counterstamps above are apparently test pieces by Bolen to test his name punches, as used on the truncations of various tokens which he signed. The Large cent is of the type of 1803, date no longer visible, and may be unique. There are two specimens of the aluminum disc in the R. B. White collection, and several others elsewhere.

| Ma-Sp 14 | (1862) | Copper | 28.3mm | — | — | — | 100. |

Obverse as reverse of Ma-Sp 7 (U.S. Arsenal). Rv: U.S. ARMORY / * / ESTABLISHED / BY / ACT OF CONGRESS / IN APRIL, / 1794. / SPRINGFIELD, MASS. Plain edge.

| Ma-Sp 16 | (1862) | Copper | 28.3mm | — | — | — | 75.00 |

Obverse as reverse of 7 (U.S. Arsenal). Rv: Liberty cap within rays. Around: UNITED STATES OF AMERICA / * LIBERTY *. Plain edge. (Wright 1173)

| Ma-Sp 17 | (1862) | Brass | 28.3mm | — | — | — | 100. |

Obverse as 14 (Arsenal). Rv: As reverse of 18 (Bolen store card). Plain edge.

| Ma-Sp 17A | (1862) | WM | 28.3mm | — | — | — | 100. |

As 17. Plain edge.

| Ma-Sp 18 | (1862) | Brass | 28.3mm | — | — | — | 100. |

Obverse: U.S. ARMORY / * / ESTABLISHED / BY / ACT OF CONGRESS / IN APRIL, / 1794. / SPRINGFIELD, MASS. Rv: As reverse of Ma-Sp 4 (J. A. BOLEN / DIE SINKER). Plain edge. (Wright 1171; Springfield 1981 sale, lot 4508)

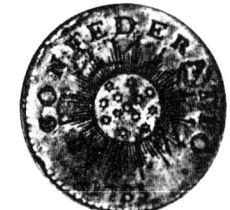 

| Rulau | Date | Metal | Size | F | VF | EF | Unc |
|---|---|---|---|---|---|---|---|
| Ma-Sp 20 | (1862) | Copper | 28.3mm | — | — | — | Unique |

Confederatio cent imitation. Rv: As Ma-Sp 4 reverse.

| Ma-Sp 22 | (1864) | Brass | 28mm | — | — | — | 350. |

J. A. BOLEN, / (ornament) / DIE SINKER AND MEDALIST. SPRINGFIELD, MASS. Rv: Radiant Phrygian (Liberty) cap at center, UNITED STATES OF AMERICA around, * LIBERTY * below. Plain edge. (Miller Mass 102B)

Only known specimen of 22 sold Oct. 30, 1982 in New York Public Library sale, lot 2718, for $352.

| Ma-Sp 24 | 1864 | Oroide | 28mm | — | — | — | 200. |

Bearded bust of Bolen left, a rosette at either side. J. A. BOLEN, above, 1864 below. Rv: As reverse of 22 (Liberty cap). Only 25 struck. (Miller Mass 103)

| Ma-Sp 25 | 1864 | Copper | 28mm | — | — | — | 200. |

As 24. Plain edge. (Fuld NC-9a). Rarity 9.

| Ma-Sp 26 | 1864 | Silver | 28mm | — | — | — | Unique |

As 24. Plain edge. (Fuld NC-9f)

| Ma-Sp 28 | 1864 | Copper | 28mm | — | — | — | 200. |

Obverse similar to 24, but smaller date and lettering. Rv: STAMP. CUTTER, / (ornament) / DIE. SINKER, / AND / MEDALIST. / SPRINGFIELD, MASS. Plain edge. Only 25 struck. (Miller Mass 105; Fuld NC-8a). Rarity 8.

| Ma-Sp 29 | 1864 | Brass | 28mm | — | — | — | 250. |

Same as 28. Plain edge. (Miller Mass 105A)

| Ma-Sp 30 | 1865 | Copper | 28mm | — | — | — | 100. |

Obverse similar to Ma-Sp 24, but 1865 date. Rv: As reverse of Ma-Sp 28. Plain edge. Only 10 struck. (Miller Mass 106)

| Ma-Sp 31 | 1865 | WM | 28mm | — | — | — | 100. |

As 30. Plain edge. Only 10 struck. (Miller Mass 107)

| Ma-Sp 32 | 1865 | WM | 28mm | — | — | — | 150. |

Obverse similar, but TWO STRUCK & DIE DESTROYED added. Plain edge. Only 2 struck. (Miller Mass 108)

| Rulau | Date | Metal | Size | F | VF | EF | Unc |
|---|---|---|---|---|---|---|---|
| Ma-Sp 34 | 1865 | Oroide | 27mm | — | — | — | 100. |

Bearded bust of Bolen left, J. A. BOLEN. at left, 1865. at right. Rv: Within oak wreath: DIE / SINKER / &c. / SPRINGFIELD / MASS / B. (tiny). Plain edge. Only 50 struck. (Miller Mass 109)

| Ma-Sp 35 | 1865 | WM | 27mm | — | — | — | 100. |

As 34. Plain edge. Only 50 struck. (Miller Mass 110)

| Ma-Sp 36 | (?) | Silver | 27mm | — | — | — | Unique |

Head of Bolen to left, tiny BOLEN under bust. J. A. BOLEN around. Rv: DIE SINKER &C. (same as Bolen number 21). Plain edge. Only 1 struck. (Miller Mass 111)

| Ma-Sp 37 | (?) | Copper | 27mm | — | — | — | 100. |

As 36. Plain edge. Only 15 struck. (Miller Mass 112)

| Ma-Sp 38 | (?) | Brass | 27mm | — | — | — | 100. |

As 36. Plain edge. Only 15 struck. (Miller Mass 113)

| Ma-Sp 39 | (?) | WM | 27mm | — | — | — | 100. |

As 36. Plain edge. Only 15 struck. (Miller Mass 114)

| Ma-Sp 41 | 1867 | Silver | 27mm | — | — | — | Unique |

Bearded bust of Bolen left, J. A. BOLEN. at left, 1867 at right. Rv: LIBERTAS AMERICANA. Plain edge. Only 1 struck. (Miller Mass 115; Bolen 32)

| Ma-Sp 42 | 1867 | Brass | 27mm | — | — | — | Unique |

As 41. Plain edge. Only 1 struck. (Miller Mass 116)

| Ma-Sp 43 | 1867 | Copper | 27mm | — | — | — | 100. |

As 41. Plain edge. (Miller Mass 116A)

| Ma-Sp 44 | 1867 | Copper | 27mm | — | — | — | 100. |

Obverse as 41 (Bolen left, 1867). Rv: As reverse of 34 (DIE SINKER in wreath). Plain edge. Only 1 copy known. (Springfield 1981 sale, lot 4508)

| Ma-Sp 45 | 1867 | WM | 27mm | — | — | — | 100. |

Same as 44. Plain edge. Only 2 specimens known. (Springfield 1981 sale, lot 4508)

| Ma-Sp 47 | 1869 | Silver | 27mm | — | — | — | Unique |

Bearded bust of Bolen left, J. A. BOLEN. at left, 1869. at right. Rv: As reverse of 34 (DIE SINKER in wreath). Plain edge. Only 1 struck. (Miller Mass 117; Bolen 217)

| Ma-Sp 48 | 1869 | Copper | 27mm | — | — | — | 100. |

As 47. Plain edge. Only 28 struck. (Miller Mass 118)

| Ma-Sp 49 | 1869 | Brass | 27mm | — | — | — | 100. |

As 47. Plain edge. Only 20 struck. (Miller Mass 119)

| Ma-Sp 50 | 1869 | WM | 27mm | — | — | — | 150. |

As 47. Plain edge. Only 3 struck. (Miller Mass 120)

| Ma-Sp 51 | 1869 | Copper | 27mm | — | — | — | 100. |

As 47. Plain edge. Only 16 struck. (Miller Mass 122)

| Ma-Sp 52 | 1869 | Silver | 27mm | — | — | — | 250. |

Obverse as 47. Rv: As obverse of Ma-Sp 56 (THE PYNCHON HOUSE). Plain edge. Only 10 struck. (Miller Mass 123)

| Ma-Sp 53 | 1869 | Copper | 27mm | — | — | — | 100. |

As 52. Plain edge. Only 95 struck. (Miller Mass 124)

| Ma-Sp 54 | 1869 | Brass | 27mm | — | — | — | 100. |

As 52. Plain edge. Only 45 struck. (Miller Mass 125)

| Rulau | Date | Metal | Size | F | VF | EF | Unc |
|---|---|---|---|---|---|---|---|
| Ma-Sp 56 | (1869) | Brass | 27mm | — | — | 20.00 | 40.00 |

View of the Old Pynchon House from the left side. Rv: THE PYNCHON HOUSE. / CALLED / THE OLD FORT. / BUILT BY / JOHN PYNCHON, / IN 1660. / TAKEN DOWN / IN 1831. / SPRINGFIELD. MASS. Plain edge.

| Ma-Sp 56A | (1869) | Copper | 27mm | — | — | 20.00 | 40.00 |

As 56. Plain edge.

| Ma-Sp 56B | (1869) | WM | 27mm | — | — | 30.00 | 50.00 |

As 56. Plain edge.

| Ma-Sp 56C | (1869) | Silver | 27mm | — | — | — | 150. |

As 56. Plain edge.

## J. CUMMINGS
### Springfield, Mass.

| Rulau | Date | Metal | Size | VG | F | VF | EF |
|---|---|---|---|---|---|---|---|
| Ma-Sp 58 | (?) | Copper | 33mm | | | | |

J. CUMMINGS / SPRINGFIELD MASS ctsp on Canada 1857 Bank of Upper Canada penny token, Breton 719.

## MOORE BROTHERS
### Springfield, Mass.

| Rulau | Date | Metal | Size | F | VF | EF | Unc |
|---|---|---|---|---|---|---|---|
| Ma-Sp 60 | (1870) | WM | 27mm | — | — | 100. | 150. |

MOORE BROTHERS / PHOTOGRAHIC / ARTISTS. / OPP / COURT SQUARE / MAIN ST. / SPRINGFIELD, MASS. Rv: PHOTOGRAPHS / MADE / AND FINISHED / IN ANY / DESIRED / STYLE OR SIZE. Plain edge. Only 400 struck. (Wright 720; Storer 1683; Miller Mass 128)

| Ma-Sp 61 | (1870) | Copper | 27mm | — | — | — | 200. |

As 60. Only 5 struck. (Miller Mass 126)

| Ma-Sp 62 | (1870) | Brass | 27mm | — | — | — | Unique |

As 60. Only 1 struck. (Miller Mass 127)

All were struck by J. A. Bolen of Springfield, Mass

## L. C. RODIER
### Springfield, Mass.

| Rulau | Date | Metal | Size | VG | F | VF | Unc |
|---|---|---|---|---|---|---|---|
| Ma-Sp 63 | 1873 | Brass | 29mm | — | — | 35.00 | — |

Large 5-pointed star. Around: L. C. RODIER'S PATENT — NOV 18. 73. (Stanley Steinberg 1982 sale)

Rodier was a gunsmith. In 1862 and in 1873 he obtained rifle patents. In 1873 the firm was called Rodier & Bates.

## SOLDIERS' FAIR
### Springfield, Mass.

| Rulau | Date | Metal | Size | F | VF | EF | Unc |
|---|---|---|---|---|---|---|---|
| Ma-Sp 65 | 1864 | — | 27mm | — | — | — | 200. |

Washington bust left, J. A. BOLEN under truncation. WASHINGTON above. Rv: SOLDIERS' / FAIR / DEC. / 1864. / SPRINGFIELD, MASS. (all within oak wreath). Plain edge. (Schenkman B5)

| Ma-Sp 67 | (1870's) | SC | 27mm | — | — | 150. | — |

Obverse as Miller Mass 17A (Beardless Lincoln right). Rv: As last. Plain edge. (DeWitt AL 1860-45(C); King 514)

| Ma-Sp 68 | (1870's) | Copper | 27mm | — | — | 10.00 | 25.00 |

Obverse as Ma-Bo 33 reverse (Apollo head). Rv: As last. (Schenkman B-3)

| Ma-Sp 68A | (1870's) | Silver | 27mm | — | — | — | 250. |

As 68. Plain edge. (Storer 1700)

## SPRINGFIELD ANTIQUARIANS
### Springfield, Mass.

| Rulau | Date | Metal | Size | VG | F | VF | Unc |
|---|---|---|---|---|---|---|---|
| Ma-Sp 69 | 1866 | Copper | 28mm | — | — | — | 40.00 |

Eagle perched on shield, to right, MASSACHUSETTS above, 1866 below. Rv: SPRINGFIELD / ANTIQUARIANS / * / JAS PARKER, / WM. H BOWDOIN, / C. B. NEWELL, / J. A. BOLEN, / J WHITCOMB, / D. K. LEE, / WM. CLOGSTON. Only 14 struck. (Wright 1034)

| Ma-Sp 70 | 1866 | WM | 28mm | — | — | — | Unique |

As last. Only 1 struck.

Struck by James A. Bolen of Springfield.

| Rulau | Date | Metal | Size | VG | F | VF | Unc |
|---|---|---|---|---|---|---|---|
| Ma-Sp 72 | 1866 | Copper | 28mm | — | — | | V. Rare |

Obverse as 69. Rv: LEXINGTON, / APRIL 19, 1775. / ******* / BALTIMORE, / APRIL 19, 1861., all within floreate circle. Plain edge.

## H. HALE
### Worcester, Mass.

| Rulau | Date | Metal | Size | VG | F | VF | EF |
|---|---|---|---|---|---|---|---|
| Ma-Wc 4 | (?) | CN | 19mm | — | — | — | — |

H. HALE ctsp on U.S. 1857 Flying Eagle cent.

| Ma-Wc 5 | (?) | Silver | 31mm | — | — | — | — |

Similar ctsp on U.S. 1855 Seated Liberty half dollar.

Gunsmith. Attribution by Stanley L. Steinberg, Malden, Mass.

## T. W. S. JOZEFA
### Webster, Mass.

| Rulau | Date | Metal | Size | VG | F | VF | Unc |
|---|---|---|---|---|---|---|---|
| Ma-Wb 3 | (?) | Brass | 29mm? | — | — | — | — |

(All incused) T W. S. JOZEFA. / WEBSTER. / MASS. Rv: ( ? ). Plain edge.

## PHENYO C. CO.
### Worcester, Mass.

| Rulau | Date | Metal | Size | VG | F | VF | Unc |
|---|---|---|---|---|---|---|---|
| Ma-Wc 12 | (1880's ?) | Brass | 28mm | — | — | 10.00 | — |

(All incused) PHENYO CAFFEIN / CURES / HEADACHE / AND / NEURALGIA / PHENYO C. CO / WORCESTER / MASS. Rv: Blank. Plain edge. (Wright 822)

| Ma-Wc 13 | (1880's ?) | Brass | 25mm | — | — | 17.50 | — |

(All incused) CHILIAN PUZZLE / REMOVE / THE RING / AND / PUT IT ON / AGAIN. Rv: Blank. Plain edge.

These two brass tags were on either end of an advertising puzzle given out by the Phenyo Caffein people. The puzzle consisted of a metal ring plus a series of wood dowels linked together with metal straps. Stanley L. Steinberg, Malden, Mass., says: "For some reason the PUZZLE tag is rarely found. It seems that many found the puzzle hard to do and were frustrated enough to destroy all but the PHENYO tag. The PHENYO tag also circulated as an advertising token."

The only known complete puzzle with tags is in the collection of Jerry Slocum, Beverly Hills, Calif.

## TOUGAS & DUPREY
### Worcester, Mass.

| Rulau | Date | Metal | Size | VG | F | VF | EF |
|---|---|---|---|---|---|---|---|
| Ma-Wc 20 | (1870's ?) | Copper | 29mm | — | — | 150. | — |

TOUGAS & DUPREY / WORCESTER / MASS. ctsp on reverse of U.S. 1853 Large cent. (Tanenbaum collection)

# MICHIGAN

## G. R. & I. R. R.
## Michigan ?

| Rulau | Date | Metal | Size | VG | F | VF | EF |
|---|---|---|---|---|---|---|---|
| Mi-NL 3 | (?) | Copper | 33mm | — | — | | 1 Known |

G. R. & I. R. R. 1/2 CORD NO. 16. Thick planchet. Plain edge. (James J. Curto coll.)

| Mi-NL 4 | (?) | Copper | 28mm | — | — | | 1 Known |
|---|---|---|---|---|---|---|---|

Similar, but 1/4 CORD NO. 16. Thick planchet. Plain edge. (James J. Curto coll.)

| Mi-NL 5 | (?) | Brass | 28mm | — | — | | 1 Known |
|---|---|---|---|---|---|---|---|

Same as last (1/4 CORD). Thin planchet. Plain edge. (James J. Curto coll.)

Assigned here tentatively. The unidentified railway could be something like 'Grand Rapids & Ionia R.R.' or 'Grand Rapids & Indiana R.R.'. However, Curto and others, including Clyde Drewing, feel it could be in Canada, since the token sizes equate with the penny and halfpenny of the 1850's and 1860's.

## M. C. R. R.
## (Michigan Central Railroad)
## Michigan

| Rulau | Date | Metal | Size | VG | F | VF | EF |
|---|---|---|---|---|---|---|---|
| Mi-NL 15 | (?) | Brass | 25mm | — | — | 75.00 | — |

M. C. R. R. / 109 (incused). Rv: 1/8 / CORD. Milled border on each side. Plain edge.

| Mi-NL 16 | (?) | Brass | 27mm | — | — | 75.00 | — |
|---|---|---|---|---|---|---|---|

As 15, but 1/4 / CORD. Plain edge.

| Mi-NL 17 | (?) | Brass | 27mm | — | — | 75.00 | — |
|---|---|---|---|---|---|---|---|

M. C. R. R. / 103 (incused). Rv: 1/2 / CORD. Plain edge. Number 9 and 50 also known.

| Mi-NL 18 | (?) | Brass | --mm | — | — | 100. | — |
|---|---|---|---|---|---|---|---|

As 15, but 1 / CORD. Plain edge.

Probably issued in the 1860's. (See "Woodburning Engine Fuel Tokens" by Clyde J. Drewing in *The Numismatist* for July, 1964)

## M. S. & N. I. R. R.
## (Michigan Southern & Northern Indiana Railroad)
## Michigan

| Rulau | Date | Metal | Size | VG | F | VF | EF |
|---|---|---|---|---|---|---|---|
| Mi-NL 22 | (1863-69) | Copper | 25mm | — | — | — | Rare |

M. S. & N. I. R. R. / (ornament) / E & N/ DIV / (ornament). Rv: 1/2 / CORD / 78 (incuse). Stars around rim on each side. Plain edge. (Drewing type 1) (The incuse numeral is the engine number; '78' was the 'E. M. Gilbert,' built by the MS& NIRR locomotive works. Other engine numbers known on this token: 7 'Pony'; 31 'Toledo'; 45 'South Bend'; 48 'Ontario'; 55 'Michigan'; 65 'E. Morrison'; 67 'J. Stroyer'; 68 'A. Havemeyer'; 72 'Falcon'; 81 'R. Gardner'; 87 'Monitor')

| Mi-NL 23 | (1863-69) | Brass | 25mm | — | — | — | Ex. Rare |
|---|---|---|---|---|---|---|---|

Same. Only known with engine numbers 7, 69 and 87. Plain edge. (Drewing type 1)

| Mi-NL 25 | (1863-69) | Copper | 23mm | — | — | Rare | — |
|---|---|---|---|---|---|---|---|

As last, but 1/4 / CORD / 24 (incuse) on reverse. Plain edge. (Drewing type 1) (Engine numbers known: 24, 77)

| Mi-NL 26 | (1863-69) | Copper | 25mm | — | — | — | Ex. Rare |
|---|---|---|---|---|---|---|---|

As last (1/4 / CORD), but ctsp W. O. EBERSOL. Plain edge. (Drewing type 1). This could have been an engine name, or the name of an engineer.

NOTE: E & N DIV = Eastern and Northern Division.

| Mi-NL 30 | (1863-69) | Copper | 23mm | — | — | — | — |
|---|---|---|---|---|---|---|---|

M. S. & N. I. R. R. / W. D. Rv: 1/2 / CORD / 20 (incused). Plain edge. (Drewing type 2) (Engine numbers known: 20 'Gov. Marcy'; 23 'Arab'; 33 'New Castle'; 35 Prairie'; 48 Ontario; 60 'Missouri'; 84 'M. L. Sykes Jr.'; 88 'Dictator')

| Mi-NL 32 | (1863-69) | Copper | 23mm | — | — | — | — |
|---|---|---|---|---|---|---|---|

As last, but 1/4 / CORD / 5 (incused) on reverse. Plain edge. (Drewing type 2) (Engine numbers known: 5 'J. M. Coffee Jr.'; 20 'Gov. Marcy'; 61 'Pacific'; 22 'Oceola')

| Mi-NL 34 | (1863-69) | Copper | 29mm | — | — | — | — |
|---|---|---|---|---|---|---|---|

As last (W. D. 1/2 CORD), but no engine number and in larger size. Plain edge. (Drewing type 3)

NOTE: W. D. = Western Division.

The Michigan Southern and Northern Indiana Railroad had stations at Elkhart and Kendallville, Ind.; Wauseon, Ohio; Lenawee Junction, Adrian and Coldwater, Mich. The "wood up" stations, where cords of wood were stored by the people who received these tokens for their work, were less than 60 miles apart.

The railroad kept money on deposit at various banks to redeem the tokens. They were worth from 90 cents to $1.25 per full cord.

The railroad's predecessor issued a shareholder report in 1850 and the railroad itself issued another in 1863 which gave numbers and names of all engines in use, as well as who built them, and the costs of fuel and maintenance.

The Michigan Southern Railway Co. and Northern Indiana Railway Co. merged in 1855 to form the MS&NIRR. In 1869 this line took over the Lake Shore Railway Co. and became the Lake Shore & Michigan Southern Railroad (LS&MSRR). In 1918 it was part of the New York Central system.

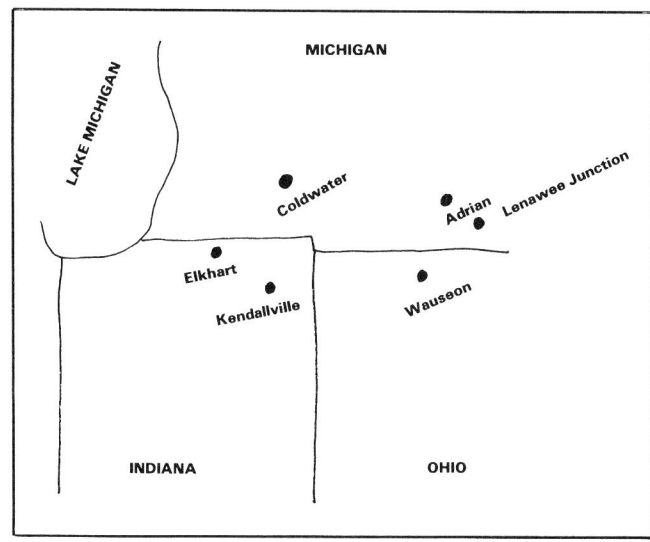

*Map of the communities served by the M.S.&N.I.R.R.*

*Typical locomotive of the woodburning era. The sketch shows "Old No. 24" of the Southern Pacific, built in 1875. Note the bulging smokestack (gradually abandoned as a style after railroads converted to coal) and the stacked wood in the tender. Cords of wood delivered to "wood-up" stations were paid for with redeemable tokens.*

## BROWN BROTHERS
### Detroit, Mich.

| Rulau | Date | Metal | Size | F | VF | EF | Unc |
|---|---|---|---|---|---|---|---|
| Mi-De 2 | (?) | Copper | 31mm | 2.50 | 3.50 | 4.50 | 6.00 |

BROWN BROTHERS / THE / CIGAR / MAKERS / * DETROIT *. Rv: THIS CHECK WILL BE REDEEMED BY ANY DEALER * / GOOD FOR / ONE / FONTELLA / CIGAR. Plain edge. (Miller Mich 1)

## D. CORNWELL BUEHLER
### Detroit, Mich.

| Rulau | Date | Metal | Size | VG | F | VF | EF |
|---|---|---|---|---|---|---|---|
| Mi-De 4 | (?) | Copper | 29mm | | | | |

D. CORNWELL BUEHLER / DETROIT ctsp on U.S. Large cent. (Hallenbeck 2.769)

## JOHN LOSCH
### East Saginaw, Mich.

| Rulau | Date | Metal | Size | VG | F | VF | Unc |
|---|---|---|---|---|---|---|---|
| Mi-ES 2 | (?) | Brass | 23mm | | | | |

(All incuse) JOHN LOSCH / GOOD FOR / 5¢ / AT BAR / E. SAGINAW. Rv: Blank. Plain edge. (Coll. John Cheramy, Victoria, Canada)

## M.B. TOUTLOFF
### Ishpeming, Mich.

| Rulau | Date | Metal | Size | VG | F | VF | Unc |
|---|---|---|---|---|---|---|---|
| Mi-Is 4 | (1874-84) | Brass | 25mm | — | — | 15.00 | — |

Pool table at bottom, THE J.M. BRUNSWICK / & / BALKE COS. Rv: GOOD FOR / 5¢ / M.B. TOUTLOFF / IN TRADE. Plain edge. (Brunswick 2353)

## J.J. DEAL
### Jonesville, Mich.

| Rulau | Date | Metal | Size | VG | F | VF | Unc |
|---|---|---|---|---|---|---|---|
| Mi-Jo 3 | (?) | Gold/Ld* | ** 57 by 22mm | — | — | Rare | — |

* Lead, gold-plated. ** Parallelogram shaped. J.J. DEAL / --- / JONESVILLE, MICH. Rv: Blank. Plain edge. (Wright 237)

## W. H. RAYNER
### Mason, Mich.

| Rulau | Date | Metal | Size | VG | F | VF | EF |
|---|---|---|---|---|---|---|---|
| Mi-MS 3 | (?) | Bronze | 23mm | 25.00 | 45.00 | — | — |

W. H. RAYNER / -- / MASON. ctsp on U.S. 1865 2-cent piece. (Rulau coll.)

A possible successor firm, Robbins B. Rayner, was in the coal, cement and roofing business circa 1917. Mason, in Ingham County, had 1,742 people in World War I.

## C. O. BROWN
### Olivet, Mich.

| Rulau | Date | Metal | Size | VG | F | VF | EF |
|---|---|---|---|---|---|---|---|
| Mi-Ov 2 | (?) | CN | 18mm | — | 30.00 | — | — |

C. O. BROWN OLIVET MICH. ctsp on U.S. 1873 nickel 3-cent piece.

# MINNESOTA

## A.E. RYAN
### Barrett, Minn.

| Rulau | Date | Metal | Size | VG | F | VF | Unc |
|---|---|---|---|---|---|---|---|
| Mn-Bt 3 | (1870) | Brass | 19mm | — | — | — | Rare |

A. E. RYAN / GENERAL MERCHANDISE / BARRETT, MINN. Rv: GOOD FOR / 5 / CTS IN TRADE. Plain edge. (Fuld NC-6b; Barnett-H&G 4635)

Although Joseph Barnett called this a Civil War token, it was shown it could not be. The first homestead in Barrett was erected in 1868.

## G. D.
### Minneapolis, Minn.

| Rulau | Date | Metal | Size | VG | F | VF | Unc |
|---|---|---|---|---|---|---|---|
| Mn-Mi 6 | (1874-84) | Brass | 24mm | — | — | 10.00 | — |

Pool table at bottom. Above, among flourishes: THE J. M. BRUNSWICK / & / BALKE COS. Rv: GOOD FOR / 5¢ / G. D. / MINNEAPOLIS. Plain edge. (Brunswick 2128)

## MINNEAPOLIS EXPOSITION
### Minneapolis, Minn.

| Rulau | Date | Metal | Size | VG | F | VF | Unc |
|---|---|---|---|---|---|---|---|
| Mn-Mi 10 | 1886 | WM | 35mm | — | — | 15.00 | 25.00 |

Liberty head right, its Phrygian cap entwined in garland of wheat and corn. Wreath of wheat and corn below and partly around. Rv: Building at center, tiny 1886 on the ground line. Above: MINNEAPOLIS EXPOSITION. On truncation of the ground: Initials M A K (the first being uncertain). Plain edge.

## POEHLER's
## Minneapolis, Minn.

| Rulau | Date | Metal | Size | VG | F | VF | Unc |
|---|---|---|---|---|---|---|---|
| Mn-Mi 20 | (?) | Brass | Oct. 28x28mm | — | — | 20.00 | — |

POEHLER'S / STORE in relief within curving depressions. 50 stamped incuse over incuse 1 ¢ between the curving depressions. Rv: P stamped incuse. Relief beaded rims within border depressions. Plain edge.

| Mn-Mi 22 | (?) | Brass | 30mm | — | — | 25.00 | — |

Similar, but 100. Plain edge.

Poehler's does not appear in the *Atlas of Minnesota*, or the 1880 Minneapolis city directory.

## ICE PALACE & WINTER CARNIVAL
## St. Paul, Minn.

| Rulau | Date | Metal | Size | F | VF | EF | Unc |
|---|---|---|---|---|---|---|---|
| Mn-SP 4 | (?) | GS | 31mm | — | — | 22.50 | 30.00 |

Castle-like building surrounded by battlemented wall, flags and pennons flying, tiny NORTHW. -- ST. WORKS under ground. At bottom: ST. PAUL. Rv: Crossed snowshoes, tobaggan, etc. at center. Around: THE ICE PALACE & WINTER CARNIVAL; below: SOUVENIR. Plain edge. Issued holed at top for suspension from light blue ribbon.

| Mn-SP 6 | 1887 | Gilt/B Sq. | 15mm | — | — | — | 12.50 |

Castle-like building at center, tiny N.W. STAMP WKS underground. Above: ST. PAUL ICE PALACE WINTER CARNIVAL. Below: 1887. Rv: Burning flame on long pole superimposed over crossed snowshoes and a sled. All arranged in diamond shape. Plain edge. Looped for suspension.

## AMERICAN HOTEL
## Winona, Minn.

| Rulau | Date | Metal | Size | VG | F | VF | EF |
|---|---|---|---|---|---|---|---|
| Mn-Wn 1 | (ca 1870 ?) | CN | 22mm | — | — | 115. | — |

AMERICAN / WINONA, MINN / HOTEL ctsp on U.S. 1866 Shield nickel. The counterstamp is struck from a die, not hand punched. (Springfield 1981 sale, lot 4564)

| Mn-Wn 2 | (ca 1870 ?) | — | — | — | — | — | — |

Similar ctsp on unspecified coins. (Brunk 6)

# MISSISSIPPI

## CLARKE & CO.
## Vicksburg, Miss.

| Rulau | Date | Metal | Size | VG | F | VF | Unc |
|---|---|---|---|---|---|---|---|
| Ms-Vi 1 | (1880's) | GS | 22mm | — | — | — | Rare |

Eagle left, landing on a drum surrounded by flags, rifles, cannon balls and rays. Rv: CLARKE & CO. / BOOKSELLERS / GOOD FOR / * 7 1/2 ¢ * / PAPER / + VICKSBURG, MISS. +. Reeded edge. (Fuld coll.)

The token's obverse is the same as that of the Wapakoneta, Ohio, Sanitary Fair and the Dunlap & Florer, Osage traders, in the 1860-70 decade. George Fuld surmises that this piece was made about 1890, but we think it likely it was struck in Cincinnati by James Murdock Jr. using an old Civil War die, earlier than 1890. Directory evidence is lacking.

However, Clarke & Co. were still listed in 1917-18 as booksellers and stationers. This is an interesting example of re-use of old dies to fill customer orders. The 7 1/2-cent denomination is very unusual.

## CROOM & HILL
## Vicksburg, Miss.

| Rulau | Date | Metal | Size | VG | F | VF | Unc |
|---|---|---|---|---|---|---|---|
| Ms-Vi 3 | (1870's) | GS | 30mm | 20.00 | 35.00 | — | — |

CROOM & HILL, HOTEL DIXIE. Rv: Numeral 50. (Miller Miss 2)

This piece was cataloged in error in *U.S. Merchant Tokens 1845-1860*. It has been shown that it emanates from the 1870's.

## PRENTIS HOUSE
## Vicksburg, Miss.

| Rulau | Date | Metal | Size | VG | F | VF | Unc |
|---|---|---|---|---|---|---|---|
| Ms-Vi 8 | (1870's?) | Brass | Oval, 43 by 26mm | — | — | — | V. Scarce |

PRENTIS HOUSE/ 100 / VICKSBURG. Rv: Blank. Plain edge. (Wright 845)

There is a similarity between this piece and that of Croom & Hill, Hotel Dixie.

# MISSOURI

## THE CONSOLIDATED KANSAS CITY SMELTING & REFINING CO.
### Kansas City, Mo.

| Rulau | Date | Metal | Size | F | VF | EF | Unc |
|---|---|---|---|---|---|---|---|
| Mo-KC 3 | 1889 | Silver | 38mm | — | 25.00 | 50.00 | 100. |

Jugate male busts right, C. KURTZ on truncation, 1889 under truncation. Around: * THE CONSOLIDATED KANSAS CITY SMELTING & REFINING CO. TO THE AMERICAN CONGRESS GREETING. Rv: Two standing females joining hands, each holding a pole topped by a Liberty cap. Around: RECIPROCITY * THE UNITED AMERICAS * COMMERCE / LOS AMERICAS UNIDAS *. Plain edge. (Hibler & Kappen 731)

This company operated mostly in Mexico. It is well known to collectors through its large number of surviving bills of exchange, drafts and other paper numismatica issued from a number of Mexican sites. In its day the firm was a giant in silver and non-ferrous metal refining, in an era when unbridled American business had deep control over much of Mexico's economy, and powerful friends in the U.S. Congress, as this piece indicates. The portraits are those of Presidents Benjamin Harrison of the U.S. and Porfirio Diaz of Mexico.

## H.C. DE SOLLAR
### Kansas City, Mo.

| Rulau | Date | Metal | Size | VG | F | VF | EF |
|---|---|---|---|---|---|---|---|
| Mo-KC 5 | (?) | Silver | 31mm | 100. | — | 175. | — |

H.C. De SOLLAR. / Kansas City. ctsp on U.S. Liberty Seated Half dollar (date worn off). Tanenbaum coll.)

De Sollar does not appear in 1870 directories.

## NATIONAL AGRICULTURAL EXPOSITION
### Kansas City, Mo.

| Rulau | Date | Metal | Size | F | VF | EF | Unc |
|---|---|---|---|---|---|---|---|
| Mo-KC 8 | 1887 | WM | 30mm | — | 20.00 | — | — |

Building at center, NATIONAL above, AGRICULTURAL / EXPOSITION / (beehive at center of laurel sprays). Rv: THE / NATIONAL / + 1887 + / AGRICULTURAL / ..*.. / EXPOSITION / KANSAS CITY, / MO. Plain edge. (Brunk coll.)

## SMITH & RIEGER
### Kansas City, Mo.

| Rulau | Date | Metal | Size | VG | F | VF | Unc |
|---|---|---|---|---|---|---|---|
| Mo-KC 11 | (1880's) | Brass | 25mm | 10.00 | 15.00 | 25.00 | 40.00 |

SMITH & RIEGER, / (ornament) / HATTERS / 554 / MAIN ST. / + / KANSAS CITY, MO. Rv: RECEIVABLE / FOR / 5 / CENTS / IN MERCHANDISE / ON ONE DOLLARS PURCHASE. Plain edge. (Miller Mo 42)

Not in 1870 *Bradstreet Directory*.

## STROUSE & BROS.
### Kansas City, Mo.
#### 1876 Centennial Tokens

Reverse type 1: VISIT / STROUSE & BROS. / THE / PEOPLE'S / CLOTHIERS / 428 MAIN ST. / KANSAS CITY, MO. (All 19mm, plain edge. None were listed by Wright, Miller or other cataloguers)

| Rulau | Obv | Rev | Metal | F | VF | EF | Unc |
|---|---|---|---|---|---|---|---|
| Mo-KC 25 | W | 1 | WM | — | — | 40.00 | 100. |
| Mo-KC 26 | X | 1 | WM | — | — | 40.00 | 100. |
| Mo-KC 26A | X | 1 | Bronze | — | — | 40.00 | 100. |
| Mo-KC 27 | Y | 1 | Bronze | — | — | 40.00 | 100. |
| Mo-KC 28 | Z | 1 | WM | — | — | 40.00 | 100. |
| Mo-KC 28A | Z | 1 | Bronze | — | — | 40.00 | 100. |

Strouse & Bros. do not appear in the 1881 directory.

## STAR SALOON
### La Clede, Mo.

| Rulau | Date | Metal | Size | VG | F | VF | EF |
|---|---|---|---|---|---|---|---|
| Mo-LC 4 | 1866 | Nickel alloy | 27mm | — | — | 150. | — |

Coronet Liberty head left, 13 stars around, 1866 below. Rv: GOOD FOR ONE DRINK / AT THE / STAR / * SALOON * / LA CLEDE, MO.

One of the two known copies appeared in the Springfield sale in Dec., 1981, as lot 4563. It is now in the Weinberg coll.

## J. B. GUM
### Mount Vernon, Mo.

| Rulau | Date | Metal | Size | VG | F | VF | EF |
|---|---|---|---|---|---|---|---|
| Mo-MV 2 | (?) | CN | 22mm | — | — | 85.00 | — |

J. B. GUM / WATCHMAKER & JEWELER / NO. 13 / MT. VERNON, MO. ctsp on U.S. 1867 Rays type Shield nickel.

Jacob B. Gum, jeweler, was still in business in 1918. He does not appear in 1870 or 1881 directories.

## JOHN KENMUIR
### St. Joseph, Mo.

| Rulau | Date | Metal | Size | F | VF | EF | Unc |
|---|---|---|---|---|---|---|---|
| Mo-Jo 6 | (1873-81) | Brass | 19mm | — | 150. | 300. | 500. |

JOHN KENMUIR / MFG. / JEWELER / ST. JOSEPH, MO. Rv: JOHN KENMUIR / WATCH / MAKER / FELIX ST. / ST. JOSEPH, MO. (Fuld Mo 880A). 5 to 10 pieces known.

This token has been listed erroneously as a Civil War token, which may account for its high price. It is clearly post-CW and may be overvalued here.

John Kenmuir was born in Lisburn, Ireland in 1831. He apprenticed in his father's manufacturing jewelry business in County Down and emigrated to America 1850. He became a manufacturing jeweler in New York and was successful. In 1863 he relocated in Leavenworth City, Kansas and became a retail clock and watch dealer.

In 1873 he moved to St. Joseph, Mo., establishing his business on Felix between 5th and 6th Streets. He was still located there in 1881. Kenmuir establied the Bell telephone in St. Joseph in 1874.

## NATIONAL RAILWAY ELECTRIC & INDUSTRIAL EXPOSITION
### St. Joseph, Mo.

| Rulau | Date | Metal | Size | F | VF | EF | Unc |
|---|---|---|---|---|---|---|---|
| Mo-Jo 15 | 1889 | WM | 38mm | — | 30.00 | 50.00 | 100. |

Building, NATIONAL RAILWAY ELECTRIC & INDUSTRIAL EXPOSITION. around, SEPT. 3RD / 1889 / * in exergue. Rv: Twelve ears of corn and KORN IS KING within central circle, ST. JOSEPH EXPOSITION / 1889 around. Plain edge.

## ANHEUSER-BUSCH
### St. Louis, Mo.

| Rulau | Date | Metal | Size | F | VF | EF | Unc |
|---|---|---|---|---|---|---|---|
| Mo-SL 3 | 1880 | CN | 29mm | — | — | 50.00 | — |

(All designs and lettering incused). Eagle on shield facing left, through large letter A, 1880 below. Rv: ANHEUSER-BUSCH / ST LOUIS. Plain edge.

(See *TAMS Journal* for Dec. 1977, page 241)

| Rulau | Date | Metal | Size | VG | F | VF | Unc |
|---|---|---|---|---|---|---|---|
| Mo-SL 2 | 1880 | Copper | 21mm | 6.00 | 10.00 | 15.00 | 50.00 |

Large A superimposed on eagle and shield, 1880 below. Rv: ANHEUSER-BUSCH / BREW'G * / ASS'N / *. Plain edge. (Miller Mo 1)

| Rulau | Date | Metal | Size | VG | F | VF | Unc |
|---|---|---|---|---|---|---|---|
| Mo-SL 2A | 1880 | Brass | 21mm | — | 20.00 | 30.00 | 75.00 |

As 2. Plain edge. (Wright 25)

## DEUTSCH FRANZOSISCHEN KRIEG
### St. Louis, Mo.

| Rulau | Date | Metal | Size | F | VF | EF | Unc |
|---|---|---|---|---|---|---|---|
| Mo-SL 8 | 1871 | Copper | 31mm | — | — | 15.00 | 35.00 |

Germania with shield and palm standing on Rhine bank, rising sun in background. DURCH EINHEIT ZUR FREIHEIT (Through unity to freedom). Rv: Oak wreath encloses: ZUR ERINNERUNG AN DEN DEUTSCH FRANZOSISCHEN KRIEG 1870 & 1871 ST. LOUIS, MO. (In commemoration of the German French War). C. STUBENRAUCH FECIT ST. LOUIS in tiny letters under Germania on obverse. Plain edge. Weight 15.21 grams.

| Rulau | Date | Metal | Size | F | VF | EF | Unc |
|---|---|---|---|---|---|---|---|
| Mo-SL 8A | 1871 | WM | 31mm | — | — | 25.00 | 50.00 |
| MI-SL 8B | 1871 | Iron | 31mm | — | — | 35.00 | 75.00 |
| Mo-SL 9 | 1871 | WM | 31.4mm | — | — | 15.00 | 35.00 |

As 8. Plain edge. (for 8A and 8B)

Similar to last, but stems on wreath are not tied together as on copper version, and there is no ribbon. Designer signature reads: C. STUBENRAUCH FECIT. Plain edge. Weight 16.35 grams.

Karl Stubenrauch was mint engraver and medalist in the Grand Duchy of Hesse-Darmstadt 1839-1848, at Darmstadt Mint. He emigrated to the U.S. and about 1850 settled in St. Louis to take up his trade. Later in the 1850's he formed the Stubenrauch & Weber partnership.

For background, see Milwaukier Friedens-Feier, Milwaukee, Wis., in this volume.

## FOURTH ST. OPERA HOUSE
### St. Louis, Mo.

| Rulau | Date | Metal | Size | VG | F | VF | Unc |
|---|---|---|---|---|---|---|---|
| Mo-SL 10 | (?) | BrassOct. | 27mm | — | — | 15.00 | — |

FOURTH ST. OPERA HOUSE / *** / J.S. EDWARDS ***** / PROP. / *** / ST. LOUIS, MO. Rv: Large 5 at center of circle of nine stars, CENTS below. (Wright 282).

## GUS'
### St. Louis, Mo.

| Rulau | Date | Metal | Size | VG | F | VF | Unc |
|---|---|---|---|---|---|---|---|
| Mo-SL 11 | (?) | BrassOct. | 24mm | — | — | 15.00 | — |

GUS' / 2 1/2 ¢ / 7' CHOUTEAU AVE. Rv: Blank. Plain edge. (Wright 407)

## HASKELL ENGRAVING CO.
### St. Louis, Mo.

| Rulau | Date | Metal | Size | F | VF | EF | Unc |
|---|---|---|---|---|---|---|---|
| Mo-SL 12 | (1884) | WM | 23mm | — | — | 200. | — |

Blaine and Logan busts jugate to right, BLAINE at left, LOGAN right. Rv: HASKELL ENGRAVING CO / (rosette) / MEDALS / CHECKS / BADGES / (rosette) / 216 PINE STREET ST LOUIS. Plain edge. Very rare; published here for the first time.

## MAURICE & HENRY
### St. Louis, Mo.

| Rulau | Date | Metal | Size | VG | F | VF | EF |
|---|---|---|---|---|---|---|---|
| Mo-SL 17 | (?) | Silver | 18mm | — | — | 100. | — |

MAURICE & HENRY / ST. LOUIS ctsp on U.S. 1872 Seated Liberty dime. (Kovacs coll.)

## CONRAD KELLERSMAN
### St. Louis, Mo.

| Rulau | Date | Metal | Size | VG | F | VF | Unc |
|---|---|---|---|---|---|---|---|
| Mo-SL 13 | 1876 | WM | 25.5mm | — | — | 40.00 | — |

Bearded head left, CONRAD KELLERSMAN 14' & HOWARD. ST. LOUIS around, 1876 below. Rv: Within wreath: GOOD / FOR ONE / 5 / CENT DRINK. Star at wreath opening at top.

This token is superbly executed, in regal European coinage fashion. First published in Missouri Numismatic Society's Journal.

## M. & ST. L. PACKET CO.
### St. Louis, Mo. (?)

| Rulau | Date | Metal | Size | VG | F | VF | Unc |
|---|---|---|---|---|---|---|---|
| Mo-SL 15 | (?) | Brass | 21mm | — | 25.00 | 50.00 | 100. |
| Mo-SL 16 | (?) | Brass | 22mm | — | 25.00 | 50.00 | 100. |

Liberty head, M. & ST. L. PACKET CO. around, BAR below. Rv: GOOD FOR ONE DRINK / 10. (TAMS maverick 9796)

Indian head, M. & ST. L. PACKET CO. around, BAR below. Rv: GOOD FOR ONE DRINK / 20. (Alpert sale, Oct. 1981, number 7)

Mississippi (or Missouri) & St. Louis Packet Co. ? Attribution by Bruce W. Smith, Fort Wayne, Ind.

## MERMOD & JACCARD JEWELRY CO.
### St. Louis, Mo.

| Rulau | Date | Metal | Size | F | VF | EF | Unc |
|---|---|---|---|---|---|---|---|
| Mo-SL 20 | 1884 | WM | 30mm | — | 10.00 | 25.00 | 35.00 |

Large building within circle. Inscription inside circle: WE CORDIALLY INVITE YOU TO VISIT OUR MAGNIFICENT ESTABLISHMENT. Outside circle: MERMOD & JACCARD JEWELRY CO. / FOURTH AND LOCUST STS. ST. LOUIS. Rv: Circular 1884 calendar. At center: DIAMONDS WATCHES SILVERWARE / FIRST QUALITIES / ONE PRICE / AND / THAT THE LOWEST. Plain edge.

## HENRY MICK
### St. Louis, Mo.

| Rulau | Date | Metal | Size | VG | F | VF | Unc |
|---|---|---|---|---|---|---|---|
| Mo-SL 22 | (1877-94) | Brass | 23mm | — | — | 25.00 | — |

GOOD FOR / 5 ¢ / HENRY MICK. Rv: BRUNSWICK / * / & CO. in circular form, small, at center of field. Plain edge. (Brunswick page 16, no number)

Henry Mick, brewer, appears in the 1870 directory.

## H.T. MOTT
### St. Louis, Mo.

| Rulau | Date | Metal | Size | F | VF | EF | Unc |
|---|---|---|---|---|---|---|---|
| Mo-SL 25 | (?) | Brass | 23mm | 7.00 | 8.50 | 14.00 | 22.50 |

Man's high boot inscribed MOTTS BIG; NO. 610 N. B'WAY. Rv: H.T. MOTT / KEEP 10¢ THIS / IN TRADE / ST. LOUIS. Plain edge.

## ST. LOUIS SAENGERFEST
### St. Louis, Mo.

| Rulau | Date | Metal | Size | F | VF | EF | Unc |
|---|---|---|---|---|---|---|---|
| Mo-SL 26 | 1872 | WM | 25mm | — | 10.00 | 18.00 | 27.50 |

Building, SAENGERFEST HALL above, 1872 / ST. LOUIS below. Rv: WM. HAGEMANN / DEN / SAENGERN / NORDAMERICA'S / JUNY 1872 / ST. LOUIS. Plain edge.

| Mo-SL 27 | 1872 | WM | 28mm | — | 10.00 | 20.00 | 35.00 |

Woman at harp to left, ST. LOUIS JUNE 1872 around. Tiny C. STUBENRAUCH ENG. in exergue. Rv: Building, 18TH NATIONAL above, SAENGERFEST in exergue. Plain edge. Mounted for suspension from blue ribbon.

| Mo-SL 28 | 1888 | Brass | 23mm | — | 8.00 | 14.00 | 25.00 |

Lyre within wreath. Rv: A REMEMBRANCE / OF THE / SAENGERFEST / AT / ST. LOUIS / * / JUNE 1888. Plain edge.

Saengerfest = A German singing festival.

## C.G. SANDERS
## St. Louis, Mo.

| Rulau | Date | Metal | Size | VG | F | VF | Unc |
|---|---|---|---|---|---|---|---|
| Mo-SL 29 | (1873-78) | WM | 25mm | 275. | 350. | 500. | 750. |

Four-mule team pulling cart loaded with wood toward right, CHEAP FUEL in exergue. Rv: C.G. SANDERS / DEALER IN / WOOD COAL / & KINDLING /3127 & 3129 / EASTON AVE / ST. LOUIS, MO. Plain edge. (Miller Mo 28)

Charles G. Sanders first appears in the city directories in 1867 as a measurer. By 1869 he had become a wood dealer. In 1872 he was at Franklin Ave. and Leffingwell, and he added coal to his inventory. In 1873 he moved to 3127 Easton. In 1878 the firm became Charles G. Sanders & Co. as he admitted Eugene F. Pushon as partner. In 1883 the addresses are given as 3137 & 3139 Easton. In 1890 Sanders is listed as a broker and apparently retired from the fuel business.

The token must date from the 1873-1878 period, before the "& Co." was added to the firm name, yet after relocation at 3127 Easton. This token was listed with a question mark as to its dating in the 1st edition of my *U.S. Merchant Tokens 1845-1860*. This is now resolved and this very rare piece is attributed to the 1866-1889 era.

## SCHNAIDER'S GARDEN
## St. Louis, Mo.

| Rulau | Date | Metal | Size | F | VF | Unc |
|---|---|---|---|---|---|---|
| Mo-SL 30 | (1885) | GS | 33mm | 20.00 | 40.00 | 65.00 |

View of buildings and gardens. At base in tiny letters: W. W. WILCOX CHICAGO. Rv: SCHNAIDER'S / (ornament) / GARDEN / (ornament) / ST. LOUIS, MO. Plain edge. (Wright 949)

| Rulau | Date | Metal | Size | | | |
|---|---|---|---|---|---|---|
| Mo-SL 30A | (1885) | Copper | 33m | — | Unique | — |

As 30. Plain edge.

| | | | | | | |
|---|---|---|---|---|---|---|
| Mo-SL 30B | (1885) | Brass | 33mm | 25.00 | 45.00 | 80.00 |

As 30. Plain edge.

Struck by W. W. Wilcox of Chicago.

| Rulau | Date | Metal | Size | VG | F | VF | Unc |
|---|---|---|---|---|---|---|---|
| Mo-SL 31 | (1880's) | Brass | 20mm | 6.00 | 10.00 | 15.00 | 25.00 |

Gothic S within open-end wreath. Rv: SCHNAIDER'S / 5 / GARDEN. Plain edge. Small 5.

| | | | | | | | |
|---|---|---|---|---|---|---|---|
| Mo-SL 31A | (1880's) | Brass | 21mm | 6.00 | 10.00 | 15.00 | 25.00 |

Similar to 31, but larger numeral 5.

| Rulau | Date | Metal | Size | VG | F | VF | Unc |
|---|---|---|---|---|---|---|---|
| Mo-SL 32 | 1886 | WM | 39mm | — | — | 30.00 | 60.00 |

Knights Templar emblem, a Maltese cross with a radiant cross-through-crown at center. IN — HOC — SIGNO — VINCES on arms of cross. Rv: SCHNAIDER'S GARDEN SOUVENIR / 23" / TRIENNIAL / K.T. / CONCLAVE / * ST. LOUIS. SEPT. 1886. *. Plain edge.

Joseph Schnaider, born in the Grand Duchy of Baden in 1832, learned the brewing art in Europe before emigrating to St. Louis in 1854. He became foreman of the Philadelphia Brewery on Morgan Street 1854-56. In 1856 he established his own business as a partnership, the Green Tree Brewery, on Second Street. This moved 1863 to larger quarters on Sidney Street, but Schnaider sold out in 1865.

Then in 1865 he built Joseph Schnaider's Brewery on Chouteau Avenue between Mississippi and Armstrong. Connected with it was Schnaider's Garden, a pleasure garden of the kind so common in Germany but then an innovation in St. Louis. The Garden became famous throughout the country for its high class musical and other entertainments and proved exceedingly profitable.

The whole business incorporated in 1879 under the name Joseph Schnaider Brewing Co. Schnaider died at age 49 in Heidelberg, Germany in 1881, where he had traveled to recover his shattered health. He left a wife and seven children. The business was continued by the company until 1889, when it was absorbed by St. Louis Brewing Assn., which closed the brewery a few years later.

## SOUTH MISSION SABBATH SCHOOL
## St. Louis, Mo.

| Rulau | Date | Metal | Size | F | VF | EF | Unc |
|---|---|---|---|---|---|---|---|
| Mo-SL 32F | 1867 | Silver | 25mm | — | 150. | 200. | — |

Building within central circle, SOUTH MISSION SABBATH SCHOOL / * ST. LOUIS MO. * around. Rv: JULY 7 1867 above radiant book, on which is inscribed: THE WAY / OF LIFE. Reeded edge. (Hartzog coll.)

The illustrated specimen is struck over a U.S. 1857 Seated Liberty quarter.

## JOEL SWOPE
## St. Louis, Mo.

**1876 Centennial Tokens**

Reverse type 1: JOEL SWOPE'S / ONE / PRICE / SHOE HOUSE / —*— / 311 N. 4TH ST. / ST. LOUIS. (All 23mm, plain edge)

| Rulau | Obv | Rev | Metal | F | VF | EF | Unc |
|---|---|---|---|---|---|---|---|
| Mo-SL 33 | A | 1 | WM | — | — | 20.00 | 50.00 |
| | (Miller Mo 36A; Wright 1082) | | | | | | |
| Mo-SL 34 | B | 1 | WM | — | — | 20.00 | 50.00 |
| Mo-SL 34A | B | 1 | Brass | — | — | — | 60.00 |
| Mo-SL 35 | E | 1 | WM | — | — | 25.00 | 60.00 |
| Mo-SL 35A | E | 1 | Brass | — | — | — | 60.00 |
| | (Miller Mo 36) | | | | | | |
| Mo-SL 36 | F | 1 | WM | — | — | — | 65.00 |
| | (Springfield 1981 sale, lot 4548) | | | | | | |
| Mo-SL 37 | G | 1 | WM | — | — | — | 60.00 |
| Mo-SL 38 | H | 1 | WM | — | — | — | 60.00 |
| Mo-SL 39 | J | 1 | WM | — | — | 25.00 | 60.00 |
| Mo-SL 40 | K | 1 | WM | — | — | — | 60.00 |

It is possible Die D (Two heads) may exist, but it has not been seen.

Seen above is Swope's "Shoe Buggy", a 19th century promotion of great effectiveness.

Swope, Levy & Co., wholesalers in boots and shoes, was established in 1865 by Joel Swope and Joseph and David Levy, at 41 No. Main St., St. Louis. In 1867 they moved to 124 No. Main St. In 1868 a new partnership was formed by Joel Swope and his brother Isaac, the latter a former Civil War sutler; this was Swope & Brother at 1012 Broadway 1868-1870.

In 1871 Joel Swope became sole proprietor, at 2012 Broadway. Later addresses of Joel Swope's were 1016 Broadway (1872); 112 No. 4th (1873-75); 311 No. 4th, the address on the tokens (1876-80). About 1881 the business became Joel Swope & Bro. when another brother, Meier Swope, joined Joel. In 1887 the firm moved to 311 No. Broadway. Joel Swope died in 1901.

Meier Swope became head of the firm, which was renamed Swope Shoe Company in 1902. It is still known by this name in business today.

## C. THIET
### St. Louis, Mo.

| Rulau | Date | Metal | Size | VG | F | VF | Unc |
|---|---|---|---|---|---|---|---|
| Mo-SL 60 | (1880's) | Brass | 23mm | — | 16.00 | 30.00 | 50.00 |

C. THIET. Rv: C. THIET / MODOC / ST. LOUIS. Plain edge.

Charles Thiet's Modoc Saloon is listed at 704 So. 4th St. in the 1881 directory.

## SHIBBOLETH LEAD MINING CO.
### Shibboleth, Mo.

| Rulau | Date | Metal | Size | VG | F | VF | Unc |
|---|---|---|---|---|---|---|---|
| .Mo-Sh 1 | (1880's) | Brass | 20mm | 20.00 | 35.00 | 50.00 | 75.00 |

SHIBBOLETH L.M. CO. (incuse) / 5¢. Rv: S.L.M. (incuse). Plain edge.

| Mo-Sh 2 | (1880's) | Brass | 30mm | 20.00 | 35.00 | 50.00 | 100. |

(All incuse) SHIBBOLETH LEAD MINING CO. / $1oo. Rv: Blank. Plain edge. (Wright 979)

The value of token study to history is demonstrated by these pieces. Without them, the saga of a town and an industry might be lost.

Type 1 appeared in a lumber camp token book recently as an unattributed item. Type 2 was called "extremely rare" by Dr. Wright in 1898. A third type of S.L.M. Co. token is reported by Mike Pfefferkorn of St. Louis, but no description is available.

Lead was discovered at Shibboleth in 1811. Mining commenced then and was conducted sporadically by various owners until at least the 1880's. A town grew up around the mines, but it had largely disappeared by 1900.

The U.S. Postal Guides for 1877-81 reveal it did not have a post office at that time. The town still appears in census records, but it is not shown on any 20th century maps. It is located in Washington County, 1.5 miles northwest of Cadet.

# MONTANA

## GREEN'S BUFFET
### Butte, Mont.

| Rulau | Date | Metal | Size | VG | F | VF | Unc |
|---|---|---|---|---|---|---|---|
| Mt-Bu 4 | (?) | Copper | 28mm | 12.50 | 17.50 | 25.00 | 40.00 |

Mine headgear and building, THE ANACONDA above, BUTTE below. Rv: BEST IN THE WEST / —.— / 12 1/2 ¢ / —.— / GREEN'S BUFFET. Plain edge.

## N. P. EXC.
### Grantsdale, Montana

| Rulau | Date | Metal | Size | VG | F | VF | EF |
|---|---|---|---|---|---|---|---|
| Mt-Gr 1 | (?) | Silver | 31mm | — | — | 95.00 | |

N.P. EXC. GRANTSDALE, MONT. ctsp on U.S. 1870 Seated Liberty half dollar.

## SCHWAB & ZIMMERMAN
### Helena, Mont.

| Rulau | Date | Metal | Size | VG | F | VF | Unc |
|---|---|---|---|---|---|---|---|
| Mt-He 20 | (1880-95) | CN | 25mm | — | — | 20.00 | — |

COSMOPOLITAN HOTEL / — BAR — / SCHWAB / AND / ZIMMERMAN / PROPRIETORS / HELENA, MONTANA. Rv: * GOOD FOR * / 12 1/2 ¢ / S AND Z / IN / * TRADE *. Plain edge. (Wright 947)

### D. M. CROWLEY
### Lewistown, Mont.

| Rulau | Date | Metal | Size | VG | F | VF | Unc |
|---|---|---|---|---|---|---|---|
| Mt-Le 4 | (?) | Alum | 25mm | — | — | 30.00 | — |

Horse standing left, ZODIAC in exergue. Rv: D. M. CROWLEY / GOOD FOR / ONE DRINK / AT THE BAR / LEWISTOWN, MONT. Plain edge. (Wright 211)

# NEBRASKA

### ROE
### Beatrice, Neb.

| Rulau | Date | Metal | Size | VG | F | VF | EF |
|---|---|---|---|---|---|---|---|
| Ne-Be 9 | (?) | Bronze | 23mm | — | 45.00 | — | — |

ROE. / BEATRICE / NEB ctsp on U.S. 1869 2-cent piece. The letters of ROE. and NEB are crude and irregular, but BEATRICE may have been incused from a letter-punch. NIFMY ctsp on reverse of coin. (Frank Kovacs coll.)

### E. E. S.
### (E. E. Sponable)
### Beatrice, Neb.

| Rulau | Date | Metal | Size | VG | F | VF | Unc |
|---|---|---|---|---|---|---|---|
| Ne-Be 13 | (1875-84) | CN Oct. | 25mm | — | — | 35.00 | — |

Pool table at center within beaded circle. Around: THE H. W. COLLENDER COS. Below: * CHECK *. Rv: Circle of 25 stars near rim. Within central circle: E. E. S. / BEATRICE / NEBR. Plain edge. (Brunswick 4003)

### HUGO F. BILZ
### Omaha, Neb.

| Rulau | Date | Metal | Size | F | VF | EF | Unc |
|---|---|---|---|---|---|---|---|
| Ne-Om 3 | (?) | Brass | 28.5mm | 4.50 | 6.00 | 7.50 | 10.00 |

Shield at center, BAR on diagonal across it. Lions as supporters, a screaming eagle as crest. HUGO F. BILZ above; * 14. & DOUGLAS ST. * below. Rv: 2 1/2 / CTS. within wreath; GOOD FOR above, IN TRADE below. Plain edge.

### J. TREITSCHKE
### Omaha, Neb.

| Rulau | Date | Metal | Size | F | VF | EF | Unc |
|---|---|---|---|---|---|---|---|
| Ne-Om 15 | (?) | Brass | 24mm | — | 7.50 | — | — |

J TREITSCHKE / GOOD FOR / 5 C / AT BAR / OMAHA. Rv: Blank. Plain edge. (Wright 1158)

# NEVADA

## MONARCH SALOON
### Carson City, Nev.

| Rulau | Date | Metal | Size | VG | F | VF | Unc |
|---|---|---|---|---|---|---|---|
| Nv-CC 4 | (1874-84) | Brass | 24mm | — | — | 15.00 | — |

Pool table within beaded central circle, THE J. M. BRUNSWICK & BALKE COS. around, CHECK below. Rv: GOOD FOR / 1 / DRINK / MONARCH SALOON. (Large M and S in Monarch Saloon.) Plain edge. (Brunswick 2252)

| Rulau | Date | Metal | Size | VG | F | VF | Unc |
|---|---|---|---|---|---|---|---|
| Nv-CC5 | (1874-84) | Brass | 24mm | — | — | 20.00 | — |

As 4, but N in SALOON in backward. Plain edge. (Brunswick 2253)

# NEW HAMPSHIRE

## KEARSARGE HOUSE
### Conway, N.H.

| Rulau | Date | Metal | Size | VG | F | VF | EF |
|---|---|---|---|---|---|---|---|
| NH-Cn 3 | (?) | Bronze | 24mm | 25.00 | — | — | — |

KEARSARGE / HOUSE in two lines ctsp on U.S. 2-cent piece of the 1864-72 period.

In 1868, the Kearsarge House, a hotel in Conway, N.H., was owned by S. D. Thompson, according to the *New Hampshire Business Directory* for that year.

## J. BROWN
### Fremont, N.H.

| Rulau | Date | Metal | Size | VG | F | VF | EF |
|---|---|---|---|---|---|---|---|
| NH-Fr 2 | (ca 1867-68) | — | — | — | — | — | — |

J. BROWN / FREMONT, N.H. ctsp on unspecified coins. (Brunk 68)

John Brown & Sons were gunsmiths in Fremont, N.H., according to the *New Hampshire Business Directory* for 1868.

## G. N. DEMOND
### Gorham, N.H.

| Rulau | Date | Metal | Size | VG | F | VF | EF |
|---|---|---|---|---|---|---|---|
| NH-Go 4 | (?) | Silver | 25mm | — | — | — | — |

G. N. DEMOND / GORHAM, NEW HAMPSHIRE ctsp on U.S. 1878 Liberty Seated quarter dollar. (Gould 79)

## C.D. ROBINSON
### Epping, N.H.

| Rulau | Date | Metal | Size | VG | F | VF | Unc |
|---|---|---|---|---|---|---|---|
| NH-Ep 1 | (1884-1900) | Brass | 24mm | — | — | 40.00 | — |

Large pool table. Above: THE / BRUNSWICK / —BALKE— / COLLENDER CO. Rv: GOOD FOR / 5¢ / C. D. / ROBINSON / EPPING N.H. / IN / TRADE. Plain edge. (Brunswick 5613)

## R. J. P. GOODWIN
### Manchester, N.H.

| Rulau | Date | Metal | Size | VG | F | VF | EF |
|---|---|---|---|---|---|---|---|
| NH-Ma 4 | (?) | Silver | 25mm | — | — | 100. | — |

R. J. P. GOODWIN, MANCHESTER, N.H. ctsp on Canada 1870 Victoria quarter dollar.

Richard J. P. Goodwin is listed as a physician in Manchester in 1868 in the *New Hampshire Business Directory*. At that time, the city had 20,107 people.

## F. W. EMERY
### Peterborough, N.H.

| Rulau | Date | Metal | Size | VG | F | VF | EF |
|---|---|---|---|---|---|---|---|
| NH-Pe 3 | (1868) | Copper | 29mm | — | — | 100. | — |

F. W. EMERY ctsp on U.S. 1851 Large Cent.

Emery was a jeweler and dealt in clocks, watches, silverware etc.
The attribution is tentative. There was also a gunsmith named F. W. Emery in Chatfield, Minn., though this latter seems unlikely this early for rural Minnesota. New Hampshire was a veritable hotbed of counterstamping activities at this time.

## P. S. & P. R. R. CO.
### (Portland, Saco and Portsmouth Railroad)
### Portsmouth, N.H.

| Rulau | Date | Metal | Size |
|---|---|---|---|
| NH-Po 5 | (?) | Copper | 29mm Unique |

P. S. & P. R. R. ctsp in one line on U.S. 1848 Large cent. (Alfred D. Hoch coll.)

## Jas. A. Morse & Co.'s
## OYSTER AND EATING HOUSE,

ALSO

Wholesale and Retail Dealers in

Imported Wines, Liquors, Ales, Porter, Cider, Tobacco and Cigars. Also, Poultry, Wild Game, Oysters, etc.

Meals furnished at all hours. Elm Street, MANCHESTER, N. H., a few doors north of the Manchester House.

---

### BURPEE & CO.,

Wholesale and Retail Dealers in

**Hard and Soft Wood,**

SPRING STREET,

Manchester, N. H.

### C. C. CLARK,
### GUNSMITH.

All kinds of Fire Arms repaired at short notice.

25 Stark Block, Manchester, N.H.

---

### O'NEIL & JONES,

Wholesale and Retail Dealers in

**Wines, Liquors and Ales.**

Also Agents for the

FINEST ALES AND PORTER

In the country. In butts, barrels, half barrels and bottles.

☞ ALL ORDERS PROMPTLY ATTENDED TO. ☜

---

### SACCALEXIS GLOSSIAN,

THE NATIVE

**Indian Doctor,**

Of the Penobscot Tribe.

He cures dyspepsia, dropsy, jaundice, canker, and all CANCER HUMORS. Call and see him.

No. 4 GRANITE BLOCK,
125 Elm St., MANCHESTER, N. H.

### Wallace's Hair Restorative

Restores gray or faded hair to its natural color, causes new hair to grow on bald heads, prevents the hair falling off from any cause, cures all diseases of the scalp, completely cleanses the head from dandruff and all matter injurious to its growth.

Every bottle warranted to do all we claim for it. Agents wanted.

F. L. WALLACE & BRO.,
*27 Hanover Street,*
*MANCHESTER, N. H.*

# NEW JERSEY

## APPLEGATES PALACE OF FLYING ANIMALS
### Atlantic City, N.J.

| Rulau | Date | Metal | Size | VG | F | VF | Unc |
|---|---|---|---|---|---|---|---|
| NJ-AC 3 | (1889-90) | Brass | 29mm | 12.50 | 16.00 | 25.00 | 75.00 |

Two donkeys facing in opposite directions, star below. WHEN SHALL WE THREE MEET AGAIN. is around. Rv: APPLEGATES / (ornament) / PALACE / — OF — / FLYING ANIMALS. Plain edge. (Wright 40; Miller Pa 22)

Recent evidence assigns a date to this piece. A similar donkey die, but only 19mm in diameter, was used in the late 1840's on the Durkee & Co. omnibus tokens of New York City. The Applegate tokens postdate the CW era.

One Pennsylvania diesinker's token (Pa-Ph 373) has the same two-donkey motif, indicating the probability that Sinkler & Davey struck the Applegate token.

Sinkler & Davey were in business in the late 1880's, according to David Gladfelter, a collector of diesinker tokens who owns one of these pieces (ex-Schenkman). They used the donkey die only 1889-90, apparently.

A "palace of flying animals" or "flying horses" is an old name for a merry-go-round. Probably Adams, Raymond et al assigned these pieces to Philadelphia in the mistaken belief they were associated with the 1876 Applegates Galleries tokens.

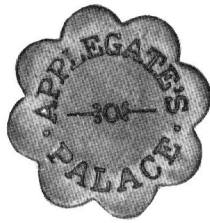

| Rulau | Date | Metal | Size | VG | F | VF | Unc |
|---|---|---|---|---|---|---|---|
| NJ-AC 6 | (1884-89) | BS | 29mm | — | — | 25.00 | — |

APPLEGATE'S / (ornament) /. PALACE. Rev: Large numeral 5. (Damia Francis coll.)

John R. Applegate, an Atlantic City, N.J., Boardwalk photographer, built a pier there at Tennessee Avenue and the Boardwalk in 1883. It was a double decker with an amusement pavilion at the far end. The pier was operated for seven seasons under Applegate's management.

## APPLEGATE'S ON THE BEACH
### Atlantic City, N.J.

| Rulau | Date | Metal | Size | VG | F | VF | Unc |
|---|---|---|---|---|---|---|---|
| NJ-AC 11 | (1884-89) | WM | 17mm | 5.00 | 7.00 | 10.00 | — |

APPLEGATE'S / ON / THE / BEACH. Rv: Blank (intaglio of obverse). (Miller Pa 27)

| Rulau | Date | Metal | Size | VG | F | VF | Unc |
|---|---|---|---|---|---|---|---|
| NJ-AC 12 | (1884-89) | Brass | 25mm | — | — | 100. | Rare |

A WALK ON / APPLEGATE'S / 5 / PIER. Rv: A RIDE ON / APPLEGATE'S / 5 / CAROUSAL. Plain edge. (Miller Pa 27A)

The series of cards issued by Applegate span a good number of years. Wayte Raymond felt Pa 22 was issued well before 1850, but this seems erroneous. Its scalloped companion, discovered only in 1977 by Rich Hartzog, is obviously much later. Another unrelated series, APPLEGATES GALLERIES (Adams Pa 23 to 25; Wright 29), was issued in 1876 in Philadelphia.

Lionel Rudduck possessed both specimens above and attributed them to Atlantic City, N.J. — not Philadelphia.

## CHARLES McGLADE MANSION
### Atlantic City, N.J.

| Rulau | Date | Metal | Size | F | VF | EF | Unc |
|---|---|---|---|---|---|---|---|
| NJ-AC 20 | 1888 | WM | 25mm | — | — | 10.00 | — |

SOUVENIR / CHARLES McGLADE / MANSION / ATLANTIC CITY / 1888. Rv: SOUVENIR / CONSTANTINE CARPENTER / DANCING / ACADEMY / PHILADELPHIA / 1888. Plain edge.

## YOUNG & CO.
### Atlantic City, N.J.

| Rulau | Date | Metal | Size | VG | F | VF | Unc |
|---|---|---|---|---|---|---|---|
| NJ-AC 31 | (?) | WM | 26mm | — | — | 20.00 | 30.00 |

Lady on horseback, YOUNG & CO. Rv: Large star, MERRY GO ROUND. Plain edge. (Wright 1293)

## YOUNG'S AMUSEMENT CO.
### Atlantic City, N.J.

| Rulau | Date | Metal | Size | VG | F | VF | Unc |
|---|---|---|---|---|---|---|---|
| NJ-AC 33 | (?) | RV | 25mm | — | — | 20.00 | 40.00 |

Lady on horseback, ATLANTIC CITY above. Rv: Shoreline scene, YOUNG'S AMUSEMENT CO. / MERRY GO / ROUND. Plain edge.

## YOUNG & McSHEA
### Atlantic City, N.J.

| Rulau | Date | Metal | Size | VG | F | VF | Unc |
|---|---|---|---|---|---|---|---|
| NJ-AC 36 | (1885) | Brass | 26mm | — | — | 20.00 | 30.00 |

Lady on horseback, ATLANTIC CITY above. Rv: Lighthouse; ship sailing; YOUNG & McSHEA'S / MERRY GO / ROUND. Plain edge. (Wright 1295)

| Rulau | Date | Metal | Size | VG | F | VF | Unc |
|---|---|---|---|---|---|---|---|
| NJ-AC 38 | 1888 | Brass | 25mm | — | — | 25.00 | — |
| | | Similar to last, but date 1888 added. Rv: Similar to last. | | | | | |
| NJ-AC 39 | (?) | RV | 25mm | — | 15.00 | 25.00 | 40.00 |
| | | Similar to last, but Gothic lettering and no date. | | | | | |
| NJ-AC 40 | (?) | BV | 25mm | — | 15.00 | 25.00 | 40.00 |
| | | As last. Plain edge. | | | | | |

In general, we have avoided listing hard rubber store cards, but make an exception in the various Young series.

John Lake Young added much to the color of Atlantic City: Bathhouses, Young's Hotel (later the Mayflower), Young's Ocean Pier (originally Applegate's, later Central Pier), Young & McShea's merry-go-round, Bleak House, Young's Apartment Hotel, Young's Million Dollar Pier.

Born in 1853 near Atlantic City, by 1885 he was a lifeguard and policeman there. In 1885 he and Stewart R. McShea, a retired Pennsylvanian, became partners in a carousel on the Boardwalk. McShea was a most religious man and was opposed to Sunday amusement activity. The city also frowned on such frivolity.

To keep the merry-go-round in the limelight seven days a week, they bought more than 100 records, mostly hymns, for the organ; and enough hymnals for one for each double seat on the carousel. The idea caught on and visitors flocked to sing hymns and ride the merry-go-round on Sundays.

## BORDENTOWN HOUSE
### Bordentown, N.J.

| Rulau | Date | Metal | Size | F | VF | EF | Unc |
|---|---|---|---|---|---|---|---|
| NJ-Bo 1 | (?) | Brass | 28mm | — | — | 25.00 | — |
| | | (All incuse) BORDENTOWN HOUSE 5 in circle. Rv: Blank. | | | | | |

Bordentown House was one of the best known hotels in New Jersey during the days of the old Camden & Amboy Railroad. It was opened to the public in 1832.

## KAIGHN'S AVE. PALACE
### Camden, N.J.

| Rulau | Date | Metal | Size | VG | F | VF | Unc |
|---|---|---|---|---|---|---|---|
| NJ-Cm 6 | (1880's ?) | Brass Oct 27mm | | — | — | 30.00 | — |
| | | KAIGHN'S AVE. PALACE OF FLYING / ANIMALS / 409-11-13 / KAIGHN AVE / CAMDEN, N.J. Rv: Incused numeral 164. | | | | | |

The term "palace of flying animals" was used to describe a merry-go-round in the early days. Applegate's Palace of Flying Animals was a well-known merry-go-round enterprise in Atlantic City, N.J. (though its tokens were thought for long to be from Philadelphia). The term apparently grew up when the earliest merry-go-rounds were said to have "flying horses."

## STOCKTON HOTEL
### Cape May, N.J.

| Rulau | Date | Metal | Size | F | VF | EF | Unc |
|---|---|---|---|---|---|---|---|
| NJ-CM 5 | 1876 | WM | 18mm | — | 5.00 | 10.00 | 15.00 |
| | | Bust of George Washington. Rv: CHILDREN'S / BALL / STOCKTON / HOTEL / CAPE MAY N.J. / 1876. | | | | | |

## WHITNEY BROS.
### Glassboro, N.J.

| Rulau | Date | Metal | Size | F | VF | EF | Unc |
|---|---|---|---|---|---|---|---|
| NJ-Gb 4 | 1869 | Copper | 19mm | 2.50 | 4.00 | 7.50 | 20.00 |
| | | Demijohn at center, WHITNEY GLASS WORKS around, *** / (leaf) N.J. (leaf) below. Rv: DUE BEARER IN M'DSE AT OUR STORE / ONE CENT / WHITNEY BROS / 1869. Plain edge. (Miller NJ 19) | | | | | |
| NJ-Gb 5 | 1869 | Brass | 19mm | 2.50 | 4.00 | 7.50 | 20.00 |
| | | As 19. Plain edge. (Wright 1240; Miller NJ 20) | | | | | |
| NJ-Gb 6 | 1869 | WM | 19mm | — | — | 12.50 | 40.00 |
| | | As 19. Plain edge. Thin flan. (Miller NJ 21) | | | | | |
| NJ-Gb 7 | 1869 | WM | 19mm | — | — | 12.50 | 40.00 |
| | | As 21, but Thick flan. (Miller NJ 22) | | | | | |
| NJ-Gb 8 | 1869 | CN | 19mm | — | — | 14.50 | 40.00 |
| | | As 19. Plain edge. (Miller NJ 22A) | | | | | |
| NJ-Gb 9 | 1869 | Silver | 19mm | — | — | — | 200. |
| | | As 19. Plain edge. (Miller NJ 18) | | | | | |
| NJ-Gb 11 | (1869) | Copper | 19mm | — | — | — | 85.00 |
| | | Obverse as 19 (demijohn). Rv: Eagle with U.S. shield on breast (Fuld CW die 1182). Plain edge. (Fuld NC-29a). Rarity 9. | | | | | |
| NJ-Gb 12 | (1869) | WM | 19mm | — | — | — | 85.00 |
| | | As 22D. Plain edge. (Fuld NC-29e). Rarity 9. | | | | | |
| NJ-Gb 13 | (1869) | Silver | 19mm | — | — | — | 200. |
| | | As 22D. Plain edge. (Fuld NC-29f). Rarity 9. | | | | | |

This firm also issued cent-denomination tokens dated 1852 (Miller NJ 16 and 17).

## BASFORD & GLENN
### Jersey City, N.J.

| Rulau | Date | Metal | Size | VG | F | VF | Unc |
|---|---|---|---|---|---|---|---|
| NJ-JC 2 | (?) | Aluminum | 24mm | — | 4.00 | — | — |
| | | BASFORD & GLENN / —*— / 2 1/2 / *— / — 5 EXCHANGE PLACE J.C. Rv: Macy & Jenkins / - - - / OLD / CLUB HOUSE / — . / — WHISKEY / . (Wright 43) | | | | | |

## THE BOSTON
### Jersey City, N.J.

| Rulau | Date | Metal | Size | VG | F | VF | Unc |
|---|---|---|---|---|---|---|---|
| NJ-JC 4 | (?) | Brass | 31mm | — | — | 20.00 | 35.00 |
| | | Radiant sun at center, a scroll above and below. Scrolls read: THE BOSTON / ONE PRICE. Rv: B.O.P.C.H. / (ornament) / 42 & 44 / NEWARK AVE. / (ornament) / JERSEY CITY. (Wright 1104) | | | | | |

Wright called this piece very rare about 1899. It was probably issued some time after the Civil War.

B.O.P.C.H. = Boston One Price Clothing House.

## DIXON CRUCIBLE CO.
### Jersey City, N.J.

| Rulau | Date | Metal | Size | VG | F | VF | Unc |
|---|---|---|---|---|---|---|---|
| NJ-JC 7 | 1876 | Graphite | 63mm | — | — | — | 250. |

DIXON'S / CARBURET OF IRON / STOVE (POT) POLISH / AMERICAN GRAPHITE / PENCILS / CENTENNIAL 1876 EXHIBITION. Rv: Bound group of graphite rods at center. DIXON CRUCIBLE CO. / ESTABLISHED / 1827 above; ORESTES CLEVELAND / PRESIDENT. / JERSEY CITY, N.J. (Wright 260)

Called the "rarest type of 1876 Centennial piece extant," this specimen is struck in graphite. Only a few pieces survive. The illustrated specimen was lot 2704 in the Bowers & Ruddy 1981 ANA sale. Dr. B.P. Wright in 1899 considered this piece rare.

## ALFRED R. SHREVE
### Mount Holly, N.J.

| Rulau | Date | Metal | Size | F | VF | EF | Unc |
|---|---|---|---|---|---|---|---|
| NJ-MH 3 | (1863-69) | Brass | 25.5mm | — | — | 10.00 | 35.00 |

A shield, inscribed with a monogram formed by the letters A.R.S. Rv: ALFRED R. SHREVE / DEALER / IN / HARDWARE / PAINTS / OILS & C / MOUNT HOLLY / N.J. (Miller NJ 23)

| NJ-MH 4 | (1863-69) | Copper | 25.5mm | — | — | 10.00 | 35.00 |
|---|---|---|---|---|---|---|---|

As NJ 23. (Wright 981; Miller NJ 24)

| NJ-MH 5 | (1863-69) | WM | 25.5mm | — | — | 10.00 | 35.00 |
|---|---|---|---|---|---|---|---|

As NJ 23.

| NJ-MH 6 | (1863-69) | WM | 25.5mm | — | — | 20.00 | 50.00 |
|---|---|---|---|---|---|---|---|

As NJ 25, but Thick flan.

## BALDWIN & SMITH
### Newark, N.J.

| Rulau | Date | Metal | Size | VG | F | VF | EF |
|---|---|---|---|---|---|---|---|
| NJ-Ne 2 | (?) | Copper | 29mm | — | 75.00 | — | — |

BALDWIN & SMITH NEWARK ctsp on U.S. 1849 Large cent.

## D. A. PIONIER JUBILAUM
### Newark, N.J.

| Rulau | Date | Metal | Size | F | VF | EF | Unc |
|---|---|---|---|---|---|---|---|
| NJ-Ne 7 | 1883 | WM | 24mm | — | — | — | — |

1863 / D. A. / PIONIER / JUBILAUM / NEWARK, N.J. / 1863. Rv: Pioneer and scene.

The German American Pioneers Society issued this token in 1883. D. A. = Deutsch Amerikanische.

## CARPENDER
### New Brunswick, N.J.

| Rulau | Date | Metal | Size | VG | F | VF | EF |
|---|---|---|---|---|---|---|---|
| NJ-NB 4 | (?) | Copper | 29mm | — | — | — | — |

CARPENDER ctsp on obverse of U.S. 1834 Large cent.

| NJ-NB 5 | (?) | Copper | 29mm | — | — | — | — |
|---|---|---|---|---|---|---|---|

Similar ctsp on reverse of U.S. 1834 Large cent.

Carpender was a wallpaper manufacturer in New Brunswick, N.J., according to Stanley L. Steinberg.

## MRS. J. SCHVERLICHOVSKY
### Perth Amboy, N.J.

| Rulau | Date | Metal | Size | VG | F | VF | Unc |
|---|---|---|---|---|---|---|---|
| NJ-PA 6 | (?) | Brass | 18mm | — | — | — | — |

Fouled anchor at center, MRS. J. SCHVERLICHOVSKY around P. A. N. J. below. Rv: GOOD FOR / * 5 ¢ * / IN TRADE. Plain edge.

## N.J.N.G. 9TH REGT. C CO.
### (New Jersey National Guard, 9th Regiment 'C' Company)
### New Jersey

| Rulau | Date | Metal | Size | F | VF | EF | Unc |
|---|---|---|---|---|---|---|---|
| NJ-Un 1 | 1881 | WM | 30mm | — | — | — | 25.00 |

Large Armory building at center, COMMEMORATIVE OF THE ARMORY FAIR / DEC 1881 above; 9TH REGT. / N.J.N.G. in exergue. Rv: Fancy monogram CCo at center, wreath and circle entirely around. Plain edge.

| NJ-Un 2 | 1881 | Brass | 30mm | — | — | — | — |
|---|---|---|---|---|---|---|---|

As last. Plain edge. (Wright 203)

(See page 192, *TAMS Journal* for October 1972)
The location of Company C's Armory has not been traced.

## N.G. OF N.J.
### (National Guard of New Jersey)
### Sea Girt, N.J.

| Rulau | Date | Metal | Size | F | VF | EF | Unc |
|---|---|---|---|---|---|---|---|
| NJ-SG 3 | 1889 | Brass | 25mm | — | — | 15.00 | — |

New Jersey state seal. Rv: ENCAMPMENT / OF / 1ST BRIGADE / N.G. OF N.J. / AT / SEA GIRT 1889.

| NJ-SG 4 | 1890 | Brass | 25mm | — | — | 15.00 | — |
|---|---|---|---|---|---|---|---|

New Jersey state seal. Rv: ENCAMPMENT OF 2ND BRIGADE / N.G. OF N.J. / AT / SEA GIRT 1890.

## WM. LINDE
### Summit, N.J.

| Rulau | Date | Metal | Size | VG | F | VF | Unc |
|---|---|---|---|---|---|---|---|
| NJ-Sm 3 | (?) | Bronze | 25mm | — | — | 100. | — |

Clockface, on center of which is: WM. LINDE / — EXPERT — / WATCHMAKER / JEWELRY & SILVER WARE / SUMMIT. / N.J. Rv: Lord's prayer, wreath at left. Plain edge.

# NEW MEXICO

## CHAS. E. BONSALL
### Albuquerque, N.M.

| Rulau | Date | Metal | Size | VG | F | VF | Unc |
|---|---|---|---|---|---|---|---|
| NM-Aq 2 | (1874-84) | CN | 24mm | — | — | 50.00 | — |

Pool table in central circle, THE J.M. BRUNSWICK & BALKE COS. around, CHECK below. Rv: CHAS. E. BONSALL, 12 1/2 ¢, ALBUQUERQUE, N.M. Plain edge. (Brunswick 2036)

## TERTIO MILLENNIAL ANNIVERSARY
### Santa Fe, N.M.

| Rulau | Date | Metal | Size | F | VF | EF | Unc |
|---|---|---|---|---|---|---|---|
| NM-SF 4 | 1883 | S/WM | 32mm | — | — | — | 75.00 |

Eagle with serpent in its claw standing on a cactus, the date MDCCCL (1850) beneath, all radiant within a shield and above a scroll which is lettered CRESCIT EUNDO. At left: 1550. At right: 1883. Around all: TERTIO MILLENNIAL ANNIVERSARY * SANTA FE N. M. JULY 2, TO AUG 3, . Rv: Old Spanish structure. In exergue: SAN MIGUEL / CHAPEL. Plain edge. (Brunk coll.)

# NEW YORK

## JAMES ACKROYD & SONS
### Albany N.Y.

| Rulau | Date | Metal | Size | VG | F | VF | Unc |
|---|---|---|---|---|---|---|---|
| NY-Ab1 | (?) | Copper | 26mm | — | — | — | — |

Tools. JAMES ACKROYD & SONS / BROADWAY AT TIVOLI / ALBANY, N.Y. / EST. 1857.

## S. CLARK
### Albany, N.Y.

| Rulau | Date | Metal | Size | G | VG | F | EF |
|---|---|---|---|---|---|---|---|
| NY-Ab 4 | (?) | Copper | 29mm | — | — | — | — |

S. CLARK ctsp on U.S. 1846 Large cent.

R.S. Clark was a rifle maker of Albany, New York.

## S. GLOCK
### Albany N.Y.

| Rulau | Date | Metal | Size | VG | F | VF | EF |
|---|---|---|---|---|---|---|---|
| NY-Ab 8 | (?) | CN | 19mm | 50.00 | — | 100. | — |

S. GLOCK / 27 GANSE-VOORT ST. / ALBANY, N.Y. ctsp on U.S. 1857-58 Flying Eagle cent.

## C.E. HORN
### Albany N.Y.

| Rulau | Date | Metal | Size | VG | F | VF | EF |
|---|---|---|---|---|---|---|---|
| Ny-Ab 11 | (?) | CN | 19mm | — | 30.00 | — | — |

C.E. HORN 58 COLUMBIA STREET ALBANY, N.Y. ctsp on obverse of U.S. 1858 Flying Eagle cent. WILL STAMP ANY NAME & ADDR ON A KEY CHECK FOR 25 CTS. ctsp on reverse of the coin. (Owen & Schmidt 1747)

This could be an important key to understanding counterstamped coins in the post-Civil War period. The 25-cent fee seems excessive by the price standards of that day.

## G.O.
### Albany, N.Y.

| Rulau | Date | Metal | Size | VG | F | VF | EF |
|---|---|---|---|---|---|---|---|
| NY-Ab 21 | (?) | Copper | 29mm | — | — | — | — |

G.O. / ALBANY / NY ctsp on U.S. 1843 Large cent.

## LOCKWOOD SEWING SCHOOL
### Auburn, N.Y.

| Rulau | Date | Metal | Size | VG | F | VF | Unc |
|---|---|---|---|---|---|---|---|
| NY-Au 11 | (1865-79) | WM | 31mm | — | — | 10.00 | — |

AUBURN / N.Y. within circular wreath at center. Around and below: LOCKWOOD SEWING SCHOOL. Rv: 24-pointed star device with blank circle at center. Plain edge. (John Stribhei coll.)

The Lockwood school is supposed to have been active in the 1860's or 1870's.

## T. KNOX
## Auburn, N.Y.

| Rulau | Date | Metal | Size | VG | F | VF | EF |
|---|---|---|---|---|---|---|---|
| NY-Au 7 | (1872) | Copper | 29mm | — | — | — | 100. |

T. KNOX / AUBURN, N.Y. ctsp on U.S. 1848 Large cent. (Tanenbaum collection; Brunk 217)

T. Knox & Brother is listed as being in the boot and shoe business in Auburn in 1872, in *Bradstreet's Register*.

## W.E. DAVIS
## Bloomfield, N.Y.

| Rulau | Date | Metal | Size | VG | F | VF | EF |
|---|---|---|---|---|---|---|---|
| NY-Bm 3 | (?) | CN | 19mm | — | — | — | — |

W. E. DAVIS / ENGINE CALENDER (sic) & TITLE MACHINE MANF'R. NO. BLOOMFIELD, N.Y. ctsp on U.S. 1863 Indian Head cent.

## TIVOLI
## Boonville, N.Y.

| Rulau | Date | Metal | Size | F | VF | EF | Unc |
|---|---|---|---|---|---|---|---|
| NY-Bo 6 | (?) | Copper | 22mm | — | 2.00 | — | — |

Eagle on a shield. Rv: TIVOLI / 5¢ / BOONVILLE. (Wright 1150)

## SHEAK, ROGERS & CO.
## Binghamton, N.Y.

| Rulau | Date | Metal | Size | VG | F | VF | Unc |
|---|---|---|---|---|---|---|---|
| NY-Bi 11 | (1883-84) | Lead | 19mm | 6.00 | 11.00 | 15.00 | — |

SHEAK, ROGERS & CO. / *. Rv: BINGHAMTON, / N.Y. / (ornament). Plain edge.

Sheak, Rogers & Co. (Andrew G. Sheak, Peter F. Sheak and Richard J. Rogers) were cigar manufacturers at 172 Washington St. and appear in Binghamton directories under that name only in 1883 and 1884. It is possible this name could have been adopted as early as 1882.

This firm traces an interesting assortment of predecessors and successors. The firm seems to trace its lineage to Michael A. Sheak in 1870; he was the principal in Sheak & Mayo, flour, feed and wholesale provisions, at 98 Washington St. 1870-77. In the latter year it became M. A. Sheak & Co. (L. M. Bowers, principal), wholesale provisions and groceries, same address. In 1879-81 the principal was Andrew G. Sheak.

The switch to the cigar manufacturing business (later the business that grew explosively in Binghamton, especially 1895-1911) occurred about 1882-83 under the Sheak, Rogers & Co. name.

In 1885 the cigar business (same address) became Sheak, Keeler & Co. (Andrew G. Sheak, Peter F. Sheak and M. J. Keeler). The former partner began his own cigar manufactory, R. J. Rogers Co., 130 State St., 1885.

In 1887 Sheak, Keeler & Co. relocated at 123 State St. In 1888 it became Sheak, Keeler Manufacturing Co. (A. G. Sheak, M. J. Keeler, L. S. Carter and H. B. Darrow). During 1889-90 Andrew G. and Peter F. Sheak seem to reentered the cigar business themselves under those names, at 123 State St. But the business must have ended then, because in 1891 A. G. Sheak is listed as a 'commercial traveler' (salesman) and P. F. Sheak as a 'clerk bds.' (possibly boardinghouse clerk), and these listings continue through 1895.

Then in 1896 appears R. E. Curtis Medicine Co. with A. G. Sheak as manager, and it is still so listed in 1904. Meanwhile Rogers' firm had become Barlow, Rogers & Simpson and, as Barlow, Rogers & Co. survived to 1901. In the latter year it became part of the American Cigar Co. (All Sheak-Rogers research by Gary Pipher, Johnson City, N.Y.)

## BROOKLYN SINGLE TAX CLUB
## Brooklyn, N.Y.

| Rulau | Date | Metal | Size | F | VF | EF | Unc |
|---|---|---|---|---|---|---|---|
| NY-Bk 5 | (?) | CN | 26mm | — | — | — | — |

Numeral 10 at center, BROOKLYN SINGLE TAX CLUB around. Rv: Same as obverse. (All lettering incuse). Plain edge. (Wright 103)

## EDWARD COGAN
## Brooklyn, N.Y.

| Rulau | Date | Metal | Size | F | VF | EF | Unc |
|---|---|---|---|---|---|---|---|
| NY-Bk 7 | (1866-75) | WM | 26mm | — | — | 300. | — |

THE / ENGLISH / "DADDY / OF THE / AMERICAN / COIN TRADE". Rv: "YOURS FAITHFULLY (script) / (monogram) / "A FOINE OULD / BROOKLYN GINTLEMAN / OF A PEPPERY / TURN OF MOIND, / HE GITS HIS / EBENAZUR UP AND / THIN HE GOES IT / BLOIND". (Miller NY 8A)

| NY-Bk 8 | (1866-75) | Silver | 26mm | — | — | 750. | — |
| NY-Bk 9 | (1866-75) | Copper | 26mm | — | — | — | 150. |

As 7. (Wright 1109; Miller NY 8). Unique.
As 7. (Miller NY 8B)

| NY-Bk 10 | (1866-75) | WM | 26mm | — | — | — | 250. |

Similar to 7, but reverse inscription ends with MOIND. (Miller NY 7)

In the 1872 directory, Cogan appears as a broker at 100 William St. His home that year was at 408 State.

Coin dealer Edward Cogan moved from Philadelphia to Brooklyn in 1865.

These tokens were reportedly issued by Isaac F. Wood of New York to honor his friend, Cogan. It is supposedly Wood's monogram — Ici. — which appears on the pieces. According to Elizabeth Steinle, So. Charleston, W. Va., a Cogan specialist, that still requires verification.

"Yours faithfully" is the closing Cogan used on all his correspondence.

Wood was a very active collector of the 1860's and 1870's. He produced the Boston Numismatic Society medal (Ma-Bo 13 in this book), and was a dedicated collector of 1876 Centennial tokens. It is not certain when he made the Cogan pieces.

All the Cogan "Daddy" pieces are rare. NY-Bk 8 in silver is probably unique. The only known specimen, in the Elizabeth

Steinle collection, is ex-Doughty, Edgar Adams, F. C. C. Boyd and John Ford.

The provenance of the Steinle specimen of NY-Bk 10 is Doughty, Boyd, Ford. The Steinle specimen of NY-Bk 7 is Edward Cogan, Cogan family, then Steinle; it is reported here for the first time. Mrs. Steinle acquired her specimen of NY-Bk 9, also unpublished, from Thomas Delorey of the ANA.

Just what the Long Island Protective and Benevolent Association Number 1 of Brooklyn and New York was must be traced, but from the token's provenance in the New York Public Library collection it can be assumed to be some sort of laborers' group.

Enlargement

## CONEY ISLAND JOCKEY CLUB
### Brooklyn, N.Y.

| Rulau | Date | Metal | Size | F | VF | EF | Unc |
|---|---|---|---|---|---|---|---|
| NY-Bk 14 | 1880 | WM | Oval, 29 by 37mm | — | — | 25.00 | 60.00 |

Jockey riding racehorse right, 1880 / TIFFANY & CO. below, all within central oval. Around: CONEY ISLAND JOCKEY CLUB / .*. Rv: MEMBERS PASS NOT TRANSFERABLE. around empty central oval. At center an incused number. Plain edge. (Illustrated specimen, the Woodring-Fuld piece, is numbered 307). Rarity 7.

| NY-Bk 15 | 1881 | WM | Oval, 29 by 37mm | — | — | 25.00 | 60.00 |

Similar to 14, but 1881. Plain edge. (Miller NY 12A)

| NY-Bk17 | 1883 | WM | Oval, 29 by 37mm | — | — | 25.00 | 60.00 |

Similar to 14, but 1883 on panel. Plain edge. (Wright 186; Miller NY 12)

## L.I.P. & B.A. No. 1
### Brooklyn, N.Y.

 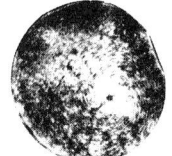

| Rulau | Date | Metal | Size | VG | F | VF | Unc |
|---|---|---|---|---|---|---|---|
| NY-Bk 27 | (1880's) | CN | 22mm | — | — | 75.00 | — |

Sailing ship within central circle. Around: L.I.P. & B.A. / No 1 OF BKLYN & N.Y. Rv: Blank. Plain edge. (N.Y. Public Library sale, Oct. 30, 1982)

## ROLLER SKATING ASSOCIATION
### Brooklyn. N.Y.

| Rulau | Date | Metal | Size | VG | F | VF | Unc |
|---|---|---|---|---|---|---|---|
| NY-Bk 40 | 1876 | Brass | 24mm | — | — | 15.00 | 40.00 |

Shoe on a roller skate, ROLLER SKATING ASSOCIATION, 1876. Rv: BROOKLYN RINK / SKATE / CHECK / * 1. Plain edge. (Miller NY 16; Wright 102)

| NY-Bk 40A | 1876 | N/Brass | 24mm | — | — | 20.00 | 45.00 |

As 40. Plain edge.

| NY-Bk 40B | 1876 | WM | 24mm | — | — | 20.00 | 45.00 |

As 40. Plain edge.

| NY-Bk 41 | 1876 | Copper | 24mm | — | — | 25.00 | 60.00 |

Obverse as last. Rv: MC CORMICK'S PARK / SKATE / CHECK. Plain edge. (Miller NY 17)

## ROXBEE & PRITCHITT
### Brooklyn, N.Y.

| Rulau | Date | Metal | Size | VG | F | VF | EF |
|---|---|---|---|---|---|---|---|
| NY-Bk 43 | (?) | Copper | 29mm | 40.00 | — | 80.00 | — |

ROXBEE & PRITCHITT / BROOKLYN ctsp on each side of U.S. 1828 Large cent. (Tanenbaum coll.)

## WILLIAMSBURGH BREWING CO.
### Brooklyn, N.Y.

| Rulau | Date | Metal | Size | VG | F | VF | Unc |
|---|---|---|---|---|---|---|---|
| NY-Bk 51 | (1875) | Brass | 23mm | 4.50 | 9.00 | 15.00 | 40.00 |

Liberty head. Rv: WILLIAMSBURGH BREWING CO. / LIMITED, / 1 / GALSS / *** Plain edge. (Miller NY 18)

## A.F. WENDT
### Buffalo, N.Y.

| Rulau | Date | Metal | Size | F | VF | EF | Unc |
|---|---|---|---|---|---|---|---|
| NY-Bf 22 | (?) | Brass | 26mm | 1.75 | 3.00 | 5.50 | 8.00 |

COMPLIMENTS / OF / A.F. WENDT / 36 / MAIN ST. Rv: Blank. Plain edge. (Wright 1720)

## WM. C. PARKER
### Chase Mills, N.Y.

| Rulau | Date | Metal | Size | VG | F | VF | Unc |
|---|---|---|---|---|---|---|---|
| NY-CM 1 | (?) | Bronze | 23mm | — | — | 100. | — |

CHASE — / WM. C. PARKER / MILLS. ctsp on reverse of U.S. 1865 2-cent piece. WM. C. PARKER ctsp on obverse of the coin. (Tanenbaum coll.)

## S. B. UNDERILL
### Chenango Forks, N.Y.

| Rulau | Date | Metal | Size | VG | F | VF | Unc |
|---|---|---|---|---|---|---|---|
| NY-CF 1 | (?) | Silver | 31mm | — | — | Rare | — |

(All script) S. B. Underill / Carriage Maker / Chenango Forks / N. Y. within ornate border, engraved on shaved reverse of U.S. 1856 Seated Liberty half dollar. Possibly unique. (Gary Pipher coll.)

Though this piece is made as a love token would be, it seems to have a merchant connotation. Carriage makers were one trade which advertised via counterstamped coins in the 1850-1880 period. It was thought better to include it then exclude it from this reference.

## FIREMEN'S TOURNAMENT
### Cobleskill, N.Y.

| Rulau | Date | Metal | Size | VG | F | VF | Unc |
|---|---|---|---|---|---|---|---|
| NY-Cb 3 | 1884 | WM | 30mm | — | — | 8.00 | — |

Fireman's hat, ladder, pike, axe and hose at center, FIREMEN'S TOURNAMENT above, COBLESKILL, NY AUG. 21, 1884 below. Rv: COBLESKILL, / ONEONTA / NORWICH, / COOPERSTOWN, / DELHI, / BAINBRIDGE, / FORT PLAIN, / SCHENEVUS, / SCHOHARIE. Plain edge. Issued holed.

All the towns named on reverse are in New York state.

## OQUAGA HOUSE
### Deposit, N.Y.

| Rulau | Date | Metal | Size | VG | F | VF | Unc |
|---|---|---|---|---|---|---|---|
| NY-Dp 4 | (?) | GS | 25mm | — | — | 30.00 | 50.00 |

OQUAGA / * / DEPOSIT / & / N.Y. / HOUSE. Rv: ** GOOD FOR ** / * 5 C * / OQUAGA / * / HOUSE. Plain edge. (Wright 791)

## BUTLER & BEE
### East Bay, L.I., N.Y.

| Rulau | Date | Metal | Size | F | VF | EF | Unc |
|---|---|---|---|---|---|---|---|
| NY-Eb 1 | 1860 (80s) | Copper | 31mm | — | — | — | 2 Known |

Imitation of Large cent. Excellently-designed Coronet Liberty head left, LIBERTY on band. Around in crude letters: BUTLER & BEE 76 E. BAY. Below: 1860. Rv: Mirror image of obverse, but struck, not intaglio. Plain edge. (R. Henry Norweb coll.)

A C. Wyllys Betts fantasy concoction, says Kenneth E. Bressett of ANACS. (See C.W. Betts under New Haven, Conn.)

## H. KNICKMAN
### East New York, N.Y.

| Rulau | Date | Metal | Size | VG | F | VF | Unc |
|---|---|---|---|---|---|---|---|
| NY-Ea 6 | (1880's) | GS | 25mm | — | — | 2.00 | — |

Liberty holding long star-spangled pennon. On four of the pennon's folds are: H. KNICKMAN / PLANK ROAD / E. N.Y. / L.I. Plain edge. Issued holed. (Fuld N.Y.-114.104.1-TR-18-GS-15 1/2-bd. no. 4, ed. no. 1-r)

This is an identification disc. Because of the PLANK ROAD wording, it was once thought to be a transportation system tag, but this is merely an address. (See also a similar disc of C.J. Lyons, Susquehanna, Pa.)

## ROBERTS DYE WORKS
### Elmira, N.Y.

| Rulau | Date | Metal | Size | VG | F | VF | EF |
|---|---|---|---|---|---|---|---|
| NY-Em 10 | (1888-89) | ? | ? | — | — | 12.00 | — |

ROBERTS DYE WORKS / 436 E. WATER ST. / ELMIRA / N.Y. ctsp on unspecified coin. (Brunk 319)

| | | | | | | | |
|---|---|---|---|---|---|---|---|
| NY-Em 12 | (1888-89) | Bronze | 21mm | — | — | — | 12.50 |

ROBERTS / DYE WORKS / 436 / E WATER ST / ELMIRA, N.Y. ctsp on Great Britain farthings. (Dates examined: 1860, 1868, 1869, 1874, 1879, 1880, 1885, 1888). Some farthings were new when stamped.

| | | | | | | | |
|---|---|---|---|---|---|---|---|
| NY-Em 12A(?) | | Copper | 21mm | — | — | — | 20.00 |

Similar ctsp on Great Britain 1885 farthing.

| | | | | | | | |
|---|---|---|---|---|---|---|---|
| NY-Em 14 | (1888-90) | Bronze | 25mm | — | — | — | 20.00 |

Similar ctsp on Great Britain 1890 halfpennies. (Most coins seen have mint luster.)

| | | | | | | | |
|---|---|---|---|---|---|---|---|
| NY-Em 16 | (1888-89) | Bronze | 31mm | — | — | — | 20.00 |

Similar ctsp on Great Britain 1889 penny.

William Roberts is listed in the 1890 *Bradstreet Directory* as a dyer, but he does not appear in the 1900, 1902 or 1905 editions. Since a number of mint-fresh 1888 farthings were used, it seems reasonable to conclude most counterstamps were applied in 1888-1889.

A hoard of these pieces came on the market some 10 years ago. Some collectors question their authenticity, but most accept them as genuine.

## J.B. WARREN
### Ithaca, N.Y.

| Rulau | Date | Metal | Size | VG | F | VF | EF |
|---|---|---|---|---|---|---|---|
| NY-It 11 | (?) | Copper | 29mm | — | — | 40.00 | — |

J.B. WARREN / ITHACA, N.Y. ctsp on U.S. Large cent. (Hallenbeck 23.525)

## H. V. PERRY
### Jamestown, N.Y.

| Rulau | Date | Metal | Size | VG | F | VF | Unc |
|---|---|---|---|---|---|---|---|
| NY-Jm 5 | 1866 | Bronze | 23mm | — | — | 75.00 | — |

H. V. PERRY / JAMESTOWN / N.Y. / 1866 ctsp on U.S. 1865 2-cent piece's shaved reverse. (Tanenbaum coll.)

Perry is listed as a gunsmith in the 1866 *Bradstreet Directory*.

## A.D. SHARPE
### Jamestown, N.Y.

| Rulau | Date | Metal | Size | F | VF | EF | Unc |
|---|---|---|---|---|---|---|---|
| NY-Jm 8 | (1884) | Brass | 15mm | — | — | 60.00 | — |

Bearded bust left, JAS G. BLAINE, all within laurel wreath. Rv: A.D. SHARPE / PEOPLES / DRY GOODS / STORE / 30 / MAIN ST. / JAMESTOWN, N.Y. Plain edge. Thin flan. Rarity 7. (Miller NY 34)

| NY-Jm 9 | (1884) | Brass | 15mm | — | — | 80.00 | — |

Bust right, GROVER CLEVELAND, all within laurel wreath. Rv: As reverse of NY-Jm 8. Plain edge. Thin flan. Rarity 8. (Miller NY 34A)

## BLACK RIVER AND UTICA RAIL ROAD COMPANY
### Jefferson County, N.Y.

| Rulau | Date | Metal | Size | VG | F | VF | Unc |
|---|---|---|---|---|---|---|---|
| NY-Jf 1 | (?) | C/L | 57mm | — | — | — | Ex. Rare |

In central circle: Landscape. Hotel in left foreground, antique train unloading freight in right foreground. Black River is shown where it empties into Lake Ontario at Dexter (?). Two vessels are seen on the river. Around, in circular "collar": BLACK RIVER AND UTICA RAILROAD COMPANY. / = *** =, Rv: Blank. Plain edge. (Wright 59)

Dr. Wright in 1898 believed his piece to be unique.

## H.E. HART
### Keeseville, N.Y.

| Rulau | Date | Metal | Size | VG | F | VF | EF |
|---|---|---|---|---|---|---|---|
| NY-Ke 4 | (?) | Bronze | 23mm | — | 75.00 | — | — |

H.E. HART / KEESEVILLE, N.Y. ctsp on U.S. 1868 2-cent piece. (Koppenhaver Aug. 1982 sale)

## L. ELDRED
### Medina, N.Y.

| Rulau | Date | Metal | Size | VG | F | VF | EF |
|---|---|---|---|---|---|---|---|
| NY-Md 4 | (?) | Copper | 29mm | — | — | — | — |

L. ELDRED / LODI / MEDINA ctsp on U.S. Large cent. (Hallenbeck 5.508)

## C. RIVINIUS
### Morrisania, N.Y.

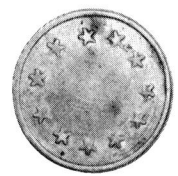

| Rulau | Date | Metal | Size | VG | F | VF | Unc |
|---|---|---|---|---|---|---|---|
| NY-Mr 1 | (1860-80) | Brass | 22mm | — | — | — | Very Rare |

C. RIVINIUS / 1 (with circle). Rv: Circle of 11 5-pointed stars. Plain edge. (Miller NY 40)

| NY-Mr 2 | (1860-80) | Brass | 22mm | — | — | — | Very Rare |

C. RIVINIUS / 1. Rv: 6-pointed star at center, border of 11 each alternating teeth and dots. Plain edge.

## S.B. & CO.
## New York, N.Y.

| Rulau | Date | Metal | Size | VG | F | VF | EF |
|---|---|---|---|---|---|---|---|
| NY-NY 3 | (?) | Copper | 29mm | — | — | 50.00 | — |

S.B. & CO. / NEW YORK ctsp on U.S. 1848 Large cent. (Tanenbaum coll.)

## BALT. & OHIO R.R.
## New York, N.Y.

| Rulau | Date | Metal | Size | VG | F | VF | Unc |
|---|---|---|---|---|---|---|---|
| NY-NY 6 | (?) | Brass | 29mm | 4.75 | 9.00 | 14.00 | 30.00 |

Horseshoe at center, HERE'S / LUCK enclosed within it. Above: BALT. & OHIO R.R. Below: OFFICE / 315 BROADWAY, N.Y. Rv: CHICAGO, CINCINNATI, ST. LOUIS, PITTSBURGH / VIA / WASHINGTON (on scroll) / TO. Plain edge. (Wright 64)

| NY-NY 6A | (?) | Copper | 29mm | — | — | 10.00 | 30.00 |
|---|---|---|---|---|---|---|---|

As 6. Plain edge.

| NY-NY 6B | (?) | Silver | 29mm | — | — | 50.00 | 100. |
|---|---|---|---|---|---|---|---|

As 6. Plain edge.

## P.T. BARNUM
## New York, N.Y.

| Rulau | Date | Metal | Size | F | VF | EF | Unc |
|---|---|---|---|---|---|---|---|
| NY-NY 10 | 1870's | Copper | 40mm | — | — | — | Ex. Rare |

Building at center, above which flies a flag labeled MUSEUM. Building inscribed AMERICAN MUSEUM on two sides. In exergue: P.T. BARNUM / PROPRIETOR. Above the building: NEW YORK. Rv: Head of Barnum in medallion. Inscribed: PHINEAS T. BARNUM. Flags and scrollwork. Flag on left reads: AMERICAN MUSEUM, NEW YORK. Inscription: THIS IMMENSE ESTABLISHMENT / CONTAINS 500,000 CURIOSITIES / INCLUDING BIRDS, BEASTS, INSECTS / FOSSILS, MINERALS, MARINE SPECIMENS, INDIAN IMPLEMENTS, SUITS OF ARMOR, STATUARY, COINS, MEDALS / CHOICE PAINTINGS, RARE ENGRAVINGS, GRAND COSMORAMA, AEREAL GARDEN / AND LECTURE ROOM IN WHICH RICH / DIVERSIFIED AND TALENTED / ENTERTAINMENTS ARE GIVEN / UNSURPASSED IN THE WORLD. ADMISSSON TO THE WHOLE / ONLY 25 CENTS. Plain edge. (Miller NY 58)

| NY-NY 11 | 1870's | WM | 40mm | — | — | — | Ex. Rare |
|---|---|---|---|---|---|---|---|

As 10. (Wright 63; Miller NY 59)

Both above struck by Allen & Moore, Birmingham, England.

| Rulau | Date | Metal | Size | F | VF | EF | Unc |
|---|---|---|---|---|---|---|---|
| NY-NY 15 | 1881 | Brass | 27mm | — | — | — | — |

Two busts jugate, facing right. GEN'L AND MRS. TOM THUMB / * SOUVENIR 1881 * Rv: P.T. BARNUM'S / GREATEST SHOW / ON / EARTH / UNITED WITH / THE / GREAT LONDON CIRCUS. (Wright 1427)

The famous P.T. Barnum's museum was located on Broadway, corner of Ann Street, and was the scene of many of Barnum's triumphs. It was here that Jenny Lind made her American debut. Adams states that the copper piece is "Ex. Rare." One white metal piece in the Fuld collection was purchased by a previous owner in 1900 who paid $6.50 for it at auction. His notation was that in white metal it was very rare at that time.

"Tom Thumb," (Charles S. Stratton) was a midget made famous by Barnum.

| NY-NY 17 | 1881 | Brass | 27mm | — | — | — | — |
|---|---|---|---|---|---|---|---|

'Chang-Yu-Sing' in Chinese characters in central circle. Around: CHANG THE GREAT CHINESE GIANT. / * SOUVENIR 1881 * Rv: Same as NY-NY 15. Plain edge.

Chang was a real giant, more than 8 feet tall. Born in Peking in 1847, his name was Chang Yu-sing. He provided an excellent counter balance of physical properties to the tiny Tom Thumb in Barnum's shows.

There are several other tokens of Tom Thumb, not directly connected to Barnum's American Museum. (See "Some Tokens of the Greatest Show on Earth," in *The Numismatist* for March 1919.

Two interesting Barnum pieces are listed below:

| NY-NY 19 | (ca 1852) | Brass | 22mm | 3.00 | 7.00 | 9.50 | 14.00 |
|---|---|---|---|---|---|---|---|

Coronet Liberty head left, 13 stars around. Rv: Stratton standing alongside two books to emphasize his tiny size. Above: GENERAL TOM THUMB. Below: 15 LBS. WEIGHT. Plain edge. (This is a game counter struck in England to use as a U.S. $5 gold piece in games, and for advertising.)

| NY-NY 20 | 1866 | Silver | 40mm | — | — | 2,000. | — |
|---|---|---|---|---|---|---|---|

Hand engraved medal. Whale spouting, ships in background. All within laurel wreath. Rv: PRESENTED / TO MY FAITHFUL / WHALE CATCHER / GEORGE MAILBOT / P.T. BARNUM / 1866. Two eyes for suspension.

Barnum exhibited three live white whales in this period, caught off Quebec. Captain Mailbot did the catching.

## BENEDICT BROS.
### New York, N.Y.

| Rulau | Date | Metal | Size | VG | F | VF | Unc |
|---|---|---|---|---|---|---|---|
| NY-NY 25 | (1866-81) | Silver | 23mm | — | — | 1 Known | |

Helmeted goddess head right, ROMA. Rv: BENEDICT BROS. / 169 & 171 / BROADWAY / N.Y. / * STERLING *. Plain edge. The flan is irregularly round in imitation of an ancient Roman coin.

The brothers were Edwin P., Fredric P. and Read Benedict. They were in business after 1853 to the 1890's. They sold watches and jewelry. They do not appear in the 1853 or 1898 directories. They are listed at 171 Broadway in the 1866 through 1890 directories, then at 171B Broadway in 1893.

## BLOOMINGDALES
### New York, N.Y.

| Rulau | Date | Metal | Size | VG | F | VF | Unc |
|---|---|---|---|---|---|---|---|
| NY-NY 30 | (?) | Brass | 28mm | 14.00 | 17.00 | 25.00 | — |

Struck rim of relief dots within recessed line on each side. Incused on obverse: BLOOMINGDALES / 637. Rv: Blank. Plain edge. Issued holed. Probably rare.

Probably a work tally for employees of Bloomingdale's department store. The stock die type of the rim design is typical of the 1880's. If a work tally, it would have been in use as a timekeeping device before introduction of the time clock system.

## J.M. BRADSTREET AND SONS
## and
## BRADSTREET, HOFFMAN & CO.
### New York, N.Y.

| Rulau | Date | Metal | Size | VG | F | VF | Unc |
|---|---|---|---|---|---|---|---|
| NY-NY 35 | 1862 | Silver | 34mm | — | — | — | 500. |

J.M. BRADSTREET AND SONS * / 247 B'WAY N.Y. / B.R. OFFICE / IN / BOSTON - BALT / PHILA. - L:VILLE / PITTS. - CHICO. / CIN. / DET / ST. LOUIS / IMPROVED / MERCANTILE AGENCY. Rv: BRADSTREET HOFFMAN & CO - 247 BROADWAY / COLLECTOR OF CLAIMS / IN / ALL PARTS / OF THE / UNITED STATES / AND / BRITISH PROVINCES / JULY 4, 1862. (Miller NY 80)

| NY-NY 36 | 1862 | Copper | 34mm | — | — | 50.00 | 100. |
|---|---|---|---|---|---|---|---|

As 35. (Wright 134; Miller NY 81)

| NY-NY 37 | 1862 | Brass | 34mm | — | — | 50.00 | 100. |
|---|---|---|---|---|---|---|---|

As 35. (Wright 133; Miller NY 82)

| NY-NY 39 | 1862 | Brass | 34mm | — | — | — | Rare |
|---|---|---|---|---|---|---|---|

Clothed, bearded bust of Lincoln left, on plain field. Rv: As reverse of 35. (BRADSTREET HOFFMAN). Plain edge. (King 560)

## H. BROWN BRO. & CO.
### New York, N.Y.

| Rulau | Date | Metal | Size | F | VF | EF | Unc |
|---|---|---|---|---|---|---|---|
| NY-NY 43 | (1876) | WM | 16mm | 5.00 | 10.00 | 15.00 | 40.00 |

Liberty Bell. Rv: H. BROWN BRO. & CO. / BOYS & / CHILDREN'S / CLOTHING / 314 GRAND ST. / NEW YORK. Plain edge. (Miller NY 134)

| NY-NY 44 | (1873-74) | WM | 26mm | 15.00 | 22.50 | 30.00 | 100. |
|---|---|---|---|---|---|---|---|

Clothed, bearded Lincoln bust right, LINCOLN above. Tiny BOLEN under bust. Rv: As 43, in larger size. Plain edge. (King 608; Miller NY 135)

| NY-NY 45 | (1875) | WM | 25mm | 5.00 | 10.00 | 15.00 | 50.00 |
|---|---|---|---|---|---|---|---|

American flag. Rv: As 44. Plain edge. (Miller NY 136)

| NY-NY 46 | (1875) | Copper | 29mm | — | — | — | Rare |
|---|---|---|---|---|---|---|---|

As 45, but struck over U.S. Large cent. Possibly unique.

## CITY OF NEW YORK AIR SHIP
### New York, N.Y.

| Rulau | Date | Metal | Size | F | VF | EF | Unc |
|---|---|---|---|---|---|---|---|
| NY-NY 50 | (1880) | Bronze | 35mm | — | 35.00 | 40.00 | 50.00 |

Balloon with large gondola, small windmill and paddle, CITY OF NEW YORK across the inflated balloon. Around: GREAT AIR SHIP CITY OF NEW YORK. Rv: DIAMETER / 150 FEET. / HEIGHT, 200 FEET. / WEIGHT WITH OUTFIT / 3½ TONS. / LIFTING POWER, / 22 TONS. / CAPACITY / OF / GAS ENVELOPE, / 375,000 CUBIC FEET. Plain edge. (N.Y. Public Library sale, Oct. 30, 1982)

| NY-NY 50A | (1880) | WM | 35mm | — | 35.00 | 40.00 | 50.00 |
|---|---|---|---|---|---|---|---|

As 50. Plain edge.

| NY-NY 50B | (1880) | Silver | 35mm | — | — | — | 100. |
|---|---|---|---|---|---|---|---|

As 50. Plain edge.

## H. CONRIED
### New York, N.Y.

| Rulau | Date | Metal | Size | VG | F | VF | Unc |
|---|---|---|---|---|---|---|---|
| NY-NY 55 | (1870's) | Silver | 25mm | — | — | 300. | — |

COMPLIMENTS OF / H. CONRIED / IRVING PLACE THEATRE ctsp on U.S. 1876-S Seated Liberty quarter. (Tanenbaum coll.)

From the late 1870's.

## DALY'S 5TH AVE. THEATRE
### New York, N.Y.

| Rulau | Date | Metal | Size | F | VF | EF | Unc |
|---|---|---|---|---|---|---|---|
| NY-NY 60 | 1876 | Silver | Rec., 76x28mm | — | — | 175. | 225. |

DALY'S 5TH. AVE. THEATRE / 200TH PERFORMANCE OF / PIQUE. / -.- / FRIDAY, JUNE 23RD.. 1876. / LADY'S / TICKET. / PIQUE. / RETAIN THIS CHECK. Rv: (hallmark: dog, anchor, Gothic 'G') / STERLING / GORHAM & CO. / SILVERSMITHS / UNION SQUARE. Plain edge. (Wright 224; Springfield 1981 sale, lot 4561)

Less than 6 pieces are known, including the Brand and Springfield collections' specimens. It is possible the B.P. Wright specimen and Springfield piece are one and the same.
Sterling silver (.925 fine) souvenir tickets for ladies for "Pique's" 200th performance at Daly's Fifth Avenue Theatre.

## DRIVING CLUB OF NEW YORK
### New York, N.Y.

 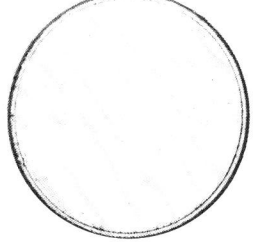

| Rulau | Date | Metal | Size | VG | F | VF | Unc |
|---|---|---|---|---|---|---|---|
| NY-NY 62 | 1885 | Silver | 34mm | — | — | Rare | |

THE DRIVING CLUB OF NEW YORK / MEMBER / (Horse galloping to left) / .1885. Rv: Blank. Plain edge. Thick flan. (Tanenbaum coll.)

Apparently this was a jockey club.

## DEAN
### New York, N.Y.

**1876 Centennial Tokens**

Reverse type 1: (All inscriptions curved) * DEAN * / CAKES / AND / CONFECTIONERY / 17 UNION SQUARE NEW YORK. (All 23mm, plain edge)

Reverse type 2: (One straight and four curved lines) DEAN / ――― / CAKES / — / AND / — / CONFECTIONERY / 17 UNION SQUARE NEW YORK. (All 23mm, plain edge)

| Rulau | Obv | Rev | Metal | FG | VF | EF | Unc |
|---|---|---|---|---|---|---|---|
| NY-NY 700 | A | 1 | WM | 5.00 | 8.00 | 15.00 | 40.00 |
| (Miller NY 194) | | | | | | | |
| NY-NY 701 | B | 1 | WM | 5.00 | 8.00 | 15.00 | 40.00 |
| (Miller NY 196; Wright 236) | | | | | | | |
| NY-NY 701A | B | 1 | Brass | — | — | 15.00 | 40.00 |
| NY-NY 702 | D | 1 | WM | — | — | 15.00 | 40.00 |
| NY-NY 703 | E | 1 | WM | — | — | 15.00 | 40.00 |
| (Miller NY 197) | | | | | | | |
| NY-NY 703A | E | 1 | Copper | — | — | — | 45.00 |
| (Miller NY 198) | | | | | | | |
| NY-NY 704 | F | 1 | WM | — | — | 20.00 | 45.00 |
| (Miller NY 199) | | | | | | | |
| NY-NY 705 | G | 1 | WM | — | — | 20.00 | 45.00 |
| NY-NY 705A | G | 1 | Copper | — | — | — | 45.00 |
| (Miller NY 195) | | | | | | | |
| NY-NY 706 | H | 1 | Copper | — | — | 20.00 | 45.00 |
| (Miller NY 200) | | | | | | | |
| NY-NY 707 | K | 1 | WM | — | — | 20.00 | 45.00 |
| NY-NY 709 | A | 2 | WM | 5.00 | 8.00 | 15.00 | 40.00 |
| (Miller NY 201) | | | | | | | |
| NY-NY 710 | B | 2 | WM | — | 10.00 | 15.00 | 40.00 |
| (Miller NY 202) | | | | | | | |
| NY-NY 711 | E | 2 | WM | — | — | 15.00 | 40.00 |
| (Miller NY 203) | | | | | | | |
| NY-NY 711A | E | 2 | Copper | — | — | 20.00 | 45.00 |
| (Miller NY 204) | | | | | | | |
| NY-NY 712 | F | 2 | WM | — | — | 20.00 | 45.00 |
| (Miller NY 205) | | | | | | | |
| NY-NY 713 | G | 2 | Copper | — | — | — | 45.00 |
| NY-NY 714 | H | 2 | Copper | — | — | 20.00 | 45.00 |
| (Miller NY 206) | | | | | | | |

There may be more unreported Dean die combinations, but the Slabaugh book of 1981 was updated by Steve Tanenbaum in 1983 before this compilation was attempted.
Charles A. Dean was a manufacturer of specialties in fine cakes and confectionery and served weddings and parties, according to the May 1, 1876 edition of *Trow's New York City Directory*.

## THE EGYPTIAN OBELISK
### New York, N.Y.

| Rulau | Date | Metal | Size | F | VF | EF | Unc |
|---|---|---|---|---|---|---|---|
| NY-NY 63 | 1880 | Copper | 34mm | — | — | — | 20.00 |

Obelisk at center, THE EGYPTIAN OBELISK above, WAS TRANSPORTED FROM EGYPT AND / ERECTED IN CENTRAL PARK, NEW YORK, 1880 below. Rv: CORNER STONE LAID BY THE GRAND LODGE F.A.M. STATE OF N.Y. / OCTOBER 9, 1880. Plain edge.

| NY-NY 63A | 1880 | Gilt Brass | 34mm | — | — | — | 20.00 |

Same as last. Plain edge.

| NY-NY 63B | 1880 | WM | 34mm | — | — | — | 22.50 |

Same as last. Plain edge.

(See "Egyptian Obelisk Explained" by Terry Trantow, in *TAMS Journal* for Dec., 1978)

## GEO. EHRET
### New York, N.Y.

| Rulau | Date | Metal | Size | VG | F | VF | Unc |
|---|---|---|---|---|---|---|---|
| NY-NY 64 | (1870's) | Brass | 23mm | — | 15.00 | 35.00 | 50.00 |

Coronet Liberty head left. Rv: GEO. EHRET / 1 / * GLASS *. Plain edge. (Miller NY 231)

## JOHN EICHLER
### New York, N.Y.

| Rulau | Date | Metal | Size | VG | F | VF | Unc |
|---|---|---|---|---|---|---|---|
| NY-NY 66 | (1870's) | Brass | 23mm | — | 15.00 | 35.00 | 50.00 |

Coronet Liberty head left. Rv: JOHN EICHLER / 1 / * GLASS *. Plain edge. (Miller NY 233)

## FARMERS' AND MECHANICS' LIFE INSURANCE CO.
### New York, N.Y.

| Rulau | Date | Metal | Size | F | VF | EF | Unc |
|---|---|---|---|---|---|---|---|
| NY-NY 70 | 1869 | Silver | 32mm | — | — | 100. | 250. |

Bust facing left, FARMERS AND MECHANICS LIFE INSURANCE CO. / NEW YORK / 1869. Rv: ONE HUNDRED THOUSAND DOLLARS / DEPOSITED / * / WITH THE / ** / NEW YORK STATE / INSURANCE / DEPARTMENT / -.- / 'I AM INSURED'. (Wright 305; Miller NY 234)

| NY-NY 71 | 1869 | Brass | 32mm | 10.00 | 16.00 | 25.00 | 50.00 |
|---|---|---|---|---|---|---|---|

As 70. (Miller NY 235)

| NY-NY 72 | 1869 | Copper | 32mm | 10.00 | 16.00 | 25.00 | 50.00 |
|---|---|---|---|---|---|---|---|

As 70. (Miller NY 236)

| NY-NY 73 | 1869 | WM | 32mm | 12.50 | 20.00 | 30.00 | 60.00 |
|---|---|---|---|---|---|---|---|

As 70. (Miller NY 237)

## 407 B.WAY
### New York, N.Y.

| Rulau | Date | Metal | Size | VG | F | VF | EF |
|---|---|---|---|---|---|---|---|
| NY-NY 80 | (?) | Silver | 24mm | — | — | 100. | — |

407 B.WAY / N.Y. ctsp on U.S. 1857 Liberty Seated quarter. (Tanenbaum coll.)

A very interesting counterstamp. It will require a great deal of luck to ascertain which merchant located at number 407 Broadway issued this piece. It probably dates from the late 1860's, or later.

## FRANKLIN & CO.
### New York, N.Y.

| Rulau | Date | Metal | Size | F | VF | EF | Unc |
|---|---|---|---|---|---|---|---|
| NY-NY 85 | 1876 | Copper | 25mm | 4.00 | 10.00 | 15.00 | 50.00 |

Liberty Bell, rayed eagle above, seven stars left, six right. CENTENNIAL / 1776 - 1876. Rv: FRANKLIN & CO. / BOYS' & / CHILDREN'S / OUTFITTING / UNION SQUARE, N.Y. Plain edge. (Wright 343; Miller NY 266A)

| NY-NY 85A | 1876 | Brass | 25mm | — | — | — | 50.00 |
|---|---|---|---|---|---|---|---|

As 85. Plain edge. Thick flan.

| NY-NY 86 | 1876 | WM | 25mm | 4.00 | 10.00 | 15.00 | 50.00 |
|---|---|---|---|---|---|---|---|

As 85. Plain edge. (Miller NY 266)

| NY-NY 88 | (1873-74) | Copper | 26mm | 15.00 | 22.50 | 30.00 | 50.00 |
|---|---|---|---|---|---|---|---|

Clothed, bearded bust of Lincoln right, LINCOLN above. Under the bust: BOLEN. Rv: As reverse of 85. Plain edge. (Miller NY 267)

| NY-NY 89 | (1873-74) | Brass | 26mm | 15.00 | 22.50 | 30.00 | 50.00 |
|---|---|---|---|---|---|---|---|

As 88. Plain edge. (King 606; Miller NY 267A)

| NY-NY 90 | (1873-74) | WM | 26mm | — | — | 35.00 | 60.00 |
|---|---|---|---|---|---|---|---|

As 88. Plain edge. (King 606; Miller NY 267B)

## FREDERICK'S PHARMACY
### New York, N.Y.
#### 1876 Centennial Tokens

Reverse type 1: GOOD FOR / * / 1 GLASS OF / SODA WATER / AT FREDERICKS / PHARMACY / COR. 60TH ST. / & SECOND AVE. N.Y. (All 23mm; plain edge)

| Rulau | Obv | Rev | Metal | F | VF | EF | Unc |
|---|---|---|---|---|---|---|---|
| NY-NY 720 | A | 1 | WM | 5.00 | 8.00 | 15.00 | 40.00 |

(Miller NY 268)

| NY-NY 720A | A | 1 | Copper | — | — | 20.00 | 45.00 |
|---|---|---|---|---|---|---|---|

Also in Bronze.

| NY-NY 720B | A | 1 | Brass | — | — | — | 45.00 |
| NY-NY 721 | B | 1 | WM | — | 8.00 | 15.00 | 40.00 |

(Miller 269)

| NY-NY 721A | B | 1 | Copper | — | — | — | 45.00 |
| NY-NY 721B | B | 1 | Brass | — | — | — | 45.00 |
| NY-NY 722 | D | 1 | Copper | — | — | — | 50.00 |

(Miller 272)

| NY-NY 723 | E | 1 | WM | — | — | 15.00 | 40.00 |

(Miller 271)

| NY-NY 723A | E | 1 | Copper | — | — | 20.00 | 45.00 |

(Miller 272)

| NY-NY 723B | E | 1 | Brass | — | — | — | 45.00 |
| NY-NY 724 | F | 1 | WM | — | — | 20.00 | 45.00 |

(Miller 273A; Wright 344)

| NY-NY 725 | G | 1 | WM | — | — | — | 50.00 |
| NY-NY 725A | G | 1 | Bronze | — | — | — | 50.00 |
| NY-NY 726 | H | 1 | WM | — | — | 15.00 | 40.00 |
| NY-NY 726A | H | 1 | Copper | — | — | — | 45.00 |
| NY-NY 727 | J | 1 | Copper | — | — | — | 50.00 |
| NY-NY 728 | K | 1 | Copper | — | — | 20.00 | 45.00 |

(Miller 274)

## FRIEDENSFEIR IM JAHRE 1871
### New York, N.Y.

| Rulau | Date | Metal | Size | F | VF | EF | Unc |
|---|---|---|---|---|---|---|---|
| NY-NY 92 | 1871 | WM | 38mm | — | — | 37.50 | — |

Standing warrior Germania with shield and sword, left, with sunrise over the (Vosges?) mountains in background, all within central circle. Around: DIE WACHT IN DEN VOGESEN. / (ornament). Rv: Within wreath: ZUR ERINNERUNG / AN DIE / FRIEDENSFEIER / IM JAHRE 1871 / NEW YORK. Plain edge. (Fred Borgmann coll.)

For an explanation of the Friedensfeier (Peace Jubilee), see Milwaukier Friedens-Feier under Milwaukee, Wis.

This Germania is somewhat different than on other 1871 Peace medalets, and she is called not Die Wacht am Rhein (The Watch on the Rhine), but Die Wacht in den Vogesen (The Watch in the Vosges).

## GLOBE FIRE INS. CO.
### New York, N.Y.

| Rulau | Date | Metal | Size | F | VF | EF | Unc |
|---|---|---|---|---|---|---|---|
| NY-NY 95 | 1876 | Copper | 25mm | 4.00 | 10.00 | 15.00 | 50.00 |

Liberty Bell. Rv: Globe at center, showing Western Hemisphere. Above: GLOBE FIRE INS. CO. Below: 176 BROADWAY N.Y. Plain edge. (Miller NY 281)

| | | | | | | | |
|---|---|---|---|---|---|---|---|
| NY-NY 96 | 1876 | Brass | 25mm | 4.00 | 10.00 | 15.00 | 50.00 |

As 95. Plain edge. (Miller NY 280)

| | | | | | | | |
|---|---|---|---|---|---|---|---|
| NY-NY 97 | 1876 | WM | 25mm | 4.00 | 10.00 | 15.00 | 40.00 |

As 95. Plain edge. (Miller NY 282)

| | | | | | | | |
|---|---|---|---|---|---|---|---|
| NY-NY 98 | (1876) | Copper | 25mm | 4.00 | 10.00 | 15.00 | 50.00 |

American flag, LONG MAY IT WAVE and 13 stars around. Rv: As 95. Plain edge. (Miller NY 283)

| | | | | | | | |
|---|---|---|---|---|---|---|---|
| NY-NY 99 | (1876) | Brass | 25mm | 4.00 | 10.00 | 15.00 | 50.00 |

As 98. Plain edge. (Miller NY 284)

| | | | | | | | |
|---|---|---|---|---|---|---|---|
| NY-NY 100 | (1876) | WM | 25mm | 4.00 | 10.00 | 15.00 | 40.00 |

As 98. Plain edge. (Wright 384; Miller NY 284A)

| | | | | | | | |
|---|---|---|---|---|---|---|---|
| NY-NY 101 | (1873-74) | WM | 25mm | 10.00 | 20.00 | 50.00 | 100. |

Clothed, bearded bust of Lincoln right, LINCOLN above, tiny BOLEN beneath bust. Rv: As 95. Plain edge. (King 609; Miller NY 285)

Types 95 and 98 are also known in bronze at same price range.

*Franconi's Hippodrome, Broadway, New York, 1853. Between 23rd and 24th Streets.*

## GREAT UNION PACIFIC TEA CO.
### New York, N.Y.

**1876 Centennial Tokens**

Reverse type 1: GREAT UNION PACIFIC / 1 lb. / COFFEE (curved) / * TEA CO. *. (All 23mm; plain edge)

Reverse type 2: 557 8TH AVE. COR. 38TH ST. / 1 lb. / COFFEE (straight) / * 368 GRAND ST. *. (All 23mm; plain edge)

*Washington Market in New York, 1869. (From Harper's Bazaar)*

Reverse type 2E. As 2, but 368 GRAND erased on die. (All 23mm; plain edge)

Reverse type 3: GREAT UNION PACIFIC TEA CO. / (numeral) / * Large letters; small numeral. (All 23mm; plain edge)

Reverse type 4: Similar to 3. Large letters; medium sized numeral. (All 23mm; plain edge)

Reverse type 5: Similar to 3. Large letters; large numeral. (all 23mm; plain edge)

Reverse type 6: GREAT UNION PACIFIC TEA COMPANY. / (numeral) / *. Small letters; medium sized numeral. (All 23mm; plain edge)

Reverse type 7: 557 8TH AVE. COR. 38TH ST. / (numeral) / * 368 GRAND ST. *. Medium sized numeral. (All 23mm; plain edge)

Reverse type 7E: As 7, but 368 GRAND erased on die. (All 23mm; plain edge)

Reverse type 8: GREAT UNION PACIFIC / 2 lb. / COFFEE. (This die is reported but has not been examined)

| Rulau | Obv | Rev | Metal | F | VF | EF | Unc |
|---|---|---|---|---|---|---|---|
| NY-NY 730 | A | 1 | WM | — | — | 15.00 | 40.00 |
| NY-NY 730 A | A | 1 | Copper | — | — | — | 45.00 |
| NY-NY 730 B | A | 1 | Brass | — | — | — | 45.00 |
| NY-NY 730 F | B | 1 | WM | — | — | 15.00 | 40.00 |
| NY-NY 730 J | E | 1 | WM | | | Not confirmed | |
| | | | (Miller Pa 186) | | | | |
| NY-NY 731 | G | 1 | WM | — | — | 15.00 | 40.00 |
| | | | Thick flan. (Miller Pa 182) | | | | |
| NY-NY 731 A | G | 1 | WM | — | — | — | 40.00 |
| | | | Thin flan. | | | | |
| NY-NY 731 B | G | 1 | Copper | — | — | — | 45.00 |
| NY-NY 732 | A | 2 | Brass | — | — | — | 50.00 |
| NY-NY 732 F | G | 2E | WM | — | 22.50 | — | — |
| NY-NY 733 | G | 3 | WM | — | — | 15.00 | 40.00 |
| NY-NY 734 | H | 4 | WM | — | — | 15.00 | 40.00 |
| | | Numeral 13. (Miller Pa 183) | | | | | |
| | | Numeral 20. | | | | | |
| NY-NY 735 | G | 5 | WM | — | — | 15.00 | 40.00 |
| | | Numeral 15. (Miller Pa 184) | | | | | |
| NY-NY 735 A | G | 5 | WM | — | — | 15.00 | 40.00 |
| | | Numeral 18. (Miller Pa 185) | | | | | |
| NY-NY 736 | A | 6 | WM | — | — | — | 40.00 |
| | | Numeral 18. | | | | | |
| NY-NY 737 | G | 7 | WM | — | — | 15.00 | 40.00 |
| | | Numeral 13. | | | | | |
| NY-NY 737 A | G | 7 | WM | — | — | 15.00 | 40.00 |
| | | Numeral 20. | | | | | |
| NY-NY 738 | G | 7E | WM | — | 22.50 | — | — |
| | | Numeral 15. | | | | | |
| NY-NY 739 | B | 8 | WM | | Not confirmed | | |
| | | (Wright 402) | | | | | |

This series is easily the most confusing and least understood of any of the Centennial card issuers. Even its location is confusing. Dr. Wright did not attribute to locale, but both Edgar Adams and Donald Miller assigned the issuer to Philadelphia. Arlie R. Slabaugh assigned it to New York City, as embossed shell cards of this issuer are reported with the New York address. However, the Great Union Pacific Tea Co. does not appear under either Philadelphia or New York in directories we have searched!

We settled on New York, with the concurrence of Steve Tanenbaum, who assembled enough of these pieces to make some sense of the series, but we will continue searching for some sort of directory verification.

In the section above, we've listed 10 separate dies (including two erasures on dies), and there well may be more. The list above is the most complete ever published, but we believe it to be representative rather than complete. Certainly many more die combinations and metal variations must have been issued, and it is likely these pieces were given out widely to customers, though all seem scarce today. Perhaps a hoard exists.

## W. D. GRIMSHAW
## New York, N.Y.

| Rulau | Date | Metal | Size | F | VF | EF | Unc |
|---|---|---|---|---|---|---|---|
| NY-NY 105 | 1867 | S/WM | 39mm | 40.00 | 60.00 | 80.00 | 100. |

Stamping press at center, STAMPED OCT. 1867 above, BY COMPRESSED AIR HAMMER below. Rv: W. D. GRIMSHAW / THOS. PROSSER / & SON / 15 GOLD ST. / NEW YORK / PAT. JAN. 10. 1865. MAY 21. 1867. Plain edge. (Miller NY 291; Wright 405)

## T. HOAG
## New York, N.Y.

### 1876 Centennial Tokens

Reverse type 1: T. HOAG / WATCHES. / CLOCKS & (on scroll) / JEWELRY (on scroll) / 1373 BROADWAY / NEW YORK. (All 23mm; plain edge)

| Rulau | Obv | Rev | Metal | F | VF | EF | Unc |
|---|---|---|---|---|---|---|---|
| NY-NY 740 | A | 1 | WM | 5.00 | 8.00 | 12.50 | 30.00 |
| | | (Wright 1454; Miller NY 341) | | | | | |
| NY-NY 741 | B | 1 | WM | — | 8.00 | 12.50 | 30.00 |
| | | (Miller 342) | | | | | |
| NY-NY 742 | E | 1 | WM | — | — | 12.50 | 30.00 |
| | | (Miller 343) | | | | | |
| NY-NY 742 A | E | 1 | Copper | — | — | 17.50 | 40.00 |
| | | (Miller 344) | | | | | |
| NY-NY 743 | F | 1 | WM | — | — | 15.00 | 35.00 |
| | | (Miller 345) | | | | | |
| NY-NY 744 | G | 1 | WM | — | — | 15.00 | 40.00 |
| | | (Miller 346A) | | | | | |
| NY-NY 745 | H | 1 | WM | — | — | — | 45.00 |
| NY-NY 745 A | H | 1 | Copper | — | — | — | 45.00 |
| | | (Miller 346) | | | | | |
| NY-NY 746 | K | 1 | WM | — | — | 15.00 | 40.00 |
| | | (Miller 346B) | | | | | |

Thomas Hoag appears in the 1876 directory.

## H. W. HOOPS
## New York, N.Y.

### 1876 Centennial Tokens

Reverse type 1: H. W. HOOPS / OLD / CONFECTIONERY / 370 BOWERY / NEW YORK. (All 23mm; plain edge)

| Rulau | Obv | Rev | Metal | F | VF | EF | Unc |
|---|---|---|---|---|---|---|---|
| NY-NY 750 | A | 1 | WM | 5.00 | 8.00 | 12.50 | 30.00 |
| | | (Miller NY 351) | | | | | |
| NY-NY 751 | B | 1 | WM | — | — | 12.50 | 30.00 |
| | | (Miller 352) | | | | | |
| NY-NY 751 A | B | 1 | Copper | — | — | — | 40.00 |
| | | (Miller 353) | | | | | |
| NY-NY 751 B | B | 1 | Brass | — | — | — | 40.00 |
| NY-NY 752 | E | 1 | WM | — | — | 12.50 | 30.00 |
| | | (Miller 354) | | | | | |
| NY-NY 753 | F | 1 | WM | — | — | 15.00 | 40.00 |
| | | (Miller 355) | | | | | |
| NY-NY 754 | G | 1 | WM | — | 8.00 | 15.00 | 40.00 |
| NY-NY 755 | K | 1 | WM | — | — | — | 40.00 |

He does not appear in the 1876 directory. A candy maker, Herman Hoops, at 270 8th Ave., does appear. There may be a connection.

## HOEFT
## New York, N.Y.

| Rulau | Date | Metal | Size | VG | F | VF | EF |
|---|---|---|---|---|---|---|---|
| NY-NY 115 (?) | | Copper | 29mm | — | — | 75.00 | — |

HOEFT / 256 CHERRY ST. / N.Y. ctsp on U.S. Large cent. (Hallenbeck 8.756)

## HUDNUT'S MINERAL
## New York, N.Y.

| Rulau | Date | Metal | Size | F | VF | EF | Unc |
|---|---|---|---|---|---|---|---|
| NY-NY 117 | (1869-81) | CN | ---mm | — | 15.00 | — | 40.00 |

HUDNUT'S MINERAL. Rv: Blank. (Miller NY 360)

Alexander Hudnut & Co. appears in 1869 as a drug store at 218 Broadway. He was here at least until 1881.
The book *Centennial — American Life in 1876* by W. P. Randel says: "Hudnut's Fountain in the Herald Building dispensed as many as 3,500 glassfuls of iced soda water on a hot day.... The $50,000 price tag for the soft drink concession at the exhibition was a measure of the popularity of the stuff."

## HUYLER'S
## New York, N.Y.

### 1876 Centennial Tokens

Reverse type 1: HUYLER'S / —*— / OLD FASHIONED / MOLASSES (on scroll) / CANDY. (on scroll) / 31 EIGHTH AVE. / AND / 869 B.WAY N.Y. (All 23mm; plain edge)

| Rulau | Obv | Rev | Metal | F | VF | EF | Unc |
|---|---|---|---|---|---|---|---|
| NY-NY 760 | A | 1 | WM | — | — | 12.50 | 30.00 |
| | | (Miller NY 361) | | | | | |
| NY-NY 761 | B | 1 | WM | — | — | 12.50 | 30.00 |
| | | Thick flan. (Wright 1466; Miller 362) | | | | | |
| NY-NY 761 A | B | 1 | WM | — | — | 12.50 | 30.00 |
| | | Thin flan. | | | | | |
| NY-NY 761 B | B | 1 | Brass | — | — | 20.00 | 45.00 |
| NY-62 | E | 1 | WM | — | — | 12.50 | 30.00 |
| NY-NY 762 A | E | 1 | WM | — | — | 12.50 | 30.00 |
| | | Thin flan. | | | | | |
| NY-NY 762 B | E | 1 | Copper | — | — | 15.00 | 35.00 |

David Huyler, baker, 31 8th Ave., appears in the 1876 directory.

| NY-NY 763 | F | 1 | WM | — | — | 15.00 | 40.00 |
|---|---|---|---|---|---|---|---|
| | | (Miller 365) | | | | | |
| NY-NY 764 | G | 1 | WM | — | — | 15.00 | 40.00 |
| NY-NY 765 | H | 1 | WM | — | — | 12.50 | 30.00 |
| | | (Miller 366) | | | | | |
| NY-NY 765 A | H | 1 | Copper | — | — | 15.00 | 40.00 |
| | | (Miller 367) | | | | | |

Huyler's also had a branch operation in Philadelphia. This famous candy maker later had special tokens at the 1904 St. Louis World's Fair.

## S. JANE'S STORE
## New York, N.Y.

| Rulau | Date | Metal | Size | VG | F | VF | EF |
|---|---|---|---|---|---|---|---|
| NY-NY 118 (?) | | Silver | 25mm | — | — | 100. | — |

s. j jane's / store / n.y. (all lower case letters) ctsp on U.S. 1873 w/Arrows quarter. (Joseph Schmidt coll.)

The first 'j' is probably a mistaken extra punch.

## JAQUITH
## New York, N.Y.

| Rulau | Date | Metal | Size | VG | F | VF | EF |
|---|---|---|---|---|---|---|---|
| NY-NY 120 (?) | | Copper | 29mm | — | — | 50.00 | — |

JAQUITH / 98 BROADWAY ctsp on U.S. Large cents. (Gould supp.; Hallenbeck 10.502)

## JEFFERSON INSURANCE COMPANY
## New York, N.Y.

| Rulau | Date | Metal | Size | F | VF | EF | Unc |
|---|---|---|---|---|---|---|---|
| NY-NY 126 | (1873-74) | WM | 26mm | 15.00 | 22.50 | 50.00 | 100. |

Clothed, bearded bust of Lincoln right, LIN-

| Rulau | Date | Metal | Size | F | VF | EF | Unc |
|---|---|---|---|---|---|---|---|
| | | COLN above. Tiny BOLEN under bust. Rv: JEFFERSON / INSURANCE / COMPANY / CAPITAL $200,000 / SURPLUS 300,000 / 111 BROADWAY / NEW YORK. Plain edge. (King 607; Miller NY 372) | | | | | |
| NY-NY 127 | (1873-74) | Brass | 26mm | — | — | — | — |
| | | As 126. Plain edge. (Miller NY 372B) | | | | | |
| NY-NY 129 | 1876 | Copper | 25mm | 5.00 | 10.00 | 15.00 | 50.00 |
| | | Liberty Bell and 13 stars, CENTENNIAL above, 1776 1876 below. Rv: As 126. Plain edge. (Wright 505; Miller NY 372A) | | | | | |
| NY-NY 129 A | 1876 | WM | 25mm | 5.00 | 10.00 | 15.00 | 40.00 |
| | | As 129. Plain edge. | | | | | |
| NY-NY 131 | (1876) | WM | 25mm | 10.00 | 15.00 | 22.50 | 50.00 |
| | | Thomas Jefferson, JEFFERSON. Rv: As 126. Plain edge. (Miller NY 372C) | | | | | |

## WILLIAM R. JENKINS
## New York, N.Y.

### 1876 Centennial Tokens

Reverse type 1: WILLIAM R. JENKINS / STATIONER, / —.— / PRINTER / & BOOKSELLER / NO. 839 / SIXTH AVE. N.Y. (All 23mm; plain edge)

| Rulau | Obv | Rev | Metal | F | VF | EF | Unc |
|---|---|---|---|---|---|---|---|
| NY-NY 770 | A | 1 | WM | 5.00 | 8.00 | 14.00 | 30.00 |
| | | | (Miller NY 373) | | | | |
| NY-NY 771 | B | 1 | WM | — | — | 14.00 | 30.00 |
| | | | (Wright 506; Miller 374) | | | | |
| NY-NY 771 A | B | 1 | Copper | — | — | 17.50 | 40.00 |
| | | | Also in Bronze. | | | | |
| NY-NY 771 B | B | 1 | Brass | — | — | 20.00 | 45.00 |
| NY-NY 772 | E | 1 | WM | — | — | 14.00 | 30.00 |
| | | | (Miller 375) | | | | |
| NY-NY 773 | F | 1 | WM | — | — | 17.50 | 40.00 |
| | | | (Miller 376) | | | | |
| NY-NY 774 | G | 1 | Copper | — | — | 20.00 | 45.00 |
| NY-NY 775 | H | 1 | WM | — | — | 17.50 | 40.00 |
| | | | (Miller 377A) | | | | |
| NY-NY 775 A | H | 1 | Copper | — | — | — | 45.00 |
| | | | (Miller 377) | | | | |
| NY-NY 776 | J | 1 | WM | — | — | — | 40.00 |

## K. KNIGHT
## New York, N.Y.

| Rulau | Date | Metal | Size | VG | F | VF | EF |
|---|---|---|---|---|---|---|---|
| NY-NY 135 | (?) | Copper | 29mm | — | 75.00 | — | — |
| | | K. KNIGHT / 5 BAXTER ST. / NEW YORK ctsp on U.S. Large cent. (Hallenbeck 11.751) | | | | | |

Several specimens were in the Maurice M. Gould collection, but unfortunately the dates on the coins were not recorded.

## RUD. KOHLER
## New York, N.Y.

| Rulau | Date | Metal | Size | VG | F | VF | Unc |
|---|---|---|---|---|---|---|---|
| NY-NY 137 | (1876) | WM | 25mm | — | 50.00 | — | — |
| | | RUD. KOHLER / 70 / 5TH / AVE / NYC ctsp on reverse of flattened Traphagen Hunter centennial token, Rulau NY-NY 851. (Tanenbaum coll.) | | | | | |

Kohler was a dealer in coins and coin books.

## TH. KRUGER
## New York, N.Y.

| Rulau | Date | Metal | Size | F | VF | EF | Unc |
|---|---|---|---|---|---|---|---|
| NY-NY 139 | 1876 | WM | 24mm | — | 7.00 | 20.00 | 40.00 |
| | | Spread eagle, BEER TICKET / 1876. Rv: GOOD FOR ONE GLASS OF BEER / AT / 440 B'WAY / RESTAURANT 285 CANAL ST., LUNCH ROOM / 564 B'WAY / LAGER BEER / STATION / TH. KRUGER-. (Wright 569) | | | | | |

## DAVID H. LANE
## New York, N.Y.

| Rulau | Date | Metal | Size | F | VF | EF | Unc |
|---|---|---|---|---|---|---|---|
| NY-NY 145 | 1875 | WM | 26mm | — | — | 50.00 | 100. |
| | | Abraham Lincoln, by Bolen. Rv: RECORDER OF DEEDS / * / 1875 / * / * DAVID H. LANE *. Plain edge. (Miller NY 416) | | | | | |
| NY-NY 147 | 1875 | Brass | 26mm | — | — | 15.00 | 50.00 |
| | | U.S. flag, 13 stars around, LONG MAY IT WAVE. Rv: As last. Plain edge. (Miller NY 416A; Wright 576) | | | | | |
| NY-NY 147 A | 1875 | Bronze | 26mm | — | — | 15.00 | 50.00 |
| | | As 147. | | | | | |

| | | | | | | | |
|---|---|---|---|---|---|---|---|
| NY-NY 149 | 1876 | Bronze | 26mm | — | — | 15.00 | 50.00 |
| | | Radiant eagle perched atop Liberty Bell. Around: ******* CENTENNIAL *******. Below: 1776 1876. Rv: As last. Plain edge. (Miller NY 416B) | | | | | |
| NY-NY 149 A | 1876 | Brass | 26mm | — | — | 15.00 | 50.00 |
| | | As 149. Plain edge. | | | | | |
| NY-NY 149 B | 1876 | WM | 26mm | — | — | 15.00 | 40.00 |
| | | As 149. Plain edge. | | | | | |
| NY-NY 149 C | 1876 | Copper | 26mm | — | — | 15.00 | 50.00 |
| | | As 149. Plain edge. | | | | | |
| NY-NY 150 | 1876 | Copper | 26mm | — | — | — | Unique |
| | | As last, but overstruck on a cut-down Large cent. The ONE CENT is clearly visible on the bell side. Struck in proof. (Bowers & Ruddy Nov. 1982 sale) | | | | | |

## FRITZ LINDINGER
## New York, N.Y.

| Rulau | Date | Metal | Size | VG | F | VF | Unc |
|---|---|---|---|---|---|---|---|
| NY-NY 153 | (1880-86) | CN | 25mm | — | — | 8.50 | — |
| | | MUTUAL CAFE / 45 / LIBERTY ST. / NEW YORK. Rv: FRITZ LINDINGER / 2 1/2 / 45 LIBERTY ST. Plain edge. (John Stribhei coll.) | | | | | |

# P.L. & CO.
# (Pierre Lorillard & Co.)
# New York, N.Y.

| Rulau | Date | Metal | Size | F | VF | EF | Unc |
|---|---|---|---|---|---|---|---|
| NY-NY 155 | 1876 | Copper | 37mm | 7.50 | 10.00 | 20.00 | 30.00 |

Monogram PL & CO within laurel wreath, 1876 breaking wreath at bottom. Rv: Large numeral 50 in circle of stars. (Miller NY 479)

| NY-NY 156 | 1876 | GS | 37mm | 7.50 | 10.00 | 20.00 | 30.00 |
|---|---|---|---|---|---|---|---|

As 155. (Wright 629; Miller NY 480)

| NY-NY 157 | 1876 | Brass | 25mm | 7.50 | 10.00 | 15.00 | 30.00 |
|---|---|---|---|---|---|---|---|

As 155, but numeral 10. (Miller NY 481)

| NY-NY 158 | 1876 | GS | 20mm | 4.00 | 6.00 | 10.00 | 30.00 |
|---|---|---|---|---|---|---|---|

Obverse as 155. Rv: Large numeral 5 in circle of 12 stars. (Miller NY 482)

| NY-NY 159 | 1876 | GS | 17mm | 4.00 | 6.00 | 10.00 | 30.00 |
|---|---|---|---|---|---|---|---|

Obverse as 155. Rv: Large numeral 1 in circle of 10 stars. (Miller NY 483)

| NY-NY 160 | 1876 | Brass | 17mm | 4.00 | 6.00 | 10.00 | 30.00 |
|---|---|---|---|---|---|---|---|

As 159.

P. (Pierre) Lorillard & Co., the famous cigarette, cigar and chewing tobacco manufacturers, are now (since 1968) a division of Loews Corporation. They are located at 200 East 42nd St. in New York City. Some of their better known cigarette brands were Old Gold, Kent, True, Newport and Spring.

Complete denomination sets in brass and GS may exist.

# MACKFELL & RICHARDSON
# New York, N.Y.

| Rulau | Date | Metal | Size | VG | F | VF | EF |
|---|---|---|---|---|---|---|---|
| NY-NY 170 | (?) | Copper | 29mm | — | — | — | — |

MACKFELL & RICHARDSON NEW YORK ctsp on U.S. Large cent. (Hallenbeck 13.500)

# R.H. MACY & CO.
# New York, N.Y.

| Rulau | Date | Metal | Size | F | VF | EF | Unc |
|---|---|---|---|---|---|---|---|
| NY-NY 173 | 1876 | Copper | 28mm | 10.00 | 20.00 | 30.00 | 100 |

Large star, numeral '7' on it. Above: R.H. MACY & CO. N.Y. Below: SODA WATER. Rv: Cupid with monkey wrench protecting soda water apparatus from a bear's attack. Tiny K. MULLER F. under Cupid and bear. JOHN MATTHEWS NEW YORK around, 1876 in exergue. Plain edge. Thick flan. (Miller NY 512)

| Rulau | Date | Metal | Size | F | VF | EF | Unc |
|---|---|---|---|---|---|---|---|
| NY-NY 174 | 1876 | Copper | 27mm | 10.00 | 20.00 | 30.00 | 100 |

As 173, but 5, 14, 18 or 36 on star instead of '7'. Plain edge. Thick flan. (Wright 645; Miller NY 513)

The reverse of both cards is that of John Matthews of New York, NY-NY 190 and 191 (which see).

# MANHATTAN WATCH CO.
# New York, N.Y.

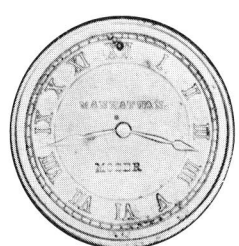 

NOTE: There are two obverse dies and two reverse dies of these tokens. Obverse (watch face) Type A has a short minute hand. Type B has a long minute hand, the hand pointing past the numerals in the border. The illustration is of Type A.

THe only difference in the reverse die is the address. Type 1 reads 234 BROADWAY, N.Y. Type 2 reads 16 PARK PLACE, N.Y.

All the Manhattan Watch Co. tokens have been made as imitation watches with a "stem winder." On a great many surviving pieces, these stem winders have been filed off, leaving the round token. To be considered in 'Unc.' condition, full stem winder must be present.

| Rulau | Date | Metal | Size | F | VF | EF | Unc |
|---|---|---|---|---|---|---|---|
| NY-NY 177 | (?) | Copper | 31mm | 5.00 | 10.00 | 15.00 | 40.00 |

Obverse A, reverse 1. Watch face, MANHATTAN on upper part of face. Rv: MANHATTAN WATCH CO. / 3/5 / SIZE OF / WATCH. / GOLD PLATE / $6.00 / NICKEL / $5.00 / + 234 BROADWAY, N.Y. +. Plain edge. (Wright 657; Miller NY 518)

| NY-NY 177 A | (?) | Brass | 31mm | 5.00 | 10.00 | 15.00 | 45.00 |
|---|---|---|---|---|---|---|---|

As 177. Plain edge. (Miller NY 519)

| NY-NY 177 B | (?) | GS | 31mm | 5.00 | 10.00 | 15.00 | 40.00 |
|---|---|---|---|---|---|---|---|

As 177. Plain edge. (Miller NY 520)

| NY-NY 178 | (?) | Brass | 31mm | 5.00 | 10.00 | 15.00 | 40.00 |
|---|---|---|---|---|---|---|---|

Obverse A, reverse 2. Short minute hand; 16 PARK PLACE, N.Y. Plain edge.

| NY-NY 178 A | (?) | GS | 31mm | 5.00 | 10.00 | 15.00 | 40.00 |
|---|---|---|---|---|---|---|---|

As 178. Plain edge.

| NY-NY 179 | (?) | GS | 31mm | 7.50 | 15.00 | 25.00 | 60.00 |
|---|---|---|---|---|---|---|---|

Obverse B, reverse 2. Long minute hand; 16 PARK PLACE, N.Y. Plain edge.

| NY-NY 181 | (?) | Gilt/GS | 31mm | — | — | — | 25.00 |
|---|---|---|---|---|---|---|---|

As 177, but ctsp 'MOSER' on lower part of watch face.

| NY-NY 182 | (?) | GS | 31mm | — | — | — | 25.00 |
|---|---|---|---|---|---|---|---|

As 177, but ctsp 'TODD / THE / JEWELER' on watch face.

It is believed additional counterstamp varieties similar to 181 and 182 will surface. These apparently were distributors of the Manhattan Watch Co. products.

## MARTINKA & CO.
### New York, N.Y.

| Rulau | Date | Metal | Size | F | VF | EF | Unc |
|---|---|---|---|---|---|---|---|
| NY-NY 185 | (1875) | S/Br | 31mm | — | 50.00 | — | 75.00 |

Magician standing on a globe, MUNDUS VULT DECIPI: DECIPIATUR. Rv: MARTINKA & CO / MANUFACTURERS / OF / FINE MAGICAL / APPARATUS / NEW-YORK / (wreath). Reeded edge.

## JOHN MATTHEWS
### New York, N.Y.

NOTE: Tokens of this design, 1863, are catalogued as Civil War tokens, Fuld NY 630-AV-Ia (Miller NY 523 to 526B)

| Rulau | Date | Metal | Size | F | VF | EF | Unc |
|---|---|---|---|---|---|---|---|
| NY-NY 190 | 1876 | Copper | 28mm | 5.00 | 7.00 | 9.00 | 12.50 |

Obverse similar to 1863 token illustration, but MATTHEWS' SODA WATER APPARATUS. above, 1876. below. Rv: Cupid with monkey wrench protecting soda water apparatus from a bear's attack. Tiny K. MULLER F. under Cupid and bear. JOHN MATTHEWS NEW YORK around, 1876 in exergue. Thick planchet. (Wright 674; Miller NY 525)

| NY-NY 191 | 1876 | Bronze | 28mm | 5.00 | 7.00 | 9.00 | 12.50 |

As 190. (Distinguishing between copper and bronze specimens is very difficult.) (Miller NY 526)

| NY-NY 195 | 1876 | Bronze | 28mm | — | — | — | 20.00 |

Obverse as reverse of 190. Rv: Blank, but '18' incused.

| NY-NY 196 | 1876 | Bronze | 28mm | — | — | — | 20.00 |

As 195, but '40,' '135,' '149,' or '180' incused.

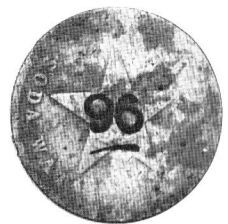

| Rulau | Date | Metal | Size | F | VF | EF | Unc |
|---|---|---|---|---|---|---|---|
| NY-NY 197 | 1876 | Bronze | 28mm | — | — | — | 20.00 |

Obv. as 195. Rv: Large star at center, SODA WATER below. '96' incused on star. Plain edge. Thick flan.

| NY-NY 199 | 1882 | S/Cop. | 45mm | 10.00 | 12.00 | 14.00 | 20.00 |

Head to right, JOHN MATTHEWS / 1808-1870. Rv: Similar to reverse of 190, 1882 in exergue. (Miller NY 527)

John Matthews founded his soda water apparatus manufactory in 1832. He held many U.S. patents.

## METROPOLITAN INSURANCE COMPANY
### New York, N.Y.

| Rulau | Date | Metal | Size | F | VF | EF | Unc |
|---|---|---|---|---|---|---|---|
| NY-NY 205 | 1865 | Copper | 27mm | 5.00 | 10.00 | 15.00 | 30.00 |

Sailing vessel to right, METROPOLITAN above, INSURANCE COMPANY below. Rv: MARINE & FIRE. / CAPITAL / $300,000 / SURPLUS / $458.321. / 108 BROADWAY / NEW YORK / 1865. (Miller NY 577)

| NY-NY 206 | 1865 | Brass | 27mm | 5.00 | 10.00 | 15.00 | 30.00 |

As 205. (Miller NY 578)

| NY-NY 207 | 1865 | Copper | --mm | 5.00 | 10.00 | 15.00 | 30.00 |

Similar to 205, but CAPITAL / $1,000,000. (Miller NY 575)

| NY-NY 208 | 1865 | Brass | --mm | 5.00 | 10.00 | 15.00 | 30.00 |

As 207. (Miller NY 576)

| Rulau | Date | Metal | Size | F | VF | EF | Unc |
|---|---|---|---|---|---|---|---|
| NY-NY 210 | 1866 | Copper | 31mm | 5.00 | 8.00 | 14.00 | 30.00 |

Obverse as 205. Rv: Similar, but legend reads: MARINE & FIRE. / CAPITAL, / $1,000,000 / ASSETS, / $1,650,000 / 108 & 110 BDWAY / NEW YORK / 1866 / DEALERS MAY PARTICIPATE IN PROFITS. Plain edge. (Miller NY 579)

| NY-NY 211 | 1866 | Brass | 31mm | 5.00 | 8.00 | 14.00 | 30.00 |

As 205. Plain edge. (Miller NY 580)

## NEW YORK TURNVEREIN
### New York, N.Y.

| Rulau | Date | Metal | Size | F | VF | EF | Unc |
|---|---|---|---|---|---|---|---|
| NY-NY 222 | 1875 | Copper | 32mm | — | 5.00 | — | — |

Insignia of the Turners Order. NEW-YORK TURNVEREIN GEGR. JUNI / 6, 1850. Rv: BAHN / FREI within wreath at center. Around: ZUR ERINNERUNG AN DIE 25 JAHR STIFTUNGS FEIER 1875. (Wright 756)

Commemorates the 25th anniversary of the founding of the New York Turners Union (Turnverein), a gymnastic association and German fraternal group.

## PARISIAN VARIETIES
### New York, N.Y.

| Rulau | Date | Metal | Size | G | VG | F | VF |
|---|---|---|---|---|---|---|---|
| NY-NY 230 | (1876) | Silver | 31mm | — | 75.00 | 100. | 150. |

PARISIAN / VARIETIES / 16. ST. & B'WAY N.Y. in three lines ctsp on U.S. 1875 half dollar. (Duffield 1500; Gould 39; Miller NY 627)

| NY-NY 231 | (1876) | Silver | 33mm | — | 75.00 | 100. | 150. |

Same ctsp on U.S. Bust type half dollar. (Gould 47)

| NY-NY 232 | (?) | Silver | 31mm | — | 75.00 | 100. | 150. |

Similar ctsp on U.S. 1874 half dollar. (Krueger coll.)

| NY-NY 232 A | (?) | Silver | 31mm | — | 75.00 | 100. | 150. |

Similar ctsp on U.S. 1873 half dollar. (Kovacs coll.)

| NY-NY 232 B | (?) | Silver | 31mm | — | 75.00 | 100. | 150. |

Similar ctsp on U.S. 1858 half dollar. (Tanenbaum coll.)

| NY-NY 234 | (?) | Silver | 39mm | — | 175. | — | 275. |

Same ctsp on U.S. Trade dollar. (Gould 47)

| NY-NY 236 | (?) | Silver | 27mm | — | 75.00 | 100. | 150. |

Same ctsp on Spanish-American 2-reales. (Gould 115)

Since the counterstamp occurs on coins of about a 60-year span (1816-1876), it is difficult to fix their probable issue date. The first counterstamps may have been applied before the Civil War, but more likely about 1876 or a bit later.

## H. J. MEYER
### New York, N.Y.

| Rulau | Date | Metal | Size | VG | F | VF | Unc |
|---|---|---|---|---|---|---|---|
| NY-NY 213 | 1880 | N/Br | 31mm | — | — | Rare | — |

H. J. MEYER / ESTABLISHED / COMMISSION / (Star) / MERCHANT / 1880 / 275 WASHINGTON ST. N. Y. CITY. Rv: BUTTER * CHEESE * EGGS / POULTRY / *** / ETC. / *. Plain edge. (Tanenbaum coll.)

## PARMELEE, WEBSTER & CO.
### New York, N.Y.

| Rulau | Date | Metal | Size | F | VF | EF | Unc |
|---|---|---|---|---|---|---|---|
| NY-NY 243 | 1868 | Silver | 21mm | — | — | — | 100. |

Bust of Grant right. Rv: PARMELEE, WEBSTER & CO. / 155 JANE ST. / PURE / 10 / ALUMINUM. Plain edge. (Miller NY 628)

| NY-NY 243 A | 1868 | Copper | 21mm | — | 10.00 | 20.00 | 40.00 |

As 243. (Miller 629)

| NY-NY 243 B | 1868 | Brass | 21mm | — | 10.00 | 20.00 | 40.00 |

As 243. (Miller 630)

| NY-NY 243 C | 1868 | WM | 21mm | — | 10.00 | 20.00 | 40.00 |

As 243. (Miller 631)

| NY-NY 243 D | 1868 | Alum | 21mm | — | — | — | — |

As 243. (Tanenbaum coll.)

## GEO. F. PHELAN
### New York, N.Y.

#### 1876 Centennial Tokens

Reverse type 1: GEO E. PHELAN / BILLIARD / (billiard table) / TABLES / 36 E. 14TH ST. N.Y. (All 23mm; plain edge)

| Rulau | Obv | Rev | Metal | F | VF | EF | Unc |
|---|---|---|---|---|---|---|---|
| NY-NY 780 | A | 1 | WM | — | — | 12.50 | 30.00 |

(Miller NY 635)

| NY-NY 780 A | A | 1 | Copper | — | — | 17.50 | 40.00 |
| NY-NY 780 B | A | 1 | Brass | — | — | 17.50 | 40.00 |

(Wright 821)

| NY-NY 781 | B | 1 | WM | — | — | 12.50 | 30.00 |

(Miller 636)

| NY-NY 781 A | B | 1 | Copper | — | — | 17.50 | 40.00 |

Also in Bronze.

| NY-NY 782 | E | 1 | WM | — | — | 12.50 | 30.00 |

(Miller 637)

| NY-NY 782 A | E | 1 | Copper | — | — | 17.50 | 40.00 |

(Miller 638)

| NY-NY 782 B | E | 1 | Brass | — | — | 20.00 | 45.00 |

| Rulau | Obv | Rev | Metal | F | VF | EF | Unc |
|---|---|---|---|---|---|---|---|
| NY-NY 783 | F | 1 (Miller 639) | WM | — | — | 17.50 | 40.00 |
| NY-NY 784 | G | 1 Also in Bronze. | Copper | — | — | 20.00 | 45.00 |
| NY-NY 785 | H | 1 Also in Bronze. | Copper | — | — | 20.00 | 45.00 |

Phelan later became part of the H. W. Collender Co. firm of billiard table manufacturers and thus, in 1884, part of the Brunswick-Balke-Collender Co. (now the Brunswick Corp.)

## W. PIMMEL
## New York, N.Y.

### 1876 Centennial Tokens

Reverse type 1: * NEW YORK SEWING MACHINE HEADQUARTERS / W. PIMMEL / GENL. AGT. / 191 / GRAND ST. N.Y. (All 23mm; plain edge)

| Rulau | Obv | Rev | Metal | F | VF | EF | Unc |
|---|---|---|---|---|---|---|---|
| NY-NY 790 | A | 1 (Miller NY 640) | WM | — | — | 14.00 | 30.00 |
| NY-NY 791 | B | 1 (Miller 641) | WM | — | — | 14.00 | 30.00 |
| NY-NY 791 A | B | 1 | Copper | — | — | 17.50 | 40.00 |
| NY-NY 791 B | B | 1 (Wright 851) | Brass | — | — | — | 40.00 |
| NY-NY 792 | E | 1 (Miller 642) | WM | — | — | 14.00 | 30.00 |
| NY-NY 793 | F | 1 (Miller 643) | WM | — | — | 17.50 | 40.00 |
| NY-NY 794 | G | 1 | WM | — | — | 17.50 | 40.00 |
| NY-NY 795 | H | 1 | WM | — | — | 17.50 | 40.00 |
| NY-NY 796 | J | 1 | WM | — | — | 20.00 | 45.00 |
| NY-NY 796 A | J | 1 | Copper | — | — | — | 45.00 |
| NY-NY 796 B | J | 1 | Brass | — | — | — | 45.00 |

## PARK THEATRE
## New York, N.Y.

| Rulau | Date | Metal | Size | F | VF | EF | Unc |
|---|---|---|---|---|---|---|---|
| NY-NY 240 | 1875 | WM | 43mm | — | 30.00 | — | 50.00 |

Accolated bust left, PRESENTED BY MR. & MRS. WM. J. FLORENCE. Rv: Wreath, within which: PARK THEATRE / DECEMBER 13, 1875 / 100DTH / NIGHT / OF THE / MIGHTY / DOLLAR. (Wright 797; Springfield 1981 sale, lot 4561)

For earlier tokens of a famous theater by this name, see Rulau's *Early American Tokens*.

## PIC-NICK & SOMMERNACHTSFEST
## New York, N.Y.

| Rulau | Date | Metal | Size | F | VF | EF | Unc |
|---|---|---|---|---|---|---|---|
| NY-NY 250 | 1876 | WM | 26mm | — | — | 50.00 | 100. |

Clothed, bearded bust of Lincoln right, LINCOLN above, tiny BOLEN beneath bust. Rv: (In 11 lines): PIC-NICK & SOMMERNACHTSFEST ABGEHALTEN VON UNIM SAENGERBUND PH. ZUIHREN DES MARSCHNER MAENNERCHOR N.Y. MONTAG 14 AUG. 1876 AUF REISTLE'S SAENGERPLATZ AD. 25 CTS. Plain edge. (King 612; Miller Pa 399)

| NY-NY 251 | 1876 | Copper | 26mm | — | 10.00 | 20.00 | 40.00 |

Liberty Bell. Rv: As 250. Plain edge. (Miller Pa 399A)

Attributed in error to Philadelphia, Pa. by Adams and Miller.

## F. PRENTICE
## New York, N.Y.

| Rulau | Date | Metal | Size | VG | F | VF | Unc |
|---|---|---|---|---|---|---|---|
| NY-NY 255 | 1867 | Silver | 32mm | — | 35.00 | 50.00 | 80.00 |

Mine buildings at center, F. PRENTICE. MINING 26 PINE ST. around, * NEW YORK * below. Rv: FIRST PRODUCT / BY / MILL PROCESS / IN THE / PAH-RANAGAT / MINING DISTRICT / NEVADA / JANY. 1867. (Wright 1582; Fonrobert 2627; Miller NY 644)

## PRUDEN'S
## New York, N.Y.

### 1876 Centennial Tokens

Reverse type 1: AT / PRUDEN'S / 66 W. 13TH ST. N.Y. / OPP. MACY'S / SCRAP PICTURES / & FIRE WORKS / — A — / SPECIALTY. (All 23mm; plain edge)

| Rulau | Obv | Rev | Metal | F | VF | EF | Unc |
|---|---|---|---|---|---|---|---|
| NY-NY 800 | A | 1 (Miller NY 646) | WM | 5.00 | 8.00 | 12.50 | 30.00 |
| NY-NY 800 A | A | 1 | Copper | — | — | 20.00 | 45.00 |
| NY-NY 800 B | A | 1 | Brass | — | — | 20.00 | 45.00 |
| NY-NY 801 | B | 1 (Miller NY 647) | WM | — | — | 12.50 | 30.00 |
| NY-NY 801 A | B | 1 (Wright 854) | Brass | — | — | 20.00 | 45.00 |
| NY-NY 802 | E | 1 (Miller 648) | WM | — | — | 12.50 | 30.00 |
| NY-NY 803 | F | 1 (Miller 649) | WM | — | — | 20.00 | 45.00 |
| NY-NY 804 | G | 1 | WM | — | — | 20.00 | 45.00 |
| NY-NY 805 | H | 1 | WM | — | — | 20.00 | 45.00 |
| NY-NY 805 A | H | 1 (Miller 650) | Copper | — | — | 22.50 | 50.00 |

Isaac C. Pruden, wholesale confectioner, appears at 66 West 13th St. in the 1876 directory.

## RICE
## New York, N.Y.

| Rulau | Date | Metal | Size | VG | F | VF | EF |
|---|---|---|---|---|---|---|---|
| NY-NY 265 | (?) | Copper | 29mm | — | — | 50.00 | — |

RICE / 194 CANAL ST. ctsp on U.S. Large cent. (Hallenbeck 18.511; Brunk 312)

The attribution to New York is purely arbitrary, based on the address. It could as well be Chicago, or another city.

# GEO. P. ROWELL & CO.
## New York, N.Y.

### 1876 Centennial Tokens

Reverse type 1: GEO. P. ROWELL & CO. / NEWSPAPER / ADVERTISING / 41 MARK ROW N.Y. (All 23mm; plain edge)

| Rulau | Obv | Rev | Metal | F | VF | EF | Unc |
|---|---|---|---|---|---|---|---|
| NY-NY 810 | A | 1 | WM | — | — | 12.50 | 30.00 |
| | | (Wright 918; Miller NY 737) | | | | | |
| NY-NY 810A | A | 1 | Brass | — | — | — | 45.00 |
| NY-NY 811 | B | 1 | WM | — | — | 12.50 | 30.00 |
| | | Thick flan. (Miller 736) | | | | | |
| NY-NY 811A | B | 1 | WM | — | — | 15.00 | 40.00 |
| | | Thin flan. | | | | | |
| NY-NY 811B | B | 1 | Copper | — | — | 15.00 | 40.00 |
| | | (Miller 735) | | | | | |
| NY-NY 811C | B | 1 | Brass | — | — | — | 45.00 |
| NY-NY 812 | C | 1 | WM | — | — | 20.00 | 45.00 |
| NY-NY 813 | D | 1 | WM | — | — | 20.00 | 45.00 |
| NY-NY 814 | E | 1 | WM | — | — | 12.50 | 30.00 |
| | | (Miller 738) | | | | | |
| NY-NY 815 | F | 1 | WM | — | — | 15.00 | 40.00 |
| | | (Miller 739) | | | | | |
| NY-NY 816 | G | 1 | WM | — | — | 15.00 | 40.00 |
| NY-NY 817 | H | 1 | WM | — | — | 15.00 | 40.00 |
| NY-NY 817A | H | 1 | Copper | — | — | 20.00 | 45.00 |
| | | (Miller 741) | | | | | |
| NY-NY 818 | J | 1 | WM | — | — | 20.00 | 45.00 |
| | | (Miller 740) | | | | | |
| NY-NY 819 | K | 1 | WM | — | — | 15.00 | 40.00 |
| NY-NY 820 | * | 1 | WM | — | — | — | 50.00 |

* Muling of the Theo. J. Harbach card, Philadelphia, with the Rowell card.

# H.G. SAMPSON
## New York, N.Y.

| Rulau | Date | Metal | Size | F | VF | EF | Unc |
|---|---|---|---|---|---|---|---|
| NY-NY 269 | 1876 | Silver | 42mm | — | — | — | 500. |

Signing of Declaration of Independence, THE / DECLARATION / OF INDEPENDENCE / 1776. Rv: Linen marker at center, inscribed N.G. SAMPSON. Above: H.G. SAMPSON, DEALER IN RARE AMERICAN & FOREIGN COINS, MEDALS & STAMPS. / COR. BROADWAY & FULTON ST. NEW YORK / 1876 / CENTENNIAL / LINEN MARKER / WHOLESALE & RETAIL. Below: MANUFACTORY, / * 91 BUSHWICK AV., BROOKLYN. * / E.D. Plain edge. (Miller NY 770)

| Rulau | Date | Metal | Size | F | VF | EF | Unc |
|---|---|---|---|---|---|---|---|
| NY-NY 269A | 1876 | Copper | 42mm | — | — | — | 150. |
| | | As 269. Plain edge. (Miller 771) | | | | | |
| NY-NY 269B | 1876 | Brass | 42mm | — | — | — | 150. |
| | | As 269. Plain edge. (Miller 772) | | | | | |
| NY-NY 269C | 1876 | WM | 42mm | — | — | — | 150. |
| | | As 269. Plain edge. (Wright 933; Miller NY 773) | | | | | |

| Rulau | Date | Metal | Size | F | VF | EF | Unc |
|---|---|---|---|---|---|---|---|
| NY-NY 270 | 1876 | Silver | 42mm | — | — | — | 500. |

Bust of Washington right at center, TO COMMEMORATE THE 100TH ANNIVERSARY OF THE above, DECLARATION OF / INDEPENDENCE below. Ornate border around all. Rv: As reverse of 269. Plain edge (Miller NY 774)

| Rulau | Date | Metal | Size | F | VF | EF | Unc |
|---|---|---|---|---|---|---|---|
| NY-NY 270A | 1876 | Copper | 42mm | — | — | — | 150. |
| | | As 270. Plain edge (Miller 775) | | | | | |
| NY-NY 270B | 1876 | Brass | 42mm | — | — | — | 150. |
| | | As 270. Plain edge. (Miller 776) | | | | | |
| NY-NY 270C | 1876 | WM | 42mm | — | — | — | 150. |
| | | As 270. Plain edge. (Miller 778) | | | | | |

# J.W. SCOTT & CO.
## New York, N.Y.

| Rulau | Date | Metal | Size | F | VF | EF | Unc |
|---|---|---|---|---|---|---|---|
| Pa-Ph 829 | (1870's) | WM | 30.6mm | — | 125. | 175. | 325. |

Confederate shield within wreath at center, Liberty cap as crest, CONFEDERATE STATES OF AMERICA above, = HALF DOL. = below. Rv: 4 ORIGINALS STRUCK BY ORDER / OF / C.S.A / IN / NEW ORLEANS / 1861 / ******* / REV. SAME AS / U.S. / (FROM ORIGINAL DIE, SCOTT). Only 500 struck.

Scott struck this token from the original Confederate half dollar reverse die, muling it with a special die of their own. The token has long been listed in R.S. Yeoman's *A Guide Book of United States Coins* (Red Book) under Confederate States of America.

### 1876 Centennial Tokens

Reverse type 1: 100 Y'RS OF NAT. IND. / 16 Y'RS / BUSINESS IN / COINS & STAMPS / —*— / J.W. SCOTT & CO. / 146 / FULTON ST. N.Y. (All 23mm; plain edge. Some Scott WM Centennial tokens were issued holed; value 15% less)

| Rulau | Obv | Rev | Metal | F | VF | EF | Unc |
|---|---|---|---|---|---|---|---|
| NY-NY 830 | A | 1 | WM | 4.00 | 7.50 | 10.00 | 20.00 |
| | | (Miller NY 801) | | | | | |
| NY-NY 830A | A | 1 | Copper | — | — | 12.50 | 25.00 |
| | | (Miller 799) | | | | | |
| NY-NY 830B | A | 1 | Brass | — | — | 15.00 | 30.00 |
| | | (Miller 800) | | | | | |

| Rulau | Obv | Rev | Metal | F | VF | EF | Unc |
|---|---|---|---|---|---|---|---|
| NY-NY 831 | B | 1 (Miller 788) | WM | — | — | 14.00 | 26.00 |
| NY-NY 831 A | B | 1 (Miller 786) | Copper | — | — | 15.00 | 30.00 |
| NY-NY 831 B | B | 1 (Miller 787) | Brass | — | — | 17.50 | 32.50 |
| NY-NY 832 | E | 1 (Miller 796) | WM | — | — | 14.00 | 26.00 |
| NY-NY 832 A | E | 1 Also in Bronze. (Miller 797) | Copper | — | — | 15.00 | 30.00 |
| NY-NY 832 B | E | 1 (Miller 795) | Brass | — | — | 17.50 | 35.00 |
| NY-NY 833 | F | 1 (Miller 791) | WM | — | — | 15.00 | 30.00 |
| NY-NY 833 A | F | 1 Also in Bronze. (Miller 789) | Copper | — | — | 17.50 | 35.00 |
| NY-NY 833 B | F | 1 (Miller 790) | Brass | — | — | 20.00 | 40.00 |
| NY-NY 834 | G | 1 Also in Bronze. | Copper | — | — | 17.50 | 35.00 |
| NY-NY 834 A | G | 1 (Miller 798) | Brass | — | — | 20.00 | 40.00 |
| NY-NY 835 | H | 1 (Miller 794) | WM | — | — | 15.00 | 30.00 |
| NY-NY 835 A | H | 1 Also in Bronze. (Miller 792) | Copper | — | — | 17.50 | 35.00 |
| NY-NY 835 B | H | 1 (Miller 793) | Brass | — | — | 20.00 | 40.00 |
| NY-NY 836 | J | 1 Also in Bronze. | Copper | — | — | 20.00 | 40.00 |
| NY-NY 837 | K | 1 | WM | — | — | 15.00 | 30.00 |
| NY-NY 837 A | K | 1 | Copper | — | — | 17.50 | 35.00 |
| NY-NY 837 B | K | 1 | Brass | — | — | 20.00 | 40.00 |

John W. Scott started his stamp and coin business in New York in 1860. Until at least World War I the Scott firm remained a giant in the coin business, and the name survives today in the Scott line of stamp catalogs (now published by others).

The Scott Centennial tokens are among the most common of these cards. They apparently were made in large variety and good quantity for distribution to customers. Since recipients were collectors, they tended to remain in numismatic channels.

Other varieties than those listed here may exist.

## SCHMITT & KOEHNE
### New York, N.Y.

| Rulau | Date | Metal | Size | VG | F | VF | Unc |
|---|---|---|---|---|---|---|---|
| NY-NY 270 | (1870's) | Brass | 23mm | — | — | — | 2 Known |

Coronet Liberty head left. Rv: SCHMITT & KOEHNE / 1 / * GLASS *. Plain edge.

This was a brewery.

## CHAS. SCHOELLER
### New York, N.Y.

| Rulau | Date | Metal | Size | VG | F | VF | EF |
|---|---|---|---|---|---|---|---|
| NY-NY 272 | (?) | Copper | 29mm | — | — | 50.00 | — |

CHAS. SCHOELLER N.Y. ctsp on U.S. Large cent. (Hallenbeck 19.517)

## SEITZ BROS.
### New York, N.Y.

| Rulau | Date | Metal | Size | VG | F | VF | Unc |
|---|---|---|---|---|---|---|---|
| NY-NY 275 | (1870's) | Brass | 23mm | 7.50 | 20.00 | 30.00 | — |

SEITZ BROS. ONE BIER. Rv: Female head. Plain edge. (Miller NY 807)

## W.C. SINCLAIR
### New York, N.Y.

| Rulau | Date | Metal | Size | VG | F | VF | EF |
|---|---|---|---|---|---|---|---|
| NY-NY 280 | (?) | Copper | 29mm | — | — | 50.00 | — |

W.C. SINCLAIR / N.Y. ctsp on U.S. 1819 Large cent. (Tanenbaum coll.; Brunk 346)

## R. SMITH
### New York, N.Y.

| Rulau | Date | Metal | Size | F | VF | EF | Unc |
|---|---|---|---|---|---|---|---|
| NY-NY 290 | (1870's) | Pewter | 23mm | — | — | — | Scrc |

Side-buttoned boot, * CUSTOM WORK * above; CORK SOLES / — * — / A SPECIALTY below. Rv: R. SMITH / BOOTS / & — / SHOES / 564 BROADWAY, N.Y. Thick planchet. Plain edge. (Wright 1005)

## SMITH & SEWARD
### New York, N.Y.

| Rulau | Date | Metal | Size | VG | F | VF | Unc |
|---|---|---|---|---|---|---|---|
| NY-NY 291 | (1889-90) | WM | 31.5mm | — | 15.00 | 22.50 | 30.00 |

Running horse. Rv: SMITH & SEWARD / MANUFACTURERS / OF / MEDALS / COINS / BADGES / 92 FULTON / 130 & 132 WILLIAM ST. / NEW YORK. Plain edge. (Miller NY 822)

| | | | | | | | |
|---|---|---|---|---|---|---|---|
| NY-NY 292 | (1889-90) | Alum | 31.5mm | — | — | 20.00 | 26.00 |

Crowned lion vampant left holding a battle axe, all within a wreath. Rv: As 291. Plain edge. (Wright 1010; Miller NY 821)

## STELLING
### New York, N.Y.

| Rulau | Date | Metal | Size | VG | F | VF | EF |
|---|---|---|---|---|---|---|---|
| NY-NY 295 | (1870's) | Silver | 25mm | — | 150. | — | 300. |

STELLING / 31 / OLD SLIP ctsp on U.S. 1854 Seated Liberty quarter dollar. (Schenkman collection)

| | | | | | | | |
|---|---|---|---|---|---|---|---|
| NY-NY 296 | (1870's) | Silver | 25mm | — | 150. | — | 300. |

Similar ctsp on U.S. 1857 Liberty Seated quarter. (Tanenbaum collection; Brunk 356)

John Stelling is listed as a liquor dealer at 31 Old Slip during the early 1870's.

## STINER TEA COMPANY
### New York, N.Y.

| Rulau | Date | Metal | Size | F | VF | EF | Unc |
|---|---|---|---|---|---|---|---|
| NY-NY 300 | (1876) | WM | 39mm | — | — | 20.00 | 50.00 |

Independence Hall, INDEPENDENCE HALL / 1776. Rv: 77 79 81 84 86 / * VESEY ST. N.Y. * / STINERS / N.Y. & CHINA / TEA / COMPANY. / M.H. MOSES & CO. / PROP'S. Plain edge. (Miller NY 838)

| NY-NY 301 | (1876) | Copper | 39mm | — | — | 20.00 | 50.00 |

As 300. (Miller NY 838A)

| NY-NY 302 | (1876) | Brass | 39mm | — | — | 20.00 | 50.00 |

As 300.

| NY-NY 303 | (1876) | Alum | 39mm | — | — | — | Unique? |

As 300. Aluminum was a very rare metal at this time.

| NY-NY 304 | (1876) | Leather | 39mm | — | — | — | Rare |

As 300.

| NY-NY 307 | (1876) | Brass | 39mm | — | — | 20.00 | 50.00 |

Liberty Bell, THE LIBERTY BELL above. Below: LEVITICUS XXV PROCLAIM LIBERTY THROUGH THE LAND UNTO ALL THE INHABITANTS THEREOF * . Rv: As 300. Plain edge. (Wright 1057)

| NY-NY 308 | (1876) | Copper | 39mm | — | — | 20.00 | 50.00 |

As 307.

| NY-NY 309 | (1876) | Bronze | 39mm | — | — | 20.00 | 50.00 |

As 307.

This firm was founded in 1840 and also issued tokens in the Merchant period before the Civil War. A Joseph Stiner & Co. Inc. were in the business of groceries, etc. in 1918.

A group of five Stiner Tea Co. pieces in proof, including the aluminum specimen, 303, and another piece struck on leather, 304, was offered by Morty Zerder, New York, in April 1982 for $1,000.

NY-NY 301 is also known in bronze.

In the 1872 directory, Joseph Stiner and Co., tea dealers, are listed in Brooklyn, N.Y., at 255 Grand and at Myrtle Ave. corner Prince.

## TRAPHAGEN, HUNTER & CO.
### New York, N.Y.

**1876 Centennial Tokens**

Reverse type 1: TRAPHAGEN, HUNTER & CO. / LEADING CLOTHIERS / FINE GOODS / AT / LOWEST / PRICES / 398, 400 & 402 / BOWERY, N.Y. (All 23mm; plain edge)

Reverse type 2: Similar, but crude lettering. (All 23mm; plain edge)

| Rulau | Obv | Rev | Metal | F | VF | EF | Unc |
|---|---|---|---|---|---|---|---|
| NY-NY 850 | A | 1 | WM | 5.00 | 8.00 | 11.00 | 20.00 |

(Miller NY 915)

| NY-NY 850 A | A | 1 | Brass | — | — | 14.00 | 30.00 |
| NY-NY 851 | B | 1 | WM | — | — | 12.50 | 25.00 |
| NY-NY 851 A | B | 1 | Brass | — | — | 20.00 | 40.00 |
| NY-NY 852 | D | 1 | WM | — | — | 15.00 | 30.00 |
| NY-NY 853 | E | 1 | WM | — | — | 12.50 | 25.00 |
| NY-NY 853 A | E | 1 | Copper | — | — | 15.00 | 30.00 |

(Miller 918)

| NY-NY 854 | F | 1 | WM | — | — | 15.00 | 30.00 |
| NY-NY 855 | G | 1 | WM | — | — | 14.00 | 30.00 |

(Miller 917)

| NY-NY 856 | H | 1 | WM | — | — | 15.00 | 30.00 |
| NY-NY 856 A | H | 1 | Copper | — | — | 17.50 | 40.00 |

(Miller 916)

| NY-NY 857 | K | 1 | WM | — | — | 15.00 | 30.00 |

(Wright 1155; Miller 915A)

| NY-NY 860 | A | 2 | WM | — | — | 15.00 | 30.00 |
| NY-NY 861 | H | 2 | WM | — | — | 15.00 | 30.00 |
| NY-NY 862 | K | 2 | WM | — | — | 15.00 | 30.00 |

## TRUCK DRIVERS B & P ASSOCIATION
### New York, N.Y. ?

| Rulau | Date | Metal | Size | VG | F | VF | Unc |
|---|---|---|---|---|---|---|---|
| NY-NY 325 | (1880's) | CN | 25mm | — | — | 75.00 | — |

Prancing horse to left within central beaded circle. Around: TRUCK DRIVERS B & P ASSOCIATION. There is a numeral, 176, stamped at bottom. Rv: Blank. Plain edge. (N.Y. Public Library sale, Oct. 30, 1982)

The Truck Drivers Benevolent and Protective Association was apparently an insurance-linked society serving early teamsters. This may have been a fraternal badge.

## TRUESDALE
### New York, N.Y.

| Rulau | Date | Metal | Size | VG | F | VF | EF |
|---|---|---|---|---|---|---|---|
| NY-NY 330 | (?) | Copper | 29mm | | | | |

TRUESDALE / N-YORK ctsp on U.S. Large cent. (Hallenbeck 20.756)

## THE UNION COFFEE CO. LIMITED
### New York, N.Y.

| Rulau | Date | Metal | Size | VG | F | VF | Unc |
|---|---|---|---|---|---|---|---|
| NY-NY 340 | (1880's) | WM | 40mm | — | 10.00 | 25.00 | 40.00 |

Female head right, ALAROMA BUNOLA around, MARY ANDERSON below. Rv: UCCo monogram at center, THE UNION COFFEE CO. LIMITED around, * NEW YORK * below. Plain edge.

| Rulau | Date | Metal | Size | VG | F | VF | Unc |
|---|---|---|---|---|---|---|---|
| NY-NY 341 | (1880's) | WM | 40mm | — | 10.00 | 25.00 | 40.00 |

Female head left, ALAROMA BUNOLA around, ADELINA PATTI below. Rv: As last. Plain edge. (Wright 1132)

Alaroma and Bunola may have been brand names of the coffee U.C. Co. sold.

The Union Coffee Co. Ltd. of New York also issued tokens in hard rubber in the 1890's depicting presidents of the U.S. These also mention Alaroma and Bunola. (See *TAMS Journal* for Oct. 1977, page 182)

Adelina Patti and Mary Anderson apparently were actresses. There are more metal tokens in this series which have not yet been reported, perhaps 10 or so. Adelina Patti-Nicolini owned Craig-y-nos Castle in Wales (see outside back cover of *TAMS Journal* for June 1977)

One contributor reports seeing 25 different in metal and various colors of hard rubber, but has no details.

## VALENTINE & COMPANY
## New York, N.Y.

| Rulau | Date | Metal | Size | F | VF | Unc | P-L |
|---|---|---|---|---|---|---|---|
| NY-NY 350 | 1882 | Alum | 35mm | — | — | 10.00 | 35.00 |

VALENTINE & COMPANY / * / NEW YORK / CHICAGO / BOSTON / PARIS / ESTABLISHED / 1832. Rv: THE STANDARD FOR QUALITY / * / VALENTINES VARNISHES (these two words share the VA, N and ES in two lines) / INCORPORATED / 1882. Plain edge. (Wright 1180)

Probably issued about 1900.

## J.W.
## New York, N.Y.

| Rulau | Date | Metal | Size | VG | F | VF | EF |
|---|---|---|---|---|---|---|---|
| NY-NY 360 | (?) | Copper | 29mm | — | — | 50.00 | — |

J.W. N-Y in relief within rectangular depression ctsp on U.S. 1820 Large cent. (Tanenbaum coll.)

The counterstamp appears to be a silversmith's hallmark of New York City.

## HORACE WATERS & SONS
## New York, N.Y.

| Rulau | Date | Metal | Size | F | VF | EF | Unc |
|---|---|---|---|---|---|---|---|
| NY-NY 364 | 1876 | WM | 24mm | 5.00 | 6.50 | 8.00 | 25.00 |

Organ of ornate design at center, small cross above organ and around: WATERS' CENTENNIAL CONCERTO ORGAN. .1876. below. Rv: HORACE WATERS & SONS / 481 / BROADWAY / NEW YORK. / PIANOS / & / ORGANS. Plain edge. (Wright 1207; Miller NY 941)

| Rulau | Date | Metal | Size | F | VF | EF | Unc |
|---|---|---|---|---|---|---|---|
| NY-NY 365 | 1876 | WM | 24mm | 5.00 | 6.50 | 8.00 | 35.00 |

As 941, but no cross above organ, which is of a different type. (Miller NY 942)

## WASHINGTON INAUGURAL CENTENNIAL
## New York, N.Y.

| Rulau | Date | Metal | Size | F | VF | EF | Unc |
|---|---|---|---|---|---|---|---|
| NY-NY 362 | 1889 | WM | 26mm | — | — | 25.00 | 40.00 |

Washington bust right, encircled by thick ornate border. Rv: — — / WASHINGTON / * / INAUGURAL / CENTENNIAL / * 1789 . 1889 * / NEW YORK CITY. Plain edge.

| | | | | | | | |
|---|---|---|---|---|---|---|---|
| NY-NY 362 F | 1889 | G/Brass | 20mm | — | — | 12.50 | 22.50 |

Washington head right, GEO. WASHINGTON FIRST PRES'T U. S. around, . 1789 . below. Rv: * CENTENNIAL OF HIS INAUGURATION / NEW YORK / APRIL 30, / 1889. Plain edge.

## HUGO WELLENKAMP
## New York, N.Y.

| Rulau | Date | Metal | Size | VG | F | VF | Unc |
|---|---|---|---|---|---|---|---|
| NY-NY 370 | (1863) | Brass | 27mm | 150. | 200. | 250. | 350. |

HUGO WELLENKAMP / COLOSSEUM / x 53 BOWERY. N.Y. x Rv: Blank (intaglio of obverse). All lettering incuse. (Miller NY 946)

Adams lists two pieces, 946 and 947, and says of 947 "Same, inscription, but different die. Brass."

There is little known of this piece or the issuer. It was not listed in the original list of New York City store cards issued in 1885, 1886 and 1887 Coin Collectors Journal. However these pieces were used in the Civil War period as several pieces are from the collection assembled and sold by Doctor George R. Bond on July 18, 1863 and stated by him to be used during the Civil War.

The Fulds were fortunate to have tokens classified by Adams as his 946 and 947. These pieces all are struck by an incuse punch. The planchets are crude, each one being different thickness and some of the edges are rough. It is believed that the punch used in striking these pieces consisted of a slot into which the word COLOSSEUM was inserted. The piece used was no doubt a very crude affair and the pressure used was varied giving different appearances to the pieces. Adams 946 is very thin. There are five minor varieties. Wellenkamp was at 57½ Bowery in 1862 and 53 Bowery in 1863.

## E. WELTECK
### New York, N.Y.

| Rulau | Date | Metal | Size | VG | F | VF | Unc |
|---|---|---|---|---|---|---|---|
| NY-NY 373 | (1876) | Brass | 23mm | — | — | | 1 Known |

Coronet Liberty head left. Rv: E. WELTECK / N.Y. / 92 CLINTON ST. Plain edge.

Ernest Welteck operated a beer parlor or a brewery.

## I.F.W.
### (Isaac F. Wood)
### New York, N.Y.

| Rulau | Date | Metal | Size | F | VF | EF | Unc |
|---|---|---|---|---|---|---|---|
| NY-NY 395 | 1877 | Brass | 21mm | — | — | 17.00 | 27.50 |

Military bust of Grant right, GENERAL U.S. GRANT around, PRESS 1869 TO '77 (on scroll) below. Rv: TO HIM THAT HATH SHALL BE GIVEN / CIVIS EDINBURGENSIS / AUG. / 31. 1877 / HER / YOUNGEST / BURGESS / I.F.W. / DES. Plain edge.

| NY-NY 395A | 1877 | Copper | 21mm | — | — | 17.00 | 27.50 |

As 395. Plain edge.

Designed by Isaac F. Woods of New York City. The dies were cut by George Hampden Lovett of the same city. Woods is also responsible for the Cogan "English Daddy" pieces of Brooklyn, N.Y., and the Boston Numismatic Society medalet, both catalogued in this reference.

## J.G. WILSON
### New York, N.Y.

| Rulau | Date | Metal | Size | VG | F | VF | EF |
|---|---|---|---|---|---|---|---|
| NY-NY 380 | (?) | Copper | 29mm | — | — | — | — |

J.G. WILSON / GAS FILTER / 39 CENTRE ST. / N.Y. ctsp on U.S. Large cent. (Hallenbeck 23.539)

## WOLFE'S SCHIEDAM SCHNAPPS
### New York, N.Y.

| Rulau | Date | Metal | Size | F | VF | EF | Unc |
|---|---|---|---|---|---|---|---|
| NY-NY 390 | (1868) | WM | 26mm | 5.00 | 10.00 | 15.00 | 35.00 |

WOLFES SCHIEDAM SCHNAPPS / FOR SALE / BY ALL / GROCERS / & / DRUGGISTS / *. Rv: DEW OF THE ALPS / AGENT / 22 / BEAVER ST. / NEW YORK. Plain edge. (Wright 1732; Miller NY 956)

At 22 Beaver St. in 1868.

## Y. & CO.
### (Yuengling & Co.)
### New York, N.Y.

| Rulau | Date | Metal | Size | F | VF | EF | Unc |
|---|---|---|---|---|---|---|---|
| NY-NY 400 | (1870's) | Brass | 22mm | 4.00 | 10.00 | 15.00 | 40.00 |

Liberty head of type of 1857 Large cent, left. Rv: Y & CO. / * 1 * / GLASS. Plain edge. (Miller NY 1006)

Yuengling & Co. were brewers in New York City and this token was good for one glass of their beer.

## ZELTNER & CO.
### New York, N.Y.

| Rulau | Date | Metal | Size | F | VF | EF | Unc |
|---|---|---|---|---|---|---|---|
| NY-NY 415 | (1870's) | Brass | 22mm | — | — | 17.50 | — |

Obverse as NY-NY 400 (Y. & CO. Liberty head). Rv: ZELTNER & CO. / * 1 * / GLASS. Plain edge. (Fuld coll.)

## W.P. DAVIS
### North Bloomfield, N.Y.

| Rulau | Date | Metal | Size | VG | F | VF | EF |
|---|---|---|---|---|---|---|---|
| NY-NB 1 | (?) | CN | 19mm | — | — | 200. | — |

W.P. DAVIS / ENGINE CALENDER / & / TILE / MACHINE / MANFR / NO. BLOOMFIELD N.Y. ctsp on reverse of U.S. 1863 Indian cent. Letter 'C' incused six times on obv. of coin. (Tanenbaum coll.)

## M.L. MARSHALL
### Oswego, N.Y.

NOTE: Tokens of this 1862 design are Civil War store cards now listed in the Fuld reference.

Morgan L. Marshall also issued 1860-dated tokens in the Merchant era and smaller, 1863-dated pieces in the Civil War period.

# OSWEGO STARCH FACTORY
## Oswego, N.Y.

| Rulau | Date | Metal | Size | VG | F | VF | Unc |
|---|---|---|---|---|---|---|---|
| NY-Os 20 | 1873 | CN | 28mm | 15.00 | 25.00 | 35.00 | 50.00 |

Cornstalk in center, OSWEGO STARCH FACTORY around, 1873. below. Rv: Eagle with drooping wings at top, ONE / BARREL FEED / T.K. in three lines below. Plain edge. Very rare.

In 1842 Thomas Kingsford invented a process of extracting starch from Indian corn or maize, and became the first person to put into successful operation the method of preparing "corn starch." He incorporated the Oswego Starch Factory in Oswego, N.Y. in 1848. By the 1870's, when the token was issued, the firm had become known as T. Kingsford & Son, Oswego Starch Factory.

A booklet published by the firm in 1876 in connection with the Centennial observances in Philadelphia, where Oswego Corn Starch (edible) and Oswego Silver Gloss Starch (for laundry) won medals, reveals that Dr. S. Willard was president of the firm at that time. Other officers included Nelson Beardsley, vice president, and A.G. Beardsley, secretary and treasurer. Thomson Kingsford was listed among the directors.

The T.K. on the 1873 token stands for Thomas Kingsford. The 'One Barrel Feed' denomination was for semi-liquid "feed starch" used as cattle feed. The token is apparently quite scarce, the author having examined only six different pieces in more than 12 years. Still, a hoard may exist somewhere.

The Oswego Starch Factory appears in the 1890 *Bradstreet Directory*, where it is revealed it had a paid-in capital of $500,000. In 1890 T. Kingsford & Son Inc. is listed as a manufacturer of starches, also. In 1899 Thomson Kingsford formed U.S. Starch Co. from his firm and many smaller ones. In 1900 U.S. Starch Co. and its rival, National Starch Co., united under the latter name. The Oswego branch of National Starch Co. appears in the 1905 and 1909 directories under T. Kingsford & Son. In 1923 it closed.

## PHOENIX KNIFE CO.
### Phoenix, N.Y.

| Rulau | Date | Metal | Size | VG | F | VF | EF |
|---|---|---|---|---|---|---|---|
| NY-Px 7 | (1886) | Silver | 18mm | — | — | 100. | — |

PHOENIX KNIFE / CO. / PHOENIX, N.Y. ctsp on U.S. 1884 Seated Liberty dime. (Gary Pipher coll.)

The Phoenix Knife Co. was no longer lised in the 1890 *Bradstreet Directory*, though a Central City Knife Co. is, which might be connected.

## SARGENT & GREENLEAF
### Rochester, N.Y.

 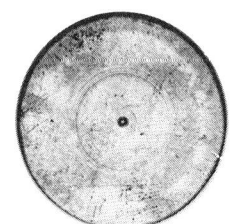

| Rulau | Date | Metal | Size | F | VF | EF | Unc |
|---|---|---|---|---|---|---|---|
| NY-Ro 9 | 1871 | S/Brass | 29mm | — | — | 35.00 | — |

(All incuse) SARGENT & GREENLEAF / PAT'D / SEP. 18. 1860 / JAN. 9. 1866 / AUG. 28. 1866 / JULY 14. 1857 / EX. 7 YEARS / JULY 14. 1871 / ROCHESTER. N.Y. Rv: Blank. Plain edge.

Sargent & Greenleaf were manufacturers of locks. Presumably the patent dates on the token are for S&L locks. The company appears in all directories through at least 1918.

## ROME BRASS & COPPER CO.
### Rome, N.Y.

 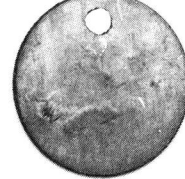

| Rulau | Date | Metal | Size | VG | F | VF | Unc |
|---|---|---|---|---|---|---|---|
| NY-Rm 14 | (?) | Brass* | 25mm | 2.50 | 3.75 | 4.75 | 11.00 |

* These pieces occur in both Brass and Copper. NO (backward N) near top center above blank central space; ROME. BRASS & COPPER. CO. around. (Number stamped in center). Rv: ROME. NEW. YORK. along bottom rim. Dentilated rims on each side. Plain edge. Issued holed. (Counterstamps examined: 3; 3 (large); 3 / NG; 4 /

| Rulau | Date | Metal | Size | VG | F | VF | Unc |
|---|---|---|---|---|---|---|---|
| | | SPRING; 9 / SPRING; 10; 10 (Rev: 6); 11 / SPRING; 14; 14 / SPRING; 14 / N.G. / HARD; 16; AR 16 (Rev: G. H, EDG); 18; 19; 20; 20 / B AND / SOFT; 22; 23 / SPRING; 24; 161; 0335) (Rulau-Miller NY 2089) | | | | | |
| NY-Rm 15 | (?) | Copper | 25mm | — | 3.75 | 4.75 | 11.00 |

Similar to 14, but N of NO is normal. There is no counterstamped numeral. Plain edge. Issued holed.

Though dates of use of these workmen's or job checks are still not known, it seems probable they were in use after, rather than before, the Civil War. Thus they will no longer be listed in our 1845-60 volume.

In 1899 the Rome Brass & Copper Co. had two mills, one for brass and one for copper, in Rome, according to city maps of that year. One rolling mill, for brass, was at Dominick and Bouck Streets, along the Mohawk River. The copper mill and its outbuildings were on both sides of the Black River Canal.

It is probable the work checks were in use in the 1860's or 1870's. They greatly resemble those of the Rome Iron Works, and the work checks in use in Connecticut and listed in *U.S. Merchant Tokens*.

## ROME IRON WORKS
### Rome, N.Y.

| Rulau | Date | Metal | Size | VG | F | VF | Unc |
|---|---|---|---|---|---|---|---|
| NY-Rm 20 | (1868-90) | Brass* | 24mm | 3.50 | 6.00 | 8.00 | 20.00 |

* These pieces occur in either Brass or Copper. NO / (blank space) / ROME IRON WORKS. Rv: ROME NEW YORK. Plain edge. Issued holed. Issued without counterstamp.

| NY-Rm 22 | (1868-90) | Brass* | 24mm | 3.50 | 6.00 | 8.00 | — |

As 20, but with various counterstamps applied. Specimens examined: 3; 5; 5 / MARKET; 9; 10 / HARD; 10 / SPRING; 14; 15 / SPRING; 16; 17; 18; 19; 21 / SOFT; 22 / NG; 30 / N.G. (Wright 913 was number 17) *These pieces occur in either Brass or Copper. Several specimens were examined with numbers 14, 16 and 18, in both metals.

Rome Iron Works was founded in 1868. It was still so named in the 1891 *Americanized Encyclopaedia Britannica*. The same firm, called Rome Iron Mills, Inc., manufactures chain link fences today at 416 Canal Street in Rome. It had 125 employees in 1980, but work is seasonal. It is owned by the Oliver family today.

## FIREMAN'S CONVENTION
### Syracuse, N.Y.

| Rulau | Date | Metal | Size | F | VF | EF | Unc |
|---|---|---|---|---|---|---|---|
| NY-Sy 6 | 1885 | WM | 24mm | — | 30.00 | — | — |

Fire engine, FIREMANS * CONVENTION *. Rv: SYRACUSE / SOUVENIR / AUG. 11-14, 1885. Plain edge. (Wright 1085)

## S.M. HENRY
### Syracuse, N.Y.

| Rulau | Date | Metal | Size | F | VF | EF | Unc |
|---|---|---|---|---|---|---|---|
| NY-Sy 9 | (?) | Brass | Oval, 32 by 19mm | — | 15.00 | — | — |

Eagle and scrollwork. S.M. HENRY / 484 BASTABLE / CITY. Rv: Blank. Plain edge. (Wright 1451)

The Bastable Block is in Syracuse, N.Y.

*Bastable Block, Syracuse, Ca. 1907*

## J H
## (John Hinkson)
## Utica, N.Y.

| Rulau | Date | Metal | Size | F | VF | EF | Unc |
|---|---|---|---|---|---|---|---|
| NY-Ut 6 | (?) | Brass | 24mm | — | — | — | — |

J 5 H / R. Rv: Blank. Plain edge. (Wright 510)

John Hinkson was a saloon proprietor, according to Dr. B. P. Wright in 1898.

## J. E. H. KELLY
## Utica, N.Y.

| Rulau | Date | Metal | Size | VG | F | VF | Unc |
|---|---|---|---|---|---|---|---|
| NY-Ut 9 | (?) | GS | Oval, 35 by 21mm | — | — | — | 2 Known |

Eagle facing left. Three scrolls beneath: J. E. H. KELLY / KELLY'S HOTEL / UTICA, N.Y. Rv: Blank. Plain edge. (Wright 541)

## W.I. MARTIN
## Utica, N.Y.

| Rulau | Date | Metal | Size | VG | F | VF | Unc |
|---|---|---|---|---|---|---|---|
| NY-Ut 11 | (?) | Copper | 35mm | — | — | — | — |
| NY-Ut 12 | (?) | GS | 29mm | — | — | — | — |
| NY-Ut 13 | (?) | GS | 29mm | — | — | — | — |
| NY-UT 14 | (?) | GS | 29mm | — | — | — | — |
| NY-Ut 15 | (?) | GS | 29mm | — | — | — | — |

NY-Ut 11: (All incused) MARTINS / 5 / 130 GENESEE ST. Plain edge.
NY-Ut 12: W.I. MARTIN / UTICA / N.Y. / 130 GENESEE ST. Rv: Same as obverse. Plain edge.
NY-Ut 13: W.I. MARTIN / 10 / 130 GENESEE ST. Rv: Same. Plain edge.
NY-Ut 14: Similar to 13, but 20. Plain edge.
NY-Ut 15: Similar to 13, but 75. Plain edge.

## WM. SEDGWICK
## Waverly, N.Y.

### 1876 Centennial Tokens

Reverse type 1: WM. SEDGWICK / WATCHMAKER / — * — / WAVERLY, N.Y. / LOOK WELL TO YOUR TIME. (All 19mm; plain edge)

| Rulau | Obv | Rev | Metal | F | VF | EF | Unc |
|---|---|---|---|---|---|---|---|
| NY-Wv 8 | X | 1 | WM | — | 7.50 | 15.00 | 40.00 |
| Pa-Wv 8A | X | 1 | Copper | — | — | 15.00 | 40.00 |
| NY-Wv 8B | X | 1 | Brass | — | — | 15.00 | 40.00 |
| NY-Wv 9 | Y | 1 | WM | — | 10.00 | 17.50 | 45.00 |
| NY-Wv 9A | Y | 1 | Copper | — | — | 17.50 | 45.00 |
| NY-Wv 10 | V | 1 | Brass | — | — | 30.00 | 55.00 |

(Miller NY 1067) on NY-Wv 8; (Miller 1067A; Wright 971) on Pa-Wv 8A; Also in Bronze on NY-Wv 9A.

These are the easiest to obtain of the 19mm tokens in the Centennial series, though all 19mm pieces are difficult in relation to the 23mm tokens.

## DEUTSCHLAND'S FRIEDENSFEIER
## Williamsburgh, N.Y.

| Rulau | Date | Metal | Size | F | VF | EF | Unc |
|---|---|---|---|---|---|---|---|
| NY-Wm 4 | 1871 | Copper | 35.4mm | — | — | — | — |

Germania with sword and shield standing on a bluff overlooking the Rhine River, a circle of dots around all. Rv: Small Iron Cross at top. Below: DEUTSCHLAND'S FRIEDENSFEIER WILLIAMSBURGH 10TEN APRIL 1871 (Germany's peace celebration). Plain edge. Weight 14.5 grams.

Designed by Emil Sigel, New York.
Williamsburgh was annexed to Brooklyn in 1855; Brooklyn became a part of New York in 1898. Long after its annexation by Brooklyn, Williamsburgh was still known by that name to its residents and others.
(See Milwaukier Friedens-Feier, Milwaukee, Wis., in this reference.)

## N. Y. N. G. 7TH REGT.
### (New York National Guard, 7th Regiment)
### New York

| Rulau | Date | Metal | Size | F | VF | EF | Unc |
|---|---|---|---|---|---|---|---|
| NY-NL 1 | 1875 | Copper | 30mm | — | — | — | — |

Battle of Bunker Hill Centennial 1775-1875. NYNG 7TH REGT. VISIT.

## N.Y & N.E.R.R
### New York ?

| Rulau | Date | Metal | Size | VG | F | VF | EF |
|---|---|---|---|---|---|---|---|
| NY-Un 20 | (?) | CN | 19mm | — | 100. | — | — |

N.Y. & N.E.R.R / .MAL (?) & PRESS CO in relief ctsp on reverse of U.S. 1861 Indian cent. Large '72' in relief on obv. of coin. (The uncertain word in ctsp is struck partly off the flan and is indistinct)

New York and New England Railroad, Engine No. 72?

## A. BELL
### Yonkers, N.Y.

| Rulau | Date | Metal | Size | VG | F | VF | Unc |
|---|---|---|---|---|---|---|---|
| NY-Yk 1 | (1880's) | Copper | 29mm | — | — | 200. | — |

(All retrograde) YONKES / (script) A. Bell / 1854 amid flourishes, in relief, ctsp on U.S. Large cent of the final type. (The plate token from the Benjamin Betts sale, 1898; it sold in a 1977 auction for $115.). Probably unique. (Miller NY 1069)

We have no evidence, but this piece's provenance and its appearance suggest it may have been another of the fantasy concoctions of C. Wyllys Betts (see examples under his name in New Haven, Conn.), and thus we assign an 1880's date to its creation.

Thanks to the kindness of Kenneth Bressett, we examined film negatives of many of Betts' concoctions from the Norweb, ANS and other holdings — all made, presumably, for his own amusement and all rare or unique. Those resembling store cards are included in this reference (see C.W. Betts and Hussey & Murray, New Haven, Conn., and Butler & Bee, East Bay, L.I., N.Y.)

## J.W. GASPER
### New York (?)

| Rulau | Date | Metal | Size | VG | F | VF | Unc |
|---|---|---|---|---|---|---|---|
| NY-Un 11 | (?) | Brass | 24mm | — | — | 8.00 | — |

NEW YORK / —*— / BAKERY. / —*— / J.W. GASPER. Rv: GOOD FOR / — 1 — / LOAF / OF / BREAD. Plain edge

# NORTH CAROLINA

## TUCKASEEGE MFG. CO.
### Gaston County, N.C.

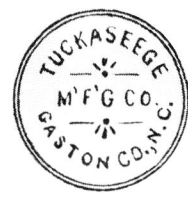 

| Rulau | Date | Metal | Size | F | VF | EF | Unc |
|---|---|---|---|---|---|---|---|
| NC-Gs 3 | (1880's) | CN | 25.5mm | 8.50 | 15.00 | — | — |

TUCKASEEGE / (ornament) / M'F'G CO / (ornament) / GASTON CO., N.C. Rv: Large 25 within rays. (Wright 1164)

## W. BONITZ
### Goldsboro, N.C.

| Rulau | Date | Metal | Size | VG | F | VF | Unc |
|---|---|---|---|---|---|---|---|
| NC-Go 1 | (1870's) | Brass | 20mm | — | — | — | 2 Known |

W. BONITZ / * / .. x .. / * / GOLDSBORO, N.C. Rv: Numeral 5 surrounded by a wreath, a star in the opening at top. Plain edge.

John Henry William Bonitz, born 1839 in Zellerfeld, Germany, came to Goldsboro 1859, buying out the general store of one Hernglaus. His brother Julius Augustus Bonitz joined him in April, 1861, and the pair also operated a printing business. Julius became a newspaperman after the Civil War, removing to Wilmington, N.C. in 1887. In the early 1870's William, as J.H.W. Bonitz was known, built the Bonitz Hotel but this burned in 1872. In 1876 he opened a restaurant, and then The Arlington (a hotel) in 1882, also known as Bonitz House. Before 1900 William moved to Wilmington, where he ran another hotel and where he died in 1913. The token is probably the work of Koehler of Baltimore.

# OHIO

## ATLANTIC BILLIARD HALL
### Cincinnati, Ohio

| Rulau | Date | Metal | Size | VG | F | VF | Unc |
|---|---|---|---|---|---|---|---|
| Oh-Ci 2 | (1866-80) | Brass | 22mm | — | — | 10.00 | — |

ATLANTIC / —*— / H. W. C. / —*— / * BILLIARD HALL *. RV: Large numeral 5 in circle of 16 stars. In tiny letters below: JAS. MURDOCK JR. 165 RACE ST CINTI O. Reeded edge.

| Oh-Ci 4 | (1880's) | Brass | 22mm | — | — | 6.50 | — |

ATLANTIC / * BILLIARD / — / * HALL * / (crossed cue sticks and four balls) / ED. L. LINZ. Rv: Nine stars in an arc above: 5 / CENTS. Plain edge.

In 1889 the Atlantic Billiard Hall, connected with an Atlantic Garden at the same location, was at 245 Vine Street. It was a combination restaurant, saloon and billiard parlor.

'H. W. C.' and Ed. L. Linz were apparently proprietors of the establishment. Dates are estimates.

## BELLEVUE HOUSE
### Cincinnati, Ohio

| Rulau | Date | Metal | Size | VG | F | VF | Unc |
|---|---|---|---|---|---|---|---|
| Oh-Ci 7 | (1876-80) | Copper | --mm | — | — | 10.00 | — |

BELLEVUE HOUSE / CINCINNATI O. Rv: 16 stars in a circle. Plain edge.

Bellevue House was at the head of the Bellevue Inclined Plane railway, which opened for traffic in 1876. Bellevue House was still in business in 1889.

(See Lookout House for a discussion of the resorts on the hills)

## BILLIGHEIMER'S BILLIARD HALL
### Cincinnati, Ohio

| Rulau | Date | Metal | Size | VG | F | VF | Unc |
|---|---|---|---|---|---|---|---|
| Oh-Ci 9 | (1880-88) | Copper | 22mm | — | — | 9.50 | — |

BILLIGHEIMER'S / BILLIARD / HALL / NOS. 210 & 212 / VINE ST / CINCINNATI, O. Rv: Large 5 in circle of 16 stars. Below: Tiny JAS. MURDOCK JR. 165 RACE ST. CIN O. Plain edge.

| Oh-Ci 10 | (1888-89) | CN | 22mm | — | — | 9.50 | — |

THE TIEMAN / BILLIARD / HALL / 210 & 212 VINE ST / CIN. O. / D. L. BILLIGHEIMER. Rv: Same as last (5 in circle of 16 stars) Plain edge.

David (or Dave) L. Billigheimer was in business with a billiard hall and saloon from 1880 to 1895 at 210 and 212 Vine St. In 1889 he was also operating another saloon at the southeast corner of John and 9th.

The tokens were struck by Murdock.

## E. J. BRAUNEIS
### Cincinnati, Ohio

| Rulau | Date | Metal | Size | VG | F | VF | Unc |
|---|---|---|---|---|---|---|---|
| Oh-Ci 12 | (1880's) | Brass | 24mm | — | — | 7.50 | — |

E. J. BRAUNEIS * / * 5 / CINCINNATI, O. Rv: ZOOLOGICAL * / 5 / GARDEN *. Plain edge. (Wright 51)

## BURNS FOLZ & SONS
### Cincinnati, Ohio

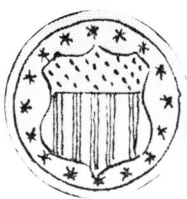 

| Rulau | Date | Metal | Size | VG | F | VF | Unc |
|---|---|---|---|---|---|---|---|
| Oh-Ci 14 | (?) | Brass | 26mm | — | — | 20.00 | — |

BURNS FOLZ & SONS / GOOD / FOR ONE / 2 / HORSE LOAD / * CINCINNATI OHIO *. Rv: U.S. shield encircled by 16 stars. Plain edge. (Wright 124)

This firm has not been traced. However, in 1889 there was one Amos Burns, contractor for unloading boats, at the southeast corner of 2nd and Broadway, who likely is connected.

This is undoubtedly a drayage check.

## LOOKOUT HOUSE
### Cincinnati, Ohio

| Rulau | Date | Metal | Size | VG | F | VF | Unc |
|---|---|---|---|---|---|---|---|
| Oh-Ci 30 | (1872-76) | Brass | 22mm | — | — | 10.00 | — |

GEO. KEMMETER & CO. / (leaf) 5 (Leaf) / CINCINNATI / * / * O *. Rv: LOOKOUT / . / HOUSE / * 5 * / JACKSON HILL. (Miller Oh 17)

| Oh-Ci 31 | (1872-76) | GS | 22mm | — | — | 12.50 | — |

As last, but numeral 20 on each side. (Miller Oh 18)

Lookout House, one of Cincinnati's hilltop resorts and beer gardens, was at the northwest corner of Locust and Mount in Mount Auburn. It was atop Jackson Hill, north of the downtown section of Cincinnati. (Mount Auburn was annexed to Cincinnati in 1870.)

Lookout House was still in business in 1889. The Mount Auburn Inclined Plane railway was opened in 1872, easing the burden of citizens to reach the summit of Jackson Hill and the Lookout House.

## RESORTS ON THE HILLS

Closely connected with the development of the inclined plane railways of Cincinnati were the famous resorts and beer gardens atop the hills which these special railways served. On the east on Mount Adams was Highland House, the largest; on the north Lookout House atop Jackson Hill, served by the Mount Auburn Inclined Plane Railway; also on the north Bellevue House served by the Bellevue Inclined Plane Railway, and on the west Price Hill House served by the Price Hill Inclined Plane Railway.

In 1877, historian Henry Howe wrote, "At the summit of these planes are immense beer gardens with mammoth buildings, where on stifling summer nights the city hive swarms out thousands upon thousands of all classes and nationalities, who thus come together and alike yield to the potent influences of music and lager."

## J. B. NEEB
### Cincinnati, Ohio

| Rulau | Date | Metal | Size | VG | F | VF | Unc |
|---|---|---|---|---|---|---|---|
| Oh-Ci 35 | (1870's) | CN | Oval, 21 by 17mm | — | — | 20.00 | — |

MOUNT AUBURN / —.— / GARDEN / —.— / * CINCINNATI *. Rv: * J. B. NEEB * / 5 / CENTS / * IN TRADE *. Plain edge.

## PRICE HILL HOUSE
### Cincinnati, Ohio

| Rulau | Date | Metal | Size | VG | F | VF | Unc |
|---|---|---|---|---|---|---|---|
| Oh-Ci 40 | (1875-80) | Br. Oct., 22mm | | — | — | 12.50 | — |

Eagle. Below, in tiny letters: JAS. MURDOCK JR. 165 RACE ST., CINT'I, O. Rv: PRICE HILL HOUSE / 5 / CENTS. / JOHN ROLF'S. Plain edge. (Wright 1602)

Price Hill House was at the top of the Price Hill Inclined Plane railway northwest of Cincinnati's downtown section. John Rolf later (1889) operated a saloon at the northwest corner of 8th and Matson Place on Price Hill.

Price Hill Inclined Plane railway was opened in 1875.

## CINCINNATI INDUSTRIAL EXPOSITION
### Cincinnati, Ohio

| Rulau | Date | Metal | Size | F | VF | EF | Unc |
|---|---|---|---|---|---|---|---|
| Oh-Ci 50 | 1870 | WM | 26mm | — | — | 15.00 | 22.50 |

Exposition building (Saengerfest Hall at center, date 1870 below. Around: * CINCINNATI INDUSTRIAL EXPOSITION. Rv: UNDER THE AUSPICES / OF THE / CHAMBER, / OF / COMMERCE / —o— / BOARD OF TRADE / & OHIO MECHANICS' / INSTITUTE. Plain edge.

(See Russ Rulau's "The Early Tokens of the Queen City, Cincinnati," in the *TAMS Journal* for April 1974.)

The very first Cincinnati Industrial Exposition is honored on this token. It was held Sept. 21 through Oct. 22, 1870, with 300,000 persons in attendance. The exposition building occupied the site of the future Music Hall in Cincinnati.

| Oh-Ci 52 | 1871 | WM | 26mm | — | — | 15.00 | 22.50 |
|---|---|---|---|---|---|---|---|

Buildings at center, INDUSTRIAL / 1871 above, EXPOSITION / . . / CINCINNATI below. Rv: CHAMBER OF COMMERCE / BOARD / OF TRADE / OHIO MECHANICS / INSTITUTE / TOTAL EXHIBITING / SPACE / 289,094. FEET. Plain edge.

| Oh-Ci 52A | 1871 | WM | 26mm | — | — | — | — |
|---|---|---|---|---|---|---|---|

As 52. Reeded edge.

The second Cincinnati Industrial Exposition, also on the site of the future Music Hall, was held Sept. 6 through Oct. 8, 1871. Though well attended, the exposition lost $14,000 which had to be repaid by its guarantors.

| Rulau | Date | Metal | Size | VG | F | VF | Unc |
|---|---|---|---|---|---|---|---|
| Oh-Ci 53 | 1871 | WM | 26mm | — | — | — | — |

Obverse as 52. Rv: UNDER THE AUSPICES OF THE / CHAMBER / OF / COMMERCE / .... / 145000 / FT / BOARD OF TRADE / & OHIO MECHANICS / INSTITUTE. Plain edge.

| Oh-Ci 54 | 1872 | WM | 31mm | — | — | 15.00 | 22.50 |
|---|---|---|---|---|---|---|---|

CINCINNATI / 1872 / (view of exposition) / INDUSTRIAL / EXPOSITION. Rv: Monogram CIE in central circle. Lettered scroll below. In two concentric lines around: BOARD OF TRADE CHAMBER OF COMMERCE / & OHIO MECHANICS INSTITUTE. Reeded edge.

| Oh-Ci 55 | 1872 | WM | 31mm | — | — | — | — |
|---|---|---|---|---|---|---|---|

Obverse similar to 54. Rv: Very large monogram CIE within 4-lobed cartouche at center. Inscription around: THE ARTS. SPACE EIGHT ACRES / OF MANUFACTURES BY ........ Reeded edge.

| Rulau | Date | Metal | Size | F | VF | EF | Unc |
|---|---|---|---|---|---|---|---|
| Oh-Ci 56 | 1872 | WM | 31mm | — | — | — | — |

Obverse as 54. Rv: Very large monogram CIE within 4-lobed cartouche at center. Inscription around: THE ARTS. SPACE EIGHT ACRES / OF MANUFACTURES BY ........ Reeded edge.

| Oh-Ci 57 | 1873 | ? | 28.5mm | — | — | — | — |
|---|---|---|---|---|---|---|---|

Obverse similar to last, but legends differ. CINCINNATI INDUSTRIAL above, * EXPOSITION * / —*— / 1873 below. Tiny W. W. SPENCER CINCINNATI along lower rim. Rv: Ohio River bridge at center, COVINGTON & CINCINNATI / BRIDGE above, * LENGTH 2200 FT. * / MAIN SPAN 1020 FT. / HIGTH (sic) 100 FT / —o— / COST $2000000. Plain edge.

 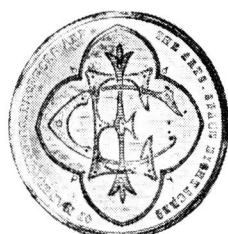

| Rulau | Date | Metal | Size | F | VF | EF | Unc |
|---|---|---|---|---|---|---|---|
| Oh-Ci 58 | 1873 | ? | 28.5mm | — | — | — | — |

Obverse as 55, but date 1873. Rv: As reverse of 56 (CIE monogram in 4-lobed cartouche). Plain edge.

| Rulau | Date | Metal | Size | F | VF | EF | Unc |
|---|---|---|---|---|---|---|---|
| Oh-Ci 59 | 1873 | GB | 28.5mm | — | — | 11.00 | 17.50 |

* CINCINNATI * / (view of exposition) / — INDUSTRIAL— / 1873. / EXPOSITION. Rv: SEAL OF CINCINNATI / JUNCTAJUVANT / (scales above crossed sword and caduceus) / * 1873. * Plain edge.

The fourth exposition was held September 3 to October 4, 1873 on the site of the future Music Hall. Another financial failure, it needed $15,000 to meet its obligations.

| Rulau | Date | Metal | Size | F | VF | EF | Unc |
|---|---|---|---|---|---|---|---|
| Oh-Ci 60 | 1874 | ? | 31mm | — | — | 10.00 | 15.00 |

Obverse similar to 57, but date 1874. Rv: Female personification of Knowledge with arms outstretched, facing. Above: MANUFACTURERS PRODUCTS & THE ARTS. In exergue: CT monogram (for diesinker C. Theiler).

| Rulau | Date | Metal | Size | F | VF | EF | Unc |
|---|---|---|---|---|---|---|---|
| Oh-Ci 61 | 1879 | WM | 31mm | — | — | 10.00 | 15.00 |

Music Hall at center, tiny MURDOCK CIN'TI below the ground line. Above: CINCINNATI INDUSTRIAL. Below: * EXHIBITION * / (beehive at center of branches). Rv: Names of sponsoring groups and 15 commissioners crowded in the field.

| Rulau | Date | Metal | Size | F | VF | EF | Unc |
|---|---|---|---|---|---|---|---|
| Oh-Ci 61A | 1879 | Copper | 31mm | — | — | 13.00 | 18.00 |

As 61

| Rulau | Date | Metal | Size | F | VF | EF | Unc |
|---|---|---|---|---|---|---|---|
| Oh-Ci 63 | 1881 | WM | 31mm | — | — | — | — |

Obverse as 61. Rv: Similar to 61, but date 1881 and some names are changed. (This token was struck by Murdock on the exposition grounds.).

| Rulau | Date | Metal | Size | F | VF | EF | Unc |
|---|---|---|---|---|---|---|---|
| Oh-Ci 64 | 1883 | WM | 31mm | — | — | — | — |

Obverse as 61 (Music Hall). Rv: ELEVENTH / CINCINNATI / INDUSTRIAL / 1883 / EXPOSITION / OF / MANUFACTURES, INVENTIONS / ART / PRODUCTS.

| Rulau | Date | Metal | Size | F | VF | EF | Unc |
|---|---|---|---|---|---|---|---|
| Oh-Ci 65 | 1884 | WM | 31mm | — | — | — | — |

Obverse as 61 (Music Hall). Rv: CINCINNATI / INDUSTRIAL / EXPOSITION / TWELFTH NATIONAL / EXHIBIT / OF / INDUSTRY & ART.

| Rulau | Date | Metal | Size | F | VF | EF | Unc |
|---|---|---|---|---|---|---|---|
| Oh-Ci 66 | 1884 | GB | 25mm | — | — | 8.00 | 11.00 |

TWELFTH / CINCINNATI (on scroll) / INDUSTRIAL (on scroll) / EXPOSITION. / 1884. Rv: LORD'S PRAYER / (Lord's prayer within central circle) / SMALLEST EVER COINED. Tiny MURDOCK — CINCINNATI at sides. Plain edge.

This piece is very similar to Murdock's reverse for the Langdon Bakery 'Widow's Mite' token (which see under Cincinnati). But the Langdon piece is much smaller!

| Rulau | Date | Metal | Size | F | VF | EF | Unc |
|---|---|---|---|---|---|---|---|
| Oh-Ci 67 | 1888 | AC Oct | 29mm | — | — | 15.00 | 22.50 |

CENTENNIAL EXPOSITION / AT CINCINNATI O. U.S.A JULY 4 TO OCT. 27 (Statue in center with dates 1788-1888) Rv: A SOUVENIR / OF THE / EXPOSITION / IN COMMEMORATION OF THE SETTLEMENT OF THE OHIO VALLEY AND THE CENTRAL STATES (old Fort Washington in center) Octagonal.

Made by Murdock.

| Rulau | Date | Metal | Size | F | VF | EF | Unc |
|---|---|---|---|---|---|---|---|
| Oh-Ci 67A | 1888 | WM | 29mm | — | — | 15.00 | 22.50 |

Octagonal

| Rulau | Date | Metal | Size | F | VF | EF | Unc |
|---|---|---|---|---|---|---|---|
| NY-NY 179 | (?) | GS | 31mm | 7.50 | 15.00 | 25.00 | 60.00 |

| Rulau | Date | Metal | Size | VG | F | VF | Unc |
|---|---|---|---|---|---|---|---|
| NY-Rm 22 | (1868-90) | Brass* | 24mm | 3.50 | 6.00 | 8.00 | — |

 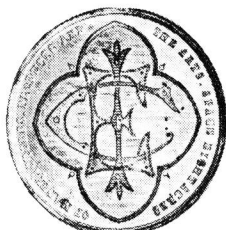  

Obverse similar to 57, but date 1874. Rv: Female personification of Knowledge with arms outstretched, facing. Above: MANUFACTURERS PRODUCTS & THE ARTS. In exergue: CT monogram (for diesinker C. Theiler).

 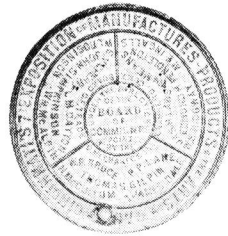

Music Hall at center, tiny MURDOCK CIN'TI below the ground line. Above: CINCINNATI INDUSTRIAL. Below: * EXHIBITION * / (beehive at center of branches). Rv: Names of sponsoring groups and 15 commissioners crowded in the field.

| Oh-Ci 61A | 1879 | Copper | 31mm | — | — | 13.00 | 18.00 |

Obverse as 61. Rv: Similar to 61, but date 1881 and some names are changed. (This token was struck by Murdock on the exposition grounds.).

| Rulau | Date | Metal | Size | F | VF | EF | Unc |
|---|---|---|---|---|---|---|---|
| Pa-Ph 181 M | 1861 | Silver | 38mm | — | — | — | 600. |

Bust left, THOMAS WILDEY above, BORN JAN. 15, 1783 / DIED OCT. 19, 1861. below. Tiny W H KEY F below truncation of shoulder. Rv: As 181. Plain edge. Only 2 specimens known. (One specimen appeared in the Levick sale, May 26, 1884; another, possibly the same one, in the Bowers & Ruddy Garrett sales 1980-81)

| Rulau | Date | Metal | Size | F | VF | EF | Unc |
|---|---|---|---|---|---|---|---|
| Pa-Ph 181 N | 1861 | Copper | 38mm | — | — | — | 75.00 |

As 181M. Plain edge. (Miller Pa 258)

| Pa-Ph 181 P | 1861 | WM | 38mm | — | — | — | 100. |

As 181M. Plain edge. (Miller Pa 250)

| Pa-Ph 182 | (?) | Brass | 29mm | — | — | 20.00 | 35.00 |

WE ALL HAVE OUR HOBBIES. Rv: As 170. Plain edge. (Miller Pa 275)

| Pa-Ph 182 A | (?) | Copper | 29mm | — | — | 20.00 | 35.00 |

As 182. (Miller 276)

| Pa-Ph 182 B | (?) | WM | 29mm | — | — | 20.00 | 35.00 |

As 182. (Miller 277)

| Pa-Ph 184 | (?) | Brass | 29mm | — | — | 20.00 | 35.00 |

DEDICATED TO COIN COLLECTORS. Rv: As 170. Plain edge. (Miller 278)

| Pa-Ph 184 A | (?) | Copper | 29mm | — | — | 20.00 | 35.00 |

As 184. (Miller 279)

| Pa-Ph 184 B | (?) | WM | 29mm | — | — | 20.00 | 35.00 |

As 184. (Miller 280)

| Pa-Ph 186 | (?) | Brass | 29mm | — | — | 20.00 | 35.00 |

Cupid. Rv: As 170. Plain edge. (Miller Pa 281)

| Pa-Ph 186 A | (?) | Copper | 29mm | — | — | 20.00 | 35.00 |

As 186. (Miller 282)

| Pa-Ph 186 B | (?) | WM | 29mm | — | — | 20.00 | 25.00 |

As 186. (Miller 283)

## WM. H. KEY (and) J.H. DIEHL
## Philadelphia, Pa.

| Rulau | Date | Metal | Size | F | VF | EF | Unc |
|---|---|---|---|---|---|---|---|
| Pa-Ph 188 | (1869-80) | Copper | 23mm | — | — | 25.00 | 50.00 |

Grecian head left, inscribed LIBERTY. Rv: WM. H. KEY / ENGRAVER / NO. 12 STH 37TH ST / PHILADELPHIA (sideways across token) / J. H. DIEHL / MANUFACTURER OF / MEDALS / NO. 728 CHESTNUT ST.,. Plain edge. (The Key and Diehl halves of the reverse read upside down in relation to each other). (Wright 251 and 549; Miller Pa 264)

| Pa-Ph 62 | (1870's) | WM | 24mm | 8.50 | 11.50 | 15.00 | 25.00 |

As 264. Plain edge. (Wright 251; Miller Pa 264A)

J.H. Diehl is listed at 728 Chestnut St. fom 1869 to 1880.

## G. KILBRIDE
## Philadelphia, Pa.

**1876 Centennial Tokens**

Reverse type 1: G. KILBRIDE / CHEMIST & / DRUGGIST / ***** / 20TH & CHESTNUT STS / ** PHILADA **. (All 23mm; plain edge)

| Rulau | Obv | Rev | Metal | F | VF | EF | Unc |
|---|---|---|---|---|---|---|---|
| Pa-Ph 980 | A | 1 | WM | — | — | 15.00 | 40.00 |
| | | | (Wright 553; Miller Pa 254) | | | | |
| Pa-Ph 981 | B | 1 | WM | — | — | 15.00 | 40.00 |
| | | | (Miller 253) | | | | |
| Pa-Ph 982 | E | 1 | WM | — | — | 15.00 | 40.00 |
| | | | (Miller 255) | | | | |
| Pa-Ph 982 A | E | 1 | Copper | — | — | 17.50 | 45.00 |
| | | | (Miller 256) | | | | |
| Pa-Ph 983 | F | 1 | WM | — | — | 20.00 | 50.00 |
| | | | (Miller 257) | | | | |
| Pa-Ph 984 | G | 1 | WM | — | — | 17.50 | 45.00 |
| Pa-Ph 985 | H | 1 | WM | — | — | 17.50 | 45.00 |
| | | | (Miller 251) | | | | |
| Pa-Ph 985 A | H | 1 | Copper | — | — | 20.00 | 50.00 |
| | | | (Miller 252) | | | | |
| Pa-Ph 986 | K | 1 | WM | — | — | 17.50 | 45.00 |
| | | | (Miller 250) | | | | |
| Pa-Ph 986 A | K | 1 | Copper | — | — | 20.00 | 50.00 |
| | | | (Miller 249) | | | | |

## JOHN W. KLINE
## Philadelphia, Pa.

| Rulau | Date | Metal | Size | F | VF | EF | Unc |
|---|---|---|---|---|---|---|---|
| Pa-Ph 200 | (1876) | Brass | 25mm | — | 10.00 | 15.00 | 50.00 |

Head of William Penn. Rv: JOHN W. KLINE 212 SOUTH 8TH ST / MANUFACTURER OF / MEDALS / TOKENS, CARDS, &C / IMPORTER & DEALER IN / COINS / MEDALS / SHELLS MINERALS / ENGRAVINGS / AND CURIOSITIES / PHILADELPHIA. Plain edge. (Miller Pa. 286)

| Pa-Ph 201 | (1876) | Copper | 25mm | — | 10.00 | 15.00 | 50.00 |

As 200. Plain edge. (Miller Pa. 287)

| Pa-Ph 202 | (1876) | WM | 25mm | — | 10.00 | 15.00 | 50.00 |

As 200. Plain edge. (Miller Pa. 288)

| Pa-Ph 202 A | (1876) | WM | 25mm | — | 10.00 | 15.00 | 50.00 |

As 202, but thin planchet. Plain edge. (Miller Pa. 289A)

| Pa-Ph 203 | (1876) | Silver | 25mm | — | — | — | 200. |

As 200. Plain edge. (Miller Pa. 289)

| Pa-Ph 203 A | (1876) | Alum | 26mm | — | — | — | 75.00 |

As 200. Plain edge.

| Pa-Ph 205 | (1876) | Copper | 25mm | — | — | — | 50.00 |

Liberty head with flowing hair left, LIBERTAS AMERICANA above, 4 JUIL 1776 in exergue. Rv: As 200. Plain edge.

| Pa-Ph 206 | (1876) | Brass | 25mm | — | — | — | 50.00 |

As 205. Thick planchet. Plain edge. (Miller Pa. 289B)

## DIETRICH KNOPPEL
## Philadelphia, Pa.

**1876 Centennial Tokens**

Reverse type 1: DIETRICH KNOPPEL / MANUFACTURER / OF / FINE / AND / PLAIN / CONFECTIONERY / 1506 MARKET ST., PHILA. (All 23mm; plain edge)

| Rulau | Obv | Rev | Metal | F | VF | EF | Unc |
|---|---|---|---|---|---|---|---|
| Pa-Ph 990 | A | 1 | Copper | — | — | 17.50 | 45.00 |
| Pa-Ph 991 | B | 1 | WM | — | — | 15.00 | 40.00 |
| | | | (Wright 1488) | | | | |
| Pa-Ph 992 | D | 1 | WM | — | — | 16.50 | 40.00 |
| Pa-Ph 993 | E | 1 | WM | — | — | 15.00 | 40.00 |
| Pa-Ph 993 A | E | 1 | Copper | — | — | 16.50 | 40.00 |
| Pa-Ph 994 | F | 1 | WM | — | — | 17.50 | 45.00 |
| Pa-Ph 995 | G | 1 | WM | — | — | 16.50 | 40.00 |
| Pa-Ph 995 A | G | 1 | Copper | — | — | 17.50 | 45.00 |
| Pa-Ph 996 | H | 1 | WM | — | — | 16.50 | 40.00 |
| Pa-Ph 996 A | H | 1 | Copper | — | — | 17.50 | 45.00 |
| Pa-Ph 997 | J | 1 | WM | — | — | 16.50 | 40.00 |

| Rulau | Obv | Rev | Metal | F | VF | EF | Unc |
|---|---|---|---|---|---|---|---|
| Pa-Ph 997 A | J | 1 | Copper | — | — | 17.50 | 45.00 |
| Pa-Ph 998 | K | 1 | WM | — | — | 16.50 | 40.00 |
| Pa-Ph 998 A | K | 1 | Copper | — | — | 17.50 | 45.00 |

This issuer was unlisted by Adams, Miller and others, though catalogued by Wright. It was reported in 1981 in Arlie R. Slabaugh's book *American Centennial Tokens and Medals* and, in Dec. 1981, in the Springfield sale, lot 4553.

## FREDERICK KNOPPEL
### Philadelphia, Pa.

#### 1876 Centennial Tokens

Reverse type 1: FRED'K KNOPPEL / MANUFACTURER / OF / FINE / CONFECTIONERY / 1208 ARCH ST., PHILA. (All 23mm; plain edge)

| Rulau | Obv | Rev | Metal | F | VF | EF | Unc |
|---|---|---|---|---|---|---|---|
| Pa-Ph 210 | A | 1 | WM | 5.00 | 8.50 | 15.00 | 40.00 |
| (Miller Pa 290) | | | | | | | |
| Pa-Ph 210 A | A | 1 | Copper | — | — | — | 50.00 |
| Pa-Ph 211 | B | 1 | WM | — | — | 15.00 | 40.00 |
| (Wright 1489) | | | | | | | |
| Pa-Ph 211 A | B | 1 | Brass | — | — | 20.00 | 50.00 |
| Pa-Ph 212 | C | 1 | WM | — | — | — | 50.00 |
| Pa-Ph 213 | D | 1 | Copper | — | — | 20.00 | 50.00 |
| (Miller 292) | | | | | | | |
| Pa-Ph 214 | E | 1 | WM | — | — | 15.00 | 40.00 |
| (Miller 293) | | | | | | | |
| Pa-Ph 215 | F | 1 | WM | — | — | 17.50 | 45.00 |
| (Miller 291) | | | | | | | |
| Pa-Ph 216 | G | 1 | WM | — | — | 16.50 | 40.00 |
| Pa-Ph 216 A | G | 1 | Copper | — | — | — | 50.00 |
| Pa-Ph 217 | H | 1 | WM | — | — | 16.50 | 40.00 |
| Pa-Ph 217 A | H | 1 | Copper | — | — | — | 50.00 |
| Pa-Ph 218 | J | 1 | WM | — | — | 16.50 | 40.00 |
| Pa-Ph 218 A | J | 1 | Copper | — | — | — | 50.00 |
| Pa-Ph 219 | K | 1 | Copper | — | — | — | 50.00 |

## JOHN LEAK
### Philadelphia, Pa.

| Rulau | Date | Metal | Size | VG | F | VF | Unc |
|---|---|---|---|---|---|---|---|
| Pa-Ph 999 | (?) | — | ---mm | 20.00 | 40.00 | 60.00 | — |

JOHN LEAK. MANUFACTURER AND ENGRAVER &C. 223 N. SECOND ST. Rv: Blank. (Miller 294 1/2)

## LINGG & BRO.
### Philadelphia, Pa.

#### 1876 Centennial Tokens

Reverse type 1: LINGG & BRO. 304 SO. 2ND ST. / WATCHES / * / AND / * / JEWELRY / * PHILA. *. Beaded inner circle. (All 23mm; plain edge)

Reverse type 2: LINGG & BRO. / WATCHES / * / AND / * / JEWELRY / 304 S. SECOND ST. PHILA. No inner circle. (All 23mm; plain edge)

Reverse type 3: As type 2, but LINGG & BRO. across center. (All 23mm; plain edge)

Reverse type 4: LINGG & BRO. On scroll: COMMEMORATION JULY 5, 1875. (All 23mm; plain edge)

Reverse type 5: Oval flan. LINGG & BRO / WATCHES / AND / JEWELRY / 304 S. SECOND ST. / PHILA. (All 25 by 20mm; plain edge)

| Rulau | Obv | Rev | Metal | F | VF | EF | Unc |
|---|---|---|---|---|---|---|---|
| Pa-Ph 220 | A | 1 | WM | 5.00 | 8.00 | 15.00 | 40.00 |
| Pa-Ph 220 A | A | 1 | Copper | — | — | 15.00 | 40.00 |
| (Miller Pa 300) | | | | | | | |
| Pa-Ph 221 | H | 1 | Copper | — | — | 15.00 | 40.00 |
| (Miller 299) | | | | | | | |
| Pa-Ph 222 | L | 1 | WM | — | — | 14.00 | 40.00 |
| (Miller 298) | | | | | | | |
| Pa-Ph 222 A | L | 1 | Copper | 5.00 | 8.50 | 15.00 | 40.00 |
| Also in Bronze. (Miller 296) | | | | | | | |
| Pa-Ph 222 B | L | 1 | Brass | — | — | — | 75.00 |
| Supposedly only 5 struck. (Wright 608; Miller 297) | | | | | | | |
| Pa-Ph 224 | A | 2 | WM | 5.00 | 8.00 | 14.00 | 40.00 |
| (Miller 301) | | | | | | | |
| Pa-Ph 225 | B | 1 | WM | — | — | 14.00 | 40.00 |
| (Miller 303) | | | | | | | |
| Pa-Ph 226 | D | 2 | WM | — | — | 15.00 | 40.00 |
| (Miller 302) | | | | | | | |
| Pa-Ph 227 | E | 2 | WM | — | — | 14.00 | 40.00 |
| (Miller 306) | | | | | | | |
| Pa-Ph 228 | F | 2 | WM | — | — | 15.00 | 40.00 |
| (Miller 307) | | | | | | | |
| Pa-Ph 229 | G | 2 | WM | — | — | 15.00 | 40.00 |
| (Miller 305) | | | | | | | |
| Pa-Ph 230 | H | 2 | WM | — | — | 14.00 | 40.00 |
| (Miller 309) | | | | | | | |
| Pa-Ph 230 A | H | 2 | Copper | — | — | 20.00 | 45.00 |
| (Miller 309A) | | | | | | | |
| Pa-Ph 230 B | H | 2 | Brass | — | — | 17.50 | 45.00 |
| (Miller 308) | | | | | | | |
| Pa-Ph 231 | J | 2 | WM | — | — | 15.00 | 40.00 |
| (Miller 304) | | | | | | | |
| Pa-Ph 232 | L | 2 | WM | — | — | 14.00 | 40.00 |
| Pa-Ph 232 A | L | 2 | Copper | — | — | 15.00 | 40.00 |
| Pa-Ph 232 B | L | 2 | Brass | — | — | 15.00 | 40.00 |
| Pa-Ph 234 | A | 3 | WM | 5.00 | 8.50 | 17.50 | 40.00 |
| (Miller 312) | | | | | | | |
| Pa-Ph 234 A | A | 3 | Copper | — | — | 20.00 | 45.00 |
| Pa-Ph 234 B | A | 3 | Brass | — | — | 20.00 | 45.00 |
| Pa-Ph 235 | B | 3 | WM | — | — | 14.00 | 40.00 |
| (Miller 313B) | | | | | | | |
| Pa-Ph 236 | D | 3 | WM | — | — | 14.00 | 40.00 |
| (Miller 311) | | | | | | | |
| Pa-Ph 237 | E | 3 | WM | — | — | 14.00 | 40.00 |
| (Miller 313A) | | | | | | | |
| Pa-Ph 238 | F | 3 | WM | — | — | 14.00 | 40.00 |
| (Miller 313C) | | | | | | | |
| Pa-Ph 239 | G | 3 | WM | — | — | 14.00 | 40.00 |
| (Miller 310) | | | | | | | |
| Pa-Ph 240 | H | 3 | WM | — | — | 14.00 | 40.00 |
| Pa-Ph 241 | J | 3 | WM | — | — | 14.00 | 40.00 |
| (Miller 313) | | | | | | | |
| Pa-Ph 243 | A | 4 | WM | — | — | 17.50 | 40.00 |
| (Miller Pa 317) | | | | | | | |
| Pa-Ph 243 A | A | 4 | Copper | — | — | 20.00 | 45.00 |
| Pa-Ph 243 B | A | 4 | Brass | — | — | 20.00 | 45.00 |
| Pa-Ph 244 | E | 4 | WM | — | — | 17.50 | 40.00 |

| Rulau | Obv | Rev | Metal | F | VF | EF | Unc |
|---|---|---|---|---|---|---|---|
| Pa-Ph 244 A | E | 4 | Copper | — | — | 20.00 | 45.00 |
| | | | (Miller 315) | | | | |
| Pa-Ph 244 B | E | 4 | Brass | — | — | 20.00 | 45.00 |
| | | | (Miller 314) | | | | |
| Pa-Ph 245 | H | 4 | WM | — | — | 17.50 | 40.00 |
| Pa-Ph 245 A | H | 4 | Copper | — | — | 20.00 | 45.00 |
| Pa-Ph 245 B | H | 4 | Brass | — | — | 20.00 | 45.00 |
| | | | (Miller 316) | | | | |
| Pa-Ph 246 | OV | 5 | WM | — | — | — | 100. |

NOTE: More than 30 mulings of obverses with each other are known. One, a muling of die A with die J in White Metal, was listed as Miller 301A. Such mulings are worth $12.50 in EF and $30.00 in Unc. See Slabaugh's reference for varieties.

ALSO NOTE: Die striations plague the Centennial series. They are not detailed in this reference.

### 1876 Centennial Tokens

Reverse type 6: LINGG & BRO. / 304 / S. SECOND ST. / WATCHES / AND / JEWELRY. (All 19mm; plain edge)

Reverse type 7: WE MAKE / THIS STYLE OF CARD / FOR / $9 PER 1000 / AT / 1029 CHESTNUT ST / PHILADA. No name on tokens. (All 19mm; plain edge)

| Rulau | Obv | Rev | Metal | F | VF | EF | Unc |
|---|---|---|---|---|---|---|---|
| Pa-Ph 248 | X | 6 | WM | — | 7.00 | 10.00 | 20.00 |
| Pa-Ph 248 A | X | 6 | Copper | — | — | 10.00 | 20.00 |
| | | | Also in Bronze. (Miller Pa 308A) | | | | |
| Pa-Ph 248 B | X | 6 | Brass | — | — | 15.00 | 25.00 |
| Pa-Ph 249 | Y | 6 | WM | — | — | 15.00 | 25.00 |
| Pa-Ph 249 A | Y | 6 | Bronze | — | — | 15.00 | 25.00 |
| Pa-Ph 250 | V | 6 | WM | — | — | 17.50 | 30.00 |
| Pa-Ph 252 | W | 7 | WM | — | — | 10.00 | 20.00 |
| Pa-Ph 253 | X | 7 | WM | — | — | 10.00 | 20.00 |
| Pa-Ph 254 | Y | 7 | WM | — | — | 10.00 | 20.00 |
| Pa-Ph 255 | Z | 7 | WM | — | — | 15.00 | 25.00 |
| Pa-Ph 255 A | Z | 7 | Copper | — | — | 15.00 | 25.00 |

## LINGG & CO.
## Philadelphia, Pa.

### 1876 Centennial Tokens

Reverse type 1: LINGG & CO. / MANUFACTURERS / OF / METALLIC / BUSINESS CARDS / MEDALS / TOKENS &C / 1029 CHESTNUT ST. PHILADA. (All 23mm; plain edge)

Reverse type 2: Similar, but Oval flan, 25 by 20mm, plain edge.

| Rulau | Obv | Rev | Metal | F | VF | EF | Unc |
|---|---|---|---|---|---|---|---|
| Pa-Ph 256 | A | 1 | WM | 5.00 | 8.00 | 15.00 | 40.00 |
| | | | (Miller Pa 323) | | | | |
| Pa-Ph 256 A | A | 1 | Copper | — | — | 20.00 | 45.00 |
| Pa-Ph 256 F | A | 1 | ** | — | — | — | 100. |
| | | | ** Purple fiber. | | | | |
| Pa-Ph 257 | B | 1 | WM | 5.00 | 8.00 | 15.00 | 40.00 |
| | | | (Miller 318) | | | | |
| Pa-Ph 257 A | B | 1 | Copper | — | — | 20.00 | 45.00 |
| | | | (Miller 320) | | | | |
| Pa-Ph 257 B | B | 1 | Brass | — | — | 17.50 | 40.00 |
| | | | (Miller 319) | | | | |
| Pa-Ph 258 | C | 1 | WM | — | — | 15.00 | 40.00 |
| | | | (Miller 318A) | | | | |
| Pa-Ph 258 A | C | 1 | Copper | — | — | 20.00 | 45.00 |
| Pa-Ph 258 B | C | 1 | Brass | — | — | 20.00 | 45.00 |
| Pa-Ph 258 F | D | 1 | WM | — | — | 20.00 | 45.00 |
| Pa-Ph 259 | E | 1 | WM | — | — | 15.00 | 40.00 |
| | | | (Miller 324) | | | | |
| Pa-Ph 259 A | E | 1 | Copper | — | — | 20.00 | 45.00 |
| Pa-Ph 260 | F | 1 | WM | — | — | 20.00 | 45.00 |
| | | | (Wright 608; Miller 326) | | | | |
| Pa-Ph 260 A | F | 1 | Copper | — | — | Not Confirmed | |
| Pa-Ph 261 | G | 1 | WM | — | — | 15.00 | 40.00 |
| Pa-Ph 261 A | G | 1 | Copper | — | — | 20.00 | 45.00 |
| Pa-Ph 262 | H | 1 | WM | — | — | 15.00 | 40.00 |
| | | | (Miller 322) | | | | |
| Pa-Ph 262 A | H | 1 | Copper | — | — | 20.00 | 45.00 |
| Pa-Ph 262 B | H | 1 | Brass | — | — | 20.00 | 45.00 |
| Pa-Ph 262 F | K | 1 | WM | — | — | 20.00 | 45.00 |
| | | | (Miller 321) | | | | |
| Pa-Ph 262 G | K | 1 | Copper | — | — | 20.00 | 45.00 |
| Pa-Ph 263 | OV | 2 | WM | — | — | 80.00 | 100. |
| | | | (Miller 326A) | | | | |

Joseph Lingg began business during the Civil War as a dealer in watches and jewelry at 1219 Prune St., Philadelphia. In the early 1870's the firm became Lingg & Bro. as Frederick Lingg joined his brother (becoming the dominant partner). They were at 1206 Pine St. and at 304 So. Second St. — the latter the address on the tokens. They apparently consolidated at the Second St. address.

About 1873 they established (or bought out) a token and medal manufacturing business at 1029 Chestnut St. Their first medalet was the 19mm (U.S. cent size) piece for the New Memorial Hall (die Z). About 1874 they produced the 23mm "double head" piece (die D) which reads I ALWAYS BUY THERE above the smiling face and I WILL IN FUTURE above the frowning face.

All the other Lingg stock obverse dies, probably produced from 1874 to 1875, were of Centennial themes. Lingg must have had some distribution arrangement with Theodore J. Harbach, the confectioner, who arranged for many other confectioners to use the cards. The Harbach token-maker cards probably were struck by Lingg.

During 1875 the Linggs sold their interest in the medallic business, and bought out Cassidy's jewelry business — probably selling to Burr & Witsil. Later this became the Centennial Advertising Medal Co., which supplied Lingg die combinations and off-metal strikes for collectors 1876-77.

It is not known why the Maryland coat of arms appears on die F. Only one issuer in Maryland, the Patapsco Fruit Butter Co. of Baltimore, used Centennial cards. Perhaps it was a mistake and the Pennsylvania arms were intended. Public Buildings, die J, is the Philadelphia City Hall, begun 1872 and completed 1901.

## DR. W. H. LOBE
## Philadelphia, Pa.

| Rulau | Date | Metal | Size | F | VF | EF | Unc |
|---|---|---|---|---|---|---|---|
| Pa-Ph 264 | (?) | WM | 24mm | — | 15.00 | 30.00 | 50.00 |

DR. W. H. LOBE / MEDICAL OFFICES / 329 / N. FIFTEENTH ST. / PHILADA. Rv: OFFICE / HOURS / 11 AM to 2 / AND / 7 to 10 PM. (Wright 613; Miller Pa. 326½)

## COUNT & COUNTESS MAGRI
## Philadelphia, Pa.

| Rulau | Date | Metal | Size | VG | F | VF | Unc |
|---|---|---|---|---|---|---|---|
| Pa-Ph 265 | 1885 | WM | 31mm | — | — | — | 40.00 |

MAGRI above a man and woman standing at center. Around border: PRESENTED BY THE COUNT & COUNTESS C.A. BRADENBURGH & CO. M'GRS. Reverse: in eleven lines, 9th & ARCH ST. MUSEUM PHILA. THE FAVORITE FAMILY RESORT FIRST APPEARANCE BEFORE PUBLIC OF COUNT AN COUNTESS MAGRI FORMERLY MRS. TOM THUMB AFTER THEIR WEDDING TOUR OF EUROPE MON. SEPT. 14, 1885. C.A. BRADENBURGH PRO & M'GR. Beaded border. Plain edge. Rarity 7. (Wright 646)

Mrs. Tom Thumb (Lavinia Warren) married Count Magri after the death of her famous husband. (See P. T. Barnum under New York City)

## MALSEED & HAWKINS
## Philadelphia, Pa.

### 1876 Centennial Tokens

Reverse type 1: * MALSEED & HAWKINS * / S.E. COR. / CLOTH / HOUSE / 8TH & MARKET STS. / *** PHILADA. ***. (All 23mm; plain edge)

| Rulau | Obv | Rev | Metal | F | VF | EF | Unc |
|---|---|---|---|---|---|---|---|
| Pa-Ph 270 | A | 1 | WM | 5.00 | 8.00 | 15.00 | 40.00 |
| | | (Miller Pa 357) | | | | | |
| Pa-Ph 271 | B | 1 | WM | — | — | 15.00 | 40.00 |
| | | Thick flan. (Miller 358) | | | | | |
| Pa-Ph 271 A | B | 1 | WM | — | — | 15.00 | 40.00 |
| | | Thin flan. | | | | | |
| Pa-Ph 271 B | B | 1 | Brass | — | — | 20.00 | 45.00 |
| Pa-Ph 272 | E | 1 | WM | 5.00 | 8.00 | 15.00 | 40.00 |
| | | (Miller 359) | | | | | |
| Pa-Ph 273 | F | 1 | WM | — | — | 17.50 | 45.00 |
| | | (Miller 360) | | | | | |
| Pa-Ph 274 | J | 1 | WM | — | — | 17.50 | 45.00 |
| Pa-Ph 275 | K | 1 | WM | — | — | 20.00 | 45.00 |
| | | (Miller 362) | | | | | |
| Pa-Ph 275 A | K | 1 | Copper | — | — | 20.00 | 45.00 |
| | | (Miller 361) | | | | | |
| Pa-Ph 275 B | K | 1 | Brass | — | — | 20.00 | 45.00 |
| | | (Wright 653; Miller 361A) | | | | | |

See also Fries, Malseed & Hawkins under Philadelphia in this reference.

## MASON & CO.
## Philadelphia, Pa.

| Rulau | Date | Metal | Size | F | VF | EF | Unc |
|---|---|---|---|---|---|---|---|
| Pa-Ph 290 | 1870 | WM | 19mm | — | 20.00 | 25.00 | 45.00 |

Washington bust facing, BORN FEB. 22, 1732 above, DIED DEC. 14, 1799 below. Rv: MASON & CO. / 1870 / COIN & STAMP / --- / DEALERS. / 139 / NO. 9TH ST. PHILA. Plain edge. (Baker 559; Fuld NC-16e; Miller Pa 363). Rarity 6. 100 struck.

| Pa-Ph 290 A | 1870 | Silver | 19mm | — | — | — | 200. |

As 290. Plain edge. Only 2 struck.

| Pa-Ph 291 | 1870 | Copper | 19mm | — | 10.00 | 15.00 | 45.00 |

As 290. Plain edge. (Baker 559; Wright 671; Fuld NC-16a) RARITY 6. 100 struck.

| Pa-Ph 292 | 1870 | Brass | 19mm | — | 10.00 | 15.00 | 45.00 |

As 290. Plain edge. (Fuld NC-16b; Miller Pa 365) 100 struck.

| Pa-Ph 293 | 1870 | Nickel | 19mm | — | — | 35.00 | 60.00 |

As 290. (Miller Pa 366) Only 20 struck.

| Pa-Ph 295 | 1870 | WM | 19mm | — | — | 200. | 300. |

Lincoln bust right, ABRAHAM LINCOLN around, 1864 below. Rv: As reverse of Pa 290. (DeWitt AL 1864-74 (B).) Tiny K below bust. (King 638) The 'K' is for diesinker William H. Key of Philadelphia. Only 2 struck.

| Pa-Ph 296 | 1870 | Brass | 19mm | — | — | 200. | 300. |

As 295. Plain edge. Only 2 struck.

| Pa-Ph 298 | 1870 | WM | 19mm | — | — | 200. | 300. |

Benjamin Franklin bust left. Rv: As 290. Only 2 struck.

| Pa-Ph 299 | 1870 | Brass | 19mm | — | — | 200. | 300. |

As 298. Only 2 struck.

Mason listed the mintages for his store cards in his journal. The order was executed by Warner and the dies cut by Key.

By 1872 Mason had moved to 907 Chestnut St.

## D. M. MURPHY
## Philadelphia, Pa.

### 1876 Centennial Tokens

Reverse type 1: D. M. MURPHY / (large numeral) / 2ND & CHRISTIAN STS. (All 23mm; plain edge)

Reverse type 2: D. M. MURPHY / 1 lb. COFFEE / 2ND & CHRISTIAN STS. (All 23mm; plain edge)

| Rulau | Obv | Rev | Metal | F | VF | EF | Unc |
|---|---|---|---|---|---|---|---|
| Pa-Ph 276 | G | 1 | WM | — | — | 17.50 | 45.00 |
| | | Numeral 13. | | | | | |
| Pa-Ph 276 B | G | 1 | WM | — | — | 17.50 | 45.00 |
| | | Numeral 15. (Wright 738; Miller 374) | | | | | |
| Pa-Ph 276 D | G | 1 | WM | — | — | 17.50 | 45.00 |
| | | Numeral 20. (Miller 375) | | | | | |
| Pa-Ph 278 | A | 2 | WM | — | — | 17.50 | 45.00 |
| | | (Miller 376) | | | | | |
| Pa-Ph 279 | G | 2 | WM | — | — | 17.50 | 45.00 |
| | | (Miller 377) | | | | | |

These pieces are very similar in style to those of the Great Union Pacific Tea Company, which see.

## NATIONAL UNION LEAGUE
## Philadelphia, Pa.

| Rulau | Date | Metal | Size | F | VF | EF | Unc |
|---|---|---|---|---|---|---|---|
| Pa-Ph 300 | 1863 | Silver | 26mm | — | — | 25.00 | 75.00 |

Facing bust of Van Buren, MARTIN VAN BUREN above, .THE PEOPLES CHOICE. below. Rv: Shield within wreath, 1863 below. Around: NATIONAL UNION LEAGUE / OF / THE / UNITED STATES. Plain edge. (DeWitt MVB-C (1).

| Pa-Ph 301 | 1863 | Copper | 26mm | — | — | 25.00 | 75.00 |

As last.

| Pa-Ph 302 | 1863 | Brass | 26mm | — | — | 25.00 | 75.00 |

As last.

| Pa-Ph 303 | 1863 | WM | 26mm | — | — | 25.00 | 75.00 |

As last.

All struck by William H. Key of Philadelphia. The shield side has been muled with many other tokens. The obverse die is Low 57 retouched.

## UNION LEAGUE
## Philadelphia, Pa.

| Rulau | Date | Metal | Size | F | VF | EF | Unc |
|---|---|---|---|---|---|---|---|
| Pa-Ph 306 | 1863 | WM | 34mm | — | — | — | 35.00 |

Scroll lettered E PLURIBUS UNUM across U.S. shield at center, separating 1776 — 1863. UNION LEAGUE / JULY 4TH above; PHILADELPHIA. below. Rv: Blank. Plain edge. Rarity 5. (Fuld NC-25e)

[132]

| Rulau | Date | Metal | Size | F | VF | EF | Unc |
|---|---|---|---|---|---|---|---|
| Pa-Ph 307 | 1863 | Silver | 34mm | — | — | — | 60.00 |

As last. Plain edge. Rarity 8. (Fuld NC-25f)

| Rulau | Date | Metal | Size | F | VF | EF | Unc |
|---|---|---|---|---|---|---|---|
| Pa-Ph 309 | 1863 | WM | 31mm | — | — | — | 40.00 |

U.S. shield above wreath at center, UNION LEAGUE above, * 1863 * below. Rv: LANCASTER / * PENNA. *. Plain edge. Rarity 7. (Fuld NC-26e)

An illogical muling.

## NINTH PRECINCT HOUSE
### Philadelphia, Pa.

| Rulau | Date | Metal | Size | F | VF | EF | Unc |
|---|---|---|---|---|---|---|---|
| Pa-Ph 315 | (1880's) | WM | 22mm | — | — | 15.00 | 40.00 |

Masonic symbol, with the ribbon bearing a legend: HONESTY, INDUSTRY, SOBRIETY, above, and below: O.V.A.M. Rv: NINTH PRECINCT / HOUSE / 126 CALLOWHILL ST. / PHILADA. / S.H. SMITH, PRO. Plain edge. (Coll. Jeff Rock, Santee, Calif.)

## PENNSYLVANIA STATE AGRICULTURAL FAIR
### Philadelphia, Pa.

| Rulau | Date | Metal | Size | F | VF | EF | Unc |
|---|---|---|---|---|---|---|---|
| Pa-Ph 320 | 1880 | Gilt/Br | 25mm | — | 25.00 | 30.00 | 50.00 |

At center a standing ram faces right, and a ewe left, while a baby lamb reclines right. In exergue: PHILA. SEP. / 1880. On scroll above is incused: INTRL. SHEEP & WOOL SHOW. Rv: Arms of Philadelphia are within a masonry capital. Atop the capital are a cow and her young bull offspring. At left: PENNSYLVANIA / STATE. At right: AGRICULTURAL / FAIR. Plain edge.

The workmanship on this medalet is outstanding, indicating it is probably a U.S. Mint product. This is one of the most beautiful medalets or tokens included in this catalog. Quite scarce; seldom seen by veteran collectors. Perhaps a dozen pieces traceable.

## PENN MUTUAL LIFE INC. COMPANY
### Philadelphia, Pa.

#### 1876 Centennial Tokens

Reverse type 1: PENN MUTUAL / LIFE / INS. COMPANY / 921 / CHESTNUT ST. / PHILA. (All 23mm; plain edge)

| Rulau | Obv | Rev | Metal | F | VF | EF | Unc |
|---|---|---|---|---|---|---|---|
| Pa-Ph 316 | A | 1 | WM | — | — | 15.00 | 35.00 |
| (Miller Pa 386) | | | | | | | |
| Pa-Ph 316 F | B | 1 | WM | — | — | 15.00 | 35.00 |
| (Miller 384) | | | | | | | |
| Pa-Ph 316 G | B | 1 | Copper | — | — | 17.50 | 40.00 |
| (Miller 383) | | | | | | | |
| Pa-Ph 316 H | B | 1 | Brass | — | — | 20.00 | 45.00 |
| Pa-Ph 317 | E | 1 | WM | — | — | 15.00 | 35.00 |
| (Miller 387) | | | | | | | |
| Pa-Ph 317 A | E | 1 | Copper | — | — | 17.50 | 40.00 |
| Pa-Ph 317 B | E | 1 | Brass | — | — | 20.00 | 45.00 |
| Pa-Ph 317 F | F | 1 | WM | — | — | 20.00 | 42.50 |
| (Wright 812; Miller 385) | | | | | | | |
| Pa-Ph 318 | G | 1 | WM | — | — | 15.00 | 35.00 |
| (Miller 388) | | | | | | | |
| Pa-Ph 318 F | H | 1 | WM | — | — | 20.00 | 45.00 |
| Pa-Ph 319 | K | 1 | WM | — | — | 20.00 | 42.50 |
| (Miller 389) | | | | | | | |

This company is still active in the insurance business.

## PFAELZER BROS.
### Philadelphia, Pa.

#### 1876 Centennial Tokens

Reverse type 1: PFAELZER BROS. / WHOLESALE / JEWELRY / 421 MARKET ST. PHILADA. (All 23mm; plain edge)

| Rulau | Obv | Rev | Metal | F | VF | EF | Unc |
|---|---|---|---|---|---|---|---|
| Pa-Ph 321 | A | 1 | WM | — | — | 15.00 | 40.00 |
| Pa-Ph 322 | B | 1 | WM | — | — | 15.00 | 40.00 |
| (Wright 818) | | | | | | | |
| Pa-Ph 322 A | B | 1 | Copper | — | — | 20.00 | 50.00 |
| Pa-Ph 322 F | E | 1 | WM | — | — | 15.00 | 40.00 |
| Pa-Ph 323 | F | 1 | WM | — | — | 17.50 | 45.00 |
| Pa-Ph 323 A | F | 1 | Copper | — | — | 20.00 | 50.00 |
| Pa-Ph 324 | H | 1 | WM | — | — | 17.50 | 45.00 |
| Pa-Ph 324 A | H | 1 | Copper | — | — | 20.00 | 50.00 |
| (Miller Pa 392) | | | | | | | |
| Pa-Ph 324 B | H | 1 | Brass | — | — | 20.00 | 55.00 |
| Pa-Ph 325 | J | 1 | WM | — | — | 17.50 | 45.00 |

## PHILADELPHIA RIFLE CLUB
### Philadelphia, Pa.

| Rulau | Date | Metal | Size | F | VF | EF | Unc |
|---|---|---|---|---|---|---|---|
| Pa-Ph 326 | 1871 | Brass | 26mm | — | — | — | 20.00 |

Target at center, letter V and eagle above. Rv: 25TH / ANNIVERSARY / PHILADELPHIA / RIFLE CLUB / AUGUST / 1871. Plain edge. (Wright 825)

This club was organized in 1846, one of the earliest rifle organizations in the country.

## A. PICARD
### Philadelphia, Pa.

#### 1876 Centennial Tokens

Reverse type 1: A. PICARD / WATCHES / AND / JEWELRY / 805 ARCH ST., PHILAD'A. (All 23mm; plain edge)

| Rulau | Obv | Rev | Metal | F | VF | EF | Unc |
|---|---|---|---|---|---|---|---|
| Pa-Ph 701 | A | 1 | WM | 5.00 | 8.00 | 14.00 | 30.00 |
| (Miller Pa 403) | | | | | | | |
| Pa-Ph 701 A | A | 1 | Copper | — | — | 17.50 | 40.00 |
| Pa-Ph 702 | C | 1 | WM | — | — | 14.00 | 30.00 |
| (Miller 401) | | | | | | | |
| Pa-Ph 702 A | C | 1 | Copper | — | — | 17.50 | 40.00 |
| Pa-Ph 702 B | C | 1 | Brass | — | — | 17.50 | 40.00 |
| (Miller 400) | | | | | | | |
| Pa-Ph 703 | E | 1 | WM | — | — | 15.00 | 35.00 |
| (Miller 403B) | | | | | | | |
| Pa-Ph 703 A | E | 1 | Copper | — | — | 17.50 | 40.00 |
| Pa-Ph 704 | F | 1 | WM | — | — | 20.00 | 45.00 |
| (Miller 403A) | | | | | | | |
| Pa-Ph 705 | G | 1 | WM | — | — | 20.00 | 45.00 |
| Pa-Ph 705 A | G | 1 | Copper | — | — | 20.00 | 45.00 |
| Pa-Ph 706 | H | 1 | WM | — | — | 17.50 | 40.00 |
| (Miller 402) | | | | | | | |
| Pa-Ph 706 A | H | 1 | Copper | — | — | 20.00 | 45.00 |
| Pa-Ph 707 | K | 1 | WM | — | — | 20.00 | 45.00 |
| (Miller 403C) | | | | | | | |

## PILGRIMAGE OF SAN FRANCISCO CLUB
### Philadelphia, Pa.

| Rulau | Date | Metal | Size | F | VF | EF | Unc |
|---|---|---|---|---|---|---|---|
| Pa-Ph 327 | 1883 | Brass | 31mm | — | — | 25.00 | — |

Cross-through-crown superimposed over Maltese cross at center. Around: PILGRIMAGE OF SAN FRANCISCO CLUB TO TRIENNIAL CONCLAVE / . 1883 . Rv: Standing pilgrim with staff facing at center. Around, in three lines: PHILADELPHIA ST. JOHN'S KADOSH ST. ALBAN CORINTHIAN AND / KENSINGTON COMMANDERIES KNIGHTS TEMPLAR. / PHILA. PA. Plain edge.

## JACOB RECH
### Philadelphia, Pa.

| Rulau | Date | Metal | Size | F | VF | EF | Unc |
|---|---|---|---|---|---|---|---|
| Pa-Ph 330 | (1873-74) | WM | 26mm | — | — | 50.00 | 100. |

Clothed, bearded bust of Lincoln right, LINCOLN above, tiny BOLEN beneath bust. Rv: JACOB RECH / FIRST CLASS / CARRIAGE / & WAGON / BUILDER / COR. OF / GIRARD AVE. & 8TH ST / PHILADELPHIA. Plain edge. (King 611; Miller Pa 404)

| Pa-Ph 332 | 1876 | Brass | 26mm | — | — | 50.00 | 100. |
|---|---|---|---|---|---|---|---|

Bust of Hayes half right, R.B. HAYES above, 1876 below. Rv: As 330. (DeWitt RBH 1876-11; Miller Pa 404A)

| Pa-Ph 333 | 1876 | WM | 26mm | — | — | 50.00 | 100. |
|---|---|---|---|---|---|---|---|

As 332. Plain edge. (DeWitt RBH 1876-11)

| Pa-Ph 335 | (1876) | Copper | 25mm | — | — | 20.00 | 50.00 |
|---|---|---|---|---|---|---|---|

American flag blowing to left, LONG MAY IT WAVE above, 13 stars to right below. Rv: As 330. Plain edge. (Wright 1590)

| Pa-Ph 337 | (1876) | Copper | 26mm | — | — | 20.00 | 50.00 |
|---|---|---|---|---|---|---|---|

Liberty bell. Rv: As 330.

Rech was in business at the same locale in 1872.

## J. REED
### Philadelphia, Pa.

#### 1876 Centennial Tokens

Reverse type 1: J. REED * ONE PRICE CLOTHING * / S. E. COR. / SECOND / & / SPRUCE / STS. / PHILAD. (All 23mm; plain edge)

| Rulau | Obv | Rev | Metal | F | VF | EF | Unc |
|---|---|---|---|---|---|---|---|
| Pa-Ph 710 | A | 1 | WM | 5.00 | 8.00 | 12.50 | 25.00 |
| Pa-Ph 711 | B | 1 | WM | — | — | 12.50 | 25.00 |
| Pa-Ph 712 | C | 1 | WM | — | — | 14.00 | 30.00 |
| (Miller 405) | | | | | | | |
| Pa-Ph 712 A | C | 1 | Copper | — | — | 17.50 | 40.00 |
| Also in Bronze. (Miller 406) | | | | | | | |
| Pa-Ph 712 B | C | 1 | Brass | — | — | 20.00 | 45.00 |
| Pa-Ph 713 | D | 1 | WM | — | — | 14.00 | 30.00 |
| Pa-Ph 714 | E | 1 | WM | — | — | 12.50 | 25.00 |
| (Miller 409) | | | | | | | |
| Pa-Ph 715 | F | 1 | WM | — | — | 17.50 | 40.00 |
| (Wright 873; Miller 410) | | | | | | | |
| Pa-Ph 716 | G | 1 | WM | — | — | 14.00 | 30.00 |
| Pa-Ph 717 | H | 1 | WM | — | — | 17.50 | 40.00 |
| (Miller 407) | | | | | | | |

Jacob Reed's Sons was established in 1824 and is still in business as a men's wear outlet. A new building was erected in 1879, shown in the next token, Pa-Ph 340, which is not part of Reed's Centennial series.

## JACOB REED'S SONS
### Philadelphia, Pa.

| Rulau | Date | Metal | Size | VG | F | VF | Unc |
|---|---|---|---|---|---|---|---|
| Pa-Ph 340 | 1879 | WM | 24mm | — | — | 7.50 | 40.00 |

A building. OUR NEW STORE / 1879. Rv: JACOB REED'S / SONS / CLOTHIERS / 2ND / & SPRUCE STS / PHILA. / ESTABLISHED 1824. Plain edge. (Wright 874)

## H. REES
### Philadelphia, Pa.

| Rulau | Date | Metal | Size | VG | F | VF | EF |
|---|---|---|---|---|---|---|---|
| Pa-Ph 343 | (?) | Copper | 29mm | 30.00 | — | 50.00 | — |

H. REES straight ctsp on U.S. Large cents. Dates examined: 1817, 1827. (Hallenbeck 18.502)

| Pa-Ph 344 | (?) | Copper | 29mm | 40.00 | — | 60.00 | — |
|---|---|---|---|---|---|---|---|

H. REES curved ctsp on U.S. 1822 Large cent. (Kovacs coll.)

| Pa-Ph 345 | (?) | Copper | 29mm | 30.00 | — | 50.00 | — |
|---|---|---|---|---|---|---|---|

H. REES / PHILA ctsp on U.S. Large cent. (Hallenbeck 18.503)

## T. ROWLAND & BROTHERS
### Philadelphia, Pa.

| Rulau | Date | Metal | Size | VG | F | VF | EF |
|---|---|---|---|---|---|---|---|
| Pa-Ph 348 | (?) | Copper | 29mm | — | — | 75.00 | — |

T. ROWLAND & BROTHERS PHILADA ctsp on U.S. Large cent. (Hallenbeck 18.764)

## N. H. RICE
### Philadelphia, Pa.

#### 1876 Centennial Tokens

Reverse type 1: CONTINENTAL / CLOTHING HALL / N. H. RICE / PROP. / 930 MARKET ST. / PHILADA., PA. (All 23mm; plain edge)

| Rulau | Obv | Rev | Metal | F | VF | EF | Unc |
|---|---|---|---|---|---|---|---|
| Pa-Ph 720 | A | 1 | WM | — | — | 14.00 | 30.00 |
| (Miller Pa 413) | | | | | | | |
| Pa-Ph 720 A | A | 1 | Copper | — | — | 15.00 | 40.00 |
| Pa-Ph 721 | B | 1 | WM | — | — | 14.00 | 35.00 |
| (Wright 882; Miller 414) | | | | | | | |
| Pa-Ph 721 A | B | 1 | Brass | — | — | 20.00 | 45.00 |
| Pa-Ph 722 | E | 1 | WM | — | — | 14.00 | 35.00 |
| (Miller 411) | | | | | | | |
| Pa-Ph 723 | F | 1 | WM | — | — | 15.00 | 40.00 |
| (Miller 412) | | | | | | | |
| Pa-Ph 724 | G | 1 | WM | — | — | 14.00 | 30.00 |
| (Miller 415) | | | | | | | |
| Pa-Ph 725 | H | 1 | WM | — | — | 15.00 | 40.00 |
| Pa-Ph 726 | J | 1 | WM | — | — | 17.50 | 40.00 |
| Pa-Ph 727 | K | 1 | WM | — | — | 15.00 | 40.00 |

## SAUSSER, DANGLER & CO.
### Philadelphia, Pa.

#### 1876 Centennial Tokens

Reverse type 1: SAUSSER / DANGLER & CO. / FINE / SEWED SHOES / 412 TO 420 / SOUTH 13TH ST. / PHILA. (All 23mm; plain edge)

| Rulau | Obv | Rev | Metal | F | VF | EF | Unc |
|---|---|---|---|---|---|---|---|
| Pa-Ph 730 | A | 1 | WM | — | — | 15.00 | 40.00 |
| (Wright 1613; Miller Pa 438) | | | | | | | |
| Pa-Ph 731 | B | 1 | WM | — | — | 15.00 | 40.00 |
| Pa-Ph 732 | E | 1 | WM | — | — | 15.00 | 40.00 |
| (Miller 439) | | | | | | | |
| Pa-Ph 733 | F | 1 | WM | — | — | 17.50 | 42.50 |
| (Miller 441) | | | | | | | |
| Pa-Ph 734 | G | 1 | WM | — | — | 17.50 | 42.50 |
| Pa-Ph 735 | H | 1 | WM | — | — | 17.50 | 42.50 |
| (Miller 442) | | | | | | | |
| Pa-Ph 736 | J | 1 | Copper | — | — | 20.00 | 45.00 |

# JOHN G. SCHMIDT
## Philadelphia, Pa.

### 1876 Centennial Tokens

Reverse type 1: JOHN G. SCHMIDT. / 1236 / POPLAR ST. / (an awl) / PHILADELPHIA / LEATHER / FINDINGS &C. (All 23mm; plain edge)

Obverse die SM: SOLE LEATHER / CALF / & GOAT SKINS. / LASTING. / MACHINE SILK / THREAD / TOOLS, UPPERS / OIL &C. (All 23mm; plain edges)

| Rulau | Obv | Rev | Metal | F | VF | EF | Unc |
|---|---|---|---|---|---|---|---|
| Pa-Ph 352 | C | 1 | Brass | — | — | 20.00 | 45.00 |
| Pa-Ph 353 | H | 1 | WM | | | Not confirmed | |
| Pa-Ph 353 A | H | 1 | Brass | — | — | 20.00 | 45.00 |
| Pa-Ph 354 | J | 1 | WM | 7.50 | 10.00 | 15.00 | 40.00 |
| | | (Miller Pa 447) | | | | | |
| Pa-Ph 354 A | J | 1 | Brass | 5.00 | 8.50 | 20.00 | 45.00 |
| | | (Miller 446) | | | | | |
| Pa-Ph 356 | SM | 1 | WM | — | — | 15.00 | 40.00 |
| | | (Miller 445) | | | | | |
| Pa-Ph 356 A | SM | 1 | Copper | — | — | 25.00 | 45.00 |
| | | (Miller 444) | | | | | |
| Pa-Ph 356 B | SM | 1 | Brass | 5.00 | 8.50 | 15.00 | 25.00 |
| | | (Wright 947; Miller 443) | | | | | |

NOTE: Pa-Ph 356B was the regular store card of Schmidt, probably issued before the other tokens were conceived. This is an interesting series, with more varieties probably awaiting discovery.

# JOS. SCHOENEMAN & CO.
## Philadelphia, Pa.

| Rulau | Date | Metal | Size | VG | F | VF | Unc |
|---|---|---|---|---|---|---|---|
| Pa-Ph 361 | (1889) | WM | 36mm | — | — | — | Scrc |

Two men in tights boxing, bare-knuckle style. Rv: JOS. / SCHOENEMAN / & CO. / PHILADELPHIA within flourishes. Plain edge. (Wright 951)

Wright reports this piece in aluminum, which needs comfirmation.

| Rulau | Date | Metal | Size | VG | F | VF | Unc |
|---|---|---|---|---|---|---|---|
| Pa-Ph 362 | (1889) | WM | 36mm | — | — | — | Scrc |

Batter awaiting baseball as an infielder watches from background. The uniform styles are Gay Nineties or earlier. Rv: Same as last. Plain edge.

| Rulau | Date | Metal | Size | VG | F | VF | Unc |
|---|---|---|---|---|---|---|---|
| Pa-Ph 363 | (1889) | WM | 36mm | — | — | — | Scrc |

Standing man riding the back of a gigantic eagle, flying right, from whose beak a ribbon reading ONWARD trails. Rv: As 361. Plain edge. (Brunk coll.)

# SCHOENEMAN LANGSTADTER & CO.
## Philadelphia, Pa.

| Rulau | Date | Metal | Size | VG | F | VF | Unc |
|---|---|---|---|---|---|---|---|
| Pa-Ph 364 | (1889) | WM | 36mm | — | — | — | Scrc |

Obverse as last (baseball game). Rv: SCHOENEMAN / LANGSTADTER / & CO. / (ornament) — PHILADELPHIA. Plain edge. (Wright 952)

# C. B. SCOTT & CO.
## Philadelphia, Pa.

### 1876 Centennial Tokens

Reverse type 1: C. B. SCOTT & CO. / MANUFR'S / AND / DEALERS IN / FURNITURE / NO. 33 / SO. SECOND ST. / PHILA. (All 23mm; plain edge)

| Rulau | Obv | Rev | Metal | F | VF | EF | Unc |
|---|---|---|---|---|---|---|---|
| Pa-Ph 740 | A | 1 | WM | — | — | 15.00 | 40.00 |
| | | (Miller Pa 449) | | | | | |
| Pa-Ph 740 A | A | 1 | Brass | — | — | 20.00 | 45.00 |
| | | (Wright 967; Miller 450) | | | | | |
| Pa-Ph 741 | B | 1 | WM | — | — | 15.00 | 40.00 |
| | | (Miller 454) | | | | | |
| Pa-Ph 741 A | B | 1 | Copper | — | — | 17.50 | 40.00 |
| Pa-Ph 742 | E | 1 | WM | — | — | 15.00 | 40.00 |
| | | (Miller 453) | | | | | |
| Pa-Ph 743 | F | 1 | WM | — | — | 17.50 | 40.00 |
| | | (Miller 455) | | | | | |

| Rulau | Obv | Rev | Metal | F | VF | EF | Unc |
|---|---|---|---|---|---|---|---|
| Pa-Ph 744 | G | 1 | WM | — | — | 17.50 | 40.00 |
| Pa-Ph 745 | H | 1 | WM | — | — | 17.50 | 40.00 |
|  |  | (Miller 452) |  |  |  |  |  |
| Pa-Ph 745 A | H | 1 | Copper | — | — | 20.00 | 45.00 |
| Pa-Ph 745 B | H | 1 | Brass | — | — | 20.00 | 50.00 |
|  |  | (Miller 451) |  |  |  |  |  |
| Pa-Ph 746 | J | 1 | WM | — | — | 20.00 | 45.00 |

## 2ND REGIMENT N.G. PA.
### Philadelphia, Pa.

| Rulau | Date | Metal | Size | F | VF | EF | Unc |
|---|---|---|---|---|---|---|---|
| Pa-Ph 372 | 1879 | Bronze | 19mm | — | 15.00 | — | — |

Crested shield of arms at center. Eagle, wings folded, head left, is the crest. Arms are those of the Pennsylvania National Guard. On a scroll below: NON SIBI SED PATRIAE (not for self but for country). Around: 2ND REGIMENT N. G. PA. / * 1840. — 1879. *. Rv: Crested, supported shield of arms of Philadelphia at center. Around: COMMEMORATION OF THE FAIR / * NOV. 10. 1879 *. Reeded edge.

Presumably the Pennsylvania National Guard was organized in 1840. This neat, well made cent-sized medalet may be a product of the U.S. Mint.

## JOHN H. SERVER
### Philadelphia, Pa.

**1876 Centennial Tokens**

Reverse type 1: JOHN H. SERVER / TOBACOO / CIGARS / AND / VARIETY STORE / 1646 S. 11TH ST. PHILA. (All 23mm; plain edge)

| Rulau | Obv | Rev | Metal | F | VF | EF | Unc |
|---|---|---|---|---|---|---|---|
| Pa-Ph 750 | A | 1 | WM | — | — | 15.00 | 40.00 |
|  |  | (Wright 1626; Miller Pa 457) |  |  |  |  |  |
| Pa-Ph 751 | B | 1 | WM | — | — | 15.00 | 40.00 |
|  |  | (Miller 456) |  |  |  |  |  |
| Pa-Ph 751 A | B | 1 | Brass | — | — | 20.00 | 45.00 |
| Pa-Ph 752 | D | 1 | WM | — | — | 15.00 | 40.00 |
|  |  | (Miller 461) |  |  |  |  |  |
| Pa-Ph 752 A | D | 1 | Brass | — | — | 20.00 | 45.00 |
| Pa-Ph 753 | E | 1 | WM | — | — | 15.00 | 40.00 |
|  |  | (Miller 458) |  |  |  |  |  |
| Pa-Ph 754 | F | 1 | WM | — | — | 20.00 | 45.00 |
|  |  | (Miller 459) |  |  |  |  |  |
| Pa-Ph 755 | G | 1 | WM | — | — | 17.50 | 40.00 |
| Pa-Ph 756 | H | 1 | WM | — | — | 17.50 | 40.00 |
|  |  | (Miller 460) |  |  |  |  |  |
| Pa-Ph 757 | K | 1 | WM | — | — | 20.00 | 45.00 |
|  |  | (Miller 460A) |  |  |  |  |  |

## SHARPLESS BROTHERS
### Philadelphia, Pa.

| Rulau | Date | Metal | Size | F | VF | EF | Unc |
|---|---|---|---|---|---|---|---|
| Pa-Ph 365 | (1875) | Brass | 29mm | 4.00 | 6.00 | 8.00 | 25.00 |

Beehive at center, SHARPLESS BROTHERS above; LATE / TOWNSEND SHARPLESS / & SONS. Rv: DRY GOODS / WHOLESALE & RETAIL / AT THEIR / NEW STORE / N.W. COR. OF 8TH & CHESTNUT. Plain edge. (Wright 944; Miller Pa 469)

| Pa-Ph 366 | (1875) | GS | 29mm | — | — | 30.00 | 50.00 |
|---|---|---|---|---|---|---|---|
|  |  | As 365. (Miller Pa 470) |  |  |  |  |  |
| Pa-Ph 367 | (1875) | Gilt | 29mm | — | — | 20.00 | 40.00 |
|  |  | As 365. (Miller Pa 471) |  |  |  |  |  |
| Pa-Ph 368 | (1875) | S/Br | 29mm | — | — | 20.00 | 40.00 |
|  |  | As 365. (Miller Pa 472) |  |  |  |  |  |
| Pa-Ph 369 | (1875) | WM | 29mm | — | 10.00 | 20.00 | 50.00 |
|  |  | As 365. (Miller Pa 473) |  |  |  |  |  |
| Pa-Ph 370 | (1875) | Silver | 29mm | — | — | 100. | 250. |
|  |  | As 365. (Miller Pa 474) |  |  |  |  |  |

According to the 1872 directory, Sharpless & Son, dry goods importers and jobbers, were located at corner 8th and Chestnut.

By 1918, there were Sharpless Brothers listed in Philadelphia as hardware dealers, but the possible successors were Sharpless & Sharpless, "men's furnishings." There was also a firm, P.E. Sharpless & Co., wholesale butter and egg merchants, with branches in other cities.

## SINKLER & DAVEY
### Philadelphia, Pa.

| Rulau | Date | Metal | Size | F | VF | Unc |
|---|---|---|---|---|---|---|
| Pa-Ph 373 | (1889-90) | Brass | 29mm | 150. | 200. | — |

Two donkeys are at center, star below. WHEN SHALL WE THREE MEET AGAIN is around. Rv: SINKLER & DAVEY / * / MANUF'S OF / FANCY METAL WORK / LABEL, CHECKS & / FANCY LETTERS. -- / 609 CALLOWHILL ST. / (arrow) PHILAD'A (arrow). Plain edge. (Miller Pa 474½)

Sinkler & Davey were diesinkers in business in Philadelphia in the late 1880's. The same obverse die (two donkeys) was used on the Applegate tokens of Atlantic City and Feely tokens of Philadelphia, and a very similar one (in reduced size) was used on the Durkee & Co. omnibus checks in New York in the 1840's. The Durkee piece may have been the model for the S&D pieces.

A successor firm, William Davey's Son, was in the stamped metal goods business in 1918.

Harry Sinkler and William H. Davey, diesinkers, are listed at the 609 Callowhill St. address only in the 1890 directory, which means they were there, probably, 1889-1890.

Therefore these pieces must be placed in the 1889-90 date frame, or just at the outer edge of our coverage in this volume.

## G. B. SOLEY
### Philadelphia, Pa.

| Rulau | Date | Metal | Size | F | VF | EF | Unc |
|---|---|---|---|---|---|---|---|
| Pa-Ph 375 | (1876) | ** | 37mm | — | — | 50.00 | 65.00 |

** Golden colored cardboard. Independence Hall at center, tiny G. B. SOLEY PHILA. below ground line. Above: BIRTH PLACE OF AMERICAN; below: INDEPENDENCE / 1776. Rv: G. B. SOLEY, 1205 CHESTNUT ST. PHILA. / MANUFACTURER / OF / (sprig) MEDALS. (sprig) / —.— / THE LORD'S PRAYER / IN SMALLEST SPACE / EVER STRUCK ON METAL. / —.— / PAPER & METALLIC / ADVERTISING / CARDS. Plain edge.

## JOHN STILZ & SON
## Philadelphia, Pa.

### 1876 Centennial Tokens

Reverse type 1: JOHN STILZ & SON / * / FINEST / CLOTHING / HOUSE / S. E. COR. 7 & MARKET / PHILADA. (All 23mm; plain edge)

| Rulau | Obv | Rev | Metal | F | VF | EF | Unc |
|---|---|---|---|---|---|---|---|
| Pa-Ph 760 | A | 1 | WM | 5.00 | 8.00 | 12.50 | 30.00 |
| (Wright 1046; Miller Pa 492) | | | | | | | |
| Pa-Ph 760 A | A | 1 | Copper | — | — | 14.00 | 37.50 |
| (Miller 491) | | | | | | | |
| Pa-Ph 760 B | A | 1 | Brass | — | — | 16.50 | 40.00 |
| Pa-Ph 761 | B | 1 | WM | — | — | 12.50 | 30.00 |
| (Miller 493) | | | | | | | |
| Pa-Ph 762 | C | 1 | WM | — | — | 15.00 | 37.50 |
| Pa-Ph 763 | E | 1 | WM | — | — | 14.00 | 37.50 |
| (Miller 495) | | | | | | | |
| Pa-Ph 764 | F | 1 | WM | — | — | 15.00 | 40.00 |
| (Miller 496) | | | | | | | |
| Pa-Ph 765 | H | 1 | WM | — | — | 14.00 | 37.50 |
| Pa-Ph 766 | K | 1 | WM | — | — | 15.00 | 40.00 |
| (Miller 497) | | | | | | | |

## G. STOKES
## Philadelphia, Pa.

| Rulau | Date | Metal | Size | F | VF | EF | Unc |
|---|---|---|---|---|---|---|---|
| Pa-Ph 380 | (1866-68) | WM | 22mm | — | — | — | — |

G. STOKES. / FINE / CLOTHING / 607 / CHESTNUT ST. PHILA. Rv: Cutaway cross-section of the Atlantic cable. Grooved edge. Planchet is 6mm thick. (Miller Pa 500; Wright 1063)

| Pa-Ph 381 | (1866-68) | Copper | 22mm | — | — | — | — |

As 380. Grooved edge. Planchet 6mm thick. Rarity 4.

Granville Stokes earlier issued an 1862-dated Civil War token. The 31mm brass token is Fuld Pa 750-T1b (Miller 498) and carries the address 609 Chestnut St.

Stokes purchased a portion of the first Atlantic cable, cut off quarter-inches in thickness and had a suitable die made for striking one side, the other side showing the arrangement of the wires. The first cable was laid, unsuccessfully, in 1858 (tokens celebrated this event even though it did not occur; these were issued by George H. Lovett of New York). The successful cable was laid by the British liner *Great Eastern*, in 1866. Probably numbers 380-381 were issued after the second cable laying between the U.S. and England.

## DR. STOUGHTON
## Philadelphia, Pa.

### 1876 Centennial Tokens

Reverse type 1: TEETH / $5 to $15 / PER SET / FILLING 75C to $1. / EXTRACTING 25C / DR. STOUGHTON / 1117 / VINE ST. (All 23mm; plain edge)

| Rulau | Obv | Rev | Metal | F | VF | EF | Unc |
|---|---|---|---|---|---|---|---|
| Pa-Ph 383 | A | 1 | WM | — | — | 20.00 | 45.00 |
| Pa-Ph 384 | B | 1 | WM | — | — | 20.00 | 45.00 |
| Pa-Ph 385 | E | 1 | WM | — | — | 20.00 | 45.00 |
| Pa-Ph 386 | F | 1 | Copper | — | — | 25.00 | 55.00 |
| Pa-Ph 386 A | F | 1 | Brass | — | — | 25.00 | 55.00 |
| Pa-Ph 387 | G | 1 | WM | — | — | 22.50 | 50.00 |
| Pa-Ph 388 | K | 1 | WM | — | — | 22.50 | 50.00 |
| (Wright 1066; Miller Pa 502) | | | | | | | |

These tokens provide a schedule of big-city dentist fees in 1876. The 25-cent extraction was without benefit of painkiller.

## JAS. THORNTON
## Philadelphia, Pa.

### 1876 Centennial Tokens

Reverse type 1: JAS. THORNTON'S / LOOKING GLASS / PICTURE FRAME / AND / BRACKET DEPOT / S. W. COR. 11 AND LOCUST ST., PHILA. (All 23mm; plain edge)

| Rulau | Obv | Rev | Metal | F | VF | EF | Unc |
|---|---|---|---|---|---|---|---|
| Pa-Ph 770 | A | 1 | WM | — | — | 12.50 | 30.00 |
| (Wright 1144; Miller Pa 521) | | | | | | | |
| Pa-Ph 771 | B | | WM | — | — | 12.50 | 30.00 |
| (Miller 520) | | | | | | | |
| Pa-Ph 771 A | B | 1 | Copper | — | — | 15.00 | 35.00 |
| (Miller 519) | | | | | | | |
| Pa-Ph 771 B | B | 1 | Brass | — | — | 17.50 | 40.00 |
| Pa-Ph 772 | D | 1 | WM | — | — | 15.00 | 35.00 |
| Pa-Ph 773 | E | 1 | WM | — | — | 15.00 | 35.00 |
| (Miller 522) | | | | | | | |
| Pa-Ph 774 | F | 1 | WM | — | — | 17.50 | 40.00 |
| (Miller 523) | | | | | | | |
| Pa-Ph 775 | G | 1 | WM | — | — | 15.00 | 35.00 |
| Pa-Ph 776 | H | 1 | WM | — | — | 15.00 | 35.00 |
| Pa-Ph 777 | J | 1 | WM | — | — | 15.00 | 35.00 |
| Pa-Ph 778 | K | 1 | WM | — | — | 17.50 | 40.00 |
| Pa-Ph 778 A | K | 1 | Brass | — | — | 20.00 | 45.00 |
| (Miller 519A) | | | | | | | |

## S. C. UPHAM
## Philadelphia, Pa.

### 1876 Centennial Tokens

Reverse type 1: S. C. UPHAM. PERFURMER. (All 19mm; plain edge)

| Rulau | Obv | Rev | Metal | F | VF | EF | Unc |
|---|---|---|---|---|---|---|---|
| Pa-Ph 780 | X | 1 | WM | — | — | 20.00 | 50.00 |
| Pa-Ph 781 | Y | 1 | WM | — | — | 20.00 | 50.00 |

S. C. Upham is well known to paper money collectors for his facsimiles of Confederate States notes. These tokens were not known to Wright, Adams, Miller and other cataloguers.

## U.S. MINT EMPLOYEES
## Philadelphia, Pa.

| Rulau | Date | Metal | Size | F | VF | EF | Unc |
|---|---|---|---|---|---|---|---|
| Pa-Ph 390 | 1879 | Brass | 25mm | 3.00 | 6.50 | 8.50 | 13.00 |

Bust left, ULYSSES S. GRANT. Tiny M on truncation of bust. Rv: Supported Philadelphia arms in center circle. STRUCK AND DISTRIBUTED IN THE MUNICIPAL PARADE (diamond) / BY THE EMPLOYES OF THE U.S. MINT / . PHILA. DEC. 16. 1879. Plain edge.

| Pa-Ph 390 A | 1879 | Gold | 25mm | — | — | —2 Known | |

As 390. Plain edge.

| Rulau | Date | Metal | Size | F | VF | EF | Unc |
|---|---|---|---|---|---|---|---|
| Pa-Ph 393 | 1882 | Brass | 25mm | 2.00 | 4.00 | 6.00 | 12.00 |

Facing bust in colonial hat, PENN 1682. Rv: Supported Pennsylvania arms in center circle. DISTRIBUTED BY EMPLOYES OF U.S. MINT DURING THE CELEBRATION. / OF PENNSYLVANIA'S BICENTENNIAL. / . OCT. 24, 1882. Plain edge.

| Rulau | Date | Metal | Size | F | VF | EF | Unc |
|---|---|---|---|---|---|---|---|
| Pa-Ph 393 A | 1882 | Gold | 25mm | — | — | 3 Known | |

As 393. Plain edge.

| Pa-Ph 393 B | 1882 | Silver | 25mm | — | — | — | — |

As 393. Plain edge.

| Rulau | Date | Metal | Size | F | VF | EF | Unc |
|---|---|---|---|---|---|---|---|
| Pa-Ph 396 | 1887 | Brass | 25mm | — | 17.50 | 25.00 | 40.00 |

Bust of U.S. Mint Director SNOWDEN right, A. LOUDON SHOWDEN / o MARSHAL o. Rv: CENTENNIAL OF THE CONSTITUTION / STRUCK / & DISTRIBUTED / IN THE / CIVIC & INDUSTRIAL / PROCESSION / SEPT. 15. / .1787-1887. Plain edge.

## VICTORIA CORDAGE WORKS
### Philadelphia, Pa.

| Rulau | Date | Metal | Size | F | VF | EF | Unc |
|---|---|---|---|---|---|---|---|
| Pa-Ph 400 | (1880's) | GB | 25mm | 3.00 | 4.00 | 5.00 | 10.00 |

Wheat stalks within a crown. TRADE MARK below. Rv: + BINDER TWINE + / VICTORIA / (radiant sun) / CORDAGE / WORKS / (radiant sun) / PHILADELPHIA / AND CORDAGE. Plain edge. (Wright 1190)

## JOHN E. VALLEE
### Philadelphia, Pa.

#### 1876 Centennial Tokens

Reverse type 1: JOHN E. VALLEE / LOCKSMITH, BELL HANGER / 1934 / GERMANTOWN AVE. (All 23mm; plain edge)

Reverse type 2: JOHN E. VALLEE / BELL HANGER / 2313 / N. EIGHTH ST. / PHILA. (All 23mm; plain edge)

| Rulau | Obv | Rev | Metal | F | VF | EF | Unc |
|---|---|---|---|---|---|---|---|
| Pa-Ph 785 | A | 1 | WM | — | — | 15.00 | 40.00 |
| | | (Miller Pa 526) | | | | | |
| Pa-Ph 786 | B | 1 | WM | — | — | 15.00 | 40.00 |
| | | (Miller 527) | | | | | |
| Pa-Ph 786 A | B | 1 | Brass | — | — | 20.00 | 45.00 |
| Pa-Ph 787 | C | 1 | WM | — | — | 15.00 | 45.00 |
| Pa-Ph 788 | D | 1 | WM | — | — | 17.50 | 40.00 |
| | | (Miller 529A) | | | | | |
| Pa-Ph 789 | E | 1 | WM | — | — | 15.00 | 40.00 |
| | | (Miller 528) | | | | | |
| Pa-Ph 790 | F | 1 | WM | — | — | 20.00 | 45.00 |
| Pa-Ph 791 | G | 1 | WM | — | — | 17.50 | 40.00 |
| | | (Miller 525) | | | | | |
| Pa-Ph 792 | H | 1 | WM | — | — | 17.50 | 40.00 |
| | | (Miller 524) | | | | | |
| Pa-Ph 793 | J | 1 | Copper | — | — | 20.00 | 45.00 |
| | | (Miller 529B) | | | | | |
| Pa-Ph 795 | A | 2 | WM | — | — | 15.00 | 40.00 |
| | | (Wright 1181 ?) | | | | | |
| Pa-Ph 796 | B | 2 | WM | — | — | 15.00 | 40.00 |
| Pa-Ph 796 F | G | 2 | WM | — | — | 17.50 | 45.00 |
| Pa-Ph 797 | H | 2 | WM | — | — | 17.50 | 45.00 |
| Pa-Ph 797 F | J | 2 | WM | — | — | 17.50 | 45.00 |
| Pa-Ph 798 | K | 2 | WM | — | — | 17.50 | 45.00 |

## C.A. WALTHER
### Philadelphia, Pa.

#### 1876 Centennial Tokens

Reverse type 1: LIBRARY ST. HALL / 412 LIBRARY ST. / PHILA. / --- / CHOICE / WINES & BEERS. / C. A. WALTHER, PROPR. (All 23mm; plain edge. Not catalogued by Slabaugh)

| Rulau | Obv | Rev | Metal | F | VF | EF | Unc |
|---|---|---|---|---|---|---|---|
| Pa-Ph 405 | J | 1 | WM | — | — | — | 100. |
| Pa-Ph 406 | K | 1 | WM | — | — | 13.50 | 25.00 |
| | | (Wright 1714; Miller Pa 529 1/2) | | | | | |

## WANAMAKER & BROWN
### Philadelphia, Pa.

| Rulau | Date | Metal | Size | F | VF | EF | Unc |
|---|---|---|---|---|---|---|---|
| Pa-Ph 410 | (1880's) | Brass | 25mm | 2.00 | 3.00 | 4.50 | 10.00 |

U.S. flag, WANAMAKER & BROWN below. Rv: Huge building at center, tiny P.L. KRIDER on exergue line. BOYS CLOTHING above, OAK HALL below. Plain edge. (Wright 1201; Miller Pa 532)

| Pa-Ph 411 | (1880's) | S/Br | 25mm | 2.50 | 3.50 | 5.00 | 10.00 |

As 410. Plain edge. (Miller Pa 532A)

| Pa-Ph 411 A | (1880's) | Copper | 25mm | — | — | — | — |

As 410. Plain edge.

Struck by Peter L. Krider of Philadelphia.

John Wanamaker (1838-1922) and Nathan Brown founded Wanamaker & Brown, clothiers, in 1861. Brown died in 1868. The firm, under William H. Wanamaker, was still in business in 1918, under the same name.

The extensive token issues of John Wanamaker Stores begin after 1890 and will be catalogued in our forthcoming reference, *U.S. Trade Tokens 1890-1913.* There are about 50 such pieces known.

## CHARLES K. WARNER
### Philadelphia, Pa.

| Rulau | Date | Metal | Size | F | VF | EF | Unc |
|---|---|---|---|---|---|---|---|
| Pa-Ph 435 | (?) | Copper | --mm | 8.00 | 14.00 | 18.00 | 50.00 |

Small bust of George Washington. Rv: 28 battles. (Miller Pa 533)

| Pa-Ph 435 A | (?) | Brass | --mm | 8.00 | 14.00 | 18.00 | 50.00 |

As 435. (Miller Pa 534)

| Pa-Ph 435 B | (?) | WM | --mm | 8.00 | 14.00 | 22.00 | 50.00 |

As 435. (Miller Pa 535)

| Rulau | Date | Metal | Size | F | VF | EF | Unc |
|---|---|---|---|---|---|---|---|
| Pa-Ph 437 | (1862-63) | Copper | 26mm | — | — | 30.00 | 75.00 |

Facing bust of Van Buren, MARTIN VAN BUREN. above, .THE PEOPLES CHOICE. below. (Obverse die of Low 57, retouched.) Rv: CHAS. K. WARNER / DEALER IN / AMERICAN & / FOREIGN / COINS / & MEDALS / 326 CHESTNUT ST., PHILA. Plain edge. (DeWitt MVB-C(3)) Only 15 struck. (Miller Pa 535A)

| Pa-Ph 437 A | (1862-63) | Brass | 26mm | — | — | 30.00 | 75.00 |
|---|---|---|---|---|---|---|---|

As 437. 15 struck. (Miller Pa 535B)

| Pa-Ph 437 B | (1862-63) | WM | 26mm | — | — | 30.00 | 75.00 |
|---|---|---|---|---|---|---|---|

As 437. 15 struck. (Miller Pa 535C)

| Pa-Ph 439 | (?) | Copper | 26mm | 8.00 | 14.00 | 18.00 | 50.00 |
|---|---|---|---|---|---|---|---|

General Peter Lyle. Rv: As 535A. Plain edge. (Miller Pa 536)

| Pa-Ph 439 A | (?) | Brass | 26mm | 8.00 | 14.00 | 18.00 | 50.00 |
|---|---|---|---|---|---|---|---|

As 439. (Miller Pa 537)

| Pa-Ph 439 B | (?) | WM | 26mm | 8.00 | 14.00 | 22.00 | 50.00 |
|---|---|---|---|---|---|---|---|

As 439. (Miller Pa 538)

| Pa-Ph 440 | (?) | Copper | 26mm | 8.00 | 14.00 | 18.00 | 50.00 |
|---|---|---|---|---|---|---|---|

THE CONSTITUTION & THE UNION. Rv: As 437. Plain edge. (Miller Pa 539)

| Pa-Ph 440 A | (?) | Brass | 26mm | 8.00 | 14.00 | 18.00 | 50.00 |
|---|---|---|---|---|---|---|---|

As 440. (Miller Pa 540)

| Pa-Ph 440 B | (?) | WM | 26mm | 8.00 | 14.00 | 22.00 | 50.00 |
|---|---|---|---|---|---|---|---|

As 440. (Miller Pa 541)

| Pa-Ph 442 | (1863) | Copper | 26mm | — | — | 30.00 | 75.00 |
|---|---|---|---|---|---|---|---|

General U.S. Grant military bust left, tiny W.H.K. below truncation. Around: LIEUT. GEN. U. S. GRANT. Rv: C. K. WARNER / (eagle) / NUMISMATIST, / 326 / CHESTNUT ST. / — / PHILADELPHIA. Plain edge. Only 15 struck. (Miller Pa 542)

| Pa-Ph 442 A | (1863) | Brass | 26mm | — | — | 30.00 | 75.00 |
|---|---|---|---|---|---|---|---|

As 442. (Miller Pa 543)

| Pa-Ph 442 B | (1863) | WM | 26mm | — | — | 30.00 | 75.00 |
|---|---|---|---|---|---|---|---|

As 442. (Miller Pa 544)

| Pa-Ph 443 | (1865) | Copper | 26mm | — | — | 30.00 | 75.00 |
|---|---|---|---|---|---|---|---|

Surrender of General Lee. Rv: As 437. Plain edge. (Miller Pa 545)

| Pa-Ph 443 A | (1865) | Brass | 26mm | — | — | 30.00 | 75.00 |
|---|---|---|---|---|---|---|---|

As 443. (Miller Pa 546)

| Pa-Ph 443 B | (1865) | WM | 26mm | — | — | 30.00 | 75.00 |
|---|---|---|---|---|---|---|---|

As 443. (Miller Pa 547)

| Pa-Ph 445 | (1868) | Copper | 26mm | — | — | 25.00 | 60.00 |
|---|---|---|---|---|---|---|---|

Bust of Horatio Seymour. Rv: As 437. Plain edge. (Miller Pa 548)

| Pa-Ph 445 A | (1868) | Brass | 26mm | — | — | 25.00 | 60.00 |
|---|---|---|---|---|---|---|---|

As 445. (Miller Pa 549)

| Pa-Ph 445 B | (1868) | WM | 26mm | — | — | 25.00 | 60.00 |
|---|---|---|---|---|---|---|---|

As 445. (Miller Pa 550)

| Pa-Ph 446 | 1862 | Copper | 26mm | — | — | 30.00 | 75.00 |
|---|---|---|---|---|---|---|---|

Monitor, 1862. Rv: As 437. Plain edge. (Miller Pa 551)

| Pa-Ph 446 A | 1862 | Brass | 26mm | — | — | 30.00 | 75.00 |
|---|---|---|---|---|---|---|---|

As 446. (Miller Pa 552)

| Pa-Ph 446 B | 1862 | WM | 26mm | — | — | 30.00 | 75.00 |
|---|---|---|---|---|---|---|---|

As 446. (Miller Pa 553)

| Pa-Ph 448 | 1860 (1865) | Copper | 27mm | — | — | 50.00 | 100. |
|---|---|---|---|---|---|---|---|

Bust of beardless Lincoln right, tiny R L PHILA under truncation of the bust. ABM: LINCOLN, REP. CANDIDATE FOR PRESIDENT around, 1860 below. Rv: Washington bust right within two-line inscription: CHAS. K. WARNER / DEALER IN / AMERICAN & / FOREIGN / MEDALS / 728 CHESTNUT ST., * PHILAD*. Plain edge. (King 601; DeWitt AL 1860-51(B); Miller Pa 554)

| Pa-Ph 448 A | 1860('65) | Brass | 27mm | — | — | 50.00 | 100. |
|---|---|---|---|---|---|---|---|

As 448. (King 601; DeWitt AL 1860-51(B); Miller 555)

| Pa-Ph 448 B | 1860('65) | WM | 27mm | — | — | 50.00 | 100. |
|---|---|---|---|---|---|---|---|

As 448. (King 601; DeWitt AL 1860-51(B); Miller 556)

The dies for 448-448B were cut by Robert Lovett Jr. of Philadelphia. It is possible they were contemporary with the date 1860 and belong in *U.S. Merchant Tokens 1845-1860*, but until evidence suggests otherwise we believe they are post-Civil War products of coin dealer Warner.

| Pa-Ph 450 | (1863) | Copper | 26mm | 8.00 | 14.00 | 18.00 | 50.00 |
|---|---|---|---|---|---|---|---|

THE UNION MUST AND SHALL BE PRESERVED around. Head of Washington on flags, Rv: As 442. Plain edge. (Miller Pa 557)

| Pa-Ph 450 A | 1863 | Brass | 26mm | 8.00 | 14.00 | 18.00 | 50.00 |
|---|---|---|---|---|---|---|---|

As 450. (Miller 558)

| Pa-Ph 450 B | 1863 | WM | 26mm | 8.00 | 14.00 | 22.00 | 50.00 |
|---|---|---|---|---|---|---|---|

As 450. (Miller 559)

| Pa-Ph 451 | 1863 | Copper | 26mm | — | — | 30.00 | 75.00 |
|---|---|---|---|---|---|---|---|

General George B. McClellan. Rv: As 442. Plain edge. Only 15 struck. (Miller Pa 560)

| Pa-Ph 451 A | (1863) | Brass | 26mm | — | — | 30.00 | 75.00 |
|---|---|---|---|---|---|---|---|

As 451. 15 struck. (Miller 561)

| Pa-Ph 451 B | (1863) | WM | 26mm | — | — | 30.00 | 75.00 |
|---|---|---|---|---|---|---|---|

As 451. 15 struck. (Miller 562)

| Pa-Ph 452 | (1864) | Copper | --mm | — | — | 30.00 | 75.00 |
|---|---|---|---|---|---|---|---|

Different head of McClellan than on 560. Rv: As 437. Plain edge.

| Pa-Ph 452 A | (1864) | Brass | --mm | — | — | 30.00 | 75.00 |
|---|---|---|---|---|---|---|---|

As 452. (Miller 564)

| Pa-Ph 452 B | (1864) | WM | --mm | — | — | 30.00 | 75.00 |
|---|---|---|---|---|---|---|---|

As 452. (Miller 565)

| Pa-Ph 454 | (?) | Copper | --mm | — | — | 20.00 | 50.00 |
|---|---|---|---|---|---|---|---|

Victoria and Albert of England. Rv: As 437. Plain edge. (Miller Pa 566)

| Pa-Ph 454 A | (?) | Brass | — | — | — | 20.00 | 50.00 |
|---|---|---|---|---|---|---|---|

As 454. (Miller 567)

| Pa-Ph 454 B | (?) | WM | --mm | — | — | 25.00 | 60.00 |
|---|---|---|---|---|---|---|---|

As 454. (Miller 568)

| Pa-Ph 455 | 1870 | Copper | 26mm | — | — | 25.00 | 60.00 |
|---|---|---|---|---|---|---|---|

U.S. flag at center, LONG MAY IT WAVE around. Rv: As 535A. Plain edge. (Miller Pa 569A)

| Pa-Ph 455 A | 1870 | Brass | 26mm | — | — | 25.00 | 60.00 |
|---|---|---|---|---|---|---|---|

As 455. (Miller 569)

| Pa-Ph 455 B | 1870 | WM | 26mm | — | — | 25.00 | 60.00 |
|---|---|---|---|---|---|---|---|

As 455. (Wright 1204; Miller Pa 569B)

| Rulau | Date | Metal | Size | F | VF | EF | Unc |
|---|---|---|---|---|---|---|---|
| Pa-Ph 457 | 1863 | Copper | 26mm | — | — | 25.00 | 60.00 |

Shield within a wreath. Around: NATIONAL UNION LEAGUE / OF / THE / 1863 / UNITED STATES. Rv: As 535A. Plain edge. Only 15 struck. (Wright 1546; Miller Pa 569C)

| Pa-Ph 457 A | 1863 | Brass | 26mm | — | — | 25.00 | 60.00 |
|---|---|---|---|---|---|---|---|

As 457. Plain edge. (Fuld NC-28b)

| Pa-Ph 457 B | 1863 | WM | 26mm | — | — | 25.00 | 60.00 |
|---|---|---|---|---|---|---|---|

As 457. Plain edge. (Fuld NC-28e)

| Pa-Ph 457 C | 1863 | CN | 26mm | — | — | — | 60.00 |
|---|---|---|---|---|---|---|---|

As 457. Plain edge. (Fuld NC-28d)

Charles K. Warner and his brother William H. Warner were sons of medalist John S. Warner, who was active as a medalist 1823-1868. Charles and William were jewelers, medalists and coin dealers until the early 20th century.

| Pa-Ph 458 | 1864 (1869) | Copper | 28mm | — | — | 50.00 | 100. |
|---|---|---|---|---|---|---|---|

Nude bust of Washington right, surrounded by two-line circular inscription: CHAS. K. WARNER, DEALER IN AMERICAN / & FOREIGN MEDALS / 728 CHESTNUT ST. / * PHILADA *. Rv: Clothed, bearded bust of Lincoln left. Around: ABRAHAM LINCOLN PRESIDENT OF THE U.S. Below: 1864. Under Lincoln's shoulder: W. H. KEY. Plain edge. (King 591; Miller Pa 800)

| Pa-Ph 458 A | 1864('69) | Brass | 28mm | — | — | 50.00 | 100. |
|---|---|---|---|---|---|---|---|

As 458. Plain edge. (King 591; Miller 801)

| Pa-Ph 458 B | 1864('69) | WM | 28mm | — | — | 50.00 | 100. |
|---|---|---|---|---|---|---|---|

As 458. Plain edge. (King 591; Miller 802)

| Pa-Ph 459 | 1864 | Brass | 28mm | — | — | 50.00 | 100. |
|---|---|---|---|---|---|---|---|

Obverse as reverse of 458 (Lincoln). Rv: C. K. WARNER / NUMISMATIST / 326 / CHESTNUT ST. / PHILADELPHIA. Plain edge. (King 592; Miller Pa 803)

| Pa-Ph 459 A | 1864 | CN | 28mm | — | — | 50.00 | 100. |
|---|---|---|---|---|---|---|---|

As 459. Plain edge. (King 592; Miller 804)

| Pa-Ph 461 | 1864 | Brass | 28mm | — | — | 50.00 | 100. |
|---|---|---|---|---|---|---|---|

Clothed, bearded bust of Lincoln left, within a circle of 31 stars. Around: ABRAHAM LINCOLN PRESIDENT OF THE U.S. ****. Below: 1864. Under Lincoln's bust: W. H. KEY. Rv: C. K. WARNER / (small eagle displayed) / NUMISMATIST / 326 CHESTNUT ST. / PHILADELPHIA. Plain edge. (King 595; Miller Pa 806)

| Pa-Ph 461 A | 1864 | WM | 28mm | — | — | 50.00 | 100. |
|---|---|---|---|---|---|---|---|

As 461. Plain edge. (King 595; Miller Pa 807)

| Pa-Ph 461 B | 1864 | Copper | 28mm | — | — | 50.00 | 100. |
|---|---|---|---|---|---|---|---|

Obverse as obverse of Pa 800 (Washington). Rv: As obverse of 461 (Lincoln in circle of 31 stars). Plain edge. (King 596; Miller Pa 809)

It is interesting to note that King's compilation, published in *The Numismatist* in 1924, was available to but apparently not fully consulted by Donald Miller in his 1962 updating of Edgar Adams' 1920 store card catalog, as Pa-Ph 458 to 461B were not mentioned. We assigned numbers 800-809. It is believed the Warner listing in the present reference catalog also fails to list all extant varieties.

Charles K. Warner was born March 29, 1845, the son of medalist John S. Warner. Charles Warner established his coin and medal business at 326 Chestnut St., Philadelphia, in 1861. During 1862-1863 he commissioned W. H. Key to strike a series of patriotic store cards bearing portraits of Van Buren, Lincoln, McClellan, Washington, etc., with his store card on the other side. Only 15 of each type were struck, and these were not sold in his coin dealership, but presented to friends. In late 1863 his store card die was modified and he continued his wide-ranging patriotic cards.

In 1869 he moved to 728 Chestnut St., where he continued issuing special store cards until 1871.

(See Albert R. Frey's "The Tokens and Medals Relating to Numismatists and Coin Dealers" in *The Numismatist* for 1903-1907).

## A. J. WEIDENER
## Philadelphia, Pa.

### 1876 Centennial Tokens

Reverse type 1: A. J. WEIDENER / 36 SO. 2ND ST., PHILA. / (ornament) / LAMPS / BRONZES & / SILVER PLATED / WARE. (All 23mm; plain edge)

| Rulau | Obv | Rev | Metal | F | VF | EF | Unc |
|---|---|---|---|---|---|---|---|
| Pa-Ph 480 | A | 1 | WM | — | — | 15.00 | 40.00 |
| (Miller Pa 570) | | | | | | | |
| Pa-Ph 481 | B | 1 | WM | — | — | 15.00 | 40.00 |
| (Miller 571) | | | | | | | |
| Pa-Ph 481 A | B | 1 | Brass | — | — | 20.00 | 45.00 |
| Pa-Ph 482 | E | 1 | WM | — | — | 15.00 | 40.00 |
| (Miller 572) | | | | | | | |
| Pa-Ph 483 | F | 1 | WM | — | — | 17.50 | 40.00 |
| (Miller 573) | | | | | | | |
| Pa-Ph 484 | G | 1 | WM | — | — | 17.50 | 40.00 |
| Pa-Ph 485 | H | 1 | WM | — | — | 17.50 | 40.00 |
| (Miller 570A) | | | | | | | |

## WHITMAN & SON
## Philadelphia, Pa.

### 1876 Centennial Tokens

Reverse type 1: WHITMAN & SON / CHOCOLATE / CONFECTIONS / BON BONS / TWELFTH & MARKET ST. / PHILA. (All 23mm; plain edge)

| Rulau | Obv | Rev | Metal | F | VF | EF | Unc |
|---|---|---|---|---|---|---|---|
| Pa-Ph 488 | A | 1 | WM | 5.00 | 8.50 | 15.00 | 40.00 |
| (Miller Pa 577) | | | | | | | |
| Pa-Ph 489 | B | 1 | WM | — | — | 15.00 | 40.00 |
| (Wright 1242; Miller 576) | | | | | | | |
| Pa-Ph 489 A | B | 1 | Copper | — | — | 17.50 | 42.50 |
| Pa-Ph 489 B | B | 1 | Brass | — | — | 20.00 | 45.00 |
| Pa-Ph 490 | E | 1 | WM | — | — | 17.50 | 42.50 |
| (Miller 578) | | | | | | | |
| Pa-Ph 491 | F | 1 | WM | — | — | 17.50 | 42.50 |
| (Miller 575) | | | | | | | |
| Pa-Ph 492 | G | 1 | WM | — | — | 17.50 | 42.50 |
| Pa-Ph 493 | H | 1 | WM | — | — | 17.50 | 42.50 |
| (Miller 575A) | | | | | | | |
| Pa-Ph 494 | K | 1 | WM | — | — | 20.00 | 45.00 |

The Whitman Sampler is still being produced. Stephen F. Whitman & Son, confectioners, were located at the southwest corner of 12th and Market, the 1872 directory reports.

## F. G. WILLIAMS & CO.
## Philadelphia, Pa.

### 1876 Centennial Tokens

Reverse type 1: DR. WILLIAMS / ANTI / DYSPEPTIC / ELIXIR / F. G. WILLIAMS & CO. / 1301-03 / MARKET ST., PHILA. (All 23mm; plain edge)

| Rulau | Obv | Rev | Metal | F | VF | EF | Unc |
|---|---|---|---|---|---|---|---|
| Pa-Ph 495 | A | 1 | WM | — | — | 17.50 | 40.00 |
| (Wright 1728; Miller Pa 580) | | | | | | | |
| Pa-Ph 496 | B | 1 | WM | — | — | 17.50 | 40.00 |
| (Miller 581) | | | | | | | |
| Pa-Ph 497 | E | 1 | WM | — | — | 17.50 | 40.00 |
| (Miller 582) | | | | | | | |
| Pa-Ph 497 F | F | 1 | WM | — | — | 20.00 | 45.00 |
| (Miller 583) | | | | | | | |
| Pa-Ph 498 | G | 1 | WM | — | — | 20.00 | 45.00 |
| Pa-Ph 498 F | H | 1 | WM | — | — | 20.00 | 45.00 |
| (Miller 579A) | | | | | | | |
| Pa-Ph 498 G | H | 1 | Copper | — | — | 22.50 | 50.00 |
| (Miller 579) | | | | | | | |

## WILSON & FENIMORE
### Philadelphia, Pa.

**1876 Centennial Tokens**

Reverse type 1: WILSON & FENIMORE / ARTISTIC / PAPER / HANGINGS / 915 / MARKET ST. / PHILA. (All 23mm; plain edge)

| Rulau | Obv | Rev | Metal | F | VF | EF | Unc |
|---|---|---|---|---|---|---|---|
| Pa-Ph 499 | A | 1 | WM | — | — | 20.00 | 45.00 |

(Wright 1729; Miller Pa 583 1/2)

## WOOD'S MUSEUM
### Philadelphia, Pa.

| Rulau | Date | Metal | Size | F | VF | EF | Unc |
|---|---|---|---|---|---|---|---|
| Pa-Ph 500 | (?) | Gold/WM | 23mm | — | 1500. | — | — |

WOODS / MUSEUM ctsp on White Metal imitation, once gold plated, of the Oregon Exchange Company 1849 $5 gold piece.

Two or three specimens are thought to exist, according to Don Kagin in *Private Gold Coins and Patterns of the United States*, where this is termed a trial piece for regular Oregon Exchange Co. gold coins. George Fuld advances the theory this was an exhibition item in Wood's Museum. One specimen appeared in the Clifford sale, March 18-20, 1982.

| | | | | | | | |
|---|---|---|---|---|---|---|---|
| Pa-Ph 502 | (1876) | Brass | 26mm | 4.50 | 8.50 | 15.00 | 40.00 |

Liberty head left, LIBERTAS AMERICANA / 4 JUIL. 1776. Rv: WOOD'S MUSEUM N. W. 9TH & ARCH / 500000 / * / CURIOSITIES / GOOD PERFORMANCE / IN LECTURE ROOM / PHILADELPHIA. Plain edge. (Miller Pa 585)

| | | | | | | | |
|---|---|---|---|---|---|---|---|
| Pa-Ph 503 | (1876) | Copper | 26mm | 4.50 | 8.50 | 15.00 | 22.50 |

As 502. Plain edge. (Miller Pa 585A)

| | | | | | | | |
|---|---|---|---|---|---|---|---|
| Pa-Ph 504 | (1876) | WM | 26mm | 4.50 | 8.50 | 15.00 | 40.00 |

As 502. Plain edge. (Miller Pa 586)

| | | | | | | | |
|---|---|---|---|---|---|---|---|
| Pa-Ph 506 | (1876) | Copper | 26mm | — | — | 20.00 | 45.00 |

Liberty Bell and 13 stars, LIBERTY BELL above, 1776 below. Rv: As 502. Plain edge. (Wright 1271; Miller Pa 586A)

## R. & G. A. WRIGHT
### Philadelphia, Pa.

| Rulau | Date | Metal | Size | VG | F | VF | Unc |
|---|---|---|---|---|---|---|---|
| Pa-Ph 510 | (1871-72) | Silver | 14mm | — | — | — | Ex. Rare |

An ornament at center. R. & G. A. WRIGHT / PHILA. Rv: GOLD / MEDAL / PERFUMERY. (Wright 1276)

Dr. Wright noted that this was the smallest card in his collection. R. and G. A. Wright, perfumers, were located at 624 Chestnut, the 1872 directory reports.

## YATES & CO.
### Philadelphia, Pa.

**1876 Centennial Tokens**

Reverse type 1: YATES & CO. / POPULAR / CLOTHIERS / LEDGER BUILDING / 6TH & / CHESTNUT STS. (All 23mm; plain edge)

| Rulau | Obv | Rev | Metal | F | VF | EF | Unc |
|---|---|---|---|---|---|---|---|
| Pa-Ph 530 | D | 1 | WM | — | 12.50 | 20.00 | 45.00 |

(Wright 1290; Miller Pa 588 1/2)

A. C. Yates and Co. also issued store cards in the Merchant period (1845-60) from Philadelphia and from Syracuse, N.Y. They were an extremely popular clothing firm in the 19th century.

## W. A. BUNTING & SON
### Pittsburgh, Pa.

| Rulau | Date | Metal | Size | F | VF | EF | Unc |
|---|---|---|---|---|---|---|---|
| Pa-Pt 2 | 1876 | | | | | | |

Building across center, TRADESMENS INDUSTRIAL above, INSTITUTE / * / 1876. Rv: W. A. BUNTING & SON / SEAL — / ENGRAVING / STEEL — STAMPS (on scroll) / STENCILS / &C. / PITTSBURGH. Plain edge.

An early and rare use of aluminum, still then a novelty.

## GREAT NORTHERN EXPOSITION
### Pittsburgh, Pa.

| Rulau | Date | Metal | Size | F | VF | EF | Unc |
|---|---|---|---|---|---|---|---|
| Pa-Pt 7 | 1883 | Brass | 21mm | — | 10.00 | 13.00 | 20.00 |

Building, PITTSBURGH above. Rv: THE GREAT / NORTHERN / * / EXPOSITION / 1883. (Wright 1114)

## GUSKY'S CLOTHIERS HATTERS
### Pittsburgh, Pa.

| Rulau | Date | Metal | Size | F | VF | EF | Unc |
|---|---|---|---|---|---|---|---|
| Pa-Pt 9 | 1887 | WM | 38mm | — | 40.00 | 50.00 | — |

St. George slaying the dragon at center. Around: SEMI-CENTENNIAL QUEEN'S JUBILEE, PITTSBURGH, PA. Below: SONS OF ST. GEORGE / JUNE 20. 1887. Rv: Within oak wreath: PRESENTED / BY / GUSKYS' / THE ONE PRICE / CLOTHIERS HATTERS / FURNISHERS / & SHOE DEALERS / 300 TO 400 / MARKET ST. / PITTSBURGH. PA. Plain edge. (Brunk coll.)

An exceptionally handsome piece, unsigned, but possibly the work of Quint in Philadelphia. Queen Victoria ascended the throne of England in 1837 and this piece commemorates the 50th anniversary of that event.

## F. A. HEISELY
### Pittsburgh, Pa.

| Rulau | Date | Metal | Size | F | VF | EF | Unc |
|---|---|---|---|---|---|---|---|
| Pa-Pt 11 | (?) | Copper | 29mm | — | — | 60.00 | — |

F. A. HEISELY ctsp on U.S. 1845 Large cent.

## PITTSBURGH EXPOSITION SOCIETY
### Pittsburgh, Pa.

| Rulau | Date | Metal | Size | F | VF | EF | Unc |
|---|---|---|---|---|---|---|---|
| Pa-Pt 25 | 1879 | S/WM | 35mm | — | — | — | 35.00 |

Building across center, PITTSBURGH EXPOSITION above, SOCIETY / 1879 / W.P.N.S. No 2 below. Rv: FOUNDED / JUNE 14TH / 1878 within central circular wreath. Around: WESTERN PENNSYLVANIA NUMSIMATIC SOCIETY / PITTSBURGH, PA. Plain edge.

## RAINBOW FIRE CO.
### Reading, Pa.

| Rulau | Date | Metal | Size | F | VF | EF | Unc |
|---|---|---|---|---|---|---|---|
| Pa-Re 8 | 1873 | WM | 32mm | — | — | 22.50 | |

Old water-pumper engine. Around: CENTENNIAL ANNIVERSARY RAINBOW FIRE CO. MARCH 17TH 1873. Rv: RAINBOW FIRE CO / INSTITUTED / MARCH 17T'/ 1773 / READING PA. (Levine Dec. 1981 sale)

## SCRANTON STOVE WORKS
### Scranton, Pa

| Rulau | Date | Metal | Size | F | VF | EF | Unc |
|---|---|---|---|---|---|---|---|
| Pa-Sc 7 | 1886 | Brass | 25.5mm | 3.00 | 5.00 | 7.00 | 15.00 |

Scroll inscribed DOCKASH MEDAL at center, around: THE SCRANTON STOVE WORKS / SCRANTON PA. Rv: Globe on a grate inscribed DOCKASH. Around: DOCKASH RANGE WORLD HUNT SOUVENIR 1886. (Wright 1127; Miller Pa 593)

## C. J. LYONS
### Susquehanna, Pa.

 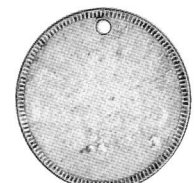

| Rulau | Date | Metal | Size | VG | F | VF | Unc |
|---|---|---|---|---|---|---|---|
| Pa-Sq 3 | (ca. 1882) | GS | 25mm | — | — | 2.00 | 3.50 |

Liberty holding long star-spangled pennon. On three of the pennon's folds are: C. J. LYONS / SUSQUEHANNA / P.A. Rv: Blank. Dentilated rims on each side. Plain edge. Issued holed.

This is a stock an identification disc. It is of the same type as the H. Knickman of East New York, N.Y., reported by the Fulds in *The Numismatist* (which see). Many of these are known.

## J. W. CLARK
### Tunkhannock, Pa.

| Rulau | Date | Metal | Size | VG | F | VF | EF |
|---|---|---|---|---|---|---|---|
| Pa-Tu 3 | (?) | CN | 22mm | — | 75.00 | | |

J. W. CLARK / TUNKHANNOCK PA ctsp on U.S. 1866 with Rays Shield nickel.

## THIRTEENTH REGIMENT N. G. PA.
### Scranton, Pa.

| Rulau | Date | Metal | Size | F | VF | EF | Unc |
|---|---|---|---|---|---|---|---|
| Pa-Sc 14 | 1880 | WM | 28mm | — | — | — | 30.00 |

Bearded male bust in Civil War uniform left, THIRTEENTH REGIMENT N.G.PA. above, ORGANIZED SEPT. 23. 1878. below. Rv: Armory at center, COMMEMORATIVE OF THE ARMORY FAIR / APRIL 1880 above, SCRANTON CITY / GUARD / ORG. AUGUST 14. 1877 below. Plain edge.

The Pennsylvania National Guard's 13th Regiment apparently grew out of the Scranton City Guard. Undoubtedly there are other Pennsylvania N.G. medalets and tokens than those included in this volume.

## SIMON & OPPENHEIMER
### Sunbury, Pa.

#### 1876 Centennial Tokens

Reverse type 1: SIMON & OPPENHEIMER, CLOTHING. (All 23mm; plain edge)

| Rulau | Obv | Rev | Metal | F | VF | EF | Unc |
|---|---|---|---|---|---|---|---|
| Pa-Sb 5 | A | 1 | WM | — | — | 25.00 | 50.00 |
| Pa-Sb 6 | G | 1 | WM | — | — | 25.00 | 50.00 |
| | | | (Miller Pa 594) | | | | |
| Pa-Sb 6A | G | 1 | Brass | — | — | — | 60.00 |

## E. T.
## (Eintracht)
### Tyrone, Pa.

| Rulau | Date | Metal | Size | F | VF | EF | Unc |
|---|---|---|---|---|---|---|---|
| Pa-Ty 2 | (1870's) | Copper | 20mm | 5.00 | 10.00 | 15.00 | 40.00 |

Similar to Pa-Ty 3 below, but numeral 5 on reverse. Plain edge.

| Pa-Ty 3 | (1870's) | GS | 20mm | 5.00 | 10.00 | 15.00 | 40.00 |

ET (script monogram) at center, EINTRACHT * above, TYRONE, PA. below. Rv: Large numeral 10 within wreath. Star above. Plain edge. (Wright 284; Miller Pa 595)

| Pa-Ty 3A | (1870's) | Brass | 20mm | 5.00 | 10.00 | 15.00 | 40.00 |

As 3. Plain edge. (Fuld coll.)

These tokens probably struck by Francis X. Koehler in Baltimore.

## SOUTH PENN HOSE COMPANY
### Pennyslvania, Location Not Known

| Rulau | Date | Metal | Size | VG | F | VF | Unc |
|---|---|---|---|---|---|---|---|
| Pa-Un 2 | 1865 | Copper | Oval 20 by 24mm | — | Rare | — | — |

Old fashioned hose cart, SOUTH PENN above, HOSE CO. below. Rv: Hose coiled around holder. Around: x INST. MARCH 27, 1846 INC'D MARCH 28 1865. Plain edge. (Wright 1019)

| Pa-Un 2A | 1865 | S Oval 20x24mm | | — | Rare | | |

As 2. Plain edge.

# RHODE ISLAND

## GEORGE FINCK
### Providence, R. I.

| Rulau | Date | Metal | Size | F | VF | EF | Unc |
|---|---|---|---|---|---|---|---|
| RI-Pr 7 | (1876) | WM | 22mm | 27.50 | 50.00 | 65.00 | 125. |

George Washington head left, 13 stars around, 1776 below. Rv: ROCHESTER HOTEL / GEORGE / FINCK / PROVIDENCE R. I. Plain edge. (Miller RI 3)

| Rulau | Date | Metal | Size | F | VF | EF | Unc |
|---|---|---|---|---|---|---|---|
| RI-Pr 8 | (1876) | Brass | 22mm | 35.00 | 65.00 | — | — |

As 7. Plain edge. (Wright 320; Miller RI 3A).

| Rulau | Date | Metal | Size | F | VF | EF | Unc |
|---|---|---|---|---|---|---|---|
| RI-Pr 9 | (1876) | Copper | 22mm | 45.00 | 80.00 | — | — |

As 7. Plain edge.

## A. A. PLASTRIDGE
### Providence, R. I.

| Rulau | Date | Metal | Size | VG | F | VF | Unc |
|---|---|---|---|---|---|---|---|
| RI-Pr 15 | Late 1860s | WM | 27mm | 10.00 | 20.00 | 35.00 | 125. |

A. A. PLASTRIDGE / (incused numeral) / MERRIAM / PROV. R. I. Rv: WHAT CHEER / (incused numeral) / EATING HOUSE. Plain edge. (Schenkman B48; R-F Srh-2; Miller RI 19)

| Rulau | Date | Metal | Size | VG | F | VF | Unc |
|---|---|---|---|---|---|---|---|
| RI-Pr 17 | (1870) | WM | 27mm | — | 6.00 | 7.50 | 10.00 |

Shield at center, within which is R. D. / 6. BY A. A. PLASTRIDGE above, PROV. R. I. below. Rv: Shield at center, within which is 12 / G. WHAT CHEER above, BAGATELLE TABLES below. Plain edge. (Wright 839; R-F Srh-1; Miller RI 20)

The first piece, RI-Pr 15, was cut by Joseph H. Merriam of Boston. There is no indication on RI-Pr 17 that Merriam prepared these dies, but it seems logical to suppose that this might be so. Both upper and lower dies of RI 17 (in excellent condition) were in the posssession of the author for about 15 years prior to 1978, when they were sold to David T. Alexander of Danbury, Conn.

Bagatelle is a modification of billiards, played on an oblong board or table. An ordinary billiard cue and nine balls, one black, four red, and four white, are used. The black ball having been placed on the upper spot, the players "string" for the lead, the winner being the one who plays his ball into the highest hole.

# SOUTH CAROLINA

## E. HENDERSON PACKING CO.
### Beaufort, S.C.

| Rulau | Date | Metal | Size | VG | F | VF | Unc |
|---|---|---|---|---|---|---|---|
| SC-Be 3 | (ca 1889 ?) | Alum Sc, 23mm | | — | 10.00 | — | |

(All incused) Large 2 1/2 at center, E. HENDERSON PACKING CO. around. Rv: Same as obverse. Incised, beaded rim on each side. Plain edge.

## HUNT PKG. CO.
### Beaufort, S.C.

| Rulau | Date | Metal | Size | VG | F | VF | Unc |
|---|---|---|---|---|---|---|---|
| SC-Be 5 | (1880's) | Brass | 20mm | — | — | 15.00 | — |

HUNT PKG. CO. / SHUCKING / CHECK / BEAUFORT S.C. Beaded rim. Rv: Blank. Plain edge.

Hunt Packing Company was a shrimp packing plant and this piece was used as a production tally during the late 1800's and possibly until about 1905. The style of check is typical of the mid-1880's.

## J. C. SEEGERS & CO.
### Columbia, S.C.

| Rulau | Date | Metal | Size | VG | F | VF | EF |
|---|---|---|---|---|---|---|---|
| SC-Co 4 | (1870's) | GS | 27mm | 30.00 | 50.00 | — | Rare |

Barrel. J. C. SEEGERS & CO. Rv: Numeral 25. Plain edge. (Miller SC 14)

| Rulau | Date | Metal | Size | VG | F | VF | EF |
|---|---|---|---|---|---|---|---|
| SC-Co 5 | (1870's) | Brass | 27mm | — | — | — | — |

As 4, but numeral 10. Plain edge.

This piece was catalogued with reserve in *U.S. Merchant Tokens 1845-1860*. It has since been determined that it postdates the Civil War.

## J. N. POOLE
### Greenville, S.C.

| Rulau | Date | Metal | Size | VG | F | VF | Unc |
|---|---|---|---|---|---|---|---|
| SC-Gr 4 | (1870's) | Brass | 19mm | — | — | — | Scarce |

Liberty head within wreath. Rv: J. N. POOLE / 5 / GREENVILLE, S.C.

# RICHARD F. MASON
## Laurens, S. C.

| Rulau | Date | Metal | Size | VG | F | VF | Unc |
|---|---|---|---|---|---|---|---|
| SC-La 5 | 1888 | Brass | 33mm | — | — | Rare | — |

RICHARD F. MASON / DEALER / IN / WATCHES, CLOCKS, / JEWELRY, SILVERWARE / SPECTACLES ETC. / - / REPAIRING A SPECIALTY / TERMS CASH / LAURENS, SO. CA. Rv: MASON'S WATCH & JEWELRY / REPAIR SHOP / WATCH CHECK / 1888 / LAURENS, SO. CA. Plain edge.

| Rulau | Date | Metal | Size | VG | F | VF | Unc |
|---|---|---|---|---|---|---|---|
| SC-La 6 | 1888 | Brass | 33mm | — | — | Rare | — |

As last, but counterstamped with various numbers between words REPAIR SHOP and WATCH CHECK on reverse. Plain edge.

Mason accounted for items left with him for repair by use of these checks. This token was written up by Melvin and George Fuld in *The Numismatist* in the early 1960's.

# SOUTH DAKOTA

## CONSTITUTIONAL PROHIBITION ORGANIZATION
### South Dakota

| Rulau | Date | Metal | Size | F | VF | EF | Unc |
|---|---|---|---|---|---|---|---|
| SD-NL 1 | 1889 | Copper | 25.5mm | — | — | 25.00 | 35.00 |

South Dakota state arms, CONSTITUTIONAL PROHIBITION ORGANIZATION. Rv: Fountain, FOR GOD, HOME & NATIVE LAND / SOUTH DAKOTA / 1889. Plain edge.

| SD-NL 2 | 1889 | Brass | 25.5mm | — | — | 25.00 | 35.00 |

As last. Plain edge.

## N. RINGROSE
### Aberdeen, S.D.

| Rulau | Date | Metal | Size | VG | F | VF | Unc |
|---|---|---|---|---|---|---|---|
| SD-Ab 2 | (1874-84) | CN | 24mm | | | | |

N. RINGROSE, 10 ¢, ABERDEEN, D.T. Rv: THE J.M. BRUNSWICK & BALKE CO. Plain edge. (Brunswick 2302)

D.T. = Dakota Territory.

## DAKOTA COMMANDERY NO. 1
### Deadwood, S.D.

| Rulau | Date | Metal | Size | F | VF | EF | Unc |
|---|---|---|---|---|---|---|---|
| SD-Dd 3 | 1880 | Tin | 33mm | — | — | 100. | — |

Cross through crown at center. DAKOTA COMMANDERY NO. 1. / VINCIT OMNIA VERITAS (truth conquers all) above; CONSTITUTED / AUG. 19, 1880. / * DEADWOOD. DAK. *. Rv: Mining buildings, MADE OF BLACK HILLS TIN / HOMESTAKE above, WM. McMAKIN & CO. / TERRAVILLES S.D. below. (Last two lines of legend uncertain)

This piece is rare. Not listed in the Fuld's article on tin medals and tokens in *The Numismatist*.

The Homestake mine at Lead, S.D., the U.S.' largest gold mine, was opened 1877 and is still in operation. Lead, tin and other metals are byproducts.

## M. JACOBS
### Lead City, S.D.

| SD-Ld 2 | (1874-84) | Brass | 24mm | — | 400. | — | — |

M. JACOBS, ONE DRINK, LEAD CITY, D.T. Rv: Pool table in central circle, THE J.M. BRUNSWICK & BALKE COS. around, CHECK below. Plain edge. (Brunswick 2184)

D.T. = Dakota Territory.

# TENNESSEE

### D.P. HENDERSON & CO.
### Chattanooga, Tenn.

| Rulau | Date | Metal | Size | F | VF | EF | Unc |
|---|---|---|---|---|---|---|---|
| Tn-Ch 4 | (1880's) | Nickel | 30mm | — | — | 30.00 | |

D.P. HENDERSON / & CO. / BOOK SELLERS, / —* — / STATIONERS, / — AND — / NEWS DEALERS. Rv: CHATTANOOGA / * 7 1/2 * / TENN. Plain edge.

Struck by James Murdock Jr. in Cincinnati. (See *The Numismatist* for Sept., 1978, page 1841)

### NORTH JELLICO COAL CO.
### Jellico, Tenn.

| Rulau | Date | Metal | Size | VG | F | VF | Unc |
|---|---|---|---|---|---|---|---|
| Tn-Je 6 | 1888 | Nickel | ---mm | — | 15.00 | 25.00 | |

Crossed pick and shovel at center, NORTH JELLICO COAL CO. around, * 1888 * below. Rv: 25.

| Tn-Je 7 | 1888 | Nickel | ---mm | — | 15.00 | 25.00 | — |

As 6, but 10.

| Tn-Je 8 | 1888 | Nickel | ---mm | — | 15.00 | 25.00 | — |

As 6, but 5.

This company was in operation until 1928. After 1903 it had up to 579 employees.

### T.C. & CO.
### Memphis, Tenn.

| Rulau | Date | Metal | Size | VG | F | VF | Unc |
|---|---|---|---|---|---|---|---|
| Tn-Me 6 | (?) | Brass | 26mm | 20.00 | 25.00 | 35.00 | 45.00 |

T.C. & CO. NO. 230. Rv: 50 DRAYAGE. (Miller Tenn 45)

### DODD & WOLFE
### Memphis, Tenn.

| Rulau | Date | Metal | Size | VG | F | VF | Unc |
|---|---|---|---|---|---|---|---|
| Tn-Me 10 | (?) | ? | ---mm | 17.50 | 25.00 | 40.00 | Rare |

DODD & WOLFE / 25 / DRAYAGE / MEMPHIS. Rv: Blank. (Wright 1398; Miller Tenn 8A)

A drayage check.

### FARGASON, CORDES & CO.
### Memphis, Tenn.

| Rulau | Date | Metal | Size | VG | F | VF | Unc |
|---|---|---|---|---|---|---|---|
| Tn-Me 13 | (1865-69) | Brass | 22mm | 22.50 | 30.00 | 45.00 | |

FARGASON, CORDES & CO / DRAYAGE / MEMPHIS — 50. Rv: MURDOCK & SPENCER / 139 / 5TH ST / CIN. O. (Wright 309; Miller Tenn 9)

| Tn-Me 15 | (1865-69) | Brass | 22mm | 22.50 | 30.00 | 45.00 | — |

Similar to Tenn 9, but '25' instead of '50'. (Miller Tenn 10)

Drayage checks. Dated on the basis of the Murdock & Spencer signature, which was in use with the 139 5th St. address only in the 1864-1869 period. These pieces have never been listed as Civil War tokens.

### W.H. & CO.
### Memphis, Tenn.

| Rulau | Date | Metal | Size | VG | F | VF | Unc |
|---|---|---|---|---|---|---|---|
| Tn-Me 18 | (?) | Brass | ---mm | — | 50.00 | — | Rare |

W.H. & CO., MEMPHIS. (Miller Tenn 52)

A drayage check. No information available.

### HALLER & ELLIS
### Memphis, Tenn.

| Rulau | Date | Metal | Size | VG | F | VF | Unc |
|---|---|---|---|---|---|---|---|
| Tn-Me 20 | (?) | ? | ---mm | — | 75.00 | — | Rare |

No description available. (Miller Tenn 26)

### COAL CREEK COAL CO.
### Coal Creek, Tenn.

| Rulau | Date | Metal | Size | VG | F | VF | Unc |
|---|---|---|---|---|---|---|---|
| Tn-Cc 2 | 1884 | Brass | ---mm | 4.50 | 8.50 | 12.00 | — |

COAL CREEK COAL CO. / 25 / * 1884 *. Rv: * C.C.C.C. * / 25 / IN MERCHANDISE / (tiny) HOEFLE & DRESSELL 179 RACE. ST. CIN. O. Plain edge.

### A.O. HARRIS & CO.
### Memphis, Tenn.

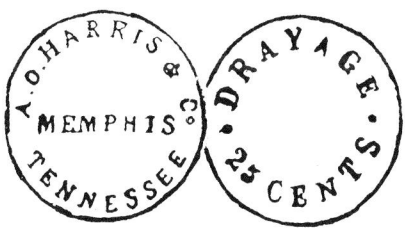

| Rulau | Date | Metal | Size | VG | F | VF | Unc |
|---|---|---|---|---|---|---|---|
| Tn-Me 22 | (?) | Brass | 28mm | 35.00 | 50.00 | 75.00 | — |

A.O. HARRIS & CO. / MEMPHIS / TENNESSEE. Rv: DRAYAGE / . 25 CENTS . Plain edge. (Wright 427; Miller Tenn 27A)

| Tn-Me 24 | (?) | Brass | 26mm(?) | 35.00 | 50.00 | 75.00 | — |

Similar to Tenn 27A, but '50' instead of '25'. (Miller Tenn 27)

Drayage checks. The entire field of Tennessee drayage checks needs research to date the issuing firms better. The checks seem to span the Merchant, Civil War and post-CW eras, and need refinement before any of them can be placed with certainty into any era.

### MEGIBBEN & BRO.
### Memphis, Tenn.

| Rualu | Date | Metal | Size | VG | F | VF | Unc |
|---|---|---|---|---|---|---|---|
| Tn-Me 28 | (?) | Brass | 22mm | 35.00 | 50.00 | 75.00 | — |

MEGIBBEN & BRO. / MEMPHIS. 50 / DRAYAGE. (Miller Tenn 29)

Drayage check.

## J.M. MERRILL & CO.
### Memphis, Tenn.

| Rulau | Date | Metal | Size | VG | F | VF | Unc |
|---|---|---|---|---|---|---|---|
| Tn-Me 30 | (?) | Brass | ---mm | 20.00 | 30.00 | 45.00 | 70.00 |

J.M. MERRILL & CO. 25 CENTS. (Miller Tenn 30)

## C. MULLER & BRO.
### Memphis Tenn.

| Rulau | Date | Metal | Size | VG | F | EF |
|---|---|---|---|---|---|---|
| Tn-Me 33 | (?) | Silver | 31mm | — | 150. | — |

C. MULLER & BRO / MEMPHIS. TENN. / IMPRVD. / SPECTACLES / MANUFACTURERS ctsp in five lines on U.S. 1855-O Half dollar.

| Tn-Me 34 | (?) | Silver | 31mm | — | 200. | — |

Similar ctsp on U.S. 1856-O Half dollar.

By 1918 a successor firm, C. Muller & Co., were in the grocery and meat business.

## NEVILS & ROSE
### Memphis, Tenn.

| Rulau | Date | Metal | Size | VG | F | VF | Unc |
|---|---|---|---|---|---|---|---|
| Tn-Me 37 | (?) | Brass | 25mm | — | 35.00 | 50.00 | — |

NEVILS & ROSE, MEMPHIS. 50 DRAYAGE. (Miller Tenn 35) A drayage check.

## PAUL & CROCKETT
### Memphis, Tenn.

| Rulau | Date | Metal | Size | VG | F | VF | Unc |
|---|---|---|---|---|---|---|---|
| Tn-Me 40 | (?) | ? | ---mm | — | 50.00 | — | — |

No information available. (Miller Tenn 36)

## J.W. SHEERER & CO.
### Memphis, Tenn.

| Rulau | Date | Metal | Size | VG | F | VF | Unc |
|---|---|---|---|---|---|---|---|
| Tn-Me 45 | (?) | Brass | 30.5mm | — | — | 20.00 | 35.00 |

J.W. SHEERER & CO * / 25 (in circle). Rv: DRAYAGE / 25 (in circle) / * CENTS *. Plain edge. (Miller Tenn 37)

| Tn-Me 46 | (?) | Brass | 30.5mm | — | — | 20.00 | 35.00 |

Similar, but '15'. (Miller Tenn 38)

| Tn-Me 47 | (?) | Brass | 30.5mm | — | — | 20.00 | 35.00 |

Similar, but '20'. (Miller Tenn 39)

| Tn-Me 48 | (?) | Brass | 30.5mm | — | — | 15.00 | 35.00 |

Similar, but '25'. (Wright 977; Miller Tenn 40)

| Tn-Me 48A | (?) | S/Br | 30.5mm | — | — | 20.00 | 35.00 |

As 48. (Miller Tenn 40A)

| Tn-Me 49 | (?) | Brass | 30.5mm | — | — | 20.00 | 35.00 |

Similar, but '50'. (Miller Tenn 41)

The Sheerer pieces seem always to occur in sets, and are seldom encountered worn.

## SOUTHWORTH & KNIGHT
### Memphis, Tenn.

| Rulau | Date | Metal | Size | VG | F | VF | Unc |
|---|---|---|---|---|---|---|---|
| Tn-Me 54 | (?) | Brass | 26mm | 20.00 | 30.00 | 40.00 | 50.00 |

SOUTHWORTH & KNIGHT. 25 DRAYAGE. (Miller Tenn 43A)

| Tn-Me 56 | (?) | Brass | 26mm | 20.00 | 30.00 | 40.00 | 50.00 |

Similar to 43A, but '50'. (Miller Tenn 43)

## WESTERN FOUNDRY
### Memphis, Tenn.

| Rulau | Date | Metal | Size | VG | F | VF | Unc |
|---|---|---|---|---|---|---|---|
| Tn-Me 60 | (?) | Brass | 22mm | — | — | — | Rare |

Circle encloses blank central space. Around: WESTERN FOUNDRY / MEMPHIS TENNESSEE. Large numeral 25 incused at center. Rv: Blank. Dentilated rim on both sides. Plain edge. Rarity 9. Fuld 600G-1bc; Wright 1226; Miller Tenn 46)

| Tn-Me 60A | (?) | Brass | 22mm | — | — | — | Rare |

(Variety described by Miller as "Large 25.") (Miller Tenn 46A)

Though Fuld calls this a Civil War store card, directory evidence is thus far lacking. Listed here with reserve.

## WILSON, LAIRD & CO.
### Memphis, Tenn.

| Rulau | Date | Metal | Size | VG | F | VF | Unc |
|---|---|---|---|---|---|---|---|
| Tn-Me 63 | (?) | Brass | 26mm | 25.00 | 35.00 | 45.00 | 60.00 |

WILSON, LAIRD & CO., MEMPHIS. 25 DRAYAGE. (Miller Tenn 49)

| Tn-Me 65 | (?) | Brass | 26mm | 25.00 | 35.00 | 45.00 | 60.00 |

Similar, but '50'. (Miller Tenn 48)

## J.M. WISWELL & CO.
### Memphis, Tenn.

| Rulau | Date | Metal | Size | VG | F | VF | Unc |
|---|---|---|---|---|---|---|---|
| Tn-Me 67 | (?) | Brass | 28mm | 15.00 | 22.50 | 27.50 | 40.00 |

J.M. WISWELL & CO. / 25 CENTS. Rv: Blank. (Miller Tenn 47)

## M. WOLF
### Memphis, Tenn.

| Rulau | Date | Metal | Size | VG | F | VF | Unc |
|---|---|---|---|---|---|---|---|
| Tn-Me 70 | (?) | Brass | 26mm | 25.00 | 35.00 | 45.00 | 60.00 |

M. WOLF, DRAYAGE CHECK. 25. (Miller Tenn 50)

| Tn-Me 72 | (?) | Brass | 26mm | 25.00 | 35.00 | 45.00 | 60.00 |

Similar, but '50'. (Miller Tenn 51)

## BEN. F. WYANT
### Memphis, Tenn.

| Rulau | Date | Metal | Size | VG | F | VF | EF |
|---|---|---|---|---|---|---|---|
| Tn-Me 74 | (?) | Silver | 31mm | — | 100. | — | — |

BEN. F. WYANT / MAY FLOWER / SALOON / NO 137 MAIN ST / MEMPHIS - TENN. in five lines ctsp on U.S. 1858-O Seated Liberty half dollar. (Schenkman collection)

## AMMIN'S BROS.
### Nashville, Tenn.

| Rulau | Date | Metal | Size | VG | F | VF | Unc |
|---|---|---|---|---|---|---|---|
| Tn-Na 1 | (?) | Br. Oct., 27mm | — | — | — | — | |

AMMIN'S BROS. / 1 QUART / NASHVILLE, TENN. Rv: Blank. Plain edge. (Wright 16)

## McKAY & LAPSLEY
### Nashville, Tenn.

McKay & Lapsley issued 1863 and 1864-dated Civil War tokens, and a related firm, D.L. Lapsley & Co. of Nashville, also issued Civil War store cards. (Respectively Fuld 690D-1a to 10d and 690C-1a to 6a). The McKay & Lapsley pieces were listed as Miller Tenn 60½ and 60½A.

## R.H. SINGLETON
### Nashville, Tenn.

| Rulau | Date | Metal | Size | F | VF | EF | Unc |
|---|---|---|---|---|---|---|---|
| Tn-Na 25 | (1866-68) | Copper | 21.5mm | 75.00 | 85.00 | 100. | 150. |
| | | Bearded Lincoln bust left, A NATION'S BENEFACTOR around, five stars below. Rv: R.H. SINGLETON / BOOKSELLER / * * * / STATIONER & / JOB PRINTER / P.O. / BUILDING / NASHVILLE. TENN. Plain edge. (King 628; Miller Tenn. 61F) | | | | | | |
| Tn-Na 26 | (1866-68) | Brass | 21.5mm | 75.00 | 85.00 | 100. | 150. |
| | | As 25. Plain edge. (Wright 987; King 628; Miller Tenn. 61A) | | | | | | |
| Tn-Na 27 | (1866-68) | CN | 21.5mm | — | — | 250. | 300. |
| | | As 25. Plain edge. Very rare. (King not listed; Miller Tenn. 61) | | | | | | |

## N.L. TARBOX & CO.
### Nashville, Tenn.

Miller Tenn 61B, Wright 1090, and a similar Tarbox piece struck over an 1864 Lincoln campaign medalet, are Civil War store cards.

## JELLICO MT. COAL & COKE CO.
### Wooldridge, Tenn.

| Rulau | Date | Metal | Size | F | VF | EF | Unc |
|---|---|---|---|---|---|---|---|
| Tn-Wo 3 | 1883 | GS | 22mm | — | — | — | — |
| | | JELLICO MT COAL & COKE CO. / 5 / MERCHANDISE / * 1883 *. Rv: 5 in circle of 16 stars. Dentilated rim on each side. Plain edge. (Caldwell 9J) | | | | | | |
| Tn-Wo 4 | 1883 | GS | ---mm | — | — | — | — |
| | | Similar, but 10. | | | | | | |
| Tn-Wo 5 | 1883 | GS | 27mm | — | — | — | — |
| | | Similar, but 25. | | | | | | |
| Tn-Wo 6 | 1883 | GS | ---mm | — | — | — | — |
| | | Similar, but 50. | | | | | | |
| Tn-Wo 7 | 1883 | GS | 38mm | — | — | — | — |
| | | Similar, but 100. | | | | | | |

Struck by J.W. Murdock & Co. of Cincinnati, Ohio. Supposedly one set in aluminum also exists but it has not been seen.
(See *The Numismatist*) for Nov. 1920, article by John H. Snow, and Dec. 1920, response by H.C. Ezekiel.)

# TEXAS

## BISMARCK SALOON
### Austin, Texas

| Rulau | Date | Metal | Size | VG | F | VF | Unc |
|---|---|---|---|---|---|---|---|
| Tx-Au 3 | (1880's) | CN | 29mm | — | — | Rare | — |
| | | Facing military bust of Otto von Bismarck at center, BISMARCK above, SALOON below. Rv: Blank. Plain edge. | | | | | | |

The Bismarck Saloon, issuer of this token, was located at 809 Congress Avenue. The famous author O. Henry (William Sidney Porter), who lived in Austin 1884-1898, is reported to have been a regular customer.
Later, another Bismarck Saloon appears at 815 Congress.

## JULES BORNEFELD
### Austin, Texas

| Rulau | Date | Metal | Size | VG | F | VF | Unc |
|---|---|---|---|---|---|---|---|
| Tx-Au 5 | (1877-96) | Brass | 21mm | — | — | 40.00 | — |
| | | Race horse standing left, PALACE SALOON / PAROLE above, * AUSTIN, TEXAS * below. Rv; JULES BORNEFELD / GOOD / FOR ONE / DRINK / (star at center of two branches). Plain edge. (Wright 1342) | | | | | | |
| Tx-Au 5A | (1877-96) | Copper | | — | — | 27.50 | — |
| | | As 5. Plain edge. | | | | | | |
| Tx-Au 5B | (1877-96) | Silver | | — | — | 60.00 | — |
| | | As 5. Plain edge. | | | | | | |

Jules Bornefeld ran the Palace Saloon at 901 Congress as early as 1877, continuing its operation until 1896. 'Parole' is a brand of rye whiskey, not the horse's name (as Dr. Wright thought).
There were a number of trial pieces of this token struck in various metals.

## COSMOPOLITAN
### Austin, Texas

| Rulau | Date | Metal | Size | VG | F | VF | Unc |
|---|---|---|---|---|---|---|---|
| Tx-Au 8 | (1883-88) | GS | 31mm | — | — | 45.00 | — |
| | | State Capitol building at center, COSMOPOLITAN above, AUSTIN / TEXAS in exergue. Rv: Old main building of University of Texas at center, GOOD FOR ONE DRINK above. Plain edge. (Wright 207) | | | | | | |
| Tx-Au 9 | (1883-88) | Brass | 31mm | — | — | 45.00 | — |
| | | Same as last. | | | | | | |
| Tx-Au 10 | (1888) | Aluminum | 31mm | — | — | 45.00 | — |
| | | Same as last. | | | | | | |

Used at the Cosmopolitan Bar in the 1883-1888 period, these beautiful tokens were made by Heidemann Mfg. Co. in San Antonio. They must have had a souvenir use in addition to their utilitarian use, which would account for their appearing in three different metals.
Aluminum did not become commercially available for token-making until 1888.

## NEFF & DUFF
### Austin, Texas

| Rulau | Date | Metal | Size | VG | F | VF | Unc |
|---|---|---|---|---|---|---|---|
| Tx-Au 15 | (1885-86) | CN | 30mm | — | — | 50.00 | — |
| | | Longhorn steer's head facing within central circle. IRON FRONT above, * AUSTIN TEXAS * below. Rv: (ornament) / NEFF & DUFF / (ornament). Plain edge. (Wright 1547) | | | | | | |

The Iron Front was the most famous of the Austin saloons, which catered to the thirsty cowboys who drove cattle to markets. The saloon was established in 1866 by Jobe and Robinson and it operated under different proprietors on the same spot until 1919.
John B. Neff and H.H. Duff were the proprietors only in 1885-1886.
The last proprietor of the Iron Front, Thomas A. "Lon" Martin, who ran the place 1905-1919, also issue a token, a cupronickel, 21mm 5-cent piece outside the scope of this work. It is worth $12.50 in VF.

## W.B. NEWTON
## Austin, Texas

| Rulau | Date | Metal | Size | VG | F | VF | Unc |
|---|---|---|---|---|---|---|---|
| Tx-Au 17 | (1880's) | GS | 29mm | — | — | 75.00 | — |

Elephant left on field of ground, WHITE above, AUSTIN, TEXAS below. Rv: W.B. NEWTON / (blank center) / * PROPRIETOR *. Plain edge.

## ST. LOUIS SALOON
## Austin, Texas

| Rulau | Date | Metal | Size | VG | F | VF | Unc |
|---|---|---|---|---|---|---|---|
| Tx-Au 20 | (1879-94) | Rubber * | 29mm | — | — | Rare | — |

BILLIE & CHARLIE / DEALERS IN / IMPORTED AND / DOMESTIC / LIQUORS & CIGARS / AUSTIN, TEXAS. Rv: GOOD FOR / * / ONE DRINK / AT THE / ST. LOUIS / SALOON. Plain edge.

* Red Vulcanite

Charles Marshall and William J. Sutor operated the St. Louis Saloon from 1879 through 1894. The token probably was issued in the early 1880's.
William J. (Billy) Sutor later was proprietor of the Hotel Sutor Bar in Austin.

## T.A. SCOTT & CO.
## Austin, Texas

| Rulau | Date | Metal | Size | VG | F | VF | Unc |
|---|---|---|---|---|---|---|---|
| Tx-Au 22 | (1886-88) | Brass | 31mm | — | — | Rare | — |

Radiant sun at center of large five-pointed star. Letters T-E-X-A-S appear in angles of the outline star. Rv: DRISKILL HOTEL BAR / T.A. SCOTT & CO. / GOOD FOR / — 1 — / DRINK / * AUSTIN, TEX. *. Plain edge.

T.A. Scott was the first proprietor of the Driskill's bar when this famous Austin hostelry opened in 1886.
The Driskill reopened in Sept. 1972, celebrating the event with a wooden token, GOOD FOR ONE FREE DRINK.

## M.E. ANDERSON
## Bastrop, Texas

| Rulau | Date | Metal | Size | VG | F | VF | Unc |
|---|---|---|---|---|---|---|---|
| Tx-Bp 1 | (ca 1882) | CN Oct., | 26mm | — | — | 27.50 | — |

GOOD FOR / * 1 * / M.E. / ANDERSON / * DRINK * (all within round beaded circle, with panels and flourishes present). Rv: Blank. Plain edge.

M.E. Anderson was listed as a saloon keeper in the 1882 *Texas Gazetteer*.

## MIDWAY SALOON
## Beeville, Texas

| Rulau | Date | Metal | Size | VG | F | VF | Unc |
|---|---|---|---|---|---|---|---|
| Tx-Be 3 | (?) | Aluminum | 30mm | — | — | 45.00 | — |

THE MIDWAY / —.— / SALOON / —.— / BEEVILLE, TEXAS. Rv: GOOD FOR / 5¢ / AT BAR. There is a recessed beaded circle inside the rim on each side. Plain edge.

## G.F. MILLS
## Beeville, Texas

| Rulau | Date | Metal | Size | VG | F | VF | Unc |
|---|---|---|---|---|---|---|---|
| Tx-Be 5 | (1880's) | Brass | 28mm | — | 7.50 | — | — |

(ornament) GOOD FOR (ornament) / 1 / SHAVE / o / G.F. MILLS (all incused). Rv: Blank. There is a recessed beaded circle inside the rim. Plain edge.

G.F. Mills owned and operated a barber shop in Beeville prior to 1890.
Comparison of this token with that of Lehm's Saloon of Brenham, Texas, reveals the basic blank checks were made by the same maker.

## EVANS & LA MOTTE
## Boerne, Texas

| Rulau | Date | Metal | Size | VG | F | VF | Unc |
|---|---|---|---|---|---|---|---|
| Tx-Bo 4 | (1880's) | Brass | 23mm | — | — | 12.50 | — |

EVANS & LA MOTTE / BOERNE. (all incused). Rv: Blank. Plain edge.

LaMotte was listed as a saloonkeeper in the 1882 *Texas Gazetteer*.

## LA VALLEE SALOON
## Boerne, Texas

| Rulau | Date | Metal | Size | VG | F | VF | Unc |
|---|---|---|---|---|---|---|---|
| Tx-Bo 8 | (1884-97) | Brass | 23mm | — | — | 12.50 | — |

(All incused). LAVALLEE / GOOD FOR / 5 / CENTS / AT BAR / SALOON. Rv: Blank. Plain edge.

L.N. LaVallee operated his saloon in Boerne at least from 1884 to 1897.

## LEHM'S SALOON
## Brenham, Texas

| Rulau | Date | Metal | Size | VG | F | VF | Unc |
|---|---|---|---|---|---|---|---|
| Tx-Bm 3 | (1880) | Brass | 28mm | — | — | 25.00 | — |

LEHM'S / GOOD FOR / 5 / CENTS / AT BAR / SALOON (all incused). Rv: Blank. There is a recessed beaded circle inside the rim. Plain edge.

Bernhard Lehman owned and operated this saloon prior to 1882.

## CHARLOTTE H. MILLER
## Brownsville, Texas

| Rulau | Date | Metal | Size | VG | F | VF | EF |
|---|---|---|---|---|---|---|---|
| Tx-Br 4 | (?) | Silver | 32.5mm | — | — | 300. | — |

CHARLOTTE H. MILLER / BROWNSVILLE / TEX. ctsp. on U.S. 1830 Bust type half dollar.

## J.L. BARNES
### Bryan, Texas

| Rulau | Date | Metal | Size | VG | F | VF | EF |
|---|---|---|---|---|---|---|---|
| Tx-By 2 | (1880-1900) | Silver | 26mm | — | — | 250. | — |

J.L. BARNES / SALOON / BRYAN TEX. cstp on U.S. 1853 Liberty Seated quarter. (Gould 6)

| Rulau | Date | Metal | Size | VG | F | VF | EF |
|---|---|---|---|---|---|---|---|
| Tx-By 3 | (1880-1900) | Silver | 31mm | — | — | 250. | — |

Similar ctsp. on U.S. 1858-O Liberty Seated half dollar. (Schenkman collection)

## H. COCKEREL
### Clarksville, Texas

| Rulau | Date | Metal | Size | VG | F | VF | Unc |
|---|---|---|---|---|---|---|---|
| Tx-Cv 3 | (1880-99) | CN | Oval 34.2 by 19.1mm | — | — | 25.00 | — |

Eagle atop U.S. shield above four folds of a scroll. On scroll, incuse, is: H. COCKEREL, / CLARKSVILLE / RED RIVER CO. / TEX. Rv: Blank. Plain edge. Holed at left as issued.

Apparently an identification tag of early vintage.

## S
### Colorado, Texas

| Rulau | Date | Metal | Size | VG | F | VF | EF |
|---|---|---|---|---|---|---|---|
| Tx-Co 2 | (1877-85) | Brass | 24mm | — | — | 40.00 | — |

Eagle displayed at center, E. PLURIBUS UNUM above, COLORADO, TEXAS. below. Rv: Large radiant 'S' within circle of alternating stars and dots.

The use of this token is unknown. It could be a merchant's token.
A Texas Ranger camp was established at Colorado in 1877, the first white settlement. A commissary could have served the camp.

## NIC. CONSTANTINE'S SALOON
### Corpus Christi, Texas

| Rulau | Date | Metal | Size | VG | F | VF | Unc |
|---|---|---|---|---|---|---|---|
| Tx-CC 4 | (?) | CN | 30mm | — | — | 45.00 | — |

NIC. CONSTANTINE'S / —.— / SALOON / CORPUS CHRISTI / TEX. Rv: GOOD FOR / ONE / * DRINK *. Plain edge.

## FRANK C. BLAINE
### Del Rio, Texas

| Rulau | Date | Metal | Size | VG | F | VF | Unc |
|---|---|---|---|---|---|---|---|
| Tx-DR 3 | (1880's) | CN | 30mm | — | 40.00 | 60.00 | Rare |

Longhorn steer's head facing in circle, tiny W.W. WILCOX at base of neck. CATTLE EXCHANGE above, * DEL RIO, TEXAS. * below. Rv: FRANK / C. / BLAINE. Plain edge.

| Rulau | Date | Metal | Size | VG | F | VF | Unc |
|---|---|---|---|---|---|---|---|
| Tx-DR 4 | (1890's) | Brass | 21mm | — | — | 12.50 | — |

FRANK C. BLAINE / DEL RIO, / TEX. Rv: GOOD FOR / 5¢ / IN TRADE. Plain edge.

The Cattle Exchange has not yet been identified. It may be a saloon.

## COW BOY'S SALOON
### Doans, Texas

| Rulau | Date | Metal | Size | VG | F | VF | Unc |
|---|---|---|---|---|---|---|---|
| Tx-Dn 2 | (?) | CN | 25mm | — | — | 60.00 | — |

Steer standing on a mound. Rv: Stars and dots form border, within which: COW BOY'S / SALOON / DOANS, TEX. Plain edge.

Also known as Doan's Store or Doan's Crossing, Doans was located in Wilbarger County on the Red River, where the Dodge City or Western Trail crossed into Oklahoma. It is said that 6,000,000 cattle crossed the Red River at this point.

## A.S. CHRISTIAN
### Elgin, Texas

| Rulau | Date | Metal | Size | VG | F | VF | Unc |
|---|---|---|---|---|---|---|---|
| Tx-El 4 | (1880's) | Brass | 19mm | — | — | 17.50 | — |

A.S. CHRISTIAN / ELGIN, TEXAS. Rv: GOOD FOR / 5¢ / AT THE BAR. Plain edge.

Elgin was founded in 1872.
Christian was probably Elgin's earliest saloonkeeper. The token was issued before 1890.

## ACME (SALOON)
### El Paso, Texas

| Rulau | Date | Metal | Size | VG | F | VF | Unc |
|---|---|---|---|---|---|---|---|
| Tx-EP 1 | (1881) | CN | 25mm | — | — | 12.50 | — |

Oval at center, within which: N.F. NEWLAND / PROP. Rose above, diamond below. Rv: GOOD FOR / 1 / ACME / * DRINK *. Plain edge.

N.F. Newland was proprietor of the Acme Saloon at its first location on South El Paso Street, about 1881.

| | | |
|---|---|---|
| Tx-EP 3 | (1895) | Ivory Cube (Die) 16x16 by 16mm — — Rare — |

Single die of six sides used in Acme's dice games. On 6-pip side: ACME. On 2-pip side: R B STEVENS. On 1-pip side: GOOD FOR / DRINK.

R.B. Stevens was proprietor of the Acme Saloon. These dice tokens were in use there on August 19, 1895, when John Wesley Hardin was gunned down from behind by "Old John" Selman. Newspaper reports say Hardin was shaking dice at the Acme bar for drinks, and as he raised his dice cup for a toss, El Paso chief constable Selman shot him in the back of the head without warning. Selman was charged with murder but was acquitted; his attorney was Albert Fall, who in the Roaring Twenties became a central figure in the Teapot Dome scandal.

----------

John Wesley Hardin (1853-1895) was known as one of the fastest gunfighters in the Southwest. He once outdrew Wild Bill Hickock in Abilene in 1871, though no gunfight resulted and the two drank together and became friends. He is reputed to have killed 40 men in his outlaw career. He killed two Union troopers at Richmond Bottoms, Texas, during the Civil War while only 12.

He became the leader of the Taylor faction against the Suttons in the Gonzales-DeWitt Counties war in 1872-1874, and killed in that was Sheriff J.W. Morgan of Cuero, gunfighter Jack Helm, and Deputy Sheriff Charles Webb of Brown County. He was reputed to have planned the murders of clan leader Bill Sutton and rancher Gabe Slaughter at Indianola.

Texas Ranger John Duncan found Hardin in hiding at Polland, Alabama and sent for Captain John Armstrong of the Rangers. They arrested Hardin in August 1887 aboard a train and Hardin served 17 years in Huntsville State Prison for the "murder" of Webb, even though witnesses said Webb attempted to shoot Hardin in the back.

Hardin was pardoned in the spring of 1894. Having studied law in prison, he opened a law office in Gonzales in Oct. 1894. In early 1895 he moved to El Paso and became a criminal lawyer. During a love affair with the wife of rustler Martin McRose he became morose and began drinking. Hardin slighted the name of policemen "Young John" Selman after Selman had arrested his mistress Mrs. McRose for carrying a gun; the tirade coming after a saloon drinking bout.

Selman's father, then the chief constable of El Paso though himself a former outlaw, shot and killed Hardin from behind in the Acme Saloon without warning. Bartender Frank Patterson told police Selman shot Hardin in the back of the head; a photograph of Hardin's body in the El Paso morgue shows bullet wounds in the right chest and right upper arm, and his face seems unmarred except for dark spots on the left eye.

----------

*San Antonio Herald-Post newspaper account on Aug. 20, 1895, says Selman fired four times. The fatal shot was to the head, it states. Hardin was shaking dice with Henry S. Brown. Proprietor R. B. Stevens of the Acme Saloon did not actually witness the killing, he said, but said employee Frank Patterson was tending the bar. Henry S. Brown said that he and Hardin were shaking dice for a quarter bet.*

## B. DOWELLS
## El Paso, Texas

| Rulau | Date | Metal | Size | VG | F | VF | EF |
|---|---|---|---|---|---|---|---|
| Tx-EP 7 | (?) | Silver | 25mm | 85.00 | — | 125. | — |

B. DOWELLS / SALOON ctsp on U.S. 1854-O quarter dollar obverse. EL PASO ctsp on reverse of coin. (All lettering is crude, as though a single-letter die punch was used laboriously)

Ben Dowell was the first mayor of El Paso, in ----------

## THE OPHIR
## El Paso, Texas

| Rulau | Date | Metal | Size | VG | F | VF | Unc |
|---|---|---|---|---|---|---|---|
| Tx-EP 14 | (1880's) | CN | 24mm | — | — | 17.50 | — |

(All legends incuse). The OHPIR / 106 (in circle) / EL PASO TEX. Rv: Within central circle: GOOD FOR / 12 1/2 / ¢ / IN TRADE. Ornament above, AT THE OPHIR below. Plain edge.

## THE PARLOR
## El Paso, Texas

| Rulau | Date | Metal | Size | VG | F | VF | Unc |
|---|---|---|---|---|---|---|---|
| Tx-EP 18 | (1888) | GS | 33mm | — | 25.00 | — | — |

Court house at center, EL PASO COURT HOUSE above, star below. Rv: Church at center. Above: GOOD FOR 1 DRINK AT THE PARLOR / EL PASO / TEX. Below: OLD CHURCH AGE 270 YEARS / PASO DEL NORTE, MEX. Plain edge.

| Tx-EP 19 | (1889) | Aluminum 33mm | — | 15.00 | — | — |
|---|---|---|---|---|---|---|

Same as last. Plain edge.

| Tx-EP 20 | (1890) | Aluminum 33mm | — | 15.00 | — | — |
|---|---|---|---|---|---|---|

Obverse as last. Rv: As last, except text under church reads: OLD CHURCH BUILT 1618 / JUAREZ, MEX.

The Paso del Norte Church was built in 1618, dating the first token exactly. Probably the third type saw the greater use as a drink check.

## B & B WHITE ELEPHANT
## Fort Worth, Texas

| Rulau | Date | Metal | Size | VG | F | VF | Unc |
|---|---|---|---|---|---|---|---|
| Tx-FW 4 | (1874-84) | Brass | 24mm | — | — | — | — |

Pool table. Above: THE / J.M. BRUNSWICK / AND / BALKE CO. Rv: GOOD FOR / 5¢ / WHITE ELEPHANT / B & B / FORT WORTH. Plain edge. (Brunswick 2381)

## BEACH HOTEL
## Galveston, Texas

| Rulau | Date | Metal | Size | VG | F | VF | Unc |
|---|---|---|---|---|---|---|---|
| Tx-Ga 2 | (1880's) | GS | 29mm | — | 7.50 | — | — |

BEACH HOTEL / 15 / GALVESTON / large 15 (the last incused). Rv: Similar, but incused; no counterstamped numeral 15. Plain edge.

The Beach Hotel burned down in 1889.

## AUG. CAMERON
## Fredericksburg, Texas

| Rulau | Date | Metal | Size | VG | F | VF | Unc |
|---|---|---|---|---|---|---|---|
| Tx-Fr 3 | (1885) | GS | 28mm | — | — | 37.50 | — |

State capitol. Rv: AUG. CAMERON / CAPITOL / —*— / —SALOON— / GOOD FOR / 10 CENTS / DRINK / * FREDERICKSBURG, TEXAS. *. Plain edge. Rarity 8. (Wright 1358).

## OPERA HOUSE WINE ROOM
### Houston, Texas

| Rulau | Date | Metal | Size | VG | F | VF | Unc |
|---|---|---|---|---|---|---|---|
| Tx-Ho 12 | (?) | GS | 28mm | — | — | — | — |
| | | (All incused) OPERA HOUSE / 15 / WINE ROOM. Rv: PAY THE / 15 / CASHIER. Plain edge. | | | | | |
| Tx-Ho 13 | (?) | GS | 28mm | — | — | — | — |
| | | As 12, but numeral 20 replaces the 15 on each side. Plain edge. (Wright 790) | | | | | |
| Tx-Ho 14 | (?) | GS | 28mm | — | — | Rare | — |
| | | As 12, but numeral 350 replaces the 15 on each side. Plain edge. | | | | | |

Dr. B.P. Wright sold a specimen of 12 on April 15, 1897 to another collector with a tag stating it was rare and from Houston. This piece was sold later to Melvin and George Fuld, who published it in *The Numismatist* in their Token Collector's Pages.

The '350' piece, number 14, was reported by Fowler and Strough in *The Trade Tokens of Texas, Supplement*, Feb. 1979.

## WHITE ELEPHANT
### Lampasas, Texas

| Rulau | Date | Metal | Size | VG | F | VF | Unc |
|---|---|---|---|---|---|---|---|
| Tx-Lm 15 | (1880) | GS | 29mm | — | — | Rare | — |
| | | Elephant standing left, WHITE above, ELEPHANT below. Rv: * WHITE ELEPHANT / (star at center of falling rays) / LAMPASAS / —*— / * TEXAS *. Plain edge. Rarity 9. | | | | | |

## BOTICA LA MALINCHE
### Laredo, Texas

| Rulau | Date | Metal | Size | VG | F | VF | Unc |
|---|---|---|---|---|---|---|---|
| Tx-La 2 | (?) | GS | 19mm | — | — | 7.50 | — |
| | | Mortar and pestle at center, BOTICA LA MALINCHE above, LAREDO, TEX. below. Rv: GOOD FOR / 6 1/4 / MEX. / IN TRADE. Plain edge. | | | | | |

'6 1/4 Mex.' was one-half real, or 6 1/4 cents U.S.

## LAREDO BEER GARDEN
### Laredo, Texas

| Rulau | Date | Metal | Size | F | VF | EF | Unc |
|---|---|---|---|---|---|---|---|
| Tx-La 7 | (?) | GS | 25mm | — | — | 12.50 | — |
| | | LAREDO / BEER / GARDEN. Rv: GOOD FOR / ONE / BEER. Plain edge. | | | | | |
| Tx-La 8 | (1889-90) | Alum | 35mm | — | 17.00 | 30.00 | — |
| | | Building at center, ANHEUSER BUSCH ST. LOUIS BEER above, LAREDO / * BEER GARDEN * below. Rv: Flying eagle with shield in its talons before a large letter A. Around: GOOD FOR ONE DRINK. Plain edge. | | | | | |

## J.C. NORIOH
### Livingston, Texas (?)

| Rulau | Date | Metal | Size | VG | F | VF | Unc |
|---|---|---|---|---|---|---|---|
| Tx-Lv 3 | (1880's) | Brass | 28mm | — | — | Rare | — |
| | | (All incused) J.C. Norioh / 6 1/4 ¢ / LIVINGSTON. Rv: Blank. Beaded, incised rim on each side. Plain edge. | | | | | |

This is a puzzling piece to place geographically. It has been described as being from Livingston, S.C., but that place did not exist at the time of this token. The 6 1/4-cent denomination would indicate the West. Other possibilities are Livingston, Tenn. and Livingston, Calif. The latter, in Merced County, had its name changed in 1881, however, to Cressey.

After checking the Postal Guides from 1877 to 1892, we chose Texas as likely. Livingston is the county seat of Polk County, and was so named in the 1877-92 period. Directory evidence for Norioh is needed.

## LATREYTE
### Houston, Texas

| Rulau | Date | Metal | Size | VG | F | VF | Unc |
|---|---|---|---|---|---|---|---|
| Tx-Ho 3 | (1892) | CN | 30mm | — | — | 40.00 | — |
| | | Building at center, POST OFFICE above, HOUSTON, TEX. below. Rv: LATREYTE on ornamental scroll across center. At bottom, in small letters: THE HEIDEMANN MFG. CO. S.A. TEX. Plain edge. (Wright N/L) | | | | | |

Jean Pierre Latreyte was born in Pau, France, May 22, 1849. At 16 he emigrated to New Orleans, working there in a saloon 1865-1871. In 1871 he moved to Houston and became a bartender at Kiam's Saloon at Travis and Preston Streets. He opened his own saloon on Congress Avenue across from the courthouse in 1875. In 1879 he opened the Sample Room Saloon on Congress and Fannin Streets.

Latreyte (now John Peter Latreyte) watched his wife Marie Matilde die in 1879. In 1882 he married a 26-year-old widow and bought into her father's hardware business. In 1891 the new post office was completed on the Sample Room's block, and in 1892 Latreyte ordered the handsome tokens depicting the new post office from Heidemann Mfg. Co. in San Antonio. He was divorced in 1894, and died while on a trip to Bourne, Texas, June 20, 1901. He had five daughters.

The Latreyte piece, though struck in 1892, belongs with the rest of the Heidemann-produced Texas pictorial tokens and thus is included in this book.

For a full treatment on Latreyte, see "Latreyte and the Sample Room Saloon" by Ernest Beerstecher, in *TAMS Journal* for August, 1977.

## THE RANCH
### Kerrville, Texas

| Rulau | Date | Metal | Size | VG | F | VF | Unc |
|---|---|---|---|---|---|---|---|
| Tx-Kr 4 | (1880's) | CN | 31mm | — | — | 25.00 | — |
| | | Steer's head at center, THE RANCH above, KERRVILLE, TEX. below. Rv: GOOD FOR / 12 1/2 ¢ / DRINK / CHAS. BARLEMANN. Plain edge. | | | | | |
| Tx-Kr 6 | (?) | Brass | 24mm | — | — | 12.50 | — |
| | | THE RANCH / (star) / KERRVILLE, TEXAS. Rv: 5¢. Plain edge. | | | | | |

## ALGONA BAR
### Llano, Texas

| Rulau | Date | Metal | Size | VG | F | VF | Unc |
|---|---|---|---|---|---|---|---|
| Tx-Ln 1 | (1880's) | CN | 30mm | — | — | 27.50 | — |
| | | Clasped hands at center, THE ALGONA / BAR above, LLANO, / TEXAS. below. Rv: GOOD FOR / —*— / 12 1/2 ¢ / —*— / DRINK. Plain edge. | | | | | |

## J.H.M. & B.
### (J.H. Muenster & Brother)
### Luling, Texas

| Rulau | Date | Metal | Size | VG | F | VF | EF |
|---|---|---|---|---|---|---|---|
| Tx-Lu 7 | (1882) | Brass | 23mm | — | — | 17.50 | — |

J.H.M. & B. / GOOD FOR / A / DRINK. Rv: Blank. Plain edge.

| Tx-Lu 9 | (1880's) | Brass | 23mm | — | — | 17.50 | — |

GOOD FOR / 1 / DRINK / J H M. & BRO. Rv: LULING. Plain edge. (All lettering incuse)

| Tx-Lu 10 | (1880's) | Brass | 23mm | — | — | 17.50 | — |

As last, but blank reverse. Plain edge.

THe Muensters operated saloons in Luling for several generations. J.H. Muenster & Brother are located there in 1882. D.C. Muenster is placed there in 1890 and 1897. S.A. Muenster operated there in 1914.

Luling was called the "the toughest town in Texas," as were Dallas, Langtry, Jacksboro, Old Tascosa and others from time to time.

| Tx-Lu 12 | (1890's) | Aluminum | 24mm | — | — | 17.50 | — |

D.C. MUENSTER / LULING, TEX. Rv: GOOD FOR / 5 / CENTS / IN TRADE. Plain edge.

## JOSEPH LIPARI
### Mexia, Texas

| Rulau | Date | Metal | Size | VG | F | VF | Unc |
|---|---|---|---|---|---|---|---|
| Tx-Mx 2 | (1874-84) | CN | 24mm | — | — | 25.00 | — |

Pool table. Above: THE J.M. BRUNSWICK / & / BALKE COS. Below: CHECK. Rv: GOOD FOR / * 1 * / JOSEPH LIPARI / DRINK. Plain edge. (Brunswick 2216)

## GEO. B. BERRY & CO.
### Mobeetie, Texas

| Rulau | Date | Metal | Size | VG | F | VF | Unc |
|---|---|---|---|---|---|---|---|
| Tx-Mb 3 | (1880's) | CN | Oct, 27mm | — | — | Rare | — |

Elephant right on mound. Rv: GOOD FOR ONE DRINK / (radiant star) / GEO. B. BERRY & CO. / (radiant star) / MOBEETIE, TEXAS. Plain edge.

Mobeetie ("Sweetwater" in Indian) was the first settlement in the Texas Panhandle. First known as Hidetown by buffalo hunters, it was established 1874 as a trading post one mile from Fort Elliott.

George B. Berry came from Kansas and opened a saloon and dance hall. Bat Masterson and Temple Houston, son of Sam Houston, both lived in Mobeetie in the early days. Bat killed his first man here in a fight over a girl.

Temple Houston, born 1860 in the governor's mansion, became in 1878 (at 18) district attorney over the vast Panhandle.

## BANK EXCHANGE
### Palestine, Texas

| Rulau | Date | Metal | Size | VG | F | VF | Unc |
|---|---|---|---|---|---|---|---|
| Tx-Pa 1 | (1874-84) | CN | 25mm | — | — | 12.50 | — |

Pool table at bottom, THE / J. M. BRUNSWICK / AND / BALKE CO. within flourishes above. Rv: GOOD FOR / 1 / AT BANK / EXCHANGE / DRINK. Plain edge.

| Tx-Pa 2 | (ca 1880) | Brass | 25mm | — | — | — | V. Rare |

Liberty head to left surrounded by a wreath. Rv: Large numeral 1 in center, REDEEMED AT BANK EXCHANGE around. (Wright 56)

Assigned to Palestine on the basis of name similarity. The term "Bank Exchange" was widely used in Texas at this period.

## J. J. MURPHY
### Palestine, Texas

| Rulau | Date | Metal | Size | VG | F | VF | Unc |
|---|---|---|---|---|---|---|---|
| Tx-Pa 4 | (1880's) | GS | 30mm | — | — | Rare | — |

Texas state capitol building. Rv: J. J. MURPHY, / GOOD FOR / *12 1/2 ¢ * / AT THE / RUBY / PALESTINE, TEXAS. Plain edge.

## W. W. CAMP
### Pecos, Texas

| Rulau | Date | Metal | Size | VG | F | VF | Unc |
|---|---|---|---|---|---|---|---|
| Tx-Pc 2 | (1880's) | Br. Oct, | 27mm | — | — | Rare | — |

Steer at center, W. W. CAMP above, PECOS, TEXAS below. Rv: 12 1/2. Plain edge.

Pecos was established in 1881 as a stop on the Texas & Pacific Railroad. It gained early fame as a hangout for fast-draw gunmen, rough and ready cowboys, numerous saloons, and the world's first rodeo (held in 1883). It is now a trading center for a large West Texas area supported by oil, irrigated farming and tourism.

## W. J. H. UMLAND
### Round Top, Texas

| Rulau | Date | Metal | Size | VG | F | VF | Unc |
|---|---|---|---|---|---|---|---|
| Tx-RT 7 | (1874-82) | Brass | 23mm | — | — | 15.00 | — |

Pool table at center, THE J. M. BRUNSWICK & BALKE CO. above, o CHECK o below. Rv: GOOD FOR / 5 ¢ / W. J. H. / UMLAND / o IN TRADE o. Plain edge.

| Tx-RT 8 | (1874-82) | Brass | 24mm | — | — | 15.00 | — |

Similar, but THE J. M. BRUNSWICK / & BALKE COS. above pool table, nothing below it. Rv: As last. Plain edge.

Umland drove a freight wagon on the old New Orleans-San Antonio road and later operated a saloon at Round Top, one of the primary stops on the route. When the railroad bypassed Round Top in the early 1880's, he moved to Carmine and opened a general mercantile business with his son-in-law, E. W. Hoppe, (Hoppe later issued tokens at Carmine).

## H. E. V. ROSENBERG
### Round Top, Texas

| Rulau | Date | Metal | Size | VG | F | VF | Unc |
|---|---|---|---|---|---|---|---|
| Tx-RT 10 | (1874-84) | CN | 24mm | — | — | 12.50 | — |

Pool table at bottom, THE J. M. BRUNSWICK / & / BALKE COS above within flourishes. Rv: GOOD FOR / 5 ¢ / H. E. / v. ROSENBERG / IN / * TRADE *. Plain edge. (Brunswick 2306)

The way the small "v." appears before Rosenberg, it must indicate the proprietor's name was H. E. von Rosenberg. He has not yet been traced.

## FRED SCHMIDT
### San Angelo, Texas

| Rulau | Date | Metal | Size | VG | F | VF | Unc |
|---|---|---|---|---|---|---|---|
| Tx-Sn 7 | (?) | Brass | 29mm | — | — | Rare | — |

Steer's head facing three-quarters right, DROP ME AT THE PARLOR SALOON above, FRED SCHMIDT below. Rv: Courthouse

| Rulau | Date | Metal | Size | VG | F | VF | Unc |
|---|---|---|---|---|---|---|---|
| | | view, SAN ANGELO, TEXAS below. Plain edge. | | | | | |
| Tx-Sn 9 | (?) | Brass | 30mm | — | — | Rare | — |

Longhorn steer head facing three-quarters right, LONGEST HORNS / IN THE / WORLD above, EIGHT FEET FROM TIP TO TIP below. Rv: Horse at left, cowboy tying roped "dogie" at right. FRED SCHMIDT above, SAN ANGELO, TEXAS below. Plain edge.

## THE ALAMO
### San Antonio, Texas

| Rulau | Date | Metal | Size | VG | F | VF | Unc |
|---|---|---|---|---|---|---|---|
| Tx-SA 1 | (1889) | GS | 32mm | — | — | 45.00 | — |

Alamo at center, CRADLE OF TEXAS LIBERTY above, ALAMO in exergue. Rv: Post office building at center, POST OFFICE above, SAN ANTONIO, TEX. below. Plain edge. (Gary Pipher coll.)

This is a muling of the Alamo die used on Tx-SA 225 (the White House Saloon piece) and on Tx-SA 72 (the Peter Jonas piece) with the Post Office die used on Tx-SA 107 (the Nentwig's Bar piece). It is undoubtedly a Heidemann Mfg. Co. product, possibly for general use in San Antonio.

## ALBERT'S SALOON
### San Antonio, Texas

| Rulau | Date | Metal | Size | VG | F | VF | Unc |
|---|---|---|---|---|---|---|---|
| Tx-SA 2 | (1880's) | GS | 32mm | — | 60.00 | 100. | — |

Mounted elk's head with 17-point antlers at center, ALBERT'S above, SALOON below. Rv: Ram's head facing, its horns and ears framing 'I O U'. Below: ONE DRINK OR CIGAR. Plain edge. (Wright N/L)

| Tx-SA 4 | (?) | WM | 31mm | 25.00 | 32.50 | 42.00 | 75.00 |
|---|---|---|---|---|---|---|---|

The Alamo at center, ALBERT'S SALOON above, THE ALAMO below. Rv: Mission at center, THE MISSION CONCEPCION above, SAN ANTONIO, / TEX. below. Plain edge.

| Tx-SA 5 | (?) | GS | 31mm | — | — | 35.00 | 80.00 |
|---|---|---|---|---|---|---|---|

As Tx-SA 4. Plain edge.

| Rulau | Date | Metal | Size | VG | F | VF | Unc |
|---|---|---|---|---|---|---|---|
| Tx-SA 7 | (1889) | Alum. | 31mm | 15.00 | 30.00 | 40.00 | 65.00 |

Mounted 78-point buck elk's head above large 5-pointed star, with T-E-X-A-S on the five points of the star. Above: ALBERT'S / — * — / SALOON. Rv: View of the Alamo at center, CRADLE OF TEXAS LIBERTY above, ALAMO in exergue. Plain edge. (Wright 12)

| Tx-SA 8 | (?) | CN | 19mm | — | — | 22.50 | — |
|---|---|---|---|---|---|---|---|

Large 6-pointed Star of David at center, ALBERT'S above, SALOON below. Rv: GOOD FOR / * 2 1/2 ¢ / IN TRADE. Plain edge.

| Tx-SA 9 | (?) | Brass | 20mm | — | — | 17.50 | — |
|---|---|---|---|---|---|---|---|

(All incuse) ALBERT'S 2 1/2. Rv: Blank. Plain edge.

Regarding Tx-SA 7, a 78-point elk's antlers was the greatest number known in Fredrich's day.

Albert Fredrich kept his well-known Albert's Saloon on Dolorosa Street. Albert's was the predecessor of another saloon, the Buckhorn, called San Antonio's most famous saloon. Fredrich, who was proud of his Jewishness at a time when this was soft-pedaled in tough Texas saloons, was the proprietor of the Buckhorn and Albert's Saloon. The Buckhorn ultimately was removed to the Lone Star Brewery grounds, where it is once more in operation as an attraction.

| Tx-SA 11 | (?) | CN | 23mm | — | — | 25.00 | — |
|---|---|---|---|---|---|---|---|

(All incused) BUCK HORN / GOOD FOR / 12 1/2 / CENTS / AT BAR / SALOON. Rv: Blank. Plain edge.

| Tx-SA 12 | (?) | Brass | 30mm | — | — | 27.50 | 35.00 |
|---|---|---|---|---|---|---|---|

Longhorn steer at center, TEXAS LONGHORN STEER above, OLD TEX / AT THE BUCKHORN below. Rv: View of the Alamo at center, THE ALAMO above, BUILT IN / 1718 / SAN ANTONIO, TEXAS. Plain edge.

## EMIL BEHRENS
### San Antonio, Texas

| Rulau | Date | Metal | Size | F | VF | EF | Unc |
|---|---|---|---|---|---|---|---|
| Tx-SA 14 | (1889-90) | CN | 25mm | — | 6.00 | 9.50 | — |

Winged Cupid riding a swan left, TRADE MARK in exergue, all within central circle. Above: * EMIL BEHRENS C.E. *. Below: PATENT ATTORNEY. Rv: SAN ANTONIO / ELECTROPLATING / WORKS / EMIL BEHRENS & CO. / MANUFACTURERS OF / LIGHT MACHINERY / MODELS & / EXPERIMENTAL / WORKS.

Emil Behrens, civil, engineer, was listed in the 1889-1890 San Antonio city directory as a civil, mechanical and electrical engineer, patent attorney, and draftsman. His token is very handsome.

## BELL & BROTHERS
## San Antonio, Texas

| Rulau | Date | Metal | Size | VG | F | VF | EF |
|---|---|---|---|---|---|---|---|
| Tx-SA 16 | 1864 | Bronze | 19mm | — | — | — | — |

BELL & BROS / (ornamentation) / SAN-ANTONIO / TEXAS ctsp on U.S. 1864 Small cent.

## J. BOSSHARDT
## San Antonio, Texas

| Rulau | Date | Metal | Size | VG | F | VF | Unc |
|---|---|---|---|---|---|---|---|
| Tx-SA 19 | (1883-85) | Brass | 23mm | — | 12.50 | 20.00 | — |

(All incused) GOOD FOR / 5 / CENTS / AT BAR / J. BOSSHARDT. Rv: Blank. Plain edge.

John Bosshardt was operating the Eureka Saloon at the corner of Navarro and Commerce Streets as early as 1883. He advertised a "free lunch every day."

## JIM BRADY & CO.
## San Antonio, Texas

| Rulau | Date | Metal | Size | VG | F | VF | Unc |
|---|---|---|---|---|---|---|---|
| Tx-SA 22 | (?) | CN | 24mm | — | — | 40.00 | — |

JIM BRADY & CO. / OFFICE BAR / MAIN PLAZA. / Rv: I. O. U. / 12 1/2 ¢ / SAN ANTONIO, TEX. Plain edge.

| Tx-SA 24 | (?) | CN | 25mm | — | — | 40.00 | — |

JIM BRADY'S / OFFICE BAR / MAIN PLAZA. Rv: I. O. U. / 12 1/2¢ / SAN ANTONIO, TEX. Plain edge. (Wright 92)

## JOHN BRADY
## San Antonio, Texas

| Rulau | Date | Metal | Size | VG | F | VF | Unc |
|---|---|---|---|---|---|---|---|
| Tx-SA 26 | (?) | GS | 30mm | — | 35.00 | 50.00 | — |

JOHN BRADY'S / (star) / PARLOR BAR / —.— / SAN ANTONIO, / TEXAS. Rv: I.O.U. / —+— / ONE / —+— / .***. BRINK .***. Plain edge.

## FRANK BROWN
## San Antonio, Texas

| Rulau | Date | Metal | Size | VG | F | VF | Unc |
|---|---|---|---|---|---|---|---|
| Tx-SA 28 | (?) | Brass | 25mm | — | 10.00 | 15.00 | — |

(All incused) FRANK BROWN / GOOD FOR / 5 LBS. / ICE / SAN ANTONIO. Rv: Blank. Plain edge. (Wright 1347)

## BUFFET BAR
## San Antonio, Texas

| Rulau | Date | Metal | Size | VG | F | VF | Unc |
|---|---|---|---|---|---|---|---|
| Tx-SA 30 | (?) | CN | 23mm | — | — | 40.00 | — |

View of the Alamo inside a star, all within a wreath. Rv: 121 / W. COMMERCE / BUFFET / BAR / SAN ANTONIO, TEX. / U.S.A. Plain edge.

## ELITE SALOON
## San Antonio, Texas

| Rulau | Date | Metal | Size | VG | F | VF | Unc |
|---|---|---|---|---|---|---|---|
| Tx-SA 38 | (1880's) | GS | 31mm | — | 35.00 | 50.00 | 85.00 |

Soldiers attacking the Alamo at center, ELITE SALOON above, FALL OF THE / ALAMO / 1836 below. Rv: Building with tall tower at center, GOOD FOR ONE DRINK above, GOV. TOWER / SAN ANTONIO, TEX. below. Plain edge. (Wright 1405)

In this unusually detailed token by the Heidemann Mfg. Co., Pres. Santa Ana's army can be seen attacking toward the Alamo in the distance. It is one of the finest of the many fine Texas pictorial tokens of this period.

## ELLSWORTH & BUCK
## San Antonio, Texas

| Rulau | Date | Metal | Size | VG | F | VF | Unc |
|---|---|---|---|---|---|---|---|
| Tx-SA 40 | (1880's) | CN | 32mm | — | — | 60.00 | — |

Mission at center, MISSION SAN JOSE. above, FOUNDED 1720. below. Rv: CATARACT BAR / * 21 * / SOLEDAD STR. / 12 1/2 / ELLSWORTH & BUCK. Plain edge. (Wright 291)

## FRED'S
## San Antonio, Texas

| Rulau | Date | Metal | Size | VG | F | VF | Unc |
|---|---|---|---|---|---|---|---|
| Tx-SA 43 | (1880's) | CN | 33mm | — | — | 45.00 | — |

Large building at center, CITY HALL above, — * — / SAN ANTONIO, TEX. below. Rv: FRED'S on ornate scroll across center. Plain edge. (Wright N/L)

## J. L. FURTNER
## San Antonio, Texas

| Rulau | Date | Metal | Size | VG | F | VF | Unc |
|---|---|---|---|---|---|---|---|
| Tx-SA 45 | (1880's) | CN | 31mm | — | — | 40.00 | — |

MAVERICK HOTEL / (star) / BAR / SAN ANTONIO / TEX. Rv: GOOD FOR ONE DRINK / OR / CIGAR / AT / J. L. FURTNER'S. Plain edge. (Wright 1422)

## GUADALUPE HOTEL
## San Antonio, Texas

| Rulau | Date | Metal | Size | VG | F | VF | Unc |
|---|---|---|---|---|---|---|---|
| Tx-SA 47 | (?) | Brass | 23mm | — | 10.00 | — | — |

GUADALUPE / HOTEL / GOOD FOR / 5 / CENTS / AT BAR. Rv: Blank. Plain edge.

| Tx-SA 48 | (?) | Brass | 23mm | — | 12.50 | — | — |

GUADALUPE HOTEL / 5 (in central circle) / BAR. Rv: Blank. Plain edge. (Wright 363)

| Tx-SA 49 | (?) | Brass | 23mm | — | 10.00 | — | — |

GUADALUPE / 5 ¢ / HOTEL. Rv: Blank. Plain edge.

| Tx-SA 50 | (?) | Brass | 28mm | — | 12.50 | — | — |

GUADALUPE / 10 ¢ / HOTEL. Rv: Blank. Plain edge.

| Tx-SA 52 | (?) | Brass | 28mm | — | 12.50 | — | — |

GUADALUPE / GOOD FOR / ONE DRINK / HOTEL. Rv: Blank.

## THE HEIDEMANN MFG. CO.
### San Antonio, Texas

| Rulau | Date | Metal | Size | VG | F | VF | Unc |
|---|---|---|---|---|---|---|---|
| Tx-SA 55 | (1880's) | CN | 33mm | — | — | 100. | 200. |

Same as obverse of Tx-SA 43 (City Hall, Fred's). Rv: THE HEIDEMANN MFG. CO / MAKERS / OF / RUBBER STAMPS / ETC / BADGES / CHECKS / SAN ANTONIO, TEX. Plain edge.

## D. & A. HEINEN
### San Antonio, Texas

| Rulau | Date | Metal | Size | VG | F | VF | Unc |
|---|---|---|---|---|---|---|---|
| Tx-SA 57 | (1889) | Alum | 30mm | — | — | 25.00 | 35.00 |

Facing military bust of Travis at center, W.B. TRAVIS above, HERO OF THE ALAMO below. Tiny COPY TD under truncation of bust. Rv: Alamo at center, THE MANHATTAN / D & A HEINEN above, THE ALAMO / ALAMO PLAZA & HOUSTON ST below. Plain edge.

| Tx-SA 59 | (?) | Alum | 23mm | — | — | 12.50 | — |

Obverse as reverse of 57 (The Alamo). Rv: GOOD FOR / CENTS 5 / AT BAR. Plain edge.

## HORNER'S
### San Antonio, Texas

| Rulau | Date | Metal | Size | VG | F | VF | Unc |
|---|---|---|---|---|---|---|---|
| Tx-SA 62 | (1880's) | GS | 25mm | — | — | 65.00 | — |

Crow perched on branch left, OLD above, WHISKEY below. GOOD FOR ONE / DRINK / AT / HORNER'S / * / SAN ANTONIO, TEX. Plain edge. (There are three varieties of this token). (Wright 1460)

| Tx-SA 63 | (1880's) | GS | Oval, 25 x 23mm | — | — | 65.00 | — |

Obverse as 62. Rv: GOOD FOR ONE / DRINK / AT HORNER'S. Plain edge.

## JONAS GARDEN
### San Antonio, Texas

| Rulau | Date | Metal | Size | VG | F | VF | Unc |
|---|---|---|---|---|---|---|---|
| Tx-SA 70 | (1882) | Brass | 23mm | — | — | — | — |

JONAS GARDEN / GOOD FOR / 5 / CENTS / AT BAR. Rv: Blank.

Peter Jonas was operating Jonas Garden at 601 Austin Street in San Antonio in 1882.

| Rulau | Date | Metal | Size | VG | F | VF | Unc |
|---|---|---|---|---|---|---|---|
| Tx-SA 72 | (1890) | Alum | 32mm | — | — | 37.50 | Rare |

Side view of courthouse, BEXAR CO. COURT HOUSE around, PETER JONAS JR. below. Rv: View of the Alamo at center, CRADLE OF TEXAS LIBERTY above, ALAMO in exergue. Plain edge. (Wright 1475)

## KLINGLER'S THEATRE
### San Antonio, Texas

| Rulau | Date | Metal | Size | VG | F | VF | Unc |
|---|---|---|---|---|---|---|---|
| Tx-SA 75 | (1880's) | CN | 25mm | — | — | — | — |

KLINGLER'S / (large 5-pointed star) / THEATRE. Rv: Large 5 in circle of 6-pointed stars. Plain edge.

| Tx-SA 77 | (1880's) | B | Oct, 25mm | — | — | — | — |

Similar, but 25. Plain edge.

Klingler's Theatre was contemporary with The Fashion, The Vaudeville, etc., popular in the 1880's and 1890's. Heidemann Mfg. Co. probably made these tokens.

## LITTLE CORNER SALOON
### San Antonio, Texas

| Rulau | Date | Metal | Size | VG | F | VF | Unc |
|---|---|---|---|---|---|---|---|
| Tx-SA 80 | (?) | CN | 24mm | — | 18.50 | 26.50 | — |

LITTLE CORER (sic) SALOON / GOOD FOR / 5 / CENTS / AT BAR. Rv: Blank. Plain edge. (Wright 611)

'Corner' was misspelled and few tokens were made, according to Dr. Wright, writing about 1898.

## McDERMOTT'S SUNSET SALOON
### San Antonio, Texas

| Rulau | Date | Metal | Size | VG | F | VF | Unc |
|---|---|---|---|---|---|---|---|
| Tx-SA 83 | (1880's) | GS | 30mm | — | — | 30.00 | — |

Sunburst at upper center, SUNSET SALOON above, 521 AUSTIN ST. / (ornament) / SAN ANTONIO, TEX. below. Plain edge.

## Mc (Ilvaine) & Pratt
### San Antonio, Texas

| Rulau | Date | Metal | Size | VG | F | VF | Unc |
|---|---|---|---|---|---|---|---|
| Tx-SA 85 | (1880's) | GS | 30mm | — | — | Rare | — |

(All incused) GOOD FOR / o / ONE DRINK / Mc & PRATT / (ornament) / SAN ANTONIO. Rv: Blank. Plain edge.

| Tx-SA 86 | (1880's) | Brass | 30mm | — | — | 30.00 | Rare |

As 85. Plain edge. (Wright 1519)

| Rulau | Date | Metal | Size | VG | F | VF | Unc |
|---|---|---|---|---|---|---|---|
| Tx-SA 88 | (1880's) | GS | 28mm | — | — | 70.00 | — |

Horse's head right. Rv: R. E. McILVAINE / —*— / 254 / W. COMMERCE / ST. / —*— / SAN ANTONIO, TEX. Plain edge. (Wright 1517)

It is believed the 'Mc' of Mc & Pratt is R. E. McIlvaine.

## MENGER HOTEL BAR
### San Antonio, Texas

| Rulau | Date | Metal | Size | VG | F | VF | Unc |
|---|---|---|---|---|---|---|---|
| Tx-SA 92 | (?) | CN | 24mm | — | — | 20.00 | — |

MENGER HOTEL / BAR / SAN ANTONIO, TEX. Rv: GOOD FOR / ONE / DRINK. Plain edge. (Wright 1520)

## F.I. MEYER
### San Antonio, Texas

| Rulau | Date | Metal | Size | VG | F | VF | Unc |
|---|---|---|---|---|---|---|---|
| Tx-SA 95 | (1889) | Alum | 30mm | — | — | Rare | — |

Eagle perched with wings upraised atop globe, across which is a scroll reading IN VINO VERITAS. Above: F.I. MEYER. Below: ALAMO PLAZA. Rv: Building at center, U.S. POST OFFICE above, SAN ANTONIO / TEXAS in exergue. Plain edge. (Wright 1522)

## MIKE & JOE'S SALOON
### San Antonio, Texas

| Rulau | Date | Metal | Size | VG | F | VF | Unc |
|---|---|---|---|---|---|---|---|
| Tx-SA 98 | (?) | CN | 25mm | — | — | 25.00 | — |

MIKE & JOE'S / (star) / SALOON / SAN ANTONIO / TEX. Rv: GOOD FOR / ONE / 12 1/2 / CENTS / DRINK. Plain edge.

## S.B. MOSSER
### San Antonio, Texas

| Rulau | Date | Metal | Size | VG | F | VF | Unc |
|---|---|---|---|---|---|---|---|
| Tx-SA 101 | (1880 ?) | CN | 25mm | — | — | 22.50 | — |

S.B. MOSSER & CO / 28 / MILITARY / PLAZA / SAN ANTONIO / TEX. Rv: GOOD FOR ONE DRINK / AT THE / REGISTER. Plain edge.

| | | | | | | | |
|---|---|---|---|---|---|---|---|
| Tx-SA 103 | (1880's ?) | CN | 25mm | — | 25.00 | — | — |

GOOD FOR ONE DRINK / (star) / AT THE / REGISTER / *. Rv: Large 6 1/4 ¢ within circle of stars and small circles. Plain edge. Scarce.

## NENTWIG'S BAR
### San Antonio, Texas

| Rulau | Date | Metal | Size | VG | F | VF | Unc |
|---|---|---|---|---|---|---|---|
| Tx-SA 107 | (1888) | GS | 31mm | — | — | 55.00 | — |

Post office building at center, POST OFFICE above, SAN ANTONIO, TEX. below. Rv: Scroll across center. On scroll: NENTWIG'S / BAR. At lower rim: (small) THE HEIDEMANN MFG. CO. S.A. TEX. Plain edge. Rarity 7.

## A. ORFILA
### San Antonio, Texas

| Rulau | Date | Metal | Size | VG | F | VF | Unc |
|---|---|---|---|---|---|---|---|
| Tx-SA 111 | (1875) | CN | 24mm | — | 35.00 | — | — |

Coronet Liberty head left within palm wreath. Rv: * GOOD FOR * / — I — / DRINK — / (ornament) / — A. ORFILA —. Plain edge. (Wright 1566)

Made by J.F.W. Dorman, Baltimore.

## MONROE PRATT
### San Antonio, Texas

| Rulau | Date | Metal | Size | VG | F | VF | Unc |
|---|---|---|---|---|---|---|---|
| Tx-SA | (1880's) | GS | 28mm | — | — | 47.50 | 80.00 |

Lady riding horse sidesaddle. Rv: MONROE PRATT / 12 1/2 ¢ / SAN ANTONIO, TEXAS. Plain edge.

| | | | | | | | |
|---|---|---|---|---|---|---|---|
| Tx-SA 116 | (1880's) | GS | 32mm | — | — | 60.00 | — |

Lady sitting sidesaddle on horseback, toward left. Rv: MONROE PRATT, / —*— / ONE / DRINK / —*— / * SAN ANTONIO, TEXAS. *. Plain edge.

| | | | | | | | |
|---|---|---|---|---|---|---|---|
| Tx-SA 117 | (1880's) | Brass | 32mm | — | — | Rare | — |

As last. Plain edge. (Wright 1581)

## PROFESSOR SALOON
### San Antonio, Texas

| Rulau | Date | Metal | Size | VG | F | VF | Unc |
|---|---|---|---|---|---|---|---|
| Tx-SA 119 | (1880's) | CN | 31mm | — | — | 60.00 | — |

Large star at upper center, PROFESSOR above, SALOON / SAN ANTONIO / TEXAS in three lines below. Rv: (Ornament) GOOD (ornament) / FOR ? ONE / — * — / (ornament) DRINK (ornament). Plain edge. (Wright 1584)

## RHEINER & GAUL
### San Antonio, Texas

| Rulau | Date | Metal | Size | VG | F | VF | Unc |
|---|---|---|---|---|---|---|---|
| Tx-SA 130 | 1880-1900 | Brass | 24mm | — | — | — | — |

R. & G. / 2 1/2. Rv: Blank. Plain edge.

| Tx-SA 132 | 1880-1900 | CN | 21mm | — | — | — | — |

R. & G. / PROP'RS. Rv: GRAND CENTRAL / POOL / CHECK. Plain edge.

| Tx-SA 133 | (1880's) | CN | 24mm | — | — | 30.00 | — |

MISSION / (ornament) / * GARDEN * / (ornament) / SALOON. Rv: GOOD FOR / ONE / * BEER * / — OR — / CIGAR. Plain edge. (Wright 1526)

| Tx-SA 134 | 1880-1900 | CN | 21mm | — | — | — | — |

RHEINER & GAUL / —.— / MISSION / GARDEN. Rv: GOOD FOR / 5¢ / — IN — / * TRADE *. Plain edge. (Wright 1596)

Mission Garden was located at 315 So. Alamo Street and was one of the "theatres" that provided amusements for the citizenry in the 1880's and 1890's. There is strong evidence linking the two R. & G. tokens to Rheiner & Gaul.

## RHEINER'S SALOON
### San Antonio, Texas

| Rulau | Date | Metal | Size | VG | F | VF | Unc |
|---|---|---|---|---|---|---|---|
| Tx-SA 136 | (1890's) | Alum Sc, 28mm | | — | — | — | 20.00 |

RHEINER'S / SALOON / DULLNIGS / CORNER. Rv: GOOD FOR / 2 1/2 ¢ / AT THE BAR. This scalloped piece has four lobes. Plain edge.

This piece is likely from a period later than that covered, but it should not be disassociated from the earlier Rheiner pieces.

## S.A. LIGHT
### San Antonio, Texas

| Rulau | Date | Metal | Size | VG | F | VF | Unc |
|---|---|---|---|---|---|---|---|
| Tx-SA 140 | (1880's) | Brass Oct 23mm | | — | — | 50.00 | — |

Large rosette at center, S.A. above, LIGHT below. Rv: Large fraction 3/4 takes up almost entire reverse. Plain edge.

The San Antonio Light is a newspaper. In 1979, when the supplement to The Trade Tokens of Texas appeared in the TAMS Journal, the authors noted that no one at the paper had any ideas what these pieces has been used for.

The beading around this stock-die type of crude brass token seems to indicate mid-1880's venue, though it could have been later. The odd denomination (if that's what the 3/4 is, would indicate some sort of tally for newsboys. The piece is probably very rare.

## A.B. SAMUELS
### San Antonio, Texas

| Rulau | Date | Metal | Size | VG | F | VF | Unc |
|---|---|---|---|---|---|---|---|
| Tx-SA 145 | (1880's) | GS | 31mm | — | — | 65.00 | — |

Large star at upper center, A.B. SAMUELS around, SAN ANTONIO, / TEXAS. below. Rv: GOOD FOR ONE DRINK / - AT - / SILVER KING / .-. Plain edge. (Wright 1610)

| Tx-SA 147 | (1880's) | CN | 31mm | — | — | 75.00 | 95.00 |

Horse's head left within horseshoe, SALOON on scroll beneath. Rv: SAMUELS & Co. / -.- / SOUTH / FLORES / ST. / -.- / SAN ANTONIO, TEX. Plain edge. (Wright 1611)

## A. SCHOLZ
### San Antonio, Texas

| Rulau | Date | Metal | Size | VG | F | VF | Unc |
|---|---|---|---|---|---|---|---|
| Tx-SA 150 | (1880's) | GS | 28mm | — | — | 50.00 | — |

Ornate two-story building at center, A. SCHOLZ, / PALM GARDEN above, * / SAN ANTONIO, TEX. below. Plain edge. (Wright 1618)

| Tx-SA 152 | (?) | Brass | 24mm | — | — | 7.50 | — |

A. SCHOLZ on scroll across center. Rv: GOOD FOR / 5¢ / IN TRADE. Plain edge.

| Tx-SA 154 | (?) | Brass | 24mm | — | — | 15.00 | — |

A. SCHOLZ'S / GOOD FOR / 5 / CENTS / AT BAR / SALOON. Rv: Blank. Plain edge.

 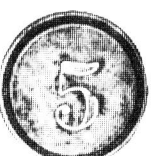

| Tx-SA 156 | (?) | Brass | 21mm | — | — | 25.00 | — |

Small palm trees on mound at bottom. Above: SCHOLZ PALM GARDEN / SAN / ANTONIO / TEX. Rv: Large numeral 5 at center. Plain edge.

| Tx-SA 158 | (1880's) | BV | 28mm | — | — | — | Rare |

A. SCHOLZ / SAN ANTONIO. Rv: GOOD FOR / 5 CENT / DRINK. Plain edge.

| Tx-SA 160 | (1890's) | Alum | 21mm | — | — | 20.00 | — |

SHOLZ (sic) PALM GARDEN / SAN / ANTONIO / TEX. Rv: GOOD FOR / 2 1/2 ¢ / IN TRADE. Plain edge.

## SOUTHERN HOTEL BAR
### San Antonio, Texas

 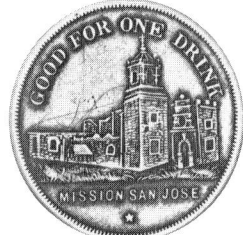

| Rulau | Date | Metal | Size | VG | F | VF | Unc |
|---|---|---|---|---|---|---|---|
| Tx-SA 164 | (1880's) | GS | 32mm | — | 25.00 | 35.00 | 45.00 |

The Alamo at center, SOUTHERN HOTEL BAR / SAN ANTONIO / TEXAS above, THE ALAMO in exergue. Rv: Mission at center, GOOD FOR ONE DRINK above, MISSION SAN JOSE below. Plain edge. (Wright 1018)

| Tx-SA 165 | (1880's) | BV | 32mm | — | — | Rare | — |

As last, but in vulcanite. Plain edge.

## DICK STRAYHORN
### San Antonio, Texas

| Rulau | Date | Metal | Size | VG | F | VF | Unc |
|---|---|---|---|---|---|---|---|
| Tx-SA 168 | (1880's) | CN | 31mm | — | — | 35.00 | |

Large diamond-shaped device at center, word THE on it. Above: NOTHING BUT THE BEST. Below: 312 WEST COMMERCE ST. Rv: DICK STRAYHORN (radiant) / (ornament) / PROPRIETOR / SAN ANTONIO / TEX. / *. Plain edge. (Wright 1640)

## ERNST STREMMEL
### San Antonio, Texas

| Rulau | Date | Metal | Size | VG | F | VF | Unc |
|---|---|---|---|---|---|---|---|
| Tx-SA 170 | (?) | Alum | 24mm | — | — | 40.00 | — |

Bust of Bismarck right, FURST OTTO VON BISMARCK around. Rv: MISMARCK SALOON / 5 / SAN ANTONIO / TEXAS / * ERNST STREMMEL. Plain edge.

## CARL STUBENRAUCH
### San Antonio, Texas

| Rulau | Date | Metal | Size | VG | F | EF | Unc |
|---|---|---|---|---|---|---|---|
| Tx-SA 173 | (1875-85) | Bronze | 28mm | — | — | 50.00 | — |

Stubenrauch bust left, CARL STUBENRAUCH GENERAL ENGRAVER & DIE SINKER around, SAN ANTONIO TEX. below. Rv: Female personification of Freedom with cornucopia leaning against a medal press. Around: MEDALS OF ALL KINDS MANUFACT'D. Plain edge.

Carl Stubenrauch had been a court engraver in Germany before emigrating to St. Louis in the 1850's. He came to San Antonio in 1875 and became the area's leading engraver, designing many beautiful tokens and medals there, and teaching his talented pupil Charles Simmang to do the same. He died about 1899.

## SUE LEE FASHION THEATRE
### San Antonio, Texas

 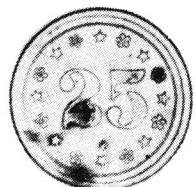

| Rulau | Date | Metal | Size | VG | F | VF | Unc |
|---|---|---|---|---|---|---|---|
| Tx-SA 175 | (1884-90) | Brass | 25mm | — | — | — | — |

SUE LEE / * FASHION * / THEATRE. Rv: Large numeral 25 encircled by 16 alternating stars and rosettes. Plain edge.

The Fashion became San Antonio's leading entertainment palace after the killing of Ben Thompson and King Fisher in 1884 put a damper on The Vaudeville.

The Sue Lee Restaurant was a short distance away, at 3 No. Flores Street. This token probably was good at both places.

## TWO BROTHERS SALOON
### San Antonio, Texas

| Rulau | Date | Metal | Size | VG | F | VF | Unc |
|---|---|---|---|---|---|---|---|
| Tx-SA 190 | (?) | Brass | 23mm | — | — | 25.00 | — |

TWO BROTHERS / GOOD FOR / 5¢ / AT BAR / SALOON (all incused). Rv: Blank. Plain edge.

| Tx-SA 192 | (1880's) | Brass | 24mm | — | — | 30.00 | — |

Clasped hands at center, TWO BROTHERS SALOON above, SAN / ANTONIO / TEX below. Rv: NO /5. Plain edge.

| Tx-SA 193 | (1889) | Alum.Oct. | 27mm | — | — | 25.00 | — |

Clasped hands at center, TWO BROTHERS BAR above, SAN ANTONIO / TEXAS below. Rv: NO. / 5. Plain edge.

| Tx-SA 195 | (1880's) | Brass | 29mm | — | — | 25.00 | — |

Clasped hands at center, TWO BROTHERS / SALOON above, SAN ANTONIO / TEXAS below. Rv: NUMBER / 1. Plain edge.

| Tx-SA 197 | (?) | Brass | 21mm | — | — | Scarce | |

Star at center, TWO BROTHERS above, BAR below. Rv: Blank. Plain edge.

| Tx-SA 199 | (1880's) | GS | 30mm | — | — | 35.00 | — |

Clasped hands across center, TWO BROTHERS / -+- / SALOON above, SAN ANTONIO / -*- / TEXAS. below. Rv: ] GOOD [ / FOR / ONE / (ornament) / ] DRINK [. Plain edge. (Wright 1695)

| Tx-SA 201 | (?) | Brass | 21mm | — | — | 20.00 | — |

TWO BROTHERS / SALOON. Rv: Large numeral 10. Plain edge.

| Tx-SA 203 | (?) | Brass | 21mm | — | — | 10.00 | — |

TWO BROTHERS / CAFE. Rv: Large numeral 10. Plain edge.

The Two Brothers issues present a confusing welter of types. They are listed here, but not necessarily in the order in which they were issued; that will require far more study.

## VAN'S CAVE
### San Antonio, Texas

| Rulau | Date | Metal | Size | VG | F | VF | Unc |
|---|---|---|---|---|---|---|---|
| Tx-SA 206 | (?) | CN | 26mm | — | — | 25.00 | — |

(All incused) VAN'S CAVE / GOOD FOR / ONE DRINK / (ornament) / SAN ANTONIO/ Rv: Blank. Plain edge.

## VAUDEVILLE THEATRE
### San Antonio, Texas

| Rulau | Date | Metal | Size | VG | F | VF | Unc |
|---|---|---|---|---|---|---|---|
| Tx-SA 208 | (1880's) | Brass | 24mm | — | — | 10.00 | — |

VAUDEVILLE / 25 / THEATRE. Rv: Large 25 at center, encircled by alternating stars and diamonds. Plain edge.

## VOLLMER SALOON
### San Antonio, Texas

| Rulau | Date | Metal | Size | VG | F | VF | Unc |
|---|---|---|---|---|---|---|---|
| Tx-SA 210 | (1885-86) | Brass | 23mm | — | — | 15.00 | — |

VOLLMER / GOOD FOR / 5 / CENTS / AT BAR / SALOON. Rv: Blank. Plain edge.

J.J. Vollmer ran a saloon at 635 Medina, according to the 1886 city directory.

## WHITE (ELEPHANT)
### San Antonio, Texas

| Rulau | Date | Metal | Size | VG | F | VF | Unc |
|---|---|---|---|---|---|---|---|
| Tx-SA 215 | (1880-1900) | CN | 25mm | — | — | 50.00 | — |

Elephant left at center, WHITE above, SAN ANTONIO, / TEXAS below. Rv: Large numeral 15 within central circle, GOOD FOR ONE DRINK around, * CENTS * below. Plain edge.

| Tx-SA 217 | (1880's) | Copper | 25mm | — | — | 75.00 | — |

As obverse of last (Elephant). Rv: The Three Graces standing nude at center, MONTAGNY below the ground under them. Plain edge. (Wright 1231)

| Tx-SA 217 A | (1880's) | WM | 25mm | — | — | Rare | — |

As 217. Plain edge.

It is not known whether Montagny is the designer of the token, or the proprietor of the White Elephant.

## WHITE HOUSE SALOON
### San Antonio, Texas

| Rulau | Date | Metal | Size | VG | F | VF | Unc |
|---|---|---|---|---|---|---|---|
| Tx-SA 225 | (1889 ?) | Alum | 31mm | — | — | 60.00 | — |

The Alamo at center, CRADLE OF TEXAS LIBERTY above, ALAMO in exergue. Rv: TAKE ME TO / THE / WHITE HOUSE / SALOON / SAN ANTONIO, TEX. Plain edge. (Wright N/L)

## KLINE'S
### Seguin, Texas

| Rulau | Date | Metal | Size | VG | F | VF | Unc |
|---|---|---|---|---|---|---|---|
| Tx-Sg 3 | (1882) | Brass | 23mm | — | — | 15.00 | — |

KLINE'S / GOOD FOR / 5 / CENTS / AT BAR / SALOON. Rv: Blank. Plain edge.

Kline appears in the 1882 *Texas Gazetteer*.

## HUGO STARCKE
### Seguin, Texas

| Rulau | Date | Metal | Size | VG | F | VF | Unc |
|---|---|---|---|---|---|---|---|
| Tx-Sg 6 | (1880's) | Brass | 29mm | — | — | 15.00 | — |

HUGO / STARCKE. Rv: GOOD FOR / 5¢ / IN TRADE / AT BAR. (AT BAR is incused). Plain edge.

Hugo Starcke ran the Sunset Saloon in Seguin in the 1880's.

## COW BOY SALOON
### Spanish Fort, Texas

| Rulau | Date | Metal | Size | VG | F | VF | Unc |
|---|---|---|---|---|---|---|---|
| Tx-Sp 2 | (1880's) | CN | 24mm | — | — | 27.50 | — |

Longhorn steer left, head facing. Rv: GOOD FOR / - A - / COW BOY / SALOON / * DRINK *. Plain edge.

Spanish Fort was an Indian village and French trappers' supply point as early as 1819.
The Cow Boy Saloon was the last oasis for thirsty cowboys coming up the Chisholm Trail, before crossing the Red River into Indian Territory (Oklahoma).
(See Doans — Doan's Crossing — on the Western, or Dodge, Trail, where a similar token was used.)

## CRYSTAL SALOON
### Waco, Texas

| Rulau | Date | Metal | Size | VG | F | VF | Unc |
|---|---|---|---|---|---|---|---|
| Tx-Wa 4 | (1874-84) | CN | 24mm | — | — | 25.00 | — |

Pool table. Above: THE J.M. BRUNSWICK / & / BALKE COS. Below: CHECK. Rv: GOOD FOR / * 1 * / CRYSTAL SALOON / * DRINK *. Plain edge. (Brunswick 2088)

# UTAH

## MODEL DAIRY
## Ogden, Utah

| Rulau | Date | Metal | Size | VG | F | VF | Unc |
|---|---|---|---|---|---|---|---|
| Ut-Og 5 | (ca 1880) | WM | Rec., 38 by 14mm | — | 100. | 175. | — |

Grasshopper left, in high relief. Rv: (all incused) MODEL DAIRY / WEST 12TH ST / OGDEN UTAH. Plain edge. (Wright 1528)

| Ut-Og 6 | (ca 1880) | WM | Rec., 38 by 14mm | — | — | — | 300. |
|---|---|---|---|---|---|---|---|

Obverse as 5. Rv: Blank. Die trial.

Rarity 8 — only about 7 or 8 pieces exist. The Fuld-Rulau specimen is pictured.
The die trial was sold by Stanley L. Steinberg in 1982 list number 87, lot 124.
The grasshopper on the token represents the "Mormon Cricket" or locust, scourge of Utah's territorial period. yet a well-known symbol to the Mormons of that day. It indicated its issuer was a Latter-Day Saints church member.
The first Polk directory for Ogden was in 1890, and there were six dairies in the city or its environs that year:

Ogden Creamery, Washington Ave. betw. 14th & 15th
Christopher Bouwers, Wilson, Ward
Isaac W. Duncan, Harrisville
James Embling, Wilson Road
West Weber Dairy, Wilson Ward
John Dowell, Wilson Ward

One of these might have been a successor. The Polk directory refers to an earlier directory, but it could not be located. (Research courtesy Donald T. Schmidt, director of library-archives division, Mormon Church historical department, Salt Lake City.)

## GALT HOUSE
## St. Joseph, Utah

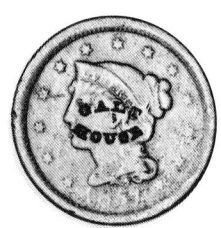 

| Rulau | Date | Metal | Size | VG | F | VF | Unc |
|---|---|---|---|---|---|---|---|
| Ut-SJ 1 | (?) | Copper | 29mm | — | — | 70.00 | — |

GALT / HOUSE ctsp on U.S. 1851 Large cent. (Brunk coll.)

The Galt House was a hotel in St. Joseph, Utah, which issued paper scrip (see NASCA sale of Jan. 10, 1983, lot 2086). This counterstamp may be associated with the scrip issue or have emanated from the same period, but this needs verification.

# VERMONT

## HOWE'S IMPROVED
## Brandon, Vt.

| Rulau | Date | Metal | Size | VG | F | VF | EF |
|---|---|---|---|---|---|---|---|
| Vt-Br 2 | (1870's) | Copper | 29mm | — | — | 75.00 | — |

HOWE'S / IMPROVED ctsp on U.S. 1848 Large cent. (Brunk coll.)

Howe's Improved Scales were manufactured by the Brandon Manufacturing Co., Brandon, Vt. This company and its agents in New York and Boston issued a large number of embossed shell cards in the 1867-1876 period (see numbers Rulau 318 to 324b in the *TAMS Journal* for April, 1961) but this is the first counterstamp reported for the firm.

## PATENT
## Windsor, Vt.

| Rulau | Date | Metal | Size | VG | F | VF | EF |
|---|---|---|---|---|---|---|---|
| Vt-Wi 4 | (?) | Silver | 27.5mm | 150. | — | 300. | — |

WINDSOR. VT. / PATENT/ ctsp on U.S. 1806 Draped Bust quarter dollar. (Collection of Dean M. Ryder, Madison, Wis.)

216    NEW HAMPSHIRE BUSINESS DIRECTORY.

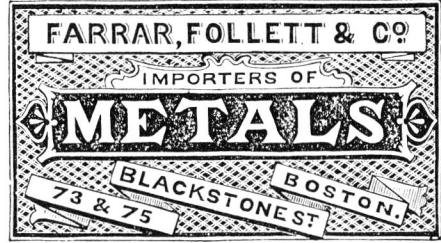

**DEALERS IN**

Tin Plate, Sheet-iron, Tin, Lead, Zinc, Copper, Hoop and Round Iron, Japanned and Stamped Ware, Tinners' Machines, Tools, &c.

## MANUFACTURERS

OF ALL KINDS OF

## IRON WIRE,

PARTICULARLY A SUPERIOR QUALITY FOR

## PAIL BAILS,

AND MAKERS OF THE CELEBRATED

## UNION BRAND TELEGRAPH WIRE,

73 and 75 BLACKSTONE STREET, BOSTON.

---

ARE OFFERED TO THE PUBLIC

## AS THE BEST IN USE,

And every Scale warranted to give entire satisfaction.

A Complete Assortment of Railroad, Hay, Coal, Portable, Counter, Druggists', and other Scales.

Together with a large variety of Beams, Spring Balances, Weights and Measures.
*Patent Alarm Money Drawers, Marvin's Fire-proof Safes.*
A large lot of Second-hand Scales for Sale at very low prices.

**HOWE SCALE CO.,**

*New England Ware-house, 131 Federal Street, Boston, Mass.*

*Two 1868 advertisements from the New Hampshire business directory of that year. Howe's Scales did not issue solid metal tokens, but issued a large number of embossed shell cards which are not included in this volume. The Parks House is reputed to have issued tokens, but they have not been located.*

[161]

## P. A. WHITNEY (and) C. A. WOODBURY
### Woodstock, Vt.

| Rulau | Date | Metal | Size | VG | F | VF | EF |
|---|---|---|---|---|---|---|---|
| Vt-Wo 6 | 1862 | Copper | 29mm | 50.00 | — | 70.00 | — |

P. A. WHITNEY / C. A. WOODBURY / WOODSTOCK / 1862 Vt. ctsp on U.S. 1847 Large cent. (Kurt Krueger coll.)

# VIRGINIA

## E. PIEPENBRING
### Alexandria, Va.

| Rulau | Date | Metal | Size | F | VF | Unc |
|---|---|---|---|---|---|---|
| Va-Al 10 | Late 1860's | Brass | 21mm | 25.00 | 37.50 | 65.00 |

E. PIEPENBRING / KOEHLER / * / ALEXDR. / VA. Rv: GOOD FOR / 2 / CENTS / KOEHLER. Plain edge. (Schenkman 1040AH2; Miller Va 1A)

| Va-Al 11 | Late 1860's | Brass | 21mm | 25.00 | 37.50 | 65.00 |

Similar to 1A, but 3 / CENTS. Plain edge. (Miller Va 1)

Edward Piepenbring was a confectioner in the late 1860's. By 1870 he was out of business. These cards probably appeared in the 1866-1869 period.

## F. H. (and) M. P.
### Bear Island, Va.

| Rulau | Date | Metal | Size | VG | F | VF | EF |
|---|---|---|---|---|---|---|---|
| Va-BI 1 | 1863 | CN | 19mm | — | 100. | — | — |

. BEAR ISLAND / F H / M P / JULY / 4 / 1863 ctsp on planed-off reverse of U.S. 1863 Indian Head cent. (Kurt Krueger coll.)

This personal piece must have some Civil War connection. July 4, 1863 was the day following the bitter three-day Battle of Gettysburg, July 1, 2 and 3, 1863. General Robert E. Lee began his retreat to Virginia on July 4, 1863, from Pennsylvania.

Bear Island is in Fairfax County, Virginia, not far from the site of the Battles of Bull Run or from the District of Columbia. It is near Lee Manor and Vienna. Bear Branch is a river rising near Vienna and flowing southward.

## COLE & FLINN
### Danville, Va.

| Rulau | Date | Metal | Size | F | VF | Unc |
|---|---|---|---|---|---|---|
| Va-Da 3 | (1876) | Tin | 23mm | — | 40.00 | 75.00 |

Bell at center, LIBERTY BELL above, 1776 below. Rv: COLE & FLINN / ONE / SODA / * DANVILLE, VA. Plain edge. (Schenkman 2040D; Miller Va 2)

Issued during the Centennial of the United States celebrations.

## DIAMOND SALOON
### Lynchburg, Va.

| Rulau | Date | Metal | Size | F | VF | Unc |
|---|---|---|---|---|---|---|
| Va-Ly 3 | 1875 | Brass | 20mm | — | 75.00 | — |

Coronet Liberty head left, 13 stars around, 1875 below. Rv: DIAMOND SALOON / 5 (in diamond) / 65, 9TH ST. / LYNCHBURG, VA. Plain edge. (Schenkman 3180I5; Miller Va 3)

Struck by the Dorman Stencil & Stamp works, Baltimore, Md.

## OFFICE RESTAURANT
### Lynchburg, Va.

| Rulau | Date | Metal | Size | F | VF | Unc |
|---|---|---|---|---|---|---|
| Va-Ly 7 | 1875 | Brass | 20mm | — | 50.00 | — |

Coronet Liberty head left, 13 stars around, 1875 below. Rv: OFFICE RESTAURANT / 5 (in circle) / 106, MAIN ST. / LYNCHBURG, VA. Plain edge. (Schenkman 3180AD5)

Struck by Dorman Stencil & Stamp Works, Baltimore, Md.

## PIEDMONT CLUB
### Lynchburg, Va.

| Rulau | Date | Metal | Size | F | VF | Unc |
|---|---|---|---|---|---|---|
| Va-Ly 9 | (1870-85) | GS | 19mm | 30.00 | — | — |

Union shield at center, * PIEDMONT CLUB * / LYNCHBURG VA. around. Rv: Numeral 10 within wreath, star at top, bow at bottom. Plain edge. (Wright 830; Schenkman 3180AF10; Miller Va 4)

This token was struck by Francis X. Koehler of Baltimore, Md.

## S.H. MARKS & CO.
## Petersburg, Va.

### 1876 Centennial Tokens

Reverse type 1: S.H. MARKS & CO. / * WHOLESALE * / AND / RETAIL / CONFECTIONERS / PETERSBURG, VA. (All 23mm; plain edge)

| Rulau | Obv | Rev | Metal | F | VF | EF | Unc |
|---|---|---|---|---|---|---|---|
| Va-Pe | A | 1 | WM | — | — | 15.00 | 40.00 |
| | | (Miller Va 15; Schenkman 3960Wa) | | | | | |
| Va-Pe 1A | A | 1 | Copper | — | — | 17.50 | 42.50 |
| | | (Schenkman 3960Wb) | | | | | |
| Va-Pe 1B | A | 1 | Brass | — | — | 17.50 | 42.50 |
| | | (Miller 15A; Schenkman 3960Wc) | | | | | |
| Va-Pe 2 | B | 1 | WM | — | — | 15.00 | 40.00 |
| | | (Miller 17; Schenkman 3960Xa) | | | | | |
| Va-Pe 2A | B | 1 | Brass | — | — | — | 42.50 |
| | | (Wright 663' Schenkman 3960Xb) | | | | | |
| Va-Pe 3 | E | 1 | WM | — | — | 17.50 | 42.50 |
| | | (Schenkman 3960Y) | | | | | |
| Va-Pe 4 | F | 1 | WM | — | — | 17.50 | 42.50 |
| | | (Schenkman 3960Y; Miller 17A) | | | | | |
| Va-Pe 5 | G | 1 | WM | — | — | 17.50 | 42.50 |
| | | (Schenkman 3960AB) | | | | | |
| Va-Pe 6 | H | 1 | WM | — | — | 17.50 | 42.50 |
| | | (Schenkman 3960AA) | | | | | |

S.H. Marks and Co., wholesale and retail confectioners, were located at 129 No. Sycamore St. They went out of business in the 1890's. Most varieties of this series were struck for collectors, in very limited numbers.

## JOSEPH KLEPPER
## Norfolk, Va.

| Rulau | Date | Metal | Size | F | VF | Unc |
|---|---|---|---|---|---|---|
| Va-No 5 | 1875 | Lead | 20mm | — | — | Rare |
| | | Coronet Liberty head left, 13 stars around, 1875 below. Rv: JOSEPH KLEPPER / 5 (on sunburst) / NORFOLK. VA. Plain edge. (Schenkman 3680AV5) | | | | |
| Va-No 6 | 1875 | Brass | 20mm | 30.00 | — | — |
| | | Similar, but numeral 10 on reverse. (Schenkman 3680AV-10) | | | | |

Joseph Klepper opened a restaurant at 139 Church St. about 1870. By 1882 his business occupied 139 thru 145 Church St., and included a billiard hall and orchestrion. In 1889 he owned a hotel, and later went into the real estate business. He died Dec. 20, 1896.

Klepper's tokens were made by Dorman Stencil & Stamp Works of Baltimore, Md.

## JAMES E. WOLFF
## Petersburg, Va.

| Rulau | Date | Metal | Size | VG | F | VF | Unc |
|---|---|---|---|---|---|---|---|
| Va-Pe 12 | 1863 | GS | 26mm | — | — | — | 100. |
| | | JAMES E. WOLFF / (tall hat) / NO. 17 / SYCAMORE ST. / PETERSBURG, VA. Rv: Shield. UNION LEAGUE 1863. (Miller Va 26) | | | | | |
| Va-Pe 13 | 1863 | WM | 26mm | — | — | — | 100. |
| | | As 12. Normal planchet. (Miller Va 27) | | | | | |
| Va-Pe 14 | 1863 | WM | 26mm | — | — | — | 100. |
| | | As 12. Thin planchet. (Miller Va 27A) | | | | | |
| Va-Pe 15 | (?) | GS | 26mm | — | — | — | 75.00 |
| | | Obverse as 12. Rv: Flag (Miller Va 28) | | | | | |
| Va-Pe 16 | (?) | WM | 26mm | — | — | — | 75.00 |
| | | As 12. (Miller Va 28A) | | | | | |
| Va-Pe 17 | (?) | GS | 26mm | — | — | — | 75.00 |
| | | As 12 (Miller Va 29) | | | | | |
| Va-Pe 18 | 1864 | Copper | 26mm | — | — | — | 100. |
| | | Obverse as 12. Rv: Abraham Lincoln. (DeWitt AL 1864-31A) (Schenkman 3960AQa; Miller Va 29½) | | | | | |
| Va-Pe 19 | 1864 | WM | 26mm | — | — | — | 100. |
| | | As 18. (King 612; Miller Va 29½A) | | | | | |

Regular Wolff store cards were issued in the 1850's and appear in my 1845-1860 reference. Items listed above are mulings from the 1867-71 period.

## J. L. WISSIN
## Portsmouth, Va.

| Rulau | Date | Metal | Size | VG | F | VF | EF |
|---|---|---|---|---|---|---|---|
| Va-Po 5 | (?) | Copper | 29mm | — | — | — | — |
| | | J.L. WISSIN PORTSMOUTH VA ctsp on U.S. Large cent. (Hallenbeck 23.513) | | | | | | |

## R. McNAMEE
## Richmond, Va.

| Rulau | Date | Metal | Size | VG | F | VF | EF |
|---|---|---|---|---|---|---|---|
| Va-Ri 8 | (1870) | Silver | 32.5mm | — | 200. | — | — |
| | | R McNAMEE / RICHD VA. ctsp on U.S. 1805 Bust type half dollar. (Schenkman collection) | | | | | | |

Robert McNamee was a dealer in surgical instruments listed in the 1870 Bradstreet directory.

## R.A. PATTERSON & CO.
## Richmond, Va.

| Rulau | Date | Metal | Size | VG | F | VF | Unc |
|---|---|---|---|---|---|---|---|
| Va-Ri 10 | 1881 | Brass | 25mm | 20.00 | 30.00 | 50.00 | — |
| | | Two-horse carriage right, RICHMOND / VA. below. Around: CHEW SHELLROAD TOBACCO / M'F'D BY R.A. PATTERSON & CO. Rv: Within central wreath: FIRST / AWARD / OF / MERIT. Around: INTERNATIONAL COTTON EXPOSITION / ATLANTA GA. 1881. Plain edge. | | | | | | |

## PIZZINI
## Richmond, Va.

### 1876 Centennial Tokens

Reverse type 1: PIZZINI, / NAPOLEON / OF / CONFECTIONERS / 807 BROAD ST. RICHMOND, VA. (All 23mm; plain edge)

| Rulau | Obv | Rev | Metal | F | VF | EF | Unc |
|---|---|---|---|---|---|---|---|
| Va-Ri 11 | A | 1 | WM | — | — | 25.00 | 45.00 |
| | | (Wright 835; Schenkman 4180AY; Miller Va 36E) | | | | | |
| Va-Ri 12 | B | 1 | WM | — | — | 30.00 | 60.00 |
| Va-Ri 12A | B | 1 | Brass | — | — | 30.00 | 60.00 |
| | | (Miller 37A; Schenkman 4180AW) | | | | | |
| Va-Ri 13 | C | 1 | WM | — | — | 30.00 | 60.00 |
| | | (Miller 36C; Schenkman 4180AV) | | | | | |
| Va-Ri 14 | D | 1 | WM | — | — | 30.00 | 60.00 |
| | | (Miller 36A; Schenkman 4180BE) | | | | | |
| Va-Ri 15 | E | 1 | WM | — | — | 30.00 | 60.00 |
| | | (Miller 37; Schenkman 4180BA) | | | | | |
| Va-Ri 16 | F | 1 | WM | — | — | 30.00 | 60.00 |
| | | (Miller 36B; Schenkman 4180BC) | | | | | |
| Va-Ri 17 | G | 1 | WM | — | — | 30.00 | 60.00 |
| | | (Schenkman 4180BB) | | | | | |
| Va-Ri 18 | H | 1 | WM | — | — | 30.00 | 60.00 |
| | | (Schenkman 4180AZ) | | | | | |
| Va-Ri 19 | J | 1 | WM | - | — | 30.00 | 60.00 |
| | | (Miller 36D; Schenkman 4180BD) | | | | | |
| Va-Ri 20 | K | 1 | WM | — | — | 30.00 | 60.00 |
| | | (Miller 36; Schenkman 4180AX) | | | | | |

Most varieties of these Centennial store cards were struck in very small quantities for collectors. Any significant demand would raise their price, as Virginia is a popular state with today's collectors.

## G. SAUER
### Richmond, Va.

| Rulau | Date | Metal | Size | VG | F | VF | Unc |
|---|---|---|---|---|---|---|---|
| Va-Ri 26 | (1870's) | Brass | 20mm | 15.00 | 20.00 | 25.00 | 40.00 |

Eagle with spread wings. Rv: G. SAUER / 5 (incuse) / RICHMOND, VA. Plain edge. (Miller Va 39; Schenkman 4180BN5)

| Va-Ri 27 | (1870's) | Brass | 20mm | 15.00 | 20.00 | 25.00 | 40.00 |
|---|---|---|---|---|---|---|---|

Similar to 26, but incused numeral 10. Plain edge. (Miller 40; Schenkman 4180BN10)

| Va-Ri 28 | (1870's) | GS | 20mm | 17.50 | 22.50 | 27.50 | 45.00 |
|---|---|---|---|---|---|---|---|

Similar to 26, but incused numeral 25. Plain edge. (Miller 41; Schenkman 4180BN25)

| Va-Ri 29 | (1870's) | Brass | 20mm | — | — | — | 45.00 |
|---|---|---|---|---|---|---|---|

Similar to 26, but no incused numeral at center. Plain edge. (Miller 38; Schenkman 4180BN25a)

## CHRIST. SCHAEFER
### Richmond, Va.

| Rulau | Date | Metal | Size | VG | F | VF | Unc |
|---|---|---|---|---|---|---|---|
| Va-Ri 31 | (1870) | Brass | 19mm | 5.00 | 9.00 | 14.00 | 20.00 |

CHRIST. SCHAEFER / ELBA / * / PARK / RICHMOND, VA. Rv: Numeral 5 within wreath, star at top. Plain edge. (Miller Va 42; Wright 936; Schenkman 4180B05)

| Va-Ri 32 | (1870) | Brass | 19mm | 5.00 | 9.00 | 14.00 | 20.00 |
|---|---|---|---|---|---|---|---|

Similar to 31, but numeral 10 within wreath. (Miller 43; Schenkman 4180B010)

Both tokens were struck by Francis X. Koehler of Baltimore, about 1870.

## UNION MANUFACTURING CO.
### Richmond, Va.

| Rulau | Date | Metal | Size | VG | F | VF | EF |
|---|---|---|---|---|---|---|---|
| Va-Ri 36 | (?) | Silver | 31mm | — | 250. | — | — |

UNION MANFG CO. / RICHMOND VA. ctsp on U.S. 1859 Seated Liberty half dollar. (Schenkman collection)

## W.L. WARING
### Richmond, Va.

| Rulau | Date | Metal | Size | F | VF | EF | Unc |
|---|---|---|---|---|---|---|---|
| Va-Ri 40 | (1860-65) | WM | 22mm | — | 75.00 | — | — |

(All incused) W.L. WARING / DRUGGIST / RICHMOND, VA. Rv: BROAD. ST / ONE / No 107 / SODA. Plain edge. The reverse inscription arranged to form a cross, at center of which is a soda glass. Crude planchet. (Wright 1203; Miller Va 44; Schenkman 4180CE)

Warren L. Waring was listed 1858-59 as part of the firm of Waring & Pearce with James H. Pearce, at 107 Broad St. In 1860 Waring was listed as a druggist at 107 Broad St. alone. No directories were published during the Civil War, and in the 1866 directory Waring no longer appears.

# WASHINGTON

## ANDERSON BROS.
### Brewster, Wash.

| Rulau | Date | Metal | Size | VG | F | VF | Unc |
|---|---|---|---|---|---|---|---|
| Wa-Br 1 | (1874-84) | Brass | 25mm | — | — | — | — |

ANDERSON BROS., 5 ¢. Rv: Pool table in center circle, THE J. M. BRUNSWICK & BALKE COS. around, CHECK below. Plain edge. (Brunswick 2010)

## BINNARD'S ELITE SALOON
### Colfax, Wash.

| Rulau | Date | Metal | Size |
|---|---|---|---|
| Wa-Co 2 | (1874-84) | CN | 25mm |

BINNARD'S ELITE SALOON, COLFAX, W.T. Rv: Pool table at bottom. Above: THE / J. M. BRUNSWICK / AND / BALKE CO. Plain edge. (Brunswick 2032)

W.T. = Washington Territory.

## M. A. CAVANAGH
### Dayton, Wash.

| Rulau | Date | Metal | Size | VG | F | VF | Unc |
|---|---|---|---|---|---|---|---|
| Wa-Dy 3 | (1877-89) | Brass | 25mm | — | 17.50 | — | — |

—*— / CHECK / —*— within central circle. Around: BRUNSWICK & COMPANY / * CHICAGO *. Rv: GOOD FOR / 1 CIGAR / M. A. CAVANAGH / DAYTON W. T. Plain edge. (Brunswick 14)

Washington Territory (W.T.) was created in 1853 out of Oregon Territory. Washington was admitted as a state in 1889.

## TOKLAS SINGERMAN & CO.
### Seattle, Wash.

| Rulau | Date | Metal | Size | F | VF | EF | Unc |
|---|---|---|---|---|---|---|---|
| Wa-Se 8 | 1888 | Copper | 35mm | 150. | 170. | 200. | — |

Washington head left, COR. FRONT & COLUMBIA ST. above, 1888 below, all within beaded central circle. Around: COMPLIMENTS OF TOKLAS SINGERMAN & CO. / * SEATTLE, W.T. *. Rv: Within laurel and oak wreath: STRICTLY / —.— / ONE PRICE / —&— / LOWEST / FIGURES. Around CLOTHIERS & GENTS FURNISHERS. (Wright 1087)

Occurs with and without a loop to attach to a leather strap for use as a fob, according to Dr. B.P. Wright and Byron Johnson. WT = Washington Territory.

## H. OBERMAN & CO.
### Centralia, Wash.

| Rulau | Date | Metal | Size | VG | F | VF | Unc |
|---|---|---|---|---|---|---|---|
| Wa-Ce 7 | (1883-89) | WM | 25mm | — | — | 20.00 | — |

Pool table at center, JACOB STRAHLE & CO BILLIARD MFRS above, 515 MARKET ST. SAN FRANCISCO, CAL. below. Rv: H. OBERMAN & CO. / GOOD FOR / 10 ¢ / IN TRADE / CENTRALIA, W.T. Plain edge. (Byron Johnson coll.)

## PEARL BAKERY
### Colfax, Wash.

| Rulau | Date | Metal | Size | VG | F | VF | Unc |
|---|---|---|---|---|---|---|---|
| Wa-Co 9 | (1880's) | Brass | 25mm | — | — | 17.50 | — |

PEARL BAKERY / COLFAX W.T. / (incuse) B. Rv: GOOD FOR / 5 / CENTS / IN TRADE. Plain edge. (Byron Johnson coll.)

## TACOMA MILL CO.
### Tacoma, Wash.

| Rulau | Date | Metal | Size | VG | F | VF | Unc |
|---|---|---|---|---|---|---|---|
| Wa-Ta 5 | (1870's) | Iron | 25mm | — | — | — | Rare |

TACOMA MILL CO. 40 ¢. (No description available)

| Rulau | Date | Metal | Size | VG | F | VF | Unc |
|---|---|---|---|---|---|---|---|
| Wa-Ta 6 | (1870's) | Iron | 30mm | — | — | — | Rare |

Similar, but 45¢.

| Wa-Ta 7 | (1870's) | Brass | Oval, 32 by 26mm | — | — | — | Rare |

Similar, but $1.

In the early 1870's the Tacoma Mill Company, unable to secure gold and silver to pay Indian laborers and provide a trading medium for settlers, decided to issue their own tokens, and set the company blacksmith to work upon them. All were crudely made, stamped with a value, and passed current over the country tributary to the mill.

This "mill coinage" is difficult to locate today. In 1937 William Hansom of the Tacoma Mill Co. presented a set of the three pieces to Tacoma's Ferry Museum, but Byron Johnson reports these are no longer there; they have disappeared. At the time of presentation of the tokens to the museum, Hansom wrote: "The honesty of the people and the absence of any blacksmith save that of the company, made the use of this money possible." (See *The Numismatist* for April, 1937, pages 299-300, for additional details)

## H.M. HART
### Whatcom, Wash.

| Rulau | Date | Metal | Size | VG | F | VF | Unc |
|---|---|---|---|---|---|---|---|
| Wa-Wt 3 | (1880's) | ? | ---mm | — | — | — | — |

H.M. HART, WHATCOM, W.T. (Description not available)

This was a pool hall, according to Byron Johnson, Seattle.

# WISCONSIN

## HOWARD & TOOLEY
### Ashland, Wis.

| Rulau | Date | Metal | Size | VG | F | VF | Unc |
|---|---|---|---|---|---|---|---|
| Wi-As 2 | (1887-94) | Brass | 25mm | — | 20.00 | 25.00 | — |

—*— / CHECK / —*— within central circle. Around: BRUNSWICK & COMPANY / * CHICAGO *. Rv: GOOD FOR / 5 ¢ / HOWARD & TOOLEY. Plain edge. (Brunswick 38)

## M. HOMS
### Eau Claire, Wis.

| Rulau | Date | Metal | Size | VG | F | VF | Unc |
|---|---|---|---|---|---|---|---|
| Wi-EC 3 | (1874-84) | CN Oct | 26mm | — | 20.00 | 25.00 | — |

CHECK at center (the first C being large and ornate). Around: THE J. M. BRUNSWICK & BALKE COS. Rv: GOOD FOR / 10 ¢ / M. HOMS / IN TRADE. Plain edge. Brunswick 2169)

## HATCH'S RESTAURANT
### La Crosse, Wis.

| Rulau | Date | Metal | Size | VG | F | VF | EF |
|---|---|---|---|---|---|---|---|
| Wi-Lx 4 | (?) | CN | 22mm | — | 75.00 | — | — |

HATCH'S / RESTAURANT / COR MAIN & 3RD STS. / LA X WIS / ctsp on U.S. 1867 Shield nickel. (Frank Kovacs coll.)

| Wi-LX 5 | (?) | CN | 22mm | — | 75.00 | — | — |

Similar ctsp on U.S. 1868 Shield nickel. (Dick Grinolds 1982 sale)

| Wi-LX 7 | (?) | CN | 22mm | — | 75.00 | — | — |

Similar ctsp on U.S. 1873 Shield nickel. (Schenkman coll.)

| Wi-LX 9 | (?) | CN | 22mm | — | 75.00 | — | — |

Similar ctsp on U.S. Shield nickel, date not legible. (Kurt Krueger Aug. 1982 sale)

## HARMON BROS.
### Manawa, Wis.

| Rulau | Date | Metal | Size | VG | F | VF | EF |
|---|---|---|---|---|---|---|---|
| Wi-Mw 2 | (1880's) | Brass | 29mm | — | 12.50 | 15.00 | — |

(All incused) HARMON BROS. / 10 / HOTEL MANAWA. Rv: Blank. Beaded, incised rim on either side. Plain edge. (TAMS maverick number 8704. Dec. 1978 TAMS Journal)

The blank style is typical of the mid-1880's. Needs directory verification. Manawa is located in central Waupaca County.

By 1918 there were two hotels in Manawa, which then had 820 population.

*F. Harbridge, "chemist, drugs and family grocer" at 148 Main Street in Racine, Wis., was a typical merchant of the area when this sketch was drawn in 1879.*

## J. W. FULLER
### Milwaukee, Wis.

| Rulau | Date | Metal | Size | VG | F | VF | EF |
|---|---|---|---|---|---|---|---|
| Wi-Mi 15 | (?) | CN | 22mm | — | 55.00 | — | |

J. W. FULLER JEWELER ctsp on U.S. 1866 Shield nickel.

## K
### Milwaukee, Wis.

| Rulau | Date | Metal | Size | F | VF | EF | Unc |
|---|---|---|---|---|---|---|---|
| Wi-Mi 22 | (1871) | WM | 25mm | — | 15.00 | 20.00 | 30.00 |

Obverse: Same as obverse of Milwaukier Friedens-Feier 1871 token (which see). Rv: GOOD FOR / 10 / CENTS / K. Plain edge. (Coll. Charles Ziegler, York, Pa.)

Apparently diesinker Marr used the German peace celebration medalet obverse die as a stock die to manufacture trade tokens. The attribution to Milwaukee is tentative.

## CHAS. KLEINSTEUBER
### Milwaukee, Wis.

| Rulau | Date | Metal | Size | F | VF | Unc |
|---|---|---|---|---|---|---|
| Wi-Mi 25 | 1867 | WM | 22mm | 20.00 | 25.00 | 40.00 |

Bearded man's head left. CHAS. KLEINSTEUBER / 18 -- 67 / * MECHANIC *. 318 STATE ST. MILWAUKEE. Plain edge. (The signature MARR appears beneath the truncation of the neck.) (Miller Wis. 8)

Struck by Mossin & Marr of Milwaukee. The same firm struck similar, 1863-dated tokens for Kleinsteuber in copper and silver (Fuld 510V-1a to 3a) in the Civil War store card series. In 1863 he was located at 24 Tamarack St.
Kleinsteuber was a manufacturer of small machinery and an engraver, stencil cutter, etc.

## MILWAUKEE INDUSTRIAL EXPOSITION
### Milwaukee, Wis.

| Rulau | Date | Metal | Size | F | VF | EF | Unc |
|---|---|---|---|---|---|---|---|
| Wi-Mi 30 | 1886 | Copper | 22mm | — | 12.50 | 15.00 | 25.00 |

Screaming eagle, wings upraised, perched on a U.S. shield. In background are train, steamship, sheaf of wheat, cogwheel, anchor, etc. Rv: (Circular inscription around rim): MILWAUKEE INDUSTRIAL EXPOSITION. SEP 1. to OCT. 16. 1886 *. The center is blank. Plain edge.

| Wi-Mi 30A | 1886 | CN | 22mm | — | Rare | — | |

As 30, but overstruck on a U.S. Shield nickel. (Mike O'Hara coll.)

| Wi-Mi 30B | 1886 | WM | 22mm | — | Rare | — | |

As 30, but overstruck on a white metal token.

## E. A. M. LEIDEL
### Milwaukee, Wis.

| Rulau | Date | Metal | Size | F | VF | EF | Unc |
|---|---|---|---|---|---|---|---|
| Wi-Mi 27 | (1886) | Brass | 22mm | — | 15.00 | 22.50 | — |

Obverse same as obverse of the Milwaukee Industrial Exposition token, Wi-Mi 30 (Screaming eagle on shield). Rv: Leidel store card. Plain edge. (Hartzog coll.)

## MILWAUKIER FRIEDENS-FEIER
### Milwaukee, Wis.

| Rulau | Date | Metal | Size | F | VF | EF | Unc |
|---|---|---|---|---|---|---|---|
| Wi-Mi 33 | 1871 | WM | 26mm | 10.00 | 15.00 | 20.00 | 30.00 |

Germania standing, with sword and imperial double-headed eagle shield in her hands, looking across the Rhine River. The signature MARR is at bottom. Rv: MILWAUKIER / FRIEDENS- / FEIER / VON / 27-29. MAI. / 1871. Plain edge.

"Milwaukier Friedens-Feier von 27-29 Mai 1871" translates from the German to: Milwaukee Peace Celebration of May 27-29, 1871. The piece honors the local celebration by Milwaukee's large Germanic population of the victory over France in the Franco-Prussian War. The representation of Germania is an early one, before the creation that year of the German Empire — thus the use of the old imperial (Austrian) double-headed eagle rather than the later German Empire single-headed eagle. Germania here is not dissimilar to her representation in the huge bronze statue *Die Wacht am Rhein* overlooking the Rhine, which was constructed later.
Marr is the engraver of the Milwaukee firm of Mossin and Marr which prepared many Civil War tokens.
By the conclusion of the Franco-Prussian War in 1871, the Germanic immigration to the United States was already a massive phenomenon. Though the immigration had not yet peaked, many German neighborhoods had already been established in American cities. Though few cities became as "German" as Milwaukee, obvious remnants of German influence still remain in many large cities such as St. Louis, Chicago and Cincinnati.
Most Germans came to the U.S. looking for better economic conditions, but many also came for greater political freedom, bringing with them strong republican and socialist sentiments.
Referring to these political malcontents, the contemporary German historian and proselytizing monarchist Dr. Moritz Busch observed that the attitudes of the immigrant Germans in America were satisfactory and "increasing in pro-German feeling." He wrote: "The war and its results far outweigh republicanism with them. It seems that our democrats must go abroad before they can feel as they ought to do." (From *Bismarck in the Franco-German War*, circa 1880.)
A number of medallic tokens have been struck here in the U.S. to celebrate the Fatherland's glorious victory and unification. They are listed in this catalog under San Francisco, St. Louis, Williamsburgh, N.Y., Milwaukee and Non-Local. Surely there must be more.
(The above footnote was written by Fred J. Borgmann, Iola, Wis.)

## SOLDIERS HOME FAIR
### Milwaukee, Wis.

| Rulau | Date | Metal | Size | VG | F | VF | Unc |
|---|---|---|---|---|---|---|---|
| Wi-Mi 42 | 1865 | Copper | 19mm | 25.00 | 40.00 | 50.00 | 85.00 |

Scroll, on which is: HONOR & / COUNTRY. Rv: MILWAUKEE / 1865 / SOLDIERS

| Rulau | Date | Metal | Size | VG | F | VF | Unc |

HOME FAIR. Plain edge. Rarity 7 (Fuld NC-17a). Issued with slot at top, probably for wear.

The Soldiers Home Fair was held in June of 1865, just three months after the end of the Civil War. The die work resembles that of Mossin & Marr of Milwaukee.

## L. A. TANTH
### Omro, Wis.

| Rulau | Date | Metal | Size | VG | F | VF | EF |
|---|---|---|---|---|---|---|---|
| Wi-Om 4 | 1881 | Copper | 29mm | — | —Unique | | |

L A TANTH / WINNEBAGO / CHAPT NO 43 / JAN 19TH 81 engraved in script on planed-off obverse of a U.S. Large cent. (Kurt Krueger coll.)

Winnebago Chapter 43 at Omro, Wis., also issued Masonic Mark pennies of its own.

## MITCHELL & LEWIS CO. LTD.
### Racine, Wis.

| Rulau | Date | Metal | Size | F | VF | EF | Unc |
|---|---|---|---|---|---|---|---|
| Wi-Ra 5 | 1884 | Alum | 38mm | — | 15.00 | 20.00 | 30.00 |

A wagon, THE OLD above, RELIABLE below. Around: MITCHELL & LEWIS CO. L'T'D. / RACINE, WIS. Rv: ESTABLISHED 1831 / THE MITCHELL / WAGON / IS THE BEST / INCORPORATED 1884. (Wright 713)

The Mitchell Wagon Co. was still manufacturing wagons in 1918, but an affiliate, Mitchell Motors Co., was making automobiles and trucks at that time.

## HENRY DAUB
### Watertown, Wis.

| Rulau | Date | Metal | Size | VG | F | VF | EF |
|---|---|---|---|---|---|---|---|
| Wi-Wa 3 | (1874-84) | Brass | 25mm | — | — | 20.00 | 25.00 |

Billiard table at bottom. Above: THE / J. M. BRUNSWICK / AND / BALKE CO. Rv: GOOD FOR / 1 / HENRY DAUB / * DRINK *. Plain edge. (Brunswick 2094)

## P. L.
### (Pahl-Links Brewery)
### (Wisconsin ?)

| Rulau | Date | Metal | Size | VG | F | VF | Unc |
|---|---|---|---|---|---|---|---|
| Wi-Un 1 | (1865-85) | Brass | 19mm | — | 15.00 | 20.00 | 30.00 |

P* L*. Rv: GOOD FOR / ONE / B'LL. SLOP / *. Plain edge.

Louis P. Pahl operated the Pahl-Links Brewery 1865-1890, according to the *Register of U.S. Breweries 1876-1976*. (See page 39, *TAMS Journal* for Feb. 1978)

## MEINERS & VILTER
### (Wisconsin ?)

| Rulau | Date | Metal | Size | VG | F | VF | Unc |
|---|---|---|---|---|---|---|---|
| Wi-Un 2 | (?) | Brass | 19mm | — | 15.00 | 20.00 | 30.00 |

MEINERS / & / VILTER. Rv: GOOD FOR / ONE / B'LL. SLOP. Plain edge.

Possibly Milwaukee.

# WYOMING

## GOBELMAN BROS.
### Carbon, Wyo.

| Rulau | Date | Metal | Size | VG | F | VF | Unc |
|---|---|---|---|---|---|---|---|
| Wy-Ca 3 | (1874-84) | Brass | 25mm | — | 25.00 | 40.00 | — |

Pool, table at bottom, THE / J. M. BRUNSWICK / AND / BALKE CO above. Rv: GOOD FOR / 1 / DRINK / GOBELMAN BROS. / MINERS SAMPLE ROOMS / CARBON, WYO. Plain edge. (Brunswick 2143)

## WYOMING CAPITAL BUILDING
### Cheyenne, Wyo.

| Rulau | Date | Metal | Size | F | VF | EF | Unc |
|---|---|---|---|---|---|---|---|
| Wy-Ch 12 | 1887 | Copper | 29mm | — | — | 25.00 | 30.00 |

Building. Rv: CORNER STONE LAYING / OF / WYOMING / CAPITAL / BUILDING / MAY 18 1887 / CHEYENNE WYO. (Wright 1280)

# NON-LOCAL

| Rulau | Date | Metal | Size | VG | F | VF | EF |
|---|---|---|---|---|---|---|---|
| NL 6 | (1865) | Copper | 23mm | — | 75.00 | — | — |

DA M. / J. W. BOOTH ctsp on reverse of U.S. 1864 2-cent piece. (Lot 574, Joseph Lepczyk auction of June 3, 1982)

This piece undoubtedly refers to the assassination of President Abraham Lincoln by actor John Wilkes Booth in April, 1865.

## HIT HIM AGAIN
### Non-Local

| Rulau | Date | Metal | Size | VG | F | EF |
|---|---|---|---|---|---|---|
| NL 9 | (?) | CN | 19mm | — | 15.00 | — |

HIT HIM AGAIN ctsp on U.S. 1858 Flying Eagle cent.

## RETURN OF PEACE
### Non-Local

| Rulau | Date | Metal | Size | F | VF | EF | Unc |
|---|---|---|---|---|---|---|---|
| NL 15 | 1871 | WM | 28mm | — | 20.00 | — | — |

Wilhelm I of Prussia in a pickelhaube (spiked helmet). Rv: IN COMMEMORATION OF THE RETURN OF PEACE 1871. Plain edge. Weight 7.65 grams.

See background under Milwaukier Friedens-Feier, Milwaukee, Wis.

## EAGLES ON MISCELLANEOUS COINS

| Rulau | Date | Metal | Size | F | VF | EF | Unc |
|---|---|---|---|---|---|---|---|
| NL 55 | (?) | CN | 22mm | — | 25.00 | — | — |

Eagle with beak to right ctsp on obverse of U.S. 1868-type Shield nickel. Similar ctsp on reverse of coin. (Stanley Steinberg 1982 sale)

# LOCATION NOT KNOWN

## M. A. ABBEY
### Location Not Known

| Rulau | Date | Metal | Size | VG | F | VF | Unc |
|---|---|---|---|---|---|---|---|
| MV 1 | (?) | Copper | 29mm | — | — | — | — |

M. A. ABBEY ctsp on U.S. Large cents of various dates. (Duffield 1431; Hallenbeck 1.500; Brunk 2)

## J. A. ABBOTT
### Location Not Known

| Rulau | Date | Metal | Size | VG | F | VF | Unc |
|---|---|---|---|---|---|---|---|
| MV 1 | (?) | — | --mm | — | — | — | — |

J. A. ABBOTT ctsp on unspecified coins. (Brunk 3)

## A. H. ALLEN
### Location Not Known

| Rulau | Date | Metal | Size | VG | F | VF | Unc |
|---|---|---|---|---|---|---|---|
| MV 1C | 1868 | Br Oval 44 x 25mm | | — | 20.00 | — | — |

A. H. ALLEN / "PAT'D 185. REIS'D 1861 / EXT'D 1868". Rv: Incused oval. Plain edge. (Wright 13)

It would be interesting to learn what it was Allen had patented in the 1850's, had the patent reissued for in 1861 and then extended in 1868.

## AMERICAN PILE CO.
### Location Not Known

| Rulau | Date | Metal | Size | VG | F | VF | EF |
|---|---|---|---|---|---|---|---|
| MV 2 | (?) | Copper | 26mm | — | — | 40.00 | — |

AMN. PILE CO. ctsp twice on obverse of Canada 1876 Large cent. AMERICAN ctsp twice on reverse of coin. (Krause coll.)

## ARNOLD
### Location Not Known

| Rulau | Date | Metal | Size | VG | F | VF | EF |
|---|---|---|---|---|---|---|---|
| MV 4 | (?) | Bronze | 19mm | — | — | 5.00 | — |

ARNOLD ctsp on U.S. 1883 Indian Head cent.

## R. E. ASHMAN
### Location Not Known

| Rulau | Date | Metal | Size | VG | F | VF | Unc |
|---|---|---|---|---|---|---|---|
| MV 6 | (1874-1884) | Brass | 25mm | — | — | 15.00 | — |

GOOD FOR / 5 ¢ / R. E. ASHMAN / IN / * TRADE *. Rv: Pool table within beaded circle. Around circle: THE J. M. BRUNSWICK & BALKE COS. / * CHECK *. Plain edge.

Not listed in *The Brunswick Token Story* by Fowler, Magnuson & White, 1977.

## ATHENEUM
### Location Not Known

| Rulau | Date | Metal | Size | VG | F | VF | Unc |
|---|---|---|---|---|---|---|---|
| MV 8 | (?) | Brass | 32mm | — | — | 3.00 | |

(All incused) ATHENEUM / 11. Plain edge.

## P. E. BALLOU
### Location Not Known

| Rulau | Date | Metal | Size | VG | F | VF | EF |
|---|---|---|---|---|---|---|---|
| MV 11 | (?) | CN | 19mm | — | — | 300. | |

P. E. BALLOU / PHRENOLOGIST ctsp on U.S. cent. (Duffield 1391)

| | | | | | | | |
|---|---|---|---|---|---|---|---|
| MV 11A | (?) | Bronze | 23mm | — | 300. | — | — |

Similar ctsp on U.S. 2-cent piece.

| | | | | | | | |
|---|---|---|---|---|---|---|---|
| MV 12 | (?) | CN | 22mm | — | 300. | — | — |

Similar ctsp on U.S. 1871 Shield nickel.

A phrenologist is one who analyzes character and development of the faculties by studying the shape and protuberances of the skull.

## PROF. ANDRE'S ALPINE CHOIR
### Location Not Known

| Rulau | Date | Metal | Size | VG | F | VF | Unc |
|---|---|---|---|---|---|---|---|
| MV 3 | (1880) | Brass | 23mm | — | — | 20.00 | |

Mustached male bust left, PROF. ANDRE'S above, * ALPINE CHOIR * below. Rv: MATRIMONIAL / NO / TIPPLER / NEED / APPLY / SOCIETY. Plain edge. Rarity 5.

Though this piece was in Dr. Wright's collection, it was not listed by him. Wright sold his specimen to C. Mathis on Sept. 25, 1900. Mathis sold his collection to Stuart Mosher, and Mosher sold it in turn to Melvin and George Fuld in 1948.

## B & H
### Location Not Known

| Rulau | Date | Metal | Size | VG | F | VF | EF |
|---|---|---|---|---|---|---|---|
| MV 9 | (?) | Copper | 29mm | — | — | — | |

B & H ctsp on U.S. Large cents of various dates. (Hallenbeck 2.005; Brunk 16)

| | | | | | | | |
|---|---|---|---|---|---|---|---|
| MV 9A | (?) | Copper | 29mm | — | — | — | |

B. & H. ctsp on U.S. Large cent. (Hallenbeck 2.006)

## BAILEY AND STOUFFER
### Location Not Known

| Rulau | Date | Metal | Size | VG | F | VF | Unc |
|---|---|---|---|---|---|---|---|
| MV 10 | (?) | Copper | 29mm | — | — | — | |

BAILEY AND STOUFFER ctsp on U.S. Large cent. (Hallenbeck 2.502)

## ED. BARRY
### Location Not Known

| Rulau | Date | Metal | Size | VG | F | VF | EF |
|---|---|---|---|---|---|---|---|
| MV 15 | (?) | Silver | 38.1mm | — | — | 75.00 | |

ED. BARRY, level and square ctsp on U.S. 1871 Seated Liberty silver dollar. (Nadin-Davis sale, Nov. 20, 1982, lot 242)

Undoubtedly a Masonic piece. Barry thus may not be a merchant.

## BLYSTONE & RHODES
### Location Not Known

| Rulau | Date | Metal | Size | VG | F | VF | Unc |
|---|---|---|---|---|---|---|---|
| MV 20 | (?) | GS | 33mm | — | — | 10.00 | — |

BLYSTONE & RHODES / 15 / -o-/ Rv: Blank. (Wright 42)

A druggist's soda check, says Dr. Wright.

## WM. L. BRADLEY
### Location Not Known

| Rulau | Date | Metal | Size | VG | F | VF | Unc |
|---|---|---|---|---|---|---|---|
| MV 22 | 1879 | Copper | 24mm | — | — | — | Rare |

* BULOW STORE * / GOOD FOR / 25 / CENTS / WM. L. BRADLEY. Rv: * THIS CHECK * / NOT / 1879 / TRANSFERABLE. Plain edge. (Wright 94)

| | | | | | | | |
|---|---|---|---|---|---|---|---|
| MV 23 | 1879 | Copper | 33mm | — | — | — | Rare |

* BULOW STORE * / GOOD FOR / 50 / CENTS / WM. L. BRADLEY. Rv: As 22. Plain edge. (Steinberg 1982 sale)

At the end of the 19th century there were two Bulows in the United States, one in Volusia County, Florida, the other in Charleston County, South Carolina. The U.S. Postal Guides for 1877 through 1881 recall there was no post office in the nation named Bulow, however.

The S.C. Bulow was near Charleston and was the larger of the two places.

The Florida Bulow was in the midst of a turpentine producing region. As late as 1918 the Bulow Turpentine Co. was active there, as a branch of Lambert & Moody, a large turpentine producer headquartered at Bunnell, Florida.

## WM. A. BRADY, THE IRISH ARAB
### Location Not Known

| Rulau | Date | Metal | Size | VG | F | VF | Unc |
|---|---|---|---|---|---|---|---|
| MV 24 | (?) | Brass | 25mm | — | — | — | |

THE IRISH ARAB / UNDER / * THE * / MANAGEMENT / * OF * WM. A. BRADY. Rv: BOBBY GAYLOR -- / * / * / IN THE * / o * / IRISH ARAB. Plain edge. (Wright 93)

## BRAKEMAN
## Location Not Known

| Rulau | Date | Metal | Size | VG | F | VF | EF |
|---|---|---|---|---|---|---|---|
| MV 26 | (1880's) | Silver | 31mm | 22.50 | — | — | — |

BRAKEMAN. In fancy lettering arched, engraved on planed-off obverse of a U.S. 1853 Arrows and Rays half dollar. (Though the obverse with date and arrows is planed off, only the 1853 eagle reverse is surmounted by rays, making identification of the exact year of the underlying coin possible.) (Rulau coll.)

The eagle side has been mounted for wear with two solder points, from which the soldered-on appurtenances have been removed. This is apparently a railroad brakeman's item, used as a fob ornament, bracelet tag, button or some other use in adorning clothing. Acquired in Houston, Texas, Jan. 31, 1982.

## V. E. BRETS
## Location Not Known

| Rulau | Date | Metal | Size | VG | F | VF | EF |
|---|---|---|---|---|---|---|---|
| MV 27 | (?) | Copper | 29mm | — | — | — | — |

VE. BRETS / . MAKER ctsp on worn-smooth U.S. Large cent. The 'S' in BRETS resembles a backward Z. (Frank Kovacs coll.)

## BRINKS
## Location Not Known

| Rulau | Date | Metal | Size | VG | F | VF | EF |
|---|---|---|---|---|---|---|---|
| MV 28 | (?) | Silver | 25mm | — | — | 20.00 | — |

BRINKS ctsp on U.S. 1877 Seated Liberty quarter. (Gould 73)

## W.J. BROADHURST
## Location Not Known

| Rulau | Date | Metal | Size | VG | F | VF | Unc |
|---|---|---|---|---|---|---|---|
| MV 30 | 1884-1900 | Br Oct. | 25mm | — | — | 15.00 | — |

GOOD FOR / 5¢ / IN TRADE / W.J. BROADHURST. Rv: Pool table, THE BRUNSWICK BALKE / COLLENDER / COMPY above, CHECK below. Plain edge.

Not listed in *The Brunswick Token Story*.

## D.B. BROWN
## Location Not Known

| Rulau | Date | Metal | Size | VG | F | VF | EF |
|---|---|---|---|---|---|---|---|
| MV 33 | (?) | Copper | 29mm | — | — | 20.00 | — |

D.B. BROWN, WARREN ctsp on U.S. Large cent. (Hallenbeck 2.763)

## H.S. BURGES
## Location Not Known

| Rulau | Date | Metal | Size | VG | F | VF | EF |
|---|---|---|---|---|---|---|---|
| MV 36 | (?) | Copper | 29mm | — | — | 30.00 | — |

H.S. BURGES ctsp on U.S. 1832 Large cent.

| MV 37 | (?) | Silver | 19mm | — | — | 35.00 | — |

Similar ctsp on U.S. 1830 dime. (Brunk 71)

| MV 38 | (?) | Copper | 29mm | — | — | 30.00 | — |

Similar ctsp (BURGES) ctsp on several different dates of U.S. Large cent. Dates examined: 1845, 1851, 1852, 1853. (Gould 10; Brunk 71) Some 25 known.

Possibility: Philadelphia. This requires more research.

## D.C. & CO.
## Location Not Known

| Rulau | Date | Metal | Size | VG | F | VF | Unc |
|---|---|---|---|---|---|---|---|
| MV 39 | (?) | Aluminum | 25mm | — | — | 5.00 | — |

Monogram D.C. & CO. Rv: RICHMOND / CO. Plain edge. (Wright 1598)

The reverse text could stand for Richmond County, which might help narrow down attribution. There are Richmond Counties in Georgia, New York, North Carolina and Virginia. Possibility: Duval Crayon Co., Port Richmond (Staten I.), N.Y.

## H. W. C.
## Location Not Known

| Rulau | Date | Metal | Size | VG | F | VF | EF |
|---|---|---|---|---|---|---|---|
| MV 700 | (?) | Copper | 29mm | — | — | — | — |

1 / H W C / P T ctsp on shaved reverse of U.S. 1848 Large cent. (Brunk 173)

| MV 701 | (?) | Copper | 29mm | — | — | — | — |

Similar ctsp on shaved reverse of U.S. 1856 Large cent.

| MV 702 | (?) | — | --mm | — | — | — | — |

2 / H W C P T ctsp on unspecified coins. (Brunk 174)

It is possible these are checks of some kind. The numerals and PT suggest possible use as dairy checks (pint).

## J.B.C.
### Location Not Known

| Rulau | Date | Metal | Size | VG | F | VF | Unc |
|---|---|---|---|---|---|---|---|
| MV 41 | (1874-84) | Brass | 25mm | — | — | 10.00 | — |

GOOD FOR / 5 ¢ / J. B. C. / IN / TRADE. Rv: Pool table. Above it: THE / J. M. BRUNSWICK / AND / BALKE CO. Plain edge.

Not listed in *The Brunswick Token Story*.

## M.C.
### Location Not Known

| Rulau | Date | Metal | Size | VG | F | VF | EF |
|---|---|---|---|---|---|---|---|
| MV 42 | (?) | Silver | 27mm | — | — | 5.00 | — |

M.C. in relief within recessed square ctsp on Spanish-American 2-reales. (Gould 415ff)

This appears to be a silversmith's hallmark. Not traced. Some possibilities.
  Metcalf B. Clark, Boston, ca. 1835
  M. Connell, Philadelphia, ca. 1800

## O.W.C.
### Location Not Known

| Rulau | Date | Metal | Size | VG | F | VF | Unc |
|---|---|---|---|---|---|---|---|
| MV 42C | (1880's) | Brass | 28mm | — | — | 2.00 | — |

(All incused) O.W.C. (large). Rv: GOOD FOR / 5 / IN TRADE. Incised, beaded rim on each side. Plain edge. (Coll. John Cheramy, Victoria, B.C., Canada)

The style of stock token is typical of the mid-1880's.

## E.E. CHILDS JR.
### Location Not Known

| Rulau | Date | Metal | Size | VG | F | VF | EF |
|---|---|---|---|---|---|---|---|
| MV 43 | (?) | Silver | 32.5mm | — | — | 100. | — |

E.E. CHILDS JR. / 16 CHAPMAN PLACE ctsp on U.S. 1825 Bust half dollar. (Gould 30)

## L. CHILDS
### Location Not Known

| Rulau | Date | Metal | Size | VG | F | VF | EF |
|---|---|---|---|---|---|---|---|
| MV 44 | (?) | — | — | — | — | 15.00 | — |

L. CHILDS ctsp on several unspecified coins. (Brunk 86)

## N.T. CLARK
### Location Not Known

| Rulau | Date | Metal | Size | VG | F | VF | EF |
|---|---|---|---|---|---|---|---|
| MV 45 | (?) | Copper | 29mm | — | 10.00 | — | — |

N.T. CLARK in relief in dentilated, recessed cartouche ctsp on U.S. 1847 Large cent. (Steinberg Feb. 1982 sale)

## COLD FRI.
### Location Not Known

| Rulau | Date | Metal | Size | VG | F | VF | EF |
|---|---|---|---|---|---|---|---|
| MV 47 | 1861 | Copper | 29mm | 25.00 | — | — | — |

COLD FRI. / FEB. 8, 1861 ctsp on U.S. Large cent. (Koppenhaver Aug. 1982 sale)

Feb 8, 1861 was indeed a Friday. Systematic climatic records date only to 1870's. It would be interesting to learn where record low temperatures were set that day.

## CONTRAHENDO ET SOLVENDO
### Location Not Known

| Rulau | Date | Metal | Size | VG | F | VF | Unc |
|---|---|---|---|---|---|---|---|
| MV 61 | 1863 | Brass | 19mm | — | — | — | 80.00 |

Large numeral 2 at center, separating o -- o. Around: CONTRAHENDO ET SOLVENDO. Below: S. P. Rv: THURSDAY / 1863. Plain edge. (Brunk coll.)

The obverse of this token is the same as the obverse of Rulau Z81 in *U.S. Merchant Tokens 1845-1860*. According to Benjamin Fauver, the 1857 token listed as Z81 was struck by Thomas Kettle in England, but the specimen above has not previously been reported in any work. It is not included by the Fuld's in *Civil War Store Cards* either.

## COLE
### Location Not Known

| Rulau | Date | Metal | Size | VG | F | VF | EF |
|---|---|---|---|---|---|---|---|
| MV 50 | (?) | CN | 19mm | — | — | 5.00 | — |

COLE ctsp on U.S. 1857 Flying Eagle cent.

## J. CONRAD
### Location Not Known

| Rulau | Date | Metal | Size | VG | F | VF | Unc |
|---|---|---|---|---|---|---|---|
| MV 54 | (1870's) | Lead | 16mm | — | 25.00 | — | — |

Society emblem at center, WOODMEN SALOON -- J. CONRAD. Rv: Wreath encloses: HALF / DIME. Around: GOOD FOR. Plain edge. (Wright 1377)

## CONSOLIDATED RACKET STORES
### Location Not Known

| Rulau | Date | Metal | Size | F | VF | EF | Unc |
|---|---|---|---|---|---|---|---|
| MV 58 | (?) | Brass | 20mm | 7.00 | 8.50 | 10.00 | 12.50 |

Nude female bust left, CASH on her coronet. CONSOLIDATED RACKET STORES / BEST VALUES. Rv: ONE / CENT in wreath; GOOD FOR above, IN MERCHANDISE below. (Wright 187)

## CONTINENTAL
### Location Not Known

| Rulau | Date | Metal | Size | VG | F | VF | EF |
|---|---|---|---|---|---|---|---|
| MV 60 | (?) | CN | 19mm | 15.00 | — | 50.00 | — |

10 (large) / CONTINENTAL (small) ctsp on U.S. 1863 Indian Head cent. (Krause coll.)

On the old envelope in which this item was located, the words 'Continental Hotel' had been inscribed.

## COOPER & DEMAREST
### Location Not Known

| Rulau | Date | Metal | Size | VG | F | VF | EF |
|---|---|---|---|---|---|---|---|
| MV 62 | (?) | Copper | 29mm | — | — | 100. | — |

COOPER & DEMAREST / 222 CANAL ST ctsp on U.S. 1848 Large cent.

New York City?

## D. H. DAY
### Location Not Known

| Rulau | Date | Metal | Size | VG | F | VF | EF |
|---|---|---|---|---|---|---|---|
| MV 64 | (?) | CN | 19mm | — | — | 5.00 | — |

D. H. DAY ctsp on U.S. 1857 Flying Eagle cent.

| MV 65 | (?) | — | --mm | — | — | 5.00 | — |

Similar ctsp on unspecified coins. (Brunk 123)

## DENGREMONT
### Location Not Known

| Rulau | Date | Metal | Size | VG | F | VF | Unc |
|---|---|---|---|---|---|---|---|
| MV 68 | 1887 | Brass | 31mm | — | — | 4.00 | 8.50 |

Boy standing, facing; bow and violin in his hands. Below: DENGREMONT. Rv: Boy standing, banner over his shoulder. On banner: FASHIONS / FOR / SPRING / 1887. Plain edge. Issued holed. (Wright 240)

## E. G. & S. M. COMPANY
### Location Not Known

| Rulau | Date | Metal | Size | VG | F | VF | EF |
|---|---|---|---|---|---|---|---|
| MV 77 | (?) | Silver | 38mm | — | — | 50.00 | — |

E. G. & S. M. COMPANY ctsp on U.S. 1872 Liberty Seated dollar. The letters are small and arched. (Gould 3)

## G. EVANS
### Location Not Known

| Rulau | Date | Metal | Size | VG | F | VF | EF |
|---|---|---|---|---|---|---|---|
| MV 83 | (?) | Bronze | 23mm | — | — | 5.00 | — |

G. EVANS ctsp on U.S. 1864 2-cent piece.

| MV 84 | (?) | — | --mm | — | — | 5.00 | — |

Similar ctsp on unspecified coins. (Brunk 140)

## FEIGENSPAN'S LAGER
### Location Not Known

| Rulau | Date | Metal | Size | VG | F | VF | EF |
|---|---|---|---|---|---|---|---|
| MV 90 | (?) | — | --mm | — | — | 150. | — |

FEIGENSPAN'S / LAGER ctsp on unspecified coins. (Brunk 142)

| MV 92 | (?) | — | --mm | — | — | 150. | — |

DRINK / FEIGENSPAN'S / LAGER ctsp on unspecified coins. (Brunk 143)

| MV 93 | (?) | Silver | 25mm | — | — | 150. | — |

Similar ctsp on U.S. 1838-1853 quarter.

Possibly Pennsylvania.

## F. F. FOSDICK
### Location Not Known

| Rulau | Date | Metal | Size | G | VG | F | EF |
|---|---|---|---|---|---|---|---|
| MV 98 | (1877) | Silver | 18mm | — | — | 15.00 | — |

F. F. FOSDICK / 77 ctsp on U.S. 1875 dime. (Steinberg coll.)

| MV 99 | (?) | Silver | 25mm | — | — | 15.00 | — |

F. FOSDICK ctsp on U.S. Liberty Seated quarter.

## J. P. FULLER
### Location Not Known

| Rulau | Date | Metal | Size | VG | F | VF | EF |
|---|---|---|---|---|---|---|---|
| MV 102 | (?) | Bronze | 19mm | — | — | 25.00 | — |

J. P. FULLER ctsp on U.S. 1866 Indian head cent.

## E. G. & SONS
### Location Not Known

| Rulau | Date | Metal | Size | VG | F | VF | EF |
|---|---|---|---|---|---|---|---|
| MV 100 | 1861 | Silver | 25mm | — | — | 25.00 | — |

E G & SONS / 1861 ctsp in a circle on U.S. 1858 Seated Liberty quarter dollar. (Harvey Gamer coll.)

## ANDY GAIER
### Location Not Known

| Rulau | Date | Metal | Size | VG | F | VF | Unc |
|---|---|---|---|---|---|---|---|
| MV 105 | 1874-84 | GS | 25mm | — | — | 15.00 | — |

GOOD FOR / 5¢ / ANDY GAIER / -- IN -- / TRADE. Rv: Pool table within beaded circle. Around cirlce: THE J.M. BRUNSWICK & BALKE COS. / * CHECK *. Plain edge.

Not listed in *The Brunswick Token Story*.

## GATES & TRASK
### Location Not Known

| Rulau | Date | Metal | Size | VG | F | VF | EF |
|---|---|---|---|---|---|---|---|
| MV 108 | (?) | Copper | 29mm | 25.00 | — | 100. | — |

GATES & TRASK ctsp on U.S. Large cent. (Dr. Sol Taylor collection)

## CHAS. D. GLADDING
### Location Not Known

| Rulau | Date | Metal | Size | VG | F | VF | EF |
|---|---|---|---|---|---|---|---|
| MV 111 | 1861 | Silver | 31mm | 40.00 | — | 60.00 | — |

CHAS. D. GLADDING (curved) / 1861 ctsp on U.S. 1854-0 with Arrows Liberty Seated half dollar. (Dr. Sol Taylor collection, Orange, Calif.)

## AICHELE GOTTLIEB
### Location Not Known

| Rulau | Date | Metal | Size | VG | F | VF | EF |
|---|---|---|---|---|---|---|---|
| MV 114 | (1880's) | Brass | 24mm | — | — | 5.00 | — |

Star in rays at center, AICHELE GOTTLIEB around, ornament at bottom. Rv: Large numeral 5 at center, circle of 13 stars around. Plain edge. (Wright 15)

Probably struck by Wright of Cincinnati.

## O. H.
### Location Not Known

| Rulau | Date | Metal | Size | VG | F | VF |
|---|---|---|---|---|---|---|
| MV 119 | (?) | Copper | Oval 26 by 19mm | 10.00 | — | — |

Fouled anchor. Heavy, beaded rim. Rv: O. H. at center, plain rim. Plain edge. (Wright 1559)

Made of two pieces of metal, the O.H. side, which is very thin, is sweated onto the anchor side.

## E. HANKS
### Location Not Known

| Rulau | Date | Metal | Size | G | VG | F | EF |
|---|---|---|---|---|---|---|---|
| MV 121 | (?) | CN | 19mm | — | — | 5.00 | — |

E. HANKS ctsp on reverse of U.S. 1859 Indian Head cent. Obverse ctsp with 8-section device. (Stanley L. Steinberg collection)

## LOTHAR HARMES
### Location Not Known

| Rulau | Date | Metal | Size | VG | F | VF | Unc |
|---|---|---|---|---|---|---|---|
| MV 122 | (?) | GS | Oct 27mm | — | — | 10.00 | — |

In a panel across the center: LOTHAR / HARMES. Roses above, ornament below. Rv: Blank. Plain edge. (Wright 425)

## E. D. HARPOLE
### Location Not Known

| Rulau | Date | Metal | Size | VG | F | VF | Unc |
|---|---|---|---|---|---|---|---|
| MV 124 | (?) | Brass | 21mm | — | — | 3.00 | — |

E. D. HARPOLE. Rv: GOOD FOR / * 6 ¼ ¢ * / IN TRADE. Plain edge.

## E. C. HATCH
### Location Not Known

| Rulau | Date | Metal | Size | VG | F | VF | EF |
|---|---|---|---|---|---|---|---|
| MV 127 | (?) | CN | 19mm | — | — | 5.00 | — |
| MV 128 | (?) | — | —mm | — | — | 5.00 | — |

E. C. HATCH ctsp on U.S. 1859 Indian Head cent.

Similar ctsp on unspecified coins. (Brunk 180)

## HOPKIN'S TRANS-OCEANIC CO.
### Location Not Known

| Rulau | Date | Metal | Size | VG | F | VF | Unc |
|---|---|---|---|---|---|---|---|
| MV 131 | (?) | Brass | 23mm | — | — | 15.00 | — |

A cartouche. An open eye at upper left. Extended hand with finger pointing to: TRAVEL / PATIENCE / PROCES. Inscription: TREWEY — THE ABSOLUTE MASTER. Rv: HOPKIN'S / TRANS- / OCEANIC COMPANY. Plain edge. (Wright 460)

## W. HUBBELL
### Location Not Known

| Rulau | Date | Metal | Size | | F | VF | |
|---|---|---|---|---|---|---|---|
| MV 134 | (?) | Copper | 29mm | — | — | 15.00 | — |
| MV 135 | (?) | Copper | 29mm | — | — | 15.00 | — |

W. HUBBELL ctsp on U.S. 1826 Large cent.

W. HUBBELL ctsp on U.S. 1835 Large cent. (three examined)

## HUNT & MOORE
### Location Not Known

| Rulau | Date | Metal | Size | VG | F | VF | EF |
|---|---|---|---|---|---|---|---|
| MV 144 | (?) | CN | 19mm | — | — | 20.00 | — |
| MV 146 | (?) | (?) | | — | — | 20.00 | — |
| MV 140 | (?) | Copper | 29mm | — | — | 20.00 | — |
| MV 142 | (?) | Copper | 29mm | — | — | 20.00 | — |
| MV 141 | (?) | Copper | 29mm | — | — | 25.00 | — |

HUNT & MOORE ctsp on U.S. 1860 Indian Head cent. (Stanley Steinberg collection)

Similar ctsp on unspecified coins. (Brunk 192)

Similar ctsp on U.S. Large cent. (Hallenbeck 8.755)

Similar ctsp on U.S. 1851 Large cent. (Stanley Steinberg 1982 sale)

Similar ctsp on U.S. 1803 Large cent.

## J. HURD
### Location Not Known

| Rulau | Date | Metal | Size | VG | F | VF | EF |
|---|---|---|---|---|---|---|---|
| MV 148 | (?) | Copper | 29mm | — | 7.50 | — | — |

J. HURD ctsp on U.S. 1832 Large cent. (Hallenbeck 8.758)

It has been suggested that J. Hurd was a Boston gunsmith, but this has not been verified.

## IRISH REPUBLIC
### Location Not Known

| Rulau | Date | Metal | Size | VG | F | VF | Unc |
|---|---|---|---|---|---|---|---|
| MV 153 | 1866 | Brass | 29mm | — | — | 150. | 300. |

Sailing ship left, dividing large F — B, IRISH above, REPUBLIC below. Rv: Clasped hands above sunrise. IRELAND / 18 (shamrock) 66 above, AMERICA below. Six stars on left, seven on right. (Wright 494)

This token is connected with the Fenian raid on Canada in May, 1866. FB equals Fenian Brotherhood. The centers of Irish agitation after the Civil War were Boston and New York.

John O'Neil was born in Ireland in 1834 and died in Omaha in Jan. 1878. He served as a Union soldier for three years, resigning in 1864 and established a pension agency in Nashville, Tenn. In 1866 he was appointed by his Irish compatriots to command the Fenian forces that invaded Canada. He invaded with a force of 1,500 men, and took control of Fort Erie. Grant arrived the next day in Buffalo with orders that no additional Fenians be allowed to cross, and with no ammunition or supplies O'Neil was forced to retreat to the U.S. Seven hundred Fenians were arrested, and after an abortive attempt to invade again in 1870, he was imprisoned for several months. He later attempted to establish an Irish colony in Nebraska.

Forrer reports that a die sinker by the name of Sewell (the medals strangely resemble the work of Scovill Mfg. Co. of Waterbury, Conn.) issued the badges shown above to members of the brotherhood. He states that the organization was set up as a Republic, and shows an illustration of the identical badge, with a suspension ribbon. After the abortive attempt of 1870, the Home Rule and Land League movements practically superseded the Fenian. The name was taken from an ancient military organization called Fionna Eirinn, said to have been instituted in Ireland in 300 B.C.

## C.O. JAMES
### Location Not Known

| Rulau | Date | Metal | Size | VG | F | VF | EF |
|---|---|---|---|---|---|---|---|
| MV 160 | 1886 | Bronze | 19mm | — | — | 5.00 | — |

1886 / C.O. JAMES ctsp on U.S. 1875 Indian Head cent. (Kurt Krueger coll.)

## L.H. JOHNSON
### Location Not Known

| Rulau | Date | Metal | Size | VG | F | VF | EF |
|---|---|---|---|---|---|---|---|
| MV 164 | 1873 | Copper | 29mm | — | — | 20.00 | — |

L.H. JOHNSON / PAT. APRIL, 1873 ctsp on U.S. Large cents. (Gould 10 bis; Hallenbeck 10.750; Brunk 198)

## C.W. KAY
### Location Not Known

| Rulau | Date | Metal | Size | VG | F | VF | EF |
|---|---|---|---|---|---|---|---|
| MV 167 | (?) | Copper | 29mm | — | — | 50.00 | — |

C.W. KAY ARTIST ctsp on U.S. Large cent. (Hallenbeck 11.500)

The name on this token needs verification. It is possible this listing is due to a mis-description for C.W. King (which see). The two Hallenbeck listings in *The Numismatist* unfortunately gave no dates on the underlying coins and thus all the Hallenbeck listings will require eventual confirmation before listings based upon them can be accepted fully.

## T. JAN. P.
### Location Not Known

 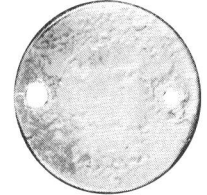

| Rulau | Date | Metal | Size | VG | F | VF | EF |
|---|---|---|---|---|---|---|---|
| MV 162 | 1879 | Copper | 25mm | — | — | 15.00 | — |

T JAN. P / 124 / 1879 ctsp on pierced, unidentifiable coin or token. (Frank Kovacs coll.)

## A.C.L. REFRESHMENT CONTRACTOR
### Location Not Known

 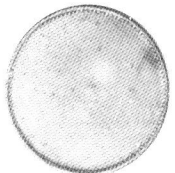

| Rulau | Date | Metal | Size | VG | F | VF | Unc |
|---|---|---|---|---|---|---|---|
| MV 178 | (1870's ?) | Brass | 23mm | 2.00 | 3.00 | 5.00 | — |

REFRESHMENT / ACL script monogram / .CONTRACTOR. Rv: Blank. Reeded edge.

This maverick reposed in the Stuart Mosher collection for years and then was sold to the Fulds about 30 years ago. Now in Rulau coll.

This piece resembles the style of Pennsylvania store cards but by F.X. Koehler of Baltimore, which see under Altoona, Johnstown and Tyrone, Pa.

## C.W. KING
### Location Not Known

| Rulau | Date | Metal | Size | VG | F | VF | EF |
|---|---|---|---|---|---|---|---|
| MV 173 | (?) | Copper | 29mm | — | — | 50.00 | — |

C.W. KING / ARTIST ctsp on U.S. Large cents of various dates. (Hallenbeck 11.503)

The term "artist" here refers to a daguerreotype artist, or early photographer. Maurice M. Gould once possessed several specimens of this counterstamp.

It is possible these tokens are earlier — from the 1850's.

| MV 174 | (?) | Silver | 25mm | — | 75.00 | — | — |

C.W. King cstp on rev. of U.S. 1856 S.L. quarter. (Brunk coll.)

## LUCY LAW
### Location Not Known

| Rulau | Date | Metal | Size | VG | F | VF | EF |
|---|---|---|---|---|---|---|---|
| MV 180 | (?) | Silver | 31mm | — | — | 25.00 | — |

LUCY LAW ctsp on U.S. 1868 Liberty Seated half dollar. (Gould 247)

## LEE & JONES
### Location Not Known

| Rulau | Date | Metal | Size | VG | F | VF | EF |
|---|---|---|---|---|---|---|---|
| MV 183 | (?) | Silver | 15.5mm | — | — | 15.00 | — |

LEE & JONES ctsp on U.S. 1838 Bust half dime.

## LION BUGGY CO.
### Location Not Known

| Rulau | Date | Metal | Size | F | VF | EF | Unc |
|---|---|---|---|---|---|---|---|
| MV 185 | (?) | Brass | 34mm | 5.00 | 7.50 | — | — |

Facing lion head, LION BUGGY CO. below. Rv: Anchor, with anchor rope around in wreath fashion. Plain edge.

## LOVETT'S PRIVATE STOCK WHISKEY
### Location Not Known

| Rulau | Date | Metal | Size | VG | F | VF | EF |
|---|---|---|---|---|---|---|---|
| MV 190 | (?) | Silver | 25mm | — | 100. | — | — |

LOVETT'S / PRIVATE STOCK / WHISKEY ctsp on a U.S. Seated Liberty 25-cent coin. (Gould 88; Gould 40; Brunk 229)

| MV 192 | (?) | Silver | 38mm | — | 150. | — | — |

Similar ctsp on U.S. 1885-O Morgan silver dollar.

| MV 193 | (?) | Silver | 38mm | — | 150. | — | — |

Similar ctsp on U.S. 1887 Morgan silver dollar. (Gould 40)

The counterstamp is late, 1878 at the earliest.

## R. LYMAN
### Location Not Known

| Rulau | Date | Metal | Size | VG | F | VF | EF |
|---|---|---|---|---|---|---|---|
| MV 196 | (?) | Copper | 29mm | — | 7.50 | — | — |

R. LYMAN in rectangular cartouche ctsp on reverse of U.S. 1825 Large cent.

## F.M.
## Location Not Known

| Rulau | Date | Metal | Size | VG | F | VF | Unc |
|---|---|---|---|---|---|---|---|
| MV 198 | (?) | Brass | 23mm | — | — | 5.00 | — |

(All incused) Tankard, wine bottle and wine glass in a line across center. Rv: GOOD FOR / A / DRINK / F M. Plain edge. (Coll. John Cheramy, Victoria, Canada)

## E.A. MANSON
## Location Not Known

| Rulau | Date | Metal | Size | VG | F | VF | EF |
|---|---|---|---|---|---|---|---|
| MV 201 | 1869 | Silver | 32.5mm | — | — | 30.00 | — |

E A MANSON / 1869 / E A MANSON ctsp on U.S. 1809 Bust half dollar. (Frank Kovacs coll.)

## E.A. MANSON (et al)
## Location Not Known

| Rulau | Date | Metal | Size | G | VG | F | EF |
|---|---|---|---|---|---|---|---|
| MV 203 | 1868 | Copper | 29mm | — | 25.00 | — | — |

E.A. MANSON / F.O. RAY / C.H. COLLEY / W.P. WENTWORTH / B.B. TUTTLE / 1868 cstp on obverse of U.S. 1843 Large cent. J.A. SMITH, JR. ctsp on reverse of the coin. (S.L. Steinberg collection)

Apparently a piece used by a maker of merchant stamps to test his punches.

## J.A. MATHEWS
## Location Not Known

| Rulau | Date | Metal | Size | VG | F | VF | EF |
|---|---|---|---|---|---|---|---|
| MV 206 | (?) | Copper | 29mm | — | — | 10.00 | — |

J.A. MATHEWS ctsp on U.S. 1848 Large cent. (Stanley Steinberg 1982 sale)

It has been suggested that Mathews was a Centerville, Ohio merchant, but this has not been confirmed.

## J.H. METZ'S HOTEL
## Location Not Known

| Rulau | Date | Metal | Size | VG | F | VF | EF |
|---|---|---|---|---|---|---|---|
| MV 209 | (?) | — | --mm | — | — | 100. | — |

J.H. METZ'S HOTEL / N.E. COR. JEFFN AV & FED. ST. ctsp on several unspecified coins. (Brunk 253)

## M. MILLER
## Location Not Known

| Rulau | Date | Metal | Size | VG | F | VF | EF |
|---|---|---|---|---|---|---|---|
| MV 211 | 1882 | Copper | 29mm | — | — | 5.00 | — |

1882 / M. MILLER / 26 ctsp on U.S. Large cent. (Hallenbeck 13.528)

## McCOLGAN & HUGHES
## Location Not Known

### 1876 Centennial Tokens

Reverse type 1: McCOLGAN & HUGHES / GOOD / FOR / 5 CTS / ★★★. (All 19mm; plain edge)

| Rulau | Obv | Rev | Metal | F | VF | EF | Unc |
|---|---|---|---|---|---|---|---|
| MV 207 | Y | 1 | WM | — | — | 250. | — |

Possibly unique; in Steve Tanenbaum coll. This issuer has escaped publication until now, 107 years after the token's appearance.

## MILLER HOUSE
## Location Not Known

| Rulau | Date | Metal | Size | VG | F | VF | EF |
|---|---|---|---|---|---|---|---|
| MV 214 | (?) | Silver | 25mm | — | — | 150. | — |

MILLER HOUSE ctsp on U.S. 1877-S Quarter dollar. (Brunk 254)

| | | | | | | | |
|---|---|---|---|---|---|---|---|
| MV 213 | (?) | Silver | 25mm | — | — | 150. | — |

Similar ctsp on U.S. 1876 quarter.

## MINERS
## Location Not Known

| Rulau | Date | Metal | Size | VG | F | VF | Unc |
|---|---|---|---|---|---|---|---|
| MV 217 | (?) | Brass | 24mm | — | — | 20.00 | — |

MINERS incuse on blank flan. Recessed dentilated rim on each side. Plain edge.

## NABOCLISH
## Location Not Known

| Rulau | Date | Metal | Size | VG | F | VF | EF |
|---|---|---|---|---|---|---|---|
| MV 222 | (?) | CN | 19mm | 8.00 | — | 15.00 | — |

NABOCLISH (in upward curved arc) / 5-pointed star ctsp on U.S. 1857 Flying Eagle cent. (Krause coll.)

## NATIONAL HORSE
## SHOW ASSOCIATION
## Location Not Known

| Rulau | Date | Metal | Size | F | VF | EF | Unc |
|---|---|---|---|---|---|---|---|
| MV 225 | 1883 | WM | 31mm | — | — | — | 35.00 |

Man with rearing horse at center, NATIONAL HORSE SHOW ASSOCIATION OF AMERICA 1883 around. Rv: Wreath at center, MEMBERS BADGE NOT TRANSFERABLE around. (Levine Dec. 1981 sale, lot 1630)

## J. MURPHY
### Location Not Known

| Rulau | Date | Metal | Size | VG | F | VF | Unc |
|---|---|---|---|---|---|---|---|
| MV 220 | (?) | Silver | 25mm | — | — | 10.00 | — |

(Hand pointing left) / J. MURPHY ctsp on shaved reverse of U.S. 1853 S.L. quarter. An ornate circular border has also been stamped on the shaved rev.

## NATIONAL NOVELTY CO.
### Location Not Known

| Rulau | Date | Metal | Size | VG | F | VF | Unc |
|---|---|---|---|---|---|---|---|
| MV 226 | (?) | CN | 25mm | — | — | 3.00 | — |

Bit for horse's mouth at center, 2 above, BITS below. Rv: NATIONAL NOVELTY CO. / GOOD FOR / 25 / IN TRADE. The token is ctsp '3' on obverse.

The '3' is curious. Does it stand for '3 bits' or 37 1/2 cents?

## OIL OF ICE
### Location Not Known

| Rulau | Date | Metal | Size | VG | F | VF | EF |
|---|---|---|---|---|---|---|---|
| MV 230 | (?) | Copper | 29mm | — | 50.00 | — | — |

OIL / OF / ICE ctsp on U.S. Large cents of several dates. (Gould 5; Hallenbeck 15.502; Brunk 278)

| | | | | | | | |
|---|---|---|---|---|---|---|---|
| MV 232 | (?) | CN | 19mm | — | 50.00 | — | — |

OIL / OF / ICE ctsp on U.S. 1857-58 Flying Eagle cents. (Gould 5)

| | | | | | | | |
|---|---|---|---|---|---|---|---|
| MV 234 | (?) | CN | 19mm | — | 50.00 | — | — |

Similar ctsp on U.S. 1859-63 Indian Head cents. (Gould 5)

| | | | | | | | |
|---|---|---|---|---|---|---|---|
| MV 236 | (?) | Bronze | 19mm | — | 60.00 | — | — |

Similar ctsp on U.S. 1869 Indian Head cent. (Kurt Krueger coll.)

| | | | | | | | |
|---|---|---|---|---|---|---|---|
| MV 238 | (?) | Bronze | 23mm | — | 60.00 | — | — |

Similar ctsp on U.S. 1865 2-cent piece.

Probably a patent medicine.

## ORDER OF THE IRON HALL
### Location Not Known

| Rulau | Date | Metal | Size | VG | F | VF | Unc |
|---|---|---|---|---|---|---|---|
| MV 241 | 1881 | WM | 40mm | — | — | Scrc | — |

Safe at center, $1,000 on its top. Above: U.P.F. Below: (on scroll) IN SEVEN YEARS. All within central circle. Outside circle: * ORDER OF THE IRON HALL * / ORGANIZED MARCH 28 - 1881. Rv: Blank. Plain edge. (Wright 1565)

## M.D. PALMER
### Location Not Known

| Rulau | Date | Metal | Size | VG | F | VF | EF |
|---|---|---|---|---|---|---|---|
| MV 246 | (?) | Silver | 38mm | — | — | 25.00 | — |

M.D. PALMER in an arc ctsp on U.S. 1871 Liberty Seated silver dollar. (Steinberg 1982 sale)

It has been suggested this might be a Chicago watchmaker.

## PAT. 1868
### Location Not Known

| Rulau | Date | Metal | Size | VG | F | VF | EF |
|---|---|---|---|---|---|---|---|
| MV 249 | 1868 | Copper | 29mm | — | — | 5.00 | — |

PAT. 1868 ctsp on U.S. Large cent. (Hallenbeck 16.502)

## PATENTED
### Location Not Known

| Rulau | Date | Metal | Size | VG | F | VF | EF |
|---|---|---|---|---|---|---|---|
| MV 251 | 1860 | Copper | 29mm | — | — | 5.00 | — |

PATENTED / JULY 3, 1860 / DEC. 7, 1858 ctsp on U.S. 1848 Large cent.

## PEACOCK
### Location Not Known

| Rulau | Date | Metal | Size | VG | F | VF | EF |
|---|---|---|---|---|---|---|---|
| MV 253 | (?) | Silver | 40mm | — | — | 100. | — |

PEACOCK ctsp on U.S. 1802 Bust type dollar. Rv: Similar ctsp on coin's reverse. (Duffield 1416)

## PHOSPHOR BRONZE
### Location Not Known

| Rulau | Date | Metal | Size | VG | F | VF | EF |
|---|---|---|---|---|---|---|---|
| MV 256 | 1871 | Copper | 28mm | — | 50.00 | — | — |

(Elephant standing left) / Phosphor-Bronze (script) / PAT. MAY 23. 71 / NOV. 14. 71 ctsp on one side of a worn-smooth unrecognizable coin. Rv: H H H engraved crudely on opposite of coin. Holed flan. Plain edge. (Rulau coll.)

## W. B. PAGE (et al)
### Location Not Known

| Rulau | Date | Metal | Size | VG | F | VF | EF |
|---|---|---|---|---|---|---|---|
| MV 244 | (?) | Copper | 29mm | — | — | 25.00 | — |

W. F. PAGE / W. B. PAGE (large) / I. C. LANE ctsp on U.S. 1827 Large cent. (Frank Kovacs coll.)

If this is a partnership, W. B. Page appears to be senior since his name is larger. This could also be a counterstamper's "test piece" used for testing customers' punches.

## PATENT
### Location Not Known

| Rulau | Date | Metal | Size | VG | F | VF | EF |
|---|---|---|---|---|---|---|---|
| MV 250 | (?) | Copper | 29mm | — | 10.00 | — | — |

PATENT ctsp five times on obverse of U.S. 1843 Large cent. Also ctsp three times on reverse of the coin. (Kovacs coll.)

## PIERCE'S ROSETTA HAIR TONIC
### Location Not Known

| Rulau | Date | Metal | Size | VG | F | EF | Unc |
|---|---|---|---|---|---|---|---|
| MV-257 | (?) | Silver | 27mm | 60.00 | — | 100. | — |

GOOD FOR / A BOTTLE / PIERCE'S / ROSETTA / HAIR TONIC ctsp on 1821 Spanish-American 2-reales (Gould 340)

| | | | | | | | |
|---|---|---|---|---|---|---|---|
| MV-257A | (?) | Silver | 27mm | 60.00 | — | 100. | — |

Similar ctsp on Spanish-American 1826-Mo 2-reales.

(Also see Dr. Darby under Boston, Mass. for Gould 325, which is a combination counterstamp of Dr. Darby and Pierce's Rosetta Hair Tonic on a Spanish-American 2-reales.)

## WOOD N. PORTER
### Location Not Known

| Rulau | Date | Metal | Size | VG | F | VF | Unc |
|---|---|---|---|---|---|---|---|
| MV 258 | 1887 | Brass | 24mm | — | 15.00 | — | — |

Pool table, THE BRUNSWICK BALKE / COLLENDER / COMPY. above, CHECK in exergue. Rv: WOOD N. PORTER / (four dots in cross form) / 1887 (scratched in) / +++. Plain edge. (Brunswick 5580)

## W.C. PUGH
### Location Not Known

| Rulau | Date | Metal | Size | VG | F | VF | EF |
|---|---|---|---|---|---|---|---|
| MV 259 | 1870 | Silver | 31mm | — | 35.00 | — | — |

IS / W.C. PUGH / (arrow, point left) 1870 (arrow, point right), ctsp on U.S. 1854 Seated Liberty half dollar.

## C. PUTNAM CAST STEEL
### Location Not Known

| Rulau | Date | Metal | Size | VG | F | VF | EF |
|---|---|---|---|---|---|---|---|
| MV 261 | (?) | Copper | 29mm | — | 10.00 | — | — |

C. PUTNAM CAST STEEL ctsp on U.S. 1802 Large cent.

## J.H.R.
### Location Not Known

| Rulau | Date | Metal | Size | VG | F | VF | Unc |
|---|---|---|---|---|---|---|---|
| MV 264 | (?) | Brass | 23mm | — | — | 3.00 | — |

(All incuse) J.H.R. / GOOD FOR / 5¢. Rv: (All incuse) D. ARMSTRONG / MAKER. Plain edge. (Coll. John Cheramy, Victoria, Canada)

## P.R.
### Location Not Known

| Rulau | Date | Metal | Size | VG | F | VF | EF |
|---|---|---|---|---|---|---|---|
| MV 266 | (?) | Copper | 29mm | — | 5.50 | — | — |

P.R. ctsp on U.S. 1822 Large cent.

## A.H. RAABE
### Location Not Known

| Rulau | Date | Metal | Size | VG | F | VF | Unc |
|---|---|---|---|---|---|---|---|
| MV 269 | 1874-84 | GS | 25mm | — | — | 15.00 | — |

GOOD FOR / 5¢ / A.H. RAABE / - IN - / TRADE. Rv: Pool table within beaded circle. Around circle: THE J.M. BRUNSWICK & BALKE COS. / * CHECK *. Plain edge.

Not listed in *The Brunswick Token Story*.

## W. REED
### Location Not Known

| Rulau | Date | Metal | Size | VG | F | VF | EF |
|---|---|---|---|---|---|---|---|
| MV 272 | (?) | Silver | 25mm | — | — | 7.50 | — |

W. REED ctsp on U.S. Liberty Seated quarter. (Clifford Mishler Coll.)

## G.E. RIDLEY
### Location Not Known

| Rulau | Date | Metal | Size | VG | F | VF | EF |
|---|---|---|---|---|---|---|---|
| MV 275 | 1871 | Silver | 38mm | — | — | — | 50.00 |

MAY 1871 / G.E. RIDLEY ctsp on U.S. 1869 Silver dollar. Reeded edge. (Hetrich coll. sale, Jan. 30, 1982, Los Angeles)

## FRED. ROLING
### Location Not Known

| Rulau | Date | Metal | Size | VG | F | VF | Unc |
|---|---|---|---|---|---|---|---|
| MV 278 | (?) | Brass | 30mm | — | — | 50.00 | — |

Clockface, hands pointing to 12 past 10, TIME / IS / MONEY on the face. Rv: FRED. ROLING / (large ornament) / N.E. COR. 5' & ELM. Plain edge. (Jim Curto coll.)

Though it resembles a Hard Times token, this piece appears to be from a much later date, perhaps the 1880's.

| Rulau | Date | Metal | Size | VG | F | VF | Unc |
|---|---|---|---|---|---|---|---|
| MV 27 | (?) | Brass | 30mm | — | — | 50.00 | — |

Obverse similar to 278, but different die. Letters and Roman numerals are larger; no beaded border near rim. Rv: (Ornament) / FRED. ROLING / (Ornament). Plain edge. (Tanenbaum coll.)

It has been suggested that the Roling cards are from Cincinnati, Ohio. This has not been verified.

## S. & H. CO.
### Location Not Known

| Rulau | Date | Metal | Size | VG | F | VF | EF |
|---|---|---|---|---|---|---|---|
| MV 280 | (?) | CN | 19mm | — | 25.00 | — | — |

S & H / CO within a heart, ctsp on U.S. 1861 Indian cent. Same ctsp on reverse. (Rulau coll.)

## N. J. SCHLOSS & CO.
### Location Not Known

| Rulau | Date | Metal | Size | F | VF | EF | Unc |
|---|---|---|---|---|---|---|---|
| MV 295 | 1889 | Gilt/C | 32mm | — | 6.00 | — | — |

Seated man and woman above Paris view, EXPOSITION UNIVERSELLE above. Rv: Fame blowing trumpet, REPUBLIQUE / FRANCAISE at left. On a tablet below the allegorical figure is: N. J. SCHLOSS & CO. Plain edge.

## L.C.S. & CO.
### Location Not Known

| Rulau | Date | Metal | Size | VG | F | VF | Unc |
|---|---|---|---|---|---|---|---|
| MV 281 | 1871 | Brass | 24mm | 2.50 | 4.00 | — | — |

Liberty head left, 13 stars around, 1871 below. Rv: L.C.S. & CO. / 5 / CENTS. (Wright 584)

## N.S. & CO.
### Location Not Known

| Rulau | Date | Metal | Size | VG | F | VF | EF |
|---|---|---|---|---|---|---|---|
| MV 283 | (?) | Silver | 38.1mm | — | — | 45.00 | — |

N.S. & CO. ctsp on U.S. 1880 Morgan silver dollar. (Frank Kovacs coll.)

## SAGADA HOCKHOUSE
### Location Not Known

| Rulau | Date | Metal | Size | G | VG | F | EF |
|---|---|---|---|---|---|---|---|
| MV 286 | (?) | Silver | 31mm | — | — | 30.00 | — |

SAGADA HOCKHOUSE ctsp on U.S. 1876 half dollar. (Gould 41)

## SAGE'S CANDY COIN
### Location Not Known

| Rulau | Date | Metal | Size | VG | F | VF | EF |
|---|---|---|---|---|---|---|---|
| MV 289 | (?) | Silver | 26mm | 75.00 | 100. | 150. | — |

SAGE'S / CANDY / COIN ctsp on U.S. 1874 Liberty Seated quarter dollar. (Gould 54; Brunk 338)

| MV 291 | (?) | Silver | 31mm | 75.00 | 100. | 150. | — |

Similar ctsp on U.S. 1874 Liberty Seated half dollar. (Gould 38)

| MV 293 | (?) | Silver | 38mm | 200. | 300. | 400. | — |

Similar ctsp on U.S. 1874 Trade dollar. (Gould 22)

## C. SCHMIDT
### Location Not Known

| Rulau | Date | Metal | Size | VG | F | VF | Unc |
|---|---|---|---|---|---|---|---|
| MV 296 | (?) | Copper | 23.5mm | — | — | 12.50 | — |

C. SCHMIDT ctsp on each side of a U.S. 1853 Half cent. (Stanley Steinberg 1982 sale)

## SELLY & F.R. LEMAN
### Location Not Known

| Rulau | Date | Metal | Size | VG | F | VF | EF |
|---|---|---|---|---|---|---|---|
| MV 280 | (?) | Copper | 29mm | — | 40.00 | — | 65.00 |

SELLY & F R LEMAN in relief within rectangular depression ctsp on U.S. 1856 Large cent. (Rulau coll.)

There is some doubt about the second name. It could be a single name — FRLEMAN, or it could be F P LEMAN, or F R LEMAIN, or possibly something else. The stamp is struck unevenly.

It appears to be a silversmith's or jeweler's hallmark and is probably important. The Rulau specimen was acquired in Dec. 1982 from the Harvey Gamer holdings.

(Kenneth Hallenbeck reports a Large cent counterstamped E. LEMAN JR. This may be connected, so is listed below.)

| MV 282 | (?) | Copper | 29mm | — | 10.00 | — | — |

E. LEMAN JR. cstp on U.S. Large cent. (Hallenbeck 12.503)

## W.A. SHEPARD & CO.
### Location Not Known

[179]

| Rulau | Date | Metal | Size | VG | F | VF | Unc |
|---|---|---|---|---|---|---|---|
| MV 303 | 1874 | Brass | 25mm | — | — | 25.00 | — |

W.A. SHEPARD & CO. / (ornament) / ESTABLISHED / MAY 3RD / 1874. Rv: COMMERCIAL BUSINESS / EXCHANGE / FROM / OCEAN TO OCEAN / 65 OFFICES. Plain edge. (Wright 1623)

## SENECA LT. CLUB
### Location Not Known

| Rulau | Date | Metal | Size | VG | F | VF | EF |
|---|---|---|---|---|---|---|---|
| MV 299 | (?) | Copper | 29mm | — | 50.00 | — | — |

SENECA / LT CLUB ctsp on U.S. 1856 Large cent. (Frank Kovacs coll.)

## A. SHARRARD
### Location Not Known

| Rulau | Date | Metal | Size | VG | F | VF | EF |
|---|---|---|---|---|---|---|---|
| MV 302 | (?) | Silver | 32.5mm | — | — | 15.00 | — |

A. SHARRARD ctsp on U.S. 1832 Half dollar. (Duffield 1420)

## SILVER BOW CLUB
### Location Not Known

| Rulau | Date | Metal | Size | VG | F | VF | Unc |
|---|---|---|---|---|---|---|---|
| MV 305 | (?) | GS | 27mm | — | — | 7.50 | — |

A. O. W. Rv: Blank. Plain edge (Wright 32)

Dr. B. P. Wright in 1898 said this was a check for the Silver "Draw" Club.

| MV 307 | (?) | GS | 25mm | — | — | 7.50 | — |

SILVER BOW / 20 / CLUB. Rv: A.W.O. across center, three stars above and three below. Plain edge. (Wright 984)

## H.W. SMITH
### Location Not Known

| Rulau | Date | Metal | Size | VG | F | VF | Unc |
|---|---|---|---|---|---|---|---|
| MV 310 | 1884-1900 | Brass | 25mm | — | — | 15.00 | — |

GOOD FOR / 2½¢ / H.W. SMITH / —.— / ON BILLIARD TABLE. Rv: Similar to Broadhurst piece in the BBC series, but hyphen between BRUNSWICK-BALKE. Plain edge.

Not listed in *The Brunswick Token Story.*

## J. T. SMITH
### Location Not Known

| Rulau | Date | Metal | Size | VG | F | VF | EF |
|---|---|---|---|---|---|---|---|
| MV 312 | (?) | CN | 19mm | — | — | 5.00 | — |

J.T. SMITH ctsp on U.S. 1859 Indian Head cent.

| MV 314 | (?) | — | — | — | — | 5.00 | — |

Similar ctsp on unspecified coins. (Brunk 350)

## SO. RIVER CUTLERY CO.
### Location Not Known

| Rulau | Date | Metal | Size | VG | F | VF | EF |
|---|---|---|---|---|---|---|---|
| MV 317 | (?) | Copper | 29mm | — | — | 50.00 | — |

SO. RIVER CUTLERY CO. ctsp on U.S. Large cent. (Hallenbeck 19.752)

## G. E. STEVENS
### Location Not Known

| Rulau | Date | Metal | Size | VG | F | VF | EF |
|---|---|---|---|---|---|---|---|
| MV 320 | (?) | CN | 19mm | — | — | 5.00 | — |

G. E. STEVENS ctsp on U.S. 1858 Flying Eagle cent.

| MV 322 | (?) | — | — | — | — | — | — |

Similar ctsp on unspecified coins. (Brunk 359)

## A. S. STILLMAN
### Location Not Known

| Rulau | Date | Metal | Size | VG | F | VF | EF |
|---|---|---|---|---|---|---|---|
| MV 325 | 1870 | Copper | 29mm | — | — | 10.00 | — |

PRESENTED BY A. S. STILLMAN 1870 ctsp on U.S. Large cent. (Hallenbeck 19.777)

## E. STILLMAN
### Location Not Known

| Rulau | Date | Metal | Size | VG | F | VF | EF |
|---|---|---|---|---|---|---|---|
| MV 327 | (?) | Copper | 29mm | — | — | 5.00 | — |

E. STILLMAN ctsp on U.S. Large cents of various dates. (Brunk 361)

| MV 329 | (?) | — | ---mm | — | — | 5.00 | — |

Similar ctsp on unspecified U.S. coins. (Brunk 361)

## STORRS & COOK
### Location Not Known

| Rulau | Date | Metal | Size | VG | F | VF | EF |
|---|---|---|---|---|---|---|---|
| MV 333 | (?) | Copper | 29mm | — | — | 10.00 | — |

STORRS & COOK ctsp on U.S. Large cent. (Hallenbeck 19.781)

## STOEHR'S LAGER BIER
### Location Not Known

| Rulau | Date | Metal | Size | VG | F | VF | EF |
|---|---|---|---|---|---|---|---|
| MV 332 | (?) | — | — | — | — | 100. | — |

DRINK / STOEHR'S / LAGER BIER ctsp on unspecified coins. (Brunk 363)

## F. R. STRANGE
### Location Not Known

| Rulau | Date | Metal | Size | VG | F | VF | EF |
|---|---|---|---|---|---|---|---|
| MV 335 | (?) | Copper | 29mm | — | — | 15.00 | — |

F. R. STRANGE in ornate cartouche ctsp on U.S. Large cent. (Stanley L. Steinberg sale of Feb. 1982; Brunk 371)

There were at least two families named Strange in the letter cutting business who made counterstamped pieces — E. W. Strange of Taunton, Mass. in the 1850's, and J. W and C. A. Strange, father and son of Bangor, Maine in the 1860's. Whether F. R. Strange is connected with either is not known at this stage.

## DANIEL SULLY
### Location Not Known

| Rulau | Date | Metal | Size | VG | F | VF | Unc |
|---|---|---|---|---|---|---|---|
| MV 338 | (?) | Brass | 31mm | — | — | Rare | — |

Standing rooster: .DANIEL SULLY. / MEDAL / FOR THE / BEST AND LONGEST / THE MILLIONAIRE. Rv: Wrench enclosing a screw; GOOD FOR / ONE. Plain edge. Rare. (Wright 1076)

This is one of the few erotic items in Dr. Wright's 1900 listing.

## SWAN HOUSE
### Location Not Known

| Rulau | Date | Metal | Size | VG | F | VF | Unc |
|---|---|---|---|---|---|---|---|
| MV 341 | (?) | Brass | 25mm | — | — | 3.00 | — |

SWAN HOUSE. Rv: Blank. Plain edge. (Wright 1079)

## TIVOLI & WALLHALLA
### Location Not Known

| Rulau | Date | Metal | Size | F | VF | EF | Unc |
|---|---|---|---|---|---|---|---|
| MV 344 | (?) | Lead | 16mm | — | — | 10.00 | — |

Within central circle: TONY. Around: TIVOLI & WALLHALLA. Rv: GOOD FOR ONE DRINK / 5 / CENTS. Plain edge. (Wright 1149)

## N. J. TRACY
### Location Not Known

| Rulau | Date | Metal | Size | VG | F | VF | EF |
|---|---|---|---|---|---|---|---|
| MV 350 | (?) | Silver | 18mm | — | 50.00 | — | — |

N. J. TRACY ctsp on U.S. 1853 dime. (Duffield 1425)

| | | | | | | | |
|---|---|---|---|---|---|---|---|
| MV 353 | (?) | Copper | 29mm | — | 40.00 | — | — |

N. J. TRACY in relief in a curved rectangular cartouche ctsp on U.S. 1850 Large cent. (Brunk 391.2)

| | | | | | | | |
|---|---|---|---|---|---|---|---|
| MV 355 | (?) | Copper | 29mm | — | — | 35.00 | — |

Similar ctsp on U.S. 1846 Large cent. MSB on rev. (Frank Kovacs coll.)

| | | | | | | | |
|---|---|---|---|---|---|---|---|
| MV 358 | (?) | Copper | 29mm | — | — | 35.00 | — |

Similar cstp on U.S. 1848 Large cent. Incuse R.L. also ctsp.

| | | | | | | | |
|---|---|---|---|---|---|---|---|
| MV 357 | (?) | Copper | 29mm | — | — | 35.00 | — |

N. J. TRACY in relief within depressed rectangle ctsp on U.S. 1851 Large cent. (Rulau coll.; Brunk 391.1)

| | | | | | | | |
|---|---|---|---|---|---|---|---|
| MV 356 | (?) | Copper | 29mm | — | — | 35.00 | — |

Similar ctsp on U.S. 1849 Large cent. (Stanley Steinberg 1982 sale; Brunk 91.1.)

| | | | | | | | |
|---|---|---|---|---|---|---|---|
| MV 359 | (?) | CN | 19mm | — | — | 30.00 | — |

Similar ctsp on U.S. 1858 Flying Eagle cent. (Frank Kovacs coll.)

| | | | | | | | |
|---|---|---|---|---|---|---|---|
| MV 361 | (?) | Silver | 18mm | — | 50.00 | — | — |

Similar ctsp on U.S. 1839 Seated Liberty dime. (Rulau coll.)

## E. P. VAUX
### Location Not Known

| Rulau | Date | Metal | Size | VG | F | VF | EF |
|---|---|---|---|---|---|---|---|
| MV 370 | (?) | CN | 19mm | — | — | 300. | — |

E. P. VAUX ctsp on U.S. 1856 Flying Eagle cent. (Duffield 1431)

| | | | | | | | |
|---|---|---|---|---|---|---|---|
| MV 371 | (?) | CN | 19mm | — | — | 15.00 | — |

E. P. VAUX ctsp on U.S. 1857 Flying Eagle cent. (John Ford coll.)

## W. & E.
### Location Not Known

| Rulau | Date | Metal | Size | VG | F | VF | EF |
|---|---|---|---|---|---|---|---|
| MV 372 | (?) | Copper | 29mm | — | — | 25.00 | — |

W & E / 25 ctsp on shaved reverse of U.S. 1856 Large cent. (Brunk coll.)

## D.W.
### Location Not Known

| Rulau | Date | Metal | Size | VG | F | VF | Unc |
|---|---|---|---|---|---|---|---|
| MV 373 | (?) | Brass | 24mm | — | — | 10.00 | — |

Lizard in an oval panel at center. Rv: No -- / D.W. Plain edge. (Wright 234)

## R. H. W. CO.
### Location Not Known

| Rulau | Date | Metal | Size | F | VF | EF | Unc |
|---|---|---|---|---|---|---|---|
| MV 374 | (?) | Brass | 27mm | — | — | 5.00 | — |

Eagle with outspread wings perched on a scroll. The numeral 1798 is incused on the scroll. Rv: (Three fleurs) .R.H.W.Co. / (three fleurs). Plain edge.

The piece appears to be a check of some sort (tool, time, waiter's, etc.). (In collection Jackson Sellwood, Collings Lakes, N.J.)

## W. W. & CO.
### Location Not Known

| Rulau | Date | Metal | Size | VG | F | VF | EF |
|---|---|---|---|---|---|---|---|
| MV 376 | (?) | Copper | 29mm | — | — | 25.00 | — |

W. W & CO ctsp on U.S. 1854 Large cent. (Frank Kovacs coll.)

## WALLIS & CORNNELL
### Location Not Known

| Rulau | Date | Metal | Size | F | VF | EF | Unc |
|---|---|---|---|---|---|---|---|
| MV 379 | 1868 | Brass | 24.5mm | — | — | 15.00 | — |

WALLIS & CORNNELL / —.— / 1868 / —.— / (five stars). Rv: ONE BAG / 20 ¢ / GRAINS. Plain edge.

Possibly Virginia, but it is apparently a maverick miller's token.

## WALTONS BITTERS
### Location Not Known

| Rulau | Date | Metal | Size | VG | F | VF | EF |
|---|---|---|---|---|---|---|---|
| MV 382 | (?) | Silver | 31mm | 75.00 | 100. | 150. | — |

WE RECOMMEND / WALTONS / BITTERS ctsp on U.S. 1855-O half dollar. (Krause coll.; Brunk 404)

| MV 383 | (?) | Silver | 31mm | — | 100. | 150. | — |

Similar ctsp on U.S. 1859 half dollar. (Gould 43)

## WELLS FARGO
### Location Not Known

| Rulau | Date | Metal | Size | VG | F | VF | EF |
|---|---|---|---|---|---|---|---|
| MV 385 | (1870's) | Copper | 34mm | — | 300. | — | — |

WELLS FARGO / U.S. / R.W.P.O. / EXPRESS ctsp on England penny of 1806-1807, date worn off.

R.W.P.O. = Railway post office. There are three pieces known. Just what use was made of this item is not known. The Wells Fargo Express Co. was one of the largest delivery and transportation companies in North America, operating all over the West as well as the East.

## WATROUS (&) CO.
### Location Not Known

| Rulau | Date | Metal | Size | VG | F | VF | EF |
|---|---|---|---|---|---|---|---|
| MV 384 | (?) | Copper | 29mm | — | — | 25.00 | — |

WATROUS . CO ctsp on reverse of U.S. 1851 Large cent. (The . could be a broken ampersand)

## ANTON WERNER
### Location Not Known

| Rulau | Date | Metal | Size | F | VF | Unc |
|---|---|---|---|---|---|---|
| MV 386 | (1884-1900) | Brass | 25mm | — | 15.00 | — |

GOOD FOR / 5 ¢ / ANTON / WERNER / IN / * TRADE *. Rv: (Brunswick-Balke-Collender check). Plain edge.

Not listed in *The Brunswick Token Story*.

## H.M. WHITBECK'S CIRCUS
### Location Not Known

| Rulau | Date | Metal | Size | VG | F | VF | EF |
|---|---|---|---|---|---|---|---|
| MV 390 | (1860's) | Silver | 27mm | — | — | 200. | — |

H.M. WHITBECK'S / CIRCUS ctsp on Spanish-American 1772 2-reales. (Schenkman collection; Brunk 412)

| MV 391 | (1860's) | Silver | 28mm | — | — | 200. | — |

Similar ctsp on Spanish-American 1788 2-reales. (Lou Rasera report)

## WILDER HOUSE
### Location Not Known

| Rulau | Date | Metal | Size | VG | F | VF | EF |
|---|---|---|---|---|---|---|---|
| MV 396 | (?) | Silver | 25mm | — | — | 35.00 | — |

WILDER HOUSE ctsp on U.S. 1857 Seated Liberty quarter. (Gould 94)

## GEORGE WILDER
### Location Not Known

| Rulau | Date | Metal | Size | VG | F | VF | EF |
|---|---|---|---|---|---|---|---|
| MV 393 | (?) | Silver | 18mm | — | — | 15.00 | — |

Eagle, GEORGE WILDER ctsp on U.S. 1887 Seated Liberty dime. (Gould 170)

## WIMAN (THE) COPPERSMITH
### Location Not Known

| Rulau | Date | Metal | Size | VG | F | VF | EF |
|---|---|---|---|---|---|---|---|
| MV 400 | (?) | Copper | 29mm | — | — | 50.00 | — |

Large eagle and WIMAN COPPERSMITH ctsp on U.S. Large cents of various dates. (Hallenbeck 23.518)

## C.H. WING
### Location Not Known

| Rulau | Date | Metal | Size | VG | F | VF | EF |
|---|---|---|---|---|---|---|---|
| MV 403 | (?) | Copper | 29mm | — | — | 10.00 | — |

C.H. WING ctsp on U.S. 1843 Large cent.

| MV 405 | (?) | | | | | | |

Similar ctsp on unspecified coins. (Brunk 420)

## G.J. WING
### Location Not Known

| Rulau | Date | Metal | Size | VG | F | VF | Unc |
|---|---|---|---|---|---|---|---|
| MV 408 | (?) | Bronze | 19mm | — | — | 5.00 | — |

G.J. WING ctsp on U.S. 1884 Indian Head cent.

| MV 410 | (?) | Bronze | --mm | — | — | 5.00 | — |

(G.) J. WING ctsp on U.S. 1864 2-cent piece.

## GEO. WOLBRECHT'S TIVOLI
### Location Not Known

| Rulau | Date | Metal | Size | VG | F | VF | Unc |
|---|---|---|---|---|---|---|---|
| MV 413 | (?) | Brass | 19mm | — | — | 10.00 | — |

Female head left, GEO. WOLBRECHT'S TIVOLI. Rv: Large numeral 5 at center, GOOD FOR ONE CTS DRINK around. Plain edge. (Wright 1260)

A drink for 5 cents in the Good Old Days!

## R.F. WRIGHT
### Location Not Known

| Rulau | Date | Metal | Size | VG | F | VF | Unc |
|---|---|---|---|---|---|---|---|
| MV 416 | (?) | Brass | 24mm | — | — | 4.50 | — |

R.F. WRIGHT / 10¢ / SILVER DOLLAR SHOP. Rv: In circle at center: AUG. KERN B.S. CO., ST. LOUIS. Plain edge. (Wright 1277)

## Y & T
### Location Not Known

| Rulau | Date | Metal | Size | VG | F | VF | EF |
|---|---|---|---|---|---|---|---|
| MV 420 | (?) | Bronze | 19mm | — | — | 50.00 | — |

Y & T in three-leaf clover with stem (repeated four times) ctsp on reverse of U.S. 1864 Indian Head cent. (Fuld NC-35a) Rarity 7.

Originally thought to have been a Civil War token, but probably issued closer to 1870.

## YANKEE BLADE
### Location Not Known

| Rulau | Date | Metal | Size | VG | F | VF | EF |
|---|---|---|---|---|---|---|---|
| MV 423 | (?) | Silver | 25mm | — | — | 20.00 | — |

YANKEE BLADE ctsp on U.S. 1853 Arrows & Rays Seated Liberty quarter. (Gould 96)

## ZIRIAX
### Location Not Known

| Rulau | Date | Metal | Size | VG | F | VF | EF |
|---|---|---|---|---|---|---|---|
| MV 440 | (?) | CN | 22mm | — | — | 8.00 | — |

ZIRIAX ctsp on U.S. 1867 Shield nickel.

## (Elephant)
### Location Not Known

| Rulau | Date | Metal | Size | VG | F | VF | Unc |
|---|---|---|---|---|---|---|---|
| MV 450 | (1880's ?) | CN | 25mm | — | — | 17.50 | — |

Elephant standing on mound to right. There are four die breaks extending inward from the rim, at 4, 5:30, 9 and 10 o'clock. Beaded inner rim border. Rv: Large 5 in a circle of 16 6-pointed rosettes. Plain edge. (Spangenberger coll.)

## M. V. Y.
### Location Not Known

| Rulau | Date | Metal | Size | VG | F | VF | EF |
|---|---|---|---|---|---|---|---|
| MV 421 | 1889 | Copper | 29mm | — | — | 10.00 | — |

M. V. Y. ctsp on obverse of U.S. 1803 Large cent. Date 1889 ctsp on reverse of the coin. (Kovacs coll.)

# MISCELLANEOUS COUNTERSTAMPS

(All on U.S. coins unless specified otherwise)

—A—

| | |
|---|---|
| A | on 1824 Large cent (rev.) |
| Large A | on 1824 Large cent (rev.) |
| A . A (relief, in oval depression with dotted rim) | on Spanish-American 1-real (worn smooth). (Possibly silversmith Allen Armstrong, Philadelphia, circa 1806) |
| A & B | on 1850's Liberty Seated dime |
| E. ABBOTT | on 1862 Indian cent |
| Z. S. ADAIR | on 1859 Indian cent |
| H. D. ADAMS | on 1853 Arrows & Rays S.L. quarter |
| V. ADAMS | on 1850 Large cent |
| F. AGNEW | on 1863 Indian cent |
| H. J. ALLEN | on 1877 S.L. half dollar (rev.) |
| ALF E. AMES (both sides) | on 1865 2-cent piece |
| A. C. ARNOLD | on 1878 Morgan silver dollar |
| J. ASHBORN | on 1838 Large cent |
| AYFR | on Spanish-American 1775-SLP-JR 2-reales (possibly AYER) |
| R. ATKIN | on 1864 2-cent piece |
| S. ATWOOD | on Large cent |

—B—

| | |
|---|---|
| B (five times) Y (twice) | on 1853 Arrows S.L. quarter |
| B. / J. (star) B. | on 1856 dime |
| A . B (relief, in toothed rect. depression) / GWH in rectangular frame (incuse) | on 1833 Large cent |
| Monogram AB | on 1823 Half cent |
| I. B (relief, in square depression) | on 1826 Large cent (Hallenbeck 9.001) |
| I. B / 6 | on 1809 Half cent |
| I. C. B. | on 1838 Large cent (rev.) |
| JB | on 1857 S.L. half dollar |
| L. K. B. inside dotted rectangle | on 1839 Large cent |
| L. M. BAILEY | on 1864 2-cent piece |
| B. K. BAKER | on 1835 Bust quarter |
| B. L. BAKER | on 1854 S.L. quarter |
| H. D. BAKER | on 1864 2-cent piece (rev.) |
| W. C. BALL | on 1857 Flying Eagle cent |
| E. BASTON (both sides) | on 1840 Large cent |
| BATH / BATH | on Half dime |
| C. W. BEAL | on 1864 2-cent piece |
| BEAN | on 1817 Large cent |
| B. C. BEARDSLEY | on 1864-S S.L. half dollar |
| H. BEEMAN (relief, in rect. depression) | on 1802 Large cent (three times) |
| C. E. BLISS | on 1851 Large cent |
| S. C. BORDEN (both sides) | on 1848 Large cent |
| BOSTON | on 1828 Half cent (Hallenbeck 2.752) |
| —do— | on 1828 Large cent |
| 1776 / BOSTON / . | on late Large cent |
| A. C. BOWE. | on 1848 Large cent |
| G. W. BOWEN. | on 1818 Large cent |
| J. A. BOYER | on 1827 Large cent |

| | |
|---|---|
| M. BRAGG. (obv. once, rev. twice) | on 1843 Large cent |
| E. BRAINARD | on 1851 Large cent |
| H. H. BREWER (both sides) | on 1866 Shield nickel |
| G. W. BRINK | on 1848 Large cent |
| BRITENBAKER | on 1837 Large cent |
| E. BROWN | on 1864 2-cent piece |
| GEO. H. BROWN | on 1824 Large cent |
| W. BROWN | on 1837 Large cent |
| BROWNE / BROWNE (both sides) | on 1862 Indian cent |
| BRUN | on 3-cent silver piece |
| G. W. BURNHAM | on 1870 Shield nickel |
| B. BUSH | on 1838 Large cent |

—C—

| | |
|---|---|
| C | on 1863 'Millions for Contractors' Civil War token |
| C & P | on 1833 Large cent |
| E. C. C. (both sides) | on 1833 Half cent (Duffield 1612) |
| M C / JUN / 3 / 1885 | on 1883 Indian cent |
| R. C. (both sides) | on 1848 Large cent |
| S C / CAST STEE(L) / S C (obv.); Handle (?) | on 1822 Large cent |
| W H C (Star) | on 1853 Arrows & Rays S.L. quarter |
| C. H. A & S O (both sides) | on 1850 Large cent |
| ELMER. M. CAMPBELL. / BIRD. S / F. R (on rev.); F R (on obv.) ch | on 1889 Liberty nickel |
| CARLETON (relief, in rect. depression, on obv.; also, four times on rev.) | on Large cent |
| J. CARLTON (obv. once, rev. twice) | on 1852 Large cent |
| F. C. CARTER | on 1819 Large cent (two specimens known) |
| H. C. CARTER | on 1856 Large cent |
| J. A. CASHMAN | on Shield nickel |
| R. CHADWI | on 1802 Large cent (die runs off flan) |
| C. A. W. / E. A. CHADWICK | on 1864 2-cent piece |
| CENT (relief) | on 1787 Connecticut cent (Duffield 1384) |
| S. E. CHAPMAN | 1883 Indian cent |
| A. CLARK (relief, in toothed rect. depression) | on 1834 Large cent |
| J. C. CLARK (twice) | on 1816 Large cent |
| J. G. CLARKSON (both sides) | on 1828 Large cent |
| I. CLEMENCE (relief, in rect. depression) on obv.; G / 9 on rev. | on 31mm copper disc |
| J. C. CLEMENT / J. K. WILSON | on 1841 Hard Times token |
| CLINTON | on 1848 Large cent |
| CNIPPES (in arc) | on 1820 Large cent |
| H. CLOUGH | on 1819 Large cent (rev.) |
| CODHAM / HANDS UP | on 1875 half dollar |
| C. COESTER (twice on obv., once on rev.) | on 1853 Large cent |
| C. COLLEY | on 1849 Large cent |
| C. COLLINS | on 1848 Large cent |
| COLUMBUS, O. | on 1876 S.L. quarter |
| S. W. Comings (six times on obv., twice on rev.) | on 1839 Large cent |
| J. CONANT | on 1824 Large cent |
| E. CONROY (both sides) | on early Large cent |
| H. M. CONVERSE | on 1863 Indian cent |
| WM H. COOPER. | on 1851 Large cent |
| D. C. CORNISH | on 1833 Large cent |
| J. W. CORTELYOU (relief, in rect. depression) | on 1821 Large cent |
| H. L. COUCH | on 1864 2-cent piece |

| | | | |
|---|---|---|---|
| A. F. CRAIN (twice) | on 1865 2-cent piece | A. H. ELWELL (twice on obv., twice on rev.) | on 1847 Large cent |
| H. CRIST | on 1876 S.L. half dollar | F. EMERSON | on 1857 Flying Eagle cent |

—D—

E M D     on 1883 Indian cent (rev.)

G. E. D.     on 1863 Indian cent

J M D     on Large cent (shaved obv.)

J. DAVIS / J. DAVIS (on obv.; once on rev.)     on 1856 S.L. quarter

JERRY / (star) / DAY     on 1859 Indian cent

P DEIB (relief, in rect. depression)     on 1828 Large cent

G. DELANO     **on Large cent (Duffield 1431)**

G. M. DEWEES (obv.); Script W . (rev.)     on 1835 (?) Large cent (the Script W . could be a Script E . if arranged vertically)

A. D. DODDS (both sides)     on 1837 Bust half dollar

J. P. DORE (both sides)     on 1865 3-cent piece

J. DOUGLASS     on 1847 Large cent

S. DOW     on 1859 Indian cent

DUNTON (obv.); T. S. F. (rev.)     on 1865 2-cent piece

C. C. DYER     on Large cents (dates worn off)(two specimens known)

E. E. DYER (both sides)     on 1826 Bust half dollar

—E—

E     on Spanish-American 1-real circa 1818

E _ B (relief, in rect. depression)     on 1833 Large cent

G. E. E.     on 1798 Bust silver dollar (Duffield 1611)

EAGLE HOTEL     on 1805 Bust dime (rev.)

E. D. EAMES     on Large cent (Hallenbeck 5.500)

A. G. EARLE     on 1849 dime

EEDS     on Spanish-American 1763-Mo-M Ferdinand VI Pillar 1-real (could be an initial missing letter, e.g. LEEDS, DEEDS, etc.)

ENNIST     on 1843 Half cent

C. W. EVERETT (both sides)     on 1845 Large cent

—F—

F     on 1870-CC S.L. silver dollar. (F under left wing of eagle)

F (serif-type, large)     on 1835 Bust dime

5. F (relief, in toothed rect. depression)(twice)     on 1825 Half cent

A F     on Spanish-American 1745-Mo-M 2-reales

E. E. FARRAR.     on 1838 Large cent

R. FAXON     on 1843-O dime

J. H. FERGUSON 33     on Large cent (Duffield 1431)

J. FISK     on 1846 Large cent

M. FLANAGAN (both sides)     on 1856 Large cent

C. FORSBERT     on 1854 S.L. quarter. (Attributed to Carl Forsberg, peanut wholesaler, Suffolk, Va.; not verified)

E. A. FOSS     on 1866/6 Indian cent

E. M. FOSS     on 1870 2-cent piece

FRENCH (four times, forming square; monogram at center)     on 1807 Large cent

. FOX     on 1846 Large cent

W. FUGE     on 1854 Large cent

FULTON.     on 1853 Large cent

C. B. FRENCH     on 1878 (7/8 tail feathers) Morgan silver dollar

S. FRY     on 1841 Large cent

—G—

C A G     on Canada Large cent (rev.)

E G G     on 1795 Bust silver dollar (Duffield 1610)

G / SHE (relief, in two rect. depressions)     on Large cent ca. 1801-03

| | |
|---|---|
| J G & | on 1885 Indian cent (rev.) |
| J. G. JR— | on Large cent ca. 1796 |
| R. S. G. (relief, in rect. depression) below (Small eagle, wings folded) (in oval depression) | on 1808 Large cent |
| W. M. G. | on 1865 Indian cent |
| WARRANTED W G | on Large cent |
| W M G | on 1828 Half cent |
| C. W. GARFIELD (both sides) | on 1842 Large cent |
| E. S. GIFFORD (twice) | on 1842 Large cent |
| J. F. GORDON | on 1834 Large cent (rev.) |
| W. G. GOURLE | on 1844 Large cent |
| H. GOULD | on 1858 Flying Eagle cent |
| M GOULDING | on 1848 Large cent |
| H. M. GREELY | on 1866 Shield nickel |
| GUTTER. | on 1847 Large cent |

—H—

| | |
|---|---|
| H | on 1858 Flying Eagle cent |
| C H | on Spanish-American 1794-LME-IJ 2-reales |
| (Two flowers) / (bunch of grapes) / C H | on Large cent (rev.) |
| C. W. H. | on 1848 Large cent |
| E H | on 1826 Half cent |
| G W H | on France 1824-W silver 5-francs |
| J. H. (very large) | on 1854 Large cent |
| J. L H (relief, in toothed rect. depression) | on Large cent |
| W. S. H. / B. S. M. / W. S. H. / B. S. M. / C. S. T. | on 1840 Large cent (shaved rev.) |
| G. HAGY (both sides) | on 1850 Large cent |
| R. HALL | on 1836 Large cent |
| G. F. HAMBLIN | on 1837 Large cent |
| J. HARP | on 1818 Large cent (rev.) |
| S. HARPER (circular) | on 1847 Large cent |
| C. HARRIS | on 1865 2-cent piece |
| P. J. HARTEL | on 1850 Large cent |
| J. HARVEY | on 1843 Large cent |
| J. W. HARVEY (both sides) | on 1858-O S.L. half dollar |
| J. W. HAWLEY | on 1807 Large cent (rev.) |
| W. H. HAYDEN | on 1860 Indian cent |
| J. HAYTON (three rimes on obv., twice on rev.) | on 1856 Large cent |
| W. C. HAZELTON / WCH. | on 1853 Large cent |
| H W HAZELTON / W.C.H. | on 1853 Large cent |
| HEATH | on 1877 half dollar |
| B. HERR | on 1832 Large cent |
| S. M. HINE | on 1839 Large cent |
| HOLME (relief, in toothed rect. depression) | on 1833 Large cent (this name is incomplete at both ends) |
| J. HOO (relief, in rect. depression) | on Bust type dime (the HOO could be HOB, HOR, HOD) |
| HOAGLAND | on 1876 S.L. quarter |
| J. HOLT (twice) | on 1798 Large cent |
| HONESTY (curved) / S. E. D. on obv.; (large incused cross) on rev. | on 1858 Flying Eagle cent |
| D. A. HOUSE (both sides) | on 1827 Large cent |
| J. K. HOUSEL (relief, within rect. depression) | on 1847 Large cent |
| E. L. HOWARD | on 1819 Large cent |
| J. HOWE JR. (both sides) | on 1858 Flying Eagle cent |
| SILAS HOWE (in arc) | on 1853 Large cent |
| T. HOWES (?) | on 1826 Large cent |
| W. H. HOYT | on 1838 Large cent |
| W. HUBBELL | on 1835 Large cent |
| P G HULL | on 1853 Arrows S.L. quarter |

| | |
|---|---|
| E. HUNT | on 1846 Large cent |
| H. S. HUNTINGTON | on 1853 Arrows & Rays S. L. quarter |
| HYDE | on 1828 Half cent |

—I—

| | |
|---|---|
| H. J. IVES (both sides) | on 1841 Large cent |

—J—

| | |
|---|---|
| J. A. J. B. (in oval frame, twice, all incused) | on 1805 Large cent |
| 04JAMES & CO. / 4 SUMMER ST. | on 1812 Large cent |
| R. A. JOHNS / R. A. JOHNSTON | on 1876 S.L. half dollar |
| C. JOHNSON | on 1840 Large cent |
| JONES | on 1863 Indian cent (Hallenbeck 10.751 ?) |

—K—

| | |
|---|---|
| K (relief, in oval depression) | on 1848 Large cent (Duffield 1598; Hallenbeck 11.000) |
| E. T. K. | on 1850 Large cent |
| G K / XXXX (obv.); (fourteen X's) on rev. | on 1848 Large cent |
| J K | on 1852 Large cent |
| L K | on 1853 Arrows half dime |
| P K | on 1851 Half cent (2 specimens examined) |
| H. KEELER | on 1807 :Large cent |
| J. P. KELLEY / R. A. B (obv.); KELLEY / R. A. B | on 1864 2-cent piece |
| T. G. KELLY (twice on obv., once on rev.) | on 1868 Shield nickel |
| G. L. KERN (twice on obv., once on rev.) | on 1851 (?) Large cent |
| J. W. KETT | on 1813 Large cent |
| W. KIDD | on 1847 Large cent |
| A. H. KING / C. F. WILLIAMS / A. H. KING (on obv.); C. F. WILLIAMS (twice, on rev.) | on 1839 Large cent |
| I. KINSEY (Both sides) | on 1794 Large cent (Hallenbeck 11.513 ?) |
| F L KIRK | on Shield nickel (rev.) |
| H. KLUGH (twice) | on 1837 Liberty/Not One Cent HTT, Low 33 |

—L—

| | |
|---|---|
| L & K | on 1864 2-cent piece |
| C. P. L. | on 1837 Hard Times token |
| T. L | on Large cent |
| W. S. LACEY | on 1840 Large cent |
| C. LANE (rev.); J C (obv.) | on 1809 Large cent |
| G. LATHAM | on 1853 Large cent |
| J. LEACH (both sides) | on 1838 Large cent |
| LEX. KY. | on Spanish-American 1813-So-FI 2-reales |
| I. LITTLE | on 1818 Large cent |
| C. R. LIVCY | on 1859 Seated Liberty quarter |
| G. S. LOCKE | on 1837 Large cent (rev.) |
| J. T. LOCKE | on Half cent (rev.) |
| S. LOGAN (both sides) | on 1840 (?) Large cent |
| R. R. LOOMIS | on 1832 Large cent |
| C. N. LORD | on 1848 Large cent |
| C. P. LORD | on 1851 Large cent |
| H. D. LORD | on 1845 S.L. dime |
| J. LOSEE | on 1887 Indian cent |
| S. LOVEJOY | on Large cent (Duffield 1431) |
| S. H. LOVEJOY | on Large cent (Duffield 1431) |
| W. A. LOWE. | on 1864 2-cent piece |
| J. W. LUNT (obv.); J. W. LUNT / A (rev.) | on 1839 Large cent |

## —M—

**M & D** on 1857 Half cent (Hallenbeck 13.002 ?)

**A N M** (relief, in rect. depression) on 1832 Large cent

**J. H. M'C** (relief, in depression) on Spanish-American 1734-Mo 2-reales

**T • M** on Large cent (Duffield 1451; Hallenbeck 20.250)

**B. W. MACKAY** on 1867 Shield nickel

**A. MACY** (both sides) on (1834) Schenk-Richards HT token, Low 164

**B. MAGINN** on 1863 Indian cent

**J. MANN** on 1820 Large cent

**D. MARC** (in open rect. cartouche) on 1843 dime

**D. W. MARTYN** (both sides) on 1851 Large cent

**G. MAYER** (relief, in rect. depression) on 181. Large cent

**D. McCANN.** on 1846 Large cent

**J. M. R. / C. McFARLIN / J. M. R.** on 1853 Large cent

**T. McAVITY / 9 WATER STREET** on England 1816 shilling

**J Mc HARG** on 1819 Large cent

**McIL WHAM** on early Large cent

**J. B. McLEAN** on 1855-O half dollar

**W. MEAD** (obv.); **J T** (rev.) on 1841 'Millions for Defence' HTT

**J. O. MEGQUIER** on Large cent (Duffield 1431)

**MELCRISTIE.** on 1855-O Seated Liberty half dollar

**MESSEN** on Flowing Hair Large cent

**F. MILLER** on 1864 Indian cent

**W. L. W. / I. B. MOLER** (rev.); **W. L. W.** (obv.) on 1876 S.L. quarter

**MOORE** on Liberty Seated quarter

**M. MOORE** on Ireland 1783 halfpenny

**P. MOREY** (both sides) on 1840 Large cent

**W MOWENS** on 1865 Indian cent

**D. MUNSON** on half dime (Duffield 1414)

## —N—

**J. F. NASON** on 1847 Large cent

**NEW YORK** on 1831 Bust dime

**do** on 1856 Large cent

**• NICHOLS** on 1863 Indian cent (shaved rev.)

**C. H. NILES** on 1837 Henry Anderson HTT, Low 107 (rev.)

**NORFOLK** on 1847 Large cent (Hallenbeck 14.754)

**JOHN / Q. (star) Z / NORRIS** (obv.); **(Three interlocking rings)** (rev.) on 1867 Shield nickel

**NORTH** on Large cent

## —O—

**A. C. OAKES** (twice) on 1834 Large cent

**B. O'NEILL** on (1833) Jackson-Donkey HTT, Low 51

**C. ORTH** on 1851 Large cent (Hallenbeck 15.750; Brunk 280)

**G. H. OSBORN** on 1845 Large cent (rev.)

**I. P. OSGOOD.** (many times, on both sides) on 1818 (?) Large cent

**THE OTTAWA** on 1889 Indian cent

**OXFORD MASS.** (obv.); **6 6 6 / OXFORD MASS** (rev.) on England Victoria Young Head halfpenny

## —P—

**P2 monogram** (rev.); **1865** (obv.) on 2-cent piece

**C. P** (relief, in toothed rect. depression) on 1827 Large cent (Hallenbeck 3.256)

| | |
|---|---|
| **O. D. PAGE** (both sides) | on 1847 Large cent |
| **S. P. PAINE** | on Large cent |
| **PALACE / G. RINGRAM / 6** (obv.); **G. RINGRAM / J. W. FLETCHER / 6 / M** (rev.) | on 1857 F.E. cent |
| **E. PARC** (relief, in rect. depression, twice, on obv.); once on rev. | on early Large cent |
| **J. PARK** | on 1854 Arrows S.L. half dime |
| **D. S. PARKER** | on 1857 F.E. cent |
| **(?) . PARKS** | on Spanish-American 1777-Mo-FM 2-reales |
| **C. S. PARNELL** (both sides) | on 1850 Large cent |
| **ORREN PEAVEY** | on Large cent (Duffield 1431) |
| **J. H. PERKINS** | on 1853 Large cent |
| **A. J. PETERSON** | on 1825 Large cent |
| **J. M. PIERCE** (both sides) | on 2-cent piece |
| **JOS. PIPPIN** | on 1869 2-cent piece |
| **H. A. PLUMB / W. R. F.** | on 1834 Large cent |
| **G. E. POND** | on 1862 Indian cent |
| **F. POOL** | on 1864 2-cent piece |
| **H. M. POOL** (obv.); **(Eagle)** (rev.) | on 1838 Large cent |
| **S. PRATT** | on 1853 A&R Seated Liberty quarter |
| **N. PRESTON** | on 1848 Large cent (rev.) |
| **A. PRICE** | on Shield nickel |

—R—

| | |
|---|---|
| **F.L.R. monogram** | on 1845 Seated Liberty quarter (Duffield 1433) |
| **G. W. R** | on Merchants Exchange HT token (holed, with W P scratched on rev.) |
| **J. RAMBO** | on 1831 Large cent |
| **B. RANGER** (obv.); **B. R.** (rev.) | on 1832 Large cent |
| **J. D. RAWSON** | on U.S. Colonial halfpenny |
| **READING, PA.** | on 1857 Flying Eagle cent |
| **W. REED** (relief, in toothed rect. depression) | on early Large cent |
| **W. A. RICE** | on 1848 Large cent |
| **F. RICHARDS** | on 1852 Large cent |
| **B. RIDLEY** | on 1868 2-cent piece |
| **C. D. RIKER** (both sides) | on 1856 Large cent |
| **G. RILEY** | on 1854 Large cent |
| **M. RINES** | on 1865 Indian cent |
| **PALACE / G. RINGRAM / 6** (obv.); **G. RINGRAM / J. W. FLETCHER / 6 / M** (rev.) | on 1857 F.E. cent |
| **ROOM / 11** | on 1863 Indian cent |
| **RUDOLPH** | on 1853 Arrows & Rays S.L. quarter |
| **J. RUST** | on 1858 Flying Eagle cent |

—S—

| | |
|---|---|
| **16 / S & L** (relief, in two rect. depressions, on rev.); **16** (relief, over last two digits of date, on obv.) | on late Large cent |
| **S & M** (three times, obv.); **S & M** (twice, rev.) | on 18(2)5 Large cent |
| **J. V. S.** | on Spanish-American 1782-Mo 2-reales |
| **P. A. S.** | on 1841 Large cent |
| **T. S. (backward) B** (relief, in toothed rect. depression) | on Large cent |
| **C. SCHMIDT** (both sides) | on 1853 Half cent |
| **F. E. SCOTT** | on 1864 2-cent piece |
| **S. F. SEAMANN** | on 1853 Large cent |
| **S. H. SEEBER** | on 1855 Large cent |
| **M. E. T. SHANNON** (script) | on 1875-S S.L. half dollar |

| | | | |
|---|---|---|---|
| **A. SHARRARD** | on 1832 Bust half dollar (Duffield 1420) | **J. T** | on 1823 Large cent |
| **C. H. SHAW** | on 1802 Large cent | **V T** | on early Large cent |
| **N. F. SHUNK** | on 1827 Bust half dollar | **TAKE A TUMBLE / MAY / 27** | on 1801 Large cent |
| **L. E. S. / SLATE.** (relief, in two rect. depressions) | on Large cent ca. 1803 | **W. M. THOMPSON** | on 1831 Large cent (rev.) |
| **W. SLEIGHT** | on 32mm worn-smooth silver coin | **S. J. TIDD** | on 1850 Large cent |
| **H. SMALLEY** | on 1877-S S.L. half dollar | **TROY, N.Y.** | on 1825 Large cent |
| **M. B. SMILEY** (both sides) | on 1822 Large cent | **J. TWIGS / 1865** (rev.); **MUTCH / MONEY** (obv.) | on 1822 Large cent |
| **C. H. SMITH** | on 1853 Arrows S.L. dime | **TWICHEL & CURTIS** (Two Suns) | on 1831 Large cent |
| **C. W. SMITH** | on Large cent (rev.) | **D. M. TYLER** | on 1856 Large cent |
| **I. D. SMITH** (twice on obv., once on rev.) | on early Large cent | **T. TYNAN** | on Large cent |

—U—

**UPPER VILLAGE / COLUMBIA / —OLD GOLD**    on Large cent (Hallenbeck 21.751)

**UPPER VILLAGE COLUMBIA / OLD / GOLD / GOLD**    on 1800 Large cent

—V—

| | |
|---|---|
| **J. A. SMITH / S. F. E.** | on 1831 Large cent |
| **W. D. SMITH** | on 1854 Large cent |
| **H. A. SPEAR** (obv.); **1866 / 8 17** (rev.) | on 1841 Large cent |
| **J. P. STADL** | on 1857 Flying Eagle cent |
| **STANTON** (relief, in rect. depression) | on 1817 Large cent |
| **C. STEVI** | on 1817 Large cent (rev.) |
| **G J. STIVERS** | on 1876 S.L. quarter |
| **H. A. STONE** | on 1859 Indian cent |
| **F. STORRS** (relief, in rect. depression) | on 1819 Large cent |
| **M. SUTTON** | on 1841 'Mint Drop' HTT, Low 68 |
| **C. SWEARER** (in arc) | on Large cent, ca. 1840's |

| | |
|---|---|
| **H. VANGORDER** | on 1846 Large cent |
| **F. E. VOIGT** | on Large cent ca. 1820 |

—W—

| | |
|---|---|
| **W** (relief, in rect. depression) | on 1842 dime |
| **Large W** (relief, in 5-pointed star depression), four hands with forefingers pointing around the star, (all incuse) | on 1860 Indian cent |
| **W.** | on 1860 gold dollar (Duffield 1447) |
| —do— | on $2½ gold piece (Duffield 1448) |
| —do— | on 1858 $3 gold piece (Duffield 1449) |
| —do— | on 1861 $5 gold piece (Duffield 1450) |

—T—

| | |
|---|---|
| **T / Eagle on globe** | on 1831 Large cent (rev.) |
| **C. T** (relief, in toothed rect. depression) | on 1805 Half cent (Hallenbeck 3.254 ?) |
| **G. H. T.** | on 1837 Henry Anderson HTT, Low 107 |

| | | | |
|---|---|---|---|
| **W & S** | on 1843 Large cent | **W. E. WHITE** | on Large cent (shaved obv.) |
| **C. E. W. / JUNE 5TH** (amid scrolls) | on 1873 S.L. half dollar | **G. WHITNEY** (both sides) | on 1819 Bust half dollar |
| **G. W** | on 1835 Half cent | **J. T. WILL** | on 1851 Large cent |
| **J W** | on 1818 Bust quarter | **F. H. WILSON** (obv.); **C. W. PATTEN** (rev.) | on 1851 Large cent |
| **J W** (both sides) | on 1832 Large cent | **WINDSOR** | on 1866 2-cent piece |
| **J. W. W.** (large) | on 1851 Large cent | **J. WINNER** | on 1817 Large cent |
| **P : W** (relief, in toothed depression) | on England 1776 halfpenny | **B. F. WISE** | on 1828 Large cent |
| **WAGNER** on Bust quarters (examined: 1814, 1818) (Duffield 1428) | | **WITHERELL / 1858** | on Large cent (shaved obv.) |
| **J. WALL** (obv.); **J. WALL** (large, rev.) | on 1840 Large cent | **G. B. WOODWARD** | on 1872 Shield nickel |
| **D. WALLWORK** | on 1870 2-cent piece | **W. L. WRIGHT** | 1852 Large cent |

—Y—

| | |
|---|---|
| **WARD** (large) on Spanish-American 1799-Mo silver 8-reales | |
| **J. P. WARE** on 1856 Large cent | **C. H. YEATON** on 1846 Large cent |
| **WARREN** (obv.); **J. WARREN** (rev.) on 1858 F.E. cent | **C. YENTES** on 1843 Large cent |
| **J. M. WATSON** (both sides) on 1852 Large cent | **I. W. YORK** on 1833 Large cent |
| **T. WEEKS** on 1824 Large cent(rev.) | **D. S. YOUNG** on 1837 Large cent |
| **H. WETTSTEIN** (both sides) on 1876 S.L. quarter | |
| **J. S. WHEELER** on 1855 Seated Liberty quarter | —Z— |
| **L. S. WHITE / open-base 8** on 1851 Large cent | **J. ZAHN** on 1873 Indian cent |

## —NUMERALS, OBJECTS—

**1 : 4**                                          on 1840 Large cent

**3** (obv.); **D** (rev.)                         on 1848 Large cent

**3** (very large)                                 on 1859 Indian cent (rev.)

**5** (both sides)                                 on 1834 Half cent

**7**                                              on 1824 Large cent

**8** (both sides)                                 on 1793 Half cent (Duffield 1460)

**9.6** (both sides)                               on 179. Large cent

**16 within divided shield**                       on 1826 Bust half dollar

**27**                                             on 1838 Large cent

**50**    on 1821 Large cent (Duffield 1590; Hallenbeck 27.007)

**1791**                                           on Large cent (Hallenbeck 27.012)

**1837**                                           on 1819/8 Large cent

**1865** (large, obv.); **P2 monogram** (rev.)     on 2-cent piece

**1876**                                           on 1876-CC Seated Liberty dime

**(Crowned, pillared Spain arms)**                 on 1802 Large cent

**(Bee) inside (Heart)**                           on 1847 Large cent

**(Standing dog)**                                 on 1843 Large cent (Duffield 1596)

**(Very early locomotive)**                        on 1839 Bust half dollar

**(Male head)** (rev., twice); once on obv.        on 1817 Large cent
                                                          (Duffield 1588)

**(Rooster)**     on 1877 Seated Liberty quarter (Duffield 1454)

**(Scepter)**          on S. Richardson N.Y.C. token, Miller 56

**Large 5-pointed star depression**     on 1857 Flying Eagle cent

**Large W** (relief, in 5-pointed star depression); four hands with forefingers pointing around the star (all incuse)     on 1860 Indian cent

**(Swan)** (relief, bold)  on Large cent (Duffield 1459; Hallenbeck 28.006)

## MORE MISCELLANEOUS COUNTERSTAMPS

**C. A** (both sides) on 1804 Half cent

**D P A / •** on 1838 Large cent

**N A** (relief, in depression; twice) on early Large cent

**N A** on 1819 Large cent (different from last)

**G B** (incuse) at center of **Toothed Diamond** (relief) on 1826 Half cent

**J B** on 1845 Large cent

**J. B. B. / & / T. D.** on 1827 Large cent

**J N B** (relief, in rect. depression; twice) on 1803 Large cent

**M. G. B.** (relief, in toothed rect. depression) on 1832 Large cent

**S B (Rosette)** on 1817 Large cent (Rosette in relief)

**N. G. BASSETT** (relief, in rect. depression) on Spanish-American 1807-Mo-TH silver 8-reales

**D S. BOOTHBY** on 1875-S S.L. 20-cent piece

**J. A. BOYER** on 1854 Large cent

**S. B. BRUSH** on 1854 S.L. half dollar

**C & B** on 1864 2-cent piece

**CH.IRA.** (relief, in rect. depression) on 1802 Large cent (could be CH.PRA.)

**A. C** on 1848 Large cent

**A G C** (incuse) / **(Vagina)** (die-struck) on 1863-S S.L. half dollar

**B. M. C** on 1828 Half cent

**C A C** on 1846 Large cent

**C. C** on 1835 Large cent

**C C** on 1816 Large cent

**J. C.** (three times on obv., once on rev.) on 1826 Large cent

**J. C.** (relief, in toothed rectangular depression) on 1821 Large cent

**S. C** (relief, in toothed rect. depression) on 1817 Large cent

**W C** (relief, in toothed rect. depression) on Large cent**V C / B C** on 1884 Indian cent (rev.)

**E. CAIN** on 1828 Half cent

**CALDWELL & SON** on 1860 Indian cent

**E. CARR** on 1816 (?) Large cent

**CHELAND** on 1847 Large cent

**CAST-STEE(L) / S. R. CLAPP.** (obv.); **E. ROBBINS** (rev.) on 1827 Large cent

**W. E. Colman.** on 1851 Large cent

**COMSTOCK** on 1866 3-cent nickel piece

**CONAN** (relief, in toothed rect. depression) on 1817 Large cent

**W. CORTON** on 1817 Large cent

**D. & (?)** on 1847 Large cent

**D x C** (relief, in toothed rect. depression) on 1819 Large cent

**A. D** on 1831 Large cent

**F A D** (D upside down) on 1847 Large cent

| | |
|---|---|
| **M. D.** | on 1840 Large cent |
| **W. J. D.** | on 1838 Large cent |
| **L. DUDLEY / CAST STEEL** | on 183. Large cent |
| **J . E** (relief, in rect. depression)(both sides) | on 1838 Large cent |
| —do— (once) | on 1822 Large cent (same punch as last) |
| **J E** (rev.); **H L B** (obv.) | on Large cent, date worn off |
| **J. M. E** (relief, in rect. depression) | on 1825 (?) Large cent |
| **N. E** | on 1821 Large cent |
| **S. E.** | on 1819 Large cent |
| **E B R H / •** | on 18.. Large cent |
| **F /** (3-pointed Rosette) | on 1881 Indian cent |
| **G. F.** | on 1855 Half cent |
| **F. GIES** (both sides) | on Civil War token, Fuld 225 AF-6a, of F. Gies |
| **S. GILKE** | on Large cent, date worn off |
| **G. E. GILMAN** | on 1853 Large cent |
| **J. GILMORE** (twice) | on 1802 Large cent |
| **D M G** | on 1835 Half cent |
| **E H G** | on Large cent, date worn off |
| **B G H** | on 1837 Hard Times token |
| **F F H** (obv.); **1876** (rev.) | on Large cent, date illegible |
| **J H •** (obv.); **•** (rev.) | on 1853 A&R half dollar (large stars) |

| | |
|---|---|
| **J. H. H.** (relief, in rect. depression) | on 1819 Large cent |
| **J. M H** | on 1826 Large cent |
| **S H** | on 1806 Half cent |
| **S. H.** | on 1856 Large cent |
| **Z P H** (both sides) | on 1816 Large cent |
| **A. HENSHAW** (relief, within rect. depression) across center. Above: **O. BENNETT** (incuse). Below: **LYONS**. | on Spanish-American 1789-Mo-FM 2-reales. (This could be U.S. or French) |
| **HORAN** | on 1817 Large cent |
| **H. I** | on 1850 Large cent |
| **J JF** (ligate) **R I** | on 1817 Large cent |
| **I O O F** (Flags)(Three rings) **F L T** (rev.); **(Tent with Guards at each side)(Three rings) F H C** (obv.) | on 1880 Indian cent (Independent Order of Odd Fellows) |
| **IN GOD WE TRUST** (curved) | on 1860-O S.L. silver dollar, reverse. (The motto occupies the same place it occupied later as part of the struck design) |
| **D. H K / 18** | on 1816 Large cent (the '18' could be '81') |
| **S. B. K** | on 1840 Large cent |
| **C. KERR** | on 1828 Large cent |
| **L.** (three times) | on 1831 Large cent |
| **C. P. L.** (twice on obv.; twice on rev.) | on 1847 Large cent |
| **I. W. L. L.** | on 1840 Large cent |
| **S. T. L.** | on 1850 Large cent |

| | |
|---|---|
| T. L. (twice) / 4 | on 1839 Large cent |
| J. LYNN / J. J. YOUNG (obv.); J. J. YOUNG / J. LYNN (rev.) | on 1866-Rays Shield nickel |
| M | on 1828 Half cent |
| M | on 1834 Large cent |
| M (Heart) G (twice) | on 1822 Large cent |
| M. B. Co (both sides) | on 1848 Large cent |
| I / AHM / I | on 1812 Large cent |
| E. P. M. | on 1847 Large cent (Hallenbeck 5.004) |
| J. H. M. | on 1840 Large cent |
| M C. M | on 1835 Large cent |
| M. O. M (both sides) | on 1838 Large cent |
| T • M (relief, in toothed rect. depression) | on 1831 Large cent |
| Mc N T | on 1848 Large cent |
| A. McLENNA (?) | on 1853 Large cent |
| (?) . MILLER | on 1803 Large cent |
| Wm H. MILLER | on 1835 Large cent (letters differ from last) |
| W. S. MILLER (both sides) | on 1866-Rays Shield nickel |
| J R H (in toothed depression) / S L MITCHELL (incuse) / J R H (in toothed depression) | on 1845 Large cent |
| S R M / 39 | on 1831 Large cent |
| Z M (relief, in toothed rect. depression) | on 1803 Large cent |
| W. MOFFATT | on 1843 Large cent |
| H T MOODY | on 1826 Large cent |
| R. E. MOOR | on 1854 Large cent |
| G. A. MORSE | on 1846 Large cent |
| J. MUIR | on 1887 Seated Liberty dime |
| G. A. MUNN | on 1837 Large cent (Hallenbeck 13.756) |
| PETER A. MURDOCH (Two stars) around edge, W W at center | on shaved reverse of 1854-Arrows dime |
| U S N | on 1886-O Morgan silver dollar |
| E. G. NEWM(A)N | on 1848 Large cent (A does not show) |
| E. NUGENT (both sides) | on 1867 2-cent piece |
| O (Cross) K | on 1833 Large cent |
| B. K. O | on 1840 Large cent |
| C. G. ORTH. | on 1853 Large cent (Hallenbeck 15.751) |
| E W P | on 1851 Half cent |
| J. V. P. (in arc) / (Masonic G-square-compass) | on Spanish-American 1783-Mo-FF 1-real |
| W. C. P | on 1803 Large cent |
| G. H. PAUL | on 1852 Large cent |
| E. PERKIN(S) | on 1845 Large cent (see *USMT 1845-1860*, pg 42) |
| S. F. PHELPS | on brass counterfeit of 1827 Large cent |
| PHILAD. | on 1820 Large cent |
| PHILADA | on 1838 (?) Large cent |
| J. H. PIERCE | on 1850 Large cent |
| W. PLACE | on 1838 Large cent |

| | | | |
|---|---|---|---|
| **S. PRESCOT** (twice) | on 1847 Large cent | **T S (Anchor or Plow)** | on 1828 Half cent (the device resembles a card-suit spade atop a rocker) |
| **R** | on 1853 Arrows & Rays S.L. half dollar | | |
| **F R** | on 1820 Large cent | **J. M. SABIN / A B** | on O-mintmarked half dollar, date illegible |
| **I. R R** | on 1817 Large cent | **J. SHORT** (in arc) | on 1851 Large cent |
| **N R** | on 1859-O Seated Liberty half dollar | **SKINI** (relief, in rect. depression) | on Large cent (S is retrograde) |
| **RR** (twice) | on 1841 Large cent (second R weak) | | |
| **S R** | on 1883-CENTS Liberty Head nickel | **L• SLACK** | on 1822 Large cent |
| **W. R.** (relief, in toothed rect. depression) | on 1844 Large cent | **JAS. . SOLT** | on 1820 Large cent |
| **R — S** | on 1844 Large cent | **STEEL / CAST** (both sides) | on 1819 Large cent |
| **W D. RAPP** (relief, in rect. depression) | on 1829 Large cent | **C. R. STICKNEY** | on 1853 Large cent |
| **S. RICE** | on 1888 Indian cent | **J. H. STIGERS** (relief, in rect. depression) | on 1826 Large cent |
| **J. RICH** | on 1855 S.L. quarter | **STROHECKER** (both sides) | on 1796 small date-large letters silver dollar |
| **RICHARDSON** | on 1829 Large cent | | |
| **S. ROGERS** | on 1832 Large cent | **N. SULWIN** (both sides) | on Large cent, date worn off |
| **J. ROHRE(R)** | on 1807 Large cent | **T** | on 1826 Large cent |
| **C. RUGG** | on 1818 Large cent | **Mc N T** | on 1848 Large cent |
| **S** (twice on obv.; once on rev.) | on 1855 Large cent | **P. H. T.** | on 1812 Large cent |
| **A O S** | on 1839 Large cent | **W. H. T.** (twice) | on 1798 Large cent |
| **J. S** | on Large cent, date worn off | **J. TEAL** | on 1829 Large cent |
| **L S** | on 1827 Large cent | **TEELBAC** | on 1853 Large cent |
| **S. S** (twice) | on Large cent | **UN-EXCELLED TRITONS** (circular) | on Seated Liberty dime (shaved obv.) |
| **T. B. S** | on 1856 Large cent | **F. A. VACHE** | on 1817 Large cent (Hallenbeck 22.500) |

| | | | |
|---|---|---|---|
| **VIENNA** (both sides) | on 1817 Large cent | **Mn WILSON** (both sides) | on 1845 Large cent |
| **F. E. VOIGD.** | on 1843 Large cent | **L. A. WINN** | on 1850 Large cent |
| —do— | on 1855 Large cent (from same die as last) | **E. WOOD** | on 1802 (?) Large cent |
| **G. H. W.** | on 1858 Flying Eagle cent | **E. K. T. Z.** | on Large cent, date worn off |
| **G. W. W.** | on 1826 Large cent | **1 3 L 7** (7 upside down) | on 1868 nickel 3-cent piece |
| **I . W / (Square-and-compass)** on Large cent of 1830's or 1840's | | **1801** | on 1818 Large cent |
| **W. D. W** | on 1832 Bust half dollar | **(X-in-circle)** | on 1816 Large cent (X in relief, circle incused) |
| **WARRANTED** (relief, in rect. depression) | on Large cent, date worn off | **(Eagle in oval)** | on 1831 Large cent (Eagle in relief, oval incused) |
| **WARRANTED** | on 1823 Large cent (different style than last) | **(8-pointed Star)** | on 1840 Large cent |
| **(?) WEBB** (relief, in toothed rect. depression) | on 1802 Large cent | **(Cross Patee within dentilated circle) and (7-Pointed Star)** | on 1829 Half cent |
| **P. WEBB** | on 1833 Large cent | **(8-spoked Wheel)** | on 1855-S S.L. half dollar |
| **WEIKER / U. S S** (obv.); **U. S. S** (rev.) on Large cent, date worn off. There never was a ship in the U.S. Navy or Coast Guard named USS Weiker, according to *Encyclopedia of U.S. Fighting Ships* (10 volumes). | | **(5-petal Flower)** | on 1877 S. L. dime |
| | | **(Ornate Anchor)** | on 1889 Liberty nickel |
| **E. WELLER** | on 1853 Large cent | **(Dog leaping right)** (relief) | on 1860 Indian cent |
| **H. WEST** (both sides) | on 1838 Large cent | **(Rosette)** | on 1841 Large cent |
| **S. WHITE** (twice) | on 1833 Large cent | **(Dagger)** (?) | on 1794 Large cent |
| **R. WIER** | on 1837 Large cent | **(Two large S's facing, two diamonds in pale between, wings above)** on 1851 Large cent (second S retrograde; all designs are outlines only) | |
| **H. T. WILCOX** | on 1844 Large cent | | |
| **WM W. WILCOX** | on 1853 Large cent | **(Crude Crown)** | on 1837 Large cent |

# Miscellaneous Love Tokens

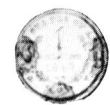

During the 1870's and 1880's, it became almost common practice to shave smooth the reverse of a U.S. silver dime or quarter (or other coin) and to engrave thereon some endearment, memorial or memento of a personal nature. Often this took the form of ornate initials or monograms, sometimes a full or partial name or nickname, occasionally a pictorial device, and, seldom, a rather complete message. The term "love token" was applied to this series of engraved pieces because of the practice of swains to honor their lady loves with such favors.

Love tokens had been used in this country from the inceptions of a national coinage, as several early 1790's specimens attest, but it became a fad of some proportion after the Civil War, and county and state fairs were places the public could encounter skilled calligraphers willing to engrave any message or initials or device on a coin — for a fee.

It is not possible to catalog such items, each of which is unique, although a very few such pieces are included within the body of this reference because of their unusual appeal or interest — mostly to show collectors what is available. Appended below is a very small sampling of some additional specimens which it would be near impossible to trace to their origins. Silver dime love tokens usually sell for $4 to $7 each (unless the device is unusual), while silver quarters command prices of $5 to $8. Generally, other coins made into love tokens are less common than the dimes and quarters. No coins seem to have escaped such treatment — gold coins of $1, $2½, $3 and $5 are seen occasionally, as well as silver dollars, Trade dollars, half dollars, Large cents and Small cents, and even the tiny silver 3-cent and half dime coins.

**Script PA within 6-point star** on U.S. 1849-O gold dollar

**Script WHA** on U.S. 1897 Barber dime

**Script AMANDA** on U.S. 1856 S.L. half dime

**Script AUNT** on U.S. 1875 dime

**Ornate BRAKEMAN** on U.S. 1853 Arrows and Rays S.L. half dollar

**Horn / BROTHER** on U.S. 1891 S.L. dime

**Script CARL** in band on U.S. 1892 Barber dime

**Script E** on U.S. 1881 Indian cent

**Script T. E. / Lighthouse and Ship at sea** on U.S. 1891 S.L. dime

**FIRST CONG. S. S. / FIRST PRIZE / REGATTA** (obv.); **WON BY / WILLIAM E. HOLMES / JULY 11. 1883** (rev.) on U.S. half dollar which has been shaved smooth on both sides and a loop attached

**Gothic G and fret border** on U.S. 1856 dime

**Gold-panning Pan / M. A. G.** on U.S. 1876 S.L. dime

**Lighthouse and Ship at sea / GEORGE** on U.S. 1891 dime (diff. scene than the T.E. piece above)

**T. H. '60 / J. L. B.** on dime-sized gold-plated base metal disc

**Monogram HHJ and ornate border** on U.S. 'CC' quarter

**Monogram MDM** on U.S. 1883 dime

**Script MAMA** on U.S. 1883 dime

**Script MAUD and Petals** on Canada 1858-1901 Young Head dime

**Script MODER and Flower** on U.S. 1834 half dime

**Script PAPA** on U.S. 1884 dime

**W. W. REVEL** on ribbon / **Gothic FBC NO. 11** on U.S. pre-1866 S.L. quarter

**Monogram IS** on U.S. 1861 dime

**Sailing Ship J.M.T.** on U.S. 1892 Barber dime

**Bird on Branch / THOMAS** on U.S. 1891 S.L. dime

**Triquetra** on British silver threepence circa 1890's (poss. Isle of Man)

## A LIBRARY INTERIOR OF THE EIGHTIES

Shown here are three views of a large library building of the 1880's (?), captured by a photographer using the old glass-plate negatives in which an emulsion coating on one side retains the light image. Three of these 10 by 8-inch glass negatives were acquired by the author in a Portsmouth, Ohio antique shop in 1981 and from the negatives glossy prints were obtained with some difficulty. Their quality is uneven — one had insufficient light penetration and appears cloudy, but the other two are excellent — showing human expressions 100 years ago very much like those of today.

These are printed here, very likely for the first time ever, to illustrate dress style and interior architecture of the period covered by the tokens in this book. The locale of the library has not been determined, but the building is very large and must have been located in a major city. Perhaps it still stands today and will be recognized?

*Interior of the reading room, from a balcony angle.*

*Ladies and gentlemen waiting to enter. Ladies first!*

*The foyer leading to the reading room. To orient your viewpoint, note the white marble bust on pedestal at the top of the stairs. Then locate this same bust at center of the reading room view. (There is a leisurely emptiness in these library views which seems strange in 1983!)*

# CANADA

## BLACKHURST & CO.
### Canada

| Rulau | Date | Metal | Size | VG | F | VF | EF |
|---|---|---|---|---|---|---|---|
| C 4 | (?) | Silver | 18mm | — | — | — | — |

BLACKHURST & CO. in tiny letters ctsp on obverse of Canada Queen Victoria young head dime, issued 1858-1901. Rv: FLORIE in ornate letters, within branches, engraved on planed-off reverse of the coin.

NOTE: The obverse has been mounted. This is a combination store card and engraved love token!

## J. B. BROWN
### Newfoundland

| Rulau | Date | Metal | Size | VG | F | VF | EF |
|---|---|---|---|---|---|---|---|
| C 8 | (?) | Silver | 33mm | — | — 75.00 | — | — |

J. B. Brown ctsp on Newfoundland 1881 50-cent piece. (Krause collection)

Unless evidence establishes otherwise, it is assumed this counterstamp was intended for Newfoundland, as "Newfie" coins of the 19th century circulated very little outside the island.

## BLACKS CHOCOLATE
### Canada ?

| Rulau | Date | Metal | Size | VG | F | VF | Unc |
|---|---|---|---|---|---|---|---|
| C 3 | (?) | Copper | 25mm | — | — | — | — |

USE / BLACKS / CHOCOLATE ctsp on Canada Large cents. (Dates examined: 1858, 1876-H). (Larry Laevens and Gregory Brunk colls.)

## T. S. DAVIES
### Canada

| Rulau | Date | Metal | Size | VG | F | VF | Unc |
|---|---|---|---|---|---|---|---|
| C 11 | (?) | Copper | 29mm | — 30.00 | — | 45.00 | |

(Fish) / T. S. DAVIES ctsp on Canada 1814 Halifax token of Hosterman and Etter, Breton 882. (Nadin-Davis March 26, 1983 sale)

## DEVINS & BOLTON
### Montreal, Canada

| Rulau | Date | Metal | Size | VG | F | VF | EF |
|---|---|---|---|---|---|---|---|
| C 16 | (1865-70) | Copper | 29mm | 10.00 | — | 22.00 | — |

DEVINS / & / BOLTON / — / MONTREAL ctsp on U.S. Large cents of various dates. (Dates examined: 1796, 1798, 1802, 1813, 1816, 1817, 1818, 1819, 1820, 1821, 1822, 1823, 1824, 1824/2, 1825, 1826, 1827, 1828, 1829, 1830, 1831, 1832, 1833, 1834, 1835, 1836, 1837, 1838, 1839, 1840, 1841, 1842, 1843, 1844, 1844/81, 1845, 1848, 1849, 1850, 1851, 1851/81, 1852, 1853, 1854, 1855, 1856). (Duffield 1398; Brunk 125)

| C 17 | (1865-70) | Copper | 28-30mm | 60.00 | — | 100. | — |

Similar ctsp on U.S. Colonial cents. (Examined: Vermont, Connecticut, Massachusetts)

| C 18 | (1867) | Copper | 29mm | — | — | — | — |

Similar ctsp, but applied upside down, on U.S. Large cents.

| C 20 | (1867) | Copper | 34mm | 10.00 | — | 22.00 | — |

Similar ctsp on Canada 1837 City Bank penny token, Breton 521.

| C 22 | (1867) | Copper | 34mm | 8.00 | — | 20.00 | — |

Similar ctsp on Canada 1837 Quebec Bank penny token.

| C 24 | (1867) | Copper | --mm | — | — | — | — |

Similar ctsp on Deanston Cotton Mill token.

| C 26 | (1867) | Brass | 28mm | 8.00 | — | 20.00 | — |

Similar ctsp on Canada 1812 halfpenny token, Breton 961.

| C 28 | (1867) | Copper | 28mm | 7.00 | — | 18.00 | — |

Similar ctsp on Canada 1837 Quebec Bank halfpenny token.

| C 29 | (1867) | Copper | 28mm | 8.00 | — | 20.00 | — |

Similar ctsp on Canada 1844 Bank of Montreal halfpenny token.

| C 30 | (1867) | Copper | 28mm | 8.00 | — | 20.00 | — |

Similar ctsp on Canada 1852 Quebec sou token.

| C 32 | (1867) | Copper | 28mm | 8.00 | — | 20.00 | — |

Similar ctsp on Canada (1835-38) Montreal sou token.

| C 36 | (1867) | Copper | 28.5mm | 12.00 | 20.00 | 30.00 | 37.00 |

Similar ctsp on U.S. Hard Times tokens of several types. (Examined: Low 10, 33, 47, 51, 58, 59). (Duffield 1254)

| C 37 | (1867) | Copper | 25mm | — | — | 30.00 | — |

Similar ctsp on U.S. 1863 Civil War token of V. Benner and Ch. Bendinger, New York City (Indian head). (Larry Laevens coll.)

| Rulau | Date | Metal | Size | VG | F | VF | EF |
|---|---|---|---|---|---|---|---|
| C 38 | (?) | Copper | 29mm | — | — | 40.00 | — |

Beaver right in relief ctsp on normal Devins & Bolton ctsp on U.S. 1847 Large cent. (Frank Kovacs coll.)

Devins & Bolton was a large druggist firm in Montreal. In the late 1860's they counterstamped almost every type of copper coin passing through their hands for advertising purposes, and their counterstamps are the most plentiful of any Canadian merchant. It is estimated that more than 600 pieces exist.

Copper coins of Ireland, Denmark, France, French Colonies, Guernsey, Norway, Portugal, St. Helena, Spain, Straits Settlements and Sweden, and British and Irish Conder tokens, and many other Canadian tokens, also received the D&B stamp.

They also attempted to issue a bronze halfpenny token which was a close copy of the Canadian regal large cent, and bore the date July 1, 1867. These were seized by Montreal Customs because of their resemblance to coin of the realm, but some are in collector hands.

## FINDLAY & McWILLIAM
### Montreal, Canada

| Rulau | Date | Metal | Size | VG | F | VF | EF |
|---|---|---|---|---|---|---|---|
| C 44 | (?) | Copper | 29mm | — | — | — | — |

FINDLAY & McWILLIAM — MONTREAL ctsp on U.S. 1836 Large cent.

| | | | | | | | |
|---|---|---|---|---|---|---|---|
| C 46 | (?) | Copper | ---mm | — | — | — | — |

Similar ctsp on Canada Nova Scotia halfpenny token of Carritt & Alport. (Duffield 1481)

## GREAT WESTERN RAILWAY
### Canada

| Rulau | Date | Metal | Size | VG | F | VF | EF |
|---|---|---|---|---|---|---|---|
| C 50 | (?) | Copper | 29mm | — | — | 1 Known | |

GREAT WESTERN / RAILWAY / CANADA ctsp on U.S. Large cent of 1841. (James J. Curto coll.)

| | | | | | | | |
|---|---|---|---|---|---|---|---|
| C 53 | (1860-75) | Brass | 33mm | — | — | 1 Known | |

(All incused) G. W. R. Rv: 1/2 CORD / 212. Plain edge. Issued holed.

| | | | | | | | |
|---|---|---|---|---|---|---|---|
| C 55 | (1860-75) | Brass | 25mm | — | — | 16 Known | |

G. W. R. / 202 (incused). Rv: HALF / CORD. Borders partially milled. Plain edge. Issued holed. (Engine numbers known: 140, 147, 168, 169, 173, 182, 193, 202, 234, 290, 302, 308, 312, 380, 408, 580)

| | | | | | | | |
|---|---|---|---|---|---|---|---|
| C 56 | (1860-75) | Brass | 25mm | — | — | 5 Known | |

(ALl incused) G W R / 205. Rv: HALF / TON. Beaded rims. Plain edge. (Engine numbers known: 205, 264, 266, 298)

The first three tokens are payment talleys for firewood delivered in cords to the "wood up" stations along the company's tracks, probably in the 1860's or early 1870's. The last is for coal.

The railroad's headquarters was in Hamilton, Ontario. The tokens may have been made at the company shops at the foot of Queen Street North. The first Great Western run, Niagara Falls to Hamilton, occurred in 1853. The GWR was amalgamated with Grand Trunk Railway in 1882. (Research by Kenneth A. Palmer, Hamilton, Canada)

## HIGBEE & McCOY
### Canada

| Rulau | Date | Metal | Size | VG | F | VF | EF |
|---|---|---|---|---|---|---|---|
| C 63 | (?) | Copper | 27mm | — | — | 75.00 | — |

HIGBEE & McCOY ctsp on Canada 1850 "Bank of Upper Canada" halfpenny token, Breton 720. (Stanley Steinberg 1981 sale)

*Typical G.W.R. Woodburner*

## J. HOOD
### Canada ?

| Rulau | Date | Metal | Size | VG | F | VF | EF |
|---|---|---|---|---|---|---|---|
| C 70 | (?) | Copper | 29mm | — | 25.00 | — | — |
| | | J. HOOD ctsp on U.S. 1849 Large cent. | | | | | |
| C 72 | (?) | Copper | 25mm | — | — | — | — |
| | | Similar ctsp on New Brunswick 1864 cent. | | | | | |
| C 74 | (?) | Bronze | 25mm | — | — | — | — |
| | | Similar ctsp on Canada 1859 large cent. | | | | | |
| C 75 | (?) | Bronze | 25mm | — | — | — | — |
| | | Similar ctsp on Canada 1888 Large cent. | | | | | |
| C 77 | (?) | Bronze | 26mm | — | — | — | — |
| | | Similar ctsp on Great Britain 1861 halfpenny. | | | | | |
| C 79 | (?) | Copper | 33mm | — | — | — | — |
| | | Similar ctsp on Essequibo & Demerara 1813 stiver. | | | | | |
| C 83 | (?) | Silver | 39mm | — | — | — | — |
| | | Similar ctsp on Great Britain 1820 George III crown. | | | | | |

All seven pieces were offered for sale in the ad of Russ Tennett, Providence, R.I., appearing in the June 1982 *Tams Journal*, page 118.

## J. W. MILLAR
### Toronto, Canada

| Rulau | Date | Metal | Size | VG | F | VF | EF |
|---|---|---|---|---|---|---|---|
| C 88 | (?) | Silver | 25mm | | | | |
| | | J. W. MILLAR / TORONTO ctsp on U.S. 1854 quarter dollar. (Koppenhaver Aug. 4, 1982 sale, lot 409) | | | | | |

## WM. JONES
### Allandale, Ontario

| Rulau | Date | Metal | Size | VG | F | VF | Unc |
|---|---|---|---|---|---|---|---|
| C 84 | (?) | Silver | 38mm | — | — | 150. | — |
| | | WM. JONES / ALLANDALE ONT. (both in curving lines) ctsp on U.S. 1878 silver dollar. (Hartzog 1980 sale) | | | | | |

## KETCHUM & CO.
### Ottawa, Canada

| Rulau | Date | Metal | Size | VG | F | VF | EF |
|---|---|---|---|---|---|---|---|
| C 85 | (?) | | --mm | | | | |
| | | KETCHUM & CO. / OTTAWA ctsp on several unspecified coins. (Brunk 204) | | | | | |

These pieces were once thought to be from Ottawa, Illinois. However, the company does not appear in the 1866, 1870, 1883 or 1889 directories.

## L. LAPOINTE
### Canada

| Rulau | Date | Metal | Size | VG | F | VF | Unc |
|---|---|---|---|---|---|---|---|
| C 86 | (?) | Copper | 28mm | — | — | — | — |
| | | L. LAPOINTE ctsp on both sides of Canada Quebec Bank halfpenny token. (Harvey Gamer coll.) | | | | | |

## Q. M. O. & O. RY.
### (Quebec, Montreal, Ottawa & Occidental Railway)
### Canada

| Rulau | Date | Metal | Size | VG | F | VF | EF |
|---|---|---|---|---|---|---|---|
| C 94 | (1860's) | Brass | ---mm | — | — | — | 1 Known |
| | | Q. M. O. & O. RY. Rv: 1/2 / CORD, NO. 11 (over 26). Plain edge. | | | | | |

(See "Woodburning Engine Fuel Tokens" by Clyde J. Drewing, in The Numismatist for July, 1964)

## T. H. ROBINSON
### Orillia, Ontario, Canada

| Rulau | Date | Metal | Size | VG | F | VF | EF |
|---|---|---|---|---|---|---|---|
| C 100 | (?) | — | --mm | — | 20.00 | 30.00 | 70.00 |
| | | T. H. ROBINSON / DRUGGIST / ORILLIA ctsp on unspecified coins. (Brunk 320) | | | | | |

## ROBINSON'S CARRIAGE WORKS
### Kingston, Ontario, Canada

| Rulau | Date | Metal | Size | VG | F | VF | EF |
|---|---|---|---|---|---|---|---|
| C 110 | (?) | — | — | — | — | 150. | — |
| | | ROBINSON'S CARRIAGE WORKS (in circle) / KINGSTON (at center) ctsp on unspecified coins. (Brunk 318) | | | | | |
| C 112 | (?) | Bronze | 26mm | — | — | 90.00 | — |
| | | Similar ctsp on Canada 1884 Large cent. (Duffield 198) | | | | | |

Robinson's Kingston Carriage Works was the business of G. W. Robinson, 233-235 Princess St., Kingston, Ontario, Canada. These counterstamps have been misattributed to Kingston, Jamaica by Ray Byrne but they are clearly Canadian.

## ROULEAU
### Canada

| Rulau | Date | Metal | Size | VG | F | VF | EF |
|---|---|---|---|---|---|---|---|
| C 120 | (ca 1858) | Copper | 29mm | — | 100. | — | — |
| | | ROULEAU ctsp on U. S. Large cent, date not visible, but probably the 1839 "Booby Head" variety with Small Letters reverse. (Rulau coll., ex-Carling Gresham) | | | | | |

| Rulau | Date | Metal | Size | VG | F | VF | EF |
|---|---|---|---|---|---|---|---|
| C 123 | (ca 1858) | Copper | 26mm | — | — | 75.00 | — |
| | | Similar ctsp on Canada "Ships, Colonies & Commerce" halfpenny token, Breton 997. (Rulau coll., ex-Halifax) | | | | | |
| C 125 | (ca 1858) | Copper | 25mm | — | — | 75.00 | — |
| | | Similar ctsp on Canada "Victoria Nobis Est" halfpenny token, Breton 982. (Duffield 1473; Brunk 324) | | | | | |
| C 127 | (ca 1858) | Copper | 27mm | — | — | 65.00 | — |
| | | Similar ctsp on Canada "Montreal Sou" token, Breton type 674-712, circa 1835-1838. (Duffield 194) | | | | | |

| Rulau | Date | Metal | Size | VG | F | VF | EF |
|---|---|---|---|---|---|---|---|
| C 129 | (ca 1858) | Copper | 27mm | — | — | 65.00 | — |

Similar ctsp on Canada "Bouquet Sou" token, Courteau 22, circa 1835-1838. (Duffield 1475)

| C 131 | (ca 1858) | Copper | 27mm | — | — | 65.00 | — |

Similar ctsp on Canada "Bank of Upper Canada" halfpenny token, Breton 720, 1850-1857. (Duffield 1474)

| C 133 | (ca 1858) | Copper | 26mm | — | — | 75.00 | — |

Similar ctsp on Canada "Prince Edward's Island" 1855 halfpenny token, Breton 918. (Rulau coll., ex-Bill Randel)

| C 140 | (?) | Copper | 28mm | — | — | Unique | ? |

JOSH ROULEAU ctsp on counterfeit Ireland George III halfpenny. (John Cheramy coll., ex-Warren Baker)

Josh Rouleau apparently was a Canadian merchant who counterstamped a good number of halfpenny-sized coppers from circulation, as all specimens seen were worn before stamping. None of the 19th century Canadian writers on tokens (Leroux, Sandham, Breton, Courteau) recorded data on counterstamped coins, though Courteau collected them, and thus Rouleau — just as Devins & Bolton of Montreal, Robinson's Carriage Works of Kingston, Ont., and Findlay & McWilliam of Montreal — long escaped collection and research.

Frank G. Duffield of Baltimore in 1919-1922 is probably the first to record any Rouleau specimens; four of them appeared in his "A Trial List of the Counterstamped Modern Coins of the World."

One member of the Rouleau clan, Charles Rouleau, married to an Indian girl who was a land beneficiary of the 1831 Prairie du Chien, Wis., Treaty, led a settlement party in 1855 and the next year founded Rulo, Kansas, on the Missouri River (originally called Rouleau). The tokens do not seem to be connected to this Rouleau, however.

Byron Johnson of Seattle, a keen numismatist and genealogist, traces some 200 families named Rouleau in Quebec Province and elsewhere in Canada, so determining the responsible merchant may prove difficult. Two articles on the Rouleau counterstamps appeared in *World Coin News* during 1980 without eliciting any specific data. The Sept. 23 and Oct. 14, 1980 issues carried the articles.

## J. VELDON
## Quebec, Canada

| Rulau | Date | Metal | Size | VG | F | VF | EF |
|---|---|---|---|---|---|---|---|
| C 160 | (?) | Copper | 34mm | — | — | — | — |

J. VELDON / QUEBEC ctsp on Nova Scotia 1856 penny token, Breton 875. (Koppenhaver Aug. 4, 1982 sale, lot 408)

## UNION STAMP FACTORY 114
## Canada

| Rulau | Date | Metal | Size | VG | F | VF | Unc |
|---|---|---|---|---|---|---|---|
| C 155 | (?) | Copper | 27mm | — | — | — | — |

BOOT & SHOE / WORKERS U... / UNION (Boot) STAMP / FACTORY 114 within shield ctsp on Canada 1820 token, Breton 1012 (rev.). In collection John Cheramy, Victoria, B.C., Canada.

# MISCELLANEOUS CANADA COUNTERSTAMPS

**AGNEW** (twice) on Canada 1855 token, Breton 919

**T. AUBRY** on U.S. 1837 Large cent

**ASHTON** on Canada 1842 token, Breton 526

**L. H. B.** on Canada 1870 25-cents

**C. S. BALL** on Canada Lesslie halfpenny token, Breton 718.

**BROWN** on Canada Lesslie 1822 twopence token, Breton 717. (Duffield 190)

**J. E. C.** on Canada 1859 Large cent

**N. C.** (relief, in toothed rect. depression) on Canada 1852 token, Breton 528

**(Card-suit Club) / (Three Anchors) / C CHENEY** (rev.); **(Club)(Anchor) / (Pipe) / (Club)** (obv.) on Canada 1859 Large cent

**D. COOK** on Canada 1844 halfpenny token, Breton 527.

**CROOK** on Newfoundland 1880 20-cents

**G. D.** on North American 1781 halfpenny token, Breton 1013.

**T. DAV...** (?) on Canada 1859 Large cent.

**SOUVENIR / DE / A. DUVAL / ST. J. P. J.** on U.S. 1835 Hard Times token, Low 99, of Lansingburgh, N.Y. (St. Jean Port Joli, Quebec)

**FRANK. / .B. / FRAZIER** (obv.); **F R** (rev.) on Nova Scotia 1840 token

**G** (large) on Canada 1837 token, Breton 522 (rev.)

**T. B. GALBRAITH** on Nova Scotia 1861 cent

**G. R. GILCHRIS** on Canada 1920 small cent

**GOODDEN** on Canada 1859 Large cent.

**J. H.** Canada 1858 10-cents

**J. F. HANLEY** on Canada 1858 10-cents

**J. HUTTON / WINDSOR** on unspecified coins (Brunk 193)

**J I** on Canada 1876-H Large cent

**S P I** (both sides) on Canada 1857 token, Breton 720

**IN SOLIS CELANIR 1869** on Canada 1857 penny token, Breton 719 (on edge)

**J** on Canada 1816 token, Breton 981

**M. JETTE** on Canada 1837 Bank of Montreal penny token. (Duffield 1468)

**J. JONES / T. AUBRY** on Canada 1850 Bank of Upper Canada penny.

**KEEP QUIET** on Canada 1884 Large cent

**H. R. KERR** on Canada 18..-H silver 25-cents (date worn)

**C G L** (relief, in small rect. depression) on 1881 Large cent (rev.)

**O. LAGACE** on Canada Quebec Bank token penny

**J. LEE** on Canada 1854 token, Breton 719

**PATd BY S. LEE APRIL 1881** on Canada 1884 Large cent

**W. F. LOW** (both sides) on Canada 1844 Bank of Montreal halfpenny token

**LYARD** on Canada 1887 Large cent (rev.)

**A. O. M. / 1904** on Canada 1901 Large cent with shaved obverse

**J. S. M.** on Canada token, Breton 522.

**MANLY** on Canada 1852 token, Breton 529

**McCAULEY** (both sides) on Canada 1859 Large cent

**W. D. McGLOGHLON** on Canada 1872-H 25-cents

**J. A. McH.** on Canada 1901 half dollar (duffield 1477)

**H Mc K** on Canada 1886 Large cent

**D. R. McRAE** (both sides) on Canada 1852 token, Breton 528

**D. MOORE** on Canada 1872-H 50-cents

**NICHOLS — HARTFORD** (twice) on Nova Scotia 1815 Starr & Shannon halfpenny token

| | | | |
|---|---|---|---|
| **F O** | on Canada 1888 Large cent | **J. F. T.** (both sides) | on Canada 1886 Large cent |
| **T. P. O.** | on Canada 1738 billon marque, Breton 508. | **U. S.** | on Canada 'Ships Colonies Commerce' halfpenny token. |
| **F. P.** | on Canada 1839 Bank of Montreal 'side view' halfpenny. | **F. UPTON** | on Nova Scotia 1832 thistle halfpenny. (Duffield 1481) |
| **H. B. P.** | on Canada brass token, obv. Breton 960, rev. Breton 1005. (Duffield 180) | **J. W.** | on Canada 1837 token, Breton 521 |
| **WM. C. PALMER** | on Canada 1872-H 25-cents | **C. R. WAGAR** (both sides) | on Canada 1859 Large cent |
| **PAQUETTE & CIE / (beaver) / MONTREAL MNFRS** | on Great Britain 1797 Cartwheel penny. (Duffield 175) | **J. H. WAKE** | on Canada 1837 token, Breton 522 |
| | | **JAS. WALD** | on Canada 1837 token, Breton 521 |
| **F. J. A. PERO** (twice) | on Canada 1842 token, Breton 526 (rev.) | **R. WATSON** | on Newfoundland 1872-H 50-cents |
| **PETERS** | on Canada 'Ships Colonies' token, Breton 997 (rev.) | **A. WHITE** | on Canada 1876-H Large cent |
| **A. J. Q. / (Three entwined rings) / (Hatchet, etc.)** | on Canada token, Breton 521 (rev.) | **H. WOODH (?)** (both sides) | on Canada 1854 token, Breton 719 |
| | | **(?) WOODS** | on Canada 1857 token, Breton 720 (rev.) |
| **R. H. & S. / 446** | on Canada 'Robert Hopwood & Son' 1852 token, Breton 898. (Duffield 343). English? | **A. C. YOUMANS** (semicircular, both sides) | on Canada 1876-H Large cent |
| **R. L. RALPH** | on Canada Montreal sou token, Breton 674. | **2** (retrograde) | on Canada 'Self Government' 1855 token, Breton 919 |
| **S** | on Canada 'Pure Copper' token, Breton 1009 | | |
| **E. SAXLUND** | on Canada 1812 halfpenny token | **OCT / JUL / 18 12** | on Canada 1882 Large cent |
| **ST. ANDREWS / CHAPTER.** | on New Brunswick 1843 penny token (Masonic) | **(Cross within circle)** | on Canada 1883-H 25-cents |
| —do— | on Nova Scotia 1856 penny token | **(Tiny Crown)** | on Canada 1882-H 25-cents |
| **T. STUART** (relief) | on Canada 1814 token, Breton 990. (Duffield 1478) | **(Large Crown)** (both sides) | on Canada 1884 Large cent |

# ENGLAND

## EMPIRE THEATRE
### England

| Rulau | Date | Metal | Size | VG | F | VF | EF |
|---|---|---|---|---|---|---|---|
| B 15 | (1880's) | Copper | 29mm | — | — | — | — |

EMPIRE THEATRE ctsp on obverse of U.S. Large cent. IMMENSE SUCCESS ctsp on reverse of the coin. (Gould 9; Hallenbeck 5.750)

| B 17 | (1880's) | Copper | 30mm | — | — | — | — |

Similar ctsp on France 1854 10-centimes. (Gould 9)

| B 18 | (1880's) | Copper | 30mm | — | — | — | — |

EMPIRE / IMMENSE SUCCESS / THEATRE ctsp on France 1863 10-centimes. (Scott type 22.210)

| B 19 | (1880's) | Copper | 30mm | — | — | 30.00 | — |

EMPIRE / IMMENSE / SUCCESS / THEATRE ctsp on Italy 1863 10-centesimi. (Krause coll.)

| B 20 | (1880's) | Copper | 30mm | — | — | — | — |

EMPIRE / IMMENSE / SUCCESS / THEATRE ctsp on Italy 1866 10-centesimi. (Stanley Steinberg 1982 sale)

| B 26 | (1880's) | Copper | 30mm | — | — | — | — |

EMPIRE / THEATRE / IMMENSE / SUCCESS ctsp on France 1872 10-centimes. (Duffield 1545)

It was never demonstrated by Maurice Gould or Kenneth Hallenbeck that this is an American counterstamp, though it seemed so to them. French copper coinage of the Second Empire enjoyed legal tender status in the U.S. until 1857, but was not an important part of the circulating medium. Ten centimes equaled one cent in face value.

J. Gavin Scott, in his 1975 book *British Countermarks on Copper and Bronze Coins*, showed that British merchants imported foreign coppers during the 1880's coin shortage, counterstamping them for advertising-small change use. French coins were especially used, but the long-obsolete U.S. Large cents also found a usage. Empire Theatre, Pears' Soap, Coleman's Mustard and May's Washing Powder are examples of 26 British counterstamps of the period.

## DUNDEE STEAM LAUNDRY
### Hawkhill, England

| Rulau | Date | Metal | Size | VG | F | VF | Unc |
|---|---|---|---|---|---|---|---|
| B 13 | (?) | WM | 39mm | — | — | 15.00 | — |

Coat of arms supported by winged griffins (?), scrolls above and below. Upper scroll reads: DEI DOMINI. Lower reads: PRUDENTIA ET CANDORE. Rv: DUNDEE / STEAM LAUNDRY (Old English lettering) / TAIT'S LANE / HAWKHILL / (tiny) S.D. CHILDS, CHICAGO, U.S.A. Plain edge. (Wright 269)

This is possibly an English token.

## G. W. ANDREWS
### England

| Rulau | Date | Metal | Size | VG | F | VF | EF |
|---|---|---|---|---|---|---|---|
| B 1 | (?) | Copper | 30mm | — | — | — | — |

G. W. ANDREWS DENTIST ctsp on France 1854 10-centimes.

| B 2 | (?) | Bronze | 21mm | — | — | — | — |

Similar ctsp on Sweden 1882 2-ore.

## B. HALL
### Bristol, England

| Rulau | Date | Metal | Size | VG | F | VF | Unc |
|---|---|---|---|---|---|---|---|
| B 35 | (?) | Copper | 36mm | — | — | — | — |

B. HALL / GLAZIER & / GLASS BENDER / BRISTOL on reverse of Great Britain 1797 Cartwheel penny. Two horse heads ctsp on obverse of the coin. (John Cheramy coll.)

## HARDING
### Ludlow, England

| Rulau | Date | Metal | Size | VG | F | VF | EF |
|---|---|---|---|---|---|---|---|
| B 40 | (?) | Copper | 27mm | — | — | 50.00 | — |

WINES. / & SPIRITS BY / HARDING / LUDLOW ctsp on unidentifiable coin (possibly Irish. Plain edge. (The second line of the ctsp is in script).

Ludlow is in Shropshire, southwest of Birmingham.

## HYMAN
### London, England

| Rulau | Date | Metal | Size | VG | F | VF | EF |
|---|---|---|---|---|---|---|---|
| B 50 | (1880's) | Copper | 25mm | — | — | — | — |

HYMAN / LONDON ctsp on France 1857 5-centimes. (Duffield 1544)

## SIR JOSIAH MASON
### England

| Rulau | Date | Metal | Size | VG | F | VF | Unc |
|---|---|---|---|---|---|---|---|
| B 62 | (?) | CN | 25mm | — | 15.00 | 19.50 | 30.00 |

Mermaid facing, admiring herself in a hand mirror, within beaded circle at center. Around: SIR JOSIAH MASON'S NICKEL ALLOY / +. Rv: . MADE OF . / .25 NICKEL / .75 COPPER / SUITABLE FOR COINAGE. Plain edge. (Wright 694)

In 1899 Dr. Wright called this piece "very rare." He added: "I do not know whether this is of American origin or not, but give it the benefit of the doubt."

The piece seems to be clearly of English origin. It may well be rare, as none of my collaborators in this book's contents are familiar with it. The workmanship is excellent.

It may emanate from the early 1860's.

## MASSEY
### Kidderminster, England

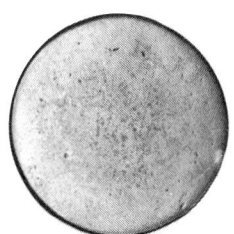

| Rulau | Date | Metal | Size | VG | F | VF | EF |
|---|---|---|---|---|---|---|---|
| B 66 | (?) | Copper | 27mm | — | — | 60.00 | — |

Wines / and Spirits / Wholesale & / Retail by ? Massey / KIDDERMINSTER ctsp on obverse of Wood's coinage piece. Plain edge. (All lines but the last are in script).

Kidderminster is in Worcestershire, southwest of and near the city of Birmingham. The S's in Wholesale and Massey are the old English type, resembling 'f'.

## LLOYD'S WEEKLY NEWSPAPER
### London, England

| Rulau | Date | Metal | Size | VG | F | VF | EF |
|---|---|---|---|---|---|---|---|
| B 58 | (?) | Copper | 36mm | — | 30.00 | — | — |

LLOYD'S WEEKLY NEWSPAPER THREE PENCE POST FREE ctsp around obverse rim of Great Britain 1797 Cartwheel penny. Rv: — LLOYD'S WEEKLY NEWSPAPER 3D POST FREE ctsp on reverse of the coin.

| Rulau | Date | Metal | Size | VG | F | VF | EF |
|---|---|---|---|---|---|---|---|
| B 58A | (?) | Copper | 29mm | — | 12.50 | — | — |

Similar ctsp on Great Britain 1807 halfpenny.

| Rulau | Date | Metal | Size | VG | F | VF | EF |
|---|---|---|---|---|---|---|---|
| B 59 | (?) | Copper | 36mm | — | 30.00 | — | — |

READ. LLOYD'S . PENNY . SUNDAY . TIMES . ctsp around obverse rim of Great Britain 1797 Cartwheel penny.

## I. COOK
### England ?

| Rulau | Date | Metal | Size | VG | F | VF | Unc |
|---|---|---|---|---|---|---|---|
| B 12 | (?) | Copper | 30mm | — | — | — | — |

I. COOK ctsp on France L'An 8-AA decime.

## A. F. KENT
### England ?

| Rulau | Date | Metal | Size | VG | F | VF | Unc |
|---|---|---|---|---|---|---|---|
| B 53 | (?) | Copper | 30mm | — | — | — | — |

A. F. KENT ctsp twice on obverse of France 1855 10-centimes. Also ctsp once on reverse of the coin.

## McNEIL
### England ?

| Rulau | Date | Metal | Size | VG | F | VF | Unc |
|---|---|---|---|---|---|---|---|
| B 70 | (?) | Copper | 25mm | — | — | — | — |

McNEIL ctsp twice on Italy 1861-M 5-centesimi.

## MILLARD
### England ?

| Rulau | Date | Metal | Size | VG | F | VF | EF |
|---|---|---|---|---|---|---|---|
| B 73 | (1880's) | Copper | 30mm | — | 7.50 | — | — |

MILLARD cstp on France 1852-A 10-centimes. (Rulau coll.)

## PEARS' SOAP
### England

| Rulau | Date | Metal | Size | VG | F | VF | EF |
|---|---|---|---|---|---|---|---|
| B 80 | (1884-85) | Copper | 25mm | — | — | — | — |

PEARS' / SOAP ctsp on France Napoleon III 5-centimes of the 1852-1857 period.

| | | | | | | | |
|---|---|---|---|---|---|---|---|
| B 83 | (1884-85) | Copper | 29mm | | | | |

Similar ctsp on U.S. Large cents of various dates.

| Rulau | Date | Metal | Size | VG | F | VF | EF |
|---|---|---|---|---|---|---|---|
| B 85 | (1884-85) | Copper | 30mm | — | — | — | — |

Similar ctsp on France Napoleon III 10-centimes of the 1852-1857 period. (Dates examined: 1853-A, 1853-B, 1853-W, 1854-K, 1855-D, 1855-BB, 1856-A, 1856-B, 1856-D)

| Rulau | Date | Metal | Size | VG | F | VF | EF |
|---|---|---|---|---|---|---|---|
| B 87 | (1884-85) | Copper | 30mm | — | — | — | — |

Similar ctsp on France Napoleon III 10-centimes of the 1861-1865 period. (Dates examined: 1861)

| Rulau | Date | Metal | Size | VG | F | VF | EF |
|---|---|---|---|---|---|---|---|
| B 89 | (1884-85) | Copper | 30mm | — | — | — | — |

Similar ctsp on France Third Republic 10-centimes of the 1870-1883 period. (Dates examined: 1872, 1872-K, 1882-A)

| Rulau | Date | Metal | Size | VG | F | VF | EF |
|---|---|---|---|---|---|---|---|
| B 90 | (?) | Copper | 30mm | — | — | — | — |

Similar ctsp on France 1882-A 10-centimes, with additional stamp: E BRISTOW, on each side. (Larry Laevens coll.)

This counterstamp is of English origin, as is the soap itself. However, Pears' Soap was advertised and sold extensively in the United States as well.

It has been reported that the Pears' Soap counterstamp also appears on coppers of Spain, Luxemburg and Italy, though principally it appears on Napoleonic 10-centime pieces of the 1852-1865 period.

Thomas J. Barratt, son-in-law of A.V.F. Pears, realized the advertising possibilities of the foreign coppers then in active circulation in England. It was not illegal to deface coins except those of the realm. In 1884-1885 he imported 250,000 pieces and had them stamped PEARS' / SOAP and placed them in circulation through commissionaires.

In 1914 Pears became a subsidiary of Lever Brothers Ltd. and in 1929 became one of the founding companies of the soap giant, Unilever NV.

(See "French and other European Coins Countermarked in England for use as Advertising Tickets in the Nineteenth Century" by J. Gavin Scott, in *Seaby's Coin & Medal Bulletin* for Dec. 1970.)

## ROBINSON
## Liverpool, England

| Rulau | Date | Metal | Size | VG | F | VF | Unc |
|---|---|---|---|---|---|---|---|
| B 94 | (?) | Copper | 33mm | — | — | — | — |

ROBINSON / LIVERPOOS ctsp on England 1806 penny. (Cheramy coll.)

## W.S.
## England

| Rulau | Date | Metal | Size | VG | F | VF | EF |
|---|---|---|---|---|---|---|---|
| B 96 | (1790's) | Copper | 29mm | — | — | — | — |

W S ctsp twice on Great Britain 1796 I. Baster halfpenny token of Devizes in Wiltshire. Reeded edge. (Diagonal reeding placed over a lettered edge) (Rulau coll.)

## SIMON
## England

| Rulau | Date | Metal | Size | VG | F | VF | EF |
|---|---|---|---|---|---|---|---|
| B 101 | (1880's) | Copper | 29mm | 10.00 | — | — | — |

SIMON ctsp on France 1853-A 10-centimes. (Rulau coll.)

## SPENCE'S PLAN
## England

| Rulau | Date | Metal | Size | VG | F | VF | EF |
|---|---|---|---|---|---|---|---|
| B 108 | (1790's) | Copper | 26.5mm | — | 50.00 | — | — |

SPENCE'S PLAN / YOU ROGUES ctsp on reverse of very worn British halfpenny token. Rv: & / FULL BELLIES ctsp on obverse of the token. Edge: PAYABLE IN LONDON LIVERPOOL OR BRISTOL. (Rulau coll.)

This unusal counterstamp is a political satire piece connected with the agitations of Thomas Spence, the London coin dealer and advocate of many political sentiments.

| B 109 | (1790's) | Copper | 26.5mm | — | 50.00 | — | — |

SPENCE'S PLAN / OR / WAR / FOREVER ctsp on worn halfpenny token.

| B 110 | (1790's) | Copper | 28mm | — | — | — | — |

FULL BELLIES / FAT BAIRNS / NO LANDLORDS ctsp on worn coin or a coin blank.

Spence had a large number of dies, which he used to impress legends on circulating coins or tokens. A few others included NO WAR PEACE AND PLENTY and READ SPENCE'S PLAN SMALL FARMS. Spence (1750-1814) was a radical revolutionary, a contemporary and friend of the French radical Marat. (See "Names in Numismatics: Thomas Spence" in *Coins* magazine of England for Jan. 1972, pg. 28)

## S.W. SILVER
## Cornhill, England

| Rulau | Date | Metal | Size | VG | F | VF | EF |
|---|---|---|---|---|---|---|---|
| B 100 | (?) | Copper | 22mm | — | — | — | — |

S.W. SILVER & CO / CLOTHIERS &C / CORNHILL ctsp on Great Britain 1799 farthing. (Cheramy coll.)

## T + C
## England

| Rulau | Date | Metal | Size | VG | F | VF | EF |
|---|---|---|---|---|---|---|---|
| B 115 | (?) | Copper | 29mm | — | — | — | — |

T + C ctsp on obverse of Great Britain 1807 halfpenny. Same ctsp on reverse of coin. (Nadin-Davis sale, Nov. 20, 1982)

## YORK HOTEL
## Sandown, England

| Rulau | Date | Metal | Size | VG | F | VF | EF |
|---|---|---|---|---|---|---|---|
| B 160 | (?) | Copper | 25mm | — | — | — | — |

REMBRIDGE / YORK HOTEL / SANDOWN ctsp on France 1863 5-centimes (Cheramy coll.)

# MISC. BRITISH COUNTERSTAMPS

| | |
|---|---|
| I A | on 1789 Anglesey Mines halfpenny token |
| L A / 4 | on England silver 18-pence bank token |
| H. B. | on Bank of England 1804 silver 5-shillings |
| H B. | on England half crown |
| H. B. (Star) L. W. (relief, in rectangular depression) | on Bank of England 1804 silver 5-shillings |
| G H B | on England 1898 farthing |
| I B (both sides) | on Anglesey Mines halfpenny token |
| W B | on England George III half crown |
| S. BAGSHAW / Crowned E | on England George III halfpenny |
| BAKER'S / CARTES DE VISITE / 28 JUBILEE ST. E. | on France Napoleon III 10-centimes (issued 1880's) |
| BALFRON FRUIT (in relief) | on British token |
| -do- | on Glasgow token |
| BORWICK'S / BAKING / POWDER | on France 1872-K 10-centimes (1880's) |
| J. BUCKLE | on England 1898 penny |
| STRAWBERRY / CABANE'S / TOOTHPASTE. | on France 1854 10-centimes (1880's) |
| L. CADMAN (four times) / BEN GALL | on England 1744 halfpenny (Duffield 1518) |
| CAST STEEL (thrice) | on Isle of Man 1798 penny |
| J. COCK / SWANSEA (obv.); GROCER (rev.) | on England 1797 Cartwheel penny |
| S. CRAIG | on Ireland 1822 halfpenny |
| WM. CUFF (relief, in crenellated rectangle) / THOMAS (incuse) | on England Charles II (1660-85) half crown (Duffield 328) |
| DEAR & SONS, GROCERS, SHANKLIN, I.W. | on France 1854 5-centimes (Isle of Wight) |
| —do— | on France 1856-W 10-centimes |
| DILLON / BRAZIER / HEREFORD | on England 1797 Cartwheel penny |
| A. DRABBER / 1 HIGH ST / MARY LE BONE / CUTLER | on England 1797 Cartwheel penny (issued 1835-53) |
| (Maltese cross) / F | on England 1799 halfpenny (Duffield 1488) |
| 1870, G. W. F. (Star) | on Great Britain 1856 Gothic silver florin. (Very ornate counterstamp) |
| I F (relief, in rectangular depression) | on England George III halfpenny |
| FEAIST'S BREAD | on France Napoleon III 10-centimes (issued 1880's) |
| A. FYFE | on England 1807 penny (Duffield 1485) |
| * F. G. * | on England 1816 shilling (Duffield 318) |
| T. G. | on England 1807 halfpenny (Duffield 1491) |
| GARDEN / GATE / HOME / BREWED / ALES | on France 1854 10-centimes (1880's) |
| P. T. GATES | on England 1853 shilling |
| GIBBSS (in circle) | on England 1811 18-pence silver bank token |
| GROS (in relief) | on England William III halfpenny |
| I H | on 1795 'Long Live the King' halfpenny token |
| S. H. (twice) | on England 1797 Cartwheel penny (for Samuel Hamer, uncle of token author S. H. Hamer)(Duffield 338) |
| B. HALL / GLAZIER / GLASSBENDER / BRISTO(L) | on England 1797 Cartwheel penny |
| HERON'S / DOUGLAS / WHISKEY | on France Napoleon III 10-centimes (1880's) |
| I N G (relief) | on Bank of England 1804 silver 5-shillings |
| J (on neck) | on England 1854 silver 4-pence |
| M KER | on England 1866 silver 3pence |
| R LOWE (twice) | on England George III threepence (worn) |
| MITCHELL / SAW MAKER / BRIGHTON | on France 1855 10-centimes (1880's) |
| MOR / GAN | on England silver 18-pence bank token |
| R. E. NISBET. (both sides) | on England 1853 halfpenny |
| Crowned P (obv.); Crowned W.H. (rev.) | on England 1799 halfpenny (Duffield 339) |
| C P (relief, in square depression) / C P (incuse) | on England William III half crown (Duffield 329) |

[211]

| | |
|---|---|
| **1860** | on England 1795 trademan's token (Duffield 1493) |
| **I P** | on England George III halfpenny |
| **I P / (Four ornaments)** | on England 1799 halfpenny |
| **(?). E. PROSSER** | on England 1873 penny (rev.) |
| **RACING / OPINION / 1D.** | on France Napoleon III 10-centimes (1880's) |
| **ROBINSON / CUTLER / OXFORD** | on England halfpennies (dates examined: 1806, 1807)(Duffield 1489) |
| -do- | on Ireland 1805 halfpenny (Duffield 1495) |
| **ROBINSON / RAZOR / MAKER / OXFORD** | on England 1797 Cartwheel penny |
| **Crowned S** | on England 1797 cartwheel penny |
| **W. SIMONS 1800** (rev.); **I B** (obv.) | on England 1797 cartwheel penny |
| **SO. SHIELDS / (Shield)** | on France 1/8-ecu (Duffield 325) |
| **STUBS** (many times, both sides) | on England 1826 penny |
| **3. OF. TEA / AND / 2 / 1 SLICE / OF. JAM.** | on England 1891 penny (rev.) |
| **(Cross) IT** (relief) | on Bank of England 1804 silver 5-shillings (the IT could indicate silversmith Joseph Taylor of Birmingham, active 1804-13) |
| **TILLEY'S / COALS / BRIGHTON** | on France 1854-K 10-centimes (1880's) |
| **J. B. V.** | on England 1862 halfpenny |
| **VOTES FOR WOMEN** | on England 1907 penny |
| **W** (serif type) | on England 1697 Charles II silver half crown |
| **(Lion) W (Male head)** (relief, in depression) | on England 1738 halfpenny (Duffield 1517) |
| **T W** (relief) / **B B B** (incuse) | on England 1813 shilling bank token (Duffield 313) |
| **WAM to JRE FEBR. 1819** | on England 1816 shilling |
| **(Kangaroo)** (relief, in small rect. depression) / **9 Ct** (relief, in small rect. depression, twice) | on England 1821 silver crown |

# IRELAND

## P. D.
## Ireland ?

| Rulau | Date | Metal | Size | VG | F | VF | EF |
|---|---|---|---|---|---|---|---|
| 16 | (?) | Copper | 28mm | — | — | — | — |

(Harp) / P . D / (two 4-leaf flowers), all within round serrated depression, ctsp on the head of George III on an English 18th century "Bungtown" halfpenny token (Wood 33; Haxby 244). (Stanley Steinberg sale list 94 of 1982)

There is a possible American connection, since many such evasion halfpence circulated on the eastern seaboard. However, the harp may well indicate Irish provenance.

## McMAHON
## Dublin, Ireland

| Rulau | Date | Metal | Size | VG | F | VF | EF |
|---|---|---|---|---|---|---|---|
| 19 | (?) | Copper | 34mm | — | 50.00 | — | — |

McMAHON / DUBLIN / CUTLER / FILL. LANE ctsp on Ireland 1820 George III-Harp penny token.

# MISCELLANEOUS IRELAND COUNTERSTAMPS

**D. ALLEN / IMPLEMENT / MAKER / MONEYMORE** on England 1797 Cartwheel penny (David Allen, Belfast, 1856-1868). 28 specimens reported.

**MR, J D (V) ALLENTIN** on worn copper coin

**J * B.** on Ireland 1760 farthing (Duffield 1549)

**O. B.** (relief, large) on Ireland George II halfpenny (Duffield 1497)

**O. B.** (relief, large, in square depression) on Ireland George II halfpenny (Duffield 1494)

**BIGGER / BOLTON / STREET CUTLER / DUBLIN** on England 1797 Cartwheel penny

**BIGGER DUBLIN** on England 1797 Cartwheel penny

—do— on worn 19th century penny token

**N W / C** (obv.); **C** (rev.) on Dublin harp token

**(CAVA)N** (obv.); **MURRAY / CAVAN** (rev.) on George III 1806 halfpenny

**P. COFFEY** on England George III halfpenny

**CHRISTIAN / COLE: ALLEY** on Ireland George III halfpenny

**W. COOKE 20** on rectangular copper piece, 20 by 17mm

**F D** on Ireland 1760 farthing (Duffield 1550)

**R. DELAHOYD** on Ireland George III halfpenny

**B. DENNIS** on Ireland 1781 halfpenny

**DISON** on Ireland 1772 halfpenny

**I. DOLLARD** on Ireland 1794 halfpenny token

**I D / (crude sailing ship) / J. DOLLARD** on Ireland halfpenny of several dates (Examined: 1775, 1781)

**B. EGAN. BIRR** on England 1797 Cartwheel twopence

**J. FITZ.P** on Ireland halfpennies (Examined: 1776, 1782)

**M. GRIFFIN** on Ireland 1782 halfpenny

**HAMBILTON** on Ireland George III halfpenny

**O : HEADEN** (relief, in engrailed rect. depression) on Ireland George III halfpenny

**T. HYNES** on Ireland George III halfpenny

**T. KELLY** on Ireland halfpence of various dates (Examined: 1781)

**CON McG.** on Voce Populi 1760 halfpenny

**O'NEILL** on Ireland 1806 farthing

**R. PARKE** (relief, in rect. depression) on Ireland George III halfpenny

**H. PERRY** on various English and Irish halfpenny tokens

**A RENFREW SOCIETY** on George II halfpenny

**SOMERVILL DOWN** on worn copper halfpenny

**PAYABLE AT MRS. SOMERVILLS DOWN** on George III halfpenny

**V. TAGART** on various Ireland halfpennies (Examined: 1782)

**Crowned R W** on Ireland token (Duffield 1551)

**L. WALTON** (obv.); **1735** (rev.) on Clifton 1735 token (Duffield 514)

**S. WILSONNS** (twice) on worn copper coin

# CEYLON

## T C
## (Tatham and Co.)
## Ceylon

| Rulau | Date | Metal | Size | VG | F | VF | EF |
|---|---|---|---|---|---|---|---|
| S 1 | (?) | Copper | 29mm | — | — | 65.00 | — |

Large T C ctsp on U.S. 1822 Large cent. (Pridmore 115)

# FRANCE

## AU GATEAU ROYAL
## France

| Rulau | Date | Metal | Size | VG | F | VF | EF |
|---|---|---|---|---|---|---|---|
| F 1 | (?) | Bronze | 31mm | — | — | — | — |

AU / GATEAU / ROYAL ctsp on Great Britain Victoria penny. (Dates examined: 1873, 1874)

| F 2 | (?) | Copper | 30mm | — | — | — | — |

Similar ctsp on France Napoleon III 10-centimes of the 1852-1857 period. (Dates examined: 1855-W, 1856-B)

It is assumed Au Gateau Royal was a restaurant, teahouse or cafe.

## EPICERIE MODERNE
## Poitiers, France

| Rulau | Date | Metal | Size | VG | F | VF | EF |
|---|---|---|---|---|---|---|---|
| F 14 | (?) | Bronze | 31mm | — | — | — | — |

EPICERIE MODERNE / POITIERS ctsp on Great Britain Victoria penny. (Dates examined: 1861, 1865, 1866, 1872, 1878, 1879)

| F 14A | (?) | Copper | 25mm | — | — | — | — |

Similar ctsp to F 14, on Spain 1868 5-centimos.

| F 15 | (?) | Bronze | 31mm | — | — | — | — |

Similar ctsp, but 'P' of EPICERIE is a question mark (?). On Great Britain penny. (Dates examined: 1862, 1872, 1892)

## LE GUANO FISON
## France

| Rulau | Date | Metal | Size | VG | F | VF | EF |
|---|---|---|---|---|---|---|---|
| F 16 | (?) | Copper | 25mm | — | — | — | — |

LE / GUANO / FISON ctsp on France 1854-BB 5-centimes.

| F 17 | (?) | Copper | 25mm | — | — | — | — |

Similar ctsp on Italy 1861-M 5-centesimi.

| F 17C | (?) | Copper | 30mm | — | 40.00 | — | — |

Similar ctsp on France 1856-A 10-centimes.

This is a French branch of the British firm Fisons Ltd., in the fertilizer business since 1840 and tracing its lineage back to 1808. The firm marketed 'Canary Guano' (with yellow canaries on the tin) until 1929.

## A. KOHLER & FILS
### France

| Rulau | Date | Metal | Size | VG | F | VF | EF |
|---|---|---|---|---|---|---|---|
| F 18 | (1907-21) | Copper | 30mm | — | — | — | — |

CHOCOLAT / A. KOHLER / & FILS ctsp on France 10-centime pieces. (Dates examined: 1864, 1902)

| F 20 | (1907-21) | Bronze | 30mm | — | — | — | — |
|---|---|---|---|---|---|---|---|

* CHOCOLAT * / KOHLER ctsp on France 1908 10-centimes.

| F 20A | (1907-21) | Bronze | 30mm | — | — | 100. | — |
|---|---|---|---|---|---|---|---|

Similar ctsp on France 1911 10-centimes.

Amedee Kohler et Fils was a Swiss firm with French and British operations. Its wholesale depot in London, 1907-21, was at 6-8 Eastcheap, London E.C. (Nestle and Anglo-Swiss Condensed Milk Co.). Then they were at 37-41 Gracechurch in 1922, but were no longer listed 1925.

## LE PICOTIN APERITIF
### France

| Rulau | Date | Metal | Size | VG | F | VF | EF |
|---|---|---|---|---|---|---|---|
| F 29 | (1885-98) | Copper | 30mm | — | — | — | — |

LE / PICOTIN / APERITIF ctsp on Italy 1866-N 10-centesimi.

| F 29A | (1885-98) | Bronze | 31mm | — | — | — | — |

Similar ctsp on Great Britain 1862 penny.

| F 29B | (1885-98) | Copper | 25mm | — | — | — | — |

Similar ctsp on Italy 1861-M 5-centesimi.

| F 30 | (1885-98) | Bronze | 31mm | — | — | — | — |

Similar ctsp, but 'P' of PICOTIN is a question mark (?). Ctsp on Great Britain penny. (Dates examined: 1860, 1861, 1862, 1863, 1866, 1867, 1873, 1874, 1876-H, 1877, 1878, 1883, 1885). This is by far the commonest counterstamp type of 19th century France.

| F 31 | (1885-98) | Bronze | 26mm | — | — | — | — |

Similar ctsp on Great Britain halfpenny. (Dates examined: 1860, 1861, 1862, 1871)

| Rulau | Date | Metal | Size | VG | F | VF | EF |
|---|---|---|---|---|---|---|---|
| F 32 | (1885-98) | Copper | 30mm | — | — | — | — |

Similar ctsp on Italy 10-centesimi. (Dates examined: 1862-M, 1863, 1866-M, 1866-N, 1866-T, 1867-H, 1867-OM, 1867-T)

| F 33 | (1885-98) | Copper | 25mm | — | — | — | — |

Similar ctsp on Italy 5-centesimi. (Dates examined: 1861, 1861-M, 1867-M)

| F 34 | (1885-98) | Copper | 30mm | — | — | — | — |

Similar ctsp on Luxemburg 10-centimes. (Dates examined: 1865, 1870)

| F 35 | (1885-98) | Copper | 30mm | — | — | — | — |

Similar ctsp on Greece 1878-K 10-lepta.

## USINE D'HARFLEUR
### France

| Rulau | Date | Metal | Size | VG | F | VF | EF |
|---|---|---|---|---|---|---|---|
| F 37 | (?) | Copper | 30mm | — | — | — | — |

USINE D'HARFLEUR in circle, with numeral 13 at center, ctsp on France 1853 10-centimes. (John Cheramy coll.)

## LESSIVE MAGIQUE
### France

| Rulau | Date | Metal | Size | VG | F | VF | EF |
|---|---|---|---|---|---|---|---|
| F 22 | (?) | Bronze | 31mm | — | — | — | — |

LESSIVE / MAGIQUE ctsp on Great Britain 1883 penny.

## VANILLAROME
### France

| Rulau | Date | Metal | Size | VG | F | VF | EF |
|---|---|---|---|---|---|---|---|
| F 39 | (?) | Copper | 30mm | — | — | — | — |

VANILLAROME ctsp on Italy 10-centesimi. (Dates examined: 1867-H, 1867-N)

## VIN DE NAPLES
### St. Gilles, France

| Rulau | Date | Metal | Size | VG | F | VF | EF |
|---|---|---|---|---|---|---|---|
| F 40 | (?) | Bronze | 31mm | — | — | — | — |

VIN DE / NAPLES PUR / 75C LA BOUTLL / FLAMENT / ST GILLES 6 / AUROY 7 BIS ctsp on Great Britain penny. (Dates examined: 1863, 1874-H)

| F 41 | (?) | Copper | 30mm | — | — | — | — |

Similar ctsp on France 1856-D 10-centimes.

## France — Miscellaneous Counterstamps

**VICTOR / ADOURDAN** on France L'An 8-A 5-centimes, Craig 135

**HENRY / A / PONT-LA-VILLE** on France 1862-A 5-centimes

**SEDAN** on France 1866 silver franc

# GERMANY

## RUDOLPH SCHRODER
## Altona, Germany

| Rulau | Date | Metal | Size | F | VF | EF | Unc |
|---|---|---|---|---|---|---|---|
| G 11 | (1876) | WM | 23mm | — | — | 20.00 | 45.00 |

Centennial die K: Capitol at center, CAPITOL AT WASHINGTON above. Rv: KAUFE DOBBINS' / ELECTRISCHE / SEIFE / DIE / BESTE VON / ALLEN / RUDOLPH SCHRODER / ALTONA. Plain edge. (Miller Pa 1)

| G 12 | (1876) | WM | 23mm | — | — | 20.00 | 45.00 |

Centennial die E: (Continental soldier) Rv: As G11. Plain edge.

Assigned by Adams, Miller and Slabaugh to Altoona, Pa. in error. Schroder distributed Dobbins' Electric Soap (Dobbins' Electrische Seife) in the Hamburg area.

# PERU

## WALLACE BARNES
## Ayacucho, Peru

| Rulau | Date | Metal | Size | VG | F | VF | EF |
|---|---|---|---|---|---|---|---|
| P 3 | (?) | Silver | 25mm | — | 85.00 | — | — |

WALLACE BARNES curved, ctsp twice on U.S. 1847 Liberty Seated quarter. The counterstamp is repeated once on reverse of the coin. (Kurt Krueger coll.)

| P 6 | (?) | Silver | 38mm | — | — | 275. | — |

WALLACE BARNES curved, ctsp on South American silver dollar. AYACUCHO PERU ctsp on edge of the coin. (ex-Rulau coll.)

| P 8 | (?) | Copper | 29mm | — | — | 50.00 | — |

WALLACE BARNES curved, ctsp on U.S. 1845 Large cent.

Some 10 pieces are known to exist. Brunk thinks these are American, not from Peru, and that the edge stamp on P 6 is not connected.

# TRINIDAD

## F.D.
## (Francois Declos)
## Trinidad

| Rulau | Date | Metal | Size | F | VF | EF | Unc |
|---|---|---|---|---|---|---|---|
| T 1 | (?) | Copper | 28mm | — | — | — | — |

Deep incuse F D ctsp on Great Britain 1790's halfpenny token, D&H Middlesex 954. (Pridmore 7A)

| T 6 | (?) | Copper | 29mm | — | — | — | — |

Similar ctsp on U.S. Large cents of various dates.

| T 2 | (?) | Copper | 28mm | — | — | 250. | — |

Similar ctsp on U.S. 1841 Hard Times token. (Brunk coll.) (Bushnell 12)

| T 3 | (?) | Bronze | 26mm | — | — | — | — |

Similar ctsp on Great Britain 1869 halfpenny. (Pridmore 7D)

| T 4 | (?) | Copper | 28mm | — | — | — | — |

Similar ctsp on Canada 1814 Nova Scotia halfpenny, Breton 880. (Pridmore 7C)

| T 5 | (?) | Copper | 28mm | — | — | — | — |

Similar ctsp on Canada 1815 Nova Scotia halfpenny, Breton 890. (Pridmore 7B)

Francois Declos, a barber, created stampee tokens (2 cents local value) by counterstamping halfpenny (cent) sized coins and tokens. In all 14 types of punchmark were used over a long period of time.

# INDEX
## (United States)

NOTE: Miscellaneous counterstamped coins are not indexed alphabetically since they are arranged alphabetically, beginning on pages 000 and 000 respectively.

### A

| Name | Page |
|---|---|
| A.C. Co. (Aughinbaugh) | 57 |
| L.A. (Asbeck) | 51 |
| Abbey, M.A. | 169 |
| Abbott, J.A. | 169 |
| Ackroyd, James & Sons | 84 |
| Acme (Saloon) | 149 |
| Adlon, J.B. | 43 |
| Ahn, J.W., Confectionery | 121 |
| Alamo, The | 153 |
| Albert's Saloon | 153 |
| Albion College | 43 |
| Algona Bar | 151 |
| Allen, A.H. | 169 |
| Allen, Dr. W.H. | 118 |
| American Hotel | 72 |
| American Hotel Bar | 17 |
| American Life Insurance Co. | 121 |
| American Pile Co. | 169 |
| Ammin's Brothers | 146 |
| Anchardoqui, C. | 17 |
| Anderson, M.E. | 148 |
| Anderson Brothers | 164 |
| Andre, Prof., Alpine Choir | 170 |
| Anheuser-Busch | 74 |
| Applegates Galleries | 122 |
| Applegates on the Beach | 81 |
| Applegates Palace of Flying Animals | 81 |
| Apollo Gardens | 60 |
| Arnold | 169 |
| Asbeck, Louis | 51 |
| Ashby, C.C. | 122 |
| Ashman, R.E. | 169 |
| Atheneum | 170 |
| Atlantic Billiard Hall | 110 |
| Aughinbaugh Canning Co. | 57 |
| Ayers, R.A. | 18 |

### B

| Name | Page |
|---|---|
| B. & B. White Elephant | 150 |
| B. & H. | 170 |
| B.L. (Baltimore Liederkranz) | 51 |
| F.B. | 47 |
| G.B. (Bauernschmidt) | 54 |
| H.C.B. (Betch) | 51 |
| J.B. | 17 |
| S.B. | 17 |
| S.B. & Co. | 89 |
| T.F.B. (Bottomley) | 58 |
| Bailey, G.L. | 50 |
| Bailey & Sawyer | 50 |
| Bailey & Stouffer | 170 |
| Baker, W.R. | 51 |
| Baker & Thomas | 28 |
| Baldwin & Smith | 83 |
| Ballou, P.E. | 170 |
| Baltimore | 51 |
| Baltimore & Ohio R.R. | 89 |
| Baltimore Festival | 51 |
| Baltimore Liederkranz | 51 |
| Baltimore Oriole Celebration | 51 |
| Bank Exchange | 152 |
| Barnes, J.L. | 149 |

### B

| Name | Page |
|---|---|
| Barnes, S.S. & Co. | 52 |
| Barnum, P.T. | 89 |
| Barry, Ed. | 170 |
| Basford & Glenn | 82 |
| Bastable Block | 108 |
| Bauernschmidt, George | 54 |
| Beach Hotel | 150 |
| Beard, Joseph Jr. | 53 |
| Bee Hive | 65 |
| Behrens, Emil | 153 |
| Bell, A. | 109 |
| Bell & Brothers | 154 |
| Bellefonte Iron Co. | 120 |
| Bellevue House | 110 |
| Benedict Brothers | 90 |
| Benesk, Casper | 44 |
| Bennett, G.W. | 47 |
| Bernard & Friedman | 59 |
| Berner, John | 39 |
| Berry, George B. & Co. | 152 |
| Betch, Charles | 51 |
| Betts, C. Wyllys | 24 |
| Bibb, The B.C. Stove Co. | 52 |
| Biggio, Lawrence | 29 |
| Billiard checks | 17, 18, 20, 23, 28, 31, 35, 39, 41, 42, 44, 48, 53, 71, 75, 78, 79, 84, 99, 110, 119, 143, 144, 150, 152, 157, 159, 164, 165, 168, 169, 171, 172, 178, 182 |
| Billigheimer's Billiard Hall | 110 |
| Bilz, Hugo F. | 78 |
| Binghurst & Kirby | 122 |
| Binnard's Elite Saloon | 164 |
| Bismarck Saloon | 147 |
| Bixby, Jotham | 17 |
| Black River & Utica R.R. Co. | 88 |
| Blaine, Frank C. | 149 |
| Blanchard, Ed. | 40 |
| Blanchard House | 39 |
| Blodgett, F. | 64 |
| Bloomingdales | 90 |
| Blystone & Rhodes | 170 |
| Boche, L. | 29 |
| Bochow, G.F. | 18 |
| Bolen, James A. | 65 |
| Bonitz, W. | 109 |
| Bonsall, Charles E. | 84 |
| Booth, J.W. | 169 |
| Bordentown House | 82 |
| Bornefeld, Jules | 147 |
| Bosshardt, John | 154 |
| Boston, The | 82 |
| Boston Numismatic Society | 59 |
| Botica La Manche | 151 |
| Bottomley, Thomas F. | 58 |
| Bowman, W.E. | 40 |
| Bradley, William L. | 170 |
| Bradstreet, J.M. & Sons | 90 |
| Bradstreet Hoffman & Co. | 90 |
| Brady, Jim & Co. | 154 |
| Brady, John | 154 |
| Brady, William A. | 170 |

### B

| Name | Page |
|---|---|
| Brakeman | 171 |
| Brauneis, E.J. | 110 |
| Brets, Ve. | 171 |
| Brinks | 171 |
| Broadhurst, W.J. | 171 |
| Brooklyn Single Tax Club | 85 |
| Brown, C.O. | 71 |
| Brown, D.B. | 171 |
| Brown, Frank | 154 |
| Brown, H. Bro. & Co. | 90 |
| Brown, J. | 79 |
| Brown, J.T. | 50 |
| Brown Brothers | 71 |
| Brown Bros. & Co. | 18 |
| Buckley, W. | 18 |
| Buehler, D. Cornwell | 71 |
| Buffet Bar | 154 |
| Buhlert & Stephany | 29 |
| Bunting, W.A. & Son | 141 |
| Burges, H.S. | 171 |
| Burnette House Annex | 118 |
| Burns, Till A. | 18 |
| Burns Folz & Sons | 110 |
| Burr, Henry W. Co. | 59 |
| Burr & Witsil | 122 |
| Burwell, Wm. & Bro. | 122 |
| Butchers N.P.A. | 29 |
| Butler & Bee | 87 |
| Byers Brothers | 36 |

### C

| Name | Page |
|---|---|
| C.C.C. & I. R.R. | 116 |
| C.C. R.R. | 22 |
| H.W.C. | 171 |
| J.B.C. | 172 |
| M.C. | 172 |
| O.W.C. | 172 |
| T.C. & Co. | 145 |
| W.A.C. | 64 |
| Cameron, Aug. | 150 |
| Camp, W.W. | 152 |
| Campbell, P.H. | 121 |
| Canalport Ave. Police Station | 29 |
| Cannon, C. | 43 |
| Carlson, Peter | 41 |
| Carpender | 83 |
| Carrollton Clothing House | 52 |
| Carson, Thomas C. | 36 |
| Casino No. 3 | 52 |
| Cassidy's | 48 |
| Cassidy's Old Established Store | 122 |
| Cavanaugh, M.A. | 164 |
| Centennial Advertising Medal Co. | 123 |
| Centennial of our Nation | 29, 40, 41 |
| Cercle de San Francisco | 19 |
| Cercle Francais | 18 |
| Cercle M.S. | 18 |
| Charroppin, E.L. | 49 |
| Chatfield, M. | 28 |
| Chicago Exposition | 30, 38 |
| Chicago Herald, The | 30 |
| Child & Bro. | 40 |

[217]

## C

| Name | Page |
|---|---|
| Childs, E.E. Jr. | 172 |
| Childs, L. | 172 |
| Childs, S.D. & Co. | 30 |
| Christian, A.S. | 149 |
| Chung Jan | 18 |
| Cincinnati Industrial Exposition | 111, 113, 115 |
| City of New York Airship | 90 |
| Clark, J.W. | 142 |
| Clark, N.T. | 172 |
| Clark, S. | 84 |
| Clarke & Co. | 72 |
| Clay, John H. | 123 |
| Cleveland Columbus Cincinnati & Indiana RR | 116 |
| Coal Creek Coal Co. | 145 |
| Cockerel, H. | 149 |
| Coffey & Harrison | 27 |
| Cogan, Edward | 85 |
| Colby, L.J. | 59 |
| Cold Fri. | 172 |
| Cole | 172 |
| Cole & Flinn | 162 |
| Colorado Central Railroad | 22 |
| Columbia Hotel | 121 |
| Concordia (Ill.) | 37 |
| Concordia (Md.) | 52 |
| Coney Island Jockey Club | 86 |
| Conklin, J.O. | 29 |
| Conrad, J. | 172 |
| Conried, H. | 90 |
| Consolidated K.C. Smelting & Refining | 73 |
| Consolidated Racket Stores | 172 |
| Constantine's, Nic., Saloon | 149 |
| Constitutional Prohibition Org. | 144 |
| Continental | 172 |
| Contrahendo et Solvendo | 172 |
| Cook, Henry | 59 |
| Cook & Sloss | 45 |
| Cooper & Demarest | 172 |
| Corn Palace | 43 |
| Cornell Watch Co. | 18 |
| Corre, A.G., Hotel Co. | 113 |
| Cosmopolitan (Bar) | 147 |
| Cotton, J.W. | 42 |
| Cotton, Willis | 42 |
| Count & Countess Magri | 131 |
| Covert, William | 123 |
| Cow Boy Saloon | 159 |
| Cow Boy's Saloon | 149 |
| Cox | 52 |
| Cragin, Isaiah L. | 123 |
| Crellin's Place | 113 |
| Crescent City Athletic Club | 48 |
| Creston Blue Grass Palace | 117 |
| Crew's Pyramidal Railway | 113 |
| Croom & Hill | 72 |
| Crowley, D.M. | 78 |
| Crystal Saloon | 159 |
| Cuddy, J. & Co. | 31 |
| Cummings, J. | 67 |
| Czarnowsky, Hy. | 23 |

## D

| Name | Page |
|---|---|
| D. Brothers | 123 |
| D.C. & Co. | 171 |
| G.D. | 71 |
| Dacosta's | 31 |
| Dakota Commandery No. 1 | 144 |
| Dallemand & Co. | 31 |
| D.A. Pionier Jubilaum | 83 |
| Daly's Fifth Avenue Theatre | 91 |
| Dana, Charles A. | 123 |
| Darby, W.H. | 119 |
| Daub, Henry | 168 |
| Davis, W.E. | 85 |
| Davis, W.P. | 105 |
| Day, D.H. | 173 |
| Deakin, W. | 31 |
| Deal, J.J. | 71 |
| Dean, Charles A. | 91 |
| Demond, G.N. | 79 |
| Dengremont | 173 |
| Deppen's Hatters | 46 |
| DePuy, Thomas | 124 |
| DeSollar, H.C. | 73 |
| Deutsch Franzosischen Krieg | 74 |
| Deutsche Friedensfeier | 19 |
| Deutschland's Friedensfeier | 108 |
| Diamond Saloon | 162 |
| Dickenson's Coin & Medal Safe | 124 |
| Diehl, J.H. | 125 |
| Diehl, J.H. & Wm. H. Key | 125 |
| Dittrich, A. | 25 |
| Dixon Crucible Co. | 83 |
| Dobbins Electric Soap | 123 |
| Dodd & Co. | 36 |
| Dodd & Wolfe | 145 |
| Dorman's Stencil & Stamp Works | 52 |
| Douglas Monument Association | 31 |
| Dowells, Ben | 150 |
| Driving Club of New York | 91 |
| Dude Saloon, The | 17 |
| Dunn, F.A. | 49 |
| Dunn, P.C., Saloon | 31 |

## E

| Name | Page |
|---|---|
| E.G. & S.M. Co. | 173 |
| E.T. (Eintracht) | 142 |
| Eagles | 169 |
| Egyptian Obelisk, The | 91 |
| Ehret, George | 91 |
| Eichler, John | 92 |
| Eintracht | 142 |
| Eldorado Saloon | 26 |
| Eldred, L. | 88 |
| Elephant | 183 |
| Elgin National Watch Co. | 37 |
| Elgin Turnverein | 38 |
| Elite Saloon | 154 |
| Ellis, William L. & Co. | 53 |
| Ellsworth & Buck | 154 |
| Emery, F.W. | 79 |
| Encampment of N.G.P. | 121 |
| Eureka (Hotel) | 19 |
| Ev. Luth. Church | 23 |
| Evans, G. | 173 |
| Evans & LaMotte | 148 |
| Evans & Watson | 124 |

## F

| Name | Page |
|---|---|
| F. & M. (and) J.R.M. | 31 |
| Falkenstein, George | 53 |
| Fargason Cordes & Co. | 145 |
| Farmers' and Mechanics' Life Ins. | 92 |
| Fatters, A. | 48 |
| Feely | 125 |
| Feigenspan's Lager | 173 |
| Fenian pieces | 22, 174 |
| Fera, George | 60 |
| Ferguson, J.H. | 125 |
| Finck, George | 143 |
| Fireman's Convention | 107 |
| Firemen's Tournament | 87 |
| First International Military Encamp. | 32 |
| Fisher, G.F. | 50 |
| Fisk, Col. James Jr. | 32 |
| Fleming, Dr. D.L. | 125 |
| Foreign Exhibition | 60 |
| Fosdick, F.F. | 173 |
| Foucar, Theo. M. | 113 |
| Founding of the City | 53 |
| 407 Broadway | 92 |
| Fourth St. Opera House | 74 |
| Frank, W. & Co. | 19 |
| Franklin & Co. | 92 |
| Franklin Fire Co. No. 13 | 125 |
| Fred's | 154 |
| Frederick's Pharmacy | 92 |
| Free Pool (Beard) | 53 |
| Freja | 38 |
| French Palace | 32 |
| Friedensfeier im Jahre 1871 | 92 |
| Fries Malseed & Hawkins | 125 |
| Fuller, J.P. | 173 |
| Fuller, J.W. | 167 |
| Furtner, J.L. | 154 |

## G

| Name | Page |
|---|---|
| G. & B. City Saloon | 119 |
| G.A.R. 19 Annual Encampment | 50 |
| G.R. & I. R.R. | 69 |
| A.J.G. | 119 |
| E.G. & Sons | 173 |
| Gaier, Andy | 173 |
| Gall, J.D. | 20 |
| Gall & Maddens | 20 |
| Galt House | 160 |
| Game counters | 19, 20, 143 |
| Gasper, J.W. | 109 |
| Gates, G.S. | 64 |
| Gates & Trask | 173 |
| Gaul, John W. | 40 |
| Gehrig, J.W. | 32 |
| Genin the Hatter | 32 |
| Gercke, J. Henry | 125 |
| Germania House | 113 |
| German Peace tokens | 19, 92, 108, 167 |
| Gerry, G. | 59 |
| Gilbert, J.W. | 126 |
| Gilcrest, V. | 118 |
| Giles Bro. & Co. | 32 |
| Gladding, Charles D. | 173 |
| Globe Fire Ins. Co. | 93 |
| Glock, S. | 84 |
| Gobelman Brothers | 168 |
| Goodwin, R.J.P. | 79 |
| Gosman & Co. | 53 |
| Gottlieb, Aichele | 174 |
| Grand Central Clothing House | 32 |
| Grand Commandery K.T. | 126 |
| Grand Hotel (Corre) | 113 |
| Gray's Bankrupt Store | 113 |
| Great Northern Exposition | 141 |
| Great Union Pacific Tea Co. | 93 |
| Green's Buffet | 77 |
| Greenwood Park | 53 |
| Gregory, B.M. | 17 |
| Greisenheim | 54 |
| Grenier's Lyceum | 33 |
| Grimshaw, W.D. | 94 |

## G

| Name | Page |
|---|---|
| Guadalupe Hotel | 154 |
| Gum, J.B. | 74 |
| Gunther's Candy | 30 |
| Gus' | 74 |
| Gusky's Clothiers Hatters | 141 |

## H

| Name | Page |
|---|---|
| E.J.H. (Hines) | 57 |
| F.H. & M.P. | 162 |
| J.H. (Hinkson) | 108 |
| J.S.H. (Hawkins) | 58 |
| O.H. | 174 |
| W.H. & Co. | 145 |
| Haas, Herman | 36 |
| Hale, H. | 68 |
| Haller & Ellis | 145 |
| Hammill, Charles W. & Co. | 54 |
| Hand, Shamgar S. | 126 |
| Hanks, E. | 174 |
| Hannah & Hogg | 33 |
| Hapgood | 60 |
| Harbach, Theo. J. | 126 |
| Harbach Brothers | 126 |
| Harbach's Christmas Tree Orn. | 126 |
| Harbach's Original Walnut Candy | 126 |
| Hardin, John Wesley | 149, 150 |
| Harmes, Lothar | 174 |
| Harmon Brothers | 165 |
| Harness & Clay | 45 |
| Harpole, E.D. | 174 |
| Harris, A.O. & Co. | 145 |
| Harrisburg Maennerchor | 120 |
| Hart's | 127 |
| Hart, H.E. | 88 |
| Hart, H.M. | 165 |
| Haskell Engraving Co. | 74 |
| Hatch, E.C. | 174 |
| Hatch's Restaurant | 165 |
| Hauschild, P. | 28 |
| Havlin Barber Shop | 113 |
| Hawkins, John S. | 58 |
| Hawley, M.C. & Co. | 35 |
| Hayward's Billiard Parlor | 41 |
| Haywood's Saloon | 26 |
| Hedlund & Olson | 26 |
| Heidemann Mfg. Co., The | 155 |
| Heinen, D. & A. | 155 |
| Heisely, F.A. | 141 |
| Henderson, D.P. & Co. | 145 |
| Henderson, E., Packing Co. | 143 |
| Henry, S.M. | 107 |
| Hensen, C.E. | 42 |
| Herman, P. Jr. | 39 |
| Hess & Speidel | 60 |
| Heyne, Herman H. | 113 |
| Hildebrand, C.S. & Co. | 42 |
| Hines, Edward J. | 47 |
| Hinkson, John | 108 |
| Hit Him Again | 169 |
| Hoag, Thomas | 94 |
| Hoeft | 95 |
| Homs, M. | 165 |
| Hoops, H.W. | 95 |
| Hopkins Trans-Oceanic Co. | 174 |
| Horn, C.E. | 84 |
| Horner's | 155 |
| Hotel de France | 27 |
| Hotel Lemhi Bar | 27 |
| Hotel Savoy | 113 |
| Howard & Tooley | 165 |

## H

| Name | Page |
|---|---|
| Howe Machine Co. | 45 |
| Howe's Improved | 160, 161 |
| Hubbell, W. | 174 |
| Hubert Mill | 22 |
| Hubert Mine | 22 |
| Hudnut's Mineral | 95 |
| Huffman, P. | 42 |
| Hughes Brothers | 119 |
| Hughes House | 127 |
| Hugo, Edward | 114 |
| Hunt Pkg. Co. | 143 |
| Hunt & Moore | 174 |
| Hurd, J. | 174 |
| Hussey & Murray | 24 |
| Huyler's | 95 |
| Hyman, N.J. | 19 |

## I

| Name | Page |
|---|---|
| Ice Palace & Winter Carnival | 72 |
| Illgen, J.F. | 28 |
| Illinois Military & Mech. Training | 33 |
| Illinois Watch Co. | 41 |
| Indiana Asbury University | 43 |
| International Exhibition | 127 |
| International Maritime Exhibition | 60 |
| Irish Republic | 174 |

## J

| Name | Page |
|---|---|
| Jackson, Samuel | 54 |
| Jacobs, M. | 144 |
| James, C.O. | 175 |
| T. Jan. P. | 175 |
| Jane's, S., Store | 95 |
| Jaquith | 95 |
| Jefferson Insurance Co. | 95 |
| Jellico Mt. Coal & Coke Co. | 147 |
| Jenkins, John H. | 47 |
| Jenkins, William R. | 96 |
| Jensch, F.A. | 33 |
| Johnson, L.H. | 175 |
| Jonas, Peter Jr. | 155 |
| Jonas Garden | 155 |
| Joslin & Park | 22 |
| Jozefa, T.W.S. | 68 |

## K

| Name | Page |
|---|---|
| K. | 167 |
| K.T. (Easton) | 120 |
| E.K. (Kelly) | 57 |
| H.N.K. (Kelley) | 58 |
| L.K. | 121 |
| Kaighn's Ave. Palace of Flying Animals | 82 |
| Kay, C.W. | 175 |
| Kearsarge House | 79 |
| Kellersman, Conrad | 75 |
| Kelley, Hezron N. | 58 |
| Kelly's | 127 |
| Kelly, Egbert | 57 |
| Kelly, J.E.H. | 108 |
| Kendall, H.N. | 27 |
| Kenmuir, John | 74 |
| Kensett | 54 |
| Kenyon, J.B. | 118 |
| Key & Co. | 127 |
| Key & Diehl | 129 |
| Kilbridge, G. | 129 |
| King, C.W. | 175 |
| Kingman & Co. | 41 |
| Kingsford, T. & Son | 106 |
| Kirtland, F.S. | 46 |
| Kittingers | 41 |
| Kleinsteuber, Chas. | 167 |

## K

| Name | Page |
|---|---|
| Klepper, Joseph | 163 |
| Kline's | 159 |
| Kline, Henry | 48 |
| Kline, John W. | 129 |
| Klingler's Theatre | 155 |
| Knickman, H. | 87 |
| Knight, K. | 96 |
| Knights of the Golden Eagle | 25 |
| Knights Templar tokens | 118, 120, 126, 134, 144 |
| Knoppel, Dietrich | 129 |
| Knoppel, Frederick | 130 |
| Knowles, A.P. | 59 |
| Knox, T. | 85 |
| Knox Brothers | 22 |
| Kohler, Rud. | 96 |
| Kohn, A. & Co. | 43 |
| Kraft & Bauer | 114 |
| Kruger, Th. | 96 |

## L

| Name | Page |
|---|---|
| L.I.P. & B.A. No 1 | 86 |
| A.C.L. Refreshment Contractor | 175 |
| P.L. & Co. (Lorillard) | 97 |
| Lane, David H. | 96 |
| Langdon Bakery | 114 |
| Laredo Beer Garden | 151 |
| Latreyte | 151 |
| LaVallee Saloon | 148 |
| Law, Lucy | 175 |
| Lawrence, A. | 64 |
| Leadville | 22 |
| Leak, John | 130 |
| Lee, George | 18 |
| Lee & Jones | 175 |
| Lehm's Saloon | 148 |
| Leidel, E.A.M. | 167 |
| Leman, E. Jr. | 179 |
| Levin, Julius & Co. | 47 |
| Levy, Jacob (Eureka) | 19 |
| Licensed Cincinnati | 114 |
| Lieuallens, J.W., Bakery | 27 |
| Linde, William | 83 |
| Lindinger, Fritz | 96 |
| Lingg & Co. | 131 |
| Lingg & Brother | 130 |
| Lion Buggy Co. | 175 |
| Lipari, Joseph | 152 |
| Litchfield S. Co. | 23 |
| Little Corner Saloon | 155 |
| Lobe, Dr. W.H. | 131 |
| Lockwood Sewing School | 84 |
| Lookout House | 110 |
| Lorillard, Pierre & Co. | 97 |
| Losch, John | 71 |
| Lovell, Thomas | 114 |
| Lovett's Private Stock Whiskey | 175 |
| Lowe, George A. | 36 |
| Lyceum Theatre | 34 |
| Lyman, R. | 175 |
| Lyon-Hall & Co. | 54 |
| Lyons, C.J. | 142 |

## M

| Name | Page |
|---|---|
| M. & St. L. Packet Co. | 75 |
| M.C. R.R. (Michigan) | 69 |
| M.R. & M. Club | 120 |
| M.S. & N.I. R.R. (Michigan) | 69 |
| F.M. | 176 |
| H.S.M. (Moody) | 41 |
| J.H.M. & B. (Muenster) | 152 |

| Name | Page |
|---|---|
| **M** | |
| Mabley & Carew | 115 |
| Macgill & Moore | 57 |
| Mackfell & Richardson | 97 |
| Macy, R.H. & Co. | 97 |
| Mallory Commission Co. | 34 |
| Malseed & Hawkins | 132 |
| Manhattan Watch Co. | 97 |
| Manson, E.A. | 176 |
| Mardi Gras | 48 |
| Marks, S.H. & Co. | 163 |
| Marshall, Morgan L. | 105 |
| Martin, W.I. | 108 |
| Martinka & Co. | 98 |
| Maryland picker chits | 58 |
| Mason & Co. | 132 |
| Mason, Richard F. | 144 |
| Masonic Temple (Boston) | 61 |
| Massachusetts Arms Co. | 64 |
| Mathews, J.A. | 176 |
| Matson, N. & Co. | 34 |
| Matthews, John | 98 |
| Mauduit & Co. | 19 |
| Maurice & Henry | 75 |
| Maxey, John J. | 35 |
| Mayer, Alf J. | 47 |
| Mayer, F.X. | 40 |
| Mayer, George L. | 47 |
| McColgan & Hughes | 176 |
| McDermott's Sunset Saloon | 155 |
| McDonald, W.C. | 42 |
| McGlade, Charles, Mansion | 81 |
| McIlvaine & Pratt | 155 |
| McKay & Lapsley | 146 |
| McLaughlin, Jas. | 118 |
| McMurray, L. & Co. | 54 |
| McNamee, R. | 163 |
| Megibben & Bro. | 145 |
| Meiners & Vilter | 168 |
| Menger Hotel Bar | 156 |
| Mermod & Jaccard Jewelry Co. | 75 |
| Merriam, Joseph H. | 61 |
| Merrill, J.M. & Co. | 146 |
| Metropolitan Insurance Co. | 98 |
| Metz's, J.H., Hotel | 176 |
| Meyer, F.I. | 156 |
| Meyer, H.J. | 99 |
| Meyer, J.J. & Co. | 55 |
| Michigan Central Railroad | 69 |
| Michigan Southern & No. Indiana R.R. | 69 |
| Mick, Henry | 75 |
| Midway Saloon | 148 |
| Mike & Joe's Saloon | 156 |
| Miller, A.F. | 27 |
| Miller, Charlotte H. | 148 |
| Miller M. | 176 |
| Miller House | 176 |
| Milligan & Son | 57 |
| Mills, G.F. | 148 |
| Milwaukee Industrial Exposition | 167 |
| Milwaukier Friedens-Feier | 167 |
| Miners | 176 |
| Minneapolis Exposition | 71 |
| Minstrel shows | 26 |
| Mitchell & Lewis Co. Ltd. | 168 |
| Model Dairy | 160 |
| Momenthy, Bruno | 55 |
| Monarch Saloon | 79 |
| Moody, H.S. | 41 |
| Moore & Brady | 55 |
| Moore Brothers | 67 |
| Morse, E.R. | 62 |
| Moser | 97 |
| Mosser, S.B. | 156 |
| Mott, H.T. | 75 |
| Muenster, J.H. & Brother | 152 |
| Muller, C. & Brother | 146 |
| Murphy, D.M. | 132 |
| Murphy, J. | 177 |
| Murphy, J.J. | 152 |
| Muschler & Willis | 28 |
| **N** | |
| N.G. of N.J. | 83 |
| N.J.N.G. 9th Regt. C Co. | 83 |
| N.P. Exc. | 77 |
| W.N. & Sons (Numsen) | 55 |
| Naboclish | 176 |
| Nalle, J. | 26 |
| National Agricultural Exposition | 73 |
| National Guard (N.J.) | 83 |
| National Guard (N.Y.) | 109 |
| National Guard (Pa.) | 121, 136, 142 |
| National Horse Show Assn. | 176 |
| National Mining & Industrial Expo. | 23 |
| National Novelty Co. | 177 |
| National Peace Jubilee | 62 |
| National Railway Electric & Ind. Expo. | 74 |
| National Union League | 132 |
| Neeb, J.B. | 110 |
| Neff & Duff | 147 |
| Nelson's Business Colleges | 115 |
| Nentwig's Bar | 156 |
| Nesbit, A. | 41 |
| Nevils & Rose | 146 |
| New Ess(ex) Saloon | 20 |
| New Resort, The | 27 |
| Newman Brothers | 19 |
| Newman's Clothing House | 120 |
| Newton, W.B. | 148 |
| Newton Wagon Co. | 28 |
| New York Clothing House | 55 |
| New York Turnverein | 99 |
| Ninth Precinct House | 133 |
| Nonpareil | 55 |
| Norioh, J.C. | 151 |
| North, Central & South American Expo. | 48 |
| North Jellico Coal Co. | 145 |
| Northwestern Dental Infirmary | 34 |
| N.W. Show Case Mfg. Co. | 34 |
| Nossaman, L.T. | 22 |
| Numsen, William & Sons | 55 |
| N.Y.N.G. 7th Regt. | 109 |
| N.Y. & N.E. R.R. | 109 |
| **O** | |
| G.O. | 84 |
| R.E.O. (Owens) | 57 |
| Oberman, H. & Co. | 165 |
| Office Restaurant | 162 |
| Oil of Ice | 177 |
| O'Neill & Co. | 56 |
| Opera House Wine Room | 151 |
| Ophir, The | 150 |
| Oquaga House | 87 |
| Order of the Iron Hall | 177 |
| Ore hauler's tokens | 22 |
| Orfila, A. | 156 |
| Orient Bar | 119 |
| Oswego Starch Factory | 106 |
| Owens, Robert E. | 57 |
| **P** | |
| P.L. (Pahl-Links) | 168 |
| P.S. & P. R.R. Co. | 79 |
| Packard, W. | 118 |
| Page, W.B. | 177 |
| Pahl-Links Brewery | 168 |
| Palmer (Mass.) | 64 |
| Palmer, M.D. | 177 |
| Palmer House | 35 |
| Parisian Varieties | 99 |
| Park Theatre | 100 |
| Parker, Ben | 49 |
| Parker, William C. | 87 |
| Parlor, The | 150 |
| Parmelee Webster & Co. | 99 |
| Patapsco Fruit Butter Co. | 56 |
| Patent | 160, 178 |
| Patented | 177 |
| Pat. 1868 | 177 |
| Patterson, R.A. & Co. | 163 |
| Paul & Crockett | 146 |
| Payton, E.L. | 115 |
| Peacock | 177 |
| Pearl Bakery | 165 |
| Penn Mutual Life Ins. Co. | 133 |
| Pennsylvania State Agricul. Fair | 133 |
| Perry, H.V. | 88 |
| Pfaelzer Brothers | 133 |
| Phelan, George E. | 99 |
| Phenyo Caffein Co. | 68 |
| Philadelphia Rifle Club | 133 |
| Phoenix Knife Co. | 107 |
| Phosphor Bronze | 177 |
| Picard, A. | 133 |
| Picker checks | 51, 57, 58 |
| Pic-Nick & Sommernachtsfest | 100 |
| Piedmont Club | 162 |
| Piedmont Exposition | 26 |
| Piepenbring, Edward | 162 |
| Pierce's Rosetta Hair Tonic | 178 |
| Pilgrimage of San Francisco Club | 134 |
| Pimmel, W. | 100 |
| Pittsburgh Exposition Society | 141 |
| Pittsburgh, Fort Wayne & Chicago R.R. | 117 |
| Pizzini | 163 |
| Plastridge, A.A. | 143 |
| Poehler's | 72 |
| Pony House | 117 |
| Poole, J.N. | 143 |
| Porter, Wood N. | 178 |
| Portland, Saco & Portsmouth R.R. | 79 |
| Post Office (Baltimore) | 56 |
| Post Office Exchange | 47 |
| Potts, W.B. | 117 |
| Pratt, Monroe | 156 |
| Prentice, F. | 100 |
| Prentis House | 72 |
| Preuser & Wellenvoss | 46 |
| Price Brothers | 56 |
| Price Hill House | 111 |
| Pringsheim | 56 |
| Probasco, Henry | 115 |
| Professor Saloon | 156 |
| Prosser, Thomas & Son (Grimshaw) | 94 |
| Pruden, Isaac C. | 100 |
| Pugh, W.C. | 178 |
| Putnam, C., Cast Steel | 178 |
| Putzel's Clothing Hall | 44 |

| Q | | |
|---|---|---|
| **Name** | | **Page** |
| Quebe, F. | | 50 |
| Quest, J.W. | | 46 |

| R | | |
|---|---|---|
| J.H.R. (Armstrong Maker) | | 178 |
| J.H.R. (Robinson) | | 51 |
| P.R. | | 178 |
| Raabe, A.H. | | 178 |
| Rainbow Fire Co. | | 142 |
| Ramsdell, C.V. | | 49 |
| Ranch, The | | 151 |
| Rayner, W.H. | | 71 |
| Rech, Jacob | | 134 |
| Reed, J. | | 134 |
| Reed, W. | | 178 |
| Reed's, Jacob, Sons | | 134 |
| Rees, H. | | 134 |
| Reid, P.J. | | 56 |
| Reinhart Brothers | | 115 |
| Resort, The | | 117 |
| Resorts on the hills | | 110 |
| Resurgens | | 26 |
| Return of Peace | | 169 |
| Rheiner's Saloon | | 157 |
| Rheiner & Gaul | | 157 |
| Rice | | 100 |
| Rice, N.H. | | 134 |
| Richards, H.M. & Co. | | 62, 63 |
| Richardson, Charles H. | | 47 |
| Richardson, C.W. | | 62 |
| Richmond, A.S. | | 50 |
| Ridge's, Dr., Food | | 62 |
| Ridley, G.E. | | 178 |
| Ringrose, N. | | 144 |
| Rivinius, C. | | 88 |
| Roberts Dye Works | | 87 |
| Robinson, Alfred S. | | 23 |
| Robinson, C.D. | | 79 |
| Robinson, John Henry | | 51 |
| Robinson Museum & Theatre | | 48 |
| Robinson & Heath | | 64 |
| Rodier, L.C. | | 67 |
| Roe | | 78 |
| Rogers & Bro. | | 64 |
| Roling, Fred. | | 178 |
| Roller Skating Association | | 86 |
| Rome Brass & Copper Co. | | 107 |
| Rome Iron Works | | 107 |
| Rosenberg, H.E.V. | | 152 |
| Rowell, George P. & Co. | | 101 |
| Rowin, T.B. | | 39 |
| Rowland, T. & Brothers | | 134 |
| Roxbee & Pritchitt | | 86 |
| Ryan, A.E. | | 71 |

| S | | |
|---|---|---|
| S | | 149 |
| S. & H. Co. | | 179 |
| E.E.S. (Sponable) | | 78 |
| L.C.S. & Co. | | 179 |
| L.R.S. (Shipley) | | 51 |
| N.S. & Co. | | 179 |
| T.J.S. (Stewart) | | 49 |
| Sagada Hockhouse | | 179 |
| Sage's Candy Coin | | 179 |
| St. Louis Saloon | | 148 |
| Salem Commandery 42, K.T. | | 118 |
| Sampson, H.G. | | 101 |
| Samuels, A.B. | | 157 |
| San Antonio Light | | 157 |
| Sanders, Charles G. | | 76 |

| S | | |
|---|---|---|
| **Name** | | **Page** |
| Sargent & Greenleaf | | 107 |
| Sauer, G. | | 164 |
| Sausser Dangler & Co. | | 134 |
| Schaefer, Christ. | | 164 |
| Schloss, N.J. & Co. | | 179 |
| Schmidt, C. | | 179 |
| Schmidt, Fred | | 152 |
| Schmidt, John G. | | 135 |
| Schmitt & Koehne | | 102 |
| Schnaider's Garden | | 76 |
| Schoeller, Charles | | 102 |
| Schoeneman, Jos. & Co. | | 135 |
| Schoeneman Langstadter & Co. | | 135 |
| Scholz, A. | | 157 |
| Schroeder, Rudolph | | 120 |
| Schutter, William H. | | 28 |
| Schuttler, Peter | | 35 |
| Schuttler & Hotz | | 36 |
| Schutzen Park | | 56 |
| Schverlikovsky, Mrs. J. | | 83 |
| Schwab & Zimmerman | | 77 |
| Schwarzenberg, H. | | 25 |
| Scott, C.B. & Co. | | 135 |
| Scott, John W. & Co. | | 101 |
| Scott, T.A. & Co. | | 148 |
| Scranton Stove Works | | 142 |
| Sea's Millinery Dept. | | 36 |
| 2nd Regt. N.G. Pa. | | 136 |
| Sedgwick, William | | 108 |
| Seegers, J.C. & Co. | | 143 |
| Seitz Brothers | | 102 |
| Selly & F.R. Leman | | 179 |
| Seneca Lt. Club | | 180 |
| Server, John H. | | 136 |
| Sharpe, A.D. | | 88 |
| Sharpless Brothers | | 136 |
| Sharrard, A. | | 180 |
| Sheak Rogers & Co. | | 85 |
| Sheep shearing tokens | | 17 |
| Sheerer, J.W. & Co. | | 146 |
| Shepard, W.A. & Co. | | 179 |
| Shibboleth Lead Mining Co. | | 77 |
| Shinn, Will J. | | 20 |
| Shipley, Larkin R. | | 51 |
| Short, Jack | | 28 |
| Shreve, Alfred R. | | 83 |
| Shriver, B.F. & Co. | | 58 |
| Shurtleff College | | 27 |
| Siebert & Vassalo | | 18 |
| Silver Bow Club | | 180 |
| Simon & Oppenheimer | | 142 |
| Sinclair, W.C. | | 102 |
| Singleton, R.H. | | 147 |
| Sinkler & Davey | | 136 |
| 6 Baltm. | | 56 |
| Smith, H.W. | | 180 |
| Smith, J.T. | | 180 |
| Smith, R. | | 102 |
| Smith & Keating | | 36 |
| Smith & Rieger | | 73 |
| Smith & Seward | | 102 |
| Snow, F.W. | | 64 |
| Society Army of the Cumberland | | 25 |
| Society Army of the Tennessee | | 25 |
| Soldiers' Fair | | 67 |
| Soldiers Home Fair | | 167 |
| Soley, G.B. | | 136 |
| Southern Exposition | | 46 |
| Southern Hotel Bar | | 158 |

| S | | |
|---|---|---|
| **Name** | | **Page** |
| South Mission Sabbath School | | 76 |
| South Penn Hose Co. | | 142 |
| South River Cutlery Co. | | 180 |
| Southworth & Knight | | 146 |
| Sovereigns of Industry | | 58 |
| Spencer, William W. | | 115 |
| Spitz, T.P. | | 64 |
| Sponable, E.E. | | 78 |
| Sprague & Blodgett | | 26 |
| Springfield Antiquarians | | 67 |
| Star Saloon | | 73 |
| Steel, C.S. | | 42 |
| Stein, E.H. | | 36 |
| Stelling, John | | 102 |
| Stevens, G.E. | | 180 |
| Steves, J.H. | | 117 |
| Stewart, Thomas J. | | 49 |
| Stillman, A.S. | | 180 |
| Stillman, E. | | 180 |
| Stilz, John & Son | | 137 |
| Stiner Tea Co. | | 103 |
| Stitely, W.S. | | 40 |
| Stockton Hotel | | 82 |
| Stoehr's Lager Bier | | 180 |
| Stokes, Granville | | 137 |
| Storrs & Cook | | 180 |
| Stoughton, Dr. | | 137 |
| Strange, C.A. | | 50 |
| Strange, F.R. | | 180 |
| Strange, J.W. | | 50 |
| Strayhorn, Dick | | 158 |
| Stremmel, Ernst | | 158 |
| Strouse & Bros. | | 73 |
| Stubenrauch, Carl | | 158 |
| Sue Lee Fashion Theatre | | 158 |
| Sully, Daniel | | 180 |
| Svea Society | | 39 |
| Swan House | | 181 |
| Swan & Anderson | | 26 |
| Sweetsir, A.D. | | 51 |
| Swenson Brothers | | 44 |
| Swope, Joel | | 76 |

| T | | |
|---|---|---|
| Tabor, A.B. | | 36 |
| Tacoma Mill Co. | | 165 |
| Tanth, L.A. | | 168 |
| Tarbox, N.L. & Co. | | 147 |
| Tarrant, Robert | | 37 |
| Terrill Brothers | | 37 |
| Tertio Millennial Anniversary | | 84 |
| Thiet, Charles | | 77 |
| Thirteenth Regiment N.G. Pa. | | 142 |
| Thomas & Robinson | | 115 |
| Thornton, James | | 137 |
| Through the Fire | | 64 |
| Tivoli | | 85 |
| Tivoli & Walhalla | | 181 |
| Todd the Jeweler | | 97 |
| Toklas Singerman & Co. | | 164 |
| Toledo Mfg. Co. | | 118 |
| Tom Thumb | | 89 |
| Tougas & Duprey | | 68 |
| Toutloff, M.B. | | 71 |
| Tracy, N.J. | | 181 |
| Traphagen Hunter & Co. | | 103 |
| Treitschke, J. | | 78 |
| Trench, Daniel G. & Co. | | 37 |
| Treusch, Charles | | 57 |
| Truck Drivers B. & P. Assn. | | 103 |

## T

| Name | Page |
|---|---|
| Truesdale | 103 |
| Tuckaseege Mfg. Co. | 109 |
| Turner, Robert & Son | 57 |
| 22 Nord-Amer. Sangerfest (1881) | 35 |
| Two Brothers Saloon | 158 |

## U

| Name | Page |
|---|---|
| Umland, W.J.H. | 152 |
| Underill, S.B. | 87 |
| Union Coffee Co. Ltd., The | 103 |
| Union League | 132 |
| Upham, S.C. | 137 |
| Urlau, William & Bro. | 119 |
| U.S. Manufacturing Co. | 57 |
| U.S. Mint Employees | 137 |

## V

| Name | Page |
|---|---|
| Valentine & Co. | 104 |
| Vallee, John E. | 138 |
| Van's Cave | 159 |
| Vaudeville, Theatre | 159 |
| Vaughan's Seed Store | 37 |
| Vaux, E.P. | 181 |
| Victoria Cordage Works | 138 |
| Vollmer Saloon | 159 |

## W

| Name | Page |
|---|---|
| W. & E. | 181 |
| D.W. | 181 |
| I.F.W. (Wood) | 105 |
| J.W. | 104 |
| R.H.W. Co. | 181 |
| W.W. & Co. | 181 |
| Wachter, M. | 40 |
| Waidner, F.A. & Co. | 57 |
| Waldron's Prescription Store | 37 |
| Wallis & Cornnell | 182 |
| Walther, C.A. | 138 |
| Walton's Bitters | 182 |
| Wanamaker & Brown | 138 |
| Waring, W.L. | 164 |
| Warner, Charles K. | 138 |
| Warren, J.B. | 88 |
| Washington City Dog Tax | 25 |
| Washington Inaugural Centennial | 104 |
| Waters, Horace & Sons | 104 |
| Watrous (&) Co. | 182 |
| Wayt Dental Co. | 46 |
| W.C. Tax | 25 |
| Weidener, A.J. | 140 |
| Weil, & Levy | 20, 21 |
| Wellenkamp, Hugo | 104 |
| Wells Fargo | 182 |
| Welteck, E. | 105 |
| Wendt, A.F. | 86 |
| Werner, Anton | 182 |
| Western Foundry | 146 |
| Whitbeck's Circus | 182 |
| White (elephant) | 159 |
| White Elephant | 151 |
| White, Leslie | 24 |
| White House Saloon | 159 |
| Whitman & Son | 140 |
| Whitney (and) Woodbury | 162 |
| Whitney Brothers | 82 |
| Whitney Sewing Machine | 42 |
| Wilder, George | 182 |
| Wilder House | 182 |
| Williams, F.G. & Co. | 140 |
| Williamsburgh Brewing Co. | 86 |
| Wilcox | 24 |
| Wilson, H. | 45 |
| Wilson, J.G. | 105 |
| Wilson & Fenimore | 141 |
| Wilson Laird & Co. | 146 |
| Wiman Coppersmith | 182 |
| Winchester | 45 |
| Wing, C.H. | 183 |
| Wing, G.J. | 183 |
| Winnett, F.G. | 64 |
| Wise, Charles | 49 |
| Wissin, J.L. | 163 |
| Wiswell, J.M. & Co. | 146 |
| Wolf, M. | 146 |
| Wolfe's Schiedam Schnapps | 105 |
| Wolbrecht's, Geo., Tivoli | 183 |
| Wolff, James E. | 163 |
| Wood, Isaac F. | 59, 85, 105 |
| Wood Engine tokens | 22, 69, 70, 116, 117, 203, 204 |
| Wood Eng. No. | 117 |
| Wood's Museum | 141 |
| World's Industrial & Cotton Cent. Expo. | 48 |
| Wright, R.F. | 183 |
| Wright, R. & G. A. | 141 |
| Wright & Son | 116 |
| Wyant, Ben. F. | 146 |
| Wyoming Capital Building | 168 |

## Y

| Name | Page |
|---|---|
| Y. & Co. (Yuengling) | 105 |
| Y. & T. | 183 |
| M.V.Y. | 183 |
| Yankee Blade | 183 |
| Yankee Robinson | 116 |
| Yates & Co. | 141 |
| Young & Co. | 81 |
| Young's Amusement Co. | 81 |
| Young & McShea | 81 |
| Young, Emily B. | 27 |
| Yuengling & Co. | 105 |

## Z

| Name | Page |
|---|---|
| Zeller, A. | 20 |
| Zeltner & Co. | 105 |
| Zimmerman, C. | 121 |
| Ziriax | 183 |

# INDEX
## (Foreign)

### A

| Name | Page |
|---|---|
| I. A. | 211 |
| L.A. | 211 |
| Adourdan, Victor | 215 |
| Agnew | 206 |
| Allen, D. | 213 |
| Allentin, J.D. | 213 |
| Andrews, G.W. | 208 |
| Ashton | 206 |
| Aubry, T. | 206 |
| Au Gateau Royal | 214 |

### B

| Name | Page |
|---|---|
| G.H.B. | 211 |
| H.B. | 211 |
| H.B. (&) L.W. | 211 |
| I.B. | 211 |
| J.B. | 213 |
| L.H.B. | 206 |
| O.B. | 213 |
| W.B. | 211 |
| Bagshaw, S. | 211 |
| Baker's Cartes de Visite | 211 |
| Balfron Fruit | 211 |
| Ball, C.S. | 206 |
| Barnes, Wallace | 216 |
| Bigger | 213 |
| Blackhurst & Co. | 202 |
| Blacks Chocolate | 202 |
| Borwick's Baking Powder | 211 |
| Brown | 206 |
| Brown, J.B. | 202 |
| Buckle, J. | 211 |

### C

| Name | Page |
|---|---|
| J.E.C. | 206 |
| N.C. | 206 |
| Cabane's Strawberry Toothpaste | 211 |
| Cadman, L. (&) Ben Gall | 211 |
| Cast Steel | 211 |
| Cavan Murray Cavan | 213 |
| Cheney, C. | 206 |
| Christian | 213 |
| Cock, J. | 211 |
| Coffey, P. | 213 |
| Cook, D. | 206 |
| Cook, I. | 209 |
| Cooke, W. | 213 |
| Craig, S. | 211 |
| Crook | 206 |
| Cuff, William | 211 |

### D

| Name | Page |
|---|---|
| F.D. | 213 |
| F.D. (Declos) | 216 |
| G.D. | 206 |
| P.D. | 212 |
| Dav..., T. | 206 |
| Davies, T.S. | 202 |
| Dear & Sons | 211 |
| Declos, Francois | 216 |
| Delahoyd, R. | 213 |
| Dennis, B. | 213 |
| Devins & Bolton | 202 |
| Dillon Brazier | 211 |
| Dison | 213 |

### D

| Name | Page |
|---|---|
| Dollard, I. | 213 |
| Dollard, J. | 213 |
| Drabber, A. | 211 |
| Dundee Steam Laundry | 208 |
| Duval, A. | 206 |

### E

| Name | Page |
|---|---|
| Egan, B. | 213 |
| Empire Theatre | 208 |
| Epicerie Moderne | 214 |

### F

| Name | Page |
|---|---|
| F. | 211 |
| G.W.F. | 211 |
| I.F. | 211 |
| Feaist's Bread | 211 |
| Findlay & McWilliam | 203 |
| Fitz. P., J. | 213 |
| Frazier, Frank B. | 206 |
| Fyfe, A. | 211 |

### G

| Name | Page |
|---|---|
| G. | 206 |
| F.G. | 211 |
| I.N.G. | 211 |
| T.G. | 211 |
| Galbraith, T.B. | 206 |
| Garden Gate Ales | 211 |
| Gates, P.T. | 211 |
| Gibbss | 211 |
| Gilchris, G.R. | 206 |
| Goodden | 206 |
| Great Western Railway | 203 |
| Griffin, M. | 213 |
| Gros | 211 |
| Guano Fison, Le | 214 |

### H

| Name | Page |
|---|---|
| I.H. | 211 |
| J.H. | 206 |
| S.H. | 211 |
| Hall, B. | 208 |
| Hall, B., Glazier | 211 |
| Hambilton | 213 |
| Hanley, J.F. | 206 |
| Harding | 208 |
| Headen, O. | 213 |
| Henry a Pont-la-Ville | 215 |
| Heron's Douglas Whiskey | 211 |
| Higbee & McCoy | 203 |
| Hood, J. | 204 |
| Hutton, J. | 206 |
| Hyman | 208 |
| Hynes, T. | 213 |

### I

| Name | Page |
|---|---|
| J.I. | 206 |
| S.P.I. | 206 |
| In Solis Celanir | 206 |

### J

| Name | Page |
|---|---|
| J. | 206, 211 |
| Jette, M. | 206 |
| Jones, J. (&) T. Aubry | 206 |
| Jones, William | 204 |

### K

| Name | Page |
|---|---|
| Keep Quiet | 206 |
| Kelly, T. | 213 |

### K

| Name | Page |
|---|---|
| Kent, A.F. | 209 |
| Ker, M. | 211 |
| Kerr, H.R. | 206 |
| Ketchum & Co. | 204 |
| Kohler, A. & Fils | 215 |

### L

| Name | Page |
|---|---|
| C.G.L. | 206 |
| Lagace, O. | 206 |
| Lapointe, L. | 204 |
| Lee, J. | 206 |
| Lee, S. | 206 |
| Lessive Magique | 215 |
| Lloyd's Weekly Newspaper | 209 |
| Low, W.F. | 206 |
| Lowe, R. | 211 |
| Lyard | 206 |

### M

| Name | Page |
|---|---|
| A.O.M. | 206 |
| J.S.M. | 206 |
| W.A.M. to J.R.E. | 212 |
| Manly | 206 |
| Mason, Sir Josiah | 209 |
| Massey | 209 |
| McCauley | 206 |
| McG., Con. | 213 |
| McGloghlon, W.D. | 206 |
| McH., J.A. | 206 |
| McK., H. | 206 |
| McMahon | 212 |
| McNeil | 209 |
| McRae, D.R. | 206 |
| Millar, J.W. | 204 |
| Millard | 209 |
| Mitchell Saw Maker | 211 |
| Moore, D. | 206 |
| Morgan | 211 |

### N

| Name | Page |
|---|---|
| Nichols | 206 |
| Nisbet, R.E. | 211 |

### O

| Name | Page |
|---|---|
| F.O. | 207 |
| T.P.O. | 207 |
| O'Neill | 213 |

### P

| Name | Page |
|---|---|
| C.P. | 211 |
| F.P. | 207 |
| H.B.P. | 207 |
| I.P. | 212 |
| Palmer, William C. | 207 |
| Paquette & Cie. | 207 |
| Parke, R. | 213 |
| Pears' Soap | 209 |
| Pero, F.J.A. | 207 |
| Perry, H. | 213 |
| Peters | 207 |
| Picotin Aperitif, Le | 215 |
| Prosser, E. | 212 |

### Q

| Name | Page |
|---|---|
| Q.M.O. & O. Ry. | 204 |
| A.J.Q. | 207 |

## R

| Name | Page |
|---|---|
| R.H. & S. | 207 |
| Racing Opinion | 212 |
| Ralph, R L. | 207 |
| Renfrew, A., Society | 213 |
| Robinson | 210 |
| Robinson Cutler | 212 |
| Robinson Razor Maker | 212 |
| Robinson, T.H. | 204 |
| Robinson's Carriage Works | 204 |
| Rouleau, Josh | 204 |

## S

| Name | Page |
|---|---|
| S. | 207, 212 |
| W.S. | 210 |
| St. Andrews Chapter | 207 |
| Saxlund | 207 |
| Schroder, Rudolph | 216 |
| Sedan | 215 |
| Silver, S.W. | 210 |
| Simon | 210 |
| Simons, W. | 212 |
| Somervill Down | 213 |
| South Shields | 212 |
| Spence's Plan | 210 |
| Stuart, T. | 207 |
| Stubs | 212 |

## T

| Name | Page |
|---|---|
| T.C. (Tatham) | 214 |
| T + C | 210 |
| I.T. | 212 |
| J.F.T. | 207 |
| Tagart, V. | 213 |
| Tatham & Co. | 214 |
| 3 of Tea | 212 |
| Tilley's Coals | 212 |

## U

| Name | Page |
|---|---|
| U.S. | 207 |
| Union Stamp Factory 114 | 205 |
| Upton, F. | 207 |
| Usine d'Harfleur | 215 |

## V

| Name | Page |
|---|---|
| J.B.V. | 212 |
| Vanillarome | 215 |
| Veldon, J. | 205 |
| Vin de Naples | 215 |
| Votes for Women | 212 |

## W

| Name | Page |
|---|---|
| W. | 212 |
| J.W. | 207 |
| R.W. | 213 |
| T.W. | 212 |
| Wagar, C.R. | 207 |
| Wake, J.H. | 207 |
| Wald, James | 207 |
| Walton, L. | 213 |
| Watson, R. | 207 |
| White, A. | 207 |
| Wilsonns, S. | 213 |
| Woodh., H. | 207 |
| Woods | 207 |

## X-Y-Z

| Name | Page |
|---|---|
| York Hotel | 210 |
| Youmans, A.C. | 207 |
| Z. | 207 |